THE BLACKWELL ENCYCLOPEDIA OF MANAGEMENT

STRATEGIC MANAGEMENT

THE BLACKWELL ENCYCLOPEDIA OF MANAGEMENT

SECOND EDITION

Encyclopedia Editor: Cary L. Cooper
Advisory Editors: Chris Argyris and William H. Starbuck

About the Editors

Editor in Chief
Cary L. Cooper is based at Lancaster University as Professor of Organizational Psychology. He is the author of over 80 books, is past editor of the *Journal of Organizational Behavior*, and Founding President of the British Academy of Management.

Advisory Editors
Chris Argyris is James Bryant Conant Professor of Education and Organizational Behavior at Harvard Business School.

William Haynes Starbuck is Professor of Management and Organizational Behavior at the Stern School of Business, New York University.

Volume Editor
John McGee is Associate Dean for the MBA Programme and Professor of Strategic Management at Warwick Business School. He has been Director of the Centre for Corporate Strategy and Change and Chair of the Marketing and Strategic Management group. He was previously at Templeton College, Oxford where he was Dean of the College, and at London Business School where he was the founding Director of the Centre for Business Strategy.

He has served on the Higher Education Funding Council Research Assessment Exercise Panels for management studies in the UK in 1996 and in 2001. He is a former President of the Strategic Management Society having been a member of its board of directors 1996–2004.

He has written extensively in the area of business economics and business strategy particularly on the evolution of industries and strategic groups analysis. His current interests are in the nature of the new information economy in which the joint effects of complexity and the pervasiveness of increasing returns create new strategic opportunities. He has also written on the emerging knowledge-based view of strategy and the implications of knowledge-intensity for the deconstruction and the reconstruction of industries and supply chains.

b

**Blackwell Encyclopedia of Management,
Second Edition: Strategic Management**
Edited by John McGee
First edition edited by Derek Channon

More explicit attention is given to
"competitive strategy" and "competitive
advantage"; the "resource-based view" is
treated fully, with recent developments
around the "knowledge-based view"; the
"new economy" is introduced, specifically
eonomics of knowledge and information and
the nature of network externalities. A new
preface by the current editor, John McGee,
acknowledges the signal contribution of
Derek Channon and outlines the key current
trends in the field of strategic management.

THE BLACKWELL ENCYCLOPEDIA OF MANAGEMENT

SECOND EDITION

STRATEGIC MANAGEMENT

Edited by
John McGee
Warwick Business School

First edition edited by
Derek F. Channon

Blackwell
Publishing

BLACKWELL PUBLISHING
350 Main Street, Malden, MA 02148-5020, USA
9600 Garsington Road, Oxford OX4 2DQ, UK
550 Swanston Street, Carlton, Victoria 3053, Australia

The right of John McGee to be identified as the Author of the Editorial Material in this Work has been asserted in accordance with the UK Copyright, Designs, and Patents Act 1988.

First published 1997 by Blackwell Publishers Ltd
Published in paperback in 1999 by Blackwell Publishers Ltd
Second edition published 2005 by Blackwell Publishing Ltd

Library of Congress Cataloging-in-Publication Data

The Blackwell encyclopedia of management. Strategic management/edited by
John McGee and Derek F. Channon
p. cm. — (The Blackwell encyclopedia of management ; v. 12)
Rev. ed. of The Blackwell encyclopedic dictionary of strategic management/
edited by Derek F. Channon. 1997.
Includes bibliographical references and index.
ISBN 1-4051-1828-8 (hardcover : alk. paper)
1. Strategic planning—Dictionaries. I. McGee, John. II. Channon, Derek F.
III. Blackwell Publishing Ltd. IV. Blackwell encyclopedic
dictionary of strategic management. V. Series.
HD30.15 .B455 2005 vol. 12
[HD30.28]
658′.003 s–dc22
[658.4′012′03]
2004018072

ISBN-13: 978-1-4051-1828-6 (hardcover: alk. paper)

ISBN for the 12-volume set 0-631-23317-2

A catalogue record for this title is available from the British Library.

Set in 9.5 on 11pt Ehrhardt
by Kolam Information Services Pvt. Ltd, Pondicherry, India

For further information on
Blackwell Publishing, visit our website:
www.blackwellpublishing.com

Contents

Preface to the First Edition

This book is the volume in the Blackwell Encyclopedia of Management devoted to the subject of strategic management. This relatively recent area of study in management stems from the 1970s, but its origins go much deeper. The literature of the subject builds upon the early pioneers of management thought, such as Urwick, Fayol, Taylor, Simon, Barnard, Chandler, and the like. Notice that nearly all of these names are from the USA. The list could be broadened to include others from Europe, such as Crozier, Woodward, Edwards, and Townsend. The field has also drawn somewhat on writers on military strategy, such as Clauzwitz, Liddell Hart, Sun Tzu, Machiavelli, and Mao Tse Tung. Not all of these conceptual thinkers are represented in this book; nor are the writers in decision theory, game theory, and such like. Regrettably, there is a finite length to any volume.

The concept of strategic management in its present form developed in the 1960s with the emergence of two very different approaches – which ultimately became complementary – at the Harvard Business School and at Carnegie Mellon. At Harvard, by recognizing that something "different" occurred at the top management level of the large corporation, and based on many of the behavioral studies by practitioners and academics such as Barnard, Drucker, Selznick, Fayol, and Urwick, case-based material was developed which attempted to explain this behavior. Eventually, in 1965, Ken Andrews articulated the concept of corporate strategy as developed at Harvard. He combined the views of Drucker and the seminal work of Alfred Chandler to define strategy as:

> The pattern of objectives, purposes or goals and major policies and plans for achieving these goals; stated in such a way as to define what business the company is in or is to be in and the kind of company it is or is to be.

In contrast, Igor Ansoff, coming from the Carnegie school and influenced by rational decision-making concepts, developed the view of strategy as the "common thread" among an organization's activities and product/markets that defined the essential nature of the business that the organization was in and planned to be in in the future.

At the same time as these two schools were developing within the academic world, in consultancy a number of important concepts were developing. Bruce Henderson and the Boston Consulting Group had developed the experience curve concept which, coupled with the observable diversification trend in large US corporations, led to the introduction of the growth share matrix, a recipe for balancing the cash flow profiles of different businesses based on expected cost advantages secured from the experience effect, the surrogate for which was subsumed to be relative market share. Similarly, Chandler's structure findings were being widely disseminated by McKinsey and Company, both amongst diversified US corporations and around the world, to introduce the profit centered (and later strategic business unit centered) form of organizational structure.

During the next decade the field developed with some dichotomy between behavioral models of strategy and analytic methods. At Harvard, interestingly, the behavioral school tended to dominate in the area now known as Business Policy, while analytic techniques, such as those of the Boston Consulting Group, found root in the marketing faculty. Ansoff visited Europe where he was instrumental in establishing a European network of scholars and helping to establish the discipline of corporate strategy there, in an environment exhibiting substantial skepticism that the area existed as a business discipline at all.

In the late 1970s, the strategic management movement in its present form was born. At perhaps the first international conference on the theme of corporate strategy, hosted by the University of Pittsburgh, it was decided by an international group of scholars that the term "Strategic Management" might be used to help coalesce the diversity between the concepts developed at Carnegie and at Harvard. Further, it was proposed that the new movement should endeavor to be truly international and embrace not only academics, but also business consultants and practitioners. This was cemented at a conference in Aix en Provence, hosted by Henry Mintzberg and attended by Dan Schendel and Derek Channon, who together with Igor Ansoff set out to create the Strategic Management Society and *Journal* in the next few years. The first international meeting of the Strategic Management Society was held in London in 1979, hosted by Hugh Parker of McKinsey and Company and Derek Channon, and attended by Dan Schendel and visitors from Harvard and around the world from business, academia, and consultancy.

The second meeting, hosted in Montreal by Henry Mintzberg, led to the creation of the Strategic Management Society. Meanwhile, Igor Ansoff, Derek Channon, and especially Dan Schendel had launched the *Strategic Management Journal*, which became and remains the leading professional journal in the area.

Since the beginning of the 1980s the area has expanded dramatically. Today it has become a leading area of management consultancy. It is a required area in the curriculum of virtually all graduate business administration and executive programs. In business, the concept of strategy is taken as an accepted norm and the search for strategic advantage has become a key element in corporate success. Notably, the work of Michael Porter in the early 1980s has built heavily upon the concepts of industrial economics, and the work of Mintzberg has challenged the analytic themes of rational economic strategy. The work of C. K. Prahalad and Gary Hamel has introduced new or modified concepts of core competence and globalization; and the consultancy industry has built upon finance theory to develop value based planning, re-engineering, benchmarking, and the like.

Seriously neglected in the literature of strategic management have been concepts from the East, and especially from Japan. This volume has, however, attempted to redress the almost total omission of the strategies, structures, and management techniques developed by Asian corporations. On average, the present major texts in the area devote less than one per cent of their content to this region, and yet in economic terms over the past several decades these countries have been the winners. Moreover, many of their management practices tend to be in almost direct contradiction of the best practices espoused in the West. We have therefore devoted a number of entries to attempting to describe and understand their management methods. While much of this discussion has been devoted to descriptions of actual practices, some attempt has also been made to show how, structurally, many of the strategies actually work. We hope this feature will add to the strategic management literature and help redress the imbalance.

The volume has also been designed to try to reflect the ideals established with the formation of the Strategic Management Society, namely to add value to the three constituencies of Academic, Business executives and Consultants, the ABCs that were the foundation of the Society. Thus, while the entries develop the theoretic concepts of the field, there is also an emphasis on the practical use of these.

Derek F. Channon

Preface to the Second Edition

It is seven years since the first edition of *The Blackwell Encyclopedia of Management: Strategic Management* was published. In his preface to that edition Derek Channon told the story of the genesis of strategic management as a conjunction of theory and practice. The theoretical impetus came from the long stream of writing at Harvard Business School and the then modern approach taken at Carnegie Tech (later Carnegie Mellon). The impetus from practice came from the prime strategy consultancies (especially Boston Consulting Group and McKinsey and Company) and from a number of the large diversified corporations among whom General Electric stands out. The field has continued to bridge theory and practice because in the final analysis strategy has to be a practical subject. Nevertheless the academic endeavor in the field of strategic management has proceeded at rapid pace to the extent that the prime journal – the *Strategic Management Journal* – is rated as one of the top academic journals in management and new strategy and strategy-related journals continue to appear.

In this new edition I have extended the range of entries to reflect the more eclectic nature of STRATEGY and to reflect the changes in the economy in terms of the growth of high-tech knowledge and its impact on the field of strategy. There is more explicit attention to COMPETITIVE STRATEGY and COMPETITIVE ADVANTAGE reflecting the extent to which this language has become the common language of strategic discourse. The RESOURCE-BASED VIEW is given much more prominence along with recent developments around knowledge and the emerging KNOWLEDGE-BASED VIEW of strategy. The inheritance of strategy from economics as firm-specific imperfections is made more explicit. The new economy is given explicit treatment, specifically economics of knowledge and information and the nature of network externalities and the implications these have for strategy-making.

The second edition of this dictionary enables us to pay tribute to the pioneering work of Derek Channon. Derek died in 2003 after a long illness. His colleagues at Manchester Business School and Imperial College Management School will miss him greatly as also will scholars and practitioners at large. Derek was a man of great energy, passion and insight. He was one of the key founders of the Strategic Management Society and a founding co-editor (along with Dan Schendel) of the *Strategic Management Journal*. He was one of the architects of the modern field of strategic management and was one those few who grandfathered the use of the term strategic management. Derek's scholarly interests were formed during his doctoral research at Harvard where he and a select few investigated multi-business firms providing empirical foundation for the then emerging study of Strategy and Structure. This set in motion a generation of empirical study and theoretical debate both in North America and in Europe. As is evident from the Preface to the First Edition, Derek was a strong champion of Japanese concepts of strategy and of management. These have become less fashionable as the Japanese economy has struggled over the last decade, but many of the distinctive Japanese characteristics of management have moved into the Western lexicon. Some like TOTAL QUALITY CONTROL have almost become anglicised in their explication but others such as SOGA SOSHA remain distinctively Japanese and are retained in this second edition because of their continuing importance in the field.

Derek made a significant and lasting mark on the field of strategic management.

John McGee

How to Use this Book

As the field of strategic management has grown in breadth and in depth I feel that it is useful to provide the reader with a map to guide their use of the entries. Figure 1 shows one conceptual framework of strategic management and the logic underlying the selection and organization of the entries.

Figure 1 is a map but it also a system model. It sets out strategy as a field of practice onto which academic research and interpretation can be mapped. Each of the elements in the diagram (e.g. over-arching direction or strategic thinking) encompasses a set of issues and generally poses a specific question.

1   Understanding the firm's over-arching *Direction* is critical. The general question being asked here is "What does the organization want to be?" The organization must develop a long-term vision of what it wants to be and takes into account the company's culture, reputation, competences, and resources in addressing that question. The vision is the core ideology of the organization, which provides the glue that binds the organization together. It encompasses a set of core values that address questions such as why the company exists and what it believes in. The core values may include such things as honesty and integrity, hard work and continuous self-improvement, strong customer service, creativity, and imagination. On the other hand, the core purpose is to do with the company's reason for being. In Walt Disney's case, it is simply stated as being to make people happy or, in Hewlett Packard's case, to make a technological contribution to the advancement and welfare of humanity. Purpose, in this sense, is very close to the mission of the organization and, as stated earlier, the vision is the core ideology which binds the organization together.

2   *Strategic thinking* This element of the strategy map advances a holistic and integrated view of the business. It asks the question of how, through analysis and strategic positioning, the firm will answer the question "Together, how will we do that?" What we seek to understand here is the

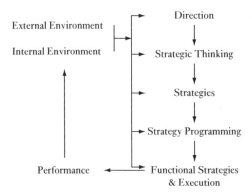

Figure 1   The strategy concepts map

relationship between the firm's positioning, resources and capabilities, and organization - the firm's strategy must be such that the elements complement and reinforce each other, i.e. the strategies are cohesive. In other words, a coordinated framework of high-level enterprise strategies is developed to achieve the vision. This brings together the best strategic thinking and analysis and widely communicates one strategic viewpoint to get everyone pulling in the same direction and to discourage unproductive behaviour.

The agreed enterprise strategy is then broken down into a range of strategies that position the organization in its markets and in its various functional activities (e.g. product strategies, distribution strategies, etc.). They emphasize strategic options and positions, and highlight them in a framework such that they work together. Obviously, strategic thinking requires a whole range of techniques and tools. These include a determination of the broad goals of the organization, thus, answering the question "What is most important?" Analysts and strategists also have to understand the sources of value creation through revenue drivers, cost drivers, and risk drivers.

This kind of framework is useful for picturing the dynamics of an industry but such frameworks do not tell the whole story. They are relatively static frameworks that make a number of assumptions, not least that all players will have perfect knowledge (everyone is aware of the extent of their power or the threat they pose) and will always exercise the power they have. To inject a more dynamic perspective, these frameworks should be seen as one part of a greater process. The strategist has to recognize the source of the power balances or imbalances, but having done that he/she needs to drill deeper into the analysis to analyze not only the sources of such threats and power but also the impact of each on the strategy process. This explains why the five forces model, central to many scholars strategy frameworks, is only a part of the systemic model presented here.

3   *Strategies* constitute the strategic framework and product goals. In its simplest terms, a strategy consists of a set of goals and a set of policies or actions to achieve those goals. Goals answer the question of "What is most important for the organization?" The strategy and process also encompasses the strategic planning process which varies from organization to organization in levels of familiarity. However, the most important element in strategic planning is to link the strategic framework and broad goals as guides and allow each of the divisions or sub-units of the organization to develop their own strategies in a coordinated fashion. That is, responsibility for strategy formulation should be devolved to the sub-units or entities within the business that have responsibility for products and services. The individual managers running those units are the ones who know the products and services, the product markets and the presence of other competitors in the market place. They can then develop a statement of what strategic positioning the organization should reasonably adopt at that level. The role of top management is to coordinate those strategies in an enterprise sense, so that it fits the overall strategic framework defined by the vision and the over-arching direction of the organization.

4   *Strategic programming* focuses on the answers to questions such as "Who, when, and how much?" In other words, assuming broad strategies are agreed, an operating plan must be developed to attack such issues as day-to-day priorities, organizational roles and responsibilities, and resource allocation with regard to budgets and systems development. Obviously, this leads to the development of a clearer, tactical plan.

5   *Functional strategies and execution* This phase of the strategy process addresses the tasks "Let's get organized and let's do it, and do it right!" In other words, the tactical part of the operating plan fills in the gaps about division plans, unit plans, and individual goals, and develops performance metrics at each level, so that monitoring of those plans can be undertaken. The executive focuses not only on the monitoring of performance and targets but the ability to adjust plans quickly and rapidly as new ideas and challenges are developed within the organization.

6   *Performance: Measurement, analysis, and purpose* In any organization, there must be a linkage to performance. The feedback that is necessary for any organization in re-framing its strategy in a

sensible way is the answer to the question "How do I do a check of performance against targets and cost?" Performance metrics are extremely important – they highlight issues such as progress towards goals and, more importantly, how certain tasks and certain strategies can be adjusted better and faster, and how change can be incorporated most effectively within the context of the organization.

7   *The internal and external environment* requires information and analysis. Obviously, changing the organization through performance monitoring and strategy adjustment is but one process in a series of feedbacks and feedback loops which are absolutely necessary in analyzing information about both internal and external environments. In the external environment, we have to question "What is happening around us?" There must be a process of data gathering and development of insight and knowledge about such issues as new technology and its impact on the business, and the potential impact of regulation and legislation on the activities of the company. The underlying national economic and macro economic conditions are also important in setting the global economic context for the organization and, at a more micro level, framing intelligence and analysis about competition, the nature and changing shape of markets and customer needs and opinions. Obviously, key success factors in this external environment enable the firm to focus on appropriate product renewal and generate knowledge and insight about new products and ideas. In the context of the internal environment, the firm needs to analyze and identify its key resources and capabilities and evaluate its impact on competitive advantage. Internal analysis also requires a process of continual investigation, discovery, and criticism leading to new ideas, new product concepts, updated financial results, and updated metrics. Information about organizational strengths and weaknesses can, in turn, lead to the continual renewal of the strategy process.

The strategy concept presented in Figure 1 is both a map, a framework, and a virtuous circle, at the core of which is a process of knowledge management which trades upon analysis of the external and internal environment, analysis of performance, analysis of strategies, and competitive updating of

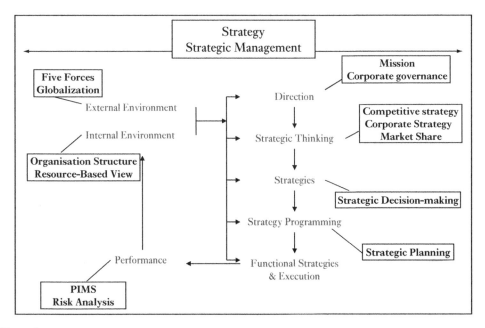

Figure 2

values and mission in order to achieve a process whereby the organization engaged in a continual debate about how it can improve and how it can frame its strategy so that the organization, itself, fits in a dynamic sense with its current and future strategic position.

The entries in this dictionary are organized around key entries which are aligned with this map (see Figure 2). This makes it possible for the reader to pursue themes through linked entries. Thus it is possible to pick out GLOBALIZATION as a key theme and pursue it and the related entries to build up a systematic view of one particular element in strategic management.

Acknowledgments

The editor and publisher gratefully acknowledge the permission granted to reproduce the copyright material in this book:

S. Nagashima, The break even point chart (figure), pp. 30–1 from *100 Management Charts*. Tokyo: Asian Productivity Organisation, 1992. Chart 5 © 1992 by Asian Productivity Organization. Reprinted with permission from the Asian Productivity Organization.

S. Nagashima, The cause and effect diagram for cost reduction (figure), pp. 38–9, from *100 Management Charts*. Tokyo: Asian Productivity Organisation, 1992. Chart 9 © 1992 by Asian Productivity Organization. Reprinted with permission from the Asian Productivity Organization.

T. Hattori, The organizational structure of Korean chaebols (figure) from "Japanese zaibatsu and Korean chaebol," p. 88 from Kae H. Chung and Hak Chong Lee (eds.), *Korean Managerial Dynamics*. New York: Praeger, 1989. © 1989 by Greenwood Publishing Group, Inc. Reproduced with permission of Greenwood Publishing Group, Inc, Westport CT.

C. W. Hofer and D. Schendel, An example of the business strength (competitive position) assessment with the weighted score approach (table), from *Strategy Formulation: Analytical Concepts*. St Paul, MN: West, 1978. © 1978. Reprinted with permission of South-Western, a division of Thomson Learning: www.thomsonrights.com.

C. W. Hofer and D. Schendel, An example of the industry (market) attractiveness with the weighted score approach (table), from *Strategy Formulation: Analytical Concepts*. St Paul, MN: West, 1978. © 1978. Reprinted with permission of South-Western, a division of Thomson Learning: www.thomsonrights.com.

D. A. Nadler, M. A. Tushman, and M. B. Nadler, Definitions of fit among components (table), from *Competing by Design: The Power of Organizational Architecture*. Oxford: OUP, 1997. © 1997 Oxford University Press. Used by permission of Oxford University Press, Inc.

Koura Kozo, table 1 and figures 1–3 from "Administrative aspects and key points of cross-functional management," from Kenji Kurogane (ed.), *Cross-functional Management*. Tokyo: Asian Productivity Organisation, 1993. © 1993 by Asian Productivity Organization. Reprinted with permission from the Asian Productivity Organization.

R. Shapiro, Moriarty, and Ross, The customer profitability matrix (figure) from "Manage customers for profits (not just sales)," from *Harvard Business Review*, 1987. © 1987 Harvard Business Review. Reprinted by permission of Harvard Business School Publishing.

A. Deaton, Luxuries, necessities and substitutes (figure), from "The measurement of income and price elasticities," from *European Economic Review*, 1975. © 1975, with permission from Elsevier.

J. Stopford, Activities overseas and structure (figure), p. 108 from *Growth and Organisational Change in the Multinational Firm*. New York: Arno Press, 1980. © 1980 J. Stopford. Reprinted by permission of John Stopford.

A. C. Hax and N. S. Majilus, Experience effects differ for different stages in the value added chain (figure) and The unsustainable experience curve effect (figure), pp. 108–26 from *Strategic Management: An Integrative Perspective*. New Jersey: Englewood Cliffs, 1984.

G. B. Allan, J. S. Hammond, The unstable experience curve effect (figure), p. 9 from *Note on the use of experience curves in competitive decision making. Case no. 175–174*. Boston: Harvard Business School, 1975. Some implications for product strategy (Table A, p. 9). © 1975 Harvard Business School Publishing. Reprinted by permission.

M. E. Porter, Porter' five forces model (figure), from *Competitive strategy: Techniques for Analyzing Industries and Competitors*. New York: Free Press: A division of Simon and Schuster, 1980. © 1980 Simon and Schuster, Inc. Reprinted by permission.

A. J. Rowe, R. O. Mason, K. E. Dickel, R. B. Mann, and R. J. Mockler, Gap analysis (figure), p. 245 from *Strategic Management*, Fourth edition. Reading, MA: Addison-Wesley, 1994. © 1994 A. J. Rowe. Reprinted by permission.

M. E. Porter, Porter's generic strategies (table and figure), in chapter 2 from *Competitive Strategy: Techniques for Analyzing Industries and Competitors*. New York: Free Press, A division of Simon and Schuster 1980. © 1980 Simon and Schuster, Inc. Reprinted by permission.

S. Goshal, table from "Global strategy: An organising framework," pp. 425–40 from *Strategic Management Journal*, 8, 1987. © 1987, John Wiley & Sons Limited. Reproduced with permission.

M. C. Bogue, E. S. Buffa, The growth/share matrix for Eastman Kodak, 1978 (figure), from *Corporate Strategic Analysis*. New York: Free Press: A division of Simon and Schuster, 1986. © 1986 Simon and Schuster, Inc. Reprinted by permission.

D. F. Channon and M. Jalland, A local umbrella company structure (figure), from *The Strategy and Structure of British Enterprise*. Cambridge, MA: Harvard Division of Research, 1973. © 1973, Macmillan. Reproduced with permission of Palgrave Macmillan.

M. E. Porter, Porter five forces frameworks (figure), from *Competitive Strategy: Techniques for Analyzing Industries and Competitors*. New York: Free Press, A division of Simon and Schuster 1980. © 1980 Simon and Schuster, Inc. Reprinted by permission.

R. J. Schonberger, The effects of JIT production (figure), from *Japanese Manufacturing Techniques*. New York: Free Press: A division of Simon and Schuster, 1985. © 1985 Simon and Schuster, Inc. Reprinted by permission.

E. Abrahamson, Print-media indicators of quality circles (figure 1), from "Management fashion," pp. 254–85, *Academy of Management Review*, 21 (1), 1996. Reprinted by permission of The Copyright Clearance Center, www.copyright.com

J. Stopford and L. T. Wells, The global matrix (figure), from *Managing the Multinational Enterprise*. New York: Basic Books, 1972. © 1972 by Basic Books, Inc. Reprinted by permission of Basic Books, a member of Perseus Books, L.L.C and Pearson Education.

D. N. Angwin and B. Saville, The growing relative importance of European cross-border acquisition activity (figure), pp. 423–35 from *European Management Journal*, 14 (4), 1997. © 1997, with permission from Elsevier.

A. J. Rowe, R. O. Mason, K. E. Dickel, R. B. Mann, and R. J. Mockler, Match of management with organizational life cycle (figure), in chapter 11 from *Strategic Management*, fourth edition. Reading, MA: Addison-Wesley. © 1994 A. J. Rowe. Reprinted by permission.

H. Mintzberg, Stages in the transition to the pure diversified form (figure), from *Mintzberg on Management*. New York: Free Press: A division of Simon and Schuster, 1989.

S. Nagashima, Pareto analysis of production cost, manufacturing expenses and expenditure (figure), pp. 36–7 from *100 management charts*. Tokyo: Asian Productivity Organisation, 1992. Chart 8 © 1992 by Asian Productivity Organization. Reprinted with permission from the Asian Productivity Organization.

Imai Masaaki, Japanese and Western PDCA cycles (figure), pp. 60–5 from *Kaizen*. New York: McGraw-Hill, 1986. © 1996 The McGraw-Hill Companies. Reproduced with permission of The McGraw-Hill Companies.

C. S. Jones, Complexity of post-take-over integration (figure), from *Successful Management of Acquisitions*. London: Derek Beattie, 1982. © 1982 by Derek Beattie Publishing.

S. Nagashima, Management analysis radar chart (figure), pp. 44–5 from *100 management charts*. Tokyo: Asian Productivity Organisation, 1992. Chart 12 © 1992 by Asian Productivity Organization. Reprinted with permission from the Asian Productivity Organization.

C. Bogan and M. English, Kodak class MEMO benchmarking M2 chart (figure) and The Xerox 12-step benchmarking process (table), pp. 58–61 from *Benchmarking for Best Practice*. New York: McGraw-Hill, 1994. © 1994 The McGraw-Hill Companies. Reproduced with permission of The McGraw-Hill Companies.

G. Stalk, P. Evans, and L. E. Shulman, Table from "Competing on Capabilities: the new Rules of Corporate Strategy," pp. 57–69 from *Harvard Business Review*, 70 (2), 1992. © 1992 Harvard Business Review. Reprinted by permission of Harvard Business School Publishing.

M. A. Peteraf, Value of a core competence (figure), from "The cornerstones of competitive advantage: a resouce-based view," pp. 179–91 from *Strategic Management Journal* 14 (2), 1993. © 1993, John Wiley & Sons Limited. Reproduced with permission.

A. A. Thompson, A. J. Strickland. "The SBU form of organizational structure from W. K. Hale (1978)," pp. 228–31 from *Strategic management*, Seventh edition. Homewood, IL: Richard D. Irwin publications, 1993.

S. Segal-Horn, Table from "Strategy in Service Organisations," from D. Faulkner and A. Campbell (eds), *The Oxford Handbook of Strategy*, Vol.1. Oxford: OUP, 2003. Table 16.4 (p. 472) by permission of Oxford University Press.

S. Segal-Horn, Indicative value chain of a hotel (figure), from "The search for core competencies in a service multinational: A case study of the French hotel Novotel," from Y. Aharoni and L. Nachum (eds), *Globalisation of Services: Some Implications for Theory and Practice*. London: Routledge, 2000. © 2000 Routledge. Reprinted by permission of Thomson Publishing Services on behalf of Routledge.

A. J. Rowe, R. O. Mason, K. E. Dickel, R. B. Mann, and R. J. Mockler, A map of the Polaroid corporation's stakeholders in 1980 (figure), pp. 134–44 from *Strategic Management*, Fourth edition. Reading, MA: Addison-Wesley, 1994. © 1994 A. J. Rowe. Reprinted by permission.

A. Thompson and A. J. Strickland, A strategic group map of the US brewing industry (figure), p. 77 from *Strategic Management*, Seventh edition. New York: Richard D. Irwin publications, 1993.

H. Mintzberg, Five basic parts of the organization (figure), from *Mintzberg on Management*. New York: Free Press: A division of Simon and Schuster, 1989.

A. J. Rowe, R. O. Mason, K. E. Dickel, R. B. Mann, and R. J. Mockler, The technology evaluation matrix (figure), pp. 116–21 from *Strategic Management,* Fourth edition. Reading, MA: Addison-Wesley, 1994. © 1994 A. J. Rowe. Reprinted by permission.

R. J. Schonberger, Total quality control (figure), p. 51 from *Japanese Manufacturing Techniques*. New York: Free Press: A division of Simon and Schuster, 1982. © 1982 Simon and Schuster, Inc. Reprinted by permission.

P. McKiernan, Extended Cyert and March Model (figure), p. 58 from *Strategies of Growth*. London: Routledge, 1992. © 1992, Routledge. Reprinted by permission of Thomson Publishing Services on behalf of Routledge.

M. E. Porter, Competitive advantage value system for a diversified form (figure), from *Competitive Strategy: Techniques for Analyzing Industries and Competitors*. New York: Free Press: A division of Simon and Schuster, 1985. © 1985 Simon and Schuster, Inc. Reprinted by permission.

M. E. Porter, The generic value chain (figure), from *Competitive Strategy: Techniques for Analyzing Industries and Competitors*. New York: Free Press: A division of Simon and Schuster, 1985. © 1985 Simon and Schuster, Inc. Reprinted by permission.

A. J. Rowe, R. O. Mason, K. E. Dickel, R. B. Mann, and R. J. Mockler, The vulnerability assessment matrix (figure), pp. 202–6 from *Strategic Management,* Fourth edition. Reading, MA: Addison-Wesley, 1994. © 1994 A. J. Rowe. Reprinted by permission.

N. M. Tichy and S. Sherman, The CRAP detector (figure), from *Control Your Own Destiny or Someone Else Will*. London: HarperCollins, 1993.

S. Nagashima, Using Lanchester theory for market domination (figure), from *100 Management Charts*. Tokyo: Asian Productivity Organisation, 1992. Chart 35 © 1992 by Asian Productivity Organization. Reprinted with permission from the Asian Productivity Organization.

P. Haspeslagh and D Jemison, Types of acquisition integration approach (figure), from *Managing Acquisitions: Creating Value Through Corporate Renewal*. New York: Free Press: A division of Simon and Schuster 1991. © 1991 Simon and Schuster, Inc. Reprinted by permission.

R. S. Kaplan and D. P. Norton, The balanced score card (figure), from "The balanced scorecard – measures that drive performance," p. 76, from *Harvard Business Review* January-February, 1990. © 1990 Harvard Business Review. Reprinted by permission of Harvard Business School Publishing.

Every effort has been made to trace copyright holders and to obtain their permission for the use of copyright material. The publisher apologizes for any errors or omissions in the above list and would be grateful if notified of any corrections that should be incorporated in future reprints or editions of this book.

About the Editors

Editor in Chief
Cary Cooper is based at Lancaster University as Professor of Organizational Psychology. He is the author of over 80 books, past editor of the *Journal of Organizational Behavior*, and Founding President of the British Academy of Management.

Advisory Editors
Chris Argyris is James Bryant Conant Professor of Education and Organizational Behavior at Harvard Business School.
William Haynes Starbuck is Professor of Management and Organizational Behavior at the Stern School of Business, New York University.

Volume Editor
John McGee is Associate Dean for the MBA Programme and Professor of Strategic Management at Warwick Business School. He has been Director of the Centre for Corporate Strategy and Change and Chair of the Marketing and Strategic Management group. He was previously at Templeton College, Oxford where he was Dean of the College, and at London Business School where he was the founding Director of the Centre for Business Strategy.

He has served on the Higher Education Funding Council Research Assessment Exercise Panels for management studies in the UK in 1996 and in 2001. He is a former President of the Strategic Management Society having been a member of its board of directors 1996–2004.

He has written extensively in the area of business economics and business strategy particularly on the evolution of industries and strategic groups analysis. His current interests are in the nature of the new information economy in which the joint effects of complexity and the pervasiveness of increasing returns create new strategic opportunities. He has also written on the emerging knowledge-based view of strategy and the implications of knowledge-intensity for the deconstruction and the reconstruction of industries and supply chains.

Contributors

Duncan Angwin
Warwick Business School

Stephanos Avgeropoulos
formerly of Imperial College, London

Michael Brocklehurst
Imperial College, London

Derek F. Channon
Late of Imperial College, London

Benita Cox
Imperial College, London

Gary Davies
Manchester Business School, University
of Manchester

Peter Dempsey
Rossmore Dempsey & Co.

Dorothy Griffiths
Imperial College, London

Alan Harrison
Cranfield School of Management

Ed Heard
Rossmore Dempsey & Co.

K. G. (Ben) Knight
Warwick University

Kevin Jagiello
Manchester Business School, University of
Manchester

Kaye Loveridge
Imperial College, London

John McGee
Warwick Business School

Gordon Mandry
Manchester Business School

Jonathan Menuhin
Hebrew University, Jerusalem

David Norburn
Imperial College, London

Taman Powell
Warwick Business School

Richard Schoenberg
Imperial College, London

Susan Segal-Horn
Open University Business School

Chris Smith
University of Adelaide

Joe Tidd
University of Sussex

David Wilson
Warwick Business School

acquisition strategy

Richard Schoenberg

Acquisition provides a rapid means of gaining an established product market position. Compared to the alternate routes for achieving growth or diversification, acquisitions overcome the relatively long time scales and potential resource constraints of internal development and do not involve the dilution of control inherent within STRATEGIC ALLIANCES.

Acquisitions may be a particularly attractive means of corporate development under certain strategic and financial conditions. In mature industries containing a number of established players, entry via acquisition can avoid the competitive reaction that can accompany attempts to enter the industry by internal development: rather than intensifying the rivalry by adding a further player, the potential competition is purchased. In other industries in which COMPETITIVE ADVANTAGE is held in assets built up over considerable periods of time, for example the back-catalogues in the record or film industries, acquisitions can immediately achieve a market position that would be virtually impossible to develop internally. The Japanese electronics company Sony, for example, has achieved this with its acquisition of CBS Records and Columbia Pictures.

Financially, acquisitive growth may be particularly attractive to a quoted company if its price : earnings ratio is relatively high compared to that of potential target companies. Under such circumstances an acquisition funded by shares may provide an immediate earnings per share enhancement to the acquiring firm. A further stimulus to the acquisition boom of the late 1980s in the UK was the existence of accounting standards that permitted acquirers to offset the goodwill element of an acquisition's cost against reserves rather than treating it as an asset that had to be depreciated over time, reducing future stated profits.

The importance of acquisitions is evidenced by the volume of activity. In 1994, US companies spent in excess of $222 billion on domestic acquisitions and a further $24 billion on cross-border transactions. Comparative figures for companies within the European Union (EU) are $67 billion and $60 billion, respectively (data source: *Acquisitions Monthly*). However, acquisitions are not without their risks: empirical studies have consistently shown failure rates approaching 50 percent, regardless of the criteria used.

A study by McKinsey and Company revealed that 43 percent of a sample of international acquisitions failed to produce a financial return that met or exceeded the acquirer's cost of capital (Bleeke and Ernst, 1993). Non-financial studies show little improvement over John Kitching's (1974) early finding that between 45 percent and 50 percent of acquisitions are considered failures or not worth repeating by the managements involved. Further support comes from Michael Porter's (1987) examination of the diversification record of large US firms over the period 1950–86. He found that 53 percent of all acquisitions were subsequently divested, rising to 74 percent for unrelated acquisitions.

As one would expect given this performance record, a significant amount of research has been conducted to examine the factors determining acquisition success or failure (see Haspeslagh and Jemison, 1991: 292–309 for a concise review of the research literature). Two key success criteria emerge. First, there must be clear opportunities to create value through the acquisition and, second, the acquired company must be effectively integrated into the new parent in a way that takes account of both strategic and human considerations. Each is discussed in turn below.

The purchase price of an acquisition typically includes a bid-premium of 30–40 percent over the previous market value of the target company. Premiums of that order in general make it difficult for acquisitions to be a financial success for the acquiring company. Many acquisitions fail because the perceived benefits of increased market share and technological, manufacturing, or market synergies fail to increase profit margins or raise turnover by the amount necessary to justify the price paid to conclude the deal. Acquisitions can only be justified in cases in which the post-merger benefits have been solidly defined. In order to successfully create value through acquisition, the future cashflow stream of the acquired company has to be improved by an amount equal to the bid-premium, plus the often overlooked costs incurred in integrating the acquisition, and the costs incurred in making the bid itself. Four basic value-creation mechanisms are available to achieve this:

1   *Resource sharing*, in which certain operating assets of the two merging companies are combined and rationalized, leading to cost reductions through economies of scale or scope. (The British pharmaceutical company Glaxo planned to save $600 million annually following its acquisition of Wellcome by combining headquarters operations, rationalizing duplicated R&D facilities onto selected sites, and adopting a single sales force in overlapping product areas.)

2   *Skills transfer*, in which value-adding skills such as production technology, distribution knowledge, or financial control skills are transferred from the acquiring firm to the acquired, or vice versa. Additional value is created through the resulting reduction in costs or improvement in market position. The effective transfer of functional skills involves both a process of teaching and learning across the two organizations, and therefore tends to be a longer-term process than resource sharing. Nevertheless, it is often the primary value-creating mechanism available in *cross-border* acquisitions, in

which the opportunities to share operational resources may be limited by geographic distance. For example, in its acquisition of the Spanish brewer Cruz del Campo, the drinks company Guinness planned to recoup the acquisition premium by using its marketing expertise to establish Cruz as a major national brand in the fragmented Spanish market.

3   *Combination benefits*. These are size-related benefits such as increased market power, purchasing power, or the transfer of financial resources. A company making a large acquisition within its existing industry, or a series of smaller ones, may succeed in raising profit margins by effecting a transformation of the industry structure. The emergence of a dominant player within the industry should reduce the extent of competitive rivalry, as well as providing increased bargaining power over both suppliers and customers for the acquiring company. The European food processing industry, for example, has consolidated rapidly through acquisitions, driven both by a desire to reduce competitive rivalry and by a belief that larger brand portfolios will help to maintain margins in the face of increasing retailer concentration. Financially based combination benefits may be available. The superior credit rating of an acquirer may be used to add value by refinancing the debt within an acquired company at a lower interest rate. In other instances in which the acquired company has been a loss-maker prior to acquisition, the associated tax credits can be consolidated to the new parent, thereby reducing the latter's tax charge.

4   *Restructuring* is applicable when the acquired company contains undervalued or underutilized assets. Here, acquisition costs are recouped by divesting certain assets at their true market value, and by raising the productivity of remaining assets. The latter may be accomplished by closing down surplus capacity, reducing head office staff, or rationalizing unprofitable product lines. Very often the two elements are combined: for example, the closure of surplus capacity may lead to a vacant factory site which can then be sold off at a premium for

redevelopment. A further form of restructuring is the concept of "unbundling." This involves acquiring an existing conglomerate (or other portfolio of businesses) the market value of which is less than the sum of the individual constituent businesses. The businesses are then sold off piecemeal, creating a surplus over the acquisition cost. Restructuring is essentially financially based, in that it does not require any strategic capability transfer between the two firms. Rather, the skill of the acquirer is in recognizing and being able to realize the true value of the targets' assets. A classic illustration of value creation through restructuring is Hanson plc's acquisition of the diversified tobacco company Imperial. Hanson paid $5 billion for Imperial and within a year had sold off its food and brewing interests, along with its London head office, for $3 billion, leaving it with the core tobacco business that generated 60 percent of Imperial's previous profits for only 40 percent of the acquisition cost.

The presence of value-creating opportunities does not in itself guarantee a successful acquisition. Plans have to be effectively implemented before the benefits can be realized in practice. This is the second area in which acquisitions frequently fail. In many instances organizational issues block the ability of the acquirer to create the planned value. Key personnel may depart following the acquisition, clashes of organizational culture may lead to mistrust and lack of communication, or inappropriate control systems may hinder the efficiency of the newly acquired firm.

Haspeslagh and Jemison's (1991) comprehensive study of the acquisition process has highlighted the fact that the appropriate form of post-acquisition integration will depend on two principal characteristics of the acquisition. First, the value-creation mechanism(s) will determine the degree of *strategic interdependence* that needs to be established between the two companies. Resource sharing and skills transfer imply high to moderate strategic interdependence respectively, while combination benefits and restructuring imply little or no interdependence. Second, the extent to which it is necessary to maintain the autonomy of the acquired company in order to preserve its distinctive skills will determine the need for *organizational autonomy*. Where critical employees are loyal to a distinctive corporate culture, as in many service businesses, it may be important to preserve that culture post-acquisition. Consideration of these characteristics suggests the appropriate form of post-acquisition strategy, as illustrated in figure 1.

Effective implementation also depends on creating an atmosphere of mutual cooperation following the acquisition. Resource sharing, skills transfer, and, to a lesser extent, combination benefits all create value through the transfer of strategic capabilities between the acquiring and acquired firms. Because of the high degree of change often involved, and the uncertainty likely to be felt by employees on both sides following the acquisition, it is critical that the acquirer works to create an overall atmosphere that is conducive to the required capability transfer. Haspeslagh and Jemison (1991) argue that there are five key ingredients to such an atmosphere:

Need for strategic interdependence

		Low	High
	High	Preservation	Symbiosis
Need for organizational autonomy			
	Low	Holding	Absorption

Figure 1   Types of acquisition integration approach (Haspeslagh and Jemison, 1991)

Table 1   Types of acquisition integration approach

Absorption integration	The aim is to achieve full consolidation of the operations, organization, and culture of both companies, ultimately dissolving all boundaries between the acquired and acquiring firms.
Symbiosis integration	The acquiring company attempts to achieve a balance between preserving the organizational autonomy of the acquired company while transferring strategic capability between the two organizations.
Preservation integration	The acquired organization is granted a high degree of autonomy, typically positioned within the acquiring organization as a stand-alone subsidiary.

1   *Reciprocal organizational understanding.* In order to work together effectively, both companies need to understand each other's history, culture, and management style. This two-way learning process is particularly important in the context of skills transfer, as the acquirer must insure that the source and origins of the sought-after skills are not inadvertently destroyed during the integration process.

2   *Willingness to work together.* Employees of both companies may have a natural reluctance to cooperate together post-acquisition. Fears over job security, changes in management style, or simple distrust of the new organization may all hinder the willingness to work together. Research suggests that the negotiation stage of an acquisition can play an important role in creating an atmosphere of cooperation. Successful implementation is more likely where there is a clear vision of the future, assurances are maintained, and concern is shown for the people involved. Post-acquisition, reward and evaluation systems also can be used to encourage cooperation.

3   *Capacity to transfer and receive the capability.* In order for skills transfer to occur, it has to be possible to accurately identify and define the skills and to actually effect their transfer. In some smaller acquisitions, for instance, it may prove difficult to transfer the acquirer's control and reporting systems, as the receiving management does not have the time both to collect substantial amounts of additional data and continue to run its business as before.

4   *Discretionary resources.* Managements need to keep in mind that acquisitions frequently

take up more managerial resource than was planned initially. Once a fuller understanding of the newly acquired company is developed post-acquisition, new opportunities and problems will often emerge that require managerial time and attention.

5   *Cause–effect understanding of benefits.* Finally, the correct atmosphere for implementation can only be generated when there is a clear understanding of how value will be created through the acquisition. Those involved in the value-creation process must understand the benefits sought and the costs involved in achieving them. The detailed knowledge about these two elements may be held at different organizational levels. Executive management will have conceptualized the benefits of acquisition, but operating management who will conduct the day-to-day implementation frequently hold the knowledge about the associated costs. Open communication between those charged with planning and implementing the acquisition becomes critical. Value can only be created when the acquisition benefits outweigh the implementation costs.

See also *post-acquisition integration*

Bibliography

Bleeke, J. and Ernst, D. (eds.) (1993). *Collaborating to Compete: Using Strategic Alliances and Acquisitions in the Global Marketplace*. New York: John Wiley.

Cartwright, S. and Cooper, C. (1992). *Mergers and Acquisitions: The Human Factor*. Oxford: Butterworth-Heinemann.

Haspeslagh, P. and Jemison, D. (1991). *Managing Acquisitions: Creating Value through Corporate Renewal*. New York: Free Press.

Kitching, J. (1964). Winning and losing with European acquisitions. *Harvard Business Review*, **52**, 124–36.

Kitching, J. (1967). Why do mergers miscarry? *Harvard Business Review*, **45**, 84–101.

Norburn, D. and Schoenberg, R. (1994). European cross-border acquisition: How was it for you? *Long Range Planning*, **27** (4), 25–34.

Porter, M. (1987). From competitive advantage to corporate strategy. *Harvard Business Review*, May/June, 43–59.

activity-based costing

Derek F. Channon

Activity-based costing (ABC) was developed to understand and control indirect costs. It also provides management with a tool that enables them to understand how costs are generated and how to manage them. By contrast, historic cost analysis tends to allocate costs according to some arbitrary formula which often fails to truly reflect actual costs.

ABC assigns costs to products and/or customers upon the basis of the resources that they actually consume. Thus an ABC system identifies costs such as machine setup, job scheduling, and materials handling. These costs are then allocated according to the actual level of activities. All overhead costs are thus traced to individual products and/or customers, as the cost to serve all customers is far from equal.

As a result, ABC forms an integral component in the STRATEGIC PLANNING process and, unlike conventional accountancy, provides a vehicle for assuming future costs rather than purely measuring past history. It allows management to identify systems, policies, or processes that operate activities and thus create cost. ABC permits management to identify actual cost drivers and address these, and so reduce fixed cost.

While ABC assigns material costs to products in the same manner as conventional accounting, it does not assume that direct labor and direct material automatically generate overhead. Rather, it assumes that products incur indirect costs by requiring resource-consuming activities, and these costs are specifically assigned rather than being estimated as a function of the direct costs.

In a traditional cost system it is usually assumed that these costs are related to volume. However, in reality some activities are not necessarily triggered by individual units but, rather, may be generated by a batch of units. For example, doubling a product's volume does not double the number of machine setups. Rather, setups are determined by the number of batches produced, and an ABC system assigns cost accordingly. Purchasing is another cost driven by batches. Traditional cost accounting allocates purchasing costs according to material cost. However, this method fails to account for the true cost of purchasing, which is directly proportional to the number of purchase orders made. ABC allocates cost according to purchase order numbers. ABC also reflects economies of scale in the factory, allocating actual costs based on setups, materials handling, warehousing costs, and the like. Such differences are illustrated in table 1.

In addition to allocating costs specifically to products, ABC assigns below-the-line costs, such as those attributable to sales, marketing, R&D, and administration. When such a sub-

Table 1 Allocation bases for traditional and ABC

Indirect cost	Traditional	ABC
Production control	Labor hours	Parts planned
Inspection	Labor hours	Inspections
Warehousing	Labor hours	Stores receipts and issues
Purchasing	Labor hours	Purchase orders
Receiving	Labor hours	Dock receipts
Order entry	Labor hours	Customer orders
Production setups	Labor hours	Production changeovers

Source: O'Guin (1991)

division is meaningful, this can be done by class or segment of customers. Usually, customer costs can vary substantially as a result of differences in the following factors:

- customer segment;
- order size;
- pre- and after-sales service levels;
- service levels;
- product size;
- distribution channel;
- geography;
- selling and marketing service .

From such an understanding of the costs to serve, management can devise policies to improve profits and reduce costs. These might operate on:

- average number of units per customer order;
- number of locations supplied;
- type and volume of sales promotions used;
- alternate pricing strategies;
- number of returns sent back;
- channels of distribution used;
- number of sales calls required;
- speed of bill payment.

An ABC system separates product- and customer-driven costs. PARETO ANALYSIS can then be used to focus on key costs on each and both dimensions concurrently, with a view to eliminating serious loss-making customer and product combinations.

Assigning Costs in an ABC System

ABC allocates all resources to either products or customers to reflect actual operations. Just as traditional accounting does this in a two-stage process, so too does ABC. However, ABC uses more cost pools and assigns costs to a wider variety of more appropriate bases. In particular, a wider choice is made of second-stage cost drivers, allowing ABC to model more complex situations in a superior way.

Activity Centers

ABC first assigns all key manufacturing and business process costs to activity centers. Being based more on actual activity measures, this analysis tends to be more rigorous than trad-

itional methods. These first-stage cost drivers are then allocated to products, as shown in figure 1. The truly differentiating feature of ABC, however, is the much greater sophistication in the treatment of second-stage drivers. Here the ABC system recognizes that many costs are not directly proportional to volume but, rather, that many are proportionate to the number of batches produced. As such, costs are assigned to batches while some, such as design engineering, are related to entire products.

Activity centers come in two groups: product-driven activity centers and customer-driven centers. Activity centers themselves are either homogeneous processes such as the punch press, machining, or assembly, or a business process such as marketing, procurement, or distribution.

Second-Stage Drivers

These are activity measures used to assign activity center costs to products or customers. In traditional cost accounting, such second-stage drivers usually consist of direct labor costs, material costs, machine hours, or other indicators of value. In ABC systems, in addition to these costs, second-stage drivers might include setup times, inspection costs, warehouse moves, sales calls, and customer orders. These drivers thus reflect how an activity center consumes cost by product and/or customers. As a result, not assigning such costs on the basis of volume can reflect the different costs of complex products or customer groups.

Hierarchical Costs

A further significant difference between ABC and traditional costing is the formal systems recognition; these costs can be stimulated at different hierarchical levels. While individual units trigger some costs, others occur at the level of the batch and even at the market segment (*see* SEGMENTATION). As a result of this recognition, ABC separates costs for management decision-making. Such hierarchical costs can also be separated by product and customer as follows.

Product-driven activities
- *Unit level*: production costs assigned once for each unit (e.g., drilling a hole).
- *Batch level*: manufacturing costs assigned once for each batch (e.g., machine setup).

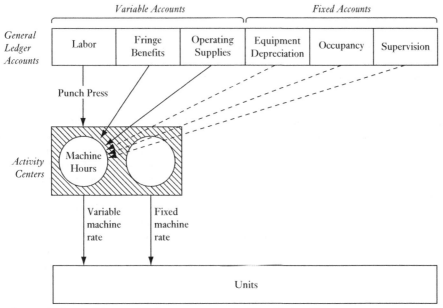

Variable Accounts   *Fixed Accounts*

By segregating the general ledger accounts flowing to parts one can create variable and fixed cost drive rates

Figure 1   Using ABC to calculate variable and fixed costs (O'Guin, 1991)

- *Product level*: costs to support the design or maintenance of a product line (e.g., product engineering and process design).

Customer-driven activities
- *Order level*: costs attributable directly to selling and delivering orders to individual customers (e.g., order entry, shipping, billing, and freight).
- *Customer level*: non-order-related costs attributable to individual customers (e.g., sales force costs, credit and collections, pre- and post-sale service costs).
- *Market level*: costs required to enter or remain in a particular market (e.g., R&D, advertising and promotion, and marketing).
- *Enterprise level*: costs required to remain in business that are unassignable to any lower level (e.g., pensions, board of management, central staff).

These might apply for higher or lower levels for a business dependent upon the cost structure of the firm; the ABC system distributes all such costs in a way that reflects actual operations.

ABC by Business Type

ABC principles have mainly been applied in manufacturing industry, but are becoming increasingly important in the service sector as cost analysis becomes an important strategic factor in a deregulated, more competitive environment.

In capital-intensive process industries, activity-based costing is very important. Many process industries utilize time-based costing as a representative of capacity utilization as a cost driver, with factors such as direct labor being assigned to a process, not a product. Process time is charged to products on the basis of machine hours. Capital costs and thus changeover costs tend to be high in process industries and should not be assigned on a volume measure such as time.

As fixed costs are so high in capital-intensive industries, high-capacity utilization is a critical determinant of business profitability. Variable pricing may well therefore be necessary and the cost of EXCESS CAPACITY needs to be calculated so that fixed costs do not incorrectly influence pricing decisions. An ABC system needs to reflect this and, in addition, the large fixed costs required to maintain the process, such as maintenance and process engineering, are annually allocated to production lines rather than being arbitrarily spread.

In some process industries, such as food and brewing, logistics costs can form an extremely large element in overall costs. Furthermore, the costs to some specific customer segments may also vary widely. Customer sales volume, location, and product mix will all affect logistics costs. This, coupled with the need for high-capacity utilization rates, can allow traditional costing systems to suggest unprofitable policies, such as the pursuit of small customers with specialist product needs. Limited production flexibility may well compound this problem. By allocating indirect costs more accurately, ABC pinpoints profitable opportunities and encourages exit from loss-making segments.

Many process industry firms actually have very primitive cost systems, offering little more than aggregate values for labor, supplies, utilities, raw materials, and the like. In addition, in many process industries the joint cost problem exists, in which a variety of products are produced as a result of a drive to produce one. ABC does not address all of these issues, and managerial decisions will need to be taken about costing system assumptions.

Service industries similarly have notoriously weak costing systems. Again, many costs (such as branch premises for a bank) are joint costs, and it may be impossible to exit part of the business without fatally damaging that part the firm wishes to retain. The use of ABC, while not providing clear answers to these problems, nevertheless identifies profitable customer and profit segments in a superior manner to traditional costing.

Designing an ABC System

The key element in designing a successful ABC system is in the choice of cost drivers. To choose these variables it is essential to identify correctly what generates activity; these activity triggers are cost drivers.

The first key principle in designing an ABC system is to keep it simple. Efforts should be concentrated on the significant costs, with the focus being on relevance rather than precision, reflecting on how the firm actually incurs cost. Moreover, many costs have no precise measures and common sense needs to be used to assign such costs in the most equitable way. Care must also be taken to avoid attempting to track every small cost, to avoid the creation of an overly expensive, complex system. All unnecessary detail increases the need for more cost drivers, which adds to the expense of designing and operating the system. Finally, keeping matters simple makes understanding easier and actually stimulates acceptance and use of the system.

Second, it needs to be recognized that each firm is somewhat individual and that the nature of costs may vary widely from company to company. As a result, different cost drivers may be employed in different corporations; thus the same type of costs may be allocated using cost drivers that are not applicable to another concern.

Third, it is imperative to understand what objectives top management wishes the cost system to support. A substantial number of decisions must therefore necessarily be made before the final design is set. Such decisions affect the choice of cost drivers, the level of system complexity, and whether or not the system is to be online.

Designing the system therefore involves the following steps:

1 Develop fully "burdened" departmental costs from the general ledger.
2 Segregate costs into product-driven or customer-driven.
3 Split support departments into major functions, each of which:
   (a) has a significant cost;
   (b) is driven by different activities.
4 Split departmental costs into function cost pools.
5 Identify activity centers.
6 Identify first-stage cost drivers.
7 Identify second-stage cost drivers on the basis of:
   (a) available data;
   (b) correlation with resource consumption;
   (c) effect on behavior.
8 Identify activity levels.

9 Choose the number of cost drivers on the basis of:
   (a) system use;
   (b) company complexity;
   (c) available resources.

ABC provides a new insight into the true profitability of products and customers by allocating indirect costs in a much more realistic way than traditional costing systems. As a result, product and customer profitability is often shown up in stark relief and in a new way, causing significant rethinking of policies and overall corporate strategy. This is especially true in industry sectors which historically have not really been required to compete vigorously. New technologies and deregulation are transforming competitive conditions in many industries, and this is leading to widespread efforts to incorporate this alternate means of costing.

Bibliography

Cooper, R. (1988). The rise of activity-based costing, part one: What is an activity-based costing system? *Journal of Cost Management* (Summer).

Cooper, R. (1990). Implementing an activity-based costing system. *Journal of Cost Management* (Spring).

Cooper, R. and Kaplan, R. S. (1991). Profit priorities from activity-based costing. *Harvard Business Review*, **69**, 130–5.

O'Guin, M. C. (1991). *The Complete Guide to Activity-Based Cost*. Englewood Cliffs, NJ: Prentice-Hall, chs. 2, 3, 4.

Rotch, W. (1990). Activity-based cost in service industries. *Journal of Cost Management* (Summer).

Turney, P. B. B. (1989). Activity-based costing: A tool for manufacturing excellence. *Target* (Summer).

advantage matrix

Derek F. Channon

During the 1970s, the Boston Consulting Group recognized that the GROWTH SHARE MATRIX had a number of limitations, in that an underlying experience effect (*see* EXPERIENCE AND LEARNING EFFECTS) was not always present and that differentiated products need not be as price-sensitive as undifferentiated or commodity products. As a result, the advantage matrix was developed, as shown in figure 1. In this system four generic environments were identified on the basis of the potential size of COMPETITIVE ADVANTAGE that could be generated, and the number of ways in which a competitor could establish a leadership position within an industry.

VOLUME BUSINESSES, STALEMATE BUSINESSES, FRAGMENTED BUSINESSES, and

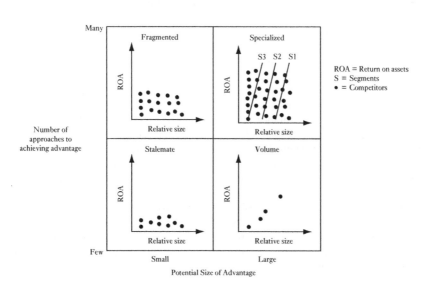

Figure 1 The BCG advantage matrix (Boston Consulting Group)

SPECIALIZED BUSINESSES are identified within this system. As shown in figure 1, only in volume businesses does the historic experience effect analysis tend to hold. In specialized businesses a relationship also exists between size and profitability within specific but different segments. In stalemate and fragmented businesses, size *per se* does not necessarily determine relative cost. Despite the BCG's modification of the growth share matrix for portfolio planning, the revised matrix is much less well known and, regrettably, the deficiencies of the original concept remain insufficiently discussed.

Bibliography

Boston Consulting Group (1974a). *Segmentation and Strategy*. Boston: Boston Consulting Group.

Boston Consulting Group (1974b). *Specialization*. Boston: Boston Consulting Group.

Rowe, A. J., Mason, R. O., Dickel, K. E., Mann, R. B., and Mockler, R. J. (1994). *Strategic Management*, 4th edn. Reading, MA: Addison-Wesley, pp. 119–22.

agency theory

Stephanos Avgeropoulos

Agency theory deals with situations in which one party (the "principal") delegates responsibility to another party (the "agent") to take decisions on its behalf. Typical agency relationships exist between shareholders and managers, employers and employees, professionals such as lawyers, doctors, or investment advisers and their clients, and elected politicians or civil servants and citizens. Delegation does not need to be explicit, and this brings into the scope of agency a wider range of transactions, such as insurance contracts, where the insurer delegates responsibility to the insured to reduce the likelihood and/or cost of the insured event occurring. Variations include multiple principals and/or multiple agents.

The establishment of an agency relationship typically increases total utility. Nevertheless, several costs are involved, including the costs of drawing up, monitoring, and enforcing the contract. Jensen and Meckling (1976) classified agency costs as follows: (1) monitoring costs, incurred by the principal to regulate the agent's behavior (including the use of incentive schemes designed to induce the agent to act in the way in which the principal would act if he/she had the information available to the agent, and also the costs of organizing multiple agents to act in unison); (2) bonding costs, incurred by the agent to assure the principal that he will not take inappropriate actions; and (3) the residual loss, which is the loss to the principal due to actions by the agent which the principal would not have undertaken (or would have undertaken differently, or actions which the principal would have undertaken but the agent did not) if he/she had the agent's information. Overall, agency costs are affected by the respective utility functions of the principal and the agent, including their risk attitudes, and the degree to which information asymmetries prevail, and a trade-off exists between monitoring costs and the residual loss.

Information asymmetries obstruct effective delegation in two principal ways. In the first case, the agent may hold information before the contract is drawn up which, if known by the principal, would influence the latter's choice. Such private information (often the rationale behind the delegation in the first place) can be withheld by the agent to increase his/her own utility from the contract. In the second case, the principal cannot accurately observe the agent's actions, either because these are difficult to distinguish from environmental factors, or because the agent again withholds information. These two cases of pre- and post-contractual difficulties are known as the hidden information (adverse selection) and hidden action (moral hazard) problems, respectively.

An important agency relationship of interest is the contract of shareholders (residual risk bearers/beneficial owners) with management (risk takers/those exercising control). In this case, shareholders may have goals such as profit maximization or value maximization, subject to a minimum level of security against variability, while management may, in addition to the above, value high levels of discretionary expenditure, sales maximization, "empire building," cost minimization, accumulation of power and prestige, promotion, and stress and effort minimization. There may be situations in which shareholders may be sufficiently dispersed so as to make the formulation and implementation of a coherent shareholder utility function difficult, in which case the agents are likely to find it easy to pursue their own objectives.

A poorly structured relationship of this sort may lead to high rates of corporate growth if managers pursue practices such as "empire building" and budget maximization; DIVERSI-FICATION, as a means of achieving growth or to reduce corporate and personal risk; allocative inefficiency, as a result of suboptimal firm size (*see* EFFICIENCY); or productive inefficiency, if, for example, an executive uses a more expensive airline at company expense to take advantage of a frequent flier scheme, the benefits of which accrue to himself personally. Shareholders can reduce the likelihood and extent of such behavior by modifying managers' interests to converge to their own, by such methods as share option and profit sharing schemes.

Most interesting in this context is the historical development and role of pension funds, mutual funds, and other like vehicles. As advances in transportation made distant markets more accessible and new technologies encouraged firms to pursue ECONOMIES OF SCALE and diversify, so firms' size and capital requirements increased. Close family or joint-stock arrangements became increasingly unsatisfactory, and stock had to be offered to a broader range of investors of increasingly lower affluence. While investors in general welcomed traded stock as a savings method that offered particu-larly good liquidity, smaller investors could only buy into few companies and found the risk of doing so too great.

As a result, intermediary vehicles such as the above started to manage portfolios of stocks on behalf of those investors who entrusted them with their funds. Beneficial stock ownership became separated from the exercise of the associated voting power (Berle and Means, 1932), and it was up to the fund managers to insure that corporate management was adequately supervised. This they did not always do, although they were capable of it, and they often preferred portfolio-based risk reduction to active involvement in the affairs of the companies. It was only recently that competition between funds started to squeeze managements to perform better, contributing to the "short-termism" of which they are sometimes accused.

Bibliography

Berle, A. A., Jr. and Means, G. C. (1932). *The Modern Corporation and Private Property*. New York: Macmillan/Commerce Clearing House.

Grossman, S. and Hart, O. (1983). An analysis of the principal and agent problem. *Econometrica*, 51, 7–46.

Jensen, M. C. and Meckling, W. H. (1976). Theory of the firm: Managerial behavior, agency costs and ownership structure. *Journal of Financial Economics*, 3, 305–60.

Williamson, O. E. (1964). *The Economics of Discretionary Behavior: Managerial Objectives in a Theory of the Firm*. Englewood Cliffs, NJ: Prentice-Hall.

balanced scorecard

Derek F. Channon

A critical element in successful strategy implementation is an appropriate management control system. Many systems do not provide the critical information required by management to assess the corporation's progress to achieving its strategic vision and objectives. The balanced scorecard is a performance measurement system developed by Kaplan and Norton which, although including financial measures of performance, also contains operational measures of customer satisfaction, internal processes, and the corporation's innovation and improvement activities, which are seen as the key drivers of future financial performance. The approach provides a mechanism for management to examine a business from the four important perspectives of:

- How do customers see the firm? (*customer perspective*)
- What does the firm excel at? (*internal perspective*)
- Can the firm continue to improve and create value? (*innovation and learning perspective*)
- How does the firm look to shareholders? (*financial perspective*)

The system also avoids information overload by restricting the number of measures used so as to focus only on those seen to be essential. The balanced scorecard presents this information in a single management report and brings together often disparately reported elements of the firm's strategic position such as short-term customer response times, product quality, teamwork capability, new product launch times and the like. Second, the approach guards against suboptimi-

zation by forcing management to examine operation measures comprehensively.

The system requires management to translate their general MISSION statements for each perspective into a series of specific measures that reflect the factors of critical strategic concern. A typical scoreboard is illustrated in table 1.

The precise scorecard design should reflect the vision and strategic objectives of the individual corporation. The key point is that the scorecard approach puts strategy and corporate vision rather than control as the key element of design and is consistent with the development of CORPORATE TRANSFORMATION techniques, cross-functional organizations, and customer–supplier interrelationships.

BUILDING THE BALANCED SCORECARD

While each organization is unique, to improve acceptance and commitment to the revised measurement system, a number of companies have sought to involve teams of managers in the design of their scorecards. This also insures that line management create a system that reflects their needs, in contrast with traditional systems, which tend to be control-driven by finance and accounting specialists. A typical scorecard design project might involve the following stages:

1 *Preparation*. Strategic business units (SBUs) should be selected for which a scorecard measurement system is appropriate. These should have clearly identifiable customers, production facilities, and financial performance measures.

2 *Interviews: first round*. Each senior SBU manager is briefed on the approach and provided with documents on the corporate

Table 1 The balanced scorecard

Goals	Measures	Goals	Measures
Financial perspective		*Customer perspective*	
Survival	Operating cashflow	New product	Percentage of sales from new products
Success	Quarterly sales growth and operating income by SBU	Speed of response	Customer measure of on-time delivery
Future prosperity	Increase market share; increase productivity; reduce capital intensity	Preferred supplier	Customer ranking survey; customer satisfaction index Market share
Internal business perspective		*Innovation and learning perspective*	
Higher productivity	Value added per employee	Technology leadership	New product design time; patent rate versus completion
	Waste as % output		No employee suggestions
	Capital intensity; machine utilization rate	Product focus efficiency	Percentage of products equal to 80% of sales; revenue per employee
Design productivity; new product introduction	Engineering efficiency – actual versus scheduled; time to market	Employee motivation	Staff attitude survey

Source: Kaplan and Norton (1990)

vision, mission, and strategy. A facilitator interviews the senior managers to obtain their views and suggestions, as well as a number of key customers to learn about their performance expectations.

3 *Executive workshop.* The top management team is brought together to begin the development of an appropriate scorecard which links measurements to strategy.

4 *Interviews: second round.* The output of the workshop is reviewed and consolidated and views are sought about the process of implementation.

5 *Executive workshop: second round.* A second workshop is then held with senior managers together with their direct subordinates and a larger group of middle managers to design the appropriate measures, link them to any change programs under way, and to develop an implementation plan. Stretch targets should also be developed for each measure, together with preliminary action programs

for their achievement. The team must also agree on an implementation program, including communication to employees, integrating the scorecard in management philosophy, and developing an appropriate information system.

6 *Implementation.* A newly formed team develops an implementation plan for the scorecard, including linking the measures to databases and information systems, communicating the system through the organization, and facilitating its introduction.

7 *Periodic review.* The scorecard should be constantly reviewed to insure that it meets the needs of management.

Bibliography

Gouillard, F. J. and Kelly, J. N. (1995). *Transforming the Corporation.* New York: McGraw-Hill.

Kaplan, R. S. and Norton, D. P. (1990). The balanced scorecard: Measures that drive performance. *Harvard Business Review*, January/February, 71–9.

Kaplan, R. S. and Norton, D. P. (1993). Putting the balanced scorecard to work. *Harvard Business Review*, September/October, 134–47.
Kaplan, R. S. and Norton, D. P. (1996). *The Balanced Scorecard*. Boston: Harvard School Press.

barriers to entry and exit

Stephanos Avgeropoulos

One of Porter's five forces (*see* INDUSTRY STRUCTURE), barriers to entry are strategies or circumstances that protect a firm from competition by making new entry difficult, or by putting potential entrants at a disadvantage. Viewed another way, barriers to entry can be considered to be the additional costs that a potential entrant must incur before gaining entry to a market. Bain (1956: 3–5) argues that entry barriers should be defined in terms of any advantage that existing firms hold over potential competitors, while Stigler (1968: 67–70) contends that, for any given rate of output, only those costs that must be borne by the new entrants but that are not borne by firms already in the industry should be considered in assessing entry barriers. The main effect of barriers to entry is that they may keep the number of companies competing in an industry small, and allow incumbents to earn supernormal profits in the long term. For them to be effective, they must, in principle, increase costs for the challenger more than they do for the incumbent.

Viewed from their function as entry-deterrent conditions, there are three broad categories of activities that lower the threat of entry, namely, structural obstacles to entry, risks of entry, and reduction of the incentive for entry. Seen from another dimension, barriers to entry can exist naturally (e.g., natural monopolies), or they can be the result of specific action by the company concerned (although this latter distinction is sometimes misleading, as competing in a naturally monopolistic industry may well be the result of strategic decision). Finally, barriers can generally be classified as either dependent on or independent of size.

SIZE-INDEPENDENT STRUCTURAL BARRIERS

Size-independent cost conditions include: government subsidies, tariffs, and international trade restrictions (anti-dumping rules, local content requirements, and quotas); regulatory policies; licensing; special tax treatment; restrictions on price competition; favorable locations; proprietary information; proprietary access to financial resources, raw materials, and other inputs; proprietary technologies, know-how, or proprietary low-cost product design; EXPERIENCE AND LEARNING EFFECTS; and proprietary access to distribution channels and markets.

To constitute credible barriers, the above need to be defensible and to continue holding in the long term. They can be obtained by encouraging government policies that raise barriers by means of trade protection, economic regulation, safety regulation (product standards and testing, plant safety, or professional body membership or accreditation requirements), or pollution control. Barriers can also be set up: by limiting access to raw materials; by exclusive ownership of the relevant assets or sources; by, for example, purchasing assets at pre-inflation prices; by tying up suppliers (by means of contracts, for example, and also by convincing them that it is risky to take on products that lack consumer recognition); by raising competitors' input costs (e.g., by avoiding passing on scale economies through suppliers and bidding up the cost of labor if they are more labor-intensive); by foreclosing alternate technologies (and obliging challengers to take defenders head-on); by investing in the protection of proprietary know-how (by means of patents, secrecy, etc.); by blocking channel access; by raising buyer SWITCHING COSTS and the costs of gaining trial (e.g., by targeting the groups most likely to try other products with discounts); or, finally, by molding of customer preferences and loyalty (e.g., through advertising and promotional activities that increase the costs that the new entrant will have to incur to attract customers), by filling product or positioning gaps, and by brand proliferation (which reduces the MARKET SHARE that will become available to the new entrant).

SIZE-DEPENDENT STRUCTURAL BARRIERS

In addition, depending on the size of the firm, other barriers may become available. ECONOMIES OF SCALE and minimum efficient scale effects, for example, force the aspiring entrant to come in on a large scale (with all the risks and costs this entails, particularly if incumbents are unable to accommodate the new entrant and are thus expected to retaliate), or accept a cost disadvantage. In addition, the absolute size of the required investment in certain industries and the fact that such investment may have to be made up front, and can be unrecoverable, limits the pool of potential entrants and may act as a deterrent for smaller potential entrants.

To make use of these barriers, scale economies can be pursued in production, if feasible. They can also be pursued in marketing and R&D, and it is in those areas where they are likely to be a more readily available tool as scale thresholds are largely determined competitively. Similarly, although the amount of capital necessary to compete in an industry is not controlled by the firm, it is possible to increase it by methods such as raising the amount of financing available to dealers or buyers, or employing more investment-intensive technologies (see INVESTMENT INTENSITY).

RISKS OF ENTRY

Once a company has decided that it can find ways in which to circumvent such barriers, it has to consider how risky its prospective industry is, and how easy it will be to survive there.

In principle, there are three industry characteristics that are said to affect this. High industry concentration makes incumbents more powerful, high investment intensity can raise the cost of failure (it may bear the risk of further financial demands, or it can simply make the firm more prone to technological obsolescence), and, finally, high advertising intensity can also act as a deterrent because of the brand loyalties and switching costs involved.

Nevertheless, high concentration is also an indication of a profitable or new industry, high investment intensity can allow the technological innovator to leapfrog incumbents, and high advertising intensity may similarly be a tool to be exploited to enter concentrated markets. As a result, there are few industry characteristics that can be depended upon as effective barriers to entry.

Instead, it may be more effective to indicate to prospective entrants that their efforts will be contested (see SIGNALING). For such indication to be effective, the incumbent must show that there are good causes for not accommodating the entrant and that the incumbent is able to fight. Upon entry, the strategies to be deployed against the new entrant must also be determined.

Starting from a consideration of the credible signals that the incumbent can use to indicate his/her intention to defend, the most effective deterrent is to make combat unavoidable upon entry (this is the most committing, and also the riskiest way, as the potential entrant may be stronger). This can be done by foreclosing or raising the cost of one's own exit routes, by means of matching competitor guarantees or anything else that increases the economic need to maintain share, such as the setting up of high fixed-cost operations, or the building up of EXCESS CAPACITY. Slow industry growth makes such signals even more credible, as it implies that the entrant cannot be accommodated without serious loss of share.

On a less committing level, any known particular threat can be delayed by signaling incipient barriers, such as by early announcement of product launches or capacity expansion.

As far as the ability to fight is concerned, the maintenance of a healthy financial state may act as a good deterrent, as well as an indication that the firm is able to expand output, cut prices, and the like.

Some methods that can be employed before entry to prepare for combat involve the establishment of blocking positions. These are for use mainly against prospective entrants that are established in other industries, but which are likely to move into the defender's markets. Protection may be achieved by setting up small business units in the main markets of such competitors, so that conflict can be threatened in those markets too, with only limited losses for the defending firm but more extensive ones for the prospective challenger. In addition, preemption can be used: this involves obtaining and maintaining a head start in critical projects that any prospective entrant would have to undertake, the size of the head start being marginally greater than the incumbent's response delay.

The response of the firm immediately upon entry is also significant. At this time, the challenger is likely to be very sensitive to new information, and its confidence dependent on early results. Causing uncertainty can help in such situations, and this can be done by disrupting test or introductory markets with high but erratic levels of marketing and sales promotion activity. Being able to introduce a new product just after a competitor has entered with an imitation of earlier products can also set him/her back, and the threat of legal action can also raise the risks, costs, and uncertainty involved, and delay entry. In any case, putting on a good defense even against entrants that are not considered particularly harmful can be useful in establishing a good track record that may help to prevent further attacks.

Finally, the role of pricing is deemed to require special attention. In principle, the threat of a price war would normally be expected to act as a deterrent, particularly in an industry with excess capacity or slow growth. Upon closer consideration, however, there may appear to be no reason for prices to be used as an entry barrier, as they can be changed easily, allowing the incumbent to enjoy high profits before entry and still be able to fight entrants with lower prices once they have entered the market. Nevertheless, limit pricing can be used to signal a cost function that is difficult to imitate, and it allows prices to act as a deterrent for higher-cost producers, at the cost of sacrificing short-run profits in order to maximize long-run profits (Salop, 1979). Having said that, however, lowering prices after entry does not necessarily indicate anticompetitive strategies, as it may be done simply to accommodate a new entrant.

Lowering the Inducement for Attack

Another method of preventing entry is to make the industry itself appear uninviting. It is difficult to deceive potential rivals completely, but some shaping of their expectations and information regarding future and current profitability may well be possible. To this effect, it is well worth publicizing realistic industry growth forecasts if it is suspected that potential challengers may be overestimating the industry's prospects, and also to make some effort to disguise large profits, as they are highly visible.

As a solution of last resort, poison pill strategies or licensing of a proprietary technology when a competing technology appears may also be effective.

Barriers to Exit

Barriers to exit are the activities and circumstances that commit a firm to its industry and its position within it.

Typical exit barriers may take the form of specialized assets, vertical integration (*see* VERTICAL INTEGRATION STRATEGY), long-term contracts with suppliers or buyers, or interrelationships and synergies (*see* SYNERGY) with other businesses, which would be adversely affected should the business unit in question be shut down.

The higher the exit barriers are, the more costly it is to abandon a market, so the stronger the incentive will be for firms to remain and compete as best they can. As a result, the barriers to exit of established firms imply that any potential entry will be contested and, as such, also act as barriers to entry for prospective entrants.

Bibliography

Bain, J. S. (1956). *Barriers to New Competition*. Cambridge, MA: Harvard University Press.

Harrigan, K. R. (1981). Barriers to entry and competitive strategies. *Strategic Management Journal*, **2**, 395–412.

Porter, M. E. (1979). How competitive forces shape strategy. *Harvard Business Review*, **57**, 2, (March/April), 137–45.

Porter, M. E. (1980). *Competitive Strategy: Techniques for Analyzing Industries and Competitors*. New York: Free Press.

Porter, M. E. (1985). *Competitive Advantage: Creating and Sustaining Superior Performance*. New York: Free Press.

Salop, S. C. (1979). Strategic entry deterrence. *American Economic Review*, **69**, 335–8.

Stigler, G. J. (1968). *The Organization of Industry*. Chicago: University of Chicago Press.

benchmarking

Derek F. Channon

In the late 1970s, the Xerox Corporation woke up to the fact that its Japanese competitors were selling copiers at prices at which Xerox could sometimes not manufacture. After realizing this, Xerox set out to understand why and to learn, from its competitors, concepts such as VALUE ENGINEERING and TEAR DOWN. Xerox also began to learn from competitors about other best practice techniques (*see* BEST PRACTICES). This has developed into the now widely practiced methodology of benchmarking, and has been extended to all elements of a business.

There are usually around ten generic categories for designing benchmarking architecture:

- customer service performance;
- product/service performance;
- core business process performance;
- support processes and services performance;
- employee performance;
- supplier performance;
- technology performance;
- new product/service development and innovation performance;
- cost performance;
- financial performance.

In designing a benchmark architecture, the first step is to design a system that enables management to achieve the organization's strategic objectives.

Second, it is necessary to create a common language for measuring performance. This should be consistent with the corporate culture.

Third, it is necessary to develop plans to collect, process, and analyze the performance measures. It is likely that while the organization possesses much of the data needed, it is not in a useful form to encourage management action. The information is collected to reflect the organization's position on a radar chart (sometimes called a "spider chart"; *see* RADAR MAPPING).

In addition to careful design of the benchmarking system architecture, other critical success factors include:

- top management support;
- benchmarking training for the project team;
- suitable management information systems;
- appropriate information technology;
- internal corporate culture;
- adequate resources.

The precise process used for benchmarking varies from company to company according to internal culture and needs. The process adopted by one of the pioneering US corporations, Xerox, used one of the more comprehensive systems, which involves 12 steps divided into five phases, and is illustrated in table 1.

Successful implementation of benchmarking systems favors simplicity. The system recommended by the Strategic Planning Institute Council on Benchmarking advocates a five-step

Table 1   The Xerox 12-step benchmarking process

Step	*Description*
Phase 1 – planning	
1	Identify what to benchmark
2	Identify comparative companies
3	Determine data collection method and collect data
Phase 2 – analysis	
4	Determine current performance gap
5	Project future performance levels
Phase 3	
6	Communicate findings and gain acceptance
7	Establish functional goals
Phase 4 – action	
8	Develop action plans
9	Implement specific actions and monitor progress
10	Recalibrate benchmarks
Phase 5 – maturity	
11	Attain leadership position
12	Fully integrate practices into processes

Source: Bogan and English (1994: 82)

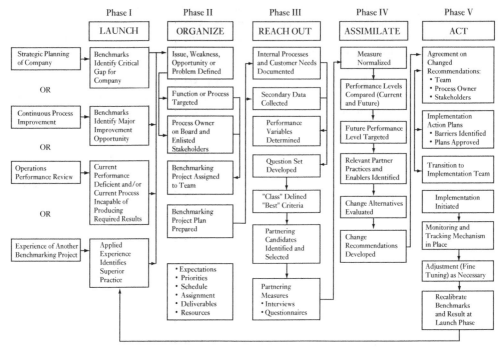

Phase I	Phase II	Phase III	Phase IV	Phase V
LAUNCH	ORGANIZE	REACH OUT	ASSIMILATE	ACT
Strategic Planning of Company	Benchmarks Identify Critical Gap for Company	Issue, Weakness, Opportunity or Problem Defined	Internal Processes and Customer Needs Documented	Measure Normalized	Agreement on Changed Recommendations: • Team • Process Owner • Stakeholders
OR		Function or Process Targeted	Secondary Data Collected	Performance Levels Compared (Current and Future)	
Continuous Process Improvement	Benchmarks Identify Major Improvement Opportunity	Process Owner on Board and Enlisted Stakeholders	Performance Variables Determined	Future Performance Level Targeted	Implementation Action Plans • Barriers Identified • Plans Approved
OR		Benchmarking Project Assigned to Team	Question Set Developed	Relevant Partner Practices and Enablers Identified	Transition to Implementation Team
Operations Performance Review	Current Performance Deficient and/or Current Process Incapable of Producing Required Results	Benchmarking Project Plan Prepared	"Class" Defined "Best" Criteria	Change Alternatives Evaluated	Implementation Initiated
OR			Partnering Candidates Identified and Selected	Change Recommendations Developed	Monitoring and Tracking Mechanism in Place
Experience of Another Benchmarking Project	Applied Experience Identifies Superior Practice	• Expectations • Priorities • Schedule • Assignment • Deliverables • Resources	Partnering Measures • Interviews • Questionnaires		Adjustment (Fine Tuning) as Necessary
					Recalibrate Benchmarks and Result at Launch Phase

Figure 1   The benchmarking process

process. This is illustrated in figure 1. These phases are explained in the following subsections.

PHASE I: LAUNCH

The launch phase requires management to decide which improvement areas have the greatest impact or potential for the corporation. These usually flow from the STRATEGIC PLANNING process, from an analysis of the corporation's internal and external best practices. Continuous monitoring should also be undertaken to identify opportunities for improvement in CORE PROCESS functions and businesses.

PHASE II: ORGANIZE

In this phase, benchmarking projects to a clear focus, a benchmarking project team is organized, and a project plan is developed.

PHASE III: REACH OUT

During the third phase the benchmarking team reaches out to understand its own and other organizations' processes. This involves:

- documentation of the process to be studied, based on customer needs;
- collection of secondary data;
- determination of variables by which to evaluate performance;
- design of a questionnaire through which to solicit performance information, both from within the corporation's own operations and from external corporations;
- collection of data;
- selection of benchmarking partners;
- on-site visits to the best-performing partners.

PHASE IV: ASSIMILATE

Best practice information is assimilated and prepared for a report for top management. Data gathered are normalized, performance gaps identified, future performance goals targeted, and implementation for changes recommended.

PHASE V: ACT

In this final phase the benchmarking team works with senior management and core process owners to develop an agreed implementation program. This leads to the development of formalized action plans, implementation schedules measurement and monitoring systems, and benchmark recalibration plans. Once this has been done, responsibility passes to an implementation benchmarking team.

Benchmarking not only is a tool in its own right, but also forms an essential component in reengineering projects (*see* REENGINEERING DISADVANTAGES; VALUE-DRIVEN REENGINEERING). The integration between these two activities is illustrated in table 2.

Bibliography

AT&T (1992). *Benchmarking: Focus on World-Class Practices*. AT&T.

Bogan, C. E. and English, M. J. (1994). *Benchmarking for Best Practices: Winning through Innovative Adaptation*. New York: McGraw-Hill.

Garvin, D. (1993). Building a learning organization. *Harvard Business Review*, 71, 78–91.

McNair, C. J. and Leibfried, K. H. J. (1992). *Benchmarking*. New York: HarperCollins.

PIMS (1993). *Benchmarking. PIMS Letter on Business Strategy*, No. 54. PIMS Europe Ltd.

Walleck, S. A., O'Halloran, D., and Leader, C. A. (1991). Benchmarking and world-class performance. *McKinsey Quarterly*, 1, 3–24.

Xerox Corporation (1987). *Leadership through Quality: Implementing Competitive Benchmarking*. Xerox Corporation Booklet, Part 1.

best practices

Derek F. Channon

This was an activity related to BENCHMARKING which formed part of the Work Out process in the US General Electric Company (GE). Historic success had led to a degree of complacency in the company and, as part of his radical campaign to modify the culture of GE, Jack Welch instituted a program of effectively benchmarking GE against a carefully selected group of companies that were also seen as excellent in terms of management practices. Nine companies, including seven major US corporations and two leading Japanese multinationals, participated in a year-long study to identify these concerns' best practices. The main findings of the

Table 2 Integrating benchmarking and reengineering

Seven-step reengineering process	Tools applied
Step 1. Identify the value-added, strategic processes from a customer's perspective.	Performance benchmark analysis (cost, quality, cycle time, etc.). Customer satisfaction benchmark analysis. Value analysis.
Step 2. Map and measure the existing process to develop improvement opportunities.	Flowcharting and process management tools. Performance measurement tools.
Step 3. Act on improvement opportunities that are easy to implement and are of immediate benefit.	Informal benchmarking for short-term solutions. Implementation planning tools.
Step 4. Benchmark for best practices to develop solutions, new approaches, new process designs, and innovative alternatives to the existing system.	Best practice benchmarking among processes and performance systems.
Step 5. Adapt breakthrough approaches to fit your organization, culture, and capabilities.	Process redesign tools. Implementation planning tools.
Step 6. Pilot and test the recommended process redesign.	Training, and pilot test techniques. Apply lessons learned from past successful pilots.
Step 7. Implement the reengineered process(es) and continuously improve.	Train employees. Implementation techniques. Use benchmarking to maintain continuous improvement process.

study were that these highly productive concerns exhibited the following characteristics:

- They managed processes rather than people.
- They used process mapping and benchmarking to identify opportunities for improvement. This involved writing down every single step, no matter how small, in a particular task.
- They emphasized continuous improvement (*see* KAIZEN) and praised incremental gains.
- They relied on customer satisfaction as the main measure of performance, so overcoming the tendency to focus on internal goals at the customer's expense.
- They stimulated productivity by introducing a constant stream of high-quality new products for efficient manufacturing.
- They treated suppliers as partners.

Bibliography

Tichy, N. M. and Sherman, S. (1993). *Control Your Own Destiny Or Someone Else Will*. London: HarperCollins, p. 205.

bidding tactics

Duncan Angwin

Launching a bid is a very expensive exercise in terms of fees to professional advisers. Experts can include investment banks, commercial banks, equity houses, lawyers, accountants, and PR advisers. How these experts are used depends upon the nature of the bid, the expertise of the protagonists, and the national/international context. The success or failure of the bid can have very widespread ramifications for all stakeholders and directly affects adviser and management credibility.

Essentially, the bidder needs to persuade the target's shareholders that it is able to produce better performance from the target company than the current management. This gives rise to *puffing* and *knocking copy*. The bidder will embark on a vigorous campaign of propaganda designed to puff up its own management abilities and knock those of the target management team. This will involve formal presentations, circulars,

and "wining and dining" key institutional shareholders, influential analysts, and financial journalists. A good example from the UK of the importance of managing the media was the acrimonious bid by Granada for Trusthouse Forte. The bid was launched on the day that the Granada group knew that Rocco Forte was on holiday, shooting game. With immediate media attention, and no one to put the Forte case, newspapers polarized the two CEOs in terms of Granada's Jerry Robinson as an industrious working-class hero versus Forte's Rocco Forte as an aristocratic hobbyist. This unjust image of Rocco Forte did considerable damage to his defense campaign.

During the 1980s, the degree of aggressive campaigning led to a string of sensational newspaper advertisements proclaiming the virtues of each position, to the extent that there are now regulations in place to tone down such campaigns.

DEFENDER TACTICS

Defense may be about trying to preserve the independence of the company or just insuring that the best price is paid. There are numerous tactics that can be used, but countries have different restrictions upon their usage.

- *Revaluation of assets*: Assets, especially property, can quickly become undervalued in companies' accounts; revaluing to a realistic level can force the bidder to raise its offer. Other types of asset, particularly intangibles, have been a particular focus of attention.
- *Improving profit forecasts*: Incumbent managements will almost certainly proclaim that they are able to produce higher levels of profit than before and will issue forecasts to this effect. There are strict rules about such forecasts, and financial advisers have to be very careful in agreeing to these new estimates. Clearly, some managements may have credibility problems in this respect, although it is worth noting the unusual case in the UK of Sketchley, the dry cleaning company, which, when approached by an unwelcome bidder, decided to show that the company was a great deal worse than the bidder anticipated – the bidder withdrew.

- *Crown jewels*: Where the bid is made for one particular asset within a business, then the sale of this asset removes the threat upon the whole business. As an example, in 1982 the American Whittaker Corporation (AWC) made a bid for the Brunswick Corporation. The latter sold its crown jewel, Sherwood Medical Industries, and AWC then withdrew.
- *Pac-man*: Although common in the US, this is rare in the UK. Nevertheless, this strategy (named after the video game), was recently employed by two breweries in the Midlands. The idea is that the target firm launches a counter-bid for the acquirer.
- *White knight*: As a last resort, the target may seek an alternative bidder who may offer a higher price, or retain the existing management.

Other tactics that may be considered, depending upon the country, are: restrictive voting rights; dual-class stocks; employee share ownership; leveraged recapitalization; poison pill; and greenmail.

See also *acquisition strategy*

Bibliography

Angwin, D. N. (2001). Mergers and acquisitions across European borders: National perspectives on pre-acquisition due diligence and the use of professional advisers. *Journal of World Business*, Spring.

Angwin, D. N. (2003). Strategy as exploration and interconnection. In S. Cummings and D. Wilson (eds.), *Images of Strategy*. Oxford: Blackwell, ch. 8.

Cartwright, S. and Cooper, C. (1996). *Acquisitions: The Human Factor*. Oxford: Butterworth-Heinemann.

blind spots

Derek F. Channon

In a remarkable number of cases, firms fail to recognize changes in competitive conditions which may severely impact their strategic position. Frequently, such blind spots fail to identify the nature of SUBSTITUTE PRODUCTS, or the entry of new competitors that may bypass the existing industry cost structure by adopting new ways of competing. These may enjoy dramatic advantages, thus negating possible historic cost positions in a stable INDUSTRY STRUCTURE achieved by high MARKET SHARE. Indeed, high market share positions may actually become a positive disadvantage, because to respond to such an attack, firms may be forced to transform the elements that had gained them their traditional COMPETITIVE ADVANTAGE.

Areas in which blind spots have been particularly common have been in newly deregulated industries, those in which channel shifts are possible and in which information technology provides the possibility of gaining substantial cost advantages. Classic examples of such blind spots would include the Merrill Lynch Cash Management Account, a product carefully designed to avoid being classified as a banking product, but in practice offering a comprehensive series of banking services, including checking, credit card, and brokerage management, and paying a superior rate of interest on all account balances. As a result, consumers withdrew their deposits from savings and loans banks and from commercial banks in the US to open such accounts, while still using these institutions for most of their personal transactions. Initially not recognizing the new form of competition, the savings and loan banks found that the cost of their deposits had risen so much that they were forced to take on increasingly risky property projects to cover their increased cost of deposits, such that by the end of the 1980s many had been forced to close, leaving the US taxpayer to pick up the bill of several hundred billion dollars.

Channel shifts have also occurred in a number of industries. IBM was forced to make dramatic price cuts in the early 1990s and to introduce a fighting brand in personal computers. As prices tumbled and new channels opened, it became impossible for IBM to retain its high-cost personal selling approach. Instead, first, companies such as Amstrad began to sell IBM-compatible machines at a deep discount to IBM through consumer electronics retail outlets. Second, new entrants such as Dell Computer opened direct marketing at an even lower cost than using retailers. As a result, IBM was forced to close its own retail outlets, cut back on its sales force overhead, and add a direct sale fighting brand.

Similarly, in Europe oil companies have dramatically lost their share of retail gasoline sales to superstores and hypermarkets. Faced with serious overcapacity, low-share oil companies were happy to supply the superstores with product, and sold increasingly under the store brand name rather than that of the oil companies. The large-share oil companies, with their heavy investment in retail gasoline outlets, have thus seen their market shares eroded by competitors able to lock in cost advantages on what for them was a marginal product.

The impact of information technology can be seen in the insurance industry where, for motor and household insurance, direct writing has transformed the industry. Traditional insurers, especially those with high market shares achieved by sales through brokers, have again been placed on the horns of a dilemma. Unable to compete because of the margins demanded by the brokers, the insurers have only reluctantly opened direct writing subsidiaries themselves for fear of alienating their traditional channels.

The careful assessment of industry boundaries, both at present and as they may be in the future, is therefore a critical element in achieving sustainable competitive advantage. The careful avoidance of blind spots is an essential ingredient in this analysis.

branding

Derek F. Channon

Branding is often viewed by consumers, both personal and institutional, as an important determinant in the purchase decision. As such, brand can add value to a product and also to its parent company. For example, products such as perfumes and cosmetics are priced heavily on the basis of brand – similar products in unbranded bottles would not command a fraction of the price. Indeed, undifferentiated products, such as vodka, can command brand-based price differentials of up to 40 percent, despite the fact that the leading brand may be chemically indistinguishable from a store private-label brand.

Today, branding has been successfully applied to almost everything, although not always with success. Furthermore, channel brands have grown significantly in importance, to the detriment of manufacturer brands. Successful brand names can also be valuable franchise properties. Name and character licensing has thus become a business valued at many billions of dollars. Clothing and accessories producers are the largest users of licensing, with fashion leaders such as Cardin, Gucci, and the like using their names to brand a wide variety of merchandise from luggage to cosmetics, in addition to clothing. Virgin is perhaps one of the widest-ranging examples of brand stretch. Having started in recorded music, Richard Branson's company initially moved into air transportation, music and computer games, stores, and cinemas, and later into soft drinks and liquor and mutual funds – many of these activities having apparently little or no relationship with one another.

Products such as toys, games, and food are also often linked back to names and characters such as Walt Disney, Power Rangers, and Jurassic Park. These tie-in linkages can often be an important ingredient in the overall economics of specific projects and enterprises. Such franchise and brand extension strategies can become key components of brand-based strategies. Harley Davidson, for example, originally the largest producer of US "heavy" motorcycles, now sees the motorcycle as essentially the ultimate fashion accessory! Today, the company franchises its name to a wide range of casual clothing, toys, motorcycle accessories, and so on.

Brand names and positioning are important strategic decisions. Successful brand development may take many years and, once developed, requires constant and steady investment. Ironically, the accountancy treatment of brands is ambiguous. Many accountants would argue that, as an intangible, a brand has no balance sheet value. Nevertheless, the value of many mergers and acquisitions has been decided on the purchaser's idea of the underlying value of brands to be acquired; as for example, in the purchase of Rowntree by Nestlé.

Among the required qualities of brand names are: (1) the need to suggest some of a product's benefits or attributes; (2) easy pronunciation (one-syllable words tend to be best, e.g., Mars, Daz, Lux, Crest); (3) a distinctive quality, such as in Firebird, Fiesta, and Canon; and (4) ease of translation into other languages, as in the case of Sony, Coca-Cola, and Shell.

Branding has also become important in institutional markets. For example, in financial services, maintenance products, and manufactured goods, products increasingly are named rather than being given a specification number.

The cost of brand support tends to be high in most markets. Unless a strong brand position can be achieved in a company's served market, therefore, a proprietary brand strategy must be questioned. Normally, unless a number one or two market position is achievable, lower-share competitors might consider exiting or becoming private-label suppliers.

Bibliography

Davidson, H. (1987). *Offensive Marketing*. Harmondsworth: Penguin, pp. 293–304.

Kotler, P. and Armstrong, G. (2004). *Principles of Marketing*, 10th edn. Upper Saddle River, NJ: Prentice-Hall.

break-even analysis

Derek F. Channon

The break-even point chart (figure 1, p. 24) shows the total cost and total revenue expected at different levels of sales volume.

For each product there is a variable cost which, when deducted from the sales value, generates a contribution. The variable cost itself can be disaggregated to identify its individual constituents. In addition, to support the product there are a number of costs which are not volume-dependent but, rather, are fixed, as shown. The volume level of sales at which the sum of unit product contributions equals the fixed cost plus the variable costs is the break-even point, as illustrated. For most businesses, there is also a desired level of profitability. This is illustrated as volume B, at which the difference between total revenue and total costs represents the profit impact target. Analysis of the chart enables management to also readily identify which cost items make up most of total expenditure, how much reduction could be made to these, and which expenses are controllable and which are not. Care should be taken in the allocation of fixed costs. Some costs which were previously considered to be fixed can be made variable by adopting techniques such as reengineering (*see* ACTIVITY-BASED COSTING; BUSINESS PROCESS REENGINEERING; REENGINEERING DISADVANTAGES; VALUE-DRIVEN REENGINEERING).

In calculating the break-even and target profits it is also important to check what these volumes represent in terms of MARKET SHARE. Such a share position should be both obtainable and sustainable at an acceptable level of cost. Frequently, firms do not undertake this check. Where substantial share gains are required to be made to achieve break-even, careful assessment should be made that this is in fact achievable. Similarly, sensitivity analysis should be undertaken on price to assess the impact on contribution margins and the consequent effect on break-even volume and market share.

Bibliography

Nagashima, S. (1992). *100 Management Charts*. Tokyo: Asian Productivity Organization, pp. 30–1.

business model

John McGee

This is a widely used term intended to provide the link between an intended strategy, its functional and operational requirements, and the performance (typically cash flows and profits) that is expected. It usually applies to single businesses where a specific COMPETITIVE STRATEGY can be identified, but it can also apply to those multibusiness portfolios that are linked by strong synergies (*see* SYNERGY) and therefore have common or similar strategies.

Chesbrough and Rosenbloom (2002) cite their experience in turning up 107,000 references to "business model" on the worldwide web while finding only three citations in the academic literature. In the usual practitioner sense, a business model is the method of doing business by which a company can sustain itself – that is, generate revenue. The business model spells out how a company makes money by specifying where it is positioned in the value chain (*see* VALUE CHAIN ANALYSIS). A more precise

24 business model

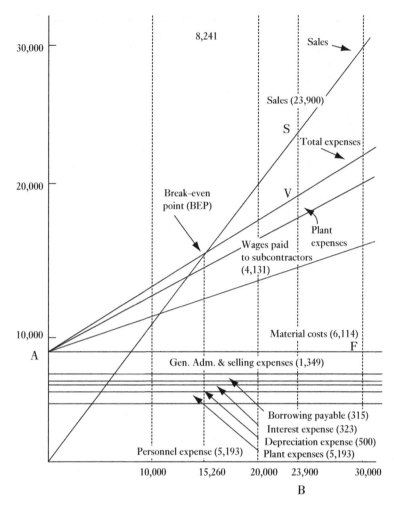

Figure 1 The break-even point chart (Nagashima, 1992)

definition has been offered by consultants KM Lab (2000): " 'business model' is a description of how your company intends to create value in the marketplace. It includes that unique combination of products, services, image and distribution that your company carries forward. It also includes the underlying organization of people and operational infrastructure that they use to accomplish their work."

Chesbrough and Rosenbloom (2002) describe the functions of a business model as:

1 to articulate the value proposition;
2 to identify a market segment (*see* SEGMENTATION);

3 to define the structure of the value chain;
4 to estimate the cost structure and profit potential;
5 to describe the position of the firm within the supply chain;
6 to formulate the strategic logic by which the firm will gain and hold advantage.

The simple Du Pont accounting identities are a good starting point for identifying a business model. Thus,

$$p = (p - c)Q - F$$

and

$$NA = WC + FA$$

where p is profits, p is price, c is variable costs, Q is quantity, F is fixed costs, NA is net assets, WC is working capital, and FA is fixed assets.

An intended strategy should have specific effects on the variables in these equations. For example, a cost leadership strategy would be expected to reduce variable costs, to increase fixed costs, and to increase fixed assets – according to the ECONOMIES OF SCALE available. Accordingly, profits and return on investment (p/NA) will be expected to increase because the rise in fixed costs and fixed assets due to the investment will be more than offset by the increase in contribution margin ($p - c$). A more ambitious business model might also specify a price reduction that will result in a volume increase through the medium of a high price elasticity and no imitation by competitors. The validity of such an assumption about lack of competitor response depends on judgments about competitor cost levels and their willingness to sacrifice margin for volume.

Similarly, a differentiation strategy would be expected to raise both costs and prices. Costs would go up because of the variable costs (such as quality and service levels) and fixed costs (such as advertising and R&D) of differentiation. Prices would be expected to increase disproportionately if the value to customers was sufficiently high to make the product price inelastic. This business model then calls for a higher margin game offset to some degree by higher fixed costs. A more ambitious model might also aim for a volume increase on the basis of higher product "value" stimulating demand (a rising demand curve rather than a negatively sloped one).

What the business model does is to articulate the logic of the intended strategy in terms of the specific operations that have to take place. With this detailed plan the consequences for cash flows can be determined and the link between (intended) strategy and (expected) performance can be established.

Beyond the obvious benefit of quantifying the strategic logic of the firm, the business model also enables sensitivity testing and risk analysis. In the case of the cost leadership example, the intention might be to reduce variable costs by a target percentage. The implications of a shortfall in cost reduction can easily be calculated and expressed in terms of the percentage change in profits in relation to a given percentage shortfall from the target cost reduction. Where the business model calls for price changes, the implications of competitor imitation or non-imitation can also be calculated.

In practice a business model can be articulated in terms of detailed plans and budgets that provide guidance to managers relating to their operational responsibilities. The logic that drives plans and budgets lies within the business model.

Bibliography

Chesbrough, H. and Rosenbloom, R. S. (2002). The role of the business model in capturing value from innovation: Evidence from Xerox Corporation's technology spin-off companies. *Industrial and Corporate Change*, 11 (3), 529–55.

Hax, A. C. and Majluf, N. S. (1984). *Strategic Management: An Integrative Perspective*. Englewood Cliffs, NJ: Prentice-Hall, ch.11.

KM Lab (2000). www.Kmlab.com/4Gwarfare.html, June 20.

Yip, G. (2004). Using strategy to change your business model. *Business Strategy Review*, 15, 2 (Summer), 17–29.

business process reengineering

Taman Powell

Business process reengineering (BPR) is an idea that grew into a fad in the early 1990s. It was started by Michael Hammer's paper (1990) and book (Hammer and Champy, 1993) on the topic. In the book, BPR is defined as "the fundamental rethinking and radical redesign of business processes to achieve dramatic improvements in critical contemporary measures of performance, such as cost, quality, service and speed."

The logic behind BPR is that many organizations are not organized in an efficient manner. They are functionally structured with many handoffs and no entity other than the CEO responsible for the end-to-end process. This disorganized approach is due to organizations evolving over time and processes evolving with them in a piecemeal manner. This occurs without anyone taking a holistic view and determining whether or not the way processes are performed makes sense.

While information technology (IT) is generally seen as the panacea for inefficiency, Hammer and Champy argue that the implementation of IT systems is largely disappointing as they tend to mechanize old ways of doing business, and therefore result only in minor improvements. Instead what is needed is a complete rethink of how the business's operations are managed.

Hammer and Champy (1993) point to the following as principles for BPR:

- Several jobs are combined into one.
- Workers make decisions.
- The steps in the process are performed in a natural order.
- Processes have multiple versions, i.e., processes are designed to take account of different situations.
- Processes are performed when it makes the most sense, e.g., if the accounting department needs pencils, it is probably cheaper for such a small order to be purchased directly from the office equipment store around the block than to be ordered via the firm's purchasing department.
- Checks and controls are reduced to the point where they make economic sense.
- Reconciliation is minimized.
- A case manager provides a single point of contact at the interface between processes.

Hybrid centralized/decentralized operations are prevalent, e.g., through a shared database decentralized decisions can be made while permitting overall coordination simply through information sharing.

From a practical standpoint, BPR is generally approached in three steps:

1   mapping of existing processes;
2   developing new processes; and
3   implementing new processes.

Some would argue that the first step should be skipped to remove the risk of contaminating the new process development by knowledge of the current approach.

Developing the new processes was generally seen as the key challenge in a BPR project. People were tasked with "discontinuous think-ing – of recognizing and breaking away from the outdated roles and fundamental assumptions that underlie operations" (Hammer, 1990), and with developing fresh new ways of operating.

Increasingly, it was realized that implementing the new processes posed the greatest challenge for BPR. It was popularly asserted that 80 percent of BPR projects failed to meet their objectives. The principal reason for this failure was neglecting people and the change process. Even Hammer noted that in hindsight he should have paid more attention to the people factors. BPR invariably resulted in massive changes to organizations. The improvements in efficiency brought about by BPR also often resulted in large redundancies. Soon BPR came to be seen as synonymous with redundancies and in turn was strongly resisted by many employees.

The other key criticism of BPR was leveled by Michael Porter (1996). He claimed that the improved efficiency brought about through BPR was a necessary but insufficient condition for success. He makes the claim that strategy is about being different from competitors, and BPR effectively focuses only on a single dimension. When all firms focus on this dimension, the level of differentiation is reduced. Additionally, there is a limit to the level of cost savings that can be achieved. This is not to say that EFFICIENCY is not important, just that efficiency is not the solution to strategy.

See also *reengineering disadvantages*

Bibliography

Hammer, M. (1990). Reengineering work: Don't automate, obliterate. *Harvard Business Review*, 68 (4), 104–12.
Hammer, M. and Champy, J. (1993). *Reengineering the Corporation: A Manifesto for Business Revolution*. New York: HarperCollins.
Porter, M. E. (1996). What is strategy? *Harvard Business Review*, 74 (6), 61–78.

business reengineering disadvantages

see REENGINEERING DISADVANTAGES

cartel

Stephanos Avgeropoulos

Producers in almost every industry face risks and uncertainties that have an adverse impact on profitability. Some of these risks are associated with the activities of competitors, so it may be possible to reduce them by overt or tacit cooperation between producers on such matters as the determination of prices and output, the marketing of new products or services, and so on. Such cooperation, if extensive, is called collusion, and the organizations that take part in it are said to be members of a cartel.

Cartels are quite distinct from oligopolies, as an oligopoly simply refers to the population of an industry by only a few competitors, for whatever reason, while a cartel is the result of conscious collusive activity in order to take advantage of opportunities for cooperation. Nevertheless, the two are interrelated, as cartels are difficult to institute and operate in non-oligopolistic environments.

METHODS

There are a number of methods of coordination, and collusion may be overt, as in the Organization of the Petroleum Exporting Countries (OPEC), or tacit, as in independently devised modes of behavior or price leadership models, whereby, for example, promises to match prices or advance price notifications insure uniformity without any communication taking place between the colluding organizations.

Turning to methods of sharing the market and the profits that it generates, a cartel can be, in principle, either profit maximizing or market sharing. A profit-maximizing cartel attempts to maximize the aggregate profits of all firms, and makes the same price and output decisions as the

multiplant firm, equating the cartel's overall marginal cost with the industry's marginal revenue. The distribution of the market between the firms is determined by marginal cost considerations, and agreement is reached between firms as to the redistribution of profits, with the firms producing most of the output (the lowest-cost ones) making payments to higher-cost firms in order to reduce the incentive of the latter to expand their output. Market-sharing cartels, on the other hand, allow each firm to maintain a set segment of the market, defined in terms of either MARKET SHARE or geographic area. The segment of the market that each firm is allowed is specified by reference to a host of factors, including historic shares and the power of each firm inside the cartel.

REQUIREMENTS FOR SUCCESS

In order for a cartel to remain successful, it must insure that it is able to defend its market from all possible threats, including the power of buyers and suppliers (*see* INDUSTRY STRUCTURE), the threat from SUBSTITUTE PRODUCTS, and the threat of entry (*see* BARRIERS TO ENTRY AND EXIT).

In addition, a cartel faces the requirement to keep its members under the terms of their agreement, so it must insure that each considers itself better off as part of the cartel than outside it. The reason why this may be difficult is that cartel-operated markets face inelastic demand (*see* ELASTICITY), so firms have an incentive to expand output beyond their allowed quotas, as this would be expected to increase their individual profitability. Precisely because demand is inelastic, limited cheating has little impact on prices, but extensive cheating can destroy the cartel. As a result, each firm will only have an incentive to cheat as long as it expects others not to cheat much; and it would prefer to keep overall cheating to low levels, as dismantling of the cartel and return to competitive conditions would be expected to make each firm worse off.

With these broad requirements in view, there are a number of factors that can enhance the stability of a cartel. These include: (1) conditions of economic and industrial growth, as a booming market can allow firms to expand output without breaching any agreement; (2) a small number of firms in the industry/cartel, as the more firms there are, the more difficult it is for cheating to be identified and exposed; (3) a slow pace of product and process innovation, as the faster this is, the more negotiations will have to be carried out; (4) similarity in producers' cost functions, as the more similar (or symmetrically differentiated) these are, the simpler coordination and the establishment of a single price will be; (5) the marketing of necessity types of products, as products facing inelastic demand do not significantly reduce profitability when prices are raised; (6) the marketing of homogeneous products, as this simplifies coordination by reducing it to the price dimension only; (7) the marketing of a small number of products, this also aiding monitoring and enforcement of the agreement; and (8) the availability of price information, to provide early warning signs of cheating.

IMPLICATIONS, DANGERS, AND BENEFITS

Cartels have significant implications in three main respects, namely, the relative power of their members and, more importantly, allocative and productive EFFICIENCY.

An immediate impact of cartel organization is that weaker firms become more important than they would be under competitive conditions. This is because every single member, whether large and profitable or small and otherwise insignificant, is able to expand output and threaten the integrity of the entire cartel. As a result, the importance of any single firm for the cartel no longer depends on its market share or profitability, as it would under competitive conditions, but on its ability to upset the delicate balance of the cartel. Therefore, larger members find it worthwhile to gain the cooperation of the smaller ones by allowing them a greater share of the market and profits than they would be able to obtain in competitive conditions.

Turning to efficiency considerations, it can be said, in principle, that collusion and cartels are undesirable, and they are often illegal too, although some survive, especially those that operate across national boundaries. The undesirability of cartels is largely based on the fact that collusion reduces the forces of competition. Cartels constrain production below the socially optimal levels, and raise prices. This transfers wealth from consumers and society to the members of the cartel, which are able to earn supernormal profits in the long run. The result is that allocative efficiency is reduced, and less of the product than is socially optimal is produced and consumed.

Restrictive practices also reduce productive efficiency. As cartel members face little competition and they are able to earn excess profits irrespective of their efforts to optimize their processes, their incentive to produce cheaply and effectively is reduced.

In addition, because of the unstable nature of such organizations, their members have to be prepared for the dissolution of the cartel and a return to more competitive production. As a result, they can often only agree to restrict output if they are each allowed to maintain their best facilities in operation. This means that, unless they all have plants of comparable technology and size, firms with inefficient plants may have to be allowed to produce while a more efficient plant that belongs to other firms remains idle. This would imply that the marginal cost of the cartel is higher than is otherwise necessary, so that productive efficiency is also compromised at the aggregate level.

CARTELS AND MONOPOLIES

The above arguments imply that the more a cartel restricts competition, the more undesirable it is. At the extreme, a monopoly would thus be the most undesirable industry organization. To keep the discussion in perspective, however, it is worth mentioning two characteristics of cartels that may on occasion compromise the validity of this last argument.

First, a cartel involves direct maintenance and administrative costs, such as the costs of negotiations and SIGNALING, and also indirect maintenance costs, such as the deviations from the lowest-cost production for the purposes of fairness to all members, as just described. Because monopolists have no such costs, it is possible to envisage a situation in which high coordination costs make a monopoly preferable to a cartel.

Second, the effect of cooperation on R&D and innovation must be considered. Technology-sharing cartels distribute the costs and risks of research, so it is possible that they may spend more on R&D than even a competitive industry would. Moreover, even if spending on research is not increased, the net consequence for growth and welfare may still remain beneficial because of the lower cost and enhanced rapidity of dissemination. In the long term, therefore, it is possible that collusion may speed productivity and output growth, and even reduce the cost of the growth process.

Bibliography

Baumol, W. J. (1992). Horizontal collusion and innovation. *Economic Journal*, **102**, 129–37.

Katz, M. L. and Ordover, J. A. (1990). R&D cooperation and competition. *Brookings Papers on Microeconomics*, 137–203.

Salop, S. C. (1986). Practices that (credibly) facilitate oligopoly coordination. In J. E. Stiglitz and G. F. Mathewson (eds.), *New Developments in the Analysis of Market Structure*. London: Macmillan, pp. 265–94.

cash cow

Derek F. Channon

A cash cow business is usually defined as one which enjoys a high relative MARKET SHARE in an industry in which the growth rate has slowed. Because of its high market share, in a traditional Boston Consulting Group (BCG) growth share matrix analysis such a business should enjoy a value-added cost advantage, relative to its competitors, assuming that an average 80 percent experience effect (*see* EXPERIENCE AND LEARNING EFFECTS) underpins the basic industry cost economics. Such businesses should supply the cash required to finance new businesses or STAR BUSINESSES should they need it, to develop market share while the industry growth rate is high.

Such businesses are extremely valuable, but are hard to manage. Psychologically, managers of such businesses often wish to invest the surplus cash flows that they are generating, as it is depressing for both management and workforce to run a business into decline. As a result, sophisticated control systems are usually required to insure that any surplus cash is extracted for redistribution within an industrial group.

Moreover, despite their growth share matrix positions, many cash cow businesses may not actually generate cash. There can be a number of reasons for this, including the following:

1 *Incorrect market definition.* In the early 1980s, the US General Electric Company appeared to enjoy high market share positions in the US electricals and electronics markets. However, these markets were globalizing (*see* GLOBALIZATION), and in world market terms US companies were rapidly losing ground to Japanese and other Far Eastern competitors.

2 *Inappropriate experience curve assumptions.* The positioning of a business on the growth share matrix assumes that a cost advantage is generated as a result of a high relative market share, with this term being used as a surrogate for superior cumulative production volume. This phenomenon may apply, but can also be circumvented when customers redefine the value chain (*see* VALUE CHAIN ANALYSIS) of their industry to gain lower cost structures. Japanese competitors with techniques such as JUST-IN-TIME production methods have been especially successful in achieving this; but competitors such as Dell Computer, Amstrad, and Schneider have successfully entered markets such as personal computers with substantially lower costs than the industry leader. Variations in channel strategy have been especially effective in achieving such cost gains.

3 *Exchange rate variations.* The advantage of high market share can be severely eroded by exchange rate variations. The rate of such movements has accelerated in recent years, causing dramatic changes in international prices that are impossible to match through normal improvements in relative productivity.

4 *Capital intensity variations.* Despite cost advantages that may exist as a result of high

market shares, high capital intensity businesses, especially those with high net working capital needs, are rarely attractive cash cows. This problem is exacerbated under conditions of moderate to high inflation. Moreover, competitors such as the Japanese have been highly successful at reducing capital intensity by just-in-time and work-in-progress stock turn improvements.

5 *Use as a market attack business.* A dangerous tactic, but one that is occasionally used, is to destroy the cash-generating ability of a competitor's market position by predatory pricing supported by cash flows from a successful business in a protected market. Japanese competitors have often been accused of such practices. For example, many Japanese products are often more expensive in the home market than in overseas markets, or competitors are excluded by the blocking of access to the distribution system. Kodak has therefore felt blocked in Japan by Fuji Film. This practice is also common in undifferentiated product markets, where the desire for capacity utilization will often lead to high capital intensity competition to erode margins by cutting price to fill the factories.

See also *growth share matrix*

Bibliography

Bogue, M. C. and Buffa, E. S. (1986). *Corporate Strategic Analysis*. New York: Free Press, chs. 2, 5.
Hax, A. C. and Majluf, N. S. (1984). *Strategic Management: An Integrative Perspective*. Englewood Cliffs, NJ: Prentice-Hall, ch. 7.
Henderson, B. D. (1973). *The Experience Curve Reviewed, IV: The Growth Share Matrix of the Product Portfolio*. Perspectives No. 135. Boston: Boston Consulting Group.
Lewis, W. W. (1977). *Planning by Exception*. Washington, DC: Strategic Planning Associates.

cash trap

Derek F. Channon

This refers to a business whose strategic position is such that it needs all the cash generated from operations to maintain its position. Such a business is not creating shareholder value and may actually be destroying it.

Cash-trap businesses tend to have a high level of capital intensity and limited or uncertain cash flows. The typical manufacturing company with typical growth rates and asset turnover must have a pre-tax profit of around 7 percent or the entire company becomes a cash trap. High growth and high capital intensity businesses require even higher margins. At maturity, such businesses will tend to convert themselves into cash traps. Such businesses have a tendency to accept that change cannot happen owing to difficulty in modifying corporate culture. Ironically, this attitude may create a window of opportunity for a new competitor that is not afraid to challenge the existing rules. This will almost invariably mean changing one or more aspects of product market positioning. For example, capital intensity can be reduced by OUTSOURCING, a technology bypass may negate experience curve expectations; a reconfiguration of the value chain (*see* VALUE CHAIN ANALYSIS) may be possible; and reengineering may be possible (*see* BUSINESS PROCESS REENGINEERING; VALUE-DRIVEN REENGINEERING).

In general, cash-trap businesses exhibit a low share and high capital intensity in markets with little or low product differentiation. In building defenses against cash-trap situations, it is important to recognize and evaluate the existing position realistically and to design countermeasures before the situation becomes irretrievable. Real cash traps destroy shareholder value and should either be changed, closed, or divested. Only a few high-share competitors in any product market can expect to avoid becoming a cash trap.

Bibliography

Henderson, B. (1972). *Cash Traps*. Boston: Boston Consulting Group.

chaebol **structure**

Derek F. Channon

The Korean *chaebol* is that country's near equivalent of the Japanese KEIRETSU STRUCTURE. Unlike the *keiretsu*, however, it is usually still managed at the top level by members of the founding family, and strategy is still set centrally, as in the prewar Japanese ZAIBATSU STRUCTURE. Furthermore, these concerns do not contain banking institutions within their structures; and although trading companies exist, they act mainly as exporting agencies rather than as in the SOGA SHOSHA.

The main reason for these differences is the late development of the Korean economy, in which industrialization took place mainly after the Korean War of the early 1950s. The industrial base left after the World War II period of Japanese colonialization was largely destroyed in the war, which also led to the division of the peninsula into North and South Korea.

After the war the South Korean economy was almost solely dependent upon the US for military and economic aid. Some import substitution projects were undertaken, but the then president, Mr. Sygman Rhee, was not especially interested in heavy government intervention. Nevertheless, the late 1950s saw the rapid development of the early *chaebol*, fueled by favorable import license concessions, access to scarce foreign exchange, and government properties seized from the Japanese. However, in 1960 the Rhee government was overthrown and the emerging *chaebol* were coerced to accept government guidance from the Ministry of Trade and Industry, in a similar manner to MITI in Japan. The position of the Korean government was also strengthened by its control over the banking industry. As a result, a partnership was developed between the *chaebol* and government, yielding a dramatic growth in the Korean economy from the 1960s to the present day.

In the 1970s, government concern at the rising economic dominance of the *chaebol* led to the introduction of laws to curb their growth. Some firms were pushed to reduce the level of family ownership by issuing their stocks on the capital market; tax payments and access to bank credits were also closely controlled. Some real estate disposals and divestments of subsidiaries by the leading 20 *chaebol* were also introduced by government. Nevertheless, industrial concentration by the top ten *chaebol* increased, and by the early 1980s these concerns held around a 25 percent share of Korea's manufacturing industry.

By the mid-1980s the Korean economy was heavily dependent upon the *chaebol*, and to restrict their activity would have been to enforce a slowdown in the nation's economic growth. There was, however, an increase in competition between the leading *chaebol*, as they came to compete for MARKET SHARE both at home and overseas. Moreover, after initially copying the evolution of Japanese industry in the postwar period, the companies began to develop their own competence in R&D, technology, marketing, and management skills. Development in industries similar to those behind the Japanese economic miracle, such as shipbuilding, heavy engineering, consumer electronics, and automobiles, formed the backbone of the emerging Korean economy. The changing nature of the *chaebol* also led to a reduction in government intervention and greater corporate independence. Nevertheless, the *chaebol* were not given control of the banking industry, as was the case with the *keiretsu*. By the late 1980s the top 30 *chaebol* groups held around 40 percent of the Korean market.

The Korean *chaebol* were much younger than their Japanese counterparts, which, prior to World War II, had developed as family-dominated *zaibatsu* groups following the Meiji Restoration and the subsequent industrialization of Japan. The oldest of the "big four" groups, Samsung, was created in 1938, while the remainder were mainly established in the 1950s. As a result, many were still owned by the families of their founders, with on average some 30 percent of listed company stock in their hands. This figure was relatively higher for the larger *chaebol* groups.

The family ownership patterns of the Korean *chaebol* have been classified into three types, as shown in figure 1. In the first of these types, ownership is direct and complete, with the founder and his family owning all the *chaebol* affiliated companies. In the second form, the family own a holding company which, in turn, owns affiliated subsidiaries: the Daewoo group is an example of this form. The third type enjoys interlocking mutual ownership, with the founding family owning the group holding company and/or some form of foundation which, in turn, owns the affiliated companies: this form is typified by the Samsung group. As the *chaebol*

Type 1: Direct ownership structure

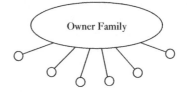

Subsidiary or affiliated companies

Type 2: Holding company structure

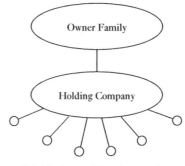

Subsidiaries or affiliated companies

Type 3: Interlocking mutual owership

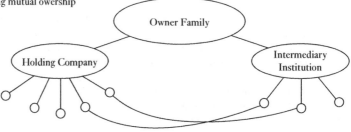

Subsidiaries or affiliated companies

Figure 1   The organizational structure of Korean *chaebols* (Hattori, 1989: 88)

evolve, the trend has been to move progressively from the first structure to the third.

While family ownership of *keiretsu* groups is generally very low, or presently nonexistent, it has been shown that more than 30 percent of the executives of the top 20 *chaebol* groups are members of the founding family. Family members thus play significant roles in the direction of the *chaebol* and, in particular, the eldest of the founder's sons is usually groomed to succeed the father when he retires. Fathers-in-law, sons-in-law, brothers, uncles, and nephews are also recruited into management.

The four leading *chaebol* are all dominated by family executives. The Samsung group has one of the highest rates of non-family member executive management, but family members still dominate the most important positions. In Hyundai the founder had seven sons, five of whom manage ten major group operations: a sixth is being groomed to succeed his father, while the founder's brother heads Hyundai Motors. In the LG group, the founder has six sons and five brothers, many of whom occupy senior positions. Daewoo, created only in 1967, is still led by its founder and, apart from his wife, no other members of the family are actively involved in management, although the future position of the founder's children is still unclear.

While family ownership is a critical factor in the management of *chaebol*, it is also important to understand that Korean tradition allows the unequal distribution of family wealth clearly in favor of the eldest son. Moreover, the Korean concept of the family is defined strictly on the basis of blood ties, whereas in Japan *zaibatsu* families could absorb non-blood-tie-related managers by adoption, marriage, or appointment. Thus, in Korea, *chaebol* successors are generally confined to family members related by blood.

In *chaebol* structures, the central office still maintains strict control over strategy and monitoring the performance of operating units. By contrast, after the elimination of the *zaibatsu* holding companies, Japanese *keiretsu* groups have a much looser system of influence over the strategies of member corporations via their presidents' councils and other integrating mechanisms.

Unlike the *keiretsu* groups, the Korean *chaebol* contain neither powerful trading companies nor significant internal financial service institutions. General trading companies within the *chaebol* only began to develop from the mid-1970s, as a result of discussions with government on how to stimulate exports. By the mid-1980s each of the major groups had created general trading companies, but the focus of these concerns was exports rather than the much wider role undertaken by the *soga shosha*. Nevertheless, by the early 1990s, the nine largest general trading companies were responsible for over 50 percent of Korean exports.

The lack of financial service institutions within the *chaebol* structure has meant that they have been forced to rely heavily on external finance to fuel their growth. In particular, they have been dependent upon government funds, which has provided the state with a major mechanism for influencing *chaebol* strategies, especially with regard to focus and diversification. Major groups have, however, been actively attempting to build their positions in the financial services sector, but these efforts are still weak by comparison with the position of the *keiretsu*.

In terms of management style, the Korean *chaebol* are more influenced by Japanese systems than by those of the West, despite the heavy US influence in the period after the Korean War and until relations with Japan were restored in the mid-1960s.

From the influences of the US and Japan, coupled with Korea's own history and traditions, Korean companies have evolved their own system of management, sometimes referred to as K-Style management. This includes top-down decision-making, paternalistic leadership, clan management, *intival* (or harmony-oriented cultural values), flexible lifetime employment, personal loyalty, seniority and merit-based compensation, and conglomerate diversification strategies.

Bibliography

Chen, M. (1995). *Asian Management Systems*. London: Routledge, chs. 12, 15.

Chang, C. S. (1988). *Chaebol*: The South Korean conglomerates. *Business Horizons*, 51–7.

Hattori, T. (1989). Japanese *zaibatsu* and Korean *chaebol*. In Kae H. Chung and Hak Chong Lee (eds.), *Korean Managerial Dynamics*. New York: Praeger, pp. 79–98.

Korean Development Institute (1982). *Ownership Structure of Korean Chaebols*. Seoul: KDI.

Lee, S. M. and Yoo, S. J. (1987a). The K-type management: A driving force of Korean prosperity. *Management International Review*, 27 (4), 68–77.

Lee, S. M. and Yoo, S. J. (1987b). Management style and practice of Korean *chaebols*. *California Management Review*, 95, 95–110.

cherry picking

Derek F. Channon

As markets mature, the opportunities to carefully segment them increase. Usually, cherry picking tends to mean that a competitor selects an upmarket segment to attack with a product/service package that is differentiable and that is perceived by customers to be superior to alternate offerings. For example, Harley Davidson motorcycles has been reborn by appealing to a particular group of dedicated enthusiasts in the US and overseas who are looking for values such as distinctiveness, individualism, and power rather than a simple means of transport. Some purchasers of expensive hi-fi systems can actually detect superior sound qualities; others buy such systems to feel good in front of their friends. Most golfers have high handicaps, but many buy expensive clubs because it makes them feel better.

Such upmarket SEGMENTATION is common and readily observed. However, it is possible to segment other market areas in which cost leadership can be combined with differentiation to achieve significant COMPETITIVE ADVANTAGE. Direct Line Insurance thus transformed the motor insurance market by offering a direct telephone service, so eliminating the need for brokers; and with a built-in cost advantage of at least 30 percent and by carefully selecting the motor risks that the company was interested in insuring, it achieved a higher level of profitability and lower risk while providing customers with lower prices and superior service quality. As a result, it has grown at over 70 percent per annum in a mature, slow-growth market.

In most markets opportunities for cherry picking exist provided that careful analysis is undertaken to identify definable segments that can be serviced in a way that creates both differentiation and sustainable competitive advantage.

Chinese family business

Michael Brocklehurst

Overseas or expatriate Chinese dominate the economies of Hong Kong, Taiwan, and Singapore and form a significant minority in economic terms in Thailand, Indonesia, Malaysia, and the Philippines. Apart from Singapore, where subsidiaries of western multinationals are very significant, the major form of business organization amongst the Chinese in these countries is the Chinese family business (hereafter CFB). Interest in the phenomenon of the CFB can be attributed to a number of factors.

First, these countries have been highly successful in terms of economic performance. This success has been achieved in a variety of different contexts vis-à-vis the state. In some cases the state has been highly supportive and interventionist, in others largely indifferent and, in some cases, even overtly hostile, to the Chinese community.

Second, on the surface at least, the CFB has achieved this success by flouting some of the nostrums of good western business practice. Firms are often small and little attention is paid to formalized management development. As Tam says: "Egalitarian employment measures, consensus decision-making, high wage homogeneity, employee empowerment and delegation are thought to be positively associated with performance. However the reverse of all these normally cherished principles is enshrined within a typical Hong Kong enterprise" (Tam, 1990: 169).

Leading on from the first and second points, there is now a growing belief that the form of business organization matters. It cannot be treated as unproblematic (as implied by early neoclassical economics). Rather, the black box, the decision-making agent, needs to be opened up and examined. Furthermore, the *context* in which the agent makes these decisions must also be considered, since such decisions are always grounded in an institutional context rather than being purely determined by market forces (Granovetter, 1985). Indeed, Whitley and Redding both argue that understanding any form of business organization (including the CFB) requires seeing it as forming part of a business system (Redding and Whitley, 1990; Whitley, 1992).

KEY FEATURES

The CFB is not coterminous with a firm. The CFB may well control a number of legally distinct firms, but it is the family that is the key decision-making unit (Tam, 1990). Nevertheless, CFBs are generally small. The structure tends to be simple and centralized on one dominant decision-maker who operates in a highly paternalist and particularist style, often bypassing middle management. Relationships and coordination are mainly hierarchic and there is little horizontal coordination. Ownership and control are usually confined to a family and business tends to be focused on a restricted range of products or markets.

Close attention is paid to cost and financial controls. COMPETITIVE ADVANTAGE is often sought by cost-cutting, by being prepared to accept low margins on a high turnover.

There are also close links with other businesses through a personalized network system (often underpinned by kinship connections). Other businesses will often contribute other elements of the value chain (components, marketing, and distribution; see VALUE CHAIN ANALYSIS) or be partners in a joint venture (see JOINT VENTURE STRATEGY) in order to reduce risk. However, each family business will retain a large degree of independence of decision-making and control. Furthermore, such arrangements are often temporary and unstable (Tam, 1990). The small scale of operation permits a high degree of strategic adaptability. However, where diversification occurs, it is generally opportunistic and undertaken to capitalize on family or network connections.

Few of the procedures covering conditions of employment are formalized or institutionalized. Recruitment and selection of non-family members is often on the basis of personal recommendation or prior acquaintance. Indeed, the use of existing employees to make recommendations insures that these employees will have a stake in the performance of the new hire. Job flexibility is the norm. Young female workers earning low wages tend to predominate in light manufacturing, textiles, and garments, particularly in Hong Kong and Taiwan (Deyo, 1989). Labor unions have little influence, partly because unions are at odds with the paternalistic ethos, and partly, in the case of Taiwan, because of state opposition.

THE INSTITUTIONAL BACKGROUND

The institutional underpinning for the CFB, which helps to explain its unique characteristics, is complex. Whitley (1992) carries a full treatment. The following aspects are of particular significance.

The state can play a number of different roles, as has already been discussed. In general, banks do not play a very significant role in the CFB; this is largely because the family wishes to retain financial control, although in Taiwan the banks have also been wary of lending to what is seen as a risky business sector.

It is also of interest to try to account for the specific values and attitudes that underpin the CFB. The key issue here is the enormous stress placed on family and kinship. The family, rather than the individual, assumes much greater importance in non-western societies as a general rule (Ferrano, 1990), but amongst the Chinese it goes even deeper; Whitley (1992) observes how this can be traced back to pre-industrial China, when the village had relatively little autonomy from the state and where very little property was held as a unit by the village; hence it was the family rather than the village that became the focus of allegiance (cf. pre-industrial Japan).

CONCLUSIONS

The high value placed on family membership is a source of both strength and weakness. On the one hand, it permits a high degree of consistency in terms of values and expected behavior of those within the business, and breeds acceptance of the paternalistic style. On the other hand, the low level of trust of non-family members inhibits the degree of delegation and restricts the size of the organization and the pool of senior managerial talent available. It also limits the loyalty that CFBs can expect from non-family employees.

The form of kinship structure, whereby family assets are equally divided amongst inheritors, and the preference for vertical over horizontal relationships, encourages fragmentation. Indeed, Wong (1985) has noted how many CFBs last for only three generations, as each brother or cousin strives to set up independently. However, this process has advantages; it insures constant revitalization and the rapid diffusion of new innovations (Tam, 1990).

In terms of long-run developments of the CFB, Deyo (1989) has noted that as CFBs move into more sophisticated sectors, training and development, and other employment practices designed to hold on to those with scarce skills, become more prevalent. Whitley (1992) observes how at present the CFB is a relatively homogeneous phenomenon compared to business systems in the UK and US, where industrialization is much more established and the system much more highly differentiated. As the CFB matures, it could be that it will become less homogeneous. Indeed, there is evidence of this in Singapore, where there is a highly qualified managerial cadre and a large multinational presence which, together, are leading to a decline in the employment of family members in the CFB (Wu, 1983).

Nevertheless, the CFB remains a powerful demonstration of how forms of business organization are embedded within a set of social institutions that make up a coherent system. Such systems sound a note of caution to those who might try to seek universal principles of managerial good practice divorced from the institutionalized context in which such practices occur.

Bibliography

Clegg, S. and Redding, G. (eds.) (1990). *Capitalism in Contrasting Cultures*. Berlin: De Gruyter.

Deyo, F. C. (1989). *Beneath the Miracle: Labor Subordination in the New Asian Industrialization*. Berkeley: University of California Press.

Ferrano, A. (1990). *The Cultural Dimension of International Business*. Englewood Cliffs, NJ: Prentice-Hall.

Granovetter, P. (1985). Economic action, social structure and embeddedness. *American Journal of Sociology*, **91**, 481–510.

Redding, G. and Whitley, R. (1990). Beyond bureaucracy: Towards a comparative analysis of forms of economic resource coordination and control. In S. Clegg and G. Redding (eds.), *Capitalism in Contrasting Cultures*. Berlin: De Gruyter.

Tam, S. (1990). *Centrifugal versus Centripetal Growth Processes: Contrasting Ideal Types for Conceptualizing the Developmental Patterns of Chinese and Japanese Firms*. Berlin: De Gruyter.

Whitley, R. (1992). *Business Systems in East Asia: Firms, Markets and Societies*. London: Sage.

Wong, S. L. (1985). The Chinese family: A model. *British Journal of Sociology*, **36**, 58–72.

Wu, Y.-Li (1983). Chinese entrepreneurs in South-East Asia. *American Economic Review*, **73**, 112–17.

Cinderella business

Derek F. Channon

Such a business is one with opportunity, but which fails to receive the resources or attention it deserves. Examples are found when such businesses are located within divisions that the corporate center has designated as mature or declining, and has therefore deprived of resources overall. In these circumstances, growth Cinderella businesses act as a threat to the existing divisional operations, as to reach their potential they require a disproportionate percentage of resources allocated to the division as a whole. In large corporations in which scale is such that small business units tend to get lost in the overall corporate structure, the position can become acute. Similarly, small-growth businesses were given little or no attention in industries such as oil when their size did not justify attention at board level and, as a result, many such DIVERSIFICATION moves by acquisition have failed.

Cinderella businesses often occur as a result of acquisition strategies (*see* ACQUISITION STRATEGY) in which firms attempt to diversify into growth markets with relatively small-scale, tentative moves, especially when moving into unrelated areas of industry. While sanctioned by the main board in large, diversified, and especially dominant business concerns (*see* DOMINANT BUSINESS STRATEGY), such moves receive little or no attention in terms of main board reporting relationships. In oil, banking, tobacco, brewing, and similar industries, diversifications by acquisition have led to the introduction of many Cinderella businesses that have received little attention from boards composed largely of executives from the original core businesses (*see* CORE BUSINESS). The problem may well be compounded by the introduction of executives from the acquiring company who have little or no understanding of the industry or needs of the small business; the imposition of parent-company bureaucratic procedures, management information, planning, and control systems inappropriate to the Cinderella organization; and the addition of overheads similar to those of the parent. As a result, many such moves have resulted in significant losses, and in some cases predator attacks on the parent concerns with a view to breaking them up and reselling the constituent businesses.

comparative advantage

Taman Powell

Comparative advantage is a term coined by the economist David Ricardo in the early part of the nineteenth century to develop the theory of international trade. But the doctrine can be applied to all forms of specialization (or territorial division of labor) and exchange, whether between persons, businesses, or nations.

Comparative advantage states that production will be maximized, and therefore everyone will be better off, if countries produce only what they have a comparative advantage in. Essentially this is a gains from specialization and trading argument. What is significant is that the argument focuses on a country's relative EFFICIENCY at production, not any absolute advantages (which would relate to a COMPETITIVE ADVANTAGE).

Let us illustrate with a simple example. Two countries, country A and country B, can each produce wine and wheat with their labor resources. For country A, it costs 15 man hours to produce a unit of wine and 30 man hours to produce a unit of wheat. For country B, it costs 10 man hours to produce a unit of wine and 15 man hours to produce a unit of wheat (table 1). This can be translated into constant units of 30 man hours (table 2).

So for country A, each unit of wheat costs 2 units of wine in terms of opportunity cost, while for country B, each 2 units of wheat cost 3 units of wine in terms of opportunity cost. Therefore, country B has a comparative advantage (versus country A) in producing wheat, since for it to produce 1 unit of wheat it foregoes the production of only 1.5 units of wine, whereas country A foregoes the production of 2 units of wine. The converse is also true in that country A has a comparative advantage (versus country B) in producing wine, since it foregoes the production of only half a unit of wheat for each unit of wine produced, while country B foregoes two-thirds of a unit of wheat.

The logic of comparative advantage would be for country A to produce only wine and country B to produce only wheat, thereby maximizing production of both products across the two countries.

There are a number of assumptions implicit in comparative advantage. Firstly, it is assumed that there is scarcity of supply, and therefore producing more of a good is beneficial. Secondly, it is assumed that the resources in each country can easily change their focus of production from one product to the other.

From a more strategic standpoint, it is also assumed that both countries are reliable in their production. If the reliability of an external country's production is doubted, and this product was important, it may be sensible for a country to continue to produce the product in which it does not have a comparative advantage to insure continuity of supply. Lastly, the comparative advantage logic also assumes that countries are aware of the accurate costing of their products. Often this is not the case (*see* ACTIVITY-BASED COSTING).

Comparative advantage is related to a number of other concepts. The reason that a country is better at producing a good than another country is to be found in the resources to which that the country has access (*see* RESOURCE-BASED VIEW). By leveraging these resources, the country is effectively focusing on its CORE COMPETENCES and OUTSOURCING the other activities. This could also be seen as the country

Table 1

	Wine	Wheat
Country A	15 man hours	30 man hours
Country B	10 man hours	15 man hours

Table 2

In 30 man hours	Wine	Wheat
Country A	2 units	1 unit
Country B	3 units	2 units

making a trade-off (*see* TRADE-OFFS) between what it does and does not want to focus on.

Bibliography

Rugman, A. L. and Hodgetts, R. M. (2003). *International Business*, 3rd edn. Upper Saddle River, NJ: Prentice-Hall, ch. 6.

competitive advantage

John McGee

In the entry on STRATEGY we draw the connection between strategy choices and profitability. There we argue that strategy choices are resource allocation decisions that enable the firm to create distinctive assets and capabilities (*see* CORE COMPETENCES; RESOURCE-BASED VIEW). These enable the firm to create imperfections in markets that are specific to itself, and therefore the firm can capture the benefits of this positioning in terms of higher prices or lower costs, or both. Figure 1 illustrates the point. A successful strategy can earn superior financial returns because it has an *unfair advantage*, that is: it creates, exploits, and defends firm-specific imperfections in the market vis-à-vis competitors. We deliberately use the term unfair advantage as a colloquial simile for competitive advantage in order to underline that such advantage is achieved in the teeth of organized opposition, both from competitors who wish to emulate the firm's success and from customers who will exercise bargaining power to achieve lower prices.

In theory, competitive advantage is the *delivering of superior value to customers and, in doing so, earning an above-average return for the company and its stakeholders*. These twin criteria impose a difficult hurdle for companies, because competitive advantage cannot be bought by simply cutting prices, or by simply adding quality without reflecting the cost premium in higher price. Competitive advantage requires the firm to be sustainably (*see* SUSTAINABILITY) different from its competitors in such a way that customers are prepared to purchase at a suitably high price. Classic perfect competition works on the basis that all products are so alike as to be commodities, and that competition takes place solely on the basis of price. The search for competitive advantage is the search for differences from competitors, and for purchase on the basis of value (i.e., the offer of an attractive performance-to-price ratio).

Competitive advantage is a statement of positioning in the market and consists of the following elements:

- a statement of competitive intent;
- outward evidence of advantage to the customer;
- some combination of:
  - o superior delivered cost position;
  - o a differentiated product;
  - o protected niches;
- evidence of direct benefits, which:
  - o are perceived by a sizable customer group;
  - o these customers value and are willing to pay for;
  - o cannot readily be obtained elsewhere, both now and in the foreseeable relevant future.

The sustainability of competitive advantage depends on the following:

- *Power*: maintaining the levels of commitments in resource terms relative to competitors.
- *Catching up*: ease of copying and nullifying the advantages.

"Real profits"

↑

Imperfections

↑

Firm-specific imperfections

↑

Distinctive assets and capabilities

↑

Strategic choices

Figure 1   Firm-specific imperfections as the source of profits

- *Keeping ahead*: productivity of one's own continuous search for enhanced or new advantages.
- *The changing game*: rate of change of customer requirements.
- *The virtuous circle*: the self-sustainability and mutual reinforcing of existing advantages.

Economists argue that competitive advantages are by their nature temporary and, therefore, decay quickly. This is to argue that product markets and the markets for underlying resources are reasonably competitive. Indeed, much of the analysis of competitive advantage is concerned with assessing just how defensible, durable, and large the advantages can be. The five forces model (Porter, 1980; *see* INDUSTRY STRUCTURE) provides a useful basis for categorizing and understanding the industry economics that lie behind competitive advantage. Notice that the barriers to entry (*see* BARRIERS TO ENTRY AND EXIT) are in essence the competitive advantages that are available in the industry. They represent the cost premiums that entrants would have to pay in order to enter the industry and compete on equal terms. In other words, these are the imperfections that the incumbents have created (or are the beneficiaries of). It is important to note that the barriers to entry may be generic, meaning that the incumbents do not have advantages over one another but have a shared advantage with a shared rent. Or the barriers may be firm-specific, implying that different incumbents are protected by different advantages and are themselves different from one another. Barriers are also entrant-specific in that different potential entrants have different assets and therefore different ways in which they might compete.

See also *national competitive advantage*

Bibliography

Besanko, D., Dranove, D., Shanley, M., and Shaefer, S. (2003). *Economics of Strategy*, 2nd edn. New York: John Wiley.

Grant, R. M. (1998). *Contemporary Strategy Analysis*, 3rd edn. Oxford: Blackwell.

McGee, J., Wilson, D., and Thomas, H. (2005). *Strategy: Analysis and Practice*. Maidenhead: McGraw-Hill.

Porter, M. E. (1980). *Competitive Strategy: Techniques for Analyzing Industries and Competitors*. New York: Free Press.

Porter, M. E. (1985). *Competitive Advantage: Creating and Sustaining Superior Performance*. New York: Free Press.

competitive market theory

John McGee

The theory of STRATEGIC MANAGEMENT was given impetus by the realization that industrial organization as a subject could be turned around to give a perspective on the rent-seeking activity of firms. This led to the notion of firms seeking market power in which rents could be protected, at least for a time, by barriers to entry (*see* BARRIERS TO ENTRY AND EXIT). These barriers were derived from the cost functions of firms, the dominant theme being the ability of firms to sustain differential cost positions through ECONOMIES OF SCALE. In the world of scale economies, where minimum efficient plant sizes are a significant fraction of the market, oligopolistic market structures prevail and are overturned principally by the growth of markets or by the advance of technology enabling the creation of new assets with more advantageous cost positions.

The notion of economies of scale is therefore fundamental to strategic management because it provides a rationale for firms to be different in terms of both asset configuration and performance. However, this is an insufficient argument on its own for the existence of diversified firms. DIVERSIFICATION requires the notion of ECONOMIES OF SCOPE. These are defined as "the cost savings realized when two different products are produced within the same organization rather than at separate organizations." They arise because the products share a common input such as plant or equipment, obtaining volume discounts on purchases (exercising monopsony power), or applying common expertise or reputation. The advantages conferred by economies of scope are not, however, inherent in the jointness of production but in the barrier to entry that protects the "original" asset. There is nothing to prevent two firms enjoying identical economies of scope if there is free competition for the underlying asset. Thus economies of scale convey the fundamental advantage that underpins superior profitability in single-product and multiple-product firms.

The discussions in strategic management textbooks about COMPETITIVE ADVANTAGE are all variations upon this same theme. The simplest articulation of the theme is the cost differential that arises in production. The more complex argument concerns knowledge assets, where the essence of the argument is the cost to reproduce knowledge and not the possession of knowledge *per se*. The subtlety in STRATEGY-MAKING resides in the variety of ways in which knowledge and expertise are acquired (which is where the cost function of knowledge acquisition is important) and then captured in products and services (the generic differentiation theme). In this almost bucolic world, the supply side and the market side are linked through some form of arm's length market exchange process. Customer desires are conveyed through the pattern of their purchasing decisions, and producers respond by adjusting the nature of their offerings. Where competition is monopolistic (or imperfect), producers may attempt to shape customer preferences and, to the extent they succeed, demand functions become downward-sloping in the conventional manner and producers can then price according to the nature of their marginal cost curves and to the price elasticities in the market. But demand and supply are mediated through a market mechanism in which product demand is independent of other products and demand is not time dependent. This latter point is crucial (*see* NETWORK EXTERNALITIES; NETWORK INDUSTRIES; NETWORKS)

measuring the relative attractiveness of its multiple businesses for investment purposes. In conjunction with McKinsey and Company, GE developed a portfolio model which differed from that of the Boston Consulting Group's GROWTH SHARE MATRIX in that it examined those variables assessed by management to be the critical success factors affecting a business. These factors were then used to identify the position of a business in a three by three matrix, each cell of which indicated a recommended investment strategy. A number of factors, the identification of which is found useful, and the matrix itself, are illustrated in figure 1.

The process of positioning a business is similar to that of the Shell directional policy matrix. The position of each business on the two composite dimensions is determined by a qualitative scoring system described in the measurement of "market attractiveness" and "competitive position." Businesses are plotted on the matrix, with their relative size indicated by the area of the circle representing each one. An alternate method of weighting each variable has been used in some companies, the values of the main PIMS variables (*see* PIMS STRUCTURAL DETERMINANTS OF PERFORMANCE) being subdivided to determine the two composite variables and then used to calculate the relative matrix position of a business.

Each cell in the matrix suggests an alternate investment strategy for the businesses contained in it, as shown. Businesses in the top left-hand corner are high in market attractiveness and

Bibliography

Baumol, W., Panzar, J., and Willig, R. (1982). Contestable markets and the theory of industry. *American Economic Review*, 72.

Saloner, G., Shepard, A., and Podolny, J. (2001). *Strategic Management*. New York: John Wiley.

competitive position–market attractiveness matrix

Derek F. Channon

During the 1970s, the US General Electric Company (GE) developed a portfolio model

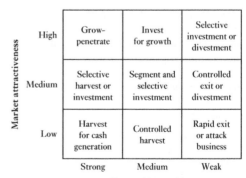

Figure 1   The market attractiveness–competitive position matrix (Channon, 1993; Stratpack Limited)

enjoy a strong competitive position: such businesses enjoy high growth and should receive priority for any investment support needed. Businesses in the grow/penetrate cell are also primary candidates for investment, in an effort to improve competitive position while growth prospects remain high. Defend/invest position businesses are in less attractive markets, but investment should be maintained as needed to defend the strong competitive position established. Businesses in the bottom left-hand corner are candidates for harvesting: the market attractiveness is low, probably indicating that growth is low, but the relative competitive position remains high. Such businesses are therefore usually producing good profits which cannot justifiably be reinvested. Surplus cash is therefore extracted for use in investing in businesses that are short of funds, or to be used to provide other types of resource.

Businesses in the center are candidates for selective investment, usually on the basis of careful market SEGMENTATION. Businesses at the bottom center and right center are candidates for withdrawal/divestment or for the pursuit of niche strategies. Businesses in the bottom right cell are both in unattractive markets and have a weak competitive position. Such businesses may well be making losses and are not likely to produce a strong positive cash flow. As a result, they are clear candidates for divestment or closure. A more sophisticated but difficult alternative is to deploy them as attack businesses against a competitor's harvest businesses, to depress their cash-generating capability. Note that each strategy also implies different objectives, and the company's management information systems and reward systems need to be tuned to reflect this.

The competitive position–market attractiveness matrix and the directional policy matrix provide more sophisticated methodologies for assessing the strategic position of a business, and can allow management to incorporate due consideration of critical variables that influence individual businesses.

COMPETITIVE POSITION

In assessing the competitive position of an individual business, a number of variables are usually taken into consideration. The calculation of relative competitive position can be operational-ized by scoring a company's position along a series of appropriate dimensions. The precise dimensions can be selected by management on the basis of their detailed knowledge of the business, and weighted according to their assessment of the relative importance of each dimension. This is illustrated in table 1. A number of such factors based on the critical variables identified in the PIMS program are used in one such system, as follows.

Competitive position measures

- *Absolute market share*: measured as a company's MARKET SHARE of its defined SERVED MARKET.
- *Relative share*: using the PIMS definition, this is defined as a percentage of the company's share divided by the sum of that of its three largest competitors.
- *Trend in market share*: the trend in the company's share over the past three years.
- *Relative profitability*: the relative profitability of the company's product as the percentage of the average of that of the three largest competitors.
- *Relative product quality*: an assessment of the relative level of the quality of a company's product compared with those of its three largest competitors, from the customer's perspective.
- *Relative price*: the relative price of a company's product as a percentage of the average of those of its three largest competitors.
- *Customer concentration*: the number of customers making up 80 percent of the company's business; the fewer the number of buyers, the greater the buyer power.
- *Rate of product innovation*: the percentage of sales from products introduced in the past three years, which indicates the degree of maturity of a business.
- *Relative capital intensity*: the capital intensity of a company's business, as a percentage of that of its three largest competitors; high relative capital intensity is usually a weakness.

Each of these factors, which may or may not be weighted, can be scored from 1 to 5, with the high score representing a very strong position and the low score a weak one. Summarizing the score for each dimension and dividing this by the

Table 1 An example of the business strength (competitive position) assessment with the weighted score approach

Critical success factors	Weight*	Rating†	Weighted score
Market share	0.10	5	0.5
SBU growth rate	×	3	—
Breadth of product line	0.05	4	0.2
Sales distribution effectiveness	0.2	4	0.8
Proprietary and key account advantages	×	3	—
Price competitiveness	×	4	—
Advertising and promotion effectiveness	0.05	4	0.2
Facilities location and newness	0.05	5	0.25
Capacity and productivity	×	3	—
Experience curve effects	0.15	4	0.6
Raw materials costs	0.05	4	0.2
Value added	×	4	—
Relative product quality	0.15	4	0.6
R&D advantages/position	0.05	4	0.2
Cash throw-off	0.1	5	0.5
Calibre of personnel	×	4	—
General image	0.05	5	0.25
TOTAL	1.00		4.3

Key: * × means that the factor does not affect the relative competitive position of the firms in that industry; † 1 = very weak competitive position, 5 = very strong competitive position.
Source: Hofer and Schendel (1978)

total possible score provides a coordinate for competitive position on the matrix.

MARKET ATTRACTIVENESS

This is assessed from data on the market/industry characteristics of a business. While the factors that determine attractiveness may vary, managerial input can be used to assess these and the relative importance of each variable by weighting them. An example is shown in table 2.

The following variables have also been found to be useful:

- *Size*: the size of a market is obviously important. However, in assessing size, careful market definition is imperative and eventually needs to be conducted on a segment-by-segment basis. The size should also be sufficiently large for the firm to make it worthwhile to provide products or services.
- *Historic growth rate*: this is useful as a guide for predicting future trends.
- *Projected growth rate*: this needs to be carefully assessed and overoptimism avoided.

Sensitivity analysis can be used to assess the impact of different growth rates.

- *Number of competitors*: the larger the number of competitors, the greater is the level of rivalry that may be expected.
- *Competitor concentration*: more concentrated markets are generally more attractive, whereas fragmented markets are usually more price competitive.
- *Market profitability*: more profitable markets are obviously more attractive.
- *Barriers to entry*: markets with high barriers to entry (*see* BARRIERS TO ENTRY AND EXIT) are more attractive than those in which the entry of new competitors is easy.
- *Barriers to exit*: high barriers to exit tend to increase competition, especially in high capital intensity industries, as competitors erode away margins in order to maintain capacity utilization.
- *Supplier power*: a small number of suppliers, e.g., of critical raw materials, reduces market attractiveness.

Table 2   An example of the industry (market) attractiveness assessment with the weighted score approach

Attractiveness criterion	Weight*	Rating[†]	Weighted score
Size	0.15	4	0.6
Growth	0.12	3	0.36
Pricing	0.05	3	0.15
Market diversity	0.05	2	0.1
Competitive structure	0.05	3	0.15
Industry profitability	0.2	3	0.6
Technical role	0.05	4	0.2
Inflation vulnerability	0.05	2	0.1
Cyclicality	0.05	2	0.10
Customer financials	0.1	5	0.5
Energy impact	0.08	4	0.32
Social	GO	4	—
Environmental	GO	4	—
Legal	GO	4	—
Human	0.05	4	0.2
TOTAL	1.00		3.38

Key: * Some criteria may be of the GO/NO GO type; † 1 = very unattractive, 5 = highly attractive.
Source: Hofer and Schendel (1978)

- *Buyer power*: a small number of large customers enhances buyer power, especially in fragmented industries, and reduces market attractiveness.
- *Degree of product differentiation*: the higher the level of differentiation, the more attractive the market is, as high differentiation tends to reduce price competition.
- *Market fit*: markets that are truly synergistic with other corporate activities enhance attractiveness (*see* SYNERGY).

Having measured the position of a business along these and any other relevant dimensions, market attractiveness is assessed by assigning a value between 1 and 5 to a business according to its relative position. If the variables are weighted, this weight should also be applied and the scores summed to arrive at an overall total. This is divided by the maximum possible score to generate the value of the market attractiveness coordinate in order to plot a business's position on the matrix.

Criticisms of the system are that it requires accurate identification of the multiplicity of variables required to position a business correctly. The weighting and numerical scoring system can deceive with its pseudo-scientific approach. There is also a desire on the part of managers to attempt to avoid the disinvest cells. Data are often not available to provide an accurate assessment of the position of a business and therefore, as a consequence, there is a tendency to drift toward the moderate score. Furthermore, it is difficult to insure consistency between the businesses. Finally, when markets change, very misleading positioning can occur in terms of market attractiveness. Thus, in GE when the electronics industry was globalizing in the 1980s, the company was often measuring its position on the basis of the US market. During the 1980s, therefore, under the leadership of Jack Welch, positioning shifted to the concept of being either number one or number two in the world, or that businesses should be sold, closed, or fixed. As a result, the portfolio of GE was dramatically changed. Nevertheless, when used well, the multivariate approach offers management a more realistic tool than the simplistic approach of the original BCG bivariate model. Moreover, such a tool can be coupled with VALUE-BASED PLANNING to provide a very sophisticated portfolio planning tool.

Bibliography

Channon, D. F. (1993). *Australia Pacific Bank Case.* Management School, Imperial College, University of London.

Hax, H. and Majluf, N. T. (1984). *Strategic Management: An Integrative Perspective.* Englewood Cliffs, NJ: Prentice-Hall.

Hofer, C. W. and Schendel, D. (1978). *Strategy Formulation: Analytical Concepts.* St. Paul, MN: West.

competitive strategy

John McGee

There can be great differences between the abilities of firms to succeed – there are fundamental inequalities between most competitors. This contrasts with the conventional economics textbook view of perfect competition, which holds that firms are essentially similar, if not the same, and that over time their performances will converge on a minimum rate of return on capital. Less efficient firms will be obliged to exit

and the more efficient firms will be subject to imitation. But the competitive strategy view of the firm is that understanding and manipulating the factors that cause these inequalities, so as to give the firm a sustainable competitive advantage, largely governs long-term business success. These factors vary widely; so different businesses, even within the same industry, often need to be doing different things. Thus, there are many strategies open to firms. The usual starting point is to recognize that strategy is the outcome of the resolution of several different, conflicting forces. These are summarized in figure 1.

Society has expectations of its business organizations. Owners, managers, and other implementers of strategy have their own personal values and ambitions. The company has strengths and weaknesses, and the industry context offers opportunities and threats. The traditional top-down view of strategy is encapsulated in the STRATEGIC PLANNING view. This involves deciding on long-term objectives and strategic direction, eliminating or minimizing

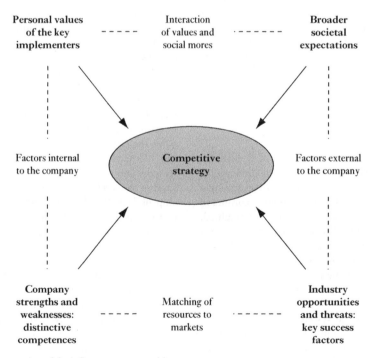

Figure 1   An overview of the influences on competitive strategy

weaknesses, avoiding threats, building on and defending strengths, and taking advantage of opportunities. But, from reading this lesson, it should be clear that, given the strategic direction, the key strategic decision is product market selection. This should be based on the existence of long-term viable business opportunities (not merely the existence of growing markets), together with the prospect of creating the relevant CORE COMPETENCES. Viable business opportunities depend on:

- the existence of valuable market segments;
- the existence of a sustainable positional advantage;
- the creation of the appropriate strategic assets.

In conducting the assessment of viable business opportunity, the term *key success factors* is often used. Intuitively, this means "What do we have to do to succeed?" Figure 2 and table 1 illustrate the process (see Grant, 1998). There is a set of key questions to ask:

- Is there a market?
- Do we have some advantage?
- Can we survive the competition?

These lead us into two pieces of analysis: the analysis of customers and demand, and the analysis of competition (summarized in figure 2). Table 1 shows how these can be put together to identify key success factors in three different industries. The key success factors represent the strategic logic(s) (there is usually more than one) available. In the steel industry, the key success factors revolve around low cost, cost efficiencies, scale effectiveness, with some scope for specialty steels. In the fashion industry, key success factors are about differentiation, coupled with an element of low cost. Differentiation has speed of response characteristics, but the industry and the market are so broad that there are distinctive segments, some of which are cost driven, while others are differentiation driven. This industry provides a good example of the multiplicity of available strategies.

In formulating competitive strategy, there are some important things to remember.

- *Resources are limited*, opportunities are infinite. The essence of strategy lies in saying "Yes" to only some of the options and, therefore, "No" to many others. TRADE-OFFS are essential to strategy – they reflect the need for choice and they purposefully limit what a company offers.
- Always factor in *opportunity costs*. A dollar invested "here" is a dollar not invested "there," or not given back to shareholders.
- The essence of strategy is choosing to perform activities *differently* than rivals.

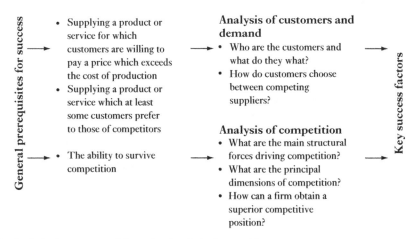

Figure 2   Analysis of customers and demand and analysis of competition

Table 1   Identifying key success factors

Industry	What do customers want? (analysis of demand) +	How do firms survive competition? (analysis of competition) =	Key success factors
Steel	Customers include automobiles, engineering, and container industries. Customers acutely price sensitive. Also require product consistency and reliability of supply. Specific technical specifications required for special steels.	Competition primarily on price. Competition intense due to declining demand, high fixed costs, and low-cost imports. Strong trade union bargaining power. Transport costs high. Scale economies important.	Cost efficiency through scale-efficient plants, low-cost location, rapid adjustment of capacity to output, low labor costs. In special steels, scope for differentiation through quality.
Fashion Clothing	Demand fragmented by garment, style, quality, color. Customers willing to pay price premium for fashion, exclusivity, and quality. Retailers seek reliability and speed of supply.	Low barriers to entry and exit. Low seller concentration. Few scale economies. Strong retail buying power. Price and non-price competition both strong.	Combine effective differentiation with low-cost operation. Key differentiation variables are speed of response to changing fashions, style, reputation with retailers/consumers. Low wages and overheads important.
Grocery Supermarkets	Customers want low prices, convenient location, and wide range of products.	Markets localized, concentration normally high. But customer price sensitivity encourages vigorous price competition. Exercise of bargaining power a key determinant of purchase price. Scale economies in operations and advertising.	Low-cost operation requires operational efficiency, scale-efficient stores, large aggregate purchases to maximize buying power, low wage costs. Differentiation requires large stores to provide wide product range and customer convenience facilities.

- In the long run, what matters is not how fast you are running, but whether you are *running faster than your competitors.*
- A company can only outperform rivals if it can establish a difference that it can sustain. So always test for the SUSTAINABILITY of your COMPETITIVE ADVANTAGE. Competitors are likely to view relieving you of your competitive advantage as their cardinal duty. Further, not all of them are likely to be stupid.
- The competitive value of individual activities cannot be separated from the whole. So, *fit* locks out imitators by creating a value chain that is stronger than its weakest link (see STRATEGIC FIT; VALUE CHAIN ANALYSIS).
- The long-run test of any strategy lies not in what it contributes to MARKET SHARE or profit margins but in what it contributes to long-term *return on investment.*
- Strategic positions should have a *time horizon* of a decade or more, not just of a single planning cycle and/or product cycle.

Bibliography

Grant, R. M. (1998). *Contemporary Strategy Analysis*, 3rd edn. Oxford: Blackwell.

McGee, J., Wilson, D., and Thomas, H. (2005). *Strategy: Analysis and Practice.* Maidenhead: McGraw-Hill.

competitor analysis

Derek F. Channon

In conducting competitor analysis, it is necessary to examine those key competitors that presently and/or in the future may have a significant impact on the strategy of the firm. Usually this means the inclusion of a wider group of organizations than the existing immediately direct competitors. In many cases, it is the failure of firms to identify the competitors that may emerge in the future that leads to BLIND SPOTS. Competitors for evaluation therefore include the following.

EXISTING DIRECT COMPETITORS

The firm should concentrate on major direct competitors, especially those growing as rapidly as or faster than itself. Care should be taken to uncover the sources of any apparent COMPETITIVE ADVANTAGE. Some competitors will not appear in every segment but rather in specific niches. Different competitors will therefore need to be evaluated at different levels of depth. Those which already do, or could have an ability to, substantially impact on core businesses (see CORE BUSINESS) need the closest attention.

NEW AND POTENTIAL ENTRANTS

Major competitive threats do not necessarily come from direct competitors, who may have much to lose by breaking up established market structures. New competitors include the following:

- firms with low barriers to entry (see BARRIERS TO ENTRY AND EXIT);
- firms with a clear experience effect (see EXPERIENCE AND LEARNING EFFECTS) or SYNERGY gain;
- forward or backward integrators;
- unrelated product acquirers, for whom entry offers financial synergy;
- firms offering a potential technology bypass to gain competitive advantage.

COMPETITOR INTELLIGENCE SOURCES

Collecting legal detailed information on actual and potential competitors is surprisingly easy if the task is approached systematically and continuously. Moreover, the level of resource needed for the task is not extensive. It is therefore, perhaps, surprising how few firms actually undertake the task and set out their strategies while being almost oblivious to the behavior of competitors. Key sources of competitive information include the following:

- Annual reports and 10 Ks and, where available, the annual reports or returns of subsidiaries/business units.
- Competitive product literature.
- Competitor product analysis and evaluation by techniques such as TEAR DOWN.
- Internal newspapers and magazines. These are useful in that they usually give details of all major appointments, staff background profiles, business unit descriptions, statements of philosophy and MISSION, new

products and services, and major strategic moves.

- Competitor company histories. These are useful to gain an understanding of competitor corporate culture, the rationale for the existing strategic position, and details of the internal systems and policies.
- Advertising. This illustrates and identifies themes, choice of media, spend level, and the timing of specific strategies.
- Competitor directories. These are an excellent source for identifying the organization's structure and strength, mode of customer service, depth of specialist segment coverage, attitudes to specific activities, and relative power positions.
- Financial and industry press. These sources are useful for financial and strategic announcements, product data, and so on.
- Papers and speeches of corporate executives. These are useful for details of internal procedures, the organization's senior management philosophy, and strategic intentions.
- Sales force reports. Although they are often biased, intelligence reports from field officers provide front-line intelligence on competitors, customers, prices, products, service quality, delivery, and so on.
- Customers. Reports from customers can be actively solicited internally or via external market research specialists.
- Suppliers. Reports from suppliers are especially useful in assessing competitor investment plans, activity levels, efficiency, and the like.
- Professional advisers. Many companies use external consultants to evaluate and change their strategies and/or structures. The knowledge of such advisers is usually useful, in that most adopt a specific pattern in their approach.
- Stockbroker reports. These often provide useful operational details obtained from competitor briefings. Similarly, industry studies may provide useful information about specific competitors within a particular country or region.
- Recruited competitor personnel. The systematic debriefing of recruited personnel provides intimate internal details of competitive activity.
- Recruited executive consultants. Retired executives from competitors can often be hired as consultants, and information about their former employers can be effectively determined by requesting their assistance in specific job areas.

COMPETITOR ANALYSIS DATABASE

In order to evaluate competitor strengths and weaknesses, systematic data collection on each actual and potential competitor is necessary. The most important competitors need to be comprehensively and continuously monitored. Competitors that pose a less immediate threat can be monitored on a periodic basis. The data to be collected should include the following:

- name of competitor or potential competitor;
- numbers and locations of operating sites;
- numbers and nature of the personnel attached to each unit;
- details of competitor organization and business unit structure;
- financial analysis of parent and subsidiaries, stock market assessment, and details of share register; potential acquirers/acquisitions;
- corporate and business unit growth rate/profitability;
- details of product and service range, including relative quality and price;
- details of SERVED MARKET share by customer segment and by geographic area (see MARKET SHARE);
- details of communication strategy, spending levels, timing, media choice, promotions, and advertising support;
- details of sales and service organization, including numbers, organization, responsibilities, special procedures for key accounts, any team selling capabilities, and the method of the sales force SEGMENTATION approach;
- details of served markets (including identification and servicing of key accounts), estimates of customer loyalty, and market image;
- details of niche markets served, key accounts, estimates of customer loyalty, and relative market image;
- details of specialist markets served;
- details of R&D spending, facilities, development themes, special skills and attributes, and geographic coverage;

- details of operations and system facilities, capacity, size, scale, age, utilization, assessment of output efficiency, capital intensity, and replacement policies;
- details of key customers and suppliers;
- details of personnel numbers, personnel relations record, relative efficiency and productivity, salary rates, rewards and sanctions policies, degree of trade unionization;
- details of key individuals within the competitor organization;
- details of control, information, and planning systems.

From such a database, the strategy of a competitor can be analyzed and assessed as to future strategic actions and suggestions can be made as to how the firm can gain and sustain competitive advantage.

ANALYZING COMPETITOR STRATEGY

The strategy of key competitors should be analyzed and evaluated with a view to assessing their relative strengths and weaknesses, in order to identify strategic alternatives for the firm. Most large firms are multibusiness and competitor strategy needs to be evaluated at several levels:

- by function – marketing, production, and R&D;
- by business unit;
- by corporation as a whole.

From this analysis likely competitor moves and responses to external moves can be assessed.

FUNCTION ANALYSIS

For each competitor business, the main functional strategies should be identified and evaluated. While all of the desirable details may not be immediately available, continuous competitor monitoring will usually permit a comprehensive picture to be built up over time. The objective is not merely to gain competitive details but to evaluate the relative position of the evaluating firms to assess competitive position, BENCHMARKING opportunities, and so on.

MARKETING STRATEGY

- What product/service strategy is adopted by each competitor relative to yours? What is the market size by product market/customer segment? What is the market share for each competitor by served market segment?
- What is the growth rate for each product/service market segment? What is the growth rate of each competitor by segment? What are the degree and trend in market segment concentration?
- What is the product/service line strategy of each competitor? Is it full line or specialist niche?
- What is the policy toward new services adopted by each competitor? What has been the rate of new product introduction?
- What is the relative service/product quality of each competitor?
- What pricing strategy does each competitor adopt by product/service line/consumer segment?
- What are the relative advertising and promotion strategies of each competitor?
- How do competitors service each product market segment?
- What are the apparent marketing objectives of each competitor?
- How quickly do competitors respond to market changes?
- How does marketing fit in competitor cultures? Has the function been the source of key executives in the past?

PRODUCTION/OPERATIONS STRATEGY

- What are the number, size, and location of each competitor's production/operations complexes? How do these compare with each other? What product range does each produce? What is their estimated capacity? What is capacity utilization?
- What is the level of each competitor's capital employed in depreciable assets? Is it owned property?
- What working capital intensity is employed in debtors, stocks, and creditors?
- How many people are employed at each unit? What salaries are paid? What is the relative productivity?
- What is the degree of trade unionization? What is the labor relations record?
- What sales are made to other internal business units? What supplies are received from other internal business units?

- What incentive/reward systems are used?
- What services are subject to OUTSOUR-CING? Is this increasing or decreasing?
- How does production fit into each competitor's organization? Has production/operations been a source of key executives?
- How flexible is each competitor to changes in market conditions? How fast has each competitor been able to respond to changes?

RESEARCH AND DEVELOPMENT STRATEGY

- Where are new services developed?
- What is the estimated expenditure level on R&D? How does this compare? How has this changed?
- How many people are employed in research, and how many in development?
- What is the recent record for each competitor in new product introductions and patents?
- Are there identifiable technological thrusts for individual competitors?
- How rapidly can each competitor respond to innovations? What sort of reaction has typically been evoked?

FINANCIAL STRATEGY

- What is the financial performance of each competitor by business in terms of return on assets, return on equity, cash flow, and return on sales?
- What dividend payout policy appears to be in place? How are cash flows in and out controlled?
- What is the calculated SUSTAINABLE GROWTH RATE on the existing equity base?
- How does the competitor's growth rate compare with the industry average? Is adequate cash available to sustain the business and allow for expansion? Do other businesses have priority for corporate funds?
- How well are cash and working capital managed?

BUSINESS UNIT STRATEGY

Each competitor also needs to be evaluated at the business unit level to see where the business fits within the overall competitor strategy. Such questions should address the role of the business unit, its objectives, organizational structure, control and incentive systems, strategic position, environmental constraints and opportunities, position of strategic business unit (SBU) head, and performance.

GROUP BUSINESS OBJECTIVES

The position of each business within a competitor's total portfolio also needs to be evaluated. Questions that may influence behavior at the business unit level include: an evaluation of overall group financial objectives, growth capability and shareholder expectations, key strengths and weaknesses, ability to change, and the nature of the overall portfolio; GENERIC STRATEGIES adopted, values and aspirations of key decision-makers, and especially the CEO; historic reactions to earlier competitive moves; and beliefs and expectations about competitors.

From this analysis, the objective is to assess likely competitor future strategies and responses to competitive moves. In most industries success is dependent on gaining an edge on competitors, and this type of evaluation is therefore as important as basic market or customer analysis.

Bibliography

Ansoff, I. (1987). *Corporate Strategy*. Harmondsworth: Penguin, ch. 8.
Channon, D. F. (1986). *Bank Strategic Management and Marketing*. Chichester: John Wiley, ch. 4.
Garner, J. R., Rachlin, R., and Sweeny, H. W. A. (1986). *Handbook of Strategic Planning*. New York: John Wiley.
Sammon, W. L. (1986). Assessing the competition: Business intelligence for strategic management. In J. R. Gardner, R. Rachlin, and H. W. A. Sweeny (eds.), *Handbook of Strategic Planning*. New York: John Wiley.

complementary products

Stephanos Avgeropoulos

In contrast with SUBSTITUTE PRODUCTS, complementary products are those which have a negative cross-price ELASTICITY of demand. As with substitutes, there can be "strong" or "weak" complements.

The strategic importance of complementarity is somewhat inferior to that of substitutability. Nevertheless, complements raise the question of a firm's scope of activities. A number of decisions have to be made by a firm engaged in the production of complementary goods, namely with respect to control over complementary products (and industries), pricing, and the combined sale of complementary goods (bundling). The most important complements are those which have a significant impact on each other's position (e.g., in terms of cost or differentiation), and those which are associated with each other by the buyer.

IMPLICATIONS FOR INVOLVEMENT IN THE INDUSTRY OF THE COMPLEMENT

There are a number of advantages that can be gained by being active in and controlling complementary products/markets, including ECONOMIES OF SCALE in marketing (as demand for one good also boosts demand for the other), and other shared activities such as logistics (see ECONOMIES OF SCOPE).

Controlling complements, however, may have its own problems. The two most important ones are that the industry of the complement may not be as attractive as that of the base good, and that the organization concerned may not have the skills, abilities, or any relevant COMPETITIVE ADVANTAGE to compete effectively in that industry.

In any case, it should be kept in mind that some complements may change over time, so the firm's involvement in the industry of the complement may not have to be as committed. Morover, full-scale operations in the complement's industry are not always necessary. Just being active in that industry may allow the firm to sufficiently influence it, so that other firms may feel obliged to follow its examples when it sets lower prices or provides a higher level of service. As a result, controlling only a relatively small share of the complement's industry may well be sufficient to considerably improve the sales and profitability of the industry with which the main interest of a company lies.

IMPLICATIONS FOR PRICING

The profitability of complementary goods may well require pricing to be pitched at levels different from those that would have been appropriate if the two products were not complements, or were not produced by the same firm.

IMPLICATIONS FOR CAPACITY PLANNING

Finally, the relationship between complementary goods may be exploited to forecast demand for one of them, given changes in the demand for the other. Similarly, if the price of one good rises or falls, demand for the other would also be expected to be affected because they are required together by the buyer and the price of the bundle is affected. These relationships can be used for capacity planning purposes, particularly where the firm controls only one of the complements.

See also cross-subsidization

Bibliography

Porter, M. E. (1985). Competitive Advantage: Creating and Sustaining Superior Performance. New York: Free Press.

conglomerate strategy

Derek F. Channon

Conglomerates are corporations that have no apparent STRATEGIC FIT between the activities of their constituent businesses. They were defined by Wrigley in the early 1970s as businesses in which no one business accounted for 70 percent of sales and in which there was no readily apparent relationship between the activities. Conglomerates are also characterized by a small central office which is heavily oriented to finance and control, plus, in addition, acquisition analysis and implementation. Such businesses were popular in the US in the late 1960s, when it was argued that it was desirable to build a portfolio of strategic businesses at different stages of the life cycle that could financially compensate one another. In the early period of the use of the GROWTH SHARE MATRIX, this strategy was strongly advocated by the Boston Consulting Group, and the success of companies such as Textron, Litton Industries, and Ling Temco Vought (LTV) seemed to support the theory.

There was no particular effort by firms adopting a conglomerate strategy to seek SYNERGY or strategic fit between businesses, with the exception of seeking out financial synergy that could be released by the purchase of companies with underutilized assets, debt capacity, complementary cash flows, and so on. Typically, acquisition screens used by conglomerates emphasized criteria such as the following:

- the ability of target companies to meet corporate targets for profitability and return on equity;
- whether an acquired business would be cash using to finance capital investment, growth, and working capital;
- the growth rate of the industry in which the acquisition operated;
- whether the acquisition was large enough to make a significant contribution to the parent;
- potential problems due to customer relations and government or regulatory constraints;
- industry vulnerability to inflation, interest rates, and local government policy.

The financial emphasis of conglomerate strategy leads such active acquisitive firms to seek out targets with the following like characteristics:

- *Asset strips*: situations in which the market capitalization is substantially less than the underlying asset value. Substantial capital gains are possible by selling off surplus assets in order to recover acquisition costs.
- *Financially distressed businesses*: businesses which can be purchased at deep discounts but which can be turned around, provided that the acquirer has the necessary management skills to implement a TURNAROUND STRATEGY. Such businesses can then be held or sold on to realize a significant gain for the acquirer.
- *Capital-short growth companies*: such companies possess attractive growth prospects but lack the financial resources to exploit their advantage.

ADVANTAGES OF CONGLOMERATE DIVERSIFICATION

There are a number of financial advantages that can be attributed to a conglomerate strategy:

- Business risk can be dispersed across a portfolio of businesses, reducing the risk from over-concentration in any one industry. While related DIVERSIFICATION also spreads risk, it is confined to industry areas

with strategic fit, whereas no such constraint applies to conglomerates.
- Capital can be invested into businesses that justify it in terms of creating shareholder value and withdrawn from cash-generating businesses. At one time, the Boston Consulting Group thus advocated a conglomerate strategy as a logical outcome of the active pursuit of a growth share portfolio strategy.
- Corporate profitability can be stabilized by investments in businesses that are traditionally counter-cyclical to each other.
- Companies with skills in identifying asset-rich situations, and with the skills to turn around ailing businesses, can create shareholder value.
- Mergers between businesses with complementary asset investment and cash flow characteristics and/or complementary capital structures can release financial synergy, so increasing shareholder value.

DISADVANTAGES OF CONGLOMERATE DIVERSIFICATION

At the same time, many conglomerates actually underperform in the market, and rather than adding to shareholder value may be worth more in breakup situations than as conglomerate corporations. Reasons for this include the following:

- The management needs of conglomerates are primarily financial and general management skills in turnaround situations. They do not possess operational business skills, nor can they be expected to. It is, therefore, noticeable that major conglomerate failures have occurred in high-technology businesses, where the central management fails to recognize projects going out of control despite sophisticated financial reporting systems.
- Without strategic fit providing operating synergy and COMPETITIVE ADVANTAGE, there is a tendency for the component businesses of a conglomerate to do no better (and sometimes worse) than the market average. In addition, tight financial controls might reduce entrepreneurial spirit in the business units while the center provides no real support other than financial.

- Counter-cyclical businesses often do not actually behave with perfect timing, so failing to smooth the corporate earnings stream.

Nevertheless, overall, there is some evidence that high acquisition rate conglomerates do successfully perform in terms of return on equity and growth rate by comparison with related diversified concerns. Furthermore, despite an apparent trend toward reduced diversification in the late 1980s and encouragement to retreat to the core businesses (see CORE BUSINESS) of the corporation, the number of conglomerates has not diminished significantly. Indeed, there has been a tendency in North America and the UK for diversification to continue, especially with the development of mixed manufacturing and service industry corporations. Meanwhile, in the Korean CHAEBOL STRUCTURE, the Japanese KEIRETSU STRUCTURE, and within the typical CHINESE FAMILY BUSINESS, the major industrial groups have virtually all continued their strategies of conglomerate diversification.

During the 1970s the number of conglomerate businesses grew sharply in the US and the trend spread to other countries, including the UK. The failure of Litton Industries and LTV, however, made the conglomerate form unattractive to the US stock market. In the boom years of the stock market in the 1980s, conglomerates again became attractive in the US, but in the late 1980s some such corporations came under predatory attack, on the basis that breaking them up might create greater shareholder value than allowing them to remain intact. This led to the belief that retreating to a core business was a more desirable strategy.

The answer, however, as to whether a conglomerate strategy is less viable than a related diversified strategy (see RELATED DIVERSIFICATION) is far from clear. There are many corporations in the developed economies which have little or no relationships between their businesses but which are highly successful financially, and are well received by the stock market. Such concerns would include US General Electric, BTR, and Hanson Trust. These companies are very highly diversified and manage the businesses within that framework.

They also operate with very tight financial control. Similarly, in Japan the *keiretsu* structure and in Korea the *chaebol* structure have become ever more diversified.

Bibliography

Channon, D. F. (1973). *The Strategy and Structure of British Enterprise*. Cambridge, MA: Harvard Division of Research.

Rumelt, R. P. (1974). *Strategy Structure and Economic Performance*. Cambridge, MA: Harvard Division of Research.

Thompson, A. A. and Strickland, A. J. (1993). *Strategic Management*. Homewood, IL: Irwin, pp. 173–7.

Wrigley, L. J. (1970). Diversification and divisional autonomy. Unpublished doctoral dissertation, Harvard Business School.

congruence

John McGee

When viewing an organization as a system, the components of the structure (see table 1) are themselves less important than the relationships among them. Moreover, the ways in which these relationships affect organizational performance are also more significant than simple structural considerations. At any given time, each organizational component maintains some degree of *congruence* with each of the others. The congruence between two components is defined as the degree to which the needs, demands, goals, objectives, and/or structures of one component are consistent with the needs, demands, goals, objectives, and/or structures of another component.

Congruence, therefore, is a matter of how well pairs of components fit together. Consider, for example, two components: the task and the individual. At the simplest level, the task presents skill and knowledge demands on individuals who would perform it. At the same time, the individuals available to do the tasks have certain characteristics – including their levels of skill and knowledge. The greater the fit between the individual's characteristics and the demands of the task to be performed, the more effective the performance is likely to be. Obviously the fit between the individual and the task involves

Table 1   Organizational components

Fit	Issues
Individual/organization	How are individual needs met by the organizational arrangements?
	Do individuals hold clear perceptions of organizational structures?
	Is there a convergence of individual and organizational goals?
Individual/task	How are individual needs met by the tasks?
	Do individuals have skills and abilities to meet task demands?
Individual/informal organization	How are individual needs met by the informal organization?
	How does the informal organization make use of individual resources consistent with informal goals?
Task/organization	Are organizational arrangements adequate to meet the demands of the task?
	Do organizational arrangements motivate behavior that is consistent with task demands?
Task/informal organization	Does the informal organization structure facilitate task performance?
	Does it help meet the demands of the task?
Organization/informal organization	Are the goals, rewards, and structures of the informal organization consistent with those of the formal organization?

Source: Nadler and Tushman (1997: 167).

more than just knowledge and skill: performance will be affected by a wide range of factors such as job fulfillment, anxiety, UNCERTAINTY, expectation of rewards, and so on. Similarly each congruence relationship has its own specific characteristics. For an overview of the critical elements of each congruence relationship, see table 1.

Bibliography

Nadler, D. A. and Tushman, M. A. (1997). A congruence model for organizational problem solving. In Michael A. Tushman and Philip Anderson (eds.), *Managing Strategic Innovation and Change: A Collection of Readings*. Oxford: Oxford University Press.

cooperative strategies

Duncan Angwin

Strategic alliances offered the possibility of overcoming the well-known difficulties involved in making acquisitions work (*see* MERGERS AND ACQUISITIONS). Strategic alliances are just one of two broad subsets of cooperative strategies, the other being collusive strategies. They may be defined as follows:

- *Collusive strategies*: Several firms in an industry cooperate to reduce industry output below the competitive level and raise prices above the competitive level (Scherer, 1980). Such strategies normally exist between firms in the same industry and may be perceived as a defensive strategy to ward off a threat from competition. Collusion (*see* CARTEL) may be deliberate, in which case it constitutes illegal price fixing (in most countries). It may, however, be tacit. In that case firms recognize a common interest in raising prices without explicit agreement being reached. This is not currently regarded as illegal.
- *Strategic alliances*: Several firms cooperate but industry output is not reduced (Kogut, 1988). Such alliances can exist between firms in different industries and can be perceived as aimed at creating and enhancing the competitive positions of the firms involved in a very competitive environment.

The term strategic alliance itself covers a multitude of different arrangements and there is no agreed typology in the literature. However, it is critical to understand the different forms in existence, as they have profound implications for the way in which the alliance is to be managed. In particular, there is an important distinction on the grounds of whether or not the partner is a competitor (note that even if the partner is a competitor, this may not mean collusion).

See also *strategic alliances*

Bibliography

Contractor, F. J. and Lorange, P. (eds.) (1988). *Cooperative Strategies in International Business*. Lexington, MA: Lexington Books.

Kogut, B. (1988). Joint ventures: Theoretical and empirical perspectives. *Strategic Management Journal*, 19 (4), 319–32.

Scherer, F. M. (1980). *Industrial Market Structure and Economic Performance*. Boston: Houghton Mifflin.

core business

Derek F. Channon

Made popular as a theme in the late 1980s, many western companies, especially in the US, found that their strategies of DIVERSIFICATION had not achieved the improvement in profit performance that was expected. Successful corporations were identified as usually having developed a "core" business around which related activities had been developed. In companies that had adopted a related diversified strategy (*see* RELATED DIVERSIFICATION), new activities had been added, usually as a result of common technology or skill, mode of marketing and distribution, and so on. Financial SYNERGY was not significantly recognized, although in practice it was an integral component, in the strategic development of some conglomerates (*see* CONGLOMERATE STRATEGY). Many such diversification moves occurred by acquisition (*see* ACQUISITION STRATEGY).

During the 1980s the initial impact of the research on corporate excellence was to indicate that successful firms were those in which some logic occurred in diversification moves. Unsuccessful acquisitions were either sold or floated off and the proceeds returned to shareholders to avoid predatory attacks on the parent.

In addition, the significant take-up of VALUE-BASED PLANNING focusing on shareholder value encouraged the divestment of businesses contributing negative value. Interestingly, these short-term pressures from the stock market, which only influenced western companies, were largely absent in Japan, where the KEIRETSU STRUCTURE provided a stability that could actually permit firms to redefine their core business on a regular basis. As a result, Japanese firms and their *keiretsu* groups increased their degree of diversification. Similar patterns of corporate development can also be observed amongst the Korean CHAEBOL STRUCTURE and large businesses owned and/or managed by Chinese in the Pacific Rim.

Bibliography

Peters, T. and Waterman, R. (1982). *In Search of Excellence*. New York: Harper and Row.

core competences

Dorothy Griffiths

Core competences are "a set of differentiated skills, complementary assets, and routines that provide the basis for a firm's competitive capacities and sustainable advantage in a particular business" (Teece, Pisano, and Shuen, 1990). They are "the specific tangible and intangible assets of the firm assembled into integrated clusters, which span individuals and groups to enable distinctive activities to be performed" (Winterschied, 1994).

The concept of core competences is associated with the RESOURCE-BASED VIEW of the firm. Rather than emphasizing (as in traditional approaches to STRATEGY) products and markets, and focusing competitive analysis on product portfolios, the resource-based approach regards firms as bundles of resources that can be configured to provide firm-specific advantages. Prahalad and Hamel (1990) characterize the difference of approach as between a "portfolio of competences versus a portfolio of businesses." The resource-based model is able to address a number of issues that mainstream strategic analysis has found difficult. Amongst these issues are DIVERSIFICATION (see Mahoney and Pandian, 1992), and the changes in competitive environment that most firms are experiencing (GLOBALIZATION, deregulation, technological change, and quality), which mean that traditional sources of COMPETITIVE ADVANTAGE are being eroded (Hamel and Prahalad, 1994).

The term "core competences" is most closely associated with the work of Hamel and Prahalad. Other terms that are used include intangible resources (Hall, 1992), strategic capabilities (Stalk, Evans, and Shulman, 1992), strategic assets (Dierickx and Cool, 1989; Amit and Schoemaker, 1993), firm resources (Barney, 1991), core capabilities (Leonard-Barton, 1992), and distinctive competences (Andrews, 1971).

Core competences are typically characterized as:

- unique to the firm;
- sustainable because they are hard to imitate or to substitute (*see* SUSTAINABILITY);
- conferring some kind of functionality to the customer (in the case of products and some services) or to the provider (in the case of other services);
- partly the product of learning and, hence, incorporating tacit as well as explicit knowledge;
- generic because they are incorporated into a number of products and/or processes.

Recognition of the potential significance of core competences for competitive advantage was stimulated by research such as that by Rumelt (1974), which showed that of nine potential diversification strategies, the two that were most successful were those that were built on an existing skill or resource base within the firm.

Hamel and Prahalad have distinguished between three types of competences: market access, integrity related, and functionally related. Market access competences bring the firm into contact with its customers; integrity-related competences enable the firm to do things to a higher level of quality, better and/or faster than its competitors; and functionally related competences confer distinctive customer benefits.

Within the literature and debate on the subject there is a division between what Klavans (1994) has characterized as technological and institutional views of competences. The former focuses on "objective" capabilities, such as Honda's knowledge of engine design, while the latter

focuses on, for example, managerial processes for organizational learning. Leonard-Barton (1992) goes further than this. She defines what she describes as a core capability, as a knowledge set that has four dimensions: employees' knowledge and skills; knowledge and skills embodied in technical systems; managerial systems that enable the creation of knowledge; and the values and norms associated with the knowledge and its creation. She argues that this fourth dimension is often ignored. In so arguing, she shares the view of, amongst others, Child (1972), that the identification of core competences is, at some level, a political process.

The concept has proved to be attractive both to industrialists and to business strategists. At a time when companies are increasingly homogeneous in terms of technologies, regulatory environments, and location, the suggestion that competitive advantage can be won through the configuration and application of corporate-level resources has great appeal. Writing in 1992, the *Economist* Intelligence Unit identified the following uses for the concept:

- to guide diversification through the identification of basic strengths;
- to drive revitalization through the identification of CORE BUSINESS areas;
- to guard competitiveness through an earlier recognition of key skills (many firms realize what they have lost through OUTSOURCING or divestment only when it is too late);
- to provide a focus and justification for R&D in the development and maintenance of core competences;
- to inform the selection of STRATEGIC ALLIANCES that build on complementary core competences;
- to balance strategic business unit (SBU) objectives with company objectives.

This relationship between the center and SBUs is a critical issue in the management of core competences. By definition, core competences exist beyond individual SBUs. They are underlying strengths that inform, support, and differentiate the firm's business across its SBUs. Since they are not the only source of competitive advantage, there is the potential for conflict and tension between SBU objectives and corporate objectives. To deploy core competences effectively requires, at some level, cross-SBU consensus on objectives and practice. For many firms who have followed the path of increasing SBU autonomy, achieving such consensus is a major challenge in the management and/or exploitation of core competences. Yet without such a consensus firms cannot exploit, maintain, and protect their competences.

Other challenges relate to the identification, development, and maintenance of core competences. There are significant difficulties involved in the identification of core competences. At one level, firms all too easily proclaim one or more core competences. This proclamation is usually the result of internal reflection rather than external comparisons, and can lead to firms attempting to protect an advantage which they subsequently find that all their competitors share. A second difficulty is the scope of core competences. One of the most widely cited examples of a competence is Honda's expertise in engines. But what exactly does this expertise consist of? The issue in identification is the level of specificity that should be employed. Is it sufficient to say Honda has a core competence in engine design, or should the identification of a core competence try to delve deeper into what it is about Honda's engine design that provides it with advantage; or, perhaps more significantly, what is it about the way in which it manages its engine design expertise that provides the advantage? This issue of scope is an obstacle for many firms in the identification of their competences. Prahalad and Hamel (1990) recommend three tests to help identify core competences. A core competence should, first, provide potential access to a wide range of markets; second, make a significant contribution to the perceived customer benefits of the end product; and, third, be difficult for competitors to imitate.

This leads to the challenges of development. Acquisitions (see ACQUISITION STRATEGY), alliances, and licensing may all play a critical role. In turn, this raises issues about the capacity of the organization to learn, but the process of learning is one of the least discussed elements of core competence management. Competences take time to develop (Dierickx and Cool, 1989), which necessitates a longer-term and committed approach to strategic direction-setting. Such an approach is often difficult in the current environment. Firms need to engage in long-term visioning about where they might want to be in 10 to 20 years' time, and about the competences that they will need to deliver this vision (Hamel and Prahalad, 1994).

The key issue in the maintenance of core competences is who "owns" them within the firm. Given that they cross SBUs, who is responsible for their continued development and use? They are all too easily lost through being taken for granted, outsourced, or starved of development resources. A related issue is their longevity: core competences do not last for ever. Firms need to review their competence portfolio on an ongoing basis in order to maintain and retain only those that continue to provide advantage.

Bibliography

Amit, R. and Schoemaker, P. J. H. (1993). Strategic assets and organizational rent. *Strategic Management Journal*, 14, 33–46.

Andrews, K. R. (1971). *The Concept of Corporate Strategy*. Homewood, IL: Irwin.

Barney, J. B. (1991). Firm resources and sustained competitive advantage. *Journal of Management*, 17, 99–120.

Child, J. L. (1972). Organizational structure, environment and performance: The role of strategic choice. *Sociology*, 6, 1–22.

Dierickx, I. and Cool, K. (1989). Asset stock accumulation and sustainability of competitive advantage. *Management Science*, 35, 1504–14.

Economist Intelligence Unit (1992). *Building Core Competences in a Global Economy*. Research Report No. 1–12. New York: *Economist* Intelligence Unit.

Hall, R. (1992). The strategic analysis of intangible resources. *Strategic Management Journal*, 13, 135–44.

Hamel, G. and Prahalad, C. K. (1994). *Competing for the Future*. Cambridge, MA: Harvard Business School Press.

Klavans, R. (1994). The measurement of a competitor's core competence. In G. Hamel and A. Heene (eds.), *Competence-Based Competition*. Chichester: John Wiley.

Leonard-Barton, D. (1992). Core capabilities and core rigidities: A paradox in managing new product development. *Strategic Management Journal*, 13, 111–25.

Mahoney, J. T. and Pandian, J. R. (1992). The resource-based view within the conversation of strategic management. *Strategic Management Journal*, 13, 363–80.

Prahalad, C. K. and Hamel, G. (1990). The core competence of the corporation. *Harvard Business Review*, 68, 79–91.

Rumelt, R. P. (1974). *Strategy, Structure and Economic Performance*. Cambridge, MA: Harvard University Press.

Stalk, G., Evans, P., and Shulman, L. (1992). Competing on capabilities: The new rules of corporate strategy. *Harvard Business Review*, 70, 57–69.

Teece, D. J., Pisano, G., and Shuen, A. (1990). *Firm Capabilities, Resources and the Concept of Strategy*. Consortium on Competitiveness and Cooperation Working Party No. 90–9. Berkeley: Center for Research in Management, University of California, Berkeley.

Winterschied, B. C. (1994). Building capability from within: The insiders' view of core competence. In G. Hamel and A. Heene (eds.), *Competence-Based Competition*. Chichester: John Wiley.

corporate governance

David Wilson

In recent years the importance of governance has become of prime concern in the strategic management of organizations of all kinds. Effective, honest, accountable, and transparent modes of governance are now sought of organizations by stakeholders of all varieties.

There is no single model of good governance. However the OECD (2004) has identified corporate governance as one of the key elements in improving economics efficiency and growth as well as enhancing investor confidence. The describes corporate governance as:

> ... involving a set of relationships between a company's management, its board, its shareholders and other stakeholders. Corporate governance also provides the structure through which the objectives of the company are set, and the means of attaining those objectives and monitoring performance are determined. Good corporate governance should provide proper incentives for the board and management to pursue objectives that are in the interests of the company and its shareholders and should facilitate effective monitoring. (OECD, 2004)

The OECD's Principles of Corporate Governance go on to say that:

> Corporate governance is only part of the larger economic context in which firms operate that includes, for example, macroeconomic policies and the degree of competition in product and factor markets. The corporate governance framework also depends on the legal, regulatory and institutional environment. In addition, factors such as business ethics and corporate awareness of the environment and societal interests of the communities in which a company operates can also have an impact on its reputation and its long-term success. (OECD, 2004)

There have been a number of recent scandals and exposes of alleged poor governance ranging from Enron, through Parmalat, to Shell. These failures expose some of the key principles and the importance of governance structures, processes, and accountabilities.

The Enron debacle was seen as a serious failure of strategists at board level. It heralded a new era of reviews and prescriptions for board behaviors and regulation. A new era, since the first code of good governance originated in the USA in 1978. There were, of course, other high profile failures in the US – Worldcom, Global Crossing, and Tyco. In Asia the economic crisis of 1997 was laid firmly at the door of poor governance by the Asian Development Bank. And, in Europe, Parmalat and Shell Oil have also been blamed for poor governance. Clearly not just a problem in US companies, nevertheless the US Business Round Table issued a report concerning the roles and composition of boards of directors of large publicly owned companies. Monks and Minow (1992) argued that the origin of this code was in response to increasingly criminal corporate behaviour and included guidelines to quell the occurrence of hostile takeovers. This focus on board behaviors and processes was essentially about the structure, composition and conduct of boards. The main points identified the chairman's main duties as:

- overseeing board members selection and succession;
- reviewing the organizations performance and allocating its funds;
- overseeing corporate social responsibility;
- adherence to the law.

It was not until 1989 that the next code of governance was issued, this time in Hong Kong by the Hong Kong Stock Exchange. This was rapidly followed in 1991 by a best practice set of guidelines issued by the Irish Association of Investment Managers (Aguilera and Cuervo-Cazurra, 2004). After this date, the Cadbury Committee Report in the UK (1992) heralded the authorship of many codes of good conduct with Aguilera and Cuervo-Cazurra (2004: 419) concluding that there were 72 codes of good governance by the end of 1999 spread across 24 industrialized and developing countries. See Table 1 for a summary.

Table 1 Numbers of codes of governance worldwide (to end 1999)

Country	Total number of codes
English-origin legal system:	
Australia	4
Canada	4
Hong Kong	4
India	2
Ireland	2
Malaysia	1
Singapore	1
South Africa	1
Thailand	1
UK	11
USA	17
French-origin legal system:	
Belgium	4
Brazil	1
France	4
Greece	1
Italy	2
Mexico	1
Netherlands	2
Portugal	1
Spain	2
German-origin legal system:	
Germany	1
Japan	2
Korea	1
Scandinavian-origin legal system:	
Sweden	2
Total countries 24	**Total codes 72**

Source: Adapted from Aguilera and Cuervo-Cazurra (2004: 423)

The codes produced under different legal systems have often been customized to particular national settings and this has reinforced the governance differences identified by Charkham (1999). However, institutions such as the World Bank and OECD are calling for common principles and common governance structures and processes, at least to a minimum level. Exogenous forces are influencing the adoption of reasonably common codes. As organizations become more a part of the global economy for example, the transmission of common practices becomes easier and, some would say, necessary. Government liberalization and the increasing influence of foreign institutional investors also force the pace for common codes and standards. In this way, exogenous pressures force countries to show that their codes of corporate governance are legitimate in the global economy.

THE CONTEXT OF CORPORATE GOVERNANCE

As early as the 1930s, Berle and Means (1932) drew attention to the growing separation of power between the executive management of major public companies and their increasingly diverse and remote shareholders. This view focused on the problem of control. The central question was to what extent could boards control executive management and thereby maintain the rights and influence of the shareholders as owners of the organization? This question has been addressed in terms of agency theory, in particular in economics. In this theory, the *agents* are corporate management, and the *principals* are the shareholders. In agency theory, the board is viewed as an alternative monitoring device, which helps to control the agents to further the interests of the principals. It is assumed in agency theory that effective boards will identify with shareholder interests and use their experience in decision-making and control to exert leverage over any self-interested tendencies of corporate management – the agents. For boards to exercise their vigilance role over the chief executive officer (CEO), the board needs power (Keasey, Thompson, and Wright, 1997). For the CEO to engage in self-interested activities there must presumably be a power imbalance between the CEO and the board.

Cadbury (2000) and Cassidy (2000) all offer accounts of the rise and rise of corporate governance as an issue in the USA and Europe since the 1980s. Central to their argument about why this issue has risen so far up the policy agenda have been:

- a succession of corporate scandals;
- performance weaknesses of many firms that could be attributed at least in part to poor governance and leadership;
- disjunctures between the compensation of CEOs and executive directors and the financial performance of the companies they manage (Conyon and Murphy, 2000).

Despite these varying accounts, it is clear that there are a common set of *endogenous* pressures and questions which revolve around the purposes, responsibilities, control, leadership, and power of boards. These questions include:

- How is oversight to be exercised over those delegated to the executive management of the firm?
- How are owner's interests to be protected?
- How are the interests of the other stakeholders such as consumers, employees, and local communities to be protected?
- Who sets the purpose and direction of the organization and ensures its accountability?
- How is power over the organization legitimised and to whom is an organization accountable and responsible?

CORPORATE GOVERNANCE IN THE UK

Modern UK corporate governance regulations began with the Cadbury Report (1992) which reviewed the financial aspects of corporate governance and led to the publication of the Code of Best Practice. This was followed by the Greenbury Committee (1995) which reviewed directors' remuneration, while the Hampel Committee on corporate governance (established in 1995 and reporting in 1998) had a broader remit that built on Cadbury and Greenbury, essentially picking up new issues that had arisen from both reports. Following the report of the Hampel Committee, the first edition of the Combined Code was published by the London Stock Exchange (LSE) Committee on Corporate Governance and was added as an appendix to the LSE Listing Rules. The code superseded all previous codes for UK-listed companies and was derived from Cadbury, Greenbury, Hampel, and the LSE's Listing Rules. The principles behind the code were those of market and self-regulation. The code was not legally enforceable, but a company was required to explain how the principles of the code had been followed and to disclose when and why they did not follow the code. If these reasons were not deemed acceptable by the stock market, it would be reflected in the company's stock price.

Since the publication of the first edition of the Combined Code, three other important reports have been published to date. These are the Turnbull Report, which provides guidelines for Directors on how to meet the Code's provisions on internal control; the Smith Report, which relates to the provisions on audit committees and auditors; and the Higgs Report, which was a review of the role and effectiveness of non-executive directors. The findings of these reports have been incorporated into the latest edition of the Combined Code (Higgs, 2003). It represents something of a capstone on the previous reports and it has had a significant impact on the structures and processes of boards in the UK. Like all previous codes, the combined code seeks to influence board structure and conduct by means of codes of practice and not through legislation. Boards are expected to comply or explain why they have not complied in their reporting mechanisms. The key requirements of the combined code are summarized in Table 2.

The reasons for not choosing a legal requirement for disclosure and relying on codes of practice, lies on the one hand, in the less than adequate provision of the legal structure in the UK to ensure good practice and, on the other, to encourage the spirit of self-regulation. For example, UK law rests on the principle that the owners (shareholders) appoint agents (directors) to run the business, and the directors report annually on their stewardship. In practice, in public limited companies (of which there are

Table 2 Key elements of the Combined Code

The main disclosures required are:
- A statement of how the board operates and which types of decisions are taken by the board and which are delegated to management.
- Number of meetings of the board and its committees including a list of annual attendance by directors.
- A description of how performance evaluation of the board, its committees and its directors is conducted.
- What steps have been taken to ensure that members of the board, especially non-executive directors, understand the views of major shareholders about their organization.
- A description of how the nomination committee works and why open advertising or an external search agency have not been used in either the appointments of a chairman or a non-executive director.
- A description of the processes and activities of the remuneration and audit committees.

The main principles of the Code are:
- Every company should be headed by an effective board which is collectively responsible for the success of the organization.
- A clear division of responsibilities. The roles of chairman and chief executive should not be exercised by the same individual and no one individual should have unfettered powers of decision. It is worth noting here that almost 10 percent of UK-listed companies have a joint chairman/chief executive (Hemscott, 2003).
- The board should include a balance of executive and independent non-executive directors.
- Transparency of all procedures.
- The board should undertake a formal and rigorous evaluation of its own performance and that of its committees and individual directors.
- All directors should be submitted for re-election at regular intervals subject to continued satisfactory performance. Refreshing the board with new members should be planned and implemented.
- Levels of remuneration should be sufficient to attract, retain and motivate directors but this should not include paying more than is necessary for this purpose. There should be a transparent policy on remuneration.
- Financial reporting should be understandable and transparent and subject to strict internal controls.

around 2,000 in the UK), there is a two-link chain of accountability. Management is accountable to directors, and directors are accountable to shareholders. PLCs registered after November 1, 1929 are legally required to have at least two directors. There is no distinction between classes of directors; for instance, between executive (inside or full-time) directors and non-executive (outside and part-time) directors. The law refers only obscurely to chairmen and barely mentions boards. This legal minimalism leads Charkham to conclude that:

> the superstructure as we know it: boards, board committees, chairmen, non-executive directors – are pragmatic adaptations. In law none is essential; to this day ICI could legally be run by two directors, like the consulate of the Roman Republic. (Charkham, 1999: 262)

Many UK boards divide the chairman and chief executive officer (CEO) roles, and the position of chairman is often part-time. Chairmen have major responsibilities in determining the size, balance, composition, and agenda of the board. They can also play a significant part in handling external relationships with key stakeholders such as government, institutional investors, regulators, and banks. Chairmen are normally appointed by non-executive directors. Non-executive directors play an increasingly important role in influencing board processes, heading up important committees of the board such as the audit or remuneration committees. Audit and remuneration committees comprise only non-executive directors and nomination committees are headed by a non-executive director or the chairman who must meet the independence criteria laid out in the Combined Code.

Bibliography

Aguilera, R. V. and Cuervo-Cazurra, A. (2004). Codes of good governance worldwide: What is the trigger? *Organization Studies*, 25 (3), 415–43.

Berle, A. A. and Means, G. C. (1932). *The Modern Corporation and Private Property*. New York: Macmillan.

Cadbury Report (1992). *Committee on the Financial Aspects of Corporate Governance*. London: Moorgate.

Cadbury, A. (2000). The corporate governance agenda. *Corporate Governance: An International Review*. 8 (1), 7–15.

Cassidy, D. P. (2000). Wither corporate governance in the 21st century. *Corporate Governance: An International Review*, 8 (4), 297–302.

Charkham, J. P. (1999). *Keeping Good Company: A Study of Corporate Governance in Five Countries*, (Second edition). Oxford: Oxford University Press.

Conyon, M. J. and Murphy, K. J. (2000). The prince and the pauper? CEO pay in the US and UK. *The Economic Journal*, 110, F640–71.

Greenbury, R. (1995). *Directors' Remuneration: Report of a Study Group Chaired by Sir Richard Greenbury*. London: Gee Publishing.

Hampel, R. (1998). *Committee on Corporate Governance: Final Report*. London, Gee Publishing

Keasey, K., Thompson, S., and Wright, M. (1997). *Corporate Governance: Economic Management and Financial Issues*. Oxford: Oxford University Press.

McGee, J., Wilson, D., and Thomas, H. (2005). *Strategy, Analysis and Practice*. Maidenhead: McGraw-Hill.

Monks, R. A. G. and Minow, N. (1992). *Power and Accountability: Restoring Balance of Power Between Corporations, Owners and Societies*. New York: Harper Business.

OECD (2004). *Principles of Corporate Governance*. www.OECD.org

corporate recovery

see TURNAROUND STRATEGY

corporate reputation

Gary Davies

Corporate reputation has been defined in two different ways, reflecting the different uses of the term in various literatures. It has been used to denote our expectations of a firm's future actions, for example, the perceived likelihood that it will defend its markets (Weigelt and Camerer, 1988; Clark and Montgomery, 1998). Or, more often, it has been used to describe the opinion or impression that we have of a firm, created, as one of the earliest definitions has it, from the "net result of the interaction of all the experiences, impressions, beliefs, feelings and knowledge that people have about a company" (Bevis, 1967). Reputation is also conceptualized as a reservoir of goodwill, a bank deposit of trust that can be drawn down by a company when its deeds are called into question. Bernstein (1985) provided a clear view of how we create such a picture. Any organization will be seen through two stereotyping filters, the first due to the economic sector of which it is a part (e.g., "all" oil companies contribute to environmental damage), and the second due to the stereotype that we have of organizations on account of their country of origin. The importance of the "country of origin" effect has been widely researched, although mainly in consumer markets (e.g., Bannister and Saunders, 1978). These two filters will have added to them an additional layer, a more detailed picture of the firm derived from direct contact with it or from absorbing media comment and advertising messages.

Our initial picture of a firm, before we have actual contact with it, is typically based upon these two stereotypes. We use these views until we receive more tangible evidence, but even objective information will still be selectively filtered through our initial stereotyping. Employees will have benefited from greater experience of the corporate culture and will have, from their induction, training, and internal communication, substantially modified any initial stereotype. The interaction between employee and customer will be influenced by the relationship between employee and customer perceptions. For example, if both trust the organization to deliver on its promises, the interaction is likely to be more pleasant, faster, and more straightforward, and therefore to incur fewer TRANSACTIONS COSTS.

For many an organization, reputation can be a useful focus for long-term planning. How it is seen by different stakeholders will determine its success in recruiting and retaining staff, in attracting and developing its customers, in gaining preferential treatment by local and national government, in being seen as an attractive company in which to invest or supply to. Where the name of the company is also its corporate brand, as with many service organizations reputation can be key to success. Loss of reputation is perceived to be one of the greatest risks facing any company in the eyes of the CEO (AON, 2004). While reputational risk management is widely understood in terms of crisis management (Mitroff, 1988), how reputation should be managed systematically and proactively is less clear. Few companies appear to have a defined budget for reputation building, even in those companies where senior managers appeared to be convinced about the existence of direct relationships between improving reputation and improving sales and profit (Davies and Miles, 1998).

The particular relevance of corporate reputation to a service business has been widely noted (e.g., Berry, Lefkowith, and Clark, 1988; Alvesson, 1990). In a service business the corporate name is often used to influence a number of different stakeholders, whereas in many manufacturing companies individual products are often marketed under their own distinctive brand names, names that are different from the corporate name. The end customer may never interact with the manufacturer directly, but is more likely to deal with a retailer or distributor that has its own reputation. In a service business the image of the organization is likely to be influenced by a direct interaction between employee and customer. Customers may well be influenced by the culture of the organization as they enter, temporarily, into it. This may explain a common claim in the reputation literature, that there is a direct link between how internal and external stakeholders see the same organization (Davies et al., 2003), to the point where some argue for the need to align or harmonize internal (corporate) and external (brand) values as an integral part of reputation management. Reputation managers certainly see their role as being concerned with managing corporate values.

There are two views on the practicality of aligning these two groups of values. Those arguing for alignment claim that any gaps between the two create a potential for crises, when external stakeholders, especially customers, suddenly realize that the image they have of the organization is very different from the reality. The competing view is that different stakeholders will have quite different requirements and that the challenge for reputation managers is to recognize these differences so that they can aim to satisfy them all. For example, Fombrun (1996) suggests that trust might be the most important issue for employees, credibility for investors, responsibility for the general community, and reliability for customers. Doyle (1998) takes a position midway between the two opposing views and argues that a tolerance zone will exist, a region of operation where not every stakeholder will be satisfied, but where no one stakeholder will feel that the organization is acting in an unacceptable way.

The allied idea that the external image of an organization can be managed by establishing a strong internal identity, through a clear vision and a strong culture, has its supporters and, if valid, offers credible links to mainstream strategic thinking. Having a strong and differentiated image in the market (the market for customers) is an accepted generic strategy (see GENERIC STRATEGIES) and brand image can act as an entry barrier (see BARRIERS TO ENTRY AND EXIT) for potential competitors who lack a clear image. If similar imagery can be used to attract better employees and influence other stakeholders positively, then reputation management has potential as a strategic framework.

One reason why the debate about reputational alignment and gaps persists is that there is no agreed method for measuring reputation. The most widely quoted approach is that of *Fortune* magazine and its ranking of America's Most Admired Companies (AMAC). Other, media-driven, rankings are produced for overall reputation, the best company to be employed by, the most socially responsible company, and so on. To produce the AMAC rankings, companies are chosen from the largest US companies (ranked by revenue) and a small number of the largest US subsidiaries of foreign-owned companies. They are sorted by industry and the ten largest selected in each industry to constitute 57 separate groups.

To create the rankings, 10,000 executives, directors, and securities analysts select the five companies they admire most, regardless of industry. The group is told to choose from a list containing the companies that ranked among the top 25 percent in the previous year's survey, the list also including companies that ranked below the first quartile overall but which finished in the top 20 percent of their industry. To create the industry lists, the executives, directors, and analysts are asked to rank companies in their own industry on eight criteria:

- quality of management;
- quality of products/services;
- innovativeness;
- long-term investment value;
- financial soundness;
- employee talent;
- use of corporate assets; and
- social responsibility.

Fortune rankings correlate with financial performance, leading to the conclusion that a relatively good reputation ranking creates relatively good financial performance. In reality, the reverse is more likely to be the causal route (financial performance creates reputation ranking) as the rankings are dependent upon measures that are directly or indirectly financial and made by those whose view of a firm will be dominated by its financial performance. Research using the *Fortune* data demonstrates the strong interlinkages between the various items in the measure (McGuire, Sundgren, and Schneeweis, 1988; Sobol and Farrelly, 1988), and the *Fortune* approach has been widely criticized as being overly dominated by the financial performance of the companies (e.g., Fryxell and Wang, 1994). Even more damning to the reputation of the use of ranking data is that Enron, in the year prior to its collapse, was ranked very highly in the AMAC rankings, particularly for innovation and the quality of its management.

Organizations may nevertheless be tempted to play "the ranking game" and adjust their strategy to suit the criteria used to create an influential ranking. The decision as to whether to enter such a game can be seen in the way business schools view the many rankings available to potential MBA students. It can force business schools to play "a game of illusion" with very intangible results, and even to choose to misrepresent themselves (Corley and Gioia, 2000). Playing the ranking game may threaten a

school's identity if they have to pretend to be what they are not or feel pressure to change to something they do not wish to be. Worse, should all schools play the ranking game, and do so more or less equally well, the same applicants would still be shared by the same providers in much the same way as before. There would be a general "blanding" rather than BRANDING, and thus less differentiation of business schools, and the MBA itself becomes commoditized. Nevertheless, rankings do matter, as those who work in the sector can attest!

Fombrun, Gardberg, and Sever (2000) propose an alternative to existing indices such as *Fortune* that could overcome some criticisms, particularly those from an academic perspective. Their measurement tool includes six dimensions drawn from an appraisal of the reputation literature. Davies et al. (2003) develop a different line of thinking drawn from the branding and organization literatures using the metaphor of company as person to assess both internal and external perspectives using a "corporate personality scale." The scale has been used to test the claimed benefits or otherwise of alignment, finding support for both perspectives on the issue. A picture emerges where early thinking about alignment and gaps appear to be generalizations that have no clear empirical support. A contingent approach appears to be the most practical where the reputation of the organization from the perspective of multiple stakeholders should be appropriately measured and an assessment made of what is important in influencing different groups, without any prejudging of the need to align internal and external values.

Reputation is an intangible asset. Various proprietary methods have been marketed to provide a valuation for a corporate brand name (Kumar, 1999), and interest in valuation has increased following the decision to allow the inclusion of valuations for intangible assets within the balance sheet (Arnold et al., 1992). If reputation is a significant, perhaps the largest, asset a company has, then how it is managed becomes important. The reputation asset is unusual in that valuation is difficult and its value can be volatile. Worse, while there may be budgets for refurbishing buildings, the maintenance of machinery, and the upkeep of land, there are few companies with budgets targeted for reputation building (Miles and Davies, 1997). Reputation management is in its infancy as a business function. Currently the norm is for a corporate communications function to be responsible for managing communication with many stakeholders, but not for advertising and other factors that may influence reputation. The corporate communications role has evolved from public relations. Being typically focused on managing media relations, it is more reactive and tactical in nature than strategic. Links to marketing (responsible for external brand values) and human relations (responsible for internal corporate values) are unclear.

Reputation can be destroyed in seconds and the need to defend it is widely accepted, but it is unclear how reputation should be built and how strong the link from reputation to financial performance really is. If such issues can be addressed convincingly, then expect reputation management to emerge as a new business function and as one approach to the STRATEGIC MANAGEMENT of organizations, especially those in the services sector.

Bibliography

Alvesson, M. (1990). Organization: From substance to image? *Organization Studies*, 11 (3), 373–94.

AON (2004). www.aon.com/uk/en/about/Publications/biennial

Arnold, J., Egginton, D., Kirkham, L., Macve, R., and Peasnell, K. (1992). *Goodwill and Other Intangibles*. London: Institute of Chartered Accountants of England and Wales.

Bannister, J. P. and Saunders, J. A. (1978). UK consumers' attitudes towards imports: The measurement of national stereotype image. *European Journal of Marketing*, 19 (November), 562–84.

Bernstein, D. (1985). *Company Image and Reality*. Eastbourne: Holt, Rinehart, and Winston.

Berry, L. L., Lefkowith, E. E., and Clark, T. (1988). In services, what's in a name? *Harvard Business Review*, September/October, 28–30.

Bevis J. C. (1967). How corporate image is used. ESOMAR Conference, Vienna.

Clark, B. H. and Montgomery, D. B (1998). Deterrence, reputations and competitive cognition. *Management Science*, 44 (1), 62–83.

Corley, K. and Gioia, D. (2000). The reputation game: Managing business school reputation. *Corporate Reputation Review*, 3 (4), 319–33.

Davies, G., Chun, R., Da Silva, R., and Roper, S. (2003). *Corporate Reputation and Competitiveness*. London: Routledge.

Davies, G. and Miles L. (1998). Reputation management: Theory versus practice. *Corporate Reputation Review*, 2 (1), 16–27.

Doyle, P. (1998). *Marketing Management and Strategy*, 2nd edn. London: Prentice-Hall.

Fombrun, C. J. (1996). *Reputation: Realizing Value from the Corporate Image*. Cambridge, MA: Harvard Business School Press.

Fombrun, C. J., Gardberg, N. A., and Sever, J. M. (2000). The reputation quotient: A multi-stakeholder measure of corporate reputation. *Journal of Brand Management*, 7 (4), 241–55.

Fryxell, G. E. and Wang, J. (1994). The *Fortune* corporate "reputation" index: Reputation for what? *Journal of Management*, 20 (1), 1–14.

Kumar, S. (1999). Valuing corporate reputation. In *Reputation Management*. London: IOD and Kogan Page.

McGuire, J. B., Sundgren, A., and Schneeweis, T. (1988). Corporate social responsibility and firm financial performance. *Academy of Management Journal*, 31 (4), 854–72.

Miles, L. and Davies, G. (1997). *What Price Reputation?* London: Haymarket Business.

Mitroff, I. I. (1988). Crisis management: Cutting through the confusion. *Sloan Management Review*, Winter, 15–20.

Sobol, M. and Farrelly, G. (1988). Corporate reputation: A function of relative size or financial performance. *Review of Business and Economic Research*, 26 (1), 45–59.

Weigelt, K. and Camerer, C. (1988). Reputation and corporate strategy: A review of recent theory and applications. *Strategic Management Journal*, 9, 443–54.

corporate strategy

Chris Smith

The importance of the study of corporate strategy stems from the fact that large businesses are increasingly large *multibusinesses*, and networks between businesses (e.g., STRATEGIC ALLIANCES) are becoming more common. This is true across the globe, from the *chaebols* of Korea (*see* CHAEBOL STRUCTURE) and the *keiretsus* of Japan (*see* KEIRETSU STRUCTURE) to the corporate sweep of America's GE and Europe's ABB. As such, it is not just ongoing COMPETITIVE STRATEGY – the long-term dynamics of serving customers better than the competition – that occupies the minds of the top managers and investors. It is also ongoing *corporate* strategy – the value gained from the mixture of businesses and how to manage those businesses to optimize that value. Corporate strategy for multibusiness firms goes far beyond the traditional ideas of the choices of which industry/markets/products to be in. Figure 1 captures the three main ideas or insights that are fundamental to corporate strategy:

- *Portfolio management*: the businesses that should make up the portfolio.
- *Growth*: the way in which profitable growth is to be achieved both through internal investment and/or external acquisitions (*see* ACQUISITION STRATEGY).
- *Relatedness*: the way in which the synergies between businesses are to be managed and exploited (*see* SYNERGY).

At the level of the business, strategy has three important dimensions: COMPETITIVE ADVANTAGE (how to compete), the key resource allocation decisions at the business level, and the organization of the business. At the corporate level there is a parallel concern with resource allocation decisions, but at the corporate level and with organization structure and process. However, the distinguishing characteristic of the multibusiness firm is that at the center it is concerned with what businesses to be in – the portfolio question. The answer is, of course, contingent on the nature of competitive advantages, but decisions about the portfolio are taken at corporate level, whereas responsibility for securing competitive advantage is at the business level.

The economics of corporate strategy revolve around the three issues in figure 1.

1   The characteristics of the portfolio expressed as its overall return and its overall risk. This allows for gains from the statistical nature of pooled variances that means that imperfectly correlated risks of the individual businesses result in lower overall risk. This is on the basis of avoiding having all one's eggs in the same basket. It should be noted that the gains from DIVERSIFICATION may mitigate disaster, but themselves do not promote competitive advantage.

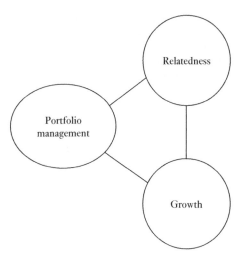

Figure 1   The three essential insights of corporate strategy

2   How synergies between businesses are captured – the idea of relatedness.
3   The growth ambitions of the firm and how these are to be achieved by internal investment and/or expansion.

There are insights and traps attached to each of these issues. Portfolio analysis arrays the strengths and weaknesses of each business. In particular the sources of cash and profit can be established and investment needs specified. Thus it is possible to assess for the portfolio what are its cash flow and profit characteristics in relation to its overall risk. However, if taken too literally, portfolio analysis can focus excessively on eliminating unprofitable, low-potential businesses and expanding high-potential businesses without attention to any underlying synergies and complementarities.

Relatedness determines whether interdependencies between businesses can create value and competitive advantage or whether each business should be treated on its own merits. The trap is that poorly performing businesses should not be maintained from "overall strength" without strong evidence of value potential from relatedness.

Sensible growth objectives and analysis identify how resources can be deployed to maintain a balance between investment, cash flow, and profits over time. Proper analysis prevents misdirected growth that focuses on growth for its own sake, leading to inappropriate timing and falling into cash traps (*see* CASH TRAP).

Corporate organization has to be consistent with the economics of the strategy. This too can be described in three parts.

1 Definition of division and business unit boundaries.
2 The intended lateral integration and coordination between business units.
3 The vertical relationships between corporate tasks and roles and line operations – the corporate–business interface.

Business unit boundaries and groupings of businesses (divisions or sectors) can be the natural and powerful way to exploit relatedness opportunities. Superior performance frequently requires that businesses be properly focused on relevant markets – that the boundaries should be drawn correctly. New boundaries should be drawn (i.e., reorganization) when the value of increasing the focus (narrowing the scope) exceeds the cost of lost relatedness benefits, and vice versa.

The corporate–business interface sets out authority and accountability in the firm. Three particular styles are commonly observed (*see* CORPORATE STYLES). STRATEGIC PLANNING involves corporate executives deeply in defining and monitoring corporate and business strategies. It is most appropriate for capital-intensive operations and highly interrelated businesses. *Strategic control* involves corporate executives in influencing business-level strategies and monitoring financial results. It is a "loose–tight" approach. *Financial control* decentralizes control of business strategy to the business and relies solely on financial control at the corporate level. It is deemed to be most appropriate for conglomerate-like strategies.

Integration mechanisms are used to balance choices made on boundaries and on the corporate-business interface. The formality of the latter two can be supplemented by less formal arrangements that can pick up related possibilities not captured within business boundaries and neglected by the corporate level need to have strong vertical controls. Therefore, self-interested lateral cooperation has a natural

place in complementing the formal organizational arrangements. More formal lateral mechanisms include centers of excellence, people transfers, transfer pricing systems, special study teams, lead business arrangements, and internal consulting. Vertical mechanisms are also possible such as intermediate levels of organization and arrangements of cross-functional authority. Strategic control styles of management typically require more explicit processes for lateral integration than other forms of control.

RESEARCH

The multidivisional firm has attracted the interest of academics and management authors. Two major questions have been the focus of research and writing:

1 *What is the additional value generated by such firms?* This is an economic question, which addresses what value is inherent in having a group of potentially stand-alone businesses under one management. Writings on this question are found mainly in academic journals and focus particularly on the value of groupings of related businesses and the associated issue of synergy.
2 *How are they best managed?* This is an organizational/strategic question, which addresses how value is optimized and, in particular, what is the role of the corporate head office in all this. This question addresses what is known as "corporate strategy" in the STRATEGIC MANAGEMENT literature.

While corporate strategy is still used by some in an all-encompassing sense, most authors now identify corporate strategy with multibusiness firms. Porter's view is typical:

> Corporate strategy, *the overall plan for a diversified company* ... concerns two different questions: what businesses the corporation should be in and how the corporate office should manage the array of business units. (Porter, 1987: 43, emphasis added)

Thus, corporate strategy is concerned with the choice of industries to compete in, the setting of an organizational context for the operations of the component business units, and managing the relationships between those businesses.

THE INHERENT VALUE OF A MULTIBUSINESS FIRM

Writers in economics and strategic management are agreed that the *economic* logic of multibusiness corporations, and hence a potential reason for their proliferation, is that the whole is worth more than the sum of its parts:

$$V_c = A_s + B_s + C_s + M_c$$

where V_c is the value of the corporation, A_s, B_s, C_s are the respective values of the stand-alone businesses A, B, and C, and M_c is the total net value of corporate membership, i.e., *membership benefits*, so:

$$V_c > A_s + B_s + C_s \text{ by the value of } M_c$$

In many cases M_c has proven to be negative. When this situation prevails, the breakup of the corporation is a financially attractive strategy, as proved by the corporate raiders–asset strippers of the 1980s.

M_c has different sources. Organizational gain, derived from the splitting of strategy and operations, has a value-logic grounded in managerial efficiency and focus. This traditional rationale, allied to the benefits of size and scale, seems an adequate explanation of the *reorganization* of growing companies from (inefficient) U-form to (efficient) M-form. However, this argument does not explain why the total value of the component businesses can be higher under a corporate umbrella than if they were stand-alone. This is a very important issue for investors, who are free to invest directly in the stand-alone businesses without the necessity of a corporate layer.

Theorists in the general area of what is known as transaction cost economics (TCE) offer some of the most persuasive ideas about the potential added value of the M-form. They propose two major categories of benefit: *governance* and *scope* advantages.

Governance.   Under this category, the corporate office takes the role of a more informed and involved investor. Unlike arm's length investors,

it is fully knowledgeable about the businesses via direct reporting and auditing mechanisms and can pressure business managers for improved performance, whilst paying market rate salaries. In a stand-alone business, a manager can take advantage of the fact that he or she controls the information flow to the investment community and can hide the true nature of any problems. In a multibusiness firm, the corporate office has all the necessary information and can sanction or replace managers of underperforming units. The corporate office also has an overview that the business manager lacks, and can thus add further information and insight to his/her decisions. In stand-alone units, business managers can maximize what has been called "on-the-job consumption," for example, making (unnecessary), spouse-accompanied, weeklong visits to desirable locations, flying first class and staying in five-star hotels. The additional corporate layer can police and prevent such dissipation of shareholders' funds. This "advantage" begs the obvious question of who guards the guards. In light of increasingly spectacular returns to directors of public companies, this is a question worth asking.

Scope.   As well as potentially dealing with the tensions between owners and managers through governance mechanisms, the multibusiness organization is argued to have value-enhancing properties, in that it can facilitate ECONOMIES OF SCOPE. *Related* businesses (those with similar markets/technologies/processes) can share specialized physical capital, knowledge, and managerial expertise. The sharing process is overseen and controlled, and disputes resolved by corporate management. With stand-alone businesses, such sharing is problematic. Potential problems include ongoing haggling, the risk of one partner exploiting the trust of the other, the risk of being let down, and the tendency for partners to try to benefit more than their input would warrant (This is an example of the "free-rider" problem and is familiar to students undertaking group work, when one member seems to get out of most of the duties, but shares in the overall assessment.) Under normal circumstances, stand-alone businesses attempt to control these problems through formal contracts and a "trading relationship." However, such sharing is not amenable to formal contract, particularly in the case of specialized organizational knowledge embodied in people. Tacit components, team embeddedness, and the uncertainty of its value make such learning particularly difficult to trade.

It is through scope economies between related businesses that corporate *synergies* (the total being more than the sum of the parts) are hypothesized to be most attainable. A relatively recent expression of scope economies has been the popularization of the concept of CORE COMPETENCES that are "the collective learning in the organization, especially how to coordinate diverse production skills and integrate multiple streams of technology" (Prahalad and Hamel, 1990: 82). The importance of core competences for multibusiness firms is that they can "*span businesses* and products within a corporation. Put differently, powerful core competencies *support several* products or *businesses*."

Prahalad and Hamel (1990), emphasizing the importance of trans-business capabilities, assert that core competences are the "central subject of corporate strategy" (p. 220) and that multibusiness companies should see themselves as a "portfolio of competencies" (p. 221) – as well as a portfolio of products and services, that is. Economies of scope are the nub of corporate strategy and the fundamental rationale for the M-form company.

See also *divisional structure; organization structure*

Bibliography

Campbell, A., Goold, M., and Alexander, M. (1995). Corporate strategy: The quest for parenting advantage. *Harvard Business Review*, March/April, 120–32.

Goold, M., Campbell, A., and Alexander, M. (1994). *Corporate-Level Strategy: Creating Value in the Multibusiness Company*. New York: John Wiley.

Porter, M. E. (1987). From competitive advantage to corporate strategy. *Harvard Business Review*, May/June, 2–21.

Prahalad, C. K. and Hamel, G. (1990). The core competence of the corporation. *Harvard Business Review*, May/June, 79–91.

Teece, D. J. (1982). Towards an economic theory of the multiproduct firm. *Journal of Economic Behavior and Organization*, 3, 39–63.

corporate styles

Chris Smith

Goold and Campbell (1987) examined high-performing corporations and concluded that the *style* of the parent is an important factor in the level of performance achieved. They examined the extent to which management styles varied along the dimensions of *planning influence* (i.e., the extent to which the corporate level became involved in the strategic and operating planning of the business; *see* STRATEGIC PLANNING) and *control influence* (i.e., the extent to which the businesses were held to budgetary and operational targets) (see figure 1).

Three styles seemed to stand out. In *financial control* companies (e.g., BTR), the center allowed a high degree of strategic and operational autonomy to the businesses (low planning influence). The budget, however, was sacrosanct and any slippage from planned performance needed swift correction, if it were not to mean the curtailment of the career of the responsible GM (high control influence). At the other end of the continuum, *strategic planning* companies (e.g., ICI) involved themselves on an ongoing basis in the strategic planning and management of the businesses (high planning control). They were more flexible if strategic contingencies caused operational performance to slip against budgeted targets, i.e., the budget was a reflection of the strategy (low control influence). In between these two extremes were the *strategic control* companies. (In

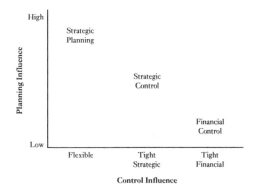

Figure 1   Parenting styles (Goold et al., 1994: 412)

a summary of this work in Goold, Campbell, and Alexander, 1994, the authors conclude that there is a continuing movement away from the *financial control* to the strategic *planning/control styles*.)

This work on styles is consistent with the view that optimizing CORPORATE STRATEGY is contingent on the appropriate organizational structures, systems, processes, etc.

> Corporate strategies that predominantly use one or other of these three roles to realize the value inherent in their resources should, according to contingency theory, align their structure, systems, and procedures according to those roles. (Collis, 1991: 7)

In accordance with this view, corporations do not need large corporate staffs if they are relying on a stand-alone influence role, whereas a coordinated and integrated staff is needed if inter-business relationships are to be a major source of value. In a similar way, the structure of business manager incentives should vary, with group-based incentives needed for inter-business-oriented corporations and stand-alone incentives appropriate for the more managerial orientations.

As well as the view that organizational structure, processes, etc. should be contingent on the corporate role, there is also the view that the optimal corporate role is contingent on the degree of *relatedness* between the business units.

To realize ECONOMIES OF SCOPE (*see* SYNERGY) from relatedness, *cooperation* between businesses is required (*see* COOPERATIVE STRATEGIES). This leads to increased centralization of functions and systems, and an increase in integrating mechanisms between businesses. The performance ambiguities inherent in sharing facilities and functions are tackled by seeking more information on a broader, less financial, range of indicators, and by business incentives based on group rather than individual performance. A value-enhancing, cooperative form may be a sustainable parenting advantage for a firm, as its unique history and social context make it idiosyncratic to the firm and, thus, more difficult to imitate.

Unrelated businesses have no opportunities for increased value from economies of scope and are argued to benefit from M-form membership due to governance benefits. Within such a framework, the corporate office of the M-form takes on the role of informed investor and runs the businesses on a *competitive* basis, as stand-alone entities that are rivals for capital, which is allocated on a "best-use" basis, consistent with external capital markets. Performance incentives are based on unambiguous, financial outputs. A summary of the proposed relationships between inherent value, basic corporate strategy, and organizational factors is shown in table 1.

In contrast to the optimism of multiple, coexistent corporate roles expressed by Porter (1987) and Goold et al. (1994), Hill (1994) points out

Table 1   Relationships between inherent value, basic corporate strategy, and organizational factors

	Source of inherent (economic) value	
	Economies of scope (related businesses)	Governance (unrelated businesses)
Basic corporate strategy	Cooperative multidivisional	Competitive multidivisional
Operating and business-level strategic decisions	Some centralization of critical functions	Complete decentralization
Inter-business integrating mechanisms	Moderate to extensive	Non-existent
Business performance appraisal	Mix of subjective and objective criteria	Primary reliance on objective financial criteria
Business incentive schemes	Linked to corporate performance	Based on business performance only

that the "radical differences" between these two types of M-form are such that

> it may be difficult for diversified firms to simultaneously realize economic benefits from economies of scope and efficient governance. ... Competitive and cooperative organizations have different internal configurations with regard to centralization, integration, control practices and incentive schemes. As a result *the internal management philosophies of cooperative and competitive organizations are incompatible.* (Hill, 1994: 312–13, emphasis added)

This means that cooperative and competitive philosophies are different strategies with different organizational and managerial arrangements. Thus, if an M-form firm is comprised of a set of businesses, some of which are related and others are not, it is faced with an economic and organizational dilemma. One resolution of this dilemma is to divest units and focus on a CORE BUSINESS grouping.

Another resolution is through the creation of another organizational level – the *division*, into which all the businesses related in a particular way (e.g., all those in the automotive components industry) are placed. In this sense, the division becomes an internal (quasi-) corporation and the divisional-level managers can focus on optimizing the relatedness of their component businesses.

Bibliography

Collis, D. (1991). Managing the multibusiness corporation. *Harvard Business Review*, Note 9-391-286.

Goold, M. and Campbell, A. (1987). *Strategies and Styles: The Role of the Center in Managing Diversified Companies*. Cambridge, MA: Blackwell.

Goold, M., Campbell, A., and Alexander, M. (1994). *Corporate-Level Strategy: Creating Value in the Multibusiness Company*. New York: John Wiley.

Hill, C. W. L. (1994). Diversification and economic performance: Bringing structure and corporate management back into the picture. In R. Rumelt, D. Schendel, and D. Teece (eds.), *Fundamental Issues in Strategy*. Boston: Harvard Business School Press, pp. 297–321.

Hoskisson, R. E., Hill, C. W. L., and Kim, H. (1993). The multidivisional structure: Organizational fossil or source of value? *Journal of Management*, **19** (2), 269–98.

Porter, M. E. (1987). From competitive advantage to corporate strategy. *Harvard Business Review*, May/June, 2–21.

corporate transformation

Derek F. Channon

The high failure rate of BUSINESS PROCESS REENGINEERING (BPR) projects has led to the development of a more subtle approach that has been called a biological model of corporate transformation, identifying the corporation as essentially an organic evolving entity. The model consists of four broad categories of activity leading to transformation. As developed by Gemini Consulting, corporate transformation is defined as "the orchestrated redesign of the genetic architecture of the corporation, achieved by working simultaneously – although at different speeds – along the four dimensions of Reframing, Restructuring, Revitalization and Renewal." These four dimensions are seen as a biological process as follows:

- *Reframing* is seen as shifting the company's perception of what it is and what it can achieve. It is designed to open the corporation's mindset and allow it to refocus.

- *Restructuring* deals with the body of the corporation and addresses competitive fitness. This activity is most akin to the BPR approach and involves similar techniques.

- *Revitalization* endeavors to link the revised corporate body to its environment, and is considered to be the factor that most clearly differentiates transformation from the perceived harshness of reengineering. The intention is not to obliterate activities but, rather, to change them positively to encourage revitalized performance.

- *Renewal* is concerned with the "people" side of transformation and with the spirit of the company. It is concerned with investment in skills and purpose to allow the company to self-regenerate with new confidence and enthusiasm; this is in contrast to reengineering projects, whose often morale-sapping impact is a major cause of failure. This activity is perhaps the most difficult to achieve, and is seen by many critics of reengineering change to be the point at which many consultants, brought in as change agents, leave their clients.

Gemini believes that 12 corporate "chromosomes" comprise the biocorporate genome, three for each of the four Rs. While each chromosome can be considered independently, they are all integrated into a total system. The chief executive officer (CEO) and the executive leadership are seen as the genetic architects of the corporation and are thus not expected to be involved in operational detail.

THE REFRAMING CHROMOSOMES

1 *Achieve mobilization.* This activity is the process of bringing together the mental energy required to initiate the transformation process. It involves moving motivation and commitment from the individual to the team, and ultimately to the total corporation.
2 *Create the vision.* The development of a corporate vision is essential to provide a shared mental framework that stretches the future dimensions of the corporation and, in human terms, provides a common sense of purpose with which people can identify. The role of the CEO in establishing such a vision is crucial.
3 *Building a measurement system.* Once the corporation is mobilized and provided with a vision, new measurement systems that allow management to monitor progress toward the future will usually be required. While often quantified, such measures will usually emphasize the strategic progress rather than the financial history. In human terms, the system should also create an identifiable sense of commitment (*see* BALANCED SCORECARD).

THE RESTRUCTURING CHROMOSOMES

4 *Construct an economic model.* This involves the systematic top-down disaggregation of a corporation in financial terms from shareholder VALUE-BASED PLANNING to ACTIVITY-BASED COSTING and service-level assessment. It provides a detailed view of how and where value is created or cost allowed in the bioanalogy of the cardiovascular system for resources to be deployed where they are needed, and redistributed from where they are not needed.
5 *Align the physical infrastructure.* This element is analogous to the corporate skeletal system and consists of the appropriate alignment of the resources of the corporation's assets, such as plants, warehouses, transportation, and equipment. While these are relatively fixed, there is also a need for continuous monitoring and, on occasion, change, as when a bone is fractured, to allow for strategic healing.
6 *Redesign the work architecture.* The work of the corporation is achieved via a complex network of processes which is identified as the work architecture. These need to be correctly configured and aligned and this process can be linked to reengineering.

THE REVITALIZATION SYSTEMS

7 *Achieve a market focus.* To Gemini, revitalization implies growth. To achieve this, customer focus provides the starting point, as developing new and perhaps undiscovered benefits that the corporation can offer to its customers leads to business growth. For the corporation, market focus provides the senses in the biological analogy.
8 *Invent new business.* Growth can also occur as the result of the development of new businesses. These can emerge from the cross-fertilization of capabilities from within the corporation, or by the introduction of activities from outside via MERGERS AND ACQUISITIONS, STRATEGIC ALLIANCES, joint ventures (*see* JOINT VENTURE STRATEGY), etc. The biological analogy of this concept can be seen as the reproductive system.
9 *Change the rules through information technology.* The strategic use of information technology can produce new ways to compete by redefining the rules of the game in many traditional industries. Biologically, the use of such technology is analogous to the nervous system.

THE RENEWAL SYSTEMS

10 *Create a reward structure.* An appropriate reward structure is seen as a major motivating force on human behavior. When the motivation system is wrongly aligned with desired behavior, it can also act as a serious demotivator and encourage undesired behavior.

11 *Build individual learning.* Corporate transformation can only successfully take place when the skills and learning of many individuals are also transformed. Individual learning promotes self-actualization of the people who constitute the corporation.

12 *Develop the organization.* Corporations are seen as needing to organize for continuous learning, enabling them to constantly adapt to an ever-changing environment in which the pace of change is often accelerating. Organizational development thus allows the corporation to evolve and fosters a sense of community amongst individuals.

Conclusion

The corporate transformation process has been applied in many corporations around the world. Such transformations frequently involve modifying the behavior of many thousands of people, often on a global basis. Such transformations take time, sometimes many years, but the end result is expected to produce transformed corporations capable of continuous adaptation to permit successful evolution.

Bibliography

Gouillard, F. J. and Kelly, J. N. (1995). *Transforming the Corporation.* New York: McGraw-Hill.

cost analysis

John McGee

The firm needs to examine the implications of its decisions for the costs of the business – the link between decision-making and costs is central to an understanding of long-run cost position and competitiveness. The guiding principle is the idea of *opportunity cost.* This is defined by Seldon and Penance (1965: 253) as "The sacrifice of alternatives foregone in producing goods or services." For example, the cost of capital for project A is the return foregone by taking project A rather than project B. It is not simply the cash cost of the funds required for project A. For an individual, the opportunity cost of a new car might be the benefits foregone by not extending the house. For a company, the opportunity cost of expansion into North America might be the return foregone by not investing in China. The notion of opportunity cost rests on the fact of scarcity, that resources are limited in relation to the possibilities that exist. Without scarcity there would be no concept of cost, and indeed economics and economic thinking would be irrelevant.

The strength and pervasiveness of the concept of opportunity cost lead us into an understanding of *relevant costs*: the costs associated with a decision are those costs that are directly affected and changed by a decision. The significance of this is that costs are decision-specific, and therefore they are unlikely to be routinely available from those costs reported in the annual accounts for the purposes of reporting to shareholders. Accounting costs are typically backward looking and relate to the firm as a whole, whereas relevant costs are decision-specific and relate to future costs. Management accounting strives to bridge this gap by taking a future perspective, although by its nature it cannot in setting budgets anticipate the characteristics of decisions that are relevant for future costs.

Many costs arise directly from the scale (volume) of operation of a business. The term *cost structure* refers to the technical conditions of production in the markets in which A and B operate. The critical issue is the balance of costs between *fixed costs*, which do not vary with output (e.g., the cost of machines or buildings or R&D spending), and *variable costs*, which do (e.g., labor costs or raw material costs). Table 1 sets out the definitions of these different cost concepts together with an example of the impact of different levels of output.

Figure 1 depicts a cost function that shows the relationship between average total cost and output. It shows how average costs vary with output. Note the shape of the average cost relationship. Average total costs fall and are at the minimum value when output is Q_1. The fall in average total costs occurs (arithmetically) because of the fall in average fixed costs.

The shape of cost curves depends critically on the specification of the relevant time period. Economists make a simple but very powerful distinction between the *short run* and the *long run*. The short run is the (short) time within

Table 1   Cost definitions and cost mechanics

1 *Output*	*2* *Total fixed* *cost*	*3* *Total* *variable cost*	*4* *Total* *cost*	*5* *Average total* *cost (4 ÷ 1)*	*6* *Average variable* *cost (3 ÷ 1)*	*7* *Average fixed* *cost (2 ÷ 1)*
100	300	100	400	4	1.0	3.00
250	300	200	500	2	0.8	1.17
400	300	300	600	1.5	0.75	0.75
500	300	400	700	1.4	0.8	0.60
560	300	500	800	1.43	0.89	0.53

Definitions: **fixed cost**: costs that do not vary with output; **variable cost**: costs that vary with output; **total cost**: fixed cost + variable cost; **average total cost**: total cost ÷ output; **average fixed cost**: fixed cost ÷ output

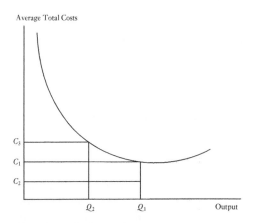

Figure 1   Technology and costs

which the fixed factors of production cannot be changed. For example, the nature of a factory and the characteristics of its production lines cannot normally be changed within a period of weeks or even months. However, over a longer period, say five years, the factory can be remodeled and the production lines rebuilt to take advantage of new technology and new working processes.

Short run cost behavior has two important characteristics. These are captured in the *law of diminishing returns*. This says that as additional amounts of variable factors of production are added to fixed factors (e.g., factory, production lines), unit costs of output will first decrease up to a point, but will then increase. The first part of this arises because the fixed costs (associated with the fixed factors of production) remain constant as output increases. Therefore unit costs will fall, and we see the importance of

attaining the "right" volumes of output where average costs are minimized. The second arises because the fixed factors imply capacity constraints on output that might in part be offset by applying more variable factors but at lower efficiencies (such as overtime rates and higher machinery maintenance costs). Thus output can only be expanded at higher marginal costs (marginal cost is the cost of producing one extra unit of output).

In the long run, all factors of production are variable. For the firm this implies investment decisions that pose the question of how much should be invested (in fixed factors like production lines) so as to minimize the cost of production in the long term. Figure 2 depicts a long run cost curve that exhibits a range in which increasing returns to scale take place (to Q_1), a range of constant returns (Q_1 to Q_2), and a range of decreasing returns to scale (beyond Q_2). In this figure the point Q_1 is called the *minimum efficient plant size* (MES).

Note that the horizontal axis is the designed scale of the plant whereas in the short run curve

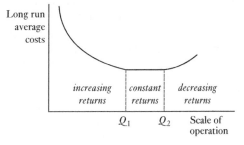

Figure 2   Long run average costs

it is the actual volume of output. Figure 3 places the short and long run curves together. The short run curve shows the costs that arise given the capital that is actually invested at that scale of plant design. Actual costs will reflect the intensity of use of that invested plant as well as the benefits of having a plant designed for that level of operation. It is possible, of course, to imagine a situation in which the plant has been designed and built to too great a scale (e.g., errors in forecasting demand), and the actual short run cost curve results in very high unit costs because the fixed costs are far too high (curve A in figure 3). ECONOMIES OF SCALE derive specifically from an optimal combination of factors of production and they can be quantified from conventional capital budgeting (net present value) calculations.

Companies that have cost functions with substantial returns to scale have a strong incentive to sell and produce the large-scale output at Q_1. If they fail to produce Q_1, average total costs will rise and this will damage their financial performance. A common source of scale economies is the opportunity to spread the fixed costs of capital, such as physical equipment like plant and buildings, or R&D spending. Scale economies usually arise from the efficient use of these fixed *firm-level* resources. There are other sources of *plant-scale* economies arising that also have an impact on average variable costs. Large-scale production enables specialization of labor to take place, increasing the productivity of the labor force and reducing average labor costs. It also enables the producer to place large orders with suppliers and negotiate quantity discounts that lower average material and component costs.

Companies A and B are both in this category. Their technology is heavily capital-intensive and, as a result, they both benefit from large-scale economies, so Q_1 is their large optimal level of output. In the long term, they are both successful in reaching this optimal scale, so they both appear in the top 25 percent of their sector's performance, and thus they enjoy a COMPETITIVE ADVANTAGE over their competitors as a result of their effective use of resources. Although this may be a critical issue in explaining the financial performance of many companies, especially in slow-growing sectors of any economy, it is not crucial to the explanation of the differences between our selected companies A and B. This is therefore not the reason for the superior long-run performance of company B. On the other hand, note that in the short run A is clearly better able to achieve the optimal scale more consistently.

Note that economies of scale are much more important in heavy manufacturing industries in which there are substantial capital requirements. Table 2 shows MES (point Q_1 in figure 2) for various industries expressed as a percentage of total output in western Europe. At one end are sectors such as steelmaking or refrigerator manufacture where scale economies are huge. At the other extreme are companies with low fixed costs where economies of scale are much less important. Carpet and shoe manufacturers are the cases shown in table 2, but service industries such as restaurants are also good examples.

MES may also change through time, an important reason for which is the benefits that can be obtained from learning from experience (*see*

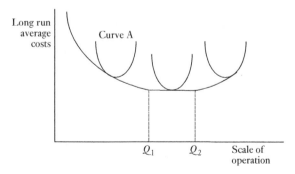

Figure 3 Short run and long run average costs

Table 2   MES as percentage of EU production

Industry	MES
Refrigerators	11
Steelmaking	10
Cigarettes	6
Carpets	0.04
Shoes	0.03

Source: Emerson (1988); Pratten (1988)

EXPERIENCE AND LEARNING EFFECTS). Learning increases a firm's *capabilities* and through time reduces average total cost as cumulative output increases. This is the *learning curve effect*. Data from the Boston Consulting Group (Conley, 1975) shows that doubling cumulative output over time reduces average total costs in a range of industries, from 30 percent in electrical components to 10 percent in oil refining. A simple way to think of this is as a dynamic economy of scale that arises from a firm learning from its experience as a producer of a particular product over several periods of time. In figure 1 the effect of the economies arising from learning is to reduce the average total cost at Q_1 (MES) from C_1 to C_2. This is another potent cause of differences in cost and profitability, but again is not important to the differences observed in firms A and B.

Another source of superior financial performance is the ability of a firm to exploit ECONOMIES OF SCOPE. Economies of scope arise when the average cost of a single product is lowered by its joint production with other products in a multiproduct firm. In figure 1 when output for each product is at Q_1 (so scale economies for each product are fully exploited), it is possible for average costs at C_2 to be even lower than C_1, if the economies of scope are also fully exploited. In practice, these scope economies can be important. A study (Pratten, 1988) of the cost effects of halving the number of products made by each producer in a selection of EU industries shows impacts that range from +3 percent in carpet manufacture to +8 percent in motor vehicles.

These scope economies may arise from the opportunity to leverage a core capability arising from knowledge and learning, organization or management skill, so as to reduce the average total cost of all products produced in a multi-product firm. A good example is the expertise that arises from technical and scientific knowledge within the firm. Exploiting this distinctive expertise by innovation and product DIVERSIFICATION lowers the average total cost of all products. Pharmaceutical manufacture and steel production are both sectors where this kind of cost economy is important. Scope economies can also arise from efficient use of resources, for example, where a number of related goods are produced using a common process. Car manufacture of a range of models is an example and part of the reason for the significant scope economies found in Pratten's study. Another source of scope economies arises from spreading the fixed cost of a network over a wider range of products. Commercial banks, for example, incur a large fixed cost from their branch networks. If they spread this cost over a large range of related corporate and retail financial products, the average total cost of each product is reduced.

Companies A and B are both able to exploit economies of scope – and do so. Hence, they build competitive advantage and appear in the top 25 percent of profits performance in their separate industries. However, for reasons outside their strategic control, scope economy opportunities are much larger in B. Its core technical competence has more uses and markets, so its product range is much larger than A's, whose core capability is in a tightly demarcated niche. This is the source of the difference in their long run performance.

A final issue of importance on the supply side in explaining differences in financial performance between industries and firms is supplier power. Powerful suppliers drive up costs and this has an impact on profits. Companies A and B are in industries in which suppliers are generally weak, with one major exception: all companies in both industries are heavy users of energy, the suppliers of which have considerable market power.

Bibliography

Conley, P. (1975). *Experience Curves as a Planning Tool.* Boston Consulting Group (pamphlet).
Emerson, M. (1988). *The Economics of 1992.* Oxford: Oxford University Press.
McGee, J., Thomas, H., and Wilson, D. (2005). *Strategy: Analysis and Practice.* Maidenhead: McGraw-Hill.

Pratten, C. (1988). A survey of the economies of scale. In *Research on the Costs of Europe*. Office for Official Publications of the European Communities, vol. 2.

Seldon, A. and Penance, F. G. (eds.) (1965). *Everyman's Dictionary of Economics*. London: J. M. Dent.

critical mass

Taman Powell

Critical mass is often confused with critical scale. Critical scale is the smallest size that is possible for a particular product or business to be viable, whether in terms of cost effectiveness (e.g., for production) or innovativeness (e.g., for R&D). Critical scale is essentially a static concept, referring to a cost optimization problem.

In contrast, critical mass is a dynamic concept with no direct link to costs. Critical mass refers to a type of "herd" behavior where people do something because they see or expect to see other people behaving similarly.

If we look at a party as an example, different people will attend depending upon the expected number of attendees. If it is expected that only 10 percent of invited people will turn up, many other people will not attend. Conversely, if it is expected that 50 percent will turn up, many additional people will attend. The relationship between expected attendance and actual attendance can be seen in figure 1, which shows the percentage of people who will attend the party if they expect a given percentage to attend.

If, for example, at any party 70 percent show up, it is clear that many attendees will be happy with the large crowd. However, some will be unhappy as they expected 90 percent to attend. If these people stay away from the next party, which results in attendance dropping to 50 percent, some of the attendees again will be unhappy as they expected close to 60 percent to be there. Similarly, some people will decide to stay away from the next gathering, which in turn causes a lower turnout. The only stable attendance level in this example is 0 percent, in which case the party dies.

The death of this series of parties could be seen as lack of interest, though this is not the case as there were a large number (around 75 percent) who were interested in attending. The issue is that critical mass was not achieved.

To solve this attendance problem we need to achieve critical mass. As can be seen in figure 1, this cannot be achieved as the attendance curve does not cross the 45° line. To overcome this issue, the attendance curve needs to be moved upwards. This can be achieved by guaranteeing the attendance of a number of people. This has been factored into figure 2 by the guaranteed attendance of nine people.

In figure 2 we can see that there are three equilibrium points: A with 9 people, B with 29 people, and C with 65 people. In this scenario, if more than 29 people attend the party, the number attending the next party will increase as the actual attendance is greater than the expected attendance. This dynamic will continue up to point C, where 65 people are

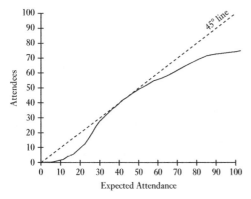

Figure 1 The relationship between expected attendance and actual attendance

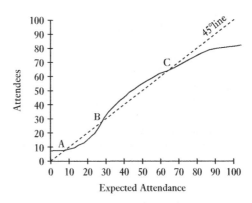

Figure 2 Achieving critical mass

attending, but will move no further unless attitudes change. Conversely, if fewer than 29 people attend the party, the number of people attending the next party will decrease as the actual attendance is lower than the expected attendance. This dynamic will continue to point A where 9 people are attending. In this scenario, critical mass is effectively achieved at point B, as this maintains the attendance at the series of parties. The dynamic of moving past point B is often called "tipping," and point B is known as the "tipping point."

In a business context, critical mass and tipping points are very important. An example could be telephones or fax machines, typical network products (see NETWORK INDUSTRIES), where adoption of the product will be slow – who wants to own the only telephone in the country? But once a certain number of telephones are sold, they start to become valuable to different people. What is important here is that at a certain point – say 5 percent of the population having a telephone – the telephone will be valuable to some people, who will go out and buy a phone, but not to others, who will not buy a phone until ownership increases. The challenge with these products is to manage adoption until ownership crosses the 45° line. After this point, it will manage itself.

Sometimes critical mass needs to be achieved rapidly as there is competition over a standard. This was the case with beta and VHS video recorders. Both products essentially provided the same service. It was uncertain which would be successful, until VHS reached critical mass and took over the industry.

A similar race for critical mass occurred with IBM PCs using the Microsoft operating system and Apple Macintosh computers. Once critical mass has been achieved by a competitor, it is extremely difficult to come back. One strategy, however, is to segment the market (see SEGMENTATION) and aim to achieve critical mass in this smaller market segment. This was the strategy that Apple adopted. When it lost the battle for the mass market, it changed its attention to focus heavily on the desktop publishing market where it had always been relatively strong. Apple achieved dominance in this market, which it maintains to this day.

It is worth noting that market conditions change (see STRATEGY CONTEXT), and with the increasing importance of the Internet and more open cross-platform software standards, Microsoft Windows PCs and Apple Macintosh computers are no longer incompatible. This has allowed Apple to change the focus of competition to its strength in industrial design and usability/user interface, without being hindered by lack of critical mass in its installed base.

Bibliography

Arthur, W. B. (1989). Competing technologies, increasing returns, and lock-in by historical events. *Economic Journal*, 99, 116–31.

Arthur, W. B. (1990). Positive feedback in the economy. *Scientific American*, 262, 92–9.

Economides, N. (1996). The economics of networks. *International Journal of Industrial Organization*, 14 (2), 675–99.

Katz, M. and Shapiro, C. (1985). Network externalities, competition and compatibility. *American Economic Review*, 75 (3), 424–40.

McGee, J., Thomas, H., and Wilson, D. (2005). *Strategy: Analysis and Practice.* Maidenhead: McGraw-Hill, ch. 12.

Shapiro, C. and Varian, H. (1999). *Information Rules: A Strategic Guide to the Network Economy.* Boston: Harvard Business School Press, ch. 7.

Shy, O. (2001). *The Economics of Network Industries.* Cambridge: Cambridge University Press, p. 113.

cross-subsidization

Stephanos Avgeropoulos

Cross-subsidization refers to using profits earned in one product market to support activities in another. It may be carried out on government instructions, such as for social reasons (the cost of postage, for example, may be set to be uniform nationwide, with the cities' traffic subsidizing rural areas), or it may be for commercial motives, using the strategy to enable a firm to compete in a market in which it would otherwise find it difficult to survive, or to otherwise enhance the combined revenue-earning potential of the two product markets, particularly if these involve COMPLEMENTARY PRODUCTS.

TYPES

There are three main cross-subsidization strategy variants, all of which price one of the goods (the base good) low to insure purchase of the other, and then price the other (more profitable) good high, to more than recoup lost revenue. The three strategies are:

- loss leadership (predominantly used in retailing, whereby the base good is priced low to attract the price-sensitive customer to the outlet, while other goods that the customer would like to buy once he or she is in the outlet are priced at more profitable levels);
- the razor and blade strategy (whereby the base product is priced low in order to lock the buyer into making subsequent purchases of the more profitably priced complementary products); and
- the trade-up strategy (whereby the base product is priced very competitively, and the buyer is expected to subsequently move up the range and buy items that are more profitable).

PRECONDITIONS

For a cross-subsidization strategy to work even with buyers who are able to see through the mechanisms, a number of conditions must hold. First, the demand for the base good must be sufficiently price sensitive to attract the customer in the first place. Then, demand for the profitable good must not be as price sensitive, so that this is purchased at the high price, and its supply must be restricted so that the firm does not end up supplying only the unprofitable good. Finally, a strong link must exist between the two, so that purchase of the base good leads to (repeated) purchase of the profitable good as well. This link typically deteriorates with time, and as products mature, cross-subsidization becomes less relevant. This is because the profitable good may become more widely available, or because SUBSTITUTE PRODUCTS are developed.

IMPLICATIONS FOR STRATEGY

As a result of the necessity for the above conditions to hold, for a company to be able to exploit the cross-subsidization potential between two products, an effort must be made to create barriers to entry (*see* BARRIERS TO ENTRY AND EXIT) into the market for the profitable good and to strengthen the connection between the base and the profitable good (e.g., by raising the SWITCHING COSTS involved). It is not important, however, to erect barriers in the market for the base good, and as long as the above conditions hold, that market may even be left to other suppliers.

Turning to pricing, the increasing difficulty that the firm will face over time in continuing to profit from the sale of goods in this way implies that prices may well need to be adjusted so that, over the long term, the profit margins for the two goods become comparable.

Bibliography

Laffont, J. J. and Tirole, J. (1990). The regulation of multiproduct firms. *Journal of Public Economics*, 43, 1–36.

Porter, M. E. (1985). *Competitive Advantage: Creating and Sustaining Superior Performance*. New York: Free Press.

customer profitability matrix

Derek F. Channon

Prices are often not determined on the basis of average production costs; in reality, different customer segments may have very different costs. Careful SEGMENTATION of the customer base can reveal that such variations in the cost to serve may vary by as much as 30 percent.

Unfortunately, normal accounting cost systems do not reveal the different costs associated with servicing different customer groups. ACTIVITY-BASED COSTING systems are much better at revealing the true costs to serve. In drawing up the customer profitability matrix illustrated in figure 1, it is important to allocate indirect costs, which are not often considered, to the maximum extent, in the following categories:

- *Pre-sale costs*. Differences occur in the buying process for different customer segments. These costs might include location,

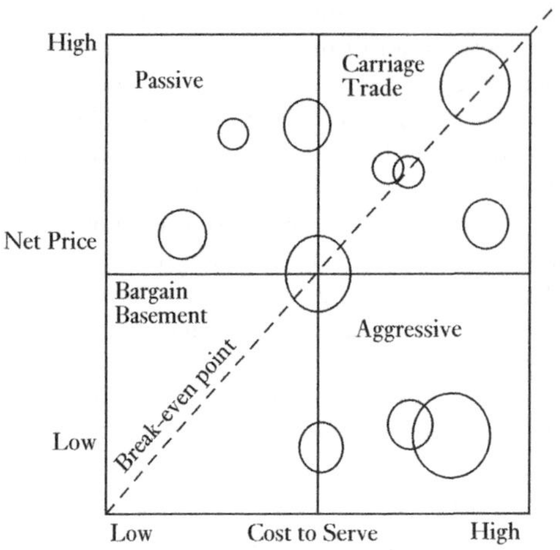

Figure 1   The customer profitability matrix (Shapiro et al, 1987)

the need for customization, and other pre-sale costs.

- *Production costs*. Customization, differences in packaging, timing, setup time, fast delivery, holding inventory, and the like can cause significant cost differences between customer segments.
- *Distribution costs*. Customer location and the mode of shipment can vary significantly between customers. These costs can be relatively easily identified, but such analysis is rarely undertaken.
- *After-sale service costs*. Costs include training, installation, repair, and maintenance costs. Many such costs are covered by warranty cover and customer claims need to be carefully analyzed to establish after-sale costs.

Having undertaken such detailed cost analysis, the actual prices charged to different customer segments, including all discounts, special offers, etc., need to be assessed, together with the volume consumed over time in terms of value (not merely volume).

The prices and costs are then plotted on the customer profitability matrix as shown in figure 1. Net price is shown on the vertical axis and cost on the horizontal. The size of each circle represents the value of each customer segment. Very large customers may be identified individually. The cross-lines represent average price and cost,

while the diagonal line shows the break-even point (*see* BREAK-EVEN ANALYSIS) at which price equals cost.

The resulting matrix shows which customer segments have high costs in relation to the prices they pay. They can be assigned to one of the four quadrants as follows:

- *Carriage trade*. High cost, high net price. Customers in this segment are willing to pay a high price for superior service. A classic example is private banking.
- *Bargain basement*. The low-cost, low net price position is less related to either service or quality. Using the above analogy, this would refer to life-line banking.
- *Passive*. Low cost, high price; less related to quality or service, and not very price sensitive either. Buying behavior is low in price sensitivity.
- *Aggressive*. High cost, low price. Such businesses enjoy high quality and service together with low price. Strong negotiators and technological leaders are often found in this category.

The matrix is then interrogated to develop strategies which help to maximize profitability. For example, Citibank in New York resegmented its check-handling business. The company found that a small number of checks represented a high level of value. These were segmented away from the volume element of check handling and processed separately, at lower cost but providing a superior level of customer service.

Strategically, a company can define itself on the basis of the type of customer it seeks to service. For example, a "Pile it high, sell it cheap" retailer such as Kwik Save would be located in the bottom left sector, while a specialist, high-price, high-cost competitor such as Harrod's would operate in the top right box. Transition from one quadrant to another may well be extremely difficult and may take a long time.

Bibliography

Shapiro, B. P., Rangan, V. K., Moriarty, R. T., and Ross, E. B. (1987). Manage customers for profits (not just sales). *Harvard Business Review*, September/October.

D

delayering

Derek F. Channon

This is the process of reducing the number of layers in the vertical management hierarchy. The concept became widely known and adopted following its introduction and development in the US General Electric Company (GE), when the incoming chief executive, Jack Welch, set about reducing the ranks of hierarchy between his office and the workplace. At the same time he eliminated many of the staff functions which had developed at GE, creating a STRATEGIC MANAGEMENT focused line function.

In companies which reengineer (*see* BUSINESS PROCESS REENGINEERING; REENGINEERING DISADVANTAGES) to an ACTIVITY-BASED COSTING system of management with a horizontal structure, the elimination of at least one layer of middle management is usually common. Companies successfully implementing such systems make use of information technology-driven management information systems which allow senior management to gain online real-time access to operations. As a result, decision-making can be speeded up, middle management does not act as an information filter, and top management can become interventionist in line operations.

Bibliography

Channon, D. F. (1995). Direct Line Insurance. In C. Baden-Fuller and M. Pitt (eds.), *Strategic Innovation: An International Casebook on Strategic Management*. London: Routledge.

Tichy, N. and Sherman, S. (1993). *Control Your Destiny Or Someone Else Will*, New York: Doubleday.

demand analysis in practice

Ben Knight and John McGee

Demand analysis is important in two ways:

1 it provides a framework for analyzing price and other influences on the sales of the firm's products; and
2 it provides a baseline for pricing products, and marketing generally, and for forecasting and manipulating demand.

Demand analysis is built around the price–quantity relationship and the many ways in which this relationship is manifested. It is easy to see how important price and volume are to the firm. Price and quantity together determine sales revenue. Sales volume dictates production volume and the scale of production operations together with the capital required for production and for working capital. Thus, volume and price fundamentally drive cash flow, profits, and return on capital (see figure 1). Consequently the extent to which price can influence volume is of great importance to the firm.

In understanding how return on capital is driven, it is helpful to consider those characteristics that shape demand (market characteristics in figure 1) and how the firm's decisions can affect the outcome. One of the enduring problems for a firm is how to avoid its activities being totally dictated by market conditions and for its own decisions to provide it with some distinctiveness in markets, thereby giving it some ability to earn profits beyond the minimum rate of return required merely to stay in business. The following characteristics of demand are particularly important:

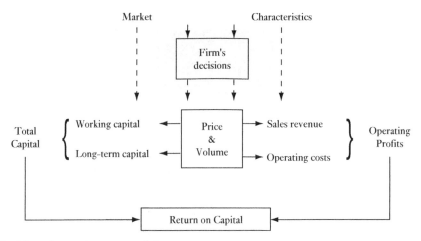

Figure 1   Price–volume and return on capital

- elasticities and the implications for revenues;
- individual versus market demand;
- final demand versus derived demand;
- producer versus consumer goods;
- durable versus perishable (non-durable) goods.

PRICE ELASTICITY AND REVENUES

Consider a product whose initial price is P_1 and whose initial sales volume is Q_1. If price is reduced to P_2 and volume increases to Q_2, we can see that on the original volume Q_1 a lower price is being earned but this is to some extent offset by the extra revenue $P_2(Q_2 - Q_1)$. The larger is the extra volume from the price cut, then the more likely it is that revenue will be greater. Thus, the higher the price ELASTICITY, the larger will be the new revenue. At the other end of the scale, if the elasticity is zero, then no

extra volume is created, and revenue will fall. When the price elasticity is one, then the price effect on the original volume $((P_1 - P_2)Q_1)$ – i.e., a fall in revenue – is exactly offset by the extra sales revenue arising from the volume increase $P_2(Q_2 - Q_1)$. Table 1 shows the general relationship between revenues and price elasticity.

INDIVIDUAL DEMAND VS. MARKET DEMAND

The demand curve for a market or any group of consumers is obtained by summing the demand curves of all the individuals concerned. This is done by summing all the quantities demanded at each price level. This submerging of individual differences may matter little if we are concerned solely with predicting total market demand at given price levels. The more stable are the individual demand curves, then the easier is the task

Table 1   Elasticity and revenue

Elasticity	Effect of price fall	Effect of price rise
Infinite (perfectly elastic)	Sell as much as can be produced	Sell nothing
Greater than 1 (elastic)	Larger sales revenue	Smaller sales revenue
1	Constant sales revenue	Constant sales revenue
Less than 1 (inelastic)	Smaller sales revenue	Larger sales revenue
0 (perfectly inelastic)	Fall in revenue proportional to fall in price	Increase in revenue proportional to increase in price

of forecasting. But, from the point of view of the pricing policy of the firm, matters are not so simple. Price is just one, albeit an important one, of the many instruments with which the product is marketed. Others include distribution channels, advertising and promotion, and support from one's own sales force as well as from retailer sales activity. To direct this marketing effort effectively, it is helpful to be able to define a target market on which the marketing effort can be focused. So the concept of market SEGMENTATION is likely to be useful, i.e., the concept of individual and group differences within the overall market demand curve. A firm may choose to treat its market in a uniform manner, spreading its marketing efforts far and wide in order to bring as much of the market within its orbit as possible. This would normally require uniform pricing and mass advertising campaigns. Alternatively, the firm might choose to adopt different price policies for different groups or segments in the market. A high price policy might be indicated for one segment and a low price for another. The success of this approach depends on the two segments being unable to communicate and/or trade with each other and being able to set up a black or gray market (such as happens with UK-sourced cars and European-sourced cars).

In economic terms a market is a group of buyers and sellers who are in sufficiently close contact for the transactions between any pair of them to affect the terms on which the others buy and sell. The existence of individual or group differences cannot be exploited if there is close contact between buyers. Firms can choose to exploit the differences in individual demand curves by pursuing product policies that enable the firm to apply a different "offer" to different segments. Thus the offer of a standard car to the mass market would result in a price level that would enable those with low price sensitivity (low price elasticity) to buy at prices lower than their reservation price (the highest price that would keep them in the market). To avoid this deadweight loss of revenue, firms devise product range policies that enable different product characteristics to be directed toward different segments. Thus, higher-income purchasers can be directed toward more expensive cars with more accessories and a higher-quality build. Lower-

income purchasers would correspondingly be directed to less well-equipped and built cars. The bigger the product range, the more the firm can cover the breadth of the market and keep potential customers within its range of offerings. But there is an extra cost of marketing and a potential loss of ECONOMIES OF SCALE in production as variety of models is increased.

FINAL DEMAND VS. DERIVED DEMAND

When demand for a product is tied to the purchase of another product, then this demand is said to be *derived*. The demand for steel is in part derived from the demand for cars and the demand for bricks is derived from the demand for houses. These are instances where the product whose demand is derived is a component part of the final product. Sometimes complementary consumption patterns cause dependence in demand. Thus the demand for film is complementary to the demand for cameras. However, the distinction between final and derived demand should not be pressed too far because in some sense all demand is derived. The demand for golf clubs is derived from a demand for leisure; the demand for washing machines is derived from demand for laundry services. Certainly, demand for all producer goods (as distinct from consumer goods) is derived, and so is the demand for labor.

Derived demand is generally supposed to have less price elasticity than final demand. This is attributable to dilution of the cost of the component by other component products whose prices are sticky. It used to be reckoned that a 10 percent rise in the price of steel would cause only a 1 percent increase in the cost of a car if all other costs remained unchanged. However, this would be a characteristic primarily of the elasticity in the short run. In the longer term there is the possibility of substitution of one raw material or component part by another. As the possibilities of substitution increas, then the price elasticity increases. Thus, glass fiber may rival steel in some applications in ship and boat building; aluminum can displace copper; and synthetic rubber can replace natural rubber.

Some products are so closely tied to the parent products that they have no distinctive demand determinants of their own, television aerials for example. Here the elasticity will be very low indeed in the short run, but such cases of fixed proportions between the parent and component products are rare. More commonly there is considerable leeway for substitution at the margin as well as more than one parent use for the product. In very many instances there is a multitude of parent uses for a product and it becomes impossible to characterize demand in terms of particular final demands. Small electric motors have no final demand of their own but to analyze their demand in terms of their thousands of parent uses would be impossibly tedious. Sulfuric acid and many other chemicals are further examples and integrated circuits provide a contemporary example.

The distinction between derived and final demand is important in understanding the determinants of demand for individual products, and where there is a stable proportional relation between the component and its parent then forecasting of demand can be done by reference to the parent.

PRODUCER GOODS VS. CONSUMER GOODS

This distinction in some ways is parallel to that between final and derived demand. However, this distinction concentrates attention on who makes the purchase decision rather than on the technological or economic relationship between the component and its parent product. There are two reasons usually cited for expecting purchase decisions of producer goods to be qualitatively different from those for consumer goods. Buyers are expected to be professional and, hence, more expert. Also, their motives for buying are expected to be purely economic and not influenced by non-monetary considerations.

It is doubtful whether the distinction between producer and consumer goods can always be maintained. How does one distinguish between cars sold to companies and those sold to private individuals? In addition, it is not at all clear that producer goods are evaluated in a cold-eyed professional way. There must be thousands of purchases by any one firm that are incidental in their impact on costs and are purchased with speed and convenience, without expensive evaluation. This of course leaves the door open for the human element in purchasing, which is supposed to be so characteristic of final consumers.

DURABLE GOODS VS. PERISHABLE (NON-DURABLE) GOODS

By definition, durable goods are not completely consumed at the time of their purchase; they yield a stream of services over time (typically measured in years rather than months). They include both consumer and producer durables. The sale of durables can be seen as replacing that part of the existing stock of durables that has worn out (i.e., replacement demand), and as that which is really new (i.e., an expansion of demand). Thus, if the existing stock of cars is 100, of which 10 wear out each year, and the normal growth in demand is 5 each year, then car production (and sales) would be 15, two-thirds of which is to meet replacement demand. If there is now an increase in demand for car stock of 3 units (less than a 3 percent increase), then production must rise to 18 (a 20 percent increase) in order to meet this increase, Relatively modest increases in demand for a stock of durables can thus result in large fluctuations in production.

In general, the demand for durable goods fluctuates differently and more violently than the demand for perishable products. The further down the chain of production, the more violent is the cutback in production when final demand falls. If economic activity were to contract by 1 percent, it would not be surprising to see contractions of 10 percent or even 20 percent in the output of the steel and metals industries. The volatility of demand for durables is not the only salient feature. Both replacement and expansion have quite distinct sets of demand determinants. When the demand for transportation as a whole goes up, then production tends to take some time to respond and used car values go up relative to scrap values. Then the scrapping rate falls and thus replacement demand also falls. So an increase in demand may initially extend the life of the existing stock and reduce replacement demand. Conversely, if the public desires fewer cars, the scrapping rate accelerates as used car prices fall relative to scrap prices. The most important factor determining replacement demand is the rate of obsolescence that determines prices in second-hand car markets. There are two elements in obsolescence. One is purely financial and requires a comparison of capital costs and running costs of a new car with the scrap value and running costs of the old car. In general, running costs rise with age to a point where the difference in running costs between new and old becomes larger than the required capital outlay. Physical deterioration lies behind these calculations and is an obvious component of obsolescence. However, it is rarely the only factor in replacement decisions. When replacement takes place before the financial criterion is satisfied, then in some other way the services of the new car are more highly valued than the services of the (apparently cheaper) old car. For consumer durables and perhaps also for producer durables as well, style, convenience, and youth play an important role in demand.

The determinants of expansion demand for durables are not, in principle, very different from those for perishables but, in practice, are much more complicated. The key to durables lies in their length of life and the purchase decision is marked by the buyer's difficulty in assessing the future. The buyer has to assess whether he or she can afford to operate it, whether its services will command a suitable price in the future, whether its price will rise or fall if he or she postpones the purchase, and so on. For durable goods not only present prices and incomes but their trends and the buyer's optimism are proper variables to consider. Expectations about technological change are also critical. Should one wait for prices to fall as technology improves (e.g., computers and video games), or might important savings be lost through delay?

Bibliography

Besanko, D., Dranove, D., Shanley, M., and Shaefer, S. (2003). *Economics of Strategy*, 2nd edn. New York: John Wiley.

Dean, J. (1951). *Managerial Economics*. Englewood Cliffs, NJ: Prentice-Hall.

Haynes, W. W. (1969). *Managerial Economics: Analysis and Cases*. Homewood, IL: Irwin-Dorsey.

McAleese, D. (2001). *Economics for Business*, 2nd edn. Upper Saddle River, NJ: Prentice-Hall.

McGee, J., Thomas, H., and Wilson, D. (2005). *Strategy: Analysis and Practice*. Maidenhead: McGraw-Hill.

demand analysis in theory

Ben Knight and John McGee

The demand side of the market is also relevant to an understanding of the "deep structure of markets," which is so critical to company performance. The first issue is the degree to which market-level product demand is responsive to changes in price.

Figure 1 shows a downward-sloping relationship of demand with product price. This market "demand curve" shows that price increases reduce the volume of demand, and vice versa. We could measure the degree of responsiveness of demand to a change in price as the:

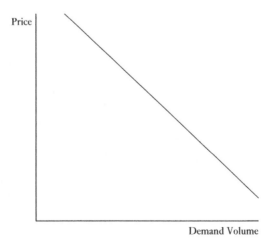

Figure 1   Market demand curve

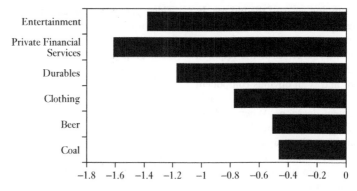

Figure 2   Luxuries, necessities, and substitutes: market price elasticities of demand (Deaton, 1975)

$$\frac{\text{change in quantity demanded}}{\text{change in price}}$$

which is the slope of the demand curve, or by:

$$\frac{\%\ \text{change in quantity demanded}}{\%\ \text{change in price}}$$

This is the measure preferred by economists, who call it the "*own price elasticity of demand*" (*see* ELASTICITY). Since demand falls when price is raised and vice versa, real-life estimates of the price elasticity are generally negative. Some examples are shown in figure 2.

WHAT FACTORS INFLUENCE THE ELASTICITY?

First, necessities like basic foodstuffs and fuel are likely to have a low elasticity and demand is therefore relatively insensitive to changes in price. Second, also important is the availability of substitutes for the product (*see* SUBSTITUTE PRODUCTS). If substitutes are readily available, an increase in price will have a much larger impact on demand. Petrol, for example, has no close substitutes. If you own a petrol-driven car, you have no alternative to petrol and, hence, the elasticity of demand for petrol will be low.

This market-level demand relationship gives rise to an aspect of the market environment over which companies have no direct control. Products like this are an attractive source of revenue for a government. Increases in the rate of tax raise prices but have little effect on the volume of sales. Because of this, raising the rate of tax has a strong positive effect on tax revenue. The result, from the firm's point of view, is that political forces over which it has no control significantly alter market prices and severely constrain its pricing strategy.

WHAT ABOUT THE FIRM-LEVEL RELATIONSHIP OF PRICE AND DEMAND?

A crucial issue here is the homogeneity of the product and the ability of the individual firm to differentiate its output from others through BRANDING, thereby reducing the threat of substitute products. If the product is difficult to differentiate, the firm will face a highly elastic demand curve, whatever the industry-level relationship looks like.

In the extreme case in which the product is completely homogeneous, the firm will face a horizontal demand curve as shown in figure 3, so that if an individual firm raises its price above P_1, the volume of demand will shrink to zero. If it lowers its price it is overwhelmed by demand. The firm in this case is a passive actor with absolutely no power over the market for its products. This is a key feature of perfect competition, in which the individual firm is a price-taker with absolutely no impact on prices. In the more normal case where some differentiation is possible, perhaps by product branding or through service excellence, the firm is able to exercise some market power and secure a degree of control. This market power extends not only to price (raising it), but also to the price elasticity, as figure 1 shows. Branding secures the

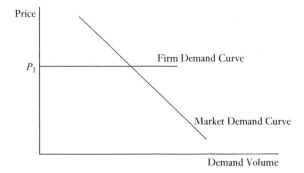

Price

P_1

Firm Demand Curve

Market Demand Curve

Demand Volume

Figure 3   Firm and market demand curves

attachment of the buyer to the individual product, so that an increase in its price will have a less
adverse effect on demand, because there is less
substitution into alternative products available
from other firms in the same market.

A good illustration of these concepts is a
branded food manufacturer like Heinz or Nestlé,
operating in the European Union (EU) or the
US. It is possible for these manufacturers to
brand the product and hence secure a price premium and improve profitability, and this is what
they have done. Since branding also has the helpful effect of reducing the price elasticity, the extra
profit margin they get is sustainable over time (*see*
SUSTAINABILITY). However, these benefits are
increasingly problematic for the branded food
manufacturers, because of the growth in supermarket retailing and hence the growth in the
buying power of their customers. Large retailers
promote their own brands, weakening the manufacturer's brand, and, as a result, demand large-
quantity discounts from branded food manufacturers who need the supermarket outlet for their
products. Clearly, the changing balance of power
(control) on the demand side of the market challenges the sustainability of an individual business's COMPETITIVE ADVANTAGE, even when
it successfully brands its products.

Consider two companies, A and B. Both sell a
difficult-to-differentiate product to powerful industrial users. As a result, it is difficult for either
to secure premium prices and the profits that go
along with them. This is characteristic of all
firms in their markets, so, in the sector ranking
of profitability, both appear in low profitability
sectors (A in paper packaging for the food indus-

try and B in metal manufacture). Some global
data for this are shown in figure 4.

A further reason for the relatively poor sectoral profits performance of A and B is the result
of the weak effect of long-run increases in national income on the demand for these products.
Both A and B have their customer base in the
rich industrial economies of North America and
the EU. In these markets, the share (or intensity,
as it is sometimes called) of the products produced by A and B in the total national sales of
all products is falling. They produce manufactured products and this sector's share of total
sales is declining, while the service sector is
expanding. Many manufacturing markets suffer
as a consequence of mature and saturated
markets. We can measure the response of
market-level sales to changes in the long-run
income of a country by calculating the long-run
income elasticity of demand. This is an analogous concept to "price elasticity."

The long-run income elasticity of demand is:

$$\frac{\% \text{ change in long-run quantity demanded}}{\% \text{ change in long-run national income}}$$

Generally, this is a positive number, so increases
in national income shift the market demand
curve upwards, as shown in figure 5, where the
initial curve D_1 is shifted to a new curve D_2 as a
result of an increase in income. Since the curve
has shifted up, more will be demanded at each
price. At a price of P_1, for example, the quantity
demanded will increase from Q_1 to Q_2. If national income falls, the opposite happens and the
quantity demanded falls.

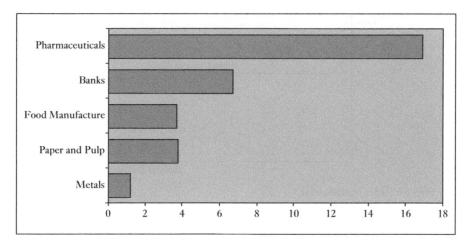

Figure 4 Return on revenues (%) in the Fortune Global 500, 2001 (www.fortune.com)

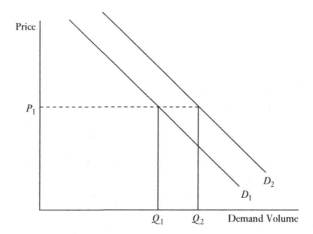

Figure 5 Market demand curve and changes in national income

Where the income elasticity is high, firms will experience large increases in market demand when over the long run incomes increase, and vice versa when it is low. In the mature economies of the EU and the US, the long-run income elasticity of demand is higher in service markets like tourism or media providers, but low in engineering and food, which are the end users of the output of companies A and B. The result is a progressive decline in the share of GDP produced in the manufacturing sector and a rise in the service sector's share. Note also the link between the long-run income elasticity and

financial performance. High income elasticities suggest that service providers or manufacturers of high-tech products like pharmaceuticals are likely to be high-performing sectors, while the traditional manufacturing sectors will do relatively badly because of low income elasticities (see figure 4). What makes it worse for manufacturers A and B is that in an earlier stage of economic development, the long-run elasticity was a good deal higher. In this period, substantial capacity was installed to meet the large long-run growth in demand. Reduction of this capacity in a stagnant manufacturing market is a slow business and this often leaves substantial surplus capacity. This adversely affects the intensity of market rivalry, driving down prices and contributing to the weak financial performance we see in figure 4.

The long-run income elasticity of market demand is clearly an important feature of markets and a key influence on financial performance. It is also largely out of the strategic control of individual firms.

Bibliography

Besanko, D., Dranove, D., Shanley, M., and Shaefer, S. (2003). *Economics of Strategy*, 2nd edn. New York: John Wiley.

Deaton, A. (1975). The measurement of income and price elasticities. *European Economic Review*.

McAleese, D. (2001). *Economics for Business*, 2nd edn. Upper Saddle River, NJ: Prentice-Hall.

McGee, J., Thomas, H., and Wilson, D. (2005). *Strategy: Analysis and Practice*. Maidenhead: McGraw-Hill.

deregulation

Stephanos Avgeropoulos

This is the abolition or considerable weakening of an existing regulatory regime (*see* REGULATION) to increase the responsiveness of a previously regulated industry to its input and/or output markets and lead to more competition.

Deregulation can take place within any one country or part thereof (such as the deregulation of the US airline industry or of London buses), across larger geographic areas (such as the telecommunications industry in Europe), or on a global basis.

Causes and Timing

Deregulation can be the result of two main developments. First, it may become desirable because of the growing inefficiencies that regulation can impose by artificially isolating markets that the growth of multinationals and the globalization of the marketplace tend to integrate. Second, it may become desirable when technological innovations make regulatory limitations obsolete; for instance, by means of fundamentally transforming cost structures or, again, redefining the boundaries of industries.

The need for deregulation, therefore, typically emerges as a result of largely external influences, although government action is usually required to permit and enact the required changes. As far as the incentives for government itself are concerned, this has to take into account not only social and EFFICIENCY considerations and the interests of consumers, but also the interests of producers, who may well have developed close political ties while regulated. According to the balance between these factors, government involvement can either be responsive (in which case it acts upon requests by powerful interest groups adversely affected by regulation, such as innovative producers or overcharged consumers), or proactive (in which case it acts before any powerful interest group expresses any desire for deregulation, this sometimes being observed in cases in which deregulation forms part of a larger government initiative, such as PRIVATIZATION). Historically, banking is one of the industries that has been deregulated as a result of innovations, whereas public utilities have been deregulated as a result of political initiative.

The Impact of Deregulation

Impact on market structure and level of competition. Deregulation has a profound impact on a firm's competitive environment. Because it reduces barriers to entry (*see* BARRIERS TO ENTRY AND EXIT), allows firms to go into related fields, and encourages new firms to develop, it increases the number of firms in the previously regulated market, and enhances competition in that market. The new firms may well bring with them cost-cutting technologies, additional capacity, and hence the ability to cut prices. At the same time, unbundling gives customers greater flexibility to make product/service and price/performance trade-offs, so their level of knowledge increases and they become more price sensitive.

An additional factor that makes the environment more competitive is that, in their effort to match new entrants, established competitors imitate new offerings without full knowledge of their own costs, thereby leading to deep price cuts.

A McKinsey study on the post-deregulation US airline, financial services, telephone, trucking, and railroad industries made some detailed observations as to the implications of these changes (Bleeke, 1990). According to the study, therefore, an industry changes immediately after deregulation when a number of new companies enter the market. Prices and profitability fall rapidly, the most attractive segments often become the least profitable, the variation in profitability between the best and worst performers widens, and many entrants go out of business or merge with stronger competitors. Waves of MERGERS AND ACQUISITIONS initially consolidate weak competitors and subsequently combine the strong, and many companies are forced to abandon many areas of activity, largely because of the increasing cost of competing in any single one of them. During this period, the overall market grows, despite any failures, and flexibility is key to survival, particularly with respect to pricing, so that all potential sources of profit are exploited. Similarly, the organization's resources need to be conserved, and large expenditures need to be considered twice, even if they are intended to lead to the introduction of cost-cutting technology.

Some five years after deregulation, the industry stabilizes and the competitive environment changes again. The weakest competitors have all gone, larger companies have learned how to compete with new rivals, and the price gap between new entrants and existing companies diminishes as the latter's cost-cutting efforts have taken effect. At this stage, the deregulated market can be assumed to have completed the phase of post-deregulation reorganization and should be considered just like any competitive industry.

Impact on the use of technology and the variety of output. Regulated industries face little competition, and they find it relatively easy to pass on increased costs to customers. This means that they need not worry so much about cost-cutting, although some regulatory regimes have shown the capability to successfully control costs (see the relevant discussion in the entry on regulation). The use of technology in regulated industries, therefore, is predominantly applied to providing higher levels of service. As deregulation puts heavy emphasis on cost-cutting, however, cost-cutting technologies are brought into the industry.

Similarly, unbundling and the removal of constraints on price and product competition lead to a broader range of offerings and affords the customer a full range of product/service and price/performance trade-offs. Lower quality at lower prices becomes an option, therefore, but when deregulation is not complete and some monopolistic elements remain (e.g., because of natural monopolies), the danger of lower quality for higher profits remains or even increases as the oversight of the regulatory authority ceases to exist.

Impact on culture, skills, and the strategic process. Turning to the organizations themselves, culture is one of the predominant variables that need to change with deregulation. The traditional attitude of regulated organizations is to accept the guidance of the regulatory authorities and so to be reactive rather than proactive. By contrast, many of the new competitors entering deregulated industry deliberately seek to gain COMPETITIVE ADVANTAGE by circumventing existing regulatory barriers (as these are weakened during the process of deregulation), and this makes proactive strategy development advisable for the incumbent companies as well. This typically demands a complete and time-consuming change in organizational culture.

In addition, while regulation requires an emphasis on political and negotiation skills to deal with the regulator, the post-deregulation market environment requires heavier emphasis on planning, marketing, and financial skills.

As a result, therefore, previously regulated companies typically go through a transitory period of weakness upon deregulation, during which the new skills are developed or brought in and assimilated.

IMPACT ON STRATEGIC OUTCOME

Diversification. Turning to the strategy innovations of the deregulated firms, these are often influenced by the kind of relationship that the firm previously enjoyed with its regulator. If this was cosy, and if the firm had focused all its activities around the regulator, DIVERSIFICATION will follow into other markets with equal or better profit potential (the reason why the firm would have avoided such diversification while regulated is that the regulator would have been unable to act to the firm's advantage in unrelated industries). Similarly, if deregulation implies that the regulator adopts a change agent role, to reduce the amount of help that it used to provide to the regulated firms, then the increasing divergence between the interests of the regulator and the regulated industry would again be expected to lead the firm into markets over which the regulator has no control.

In addition to product market diversification, geographic diversification also takes place with deregulation, for the same reasons. Moreover, this can be due to the fact that the regulated firm is now free to go abroad (and has the incentives to do so), or it may be that a particular deregulation is coordinated internationally (e.g., European deregulation in telecommunications).

Alliances and acquisitions. Where deregulation opens up new markets, either by means of the combination of technologies or by allowing companies to enter foreign markets, alliances (*see* STRATEGIC ALLIANCES), JOINT VENTURES, and acquisitions are often pursued as a means of acquiring missing skills or rapidly building MARKET SHARE.

SUCCESSFUL POST-DEREGULATION STRATEGIES

As most of the above industry-wide changes have been observed to take place in every deregulated industry, it is reasonable to expect that a number of generic responses to deregulation will exist. Indeed, three studies (Bleeke, 1983, 1990; Channon, 1986) have identified several such strategies, and the indicative rationalization of their findings that follows is intended to act only as an introduction to the illuminating studies themselves.

In essence, the studies have observed that the industry is too volatile during the first five years of deregulation for any particular strategy to be successful, even if a company prepared early enough so that it could have such a strategy in place. Instead, as has already been mentioned, flexibility and opportunism are necessary, while working toward positioning the company for the time when the initial five-year period expires. At the end of that period, most successful companies are found to have positioned themselves in one of the following ways.

Broad-based distribution strategies. Firms that adopt strategies of this kind market a wide range of products over wide geographic areas, nationwide or globally. Each market can often only accommodate a small number of such competitors although, in the early stages of deregulation, many companies contend for such a positioning. Essential requirements for success as a broad-based distributor include: (1) the integration of operations and marketing across the entire area served (as loose regional affiliations are inadequate for achieving the broad service and information coverage required, and for the purposes of unified marketing); (2) the availability of cost information that allows price adjustment according to the sensitivity of specific segments, as competition dictates (*see* ELASTICITY); and (3) the development of a full service perspective, as regulations permit.

Cost-focused strategies. The second strategy is of low-cost production of a narrow range of products. Again, because of economies of scale and the like, there is only space for few low-cost producers at equilibrium. While, therefore, this is a strategy much favored by new entrants immediately after deregulation (because they may have cost advantages over incumbents), many subsequently migrate to adopt specialty or segment-focused strategies, leaving behind them, ironically, a much less profitable industry. Migration may be initiated by a realization that their own costs are rising, because yet lower-cost competitors enter the market, or because they have attacked incumbents or broad-based competitors in their key markets who, in turn, being more powerful, have waged costly price wars against them. Success as a low-cost provider requires paramount emphasis on cost reduction, often brought about as much by streamlining and the use of technology as by the identification of innovative methods to eliminate entire stages of the value chain (e.g., by the use of direct mail to substitute retail selling). The lack of structural costs gives entrants a strong advantage over incumbents, as does their lack of established commitments, particularly in customer relations-based service businesses, which allows them to select the segments they wish to serve, and to price competitively in those segments knowing that, if established firms followed suit, they would be cannibalizing the profitability of their existing operations. In addition, marketing is based on price, with minimal or no service offered.

Segment-focused strategies. The third strategy provides premium or expensive services at premium prices. There are a number of segment-focused strategy variants. Some have appeared later on in the deregulation process (as technology permitted), and some are found more in some industries than in others. In principle, segment-focused strategies require companies to be able to identify the right segment(s). In addition, the establishment of a close relationship with customers (e.g., by the means of customer databases), bundling, and increasing product complexity and added features can be helpful in reducing customers' price sensitivity and providing opportunities to cross-sell additional products. Each of the segment-focused strategies is now discussed individually.

- *Speciality (niche) strategies.* A niche positioning (focusing upon either product or geography) can be chosen by companies too small to attempt national or global strategies. Niche competitors sometimes turn out to be broad-based competitors that have retrenched back to their core skills, so they are often well equipped to hold on to their markets, particularly if their niche is customer/product oriented rather than geographically defined. Niche strategies are relatively high risk and high return, by virtue of their specialization and their focus on some particular product or geographic area. Innovative segmentation and the development and marketing of products for these segments is necessary for the successful implementation of these strategies.

- *Composite service strategies.* The composite service strategy was first observed in the financial services industry, in which some firms rebundled products and services in innovative ways, striving for synergies (*see* SYNERGY). In this category, one should also place firms that provide information to customers so that they can make a more informed choice as to the product they require after deregulation has opened the way to a multitude of product/service and price/performance trade-offs. The success of such strategies is often associated with the ability to create added value by such rebundling. An established customer base, the credibility to offer the services in question, an alternative delivery system, and a low-cost structure relative to traditional suppliers of similar services (although the rebundlers are themselves not necessarily price cutters) are also associated with success.

- *Global service strategies.* The global service strategy is pursued by firms that sell high

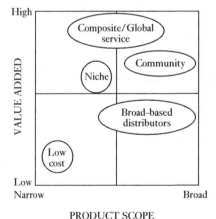

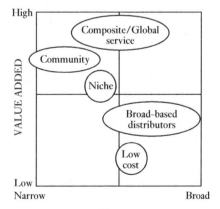

Figure 1   Strategies under deregulation

value-added services to selected multi-national and other large customers. The strategy requires sophisticated integrated delivery systems, coupled with the provision of a considerable level of personalized service. There are relatively few customers for such firms, and the amount of business required to make them profitable means that only a handful of global service firms can populate each industry worldwide.

• *Community strategies.* The final segment-focused strategy aims for the provision of a broad range of products to largely undifferentiated customers in small, protected geographic markets. A high level of service is provided to achieve customer loyalty, and a premium is charged for it. The markets in which these firms operate are too small to be tempting for larger competitors. Broad-based distributors and low-cost producers find it uneconomic to reach the small customer bases, and specialty companies are kept away by virtue of the local market being unsophisticated and offering little scope for segmentation. Customer loyalty provides an additional layer of protection. Overall, community firms can earn healthy profits, particularly if some regulation remains in place, provided that they do not try to expand into areas which are also served by larger firms. The strategies remain vulnerable in the long term, however, and community firms are threatened if some development allows more open entry into their markets. Having said that, community firms are sometimes found cooperating with potential predators, e.g., by buying from larger specialist concerns prevented from developing national strategies. Finally, competition and price reductions in adjacent markets can adversely influence community firms, which may be obliged to lower prices even though they face no direct challenge. In order to succeed, community firms require a very high market share. In addition, they must price selectively, according to the level of competition that is faced in each product line, they must stress personal service, watch costs and productivity and avoid complacency, and perhaps develop ties with larger firms. Growth comes from entry into other com-

munity markets, particularly those vacated by larger competitors.

Shared utility strategies. Finally, shared utilities are firms that specialize in activities which are expensive for the smaller firms, yet essential for their competitive survival (e.g., the provision of financial information). They undertake these activities on behalf of the smaller firms and, as economies of scale are achieved by virtue of the size of the combined activities, they provide these services at a cost that is very advantageous to the buyer firms. As with community firms, market share is very important, so there is only space for very few shared utilities in each industry. Their existence makes it possible for many small firms to populate a market that would otherwise be oligopolistic, so they can enhance competition in an industry and earn good profits by doing so. Common elements of success in shared utilities include the ability to identify the appropriate activities (which cannot be activities core to the value chains of the prospective customers), and the ability to be effective and cheap in undertaking them. Servicing some key players and becoming the industry standard is also important at the early stages, and this can determine whether or not the service will catch on.

CHOICE OF POST-DEREGULATION STRATEGY

From this brief description of the most commonly encountered post-deregulation strategies, it should be possible to select a shortlist of appropriate strategies for any particular firm.

It should also be evident, however, that the choice is fairly deterministic, both for incumbents and new entrants, at least for the early years after deregulation. Morover, given the few strategies that incumbents can choose from, it is possible that more will strive to pursue a certain strategy than the market will accommodate. In this sense, regulated markets that were made up of few large firms may have an easier transition, although the accumulation of market power also tends to make such firms inflexible, and it is harder for them to adjust to the competitive environment.

Impact on structure. Turning to organizational structure, diversification and a newly competitive environment both result in a strong trend toward organizational restructuring, this mainly involving divisionalization and the setting up of a series of customer-oriented marketing units to deal with the increased range of services and products offered.

In addition, particularly where deregulation takes place in conjunction with privatization and involves the setting up of a competitive market starting from a single organization, the incumbent organization may have to be split into a number of competing enterprises, horizontally or vertically; or, alternatively, third parties may be given the right to establish new companies and compete.

Overall impact on performance.   Having already discussed the effect that deregulation has on prices (and the ways in which this can be moderated), the impact on performance should follow. Overall, however, it is not possible to evaluate the likely impact of deregulation on any particular firm without consideration of the actions that any such firm takes to prepare for and react to deregulation. In the long term, performance may either increase or fall, because while regulation is expected to assure a reasonable stream of profits for all, deregulation opens the way to both very low and much higher levels of profits.

In the short term, the profits of established competitors are very often under threat, and profitable national monopolies are likely to face a difficult time adjusting to their new environment, particularly if all regulatory protection is removed at once. Initially, profits tend to fall, until reorganization and change of culture for competition are complete. At this point, a longer-term danger exists if the organization overlooks important environmental changes (*see* BLIND SPOTS), and this may well determine whether it survives in the competitive environment. If it adjusts, a whole new range of opportunities for considerably higher turnover are open to it, both nationally and internationally. Otherwise, if it remains largely unchanged in its culture and organization, it is likely to perish. A third possibility that is sometimes observed is that an organization appears to be adjusting well but, for a number of reasons, makes the wrong choices in the product market. This can also compromise performance.

Bibliography

Bleeke, J. A. (1983). Deregulation: Riding the rapids. *McKinsey Quarterly*, Summer, 26–44.

Bleeke, J. A. (1990). Strategic choices for newly open markets. *Harvard Business Review*, **68**, 5 (September/October), 158–66. Reprinted in *McKinsey Quarterly* (1991), **1**, 75–89.

Channon, D. F. (1986). *Global Banking Strategy*. Chichester: John Wiley, ch. 9.

Mahimi, A. and Turcq, D. (1993). The three faces of European deregulation. *McKinsey Quarterly*, **3**, 35–50.

Mahon, J. F. and Murray, E. A., Jr. (1981). Deregulation and strategic transformation. *Journal of Contemporary Business*, **9** (2), 123–38.

design school

Taman Powell

The design school is one of the ten STRATEGIC MANAGEMENT schools of thought coined by Mintzberg, Ahlstrand, and Lampel (1998). The design school views strategy formation as a process of conception where the central challenge is to establish a fit between the firm's qualities and the opportunities present in the environment.

The design school endorses a prescriptive view of strategy formulation, being potentially more concerned with how strategy should be formulated rather than how it actually is. The other schools proposed by Mintzberg fall into three groupings:

- *Prescriptive*: The design, planning, and positioning schools.
- *Descriptive*: The entrepreneurial, cognitive, learning, power, cultural, and environmental schools.
- *Configuration*: The configuration school.

The design school sees the CEO as being responsible for strategy development. She follows a deliberate process with her top-level management to develop a strategy that is based on thorough and deliberate analysis. This strategy is explicit, and is implemented by the organization.

There are a number of criticisms of the design school. Central among these is that it assumes that thought should lead action, and indeed, that thinking work should be separated from doing work. This segregation can pose problems, as noted by James Brian Quinn (1978): "It is virtually impossible for a manager to orchestrate all internal decisions, external environmental events, behavioral and power relationships, technical and informational needs, and actions of intelligent opponents so that they come together at a precise moment."

Even if the strategy is perfect at a point in time, the rigidity promoted by the design school has a tendency to encourage inflexibility that may limit opportunities to the firm. This is particularly the case in more dynamic environments.

The design school also does not leverage the abilities and ideas of employees, as they are not included in the development of the strategy. It effectively sees the knowledge of front-line employees as not being strategically relevant. This is clearly not the case, as has been aptly demonstrated by programs such as employee suggestions.

Separating design from implementation also runs the risk of damaging learning in the organization. This is because it is often the front-line personnel tasked with the implementation who generally have the detailed knowledge acquired from implementing the strategy, yet they are not involved in the formulation of the next strategy, effectively severing any form of feedback.

Bibliography

Mintzberg, H., Ahlstrand, B., and Lampel, J. (1998). *Strategy Safari*. Hemel Hempstead: Prentice-Hall.

Quinn, J. B. (1978). Strategic change: "Logical incrementalism." *Sloan Management Review*, **20** (1), 7–21.

differentiation

see BRANDING; DEMAND ANALYSIS IN PRACTICE; DEMAND ANALYSIS IN THEORY

diversification

Derek F. Channon

Most companies begin as single business concerns (*see* SINGLE BUSINESS STRATEGY) serving a local regional market. In the early years of corporate development, most companies operate with a limited product range. While the initial market offers scope, expansion may still come from market and/or geographic growth. The great majority of companies either choose, or are forced, to limit their growth aspirations.

Those corporations which choose, or are presented with opportunities, to develop tend to do so by diversification as and when their original strategies mature. The evolution of strategic development has led to the development of a number of models, based especially on the work of Chandler. On the basis of his observations, Scott produced an early model of corporate growth, shown in figure 1. In this model, companies evolved from the single business phase to an integrated structure, and finally to a related or unrelated diversified strategy, which, as indicated by Chandler, was managed by a multidivisional structure. In refinements of this stages of corporate growth model, the product market/geographic diversification strategies amongst large corporations, initially in the US, and in manufacturing industry were examined. This was later extended to cover other major developed country economies and to embrace service industries and, more recently, combinations of service and manufacturing concerns, as these developed from the 1970s onward. This research indicated that there were some industries which had difficulty in diversifying substantially, because of their cash flow-generating characteristics and the need to invest in all aspects of the business in order to maintain an integrated flow of product. These were concerns that had adopted a DOMINANT BUSINESS STRATEGY, which corresponded with Scott's stage II corporations. Normally, a major trauma, such as the first oil-price shock for oil companies or the impact of PRIVATIZATION for utilities concerns, was necessary for such firms to have the funds or the will to move to a fully diversified mode, by adopting either a related diversified strategy (*see* RELATED DIVERSIFICATION) or a CONGLOMERATE STRATEGY. The definition of each of these categories is dealt with at length elsewhere; however, financial relatedness tends to be neglected, and moves that embrace this variable tend to be classified as

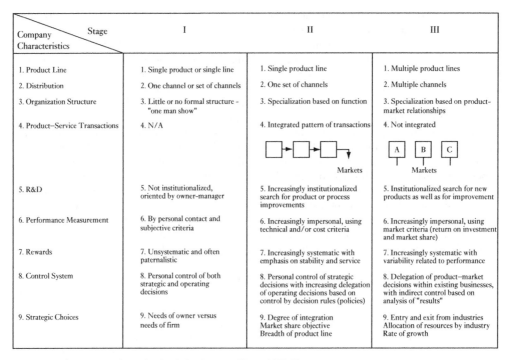

Company Characteristics \ Stage	I	II	III
1. Product Line	1. Single product or single line	1. Single product line	1. Multiple product lines
2. Distribution	2. One channel or set of channels	2. One set of channels	2. Multiple channels
3. Organization Structure	3. Little or no formal structure - "one man show"	3. Specialization based on function	3. Specialization based on product–market relationships
4. Product–Service Transactions	4. N/A	4. Integrated pattern of transactions	4. Not integrated
5. R&D	5. Not institutionalized, oriented by owner-manager	5. Increasingly institutionalized search for product or process improvements	5. Institutionalized search for new products as well as for improvement
6. Performance Measurement	6. By personal contact and subjective criteria	6. Increasingly impersonal, using technical and/or cost criteria	6. Increasingly impersonal, using market criteria (return on investment and market share)
7. Rewards	7. Unsystematic and often paternalistic	7. Increasingly systematic with emphasis on stability and service	7. Increasingly systematic with variability related to performance
8. Control System	8. Personal control of both strategic and operating decisions	8. Personal control of strategic decisions with increasing delegation of operating decisions based on control by decision rules (policies)	8. Delegation of product–market decisions within existing businesses, with indirect control based on analysis of "results"
9. Strategic Choices	9. Needs of owner versus needs of firm	9. Degree of integration Market share objective Breadth of product line	9. Entry and exit from industries Allocation of resources by industry Rate of growth

Figure 1   Three stages of organizational development (Scott, 1971: 7)

unrelated. Nevertheless, it can be argued that the combination of a cash-generating business such as gambling with investment in hotels represents a clear way to achieve financial SYN-ERGY.

The strategic evolution of the top 200 British corporations is shown in figure 2. In this sample no differentiation has been made between service and manufacturing concerns; state-owned enterprises have been included, as have service industries without "turnover" measures. Historically, most such research has used classifications such as Fortune 500, which was traditionally biased toward manufacturing, to identify the sample for evaluation.

The evolutionary trend has clearly been from undiversified strategies to more diversified concerns. Until 1980 the number of single business companies declined steadily, from 34 percent in 1950 to only 2 percent in 1980. This attrition occurred as a result of companies diversifying or being acquired by more diversified corporations. Those enterprises remaining in the category

were those involved in highly successful industries, such as high-share food retailers, or those protected from stock market pressures by enjoying mutual ownership, such as some building societies and life insurance concerns. During the late 1980s, the number of single business concerns increased. This was a function of the process of privatization, which created a number of large new firms in the utilities industry, particularly in water and electricity supply. Interestingly, these newly created public companies were, in most cases, seeking to diversify by geography and partially by vertical integration (*see* VERTICAL INTEGRATION STRATEGY).

Many firms diversify initially by limited moves through an ACQUISITION STRATEGY into new activities to become dominant business concerns. For most, this is a transitory step toward full diversification. There remains, however, a stable core of dominant business concerns which lack either the financial resources or the product market/technological skills to break out

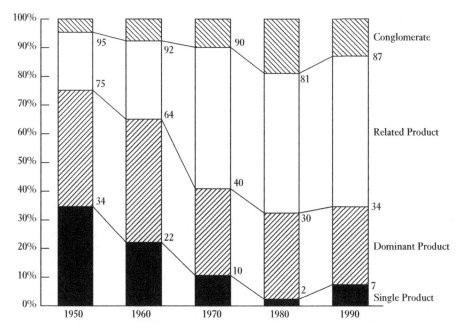

Figure 2 Diversification in the top 200 UK companies, 1950–1990 (Channon, 1973; Times 1000; *Annual Reports*, 1980–90)

from the position. Such firms tend to be involved in high capital intensity, low differentiation businesses, in which free cash flows are inadequate to provide the funds to move into new markets.

Most firms that diversify do so by acquisition, by purchasing businesses in areas that appear to be related to the original CORE COMPETENCES of the firm. However, this strategy is often flawed by the failure to clearly identify relatedness, by inexperience in acquisition (and in particular post-acquisition) procedures, and by a lack of attention by top management, as reflected in the board structure, to achieving the expected synergy. Nevertheless, by 1990 the number of related diversified corporations amongst the top 200 British firms had increased from 20 percent in 1950 to a level of 53 percent.

The number of large British firms that could be classified as conglomerates in 1990 showed a reduction from the 19 percent identified in 1980. The number of unrelated diversified concerns had grown to this level consistently from 1950 onward. Although the trend observed in the UK was not as marked as in the US, the pattern was

similar. During the 1980s, the reduction in the number of conglomerate strategies came about because some companies reduced their product market scope, there were acquisitions and breakups of highly diversified concerns, and the makeup of the top 200 companies was influenced by the addition of the substantial number of newly privatized concerns.

Overall, based on the UK experience, and supported by research in other developed economies (albeit over a lesser period of time, and less concerned with service businesses), there is clear evidence that enterprises grow, at least in part, by diversification by product and/or geography.

The process of diversification has largely occurred through acquisition, especially in the West. In recent times, stock market and external pressures have led some companies to reduce their product market scope by DIVESTMENT, although others have continued to diversify. In the absence of similar pressures, Asian corporations seem to have successfully continued to diversify. Despite the evolutionary trend toward diversification, there is strong evidence that many of those using such moves are unsuccessful. The reasons for this include the following:

- *Lack of integration capacity.* Many diversifiers do not possess the managerial skills to successfully integrate new activities.
- *Lack of board attention.* In many companies, especially those breaking out from dominant business positions, little attention is paid at board level to new business ventures.
- *Misunderstandings about relatedness.* Many moves into apparently related industries turn out not to be; for example, brewing companies might have diversified into hotels as a way of selling more beer, without recognizing that sales of alcohol were a small component in successful hotel operation.
- *Inexperience with acquisitions.* Most diversifications occur as a result of acquisitions. Unfortunately, the majority of companies available for purchase tend to suffer from some weakness, which usually needs correction. This in turn requires a skillful post-acquisition TURNAROUND STRATEGY, which companies diversifying themselves out of relative weakness rarely possess. As a result, acquisitions may well not generate the performance that was expected.
- *Clash of corporate cultures.* Each organization has a unique culture. It is imperative that the disparate cultures of organizations attempting to merge are sufficiently compatible to avoid dysfunctional organization side-effects.
- *Incorrect market identification.* Not necessarily the same as problems with relatedness, this error may occur in particular with unrelated diversification moves in which apparently attractive entries are made into markets that turn out to be much less attractive. For example, many manufacturing firms in mature markets attempted to enter the financial services market, often with disastrous consequences.
- *Difficulties of synergy release.* It has been shown that while synergy is relatively easy to identify in theory, it is extremely difficult to release in practice, with the possible exception of financial synergy.
- *Move too small.* Many firms embarking on diversification moves for the first time tend to adopt a timid approach, making only a relatively small move. Apart from not achieving COMPETITIVE ADVANTAGE in the industry sector into which the firm diversifies, small moves also suffer from a lack of board attention and difficulties of integration.
- *Inadequate functional skills.* These can be related to several of the other reasons for failure. If the diversifying firm lacks the critical success-factor core skills, these must be rapidly imported or the move may well fail.
- *Imposition of wrong style of management.* Diversification often involves entry into a new industry, in which the style of management may be quite different from that of core businesses (*see* CORE BUSINESS). Top management often fails to recognize such differences, and endeavors to introduce a culture, values, and control systems which, while relevant to the core business, are wholly inappropriate to the diversification.

Overall, diversification by product and by geography seems to be a natural process of evolution. The parameters that define the boundaries are not yet clearly delineated. Interestingly, while Chandler puts forward the proposition that structure follows strategy, the ultimate degree of diversification that can be achieved by the firm may be driven by structure. Is the KEIRETSU STRUCTURE espoused by major Japanese and Korean entities superior to the strategic business unit (SBU) structure used by western corporations, in which failing units are candidates for divestment, superior or otherwise? Time may tell.

Bibliography

Chandler, A. D. (1962). *Strategy and Structure: Chapters in the History of the Industrial Enterprise.* Cambridge, MA: MIT Press.

Channon, D. F. (1973). *Strategy and Structure of British Enterprise.* Cambridge, MA: Harvard Division of Research.

Channon, D. F. (1978). *The Service Industries: Strategy, Structure and Financial Performance.* London: Macmillan.

Rumelt, R. (1974). *Strategy Structure and Financial Performance.* Cambridge, MA: Harvard Division of Research.

Scott, B. R. (1971). Stages of corporate development. Unpublished paper, Harvard Business School.

Wrigley, L. (1971). Divisional autonomy and diversification. Unpublished doctoral dissertation, Harvard Business School.

divestment

Derek F. Channon

In the late 1980s, divestment strategies became more common as a result of stock market pressures being applied to highly diversified corporations (*see* DIVERSIFICATION). Such firms, which had largely expanded by acquisition into unrelated product markets (*see* ACQUISITION STRATEGY), were seen by acquisitive predators as candidates for breakup, as the sale of the constituent businesses would produce a substantial surplus over the market capitalization plus a bid premium. The activities of predators were also supported by stock market arbitrageurs, some commercial banks, and fund managers. In addition, bids for such companies could be orchestrated by specialist investment bankers, who would bid for such companies with a view to subsequently breaking them up. These pressures also led a number of companies to break up their own businesses to avoid the attention of predators. Again, commercial and investment banks, management consultants, and other market operators might initiate such breakups.

Other reasons for divestment include: differences in cultural fit (e.g., moves by pharmaceutical or tobacco companies into cosmetics); failure of businesses to fit with revised parent-company strategies introduced by new leaders (e.g., US General Electric transformed its portfolio of activities during the 1980s following the appointment of a new chief executive in 1981); businesses being divested or liquidated if they make a negative contribution to shareholder value following the adoption of a VALUE-BASED PLANNING system; and, finally, businesses that are identified as having weak portfolio positions.

Divestiture can result from the sale or liquidation of an existing business. The first of these policies was preferred, as the parent could hopefully rid itself of any liability for the divested activity. Such a move might take place by an outright sale to a third party, for whom the activity might be beneficial by, for example, increasing MARKET SHARE, adding new COMPLEMENTARY PRODUCTS, improving distribution access, and importing new technologies. Selling such a business to existing management, usually via a leveraged buyout strategy (*see* LEVERAGED BUYOUTS) was also often an attractive alternative. Liquidation was the most messy and usually least preferred method of business disposal. Such a move could result in hardships for displaced employees, expensive plant closures, image problems for the corporate parent, and potential litigation from injured parties.

While there has been some increase in divestiture as a result of stock market pressures, overall many corporations increased their level of diversification during the 1980s and early 1990s, although they may well have substantially adjusted their portfolio of businesses by a mix of sales and purchases.

Bibliography

Bowman, C. and Asch, D. (1987). *Strategic Management*. Basingstoke: Macmillan.

Rowe, A. J., Mason, R. O., Dickel, K. E., Mann, R. B., and Mockler, R. J. (1994). *Strategic Management*, 4th edn. Reading, MA: Addison-Wesley, pp. 439–40.

Thompson, A. A. and Strickland, A. J. (1993). *Strategic Management*. Homewood, IL: Irwin, pp. 178–81.

Toy, S. (1985). Splitting up. *Business Week*, 50–5.

divisional structure

Derek F. Channon

In his classic study of the evolution of large-scale US corporate enterprise, Chandler (1962) observed that as large corporations evolved, they became more complex. He reported, for example, that the natural development of the railroads made it impossible to centralize all decision-making. Decentralization was essential because communication systems were inadequate for information to be passed in time for the center to influence or make decisions.

Chandler noted that there was a natural tendency for some firms to diversify: he explored in depth the evolution of four major US corporations, the Du Pont Corporation, Standard Oil (later Exxon), General Motors, and Sears Roebuck, and observed how in the late 1920s a new organizational form developed in these concerns. Led by the Du Pont Corporation, these firms all found that the growing complexity of the organization made a FUNCTIONAL STRUCTURE inefficient and unwieldy. As a result, these firms developed a divisional form of organization in which operations were subdivided into a series of multifunctional units. The role of the central office changed to one of supervision and coordination of the organizational units, which were operationally autonomous, and the establishment of overall strategy. While this structure, shown in figure 1, became the key organizational form for diversified companies (*see* DIVERSIFICATION) and was spread around the world by US corporations, and especially by US consultants McKinsey and Company, the Mitsubishi ZAIBATSU STRUCTURE in Japan had developed in a very similar fashion some 15 years earlier.

The new structure broke the organization up in a way which provided divisional management with all the ingredients to operate as a complete business that could be measured in terms of profit performance. It made it easier for central management to establish investment policy, apply rewards and sanctions based on performance, and establish alternative strategies for different divisions; perhaps most of all, it helped to develop a cadre of general managers, which facilitated the strategy of further diversification. Functionally organized companies seriously lacked the capability to diversify because, apart from the CEO, they did not develop such general managers. The central office could also develop a sophisticated service function, especially in finance and planning.

In the postwar period the divisional structure spread rapidly throughout US industry, and as many of these firms began to move overseas, particularly into the developed countries of Europe, it gave them a dramatic advantage by comparison to the functional or holding company structures more normal in Europe. Servan Schreiber (1969) described this as the "American challenge" and noted that it was the div-

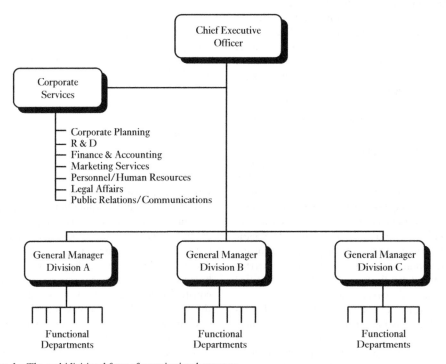

Figure 1   The multidivisional form of organizational structure

isional form of organization that was the secret of the success of American corporations in penetrating European markets.

Throughout the 1970s in manufacturing industry around the world, the divisional form of organization became widely accepted in diversified corporations. As observed by Chandler (1962), in related product diversified and geographically diversified corporations the divisions were supported by a large central office, with sophisticated staff units charged with insuring interdivisional coordination where necessary; for example, insuring efficient management of interdependency for products such as feedstocks and the like, coordinating corporation-wide services in specialist areas such as computing, and providing an overall perspective via STRATEGIC PLANNING and finance. Some central management of human resources and legal and external affairs was also normal.

The role of the board in the divisional organization was to set and monitor strategy, to measure and evaluate the performance of the divisions, to assign resources, to establish management information and control systems, to design and implement reward and sanction systems, and to make key appointments. The constitution of the board consisted usually of the chairman and chief executive, together with executives concerned with finance, often planning and human resource management, plus non-executive directors. In many, but not all, divisional structures, the general managers of major divisions were also included as members of the board.

In the late 1960s, the development of conglomerate businesses (see CONGLOMERATE STRATEGY) challenged the concept of the large central office. The new conglomerates operated a wide range of unrelated businesses, organized as product divisions, but the central office of such corporations was very small. The primary functions of the central office in these corporations were the establishment of overall strategy, acquisition search and purchase, post-acquisition rationalization, and tight financial monitoring of divisional performance. Some also had a number of general operating managers attached to the center who were capable of evaluating the operating activities of divisions placed under their control. The rationale for this small central office system was that there was deliberately no SYNERGY, other than financial, between the operating divisions; hence there was no need for central interdivisional coordination, R&D, and the like. This system appeared to be very successful for many years, especially when the overall technology requirements of the corporation were limited. However, failure occurred at Litton Industries when a number of major technological projects went out of control simultaneously. This caused a serious loss of stock market confidence in conglomerates, although in reality the financial performance of the group, when well managed, remained superior to that of related diversified businesses.

In the 1980s and 1990s, superior information technology and the trend toward DELAYERING extended the concept of the small central office to most forms of diversified corporations while, despite some moves back to core businesses (see CORE BUSINESS), many conglomerates remain.

The choice as to whether a geographic or product division system was adopted was a function of the degree of product complexity. As product diversity increased, there was a clear move toward the adoption of a product division system. Industries such as food, where strong local needs made the establishment of uniform product and marketing strategies difficult, were somewhat of an exception. Geographic divisions were common in such cases: production and products themselves were therefore localized and the need to establish centralized product divisional management had less value. By the late 1970s, most large diversified firms in the US and UK had found and adopted the multidivisional form, and a substantial number were endeavoring to operate this in conjunction with a portfolio system of management, the most commonly used of which was the GROWTH SHARE MATRIX. The same trend was found amongst the major corporations of other leading European countries; however, the degree of penetration of the divisional form was less developed and holding companies were still common, in part due to the complex shareholding patterns found in many European groups. These made it difficult to establish a common central office to set strategy for quasi-independent subsidiaries, in which minority shareholdings might hold considerable influence.

In the late 1970s, it also became recognized that the makeup of a division itself might be suboptimal. For example, in large divisions some activities might be growing rapidly while the main activities might be in decline. Since the corporate strategic resource allocation objectives and performance measurement tended to be established at the divisional level, such a growth business might be treated as a CINDERELLA BUSINESS. At the US General Electric Company (GE), therefore, it became recognized that the division did not necessarily represent the appropriate breakdown of the corporation. Hence, from the development of the PROFIT IMPACT OF MARKET STRATEGY (PIMS) program, and in conjunction with McKinsey and Company, the strategic business unit (SBU) structure was developed. The SBU then became the lowest-level planning unit in GE. A large division could therefore consist of several SBUs, each of which might be assigned a different strategic objective, performance measure, and dedicated resources, irrespective of the overall expected performance of the division itself. With this structure it was also possible to transfer some of the historic central staff functions to the divisional level and so reduce the size of the central office.

The divisional form was also important in the development of international strategy. As well as increasing the degree of product diversity, many corporations had developed international operations. The early multinationals tended to emerge from the European colonial powers, who established overseas operations in their colonies. British companies, for example, set up operations in the old empire; French and Dutch companies acted similarly. These concerns operated essentially as stand-alone units, since communications were inadequate to permit any central office control over operations. There was also no coordinated R&D, and the industries concerned tended to be either low-technology, such as food, or to involve the gathering of raw materials such as oil. The holding company structure was therefore the norm for such corporations, with central office control usually being exercised by the annual visit of a senior main board director.

After World War II, by contrast, major US corporations began to develop their overseas activities. Unlike the early Europeans, the US corporations moved to penetrate the developed economies, and especially western Europe. Moreover, it was the technology-led concerns in computing, chemicals, and the like which decided to go multinational. These firms were amongst the earliest to adopt the divisional form of organization.

In the early stages of internationalization, such firms normally established a separate international division. Exports from all domestic product divisions passed through such an export division. As international activities developed, however, it became normal not only to establish overseas sales organizations, but also to set up production facilities. In the early phases of this process the establishment of geographic divisions tended to be common. Further development of overseas production facilities, coupled with growing product complexity, caused tension between overseas geographic divisions and domestic product-based divisions. As a result, there was pressure to insure coordination between all similar product activities and to develop worldwide product research facilities. The possibility of interplant cross-border product and feedstock interchange therefore led to the movement toward the creation of worldwide product divisions. The boundaries between these three divisional variants were mapped by Stopford and Wells (1972) and are shown in figure 2.

From the early 1970s, there was also a growing trend in some industries to move to truly global rather than regionally oriented strategies. Products and components could be produced in one region and shipped around the world for assembly before being sold in a third region. This trend to complexity in both product and geography led to the development of an even more complex organizational form, the MATRIX STRUCTURE, which usually divided the corporation into a combination of both geographic and product divisions. In this structure, multiple reporting relationships were common, in which country executives reported to both area and product divisions.

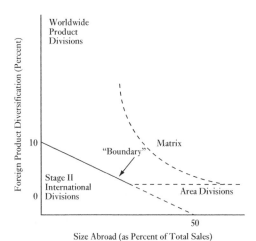

Figure 2   Activities overseas and structure (Stopford, 1980: 108)

The divisional organizational form has been an extremely important structural development in the management of the modern corporation. While the structure has continued to evolve, the basic premise remains, and its widespread adoption around the world has been a major element in the development of the strategy and structure of the diversified enterprise.

Bibliography

Chandler, A. D. (1962). *Strategy and Structure: Chapters in the History of the Industrial Enterprise*. Cambridge, MA: MIT Press.

Channon, D. F. (1973). *The Strategy and Structure of British Enterprise*. Cambridge, MA: Harvard Division of Research.

Dyas, G. P. and Thanheiser, H. T. (1976). *The Emerging European Enterprise*. London: Macmillan.

Rumelt, R. P. (1974). *Strategy, Structure and Economic Performance*. Cambridge, MA: Harvard University Press.

Schreiber, J. J. S. (1969). *The American Challenge*. New York: Aran Books.

Stopford, J. (1980). *Growth and Organizational Change in the Multinational Firm*. New York: Arno Press.

Stopford, J. and Wells, L. T. (1972). *Management and the Multinational Enterprise*. London: Longman.

Williamson, O. E. (1985). *The Economic Institutions of Capitalism*. New York: Free Press.

dog businesses

Derek F. Channon

Such businesses are defined as those in which the growth rate is slow and the relative MARKET SHARE is low compared to the leading competitor. Because of this low share, such businesses are often expected to have a higher cost structure than industry leaders. Moreover, to gain share in a mature environment is difficult and extremely expensive. The recommended strategy for such weak businesses is therefore seen as DIVESTMENT or rapid harvesting. While this may be so, care should be taken to insure that the cashflow prospects are as poor as the GROWTH SHARE MATRIX model suggests. Often, low capital intensity dog businesses can be fruitful cash generators, and harvesting can often be extended.

Divestment is the practice of selling businesses which appear not to fit with prevailing strategy. This was a recommended strategy for dog businesses. In addition, during the late 1970s and early 1980s acquisition strategies (*see* ACQUISITION STRATEGY) were popular and a further wave of predatory purchases occurred, often fueled by commercial and investment banks. In addition, unlike earlier such movements in the 1960s, such purchases became increasingly cross-border as the major world capital markets globalized. In the late 1980s and early 1990s this practice became less popular, as some of the emerging conglomerates themselves came under attack (*see* CONGLOMERATE STRATEGY), forcing divestments to reduce stock market vulnerability, increase shareholder value, and encourage the retreat to core businesses (*see* CORE BUSINESS). Many corporations did indeed sell activities that were considered non-core; for example, BAT disposed of its retail businesses to avoid an unwanted predator attack, ICI split in two with the flotation of its pharmaceutical business, and Sears Roebuck and Xerox spun off their financial services businesses. Other companies such as Hanson Trust, BTR, and US General Electric Company increased their overall degree of DIVERSIFICATION while also selling many businesses that did fit financially and/or strategically into their overall CORPORATE STRATEGY.

dominant business strategy

Derek F. Channon

Such businesses were defined empirically by Wrigley and others as those in which at least 70 percent of sales were accounted for by one key business. Dominant business corporations tended to be of several types. First, they were identifiable as being in an unstable transitory phase between single businesses and fully diversified enterprises. Second, they had developed naturally one key business which was so large that DIVERSIFICATION to a more diversified classification was difficult: such concerns included the oil companies, which despite their efforts found it difficult to find other activities that matched the main business. Third, there were companies which were trapped as dominant businesses: these businesses, including steel and other metal producers, tended to be high in capital intensity so that their cash flow-generating capacity was inadequate to both support the existing business and provide funds for diversification. Fourth, there were concerns in which one business had grown so rapidly that they had moved from a related diversified strategic position (*see* RELATED DIVERSIFICATION) back to a dominant business position: IBM, in which for a period mainframe computers dominated, provides an example.

It had proved very difficult for many dominant businesses to diversify successfully. Despite having many of the STRATEGIC MANAGEMENT skills at the center, such firms tended to operate as integrated Stage II businesses. As a result, they lacked the general management skills needed to manage a multibusiness corporation. Moreover, in the case of concerns such as oil companies, the size and scale of the main activity was such as to leave attempted diversifications without champions at board level, because of the tendency for such firms to attempt to impose the corporate culture of the CORE BUSINESS on diversifications, irrespective of whether or not this was appropriate.

The definition of the dominant business firm was subsequently refined by Rumelt (1974) to provide a measure of the degree of relatedness and vertical integration (*see* VERTICAL INTEGRATION STRATEGY) involved with a strategy. While the primary definition remained, four subdivisions of the dominant business form were identified:

- *Dominant–vertical.* These are vertically integrated firms that produce and sell a variety of end products, no one of which contributes more than 95 percent of sales.
- *Dominant–constrained.* These are non-vertical dominant business firms that have diversified by building on some particular strength, skills, or resource associated with the original dominant activity. In such firms the preponderance of diversified activities are all related one to another and to the dominant business.
- *Dominant–linked.* These are non-vertical dominant business firms that have diversified by building on several different strengths, skills, or resources or by building on new strengths, skills, or resources as they are acquired. In such firms the preponderance of the diversified activities are not directly related to the dominant business but each is somehow related to another of the firm's activities.
- *Dominant–unrelated.* These are non-vertical dominant business firms in which the preponderance of the diversified activities are unrelated to the dominant business.

Bibliography

Channon, D. F. (1973). *The Strategy and Structure of British Enterprise*. Cambridge, MA: Harvard Division of Research.

Rumelt, R. P. (1974). *Strategy, Structure and Economic Performance*. Cambridge, MA: Harvard Division of Research.

Scott, B. L. (1970). Stages of corporate development. Unpublished paper, Harvard Business School.

Wrigley, L. (1970). Divisional autonomy and diversification. Unpublished doctoral dissertation, Harvard Business School.

downsizing

Derek F. Channon

Ironically seldom discussed in the context of reengineering (*see* BUSINESS PROCESS REENGINEERING) and indeed denied, but nevertheless a common consequence, downsizing refers to a head-count reduction which usually occurs as a result of attempts to achieve radical shifts in productivity. These transformations have tended to result in head-count cuts of around 25 percent against initial stretch targets of 40 percent. In particular, downsizing has occurred with white-collar workers as a result of improved information technology, this having led to savage reduction in corporate staff (*see* DELAYERING). Over 85 percent of Fortune 1000 firms downsized between 1987 and 1991, with more than 50 percent downsizing in 1990 alone, when almost a million American managers lost their jobs. Similar trends have also occurred in Europe. Only in Japan has the philosophy of permanent employment been largely maintained, although even there pressures have been mounting, recruitment has been sharply cut back, excess workers have been transferred to subsidiaries or suppliers, and firms have been forced to diversify in efforts to maintain employment.

Nevertheless, downsizing is not necessarily a reactive and negative phenomenon but, rather, can be part of the process of "right sizing," whereby the head count employed is appropriate for the firm to gain or maintain COMPETITIVE ADVANTAGE. This is the outcome of the Japanese KAIZEN practice in which costs are continuously reduced and the workforce is actually redeployed to new activities.

Unfortunately, however, when a firm suffers a serious decline in profits, downsizing occurs as a first-response cost-cutting device. It is often not necessarily the most appropriate response, but it occurs because the firm has failed to monitor changes in its external environment and is faced with unexpected cost pressures, resulting from poor quality, inflexibility, obsolescent strategies, failure to develop new products, technology bypasses, and failure to monitor the appropriate competitors. The workforce therefore tends to suffer as a result of managerial failures rather than through any fault of its own.

Furthermore, the downsizing exercise itself does not address the underlying causes of strategic failure; moreover, the reduction in morale caused by downsizing, the probable future resistance to change, and the loss of faith in management can in the long term far outweigh the short-term reduction in cost. The actual process can also prove costly, notably in those countries in which social legislation makes redundancy terms especially expensive.

It is important therefore to gain employee commitment, rather than compliance, to the need for continuous cost reduction. Japanese companies have achieved this by their policy of permanent employment. While kaizen policies are common, the response of the Japanese workforce to *endaka*, the rapid appreciation of the yen, has been to double efforts to cut costs; for example, by dramatically increasing employee suggestions.

There are also alternatives to downsizing. As in Japan, most western companies stop hiring. Many encourage early retirement or do not replace leavers. Other strategies might include OUTSOURCING, job sharing, restricted overtime, short-time working, and switches to part-time working. Salary cuts are used infrequently (but not for top management in Japan).

When downsizing becomes inevitable, it is important that it is done effectively. A number of conclusions on how this should be achieved have been identified:

- couple productive restructuring with downsizing, either concurrently or in immediate sequence;
- continue top-down and bottom-up downsizing;
- pay special attention to both employees who lose their jobs and those who do not;
- insure that adequate advance notice is provided and involve the workforce in the process;
- downsize not only inside the firm but within the firm's external network;
- keep your head – and your heart and soul – during a crisis;
- insure that early warning systems are in place to avoid future BLIND SPOTS;

- create and sustain an information-porous organization;
- use competitive BENCHMARKING to insure that you do not suddenly wake up to find that you are no longer competitive.

Bibliography

Cameron, K. S., Freeman, S. J., and Mishra, A. K. (1991). Best practices in white collar downsizing: Managing contradictions. *Academy of Management Executive*, 57–73.

Collins, R. S., Oliff, M. D., and Vollman, T. E. (1991). *Manufacturing Restructuring: Lessons for Management.* Manufacturing 2000 Executive, Report No. 2. Lausanne, IMD.

Henkoff, R. (1990). Cost cutting, how to do it right. *Fortune*, 26–33.

Vollman, T. and Brazas, M. (1993). Downsizing. *European Management Journal*, 11, 18–28.

E

economies of scale

John McGee

The microeconomics of strategy is built initially on an understanding of the nature of costs. Cost for economists is essentially opportunity cost, the sacrifice of the alternatives foregone in producing a product or service. Thus, the cost of a factory building is the set of houses or shops that might have been built instead. The cost of capital is the interest that could have been earned on the capital invested, had it been invested elsewhere. In practice, money prices may not reflect opportunity costs, because of uncertainty, imperfect knowledge, natural and contrived barriers to movements of resources, taxes and subsidies, and the existence of externalities (spillover effects of private activities onto other parties; for example, pollution imposes costs on more than just the producer of pollution). Opportunity cost provides the basis for assessing costs of managerial actions, such as in "make or buy" decisions, and in all those situations where alternative courses of action are being considered.

Costs are also collected and reported routinely for purposes of both stewardship and control. The behavior of these costs in relation to the scale of output is of much importance. We see, for example, that BREAK-EVEN ANALYSIS is based on the extent to which costs vary in relation to output (in the short term) or are fixed in relation to output. The distinction between fixed and variable costs has implications for the flexibility a firm has in pricing to meet competitive conditions. Thus, one would always wish to price above variable cost per unit, in order to maintain positive cash flow. Fixed costs in this example are *sunk* costs; they are paid and inescapable, and the only relevant costs are those that are affected by the decision under consideration. It is the behavior of costs in the long term that has strategic implications for firms and for the structure of industries. The long term is the time horizon under consideration and affects what is considered to be "fixed." In the very long term, all economic factors are variable, whereas in the very short term, nearly all economic conditions are fixed and immutable. An economy of scale refers to the extent to which unit costs (costs per unit of output) fall as the scale of the operation (e.g., a factory) increases, (in other words, as more capital-intensive methods of operation can be employed).

In figure 1 we can see that Plant 1 exhibits increasing returns to scale or, simply, economies of scale. By contrast, Plant 2 shows decreasing returns to scale, diseconomies of scale. The strategic significance of economies of scale depends on the minimum efficient plant size (MES). This is important in relation to market size. The higher the ratio of MES to market size, the larger the share of the market taken by one plant, and the more market power that can be exercised by the firm owning the plant.

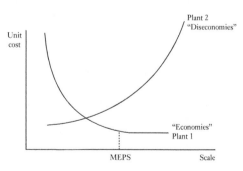

Figure 1   Minimum efficient plant size

Table 1   Minimum efficient scale for selected industries in the UK and US

Industry	% increase in average costs at ½ MES[a]	MES as % of market in	
		UK	US
Cement	26.0	6.1	1.7
Steel	11.0	15.4	2.6
Glass bottles	11.0	9.0	1.5
Bearings	8.0	4.4	1.4
Fabrics	7.6	1.8	0.2
Refrigerators	6.5	83.3	14.1
Petroleum refining	4.8	11.6	1.9
Paints	4.4	10.2	1.4
Cigarettes	2.2	30.3	6.5
Shoes	1.5	0.6	0.2

[a] This gives a measure of the sensitivity of costs across the range of plant sizes.
Source: Scherer and Ross (1990), tables 3.11 and 3.15

Table 1 contains estimates from the work of Scherer and Ross (1990). The final two columns show the ratio of MES to market size for the various industries in the US and the UK. It is evident, for example, that industry X will be much more *concentrated* than industry Y (it will have many fewer players), because economies of scale are so much bigger in relation to the market size.

The major sources of economies of scale are usually described as:

- indivisibilities and the spreading of fixed costs;
- the engineering characteristics of production.

Indivisibility means that an input cannot be scaled down from a certain minimum size and can only be scaled up in further minimum size units. Thus, costs per unit diminish after the initial investment until a further new block of investment is required. The original examples of "specialization" (the term coined by Adam Smith) were often engineering in nature. As volumes go up, it is usually cheaper to make work tasks more specialized – as exemplified dramatically in Henry Ford's mass production assembly-line operations in the first decade of the twentieth century. Economies of scale also arise because of the physical properties of pro-

cessing units. This is exemplified by the well-known cube-square rule. Production capacity is usually determined by the volume of the processing unit (the cube of its linear dimensions), whereas cost more often arises from the surface area (the cost of the materials involved). As capacity increases, the average cost decreases, because the ratio of surface area to cube diminishes. (For a full discussion of economies of scale, see Besanko et al., 2003.)

These general principles apply to functional areas other than production. In marketing, there are important indivisibilities that arise out of BRANDING and the creation of reputation effects. There are important scale effects in advertising, as the costs of campaign preparation can be spread over larger (e.g., global) markets. Research and development requires substantial minimum investments – another indivisibility – in advance of production, and the costs of R&D therefore fall as sales volumes increase. Purchasing in bulk exhibits economies of scale, in that the price per unit falls as the number of purchased items goes up. Sometimes this is because of monopolistic buying power (e.g., supermarkets in the UK). But each purchase does have a certain element of fixed costs attached to it (writing contracts, negotiation time, setting up production runs) and these may be significant.

The experience curve, sometimes called the learning curve, has similar strategic implications.

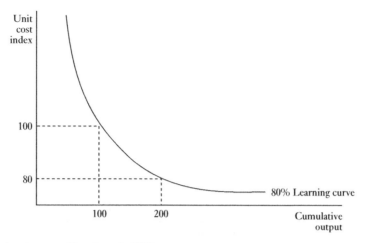

Figure 2   The learning curve (Besanko et al., 2003)

The experience curve is an empirical estimate of the proportion by which unit costs fall as experience of production increases. An 80 percent experience curve arises when costs fall to 80 percent of their previous level after production has doubled (see figure 2). Strategically, this means that a firm which establishes itself first in the market and manages to build a cost advantage by being twice the size of its nearest competitor would have a 20 percent production cost advantage over this competitor if an 80 percent experience curve existed. EXPERIENCE AND LEARNING EFFECTS arise where there are complex, labor-intensive tasks. The firm can facilitate learning through management and supervisory activities and coaching. It can also use incentives to reward learning.

In general, economies of scale and experience effects provide the basis in terms of cost advantage for those strategies that depend on cost leadership. The objective of cost leadership strategies is to realize a price discount to the customer and/or a margin premium that reflects the size of the cost advantage. Cost advantages are also available through vertical integration (*see* VERTICAL INTEGRATION STRATEGY) and the exercise of buying power.

The example in table 2 is taken from a case study on Du Pont's attempt in the 1970s to dominate the market for titanium dioxide in the US by virtue of its superior cost position. The cost advantage is based on economies of scale, on experience effects, on vertical integration, and on lower raw material prices. In total, the cost advantage over typical competitors is around 40 percent. As a result, the competitors were unable to stop Du Pont building scale-efficient new plant to take advantage of market growth – a classic example of a preemptive strategy. Similar arguments lay behind the analysis of the rapid growth of Japanese companies in the 1970s. Significant economies of scale gave the opportunity for lower prices, the building of MARKET SHARE, even lower costs, and the gradual dominance of markets. In general, the analysis of *first-mover advantage* relies on the existence of significant scale and experience effects, a price-sensitive market, and the willingness to commit capital ahead of competition.

SOURCES OF ECONOMIES OF SCALE

Division of labor. Economies of scale figure prominently in modern discussion of the appropriate size of industrial plants. The phenomenon itself has long been recognized, and Adam Smith on pin making provided the first classic description:

> one man draws out the wire, another straightens it, a third cuts it, a fourth points it, a fifth grinds it at the top for receiving the head; to make the head requires two or three different operations: to put it on is a peculiar business, to whiten the pins is another; it is even a trade by itself to put them

Table 2   Du Pont's calculation of its cost advantage

	Limenite chloride	Rutile chloride (1972 cents/lb)	Difference
From exhibit 3	18.80	21.50	−2.70
Less depreciation	−3.00	−2.50	−0.50
Capital charge	6.80	5.60	1.20
	22.60	24.60	−2.00
Learning effect	−4.75	0.00	−4.75
Scale effect	−3.75	0.00	−3.75
Integration effect	−1.30	0.00	−1.30
Capacity effect	1.30	1.00	0.30
Cost per lb	14.10	25.60	−11.50

capital charge = investment requirements per lb multiplied by hurdle rate (say 15 percent)
learning effect = 79 percent learning curve and double the experience
scale effect = 85 percent doubling effect and twice the scale
capacity effect = differences in capacity utilization

Source: Du Pont (1984), exhibits 2 and 3

into the paper; and the important business of making a pin is, in this manner, divided into about eighteen distinct operations, which, in some manufactories, are all performed by distinct hands.... I have seen a manufactory of this kind where ten men ... could, when they exerted themselves, make among them ... upwards of forty-eight thousand pins in a day.... But if they had all wrought separately and independently, and without any of them having been educated to this peculiar business, they certainly could not each of them have made twenty, perhaps not one pin in a day. (Adam Smith, *An Inquiry into the Nature and Causes of the Wealth of Nations*, 1776)

In this famous passage Adam Smith describes an improvement in labor productivity in excess of 15,000 percent. He is describing the *division of labor* (also called *specialization*) which came to Britain with the industrial revolution of the eighteenth and nineteenth centuries, bringing with it the development and organization of specialized factory trades and an increase in the use of machinery. In Smith's view, these great increases in the productivity of labor were due directly to three consequences of the division of labor: an increase in the dexterity and skill of individual workers due to specialization in one trade; the saving of time lost in moving labor from one type of work to another; and (in his words) "the invention of a great number of machines which facilitate and abridge labor, and enable one man to do the work of many."

The passing of two centuries has not diminished the force of Adam Smith's observations. The assembly line of an automatic plant provides a classic illustration of the impact of labor specialization. The extent of specialization depends technically on the scale of automation and the amount of capital invested in machinery. The greater the automation, the more can a worker specialize in one operation, e.g., a left wheel nut tightener (Scherer's example, 1970). At a rate of output of 500 cars per day, the left wheel nut tightener can be fully employed. But in a smaller plant where output is only 250 cars per day, he will be idle for half the time and may be assigned other jobs. However, this inspires losses in his EFFICIENCY as he moves to another work location (or as the work flow is rerouted to come to his position), or as he changes his mental gear and finds the correct tool and adopts a different work technique. In general larger firms can enjoy more specialization than smaller ones, but in any firm even the extent of the division of labor is restricted by the size of the market.

Identical principles apply in the use of specialized machinery. Machines can be designed to perform a range of specific tasks at high speed with great reliability and considerable savings in time and labor. Such machinery is of little value to the small-scale producer because it cannot be scaled down to her output levels and would be idle for much of the time. Likewise, their preparation for a production run requires much setup time and cost which are only recouped over long production runs. In general, smaller firms must use slower, more labor-intensive machine tools. Nowhere is this more sharply illustrated than in the comparison between the labor productivity of Japanese motorcycle factories (about 200 bikes per man year) and the factories of North America and western Europe (about 20 bikes per man year) (HMSO, 1970). Due in part to its privileged access to the large and growing Japanese and Asian markets in the 1950s and 1960s, the Japanese industry developed a scale of automation unknown in other countries where the market was more specialized and limited in size.

The benefits of division of labor are fairly obvious and can be summarized thus:

- increase in output at lower unit costs;
- increased use of machinery;
- increased possibility of improvement and quality control;
- the saving of time and tools through the avoidance of moving labor from place to place or the need to own general purpose equipment.

For the individual worker there are also several advantages (although productivity gains may have to be shared among the entire labor force): hours of work may be shortened, and work may be lightened. Against this there are problems arising from the loss of traditional skills and pride in workmanship, and monotony and strain imposed by the speed of the production line. For the firm there are clear difficulties that arise from the complexity of administration of such large units of production and the risk of failure of production from whatever cause when production is concentrated in one plant.

The cube law. Along with specialization of labor and of capital equipment goes the capital cost savings on large items of machinery due to the operation of the so-called *cube law*. The volume of a vessel (which for process plant determines the volume of output) is roughly proportional to the cube of its radius, while its surface area (where the cost is to be found) is proportional to the square. Thus, as the volume capacity of a plant increases, the material requirements and hence its capital cost tend to rise as the two-thirds power of the output capacity. There is considerable empirical support for the existence of this "two-thirds" rule, which is used by engineers in estimating the cost of new process equipment.

Economies of massed reserves. Another benefit of size comes from the *economy of massed reserves* (Robinson, 1958). This rests on the law of large numbers on which the entire insurance industry is based. To preserve continuity of production, the firm must insure itself against the consequences of machine breakdown by maintaining a reserve of EXCESS CAPACITY. The larger the firm and the more identical (or similar) machines it uses, the smaller the proportion required of spare capacity. Such economies exist for stockholding, financial assets, labor, and service department staffing.

Firm-level economies of scale. We should also distinguish between scale economies achievable at the plant level and those achievable at the level of the firm itself. Division of labor and the operation of the cube law each apply at the level of the plant. The economy of massed reserves can apply at both levels. Generally, it is relatively easy to specify and estimate the scale economies at plant level because they rest on technical, engineering considerations. Firm-level economies are more difficult to identify with such clarity and are, surprisingly, more difficult to achieve. But they are, in theory at least, the basis for much merger activity.

The costs incurred by the firm as distinct from the plant can be grouped broadly as: managerial and administrative, research and development, transportation and distribution, and marketing. Where the firm operates many plants and particularly when there is some degree of horizontal and/or vertical integration, then the firm-level economies can be of great potential significance. Administrative economies can arise through the traditional division of labor and substitution of labor by capital-intensive equipment, e.g., word-processing equipment replacing typists, automatic document coding and transferral replacing clerks. Financial economies are available by reducing the level of stocks and work in progress relative to the rate of production. Marketing economies are available in advertising to mass markets and using a common sales force to purvey a product line. Risks can be spread in R&D by managing a portfolio of projects rather than a single or few projects. The pooling of risks arises through pooling financial resources across markets with different cyclical characteristics.

Barry Supple (1977) has placed economies of scale in the context of business history and development of large-scale enterprise:

> the specific factors responsible for this trend to large-scale enterprise have varied markedly. The economies of scale in their conventional sense – the unit cost reduction derived from large accumulations of capital equipment, advanced and expensive technology, specialization of functions, bulk purchasing and distribution – played an obvious part. . . . At the same time, however, the emergence of the giant firm was also a function of financial considerations (stock market buoyancies in particular increased the probability and profitability of mergers and flotation) and of market vicissitudes and ambitions. The desire to protect investments and market shares, the ambition to secure market control and stability of sales, the pressure to mitigate competition and to expand sales and profit margins – all illustrate the range, from defensive to offensive, of policies involved, as well as the overall importance of market strategies in the history of large-scale enterprise. And, in the event, many of the most spectacular instances of big business (with Courtauld's, Lever Brothers, Austin Morris) rested as much on product differentiation as on "pure" cost advantages.

Supple's comments reinforce the earlier statement that the size and the nature of the market place some limits of the extent to which unit costs can continue to fall. Apart from market size, there are other limitations to the extent of economies of scale.

The first relates to the way in which specialized but indivisible units of equipment dovetail in the production process. At some point a stage is reached at which further cost reductions are not possible because all units of equipment are being used at their optimum rates. Any expansion of output in units less than that required for replication of existing equipment will cause unit costs to rise.

A second set of assertions about the management process is probably more significant in bringing potential technical economies to an end. The general hypothesis is that the management of sufficiently large units entails rising unit costs. One variant of this ascribes the problem to the relatively fixed input of senior management time as the scale of operation grows. The cost of communication rises very rapidly, usually evidenced by large numbers of middle managers, staff, and so on. The consequence of these managerial and coordination problems is upward pressure on costs until diseconomies of large-scale management eventually overpower the technical economies of scale. A concrete analogy is the rise in transport and distribution costs as production is increasingly centralized to obtain production economies. To service a network of distribution points from one central production point entails higher distribution costs than the servicing of smaller numbers of distribution points from a number of decentralized production facilities.

The organization of large-scale management has become highly specialized. Specialized staff functions that supply information for decision-making to line executives have been used quite effectively. Communication spurred on by rapid technological developments has been simplified and cheapened beyond our recent expectations. Control techniques based on management accounting, budgetary control, and cash flow analysis have been brought to a high state of perfection. Information technology and systems permit the storage, retrieval, and analysis of vast amounts of information. These changes in the technology of management, together with more sophisticated views of organizational structure, allow the management of large scale to become more and more effective.

Notwithstanding the state of the managerial art, the potential for achieving cost savings through larger plant and from size has often been frustrated by circumstances. Examples (HMSO, 1978) are the difficulty of phasing out of obsolete plant in the steel industry in the face of slow-growing demand and political difficulties. The motor industry in Britain also has a large number of plants in relation to the numbers of cars produced. Similarly, the merging of the manufacturing facilities of the aircraft industry and the development of a coherent commercial strategy has taken undue time. However, scale economies are not always frustrated by practical difficulties. More encouraging results have been seen in electricity generation, the restructuring of the bearings industry, and the change of scale in the brewing industry. The limits to the realization of technical economies might be summarized as follows:

- diseconomies of scale in distribution;
- the complexity of large-scale management, which requires high investment cost and accumulated experience to reduce it;
- the need to maintain product differentiation and flexibility in the face of changing tastes;
- the industrial relations problems in managing large plants.

See also *cost analysis; economies of scope*

Bibliography

Besanko, D., Dranove, D., Shanley, M., and Shaefer, S. (2003). *Economics of Strategy*, 2nd edn. New York: John Wiley.

Du Pont (1984). *Titanium Dioxide (A)*. Harvard Business School Case Study 9-385-40. Boston: Harvard Business School.

Her Majesty's Stationery Office (HMSO) (1970). *The British Motorcycle Industry*. London: HMSO.

Her Majesty's Stationery Office (HMSO) (1978). *Review of Monopolies and Mergers*. Cmnd 7198. London: HMSO.

McGee, J., Thomas, H., and Wilson, D. (2005). *Strategy: Analysis and Practice*. Maidenhead: McGraw-Hill.

Robinson, E. A. G. (1958). *The Structure of Competitive Industry*. Chicago: University of Chicago Press.

Scherer, F. M. (1970). *Industrial Market Structure and Economic Performance*. New York: Rand McNally.

Scherer, F. M. and Ross, D. (1990). *The Economics of Multiplant Operations*. Cambridge, MA: Harvard University Press.

Supple, B. (1977). *Essays in British Business History*. Oxford: Oxford University Press.

economies of scope

John McGee

A source of superior financial performance is the ability of a firm to exploit economies of scope. These arise when the average cost of a single product is lowered by its joint production with other products in a multiproduct firm. In figure 1 when output for each product is at Q_1 (so scale economies for each product are fully exploited), it is possible for average costs at C_2 to be even lower than C_1, if the economies of scope are also fully exploited. In practice, these scope economies can be important. A study (Pratten, 1988) of the cost effects of halving the number of products made by each producer in a selection of EU industries shows impacts that range from $+3$ percent in carpet manufacture to $+8$ percent in motor vehicles. These scope economies may arise from the opportunity to leverage a core *capability* (*see* CORE COMPETENCES) arising from knowledge and learning, organization or management skill, so as to reduce the average total cost of all products produced in a multiproduct firm. A good example is the expertise that arises from technical and scientific knowledge within the firm. Exploiting this distinctive expertise by innovation and product diversifi-

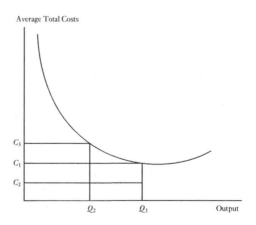

Figure 1   Economies of scope

cation lowers the average total cost of all products. Pharmaceutical manufacture and steel production are both sectors where this kind of cost economy is important. Scope economies can also arise from efficient use of *resources*, for example, where a number of related goods are produced using a common process. Car manufacture of a range of models is an example and part of the reason for the significant scope economies found in Pratten's study. Another source of scope economies arises from spreading the fixed cost of a network over a wider range of products. Commercial banks, for example, incur a large fixed cost from their branch networks. If they spread this cost over a large range of related corporate and retail financial products, the average total cost of each product is reduced.

In contrast to ECONOMIES OF SCALE, economies of scope refer to increased variety in operations, not higher volume of output. Economies of scope therefore emerge where unit costs fall because of the occurrence of common resources and/or knowledge being applied to the production of more than one product. Such common resources could be, for example, the result of shared distribution, advertising, purchasing, and similar activities. Together with CROSS-SUBSIDIZATION, economies of scope could allow the monopolization of a perfectly competitive industry.

Economies of scope can therefore be an active component of strategy development when the application of centralized management leads to lower costs. Ironically, some financially oriented acquisitive conglomerates may be relatively more successful in achieving such economies than many related diversified concerns (*see* RELATED DIVERSIFICATION). Indeed, diseconomies of scope can also readily occur when endless DIVERSIFICATION adds to managerial bureaucracy or when a failure occurs in strategy implementation, such as when like concerns fail to integrate. This is especially common when moves aimed at achieving STRATEGIC FIT fall down, usually on cultural and/or organizational grounds.

One of the main dimensions of strategic choice (*see* GENERIC STRATEGIES) revolves around the notion of *scope*. We have described economies of scope as arising when the average cost of a single product is lowered by its joint production with other products in a multiproduct firm. This is based on the indivisibility of certain resources. For example, knowledge is indivisible in the sense that it cannot be divided into pieces, some of which you choose to have and some of which you choose not to have. Knowing about aluminum means that you will have knowledge relevant to airframe manufacture and to pots and pans. Economies of scope arise when your knowledge or other indivisible resource can be applied in multiple directions without using up that resource. Thus scope becomes interesting strategically. A firm may choose to operate with broad scope (such as Ford in the automobile assembly industry covering a very wide product range as well as the globe). Conversely, a firm may choose to operate on a very narrow scope (such as Morgan, which covers only a particular part of the sports car market). The choice of broad scope suggests a calculation about available economies of scope in such a fashion that, once chosen, it is a commitment that cannot readily be reversed. The choice of narrow scope suggests an alternative calculation that the benefits of assets and other resources and capabilities focused in specific ways create differentiation and/or cost advantages of a different sort.

Bibliography

Thompson, A. A. and Strickland, A. J. J. (1993). *Strategic Management: Concepts and Cases*, 7th edn. Homewood, IL: Irwin, pp. 171–2.
Pratten, C. (1988). A survey of the economies of scale. In *Research on the Costs of Europe*. Office for Official Publications of the European Communities, vol. 2.

economies of substitution

John McGee

ECONOMIES OF SCOPE exist when the cost of joint production of two outputs is less than the cost of producing each output separately (Panzer and Willig, 1981). One course for economies of scope is the ability of a firm to use its technical competences across different products without congestion (Teece, 1980). In the area of microelectronics it is possible to realize economies of scope between software and hardware products.

Open systems require knowledge of how hardware and software products can be integrated across different vendors' systems. Specifically, software knowledge is essential to design hardware, and vice versa (Langowitz, 1987). However, there are limits to the economies that scope can offer. Eventually, as the demands for sharing know-how increase, bottlenecks in the form of over-extended scientists, engineers, and other technical personnel occur.

Whereas economies of scope refers to a process of extending know-how horizontally across products, we can also see that there is a way of achieving economies vertically within a product structure. This is the notion of economies of substitution. This observes that technological progress can be made by substituting only certain components of a multicomponent system while retaining others. Economies of substitution exist when the cost of designing a higher-performance system through the partial retention of existing components is lower than the cost of designing the system afresh.

This substitution effect arises from two causes. As a result of time lags in the evolution of different system components, site performance improvements can be attained by advances in specific components while the capabilities of other components are not yet exhausted. New components can be integrated into existing systems if components conform to standardized interface specifications. Thus, where there is *modularity* in design, then intertemporal substitution of components can occur.

A second perspective recognizes the hierarchical organization of components (Clark, 1985; Hughes, 1987). Component choices at any level of the hierarchy outline operational boundaries for lower-order components and subsystems. At the apex of the hierarchy it is possible to choose components whose capabilities are not fully exploited at the design stage. These unused technological capabilities in higher-order components give designers the latitude to increase system performance through innovations in lower-order components. System *upgradeability* can take place while also backward compatibility can be maintained.

Together modularity and upgradeability result in modular upgradeability. Modularity provides system designers with the flexibility to substitute only certain system components while retaining others. Upgradeability provides designers with the opportunity to work on an established knowledge platform thereby preserving their core knowledge base. Together they permit the improvement of system performance at low cost while maintaining backward compatibility (i.e., preserving the existing knowledge base).

Conventional approaches to innovation involved custom design of key systems components and restricting access to proprietary technical knowledge. By contrast, the modern approach is to encourage multisystem compatibility by employing standard, off-the-shelf components and by providing other firms with easy access to technologies. Thus, connected open networks have replaced unconnected closed networks. In such an environment firms compete by continually innovating and by sponsoring new technologies.

Whereas economies of scope represent a lateral extension of core technologies and knowledge base, economies of substitution represent a vertical enhancement on technology platforms that have unexploited capabilities. Scope establishes compatibility between system components whereas substitution insures upgradeability and backward compatibility.

Examples of these effects have been examined in the workstation market (Langowitz, 1987; Garud and Kumaraswamy, 1993), in telecommunications, office automation and consumer electronics, and quite generally in the computer industry (Gable, 1987).

Bibliography

Astley, G. W. and Rajam, C. (1987). The relevance of Porter's generic strategies for contemporary technical environments: A Schumpeterian view. Paper presented at the annual meeting of the Academy of Management, New Orleans, LA.

Clark, K. B. (1985). The interaction of design hierarchies and market concepts in technological evolution. *Research Policy*, **14**, 235–51.

Gable, H. L. (1987). Open standards in the European computer industry: The case of X/OPEN. In H. L. Gable (ed.), *Product Standardization and Competitive Strategy*. New York: Elsevier Science, pp. 91–123.

Garud, R. and Kumaraswamy, A. (1993). Changing competitive dynamics in network industries: An exploration of Sun Microsystems' open systems strategy. *Strategic Management Journal*, 14 (5), 351–70.

Hughes, T. P. (1987). The evolution of large technological systems. In W. E. Bijker, T. P. Hughes, and T. J. Pinch (eds.), *The Social Construction of Technological Systems*. Cambridge, MA: MIT Press.

Langowitz, N. (1987). *Sun Microsytems Inc. (A)*. Harvard Business School Case Study 9-686-133, revised. Boston: Harvard Business School.

Panzer, J. C. and Willig, N. D. (1981). Economies of scope. *American Economic Review*, 71, 268–77.

Teece, D. J. (1980). Economies of scope and the scope of the enterprise. *Journal of Economic Behavior and Organization*, 1, 223–47.

economizing

John McGee

The contrast between strategizing and economizing was first developed and given a theoretical grounding by Oliver Williamson (1991). Observing that business strategy is a highly complex subject that spans the functional areas of business and involves also the disciplines of economics, politics, organization theory, and some aspects of law, Williamson nevertheless argued that its substantive aspects could be clustered under two headings, namely, strategizing and economizing. The first has had much wider currency in the academic discussion and in practitioner debate: it works from the premise that firms can and do develop positions of market power in order to deal with the pressing problems of competition. However, Williamson argues that economizing is the more fundamental because strategizing efforts will rarely prevail if firms are burdened by significant cost excesses in their business functions or in any of their internal governance functions. Because economizing is more fundamental, Williamson has coined (or, more properly, rediscovered) the aphorism that *economy is the best strategy*.

Economizing is essentially about cost minimization. Economists treating the firm as a simple (black box) production function use the term technical efficiency to indicate firms that operate on the cost function as opposed to above it, where they would be regarded as technically inefficient. In this view consumers and producers automatically operate through the price system and the motivation of profit maximization so that technical efficiency can be maintained. But this is an egregious simplification (according to Williamson). The sources of cost inefficiency are due to inferior internal organization and maladapted operations. Differences in profits in two firms in the same industry using the same technology selling to the same customers are probably due to one firm working "smarter" with better organizational form, better internal incentives and controls, and better alignment of contractual interfaces, both inter-firm and intra-firm.

In addition to this more subtle (than technical efficiency) analysis of bureaucracy and waste, economizing is also about more effective adaptation to change. The early economic approaches (e.g., Hayek) offered the price system as the supremely important mechanism for communicating information and inducing change. But the early literature on internal organization (Barnard) held that the main concern of organization was to adapt to changing circumstances by the process of adapting internal organization. Both forms of adaptation are needed. The price system provides for autonomous changes by consumers and producers responding independently to price changes. In addition, some changes require more complex coordinated responses such as coordinated investments and coordinated internal realignments. These call for conscious, deliberate, and purposeful efforts to craft adaptive internal coordinating mechanisms. Thus complex contracting and internal organization economics are implicated.

In this view, economizing is not only fundamental but complex. It requires organizational characteristics that may be developed differentially between firms and, as such, may be the basis of significant and sustainable differences resulting in performance differences. That is, they can be the basis of COMPETITIVE ADVANTAGE and provide a foundation for understanding the nature of the RESOURCE-BASED VIEW of the firm and the nature of CORE COMPETENCES.

The above explanation is drawn from Williamson's well-known paper in the *Strategic Management Journal* where he argues that his economizing approach to strategy is based on transaction cost economics. Later approaches (e.g., Besanko et al., 2003) offer the same approach expressed in terms of technical efficiency and agency efficiency.

Technical efficiency is in part the cost minimization approach given above but more broadly refers to the choice of the least-cost production processes (e.g., through ECONOMIES OF SCALE and specialization). Agency efficiency refers to the extent to which the exchange of goods and services in the vertical chain has been organized so as to minimize coordination, agency, and TRANSACTIONS COSTS. The optimal vertical organization minimizes technical and agency inefficiencies. Thus it allows for TRADE-OFFS between vertical integration (*see* VERTICAL INTEGRATION STRATEGY) and market exchange. To the extent that the market is superior for minimizing production costs (allowing advantage to be taken of internal economies of scale and ECONOMIES OF SCOPE) and vertical integration is superior for minimizing transactions costs (by retaining these costs within the firm), the trade-offs between the two costs are normal and inevitable. Failure to handle these effectively can result in higher production costs, bureaucracy, waste, breakdowns in exchange, and litigation. This approach gives rather greater weight to vertical integration than to internal organization but achieves the same result in showing the importance of economizing in business strategy.

Bibliography

Barnard, C. (1938). *The Functions of the Executive*. Cambridge, MA: Harvard University Press; 15th printing, 1962.

Besanko, D., Dranove, D., Shanley, M., and Shaefer, S. (2003). *Economics of Strategy*, 2nd edn. New York: John Wiley.

Hayek, F. (1945). The use of knowledge in society. *American Economic Review*, 35 (September), 519–30.

Williamson, O. (1991). Strategizing, economizing and economic organization. *Strategic Management Journal*, 12, special issue (Winter), 75–94.

efficiency

Stephanos Avgeropoulos

There are many kinds of efficiency, namely, allocative efficiency, productive (technical) efficiency, X-efficiency, and Y-efficiency. These terms are discussed in more detail below. Pareto efficiency is discussed elsewhere (*see* PARETO ANALYSIS).

ALLOCATIVE EFFICIENCY

This refers to the efficient allocation of resources between the production of different products (by different firms), and is said to be achieved when an output mix is produced which is regarded as "socially desirable." Allocative efficiency is, therefore, more of a macroeconomic concern and less relevant for the individual firm, although it can also be used to consider matters such as the appropriate ratio of human to mechanical capital.

In contrast with X-inefficiency, which places society inside its production possibility boundary, allocative inefficiency places society at the wrong point on the boundary. In the simplest economic models, allocative efficiency can be achieved when prices equal the marginal cost of production. Inefficiency usually occurs as a result of distorted signals in a market economy, which themselves can be the result of EXTERNALITIES or anticompetitive behavior.

The measurement of allocative efficiency requires marginal cost information, which is often not available. This means that the effort to measure allocative efficiency is often not made, particularly as the incentives for the individual firm to do so are limited. The absence of competition or potential competition, however, is typically associated with high levels of allocative inefficiency.

PRODUCTIVE EFFICIENCY

A firm is said to be productively efficient when it employs the least-cost combination of input factors to produce a given output (see X-efficiency, below).

An economy is said to be productively efficient if two conditions are fulfilled, namely, that each firm is on its relevant cost curve (i.e., it is X-efficient), and that all firms have the same level of marginal cost (i.e., the marginal cost of producing the last unit of output is the the same for every firm in the industry).

X-EFFICIENCY

This term, coined by Professor Harvey Leibenstein, refers to departures from the lowest-cost method of producing some given level of output and describes the effects of individuals being selectively rational and making decisions that involve less than complete concern for all constraints and opportunities, i.e., agents who do not constantly act as maximizers.

There are three main components of X-efficiency: intra-plant motivational efficiency, external motivational efficiency, and non-market input efficiency.

There are also four main sources of X-inefficiency. The first has to do with incomplete contracts for labor; one form of X-inefficiency, for example, is the result of a poor agency relationship (*see* AGENCY THEORY), and a significant component of organizational slack can include overstaffing and spending on prestige buildings and equipment. The second is relevant when not all factors of production are marketed, which includes motivational matters (it considers, for example, inefficient behavior as a result of employee attitudes to effort, and to the search for, and utilization of, new information – an example might be when employees are too hungry or unmotivated to concentrate on their tasks). The third source of X-inefficiency centers on a production function which is not completely specified or known. Finally, X-inefficiency may be the result of tacit cooperation between competing firms as a result of interdependence and uncertainty, or of imitation, and in this case the extent of X-inefficiency is assumed to increase with market power, for reasons that include a relaxation in cost controls.

X-efficiency can be affected, among other things, by factors such as the exploitation of any ECONOMIES OF SCALE that may be available.

As a result of X-inefficiency, higher costs lead to reduced competitiveness. Leibenstein (1966) found that "X-inefficiency exists, and that improvement in X-efficiency is a significant source of increased output."

Y-EFFICIENCY

This term was coined by Michael Beesley (1973). In contrast to X-efficiency, Y-efficiency refers to the revenue side of a firm's activities. A firm is said to be Y-inefficient if it fails to expand its markets (e.g., through efficient market research and promotion) to the extent required for profit maximization.

Like X-inefficiency, Y-inefficiency is sometimes assumed to be nurtured by the lack of competitive pressures on the firm, which lead to insufficient incentives to develop new markets.

Considerations of Y-efficiency have implications for the scale and scope of a firm's activities (see, e.g., DIVERSIFICATION).

Bibliography

Beesley, M. E. (1973). Mergers and economic welfare. In *Mergers: Take-Overs and the Structure of Industry*. Reading No. 10. London: Institute of Economic Affairs.

Leibenstein, H. (1966). Allocative efficiency vs. X-efficiency. *American Economic Review*, 56 (3), 392–415.

Leibenstein, H. (1975). Aspects of the X-efficiency theorem of the firm. *Bell Journal of Economics*, 6 (2), 580–606.

elasticity

Stephanos Avgeropoulos

Elasticities are simple measures that indicate the change in one quantity as a result of a change in another, *ceteris paribus*.

Early work on demand measurement and price elasticity looked at agricultural products. These studies were useful because of the large price variations observed, which were caused by fluctuating crop yields combined with competitive market conditions, and which troubled farmers and the general population alike. They were made possible precisely because of these reasons, i.e., because of widely fluctuating prices and quantities.

There are a variety of elasticities, and a new one can be defined for any two variables where one affects the other. Frequently used elasticities consider how the demand or supply functions are affected by their individual determinants. The price elasticity of demand can be calculated, for example, to indicate the sensitivity in the demand for a product to variations in its price. In general, demand elasticities tend to rise as quantity held rises. If one has no shoes, for example, the demand for the first pair will be quite insensitive to price; when one already has a few pairs, however, one is expected to become

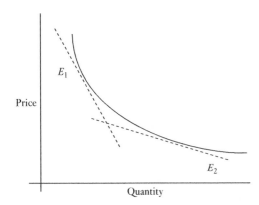

E_1

Price

E_2

Quantity

Figure 1 Price elasticity and the demand curve

more price sensitive (for the same level of income, and funds to spend on shoes). Elasticity, therefore, changes according to the point on the demand curve at which one lies: here the number of shoes already owned (see figure 1).

TYPES OF ELASTICITY

Strictly speaking, elasticity can be measured at any point on the relevant curve and specifies the change in one variable that would result from an infinitesimal change in another. This is called the point elasticity, and it is used when one is dealing with curves expressed using mathematical functions.

In practice, however, where the relevant function may not be fully specified, elasticities are measured using discrete data (e.g., by varying the price by, say, 5 percent and observing the change in the quantity demanded). In this case, ranges – rather than points – are more useful. Arc elasticity, therefore, is defined in order to measure the relative responsiveness of one variable to a discrete change in another. One can consider, for example, the arc price elasticity of demand.

Finally, there are cross-elasticities, where the responsiveness of a relevant quantity for one product is measured for a change in a quantity relating to a second product. For example, the cross-advertising elasticity of demand for product A with reference to product B will indicate how advertising expenditure for product B affects the demand for product A.

In the following discussion, some of the elasticities that are more frequently encountered in practice will be considered.

ELASTICITIES OF DEMAND

Elasticities of demand can be considered with reference to any of the variables in the demand function. Typically, these include price, advertising, income, and price expectations. Demand is said to be elastic when elasticity is greater than 1, and inelastic when it is below 1. In the (theoretically encountered) extremes, a perfectly elastic demand is associated with a horizontal demand curve, and a perfectly inelastic demand with a vertical curve. By (confusing) convention, the absolute value of demand elasticities is sometimes reported.

Price elasticity of demand. This is probably the most widely used elasticity. The mathematical formula for the arc price elasticity of demand is as follows:

$$E_p = \frac{\Delta Q/Q}{\Delta P/P} = \frac{\Delta Q}{\Delta P} \cdot \frac{P}{Q}$$

where P is price and Q is quantity. If ? is replaced throughout by the partial differential operator (∂), then the formula for the point price elasticity is obtained:

$$E_p = \frac{\partial Q/Q}{\partial P/P} = \frac{\partial Q}{\partial P} \cdot \frac{P}{Q}$$

By convention, products with elastic demand (products whose price elasticity is greater than 1) are said to be luxuries, while products with inelastic demand (those with elasticities below 1) are said to be necessities.

A number of factors are associated with higher price elasticity. One important determinant is the extent to which a product is a luxury, as necessities have demand that is less elastic than luxuries (status symbols may well have a higher value for some people the more expensive they get, but this does not affect the shape of the downward-sloping demand curve, as there would always be enough other people who would be willing to purchase the good if its price fell further). Another factor is the availability of SUBSTITUTE PRODUCTS, as buyers of products for which no good substitutes exist tend to have fewer options than to buy the specific product. A third factor is the proportion of the buyer's income spent on the product; goods and services that account for only a small proportion of total expenditure tend to have more inelastic demands. The information available for the purchase is also relevant: the price elasticity of demand will be relatively high for search products, since consumers know exactly what they are purchasing and leap at the chance to buy the product at a lower than normal price (on the contrary, the price elasticity of demand will be relatively inelastic for experience and credence products). Finally, demand is usually more elastic in the long run than in the short run, as consumers take time to adjust their consumption patterns to changes in prices and to find alternatives.

As far as the firm is concerned, in order to maximize revenue it needs to be aware of the demand curves that it is facing and of the elasticities of its buyers. An increase in the price (P) of a product that faces inelastic demand will raise total revenue, while an increase in the price of a product that faces elastic demand will reduce total revenue. The relationship between marginal revenue (MR) and price elasticity (E_p) can be expressed as follows:

$$MR = P(1 + \frac{1}{E_p})$$

This expression is derived from the definitions of the two quantities. Total revenue is maximized where marginal revenue is zero, which is where elasticity is equal to unity.

Cross-price elasticity of demand.   This is given by:

$$E_{XY} = \frac{\Delta Q_X / \Delta Q_X}{\Delta P_Y / P_Y} = \frac{\Delta Q_X}{\Delta P_Y} \cdot \frac{\Delta P_Y}{Q_X}$$

Cross-elasticities are generally not symmetrical; i.e., the change in demand for product X caused by a change in the price of product Y may not be equal to the change in demand for product Y generated by a change in the price of product X.

Cross-price elasticities have implications for product line pricing and are useful in determining optimal policies with reference to prices and quantities for various demand levels and/or other considerations such as competitor actions (e.g., price changes). Also, if prices are set competitively and are driven by the market, they can be useful in determining demand. Good cross-price elasticity measurements can also be used to indicate whether two products are complements (*see* COMPLEMENTARY PRODUCTS), substitutes, or neither.

Advertising elasticity of demand.   The advertising elasticity of demand for a product measures the responsiveness of the quantity demanded to a change in the advertising budget for that product.

Such responsiveness can come about primarily in two main ways. First, advertising shifts the product's demand curve to the right by bringing the product to the attention of more people and increasing people's desire for the product; and, second, it makes the demand for the product less price elastic by such means as enhanced brand loyalty.

A positive relationship between advertising and the quantity demanded is expected, but the responsiveness of sales to advertising is also expected to decline as advertising expenditure continues to rise. The advertising elasticity of demand for experience and credence goods is relatively high, because consumers may be persuaded to try these products by advertisements that emphasize attributes such as the product's brand name.

As far as the usefulness of that elasticity for the firm is concerned, it can help to determine the optimal advertising level. Dorfman and Steiner (1954) first showed that the profit-maximizing ratio of advertising expenditure to sales revenue (the advertising to sales ratio) is given by the ratio of advertising elasticity to price elasticity. In essence, this means that the higher the advertising elasticity, and the lower the price elasticity, the higher will be the profit-maximizing advertising budget as a proportion of sales revenue.

Cross-advertising elasticity of demand.   This measures the responsiveness of the sales of product X to a change in the advertising effort directed at another product, Y. It is negative between substitutes and positive between complements.

Income elasticity of demand.   The income elasticity of demand may be defined as the change in quantity demanded divided by the change in consumer income, *ceteris paribus*.

Three laws of economics are relevant to a discussion of this elasticity. First, the income effect stipulates that when the price of some commodity falls, the real income of the consumer rises, so he or she is likely to purchase more goods. Second, the substitution effect suggests that a fall in the price of a good makes it less expensive in relation to other goods, leading the rational consumer to switch some portion of his or her total expenditure from the relatively lower-priced items to the relatively higher-priced ones. Finally, Engel's law suggests that the percentage of income spent on food (necessities) decreases as income increases.

By convention, goods with a positive income elasticity of demand are called normal goods (demand for them increases as income increases), and those with a negative elasticity are called inferior goods (demand for them falls as income increases, through a negative income effect).

The income elasticity of demand is a function of whether the good is a necessity or a luxury, whether the good is inferior (in which case a negative income effect applies), and also the level of income itself (as poor people respond differently than rich people).

A firm can use this elasticity to plan for capacity according to its forecasts for economic growth. If the income elasticity for its product is positive (normal good), then demand for the product will grow more rapidly as the economy grows (as consumer income rises), and it will fall more rapidly than consumer income when the economy is recessing. Demand for an inferior good, on the other hand, will fall as GNP rises, and yet increase during economic downturns.

Advertising efforts can become more effective by focusing on those potential customers whose buying patterns are likely to be affected. For example, knowledge of which products will be demanded by people with rising income (such as professionals) and which will not may be the key to better sales. Similarly, elasticities can be used to determine the location of outlets, with normal goods being sold in areas with rising income, while inferior goods are marketed in areas where the standard of living is falling.

(Price) elasticity of price expectations. Finally, the elasticity of price expectations is defined as the change in future prices expected as a result of current price changes. When this exceeds unity, it indicates that buyers expect future prices to rise (or fall) more than current prices have changed.

This elasticity is particularly useful in estimating demand in an inflationary environment. A positive coefficient, particularly if it is greater than unity, suggests that current price increases may shift the demand function to the right, which may result in the same or greater sales at the higher prices while consumers try to beat the expected price increases by building up stocks. Eventually, however, the large inventory accumulated by the consumers, or a competitor's reactions, will tend to lower the elasticity, perhaps even turning it negative, and will result in shifting the demand curve to the left.

PRICE ELASTICITY OF SUPPLY (PRODUCTION ELASTICITY)

Turning to the supply function, the price elasticity of supply is defined as the ratio of the change in output resulting from a change in the amount of some variable input employed in the production of a good. There can be, for example, a labor price elasticity of supply. This is equivalent to the ratio of the marginal to the average product for that input.

In general, the price elasticity of supply depends on how costs respond to output changes, including how easily producers can shift from the production of other commodities. Elasticity typically increases with time, as it becomes easier to switch between the production of other goods.

Bibliography

Dorfman, R. and Steiner, P. (1954). Optimal advertising and product quality. *American Economic Review*, **44**, 826–36.

Naylor, T. H., Vernon, J. M., and Wertz, K. L. (1983). *Managerial Economics: Corporate Economics and Strategy*. New York: McGraw-Hill, pp. 230–2.

electronic data interchange

Benita Cox

Electronic data interchange (EDI) is the electronic exchange of structured information (invoices, orders, etc.) between different organizations, using a standard format. It is this use of standards that differentiates EDI from traditional computer communications and enables the use of a common, shared network by many organizations, thus avoiding the need for separate links between individual organizations' computer systems, with associated high costs. A key characteristic of EDI is that the information transferred must be directly usable by the recipient's system without manual intervention. This reduces operating costs, administrative errors, and delivery delays.

The widespread use of EDI in industry means that it is no longer a discretionary expenditure. Pressure by large organizations to trade electronically has resulted in the need to conform to EDI networks to retain customers and suppliers. The primary business benefits of EDI are clearly operational. However, its potential extends beyond merely impacting the operational level to include possibilities for redefining the boundaries between organizations, increasing competitive edge, and providing new business opportunities.

The Tradenet system introduced by the Singapore government is an example of the strategic use of EDI at a national level. Tradenet was introduced to enable ships using the Port of Singapore to reduce turnaround time. It links the Port Authority with government agencies, traders, transport companies, shipping lines, freight forwarders, and airlines, using a common document. On arrival at the port the shipper enters the cargo details into the system and transmits them via the Port Authority to the appropriate government agencies for clearance. The result is that appropriate approvals may be received in 15 minutes, rather than the two days taken previously.

The most widely cited benefits of EDI are as follows:

- *New ways of carrying out business.* EDI enables an organization to change the way in which it performs business functions internally and to redefine its relationships with the external environment. For example, by speeding up the ordering process and reducing the time between receiving an order and dispatching the goods, through EDI, a company may change its focus from that of product driven to being more customer centered, with emphasis being placed on the timely provision of goods and services to the client.

- *Internal efficiency gains.* The automated exchange of operational information results in a reduction in paperwork and clerical processing. By eliminating manual input, EDI reduces the need for rekeying of data and the opportunity for mistakes. It also cuts the time delays that accompany traditional inter-company communications, resulting in significant cost savings and improved cash flow. R. J. R. Nabisco estimated that processing and paper purchase order cost the company $70 per order, whereas processing an EDI order cost 93 cents.

- *Control over stock-holding levels.* The provision of timely and accurate information on stocks which are in low supply facilitates "quick response" and JUST-IN-TIME manufacturing, by reducing stock-holding levels and integrating ordering and inventory management systems.

- *Control over relationships with suppliers.* EDI may be used to strengthen an organization's hold over its suppliers or to share information with them to mutual advantage. Online access to multiple suppliers provides the opportunity to assess which suppliers have the appropriate stock available and at what price, enabling negotiation of prices and insuring the best deal. The provision of immediate feedback on a range of information, such as quality defects, may also be used to increase the power of the purchaser. Alternately, information may be shared to provide more collaborative structures and practices, enabling suppliers and their customers to align their operations. For example, suppliers may electronically monitor stock at the shop-floor level and deliver new stock when the quantities of the product fall below minimum levels, thus bypassing warehousing requirements. Packaging of goods may be done in a way which correlates with the way in which products are displayed on the shelves, in addition to considering which suppliers have the appropriate stock available and at what price.

- *Improved customer relationships.* The provision of EDI facilities may enhance the image of a company with its customers.

Many companies are beginning to insist on EDI trading; for example, the automotive industry. The formation of the Organization for Data Exchange by Tele-Transmission in Europe (ODETTE) links vehicle and component manufacturers in many European countries.

The role of standards has been paramount to the success of EDI. Standards may be agreed at any of a number of levels: international, national, industry sector, or regional. They define trading documents in an agreed format by data items (such as customer name, address, and article number) and by grouping these items in the form of messages (such as invoices). Once all partners have agreed a common standard, this obviates the need for conversion of the documentation by each recipient to meet their internal systems requirements. The basis for an international standard – EDIFACT – has been agreed. However, in addition to EDIFACT there are a number of industry-specific standards. These include SWIFT (Society of Worldwide Inter-bank Financial Telecommunications), which enables banks to send payment instructions to each other in a standardized format. Another, TRADACOMS, is a comprehensive set of EDI standards, covering invoices, orders, delivery notes, and the like. It is the most widely used standard in the UK.

Bibliography

Earl, M. J. (1992). Putting information technology in its place: A polemic for the nineties. *Journal of Information Technology*, 7, 100–8.

emergent strategy

See STRATEGY-MAKING

excess capacity

Stephanos Avgeropoulos

A plant or firm is said to have excess capacity when it has production capacity available for use which is more than sufficient to satisfy current demand. This can either be due to market imperfections, or it can be pursued for strategic purposes, to improve a firm's competitive standing.

As far as the former family of causes is concerned, excess capacity is a result of the absence of a market mechanism which balances demand and supply in the short run. The main factors that inhibit perfect alignment of the level of utilization with its determinants include:

1   demand uncertainty (a firm may prefer to sustain some excess capacity rather than be found to be unable to meet demand when this peaks);
2   the lumpiness and indivisibilities of capacity increases (which cause a sawtooth pattern of utilization unless firms coordinate supply by agreeing time variations in market shares);
3   unexploited ECONOMIES OF SCALE (which may make it optimal to operate larger plant at less than full capacity rather than smaller plant at full capacity);
4   the reluctance of firms to reduce their presence in a market, which induces them to accept considerable excess capacity before scrapping equipment (this being the result of the irreversibility of many exiting decisions);
5   the cost of backlogging; and
6   market concentration (perhaps because of better supply coordination or more scope for reallocation of capacity across products).

Turning to the strategic use of excess capacity, this can serve as a barrier to entry (*see* BARRIERS TO ENTRY AND EXIT) to rivals that plan to enter the industry or increase their share in it. This can be done by signaling that the firm is prepared to counter the efforts of such rivals by raising output and reducing prices (*see* SIGNALING): the use of excess capacity makes such threats more credible, particularly if the investment that is made toward it is sunk and irreversible, and if any economies of scale are available. This is because the challenger would then be likely to expect that the excess capacity will, indeed, be used against it (Spence, 1977). Even then, however, there are circumstances in which excess capacity does not serve as a credible threat, and the incumbent may be better off accommodating the entrant (Dixit, 1980).

Evidence shows that, in general, strategic factors are the cause of excess capacity in a minority of industries only, and these predominantly tend to experience high growth and market undifferentiated products. Some survey work has suggested that the cost of responding to competitive threats such as copied products may normally be too high to justify any response and, even when a response is deemed necessary, that the availability of superior strategic weapons such as product differentiation may obviate the need for strategic excess capacity (Driver, 1994).

Bibliography

Baumol, W. J. and Willig, R. D. (1981). Fixed costs, sunk costs, entry barriers and sustainability of monopoly. *Quarterly Journal of Economics*, 405–31.

Dixit, A. K. (1980). The role of investment in entry deterrence. *Economic Journal*, **90** (March), 95–106.

Driver, C. (1994). Excess capacity: Theory and evidence using micro-data. Working paper, Management School, Imperial College.

Gilbert, R. and Lieberman, M. (1987). Investment and coordination in oligopolistic industries. *RAND Journal of Economics*, **18** (2), 17–33.

Spence, M. (1977). Capacity, investment and oligopolistic pricing. *Bell Journal of Economics*, 8, 534–44.

Sutton, J. (1991). *Sunk Costs and Market Structure: Price Competition, Advertising and the Evolution of Concentration*. Cambridge, MA: MIT Press.

experience and learning effects

Stephanos Avgeropoulos

Costs per unit of output may be reduced for technological and organizational reasons as a result of producing a large output rather than a small one. If such cost reduction is linked to the level of cumulative output, then the firm is said to be enjoying the experience, or learning, effect, sometimes also referred to as learning by doing (Arrow, 1962), the progress curve, or the improvement curve. If the cost reduction is linked to the number of units produced per unit of time, then ECONOMIES OF SCALE are involved. ECONOMIES OF SCOPE refer to cost reduction that is the effect of production in a large organ-

ization that administers many lines of production. These effects are interlinked in practice, but merit individual treatment for analytic purposes.

THE LEARNING EFFECT

Cost reduction as a result of growth in cumulative output has been documented at least as early as in 1925, when it was observed in relation to the direct labor costs of aircraft manufacturing. When discussed in the context of direct labor costs, this cost reduction is referred to as the learning effect. Put simply, learning improves labor productivity; i.e., the more units employees will produce, the more ways they will find to produce them faster and cheaper. This may be because repetition allows workers to discover improvements and short cuts that increase their EFFICIENCY.

THE EXPERIENCE EFFECT

During the mid-1960s, such cost reductions were also explicitly observed by Bruce Henderson at the Westinghouse Corporation, where he was a consultant. A consensus then emerged that such cost reductions applied not only to the labor portion of manufacturing costs, but also to costs incurred at every stage of what is today called the value chain (*see* VALUE CHAIN ANALYSIS), including marketing and R&D costs, and overhead. Bruce Henderson, together with the Boston Consulting Group (BCG), studied the concept in detail, and ways were found in which to utilize it for strategic decision-making.

The experience curve specifies that, for every doubling in cumulative output, unit costs of value added net of inflation will fall by a fixed percentage α, typically 20 percent. This means that the concept can be used to predict costs further down in time. If C_t and C_0 are the costs at times t and 0, respectively, and P_t and P_0 are accumulated volume of production at times t and 0, the following relationship holds:

$$C_t = C_0 \left(\frac{P_t}{P_0}\right)^{-\alpha}$$

The curve is plotted using a grid, with inflation-adjusted cost per unit on the vertical axis, and accumulated volume of production, measured in

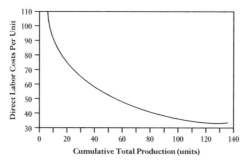

Figure 1 Typical experience curve (linear scales)

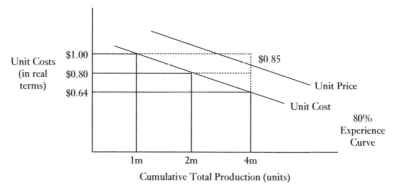

Figure 2 Typical experience curve drawn on logarithmic scales. As cumulative volume grows, there is a real decline in product cost, which can lead to cost leadership pricing strategies

units produced, on the horizontal axis (see figure 1). Plotted on logarithmic scales, the experience curve becomes a straight line, as shown in figure 2.

It is worth observing here that the curve can be drawn on a marginal as well as an average basis, as the two only differ by a constant proportion in a straight line. This is convenient, as unit costs are typically measured over a small portion of total production. More importantly, price and profit are concepts best examined marginally. As a consequence, much experience curve calculation is often undertaken on a marginal basis.

For the curve to be meaningful, it is important to define products accurately and consistently. The BCG recommends that these are defined in terms of perceived value to the customer, which implies that the same experience curve would continue to apply for product innovations that

continue to serve the same customer requirements.

SOURCES OF EXPERIENCE

There are two points that should now be made clear. First, each cost element in an end product (stage in the value chain) has its own experience curve, and it is the aggregation of these curves that makes up the average experience curve for that product. As a result, the curve for the product will tend to be an approximation (see figure 3).

Second, the experience curve concept does not specify any sources of cost reduction. It simply observes the fact of the cost reduction, leaving the rest open to debate. However, factors such as economies of scale, economies of scope, the learning effect, work specialization, new production methods and processes (these are particularly important in capital-intensive

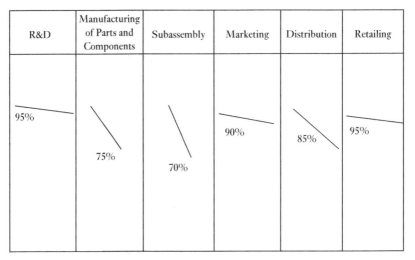

Figure 3   Experience effects differ for different stages in the value-added chain (Hax and Majluf, 1984)

industries; *see* INVESTMENT INTENSITY), product standardization (which allows the repetition of tasks inherent in experience building), product redesign and/or substitution effects (as experience is gained with the product, it can be redesigned to conserve material or use cheaper substitute materials, or to allow greater efficiency in manufacture and the like), and changes in the resource mix are among the many potential sources available for exploitation. Moreover, experience may also be gained by sharing value chain activities between a number of products, so that a common experience base is developed, and also in prioritizing value chain activities, such as by finding the optimal balance between R&D and advertising. All of these are more than sufficient to justify the cost reductions observed.

Turning to circumstances that seem to encourage experience building, this is greater (by definition) when production starts – as it doubles from the first unit to the second, and then again to the fourth – but at the thousandth unit, say, another thousand would have to be produced for experience to double once more. Ultimately, when production processes mature, the differences become much smaller.

Also, experience building appears to be greatest in situations where new and advanced technology is involved, and where the capital input dominates the production function, although this is not a matter of consensus. In addition, the lower the employee turnover is, the fewer employee interruptions there are, and the greater the ability of the firm is to transfer knowledge from the production of other similar products, the steeper the curve is.

Experience-related cost benefits are not automatic; instead, they can be achieved through constant efforts.

DETERMINATION OF A CURVE'S
CHARACTERISTICS

To use the experience curve proactively and to measure a company's own slope and that of competitors, such as for the purposes of pricing, involves an accurate determination of a number of variables including the moment in time at which experience started to be built up and the volumes involved. In addition, discontinuities such as changes in technology or major product line renovations must be taken into account. Frequently, many calculations regarding competitors' curves cannot be performed directly, and proxies such as MARKET SHARE must be used, perhaps implying that more discontinuities will have to be taken into account.

In addition, as has already been mentioned, it is important for the accurate determination of the curve's characteristics that the entire value chain is considered, and not just the market share of the end product. This is necessary not just because each activity will have its own experience curve, the aggregation of which will determine the firm's overall slope, but also because decisions on the product mix of multi-product firms may result in the accumulation of different volumes at each stage. Many firms finding themselves displaced from a dominant position have observed, in retrospect, that their definition of dominance was a narrow one.

IMPLICATIONS FOR STRATEGY

An appropriate experience effect-based strategy for a particular firm depends, among other things, on the firm's current position, the product's life-cycle stage, the firm's resources relative to competitors, its time horizon, its information about the market, and its current and anticipated cost functions.

The experience concept suggests that, for a firm with a suitably long time horizon, the present value of its profits can be maximized by building up market share as rapidly as possible to attain relative cost advantages.

In order for such a strategy to be successful, the model stipulates that the firm should only attempt to enter a market if it has the capability for leadership, and that the market it attempts to enter is a growing one, as this makes the acquisition of market share easier (competitors may not resent losing relative share as much as absolute share, and they may not even be aware that they are losing relative share if their information about the market is inadequate). Then, once the firm has decided to enter the market, it should do so as rapidly as possible, to prevent other firms from

gaining more experience. These concepts have also given rise to the development of the GROWTH SHARE MATRIX, again by the BCG.

A question that arises in a discussion of the experience curve is whether it is possible to attack a competitor that has accumulated considerable experience. Indeed, the cost differential which such a competitor is likely to have achieved makes a head-on attack to achieve similar market share difficult. However, if one looks at the concept more closely, it should become clear that it is not just the market share of the end product that is important, but that of all of the activities in the value chain. A good distribution organization, for example, perhaps shared by many different products, may well be sufficient to attack a low-cost producer that only produces a single product, or that has neglected its logistics. Similarly, "changing the rules of the game" may be possible using a new technology, or by means of practices such as JUST-IN-TIME production or total quality management, which, although relatively easy to imitate, can allow the entrant to reduce costs and enter the market on a comparable cost basis.

A related danger faced by companies that rely heavily on the experience effect to retain their leadership is that some experience cannot be constrained within the boundaries of single companies and tends to diffuse into entire industries, for example, through employee mobility or specifications for equipment ordered from outside suppliers. Similarly, some innovations may come from outside the industry, thereby being available to all competitors. In general,

Competitive Position	Product Life Stage		
	Growth	Maturity	Decline
Leader (high share)	Reduce prices to discourage new competitive capacity Use own capacity fully	Hold market share by improved quality, increasing sales effort, advertising	Maximize cash flow by reducing investment and advertising, R&D, etc., expenses (market share will decline)
Follower (low share)	Invest to increase market share Concentrate on a segment that can be dominated	Withdraw from the market, or hold share by keeping prices and costs below those of the market leaders	Withdraw from the market

Figure 4   Some implications for product strategy (Allan and Hammond, 1975: 9)

therefore, industry-wide learning and imitation may make relative cost advantages estimated on the basis of experience building too optimistic, with all the dangers that this involves.

IMPLICATIONS FOR PRICING

Assuming that a firm has decided to go down the experience curve, it may use pricing to assist it to do so more rapidly. This can be done by setting prices on the basis of expected, rather than current, costs, so that the market can be developed and market share built up faster, as the experience of Texas Instruments during the 1970s showed. This will typically have an adverse impact on current profits, although – if the firm is lucky – its efforts will be facilitated if some of its competitors have a shorter horizon, and are not so insistent on retaining their relative share.

Having said that, it should be observed that the experience effect predicts a path for costs, not prices. In most cases, including Japanese companies, prices tend to follow costs throughout the different stages of the development of a new product in a reasonably competitive market. In a small number of cases typically observed in countries such as the US, however, a very distinct relationship has been observed between the two.

According to this pattern, the firm has three options that can be pursued during the development phase. First, it may set a fairly high price, to impose a monopolistic rent and enjoy a mono-polistic profit. Alternatively, it may set a price close to costs, to deter potential entrants (*see* SIGNALING), or it may even price below cost, as just discussed. In fact, this latter choice is the most commonly observed pattern. Soon afterwards, in the phase during which demand is typically greater than supply, costs fall while prices remain firm under a "price umbrella" supported by the market leader. This is a profitable period for all, and many entrants are lured into the market and build up capacity. The beginning of the third, shakeout, period is marked by the decision by some competitor to reduce prices in order to gain share. Prices then start to tumble, falling faster than costs, and driving marginal producers out of the market. The industry begins to reorganize itself for greater emphasis on efficiency, by means of recombination or otherwise. Market shares change, and sometimes leaders too, and this continues until margins are restored to reasonable, positive levels, which indicates the beginning of the stability phase. The four stages are depicted in figure 5.

LIMITATIONS

A factor that limits the applicability of the experience curve concept is the type of product involved. When specialty (as opposed to commodity) products are involved, there may exist opportunities for differentiation that can induce the consumer to pay a premium, thereby making

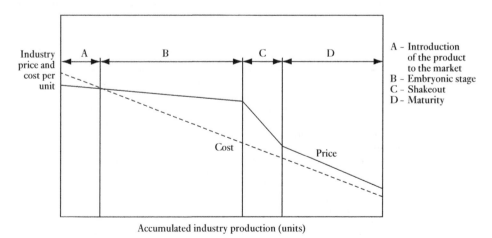

Figure 5   The unstable experience curve effect (Hax and Majluf, 1984)

cost a less relevant factor for profitability (*see* GENERIC STRATEGIES). Moreover, the experience curve model is not well suited to explain the viability of smaller businesses.

Finally, an important danger in using the experience curve model blindly lies in product and process obsolescence, as these can make the experience curve irrelevant before it can be fully exploited. When striving for cost reduction, therefore, a firm should keep in mind that it may need to maintain a regularly updated product range, as well as flexible production facilities, and both of these are likely to limit the scope for experience building. Too much emphasis on economies may impair the ability of the firm to respond in a flexible way to technological advances, environmental changes, and innovations taking place outside the firm; and, similarly, it may prevent the realization of product differentiation to capture a wider range of customers – often more profitable ones too.

THE EXPERIENCE CURVE AND THE PIMS PROGRAM

For a discussion on the experience curve to be complete, the PROFIT IMPACT OF MARKET STRATEGY (PIMS) program needs to be mentioned (*see* PIMS STRUCTURAL DETERMINANTS OF PERFORMANCE). These studies have looked at market share and profitability, and also at variables such as operating expense ratios, relative quality, capital intensity in different market positions, profit margins, and so on. In principle, the PIMS data have confirmed the experience effect data, but PIMS has added a further dimension to the discussion. Therefore, Buzzell, Gale, and Sultan (1975) and others have found that market leadership not only makes a positive contribution to profitability through lower costs, as the experience effect specifies, but also has a strong association with perceived quality. This enables the market leader (but not any followers) not only to have lower costs, but to charge higher prices too.

Bibliography

Allan, G. B. and Hammond, J. S. (1975). *Note on the Use of Experience Curves in Competitive Decision-Making*. Case No. 175-174, Harvard Business School. Boston: Intercollegiate Case Clearing House/Cranfield, UK: Case Clearing House.

Arrow, K. J. (1962). The economic implications of learning by doing. *Review of Economic Studies*, **29** (3). Reprinted 1970 in Perspectives series. Boston: Boston Consulting Group.

Boston Consulting Group (1982). *Perspectives on Experience*. Boston: Boston Consulting Group.

Buzzell, R. D., Gale, B. T., and Sultan, R. G. (1975). Market share: A key to profitability. *Harvard Business Review*, **53**, (1), 97–107.

Hax, A. C. and Majluf, N. S. (1984). *Strategic Management: An Integrative Perspective*. Englewood Cliffs, NJ: Prentice-Hall.

Henderson, B. D. (1980). *The Experience Curve Revisited*. Perspectives series. Boston: Boston Consulting Group.

Henderson, B. D. (1984). The application and misapplication of the experience curve. *Journal of Business Strategy*, **4** (3), 3–9.

Hirschman, W. B. (1964). Profit from the learning curve. *Harvard Business Review*, **42** (1), 125–39.

externalities

Stephanos Avgeropoulos

The production and/or consumption of some products may give rise to some harmful or beneficial effects that are borne by organizations or people not directly involved in such production or consumption. Such side-effects are called externalities, spillovers, or external costs.

Early works on externalities include Sidgwick (1887) and Marshall (1890). A few years later, Pigou (1920) considered the legal implications of externalities, and determined that where externalities exist in the form of social costs, it is efficient for common law to be applied so as to force the internalization of such externalities. Coase (1937), however, disagreed with this view, claiming that some externalities are sometimes self-correcting, and suggested that holding the party that created the externality liable under common law is not necessarily efficient; instead, efficiency would be best achieved by balancing costs and benefits, in which the role of causality was not decisive.

TYPES

Externalities can be categorized along a number of dimensions. The first is whether they are negative or positive, according to whether the party that is affected by them benefits or suffers.

Second, externalities can be production or consumption based, according to their source. Third, there are technological and pecuniary externalities. Technological ones, the most common kind, simply relate to the indirect effect of a consumption or production activity on the consumption or production of a third party. Pecuniary externalities, on the other hand, work through the price system when prices play additional roles other than equating demand and supply, such as when they transmit information in an asymmetric information environment, or when they are affected by some party, in which case this change also affects the welfare of other parties (e.g., one industry's increasing consumption of petroleum affects another industry's welfare through the higher petroleum prices).

Turning to examples of some types of externalities, external costs of production may include oil spills, or the impact of extensive farming on wildlife. External costs of consumption, on the other hand, may include the impact on non-smokers of smoking in public places, or the effect of a neighbor's decision to plant trees, whose roots may travel beyond the boundaries of the land on which they are planted and cause damage to nearby properties.

External benefits of production, on the other hand, may come in the form of lower training costs when a worker goes to work for another firm, improvements to regional infrastructure, such as rail facilities, which may result from the needs of one firm but subsequently be used by others, or the growth in peripheral supplier businesses, or technology spillovers, which can often explain the clustering of similar firms in certain geographic areas. Similarly, external benefits of consumption may include the existence of a well-maintained garden, which increases the value of neighboring properties, or the installation of a new, quieter air conditioner.

Sources

Externalities arise primarily because of an incomplete definition of property rights in the law. For example, they enable an industry that pollutes its environment through the use of its assets to pass on the costs of cleaning up to the rest of the community.

Consequences

Externalities, which are identified by discrepancies between social and private costs, typically lead to market failure. The most commonly encountered implication of externalities is the misallocation of resources by the market mechanism, i.e., allocative inefficiency (*see* EFFICIENCY). This typically comes about in two distinct ways. First, externalities may cause a deviation in the prices of goods from the marginal cost of producing them and, second, externalities in the form of information spillovers may lead firms to invest at suboptimal levels, if they have reason to believe that they will be unable to recoup the full cost of, say, some R&D investment.

Solutions

A number of solutions exist to reduce the impact of externalities. These include prohibition, directives, or other regulation to eradicate or limit activities that generate externalities. For example, cars may only be permitted to be driven for up to a set number of days per week, or a requirement may be imposed for safety devices such as seat belts to be installed, in order to reduce fatal accidents.

Another method, which is more suited to dealing with production externalities of non-public goods, is forced internalization, whereby the party that generates the externality is forced to deal with it itself, effectively eradicating the externality, which becomes part of the producer's own set of constraints. A company that pollutes a river may be obliged, for example, to acquire or merge with another company that makes heavy use of the polluted water further downstream. A rather less radical method of forcing internalization is by means of financial transactions such as (Pigovian) taxes (or subsidies, as appropriate), or the marketing of externality generation rights, i.e., the artificial creation of a market for the externality.

Finally, as has been shown by Coase, it may be possible to reduce the harm caused by externalities if the parties involved cooperate voluntarily. An example may be the situation in which a city that suffers from airborne pollution pays the offending factory to install improved equipment or relocate.

As far as a choice between the above methods is concerned, each is likely to have different enforcement costs and a different probability of evasion, so the specific circumstances will dictate the most appropriate one. In principle, it is more efficient not to eradicate the externality but to limit it to the point at which the benefit from any further marginal reduction equals the cost of any such reduction.

Bibliography

Arrow, K. (1969). The organization of economic activity: Issues pertinent to the choice of market vs. non-market allocation. In *The Analysis and Evaluation of Public Expenditure: The PPB System*. 91st US Congress, 1st Session, Joint Economic Committee. Washington, DC: US Government Printing Office, pp. 47–64.

Coase, R. H. (1937). The nature of the firm. *Economica*, 4 (November), 386–405.

Coase, R. H. (1960). The problem of social cost. *Journal of Law and Economics*, 3, 1–44.

Marshall, A. (1890). *Principles of Economics*. London and New York: Macmillan; 8th edn, 1948.

Pigou, A. C. (1920). *The Economics of Welfare*. London: Macmillan; reprinted London: Macmillan/New York: St. Martin's Press, 1952.

Shapley, L. and Shubik, M. (1969). On the core of an economic system with externalities. *American Economic Review*, 59, 687–9.

Sidgwick, H. (1887). *Principles of Political Economy*, 2nd edn. London and New York: Macmillan.

F

first-mover advantage

Derek F. Channon

The timing of strategic moves may be critical for success as a result of the positive advantages accruing to first movers. Being first has a significant payoff when:

1 it enhances the firm's image and reputation with buyers;
2 early entry can tie up key raw material sources, new technologies, distribution channels, etc., so as to shift the cost boundaries of a business or industry;
3 first-time operators build customer loyalty which is hard to dislodge;
4 it constitutes a preemptive strike which is difficult to copy.

The use of IT has been a major mechanism for achieving long-term first-mover advantages, which have been very difficult to overcome by follower competitors. Examples would include American Hospital Supply's ordering systems for hospitals, the American Airlines flight booking system, Merrill Lynch's Cash Management Account, and Direct Line Insurance's motor insurance operation.

For such success it is necessary to:

- redefine the business to use IT to fundamentally transform the existing way of operating, usually to provide a superior quality of service at a significantly reduced cost;
- be first to introduce new systems, including the necessary investment to achieve rapid growth to preempt the position of any followers;
- exploit first-mover advantage to achieve customer loyalty to a brand position, which will remain after competitors attempt to follow.

However, being first is no guarantee of success. Indeed, it may involve much greater risk than being an early follower. First-mover disadvantages occur when:

- pioneering is expensive and experience effects are low (*see* EXPERIENCE AND LEARNING EFFECTS);
- technological change is so rapid that early investments rapidly become obsolete;
- copying is easy and customer loyalty is fickle; and
- the skills and know-how of first movers are easy to replicate.

It is therefore extremely important to assess the critical timing for market entry, and to insure that adequate resources are available and are deployed to preempt early competitive moves.

Bibliography

Porter, M. E. (1980). *Competitive Strategy: Techniques for Analyzing Industries and Competitors.* New York: Free Press.

Thompson, A. J., Jr. and Strickland, A. J. (1993). *Strategic Management.* Homewood, IL: Irwin.

five forces model

see INDUSTRY STRUCTURE

fragmented businesses

Derek F. Channon

In fragmented businesses, there is little or no correlation between size and profitability: examples include restaurants, specialist engineering, and chemical specialties. In such industries, ECONOMIES OF SCALE may well be outweighed by the costs of complexity; and COMPETITIVE ADVANTAGE can be achieved by uniqueness independent of size, such as through customer focus, geographic concentration, design, and patent protection. When no specific competitor dominates, factors such as these tend to be more important than relative competitive position. To counter such unique advantages, it has been advocated that the creation of specific segments be used to promote standardization of design and geographic coverage, and reductions in uniqueness can be used to reduce or eliminate the strategic advantage of smaller fragmented competitors.

See also *advantage matrix*

Bibliography

Boston Consulting Group (1974). *Segmentation and Strategy*. Boston: Boston Consulting Group.

Boston Consulting Group (1974). *Specialization*. Boston: Boston Consulting Group.

Rowe, A. J., Mason, R. O., Dickel, K. E., Mann, R. B., and Mockler, R. J. (1994). *Strategic Management*, 4th edn. Reading, MA: Addison-Wesley, pp. 119–22.

functional structure

Derek F. Channon

In the single-business firm, the natural way to divide up the various activities is to organize by specialist function, as shown in figure 1, in which is illustrated a typical functional structure for a small to medium manufacturing business. At the top is a board, usually composed of the senior managers of the specialist functions together with a chairman and chief executive. In many companies the personnel and R&D function heads are not included on the board, and operate predominantly in line support roles. Human resource management and R&D are thus often excluded from the formulation of strategy. The board may or may not contain non-executive directors. As a result of investor and political pressure, the presence of non-executive directors is becoming the norm in public companies. However, in many smaller concerns and those that are privately owned, non-executives may still be excluded.

Depending upon the size of the business, the marketing and finance functions may be fully developed or the company may essentially operate a sales function and an accounting function. In smaller concerns, the accounting function may also be responsible for the company secretary and for legal aspects of the preparation of budgets and plans. Medium-term corporate plans, which tend to be financial in orientation, may also be developed.

As such firms grow larger, the functions become more fully developed. Research and development, which in smaller companies often tends to be subordinate to the production function, develops into a full-blown function. Finance and accounting tend to become separated. Marketing is introduced and tends to become superordinate to the sales function. A separate company secretary position is often established and a specialist corporate planner is introduced. While such companies may still be essentially single business, it is common that

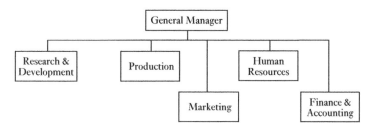

Figure 1   Functional organizational structures

multisite operations may commence, and the production function may therefore develop to involve several site managers, with an overall production manager located at the primary central site. Similarly, the sales function is often changed by the effort to open new markets, and especially export markets overseas. The introduction of an additional export sales manager is thus also likely as overseas sales expand and distribution is established, usually via the use of agents or distributors in the early stages.

The functional structure is also very effective in managing the single business in the service industry sector. In retailing, for example, a similar structure would be found, although "production" as a function is not normally present, being replaced by a function usually known as "operations." This essentially refers to distribution system management and the management of stores. These are usually grouped geographically and handled by regional managers. Merchandising and buying are other critical functions which essentially replace marketing.

The functional structure is the logical pattern for dividing up the activities of the business, provided that it is not too complex, either by product or by geography. Even when a single-business firm expands geographically, it is possible to retain a form of functional structure in many cases, provided that production is not distributed but remains centralized.

Major problems arise with the functional structure as the firm diversifies by product and/or geography, where the latter also contains production facilities. When these new strategic moves occur, a number of structural variants tend to be invoked, including the introduction of the functional holding company, the holding company (*see* HOLDING COMPANY STRUCTURE), the area division, and the product division (*see* DIVISIONAL STRUCTURE). It is extremely unusual that firms move from a functional to a MATRIX STRUCTURE, an SBU structure, or a customer-based structure, these usually being found in large, complex organizations.

Apart from problems of handling DIVERSIFICATION, problems associated with the functional form include: a failure to develop general management skills; difficulties in functional coordination; potential over-specialization; that profit responsibility is forced to the top; that it may lead to functional empire building; and that there may be a tendency to prevent entrepreneurship and reconfiguration of the value chain (*see* VALUE CHAIN ANALYSIS).

Bibliography

Chandler, A. D. (1962). *Strategy and Structure: Chapters in the History of the Industrial Enterprise*. Cambridge, MA: MIT Press.

Channon, D. F. (1973). *The Strategy and Structure of British Enterprise*. Cambridge, MA: Harvard Division of Research.

Thompson, A. A. and Strickland, A. J. J. (1993). *Strategic Management: Concepts and Cases*, 7th edn. Homewood, IL: Irwin, pp. 223–5.

G

gap analysis

Derek F. Channon

The first step in strategic analysis is the establishment of the corporate MISSION, which can then be translated into a series of quantifiable objectives. These will normally be at least partially financial, but a number are likely to be strategic. The corporate objectives can then be compared with an extrapolated performance for the corporation, generated from the sum of the expectations of the business units.

A comparison of the objectives and the expected business outcomes will usually lead to a performance gap between the two. Gap analysis is concerned with why the gap occurs and the development of measures for reducing or eliminating it. This might be achieved by changing the objectives, or by changing strategy at the level of the businesses. The forecast is initially developed subject to four key assumptions:

1 The corporation's portfolio of businesses remains unchanged.
2 Competitive success strategies in the firm's products and markets will continue to evolve as in the past.
3 The demand and profitability opportunities in the firm's marketplaces will follow historic trends.
4 The corporation's own strategies in the respective businesses will follow their historic pattern of evolution.

The first step in gap analysis is to consider revising the corporate objectives. Should expected outcomes from the businesses exceed aspirations, the objectives can be revised upward. When aspirations substantially exceed possible performance, it may be necessary to revise the objectives downward.

When, after such adjustments, a significant gap still remains, new strategies need to be developed to eliminate the gap. To forecast sales increases likely to result from the introduction of alternative growth strategies for each business, managers can estimate the following measures of market structure:

- industry market potential (IMP);
- relevant industry sales (RIS);
- real market share (RMS).

The IMP is estimated as shown in figure 1. It is assumed, first, that all customers who might reasonably use the product will do so; second, that the product will be used as often as possible; and, third, that the product will be used to the fullest extent. The IMP therefore represents the maximum possible unit sales for a particular product. The difference between this value and current sales represents the growth opportunity for each product. The RIS equals the firm's current sales plus competitive gaps, and the RMS equals sales divided by the RIS.

Four components then contribute to the gap between the firm's sales potential and its actual performance, as follows:

- *Product line gap.* Closing this gap involves completing a product line, in either width or depth, and introducing new or improved products.
- *Distribution gap.* This gap can be closed by expanding distribution coverage, intensity, and exposure.
- *Change gap.* Using this strategy, the firm endeavors to encourage non-users to try the product and to encourage existing users to consume more.
- *Competitive gap.* This gap can be closed by improving the firm's position through

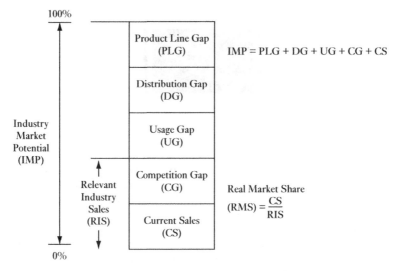

Figure 1   Gap analysis (Rowe et al., 1994: 245)

taking extra MARKET SHARE from existing competitors.

If the expected gap cannot be closed by decreasing industry market potential or gaining additional market share, attention may be shifted to assessing the firm's portfolio of businesses with a view to modifying it to add higher-growth activities and/or divesting low-growth businesses (*see* DIVESTMENT).

Bibliography

Ansoff, I. (1987). *Corporate Strategy*. Harmondsworth: Penguin.
Drucker, P. (1989). *The New Realities*. London: Mandarin, pp. 202–3.
Rowe, A. J., Mason, R. O., Dickel, K. E., Mann, R. B., and Mockler, R. J. (1994). *Strategic Management*, 4th edn. Reading, MA: Addison-Wesley, pp. 240–6.
Weber, J. A. (1977). Market structure profile and strategic growth opportunities. *California Management Review*, **20** (1).

generic strategies

John McGee

Competitive forces on industries, supply chains, and markets suggest that firms can have substantial problems in identifying and responding to the economic forces that surround them (see figure 1). However, some firms very deliberately set out to countervail these forces and create space within which they can earn profits at a higher rate than their industry confrères. This is the essence of strategy, the creation of space within which discrete and distinctive actions can secure improved positioning within markets and greater performance.

Competitive position can be improved in two basic ways. A firm might enjoy cost advantages that its rivals will find difficult to imitate. Or a firm might create a differentiated product that its rival might find difficult to imitate. The essence of perfect competition is that imitation will be easy, not too costly, and speedy. Any differences that emerge will be competed away very quickly. The introduction of an extra feature on a car (such as rear parking sensors) is generally easy to copy. However, to offer hybrid motors (electric plus gasoline, such as in the Toyota Prius) is much more difficult to copy in terms of quality, cost, and speed of imitation. Firms with distinctive cost advantages will typically have built up ECONOMIES OF SCALE and ECONOMIES OF SCOPE over a long period of time and rivals may find it difficult to attain the same low costs. The very well-known report on the British motorcycle industry (HMSO, 1970) identified huge scale economies in Japanese motorcycle factories compared to the traditional craft-based production processes of European

Supplier/buyer power

- Relative concentration

- Relative importance of product to the provider and the user

- Credible threat of vertical integration

- Substitution possibilities

- Control of information

- Switching costs

Barriers to entry

- Scale economies and experience

- Product differentiation

- Capital requirements

- Switching requirements

- Access to distribution

- Scale-independent cost advantages

- Level of expected retaliation

Intensity of rivalry *High if...*

- Several equally strong players
- Low/no growth in market
- High fixed costs and cyclical demand
- Few changes for differentiation
- Large-scale capacity increments
- Different "culture" of players
- High strategic stakes
- Major exit barriers

Pressure from substitutes

- Benefits not product features
- Sideways competition
- Comparative price/performance
- Comparative technology life cycle
- What business are you in?
- Backing by rich competitor

Figure 1 Behind the competitive forces

and US producers. This kind of cost advantage is inherently difficult to replicate and would take a very long time if it were judged even sensible to try to emulate.

The other main dimension of strategic choice revolves around the notion of *scope*. Economies of scope arise when the average cost of a single product is lowered by its joint production with other products in a multiproduct firm. This is based on the indivisibility of certain resources. For example, knowledge is indivisible in the sense that it cannot be divided into pieces, some of which you choose to have and some of which you choose not to have. Knowing about aluminum means that you will have knowledge relevant to airframe manufacture and to pots and pans. Economies of scope arise when your knowledge or other indivisible resource can be applied in multiple directions without using up that

resource. Thus scope becomes interesting strategically. A firm may choose to operate with broad scope (such as Ford in the automobile assembly industry covering a very wide product range as well as the globe). Conversely, a firm may choose to operate on a very narrow scope (such as Morgan, which covers only a particular part of the sports car market). The choice of broad scope suggests a calculation about available economies of scope in such a fashion that, once chosen, it is a commitment that cannot readily be reversed. The choice of narrow scope suggests an alternative calculation that the benefits of assets and other resources and capabilities focused in specific ways create differentiation and/or cost advantages of a different sort. Figure 2 illustrates these generic strategies.

See also *global strategies*

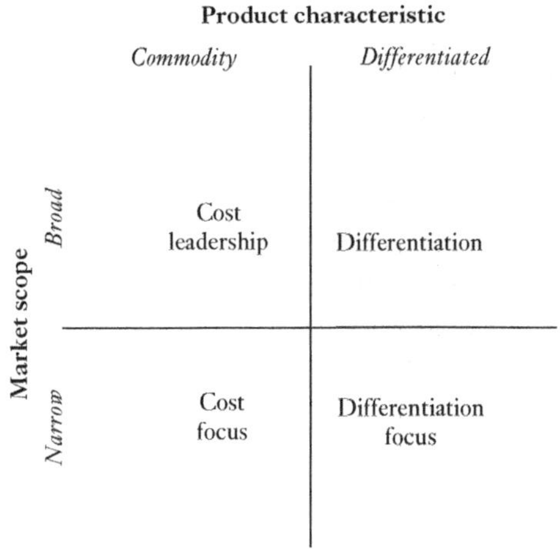

Product characteristic

Figure 2   Porter's generic strategies (Porter, 1980: ch. 2)

Bibliography

Her Majesty's Stationery Office (HMSO) (1970). *The British Motorcycle Industry*. London: HMSO.

Porter, M. E. (1980). *Competitive Strategy: Techniques for Analyzing Industries and Competitors*. New York: Free Press.

global strategic advantage

John McGee

GLOBALIZATION AND THE VALUE CHAIN

The key strategic choices in globalization revolve around local differentiation versus global standardization. These might be seen as polar opposites, but more usually the question is how to secure the right blend between the two. What would this mean for how we conduct our business?

Figure 1 enables us to think of the implications of global choices in terms of how we manage the activities in the value chain, where we locate them, and how we coordinate the whole chain. The opportunity for global standardization occurs when:

- Upstream value chain activities can be decoupled from downstream activities and, in particular, from buyer locations.

- These activities are a large part of total costs.
- Scale effects are important in these activities.

We see that these conditions hold with automobiles. Production does not need to be close to the customer, nor even to the sales channel. Assembly is a very large part of the cost and there are very big scale economies (*see* ECONOMIES OF SCALE). Conversely, multidomestic industries exist where:

- Downstream activities are tied to buyer locations and market-specific entry barriers can be created.
- These activities are a large part of total costs.

These are situations where the competitive advantages (*see* COMPETITIVE ADVANTAGE) reside primarily with the downstream, and the focus of strategic attention lies with managing its capacity to differentiate the product offering. This is typical of retailing, many service operations such as investment banking, and consumer packaged goods.

The possibility for globalization usually means that the value chain has to be partitioned in some way. The key strategic dimensions of choice are:

- Where to perform each activity in the value chain – the *configuration* question.
- How to link similar activities wherever they are located.
- How to coordinate all the activities in the value chain – the *coordination* question.

The degree of coordination is in general dependent on how globally standardized the product is, or conversely how varied the local market conditions are. Table 1 summarizes the kinds of high and low coordination patterns that might be observed. The contrast between high and low degrees of coordination stems from the balance between the two types of competitive pressure that are evident in global markets: pressures for cost reductions and EFFICIENCY, and pressures for local responsiveness. Typically, local differentiation requires low coordination, as each country operation contains much of the value chain that it needs, and those inputs it does need, such as components, will be relatively

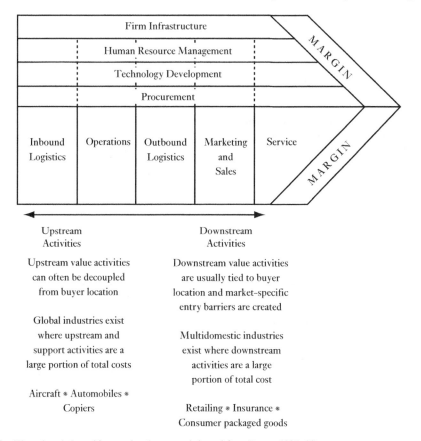

Figure 1   The value chain and international strategy (adapted from Porter, 1985: 46)

standardized. Pressures for global efficiency usually mean that there is product standardization and close integration of production and service delivery across all the value chain activities, which themselves will have been located in the lowest-cost regions/countries.

The tension between the pressures for efficiency and for local responsiveness is a constant concern for multinational companies. The efficiency dimension can be seen as pressures for global coordination and integration. This is a subtle restatement of cost and efficiency pressures, coupled with product standardization, taking account of the variety and diversity that take place at the margin around simple standardization. The pressures for national or local responsiveness represent a complex aggregate of differentiating forces, namely, differences in

consumer tastes and preferences, differences in local infrastructures and traditional practices, differences in distribution channels and other forms of access to markets, and host government demands.

SOURCES OF COMPETITIVE ADVANTAGE

Whereas CORPORATE STRATEGY is about exploiting ECONOMIES OF SCOPE across the business units of the corporation, global strategy requires the exploitation of economies of scale, scope, knowledge, and learning across national boundaries. Ghoshal (1987) provides an excellent framework (see table 2) for understanding the sources of advantage that can spring from globalization and the strategic objectives that can be pursued. Ghoshal refers to this framework as a mapping of means and ends. The means are the

Table 1   Coordination across international markets

Reasons for high coordination	Reasons for low coordination

• Share know-how and learning
• Reinforce brand reputation
• Supply identical differentiation worldwide
• Differentiate from local buyers by meeting their needs anywhere
• Seek bargaining counters with governments
• Respond to competitors' flexibility
	• Respond to diverse local conditions
	  o product needs
	  o marketing systems
	  o business practices
	  o raw material sources
	  o infrastructure
	• Circumvent government restrictions on flow of goods or information
	• Avoid high coordination costs
	• Acknowledge organizational difficulties of achieving coordination across subsidiaries

Table 2   Global strategy: sources of competitive advantage

Strategic objectives	National differences	Scale economies	Scope economies
Achieving efficiency in current operations	Benefiting differences in factor costs – wages and cost of capital	Expanding and exploiting potential scale economies in each activity	Sharing of investments and costs across products, and businesses
Managing risks	Managing different kinds of risks arising from market policy-induced changes in comparative advantages of different countries	Balancing scale with strategic and operational flexibility	Portfolio diversification and risks and options and side bets
Innovation, learning, and adaptation	Learning from societal differences in organizational and managerial processes and systems	Benefiting from experience-based cost reduction and innovation	Shared across organizational components in different markets or businesses

Source: Ghoshal (1987)

sources of advantage and the ends are the strategic objectives. The goals are an elegant articulation of three contrasting but complementary themes.

- *Achieving efficiency* is the dominant perspective in STRATEGIC MANAGEMENT, where the objective is to maximize the value of the ratio between outputs and inputs. The basic strategies of cost leadership and differentiation are both maximizers in this sense, cost strategies reducing the value of inputs and

differentiation strategies increasing the exchange value of the outputs.
- The notion of *managing risks* gets far too little attention in the academic and business literatures. Ghoshal identifies several different categories of risk:
  - o   macroeconomic risks;
  - o   political or policy risks;
  - o   competitive risks; and
  - o   resource risks.
- *Innovation, learning, and adaptation* are an outcome of resource-based thinking. Here

Ghoshal makes an interesting argument that increasing geographic scope ("globalization") is in effect an exposure to diversity and variety. The twin pressures of managing for efficiency and for local variety impose a greater need to innovate, to learn, and to adapt than is faced by a purely domestic firm.

Ghoshal maintains there are three fundamental tools for building global competitive advantage.

- The first is to exploit the differences in input and output markets in different countries. This is to exploit COMPARATIVE ADVANTAGE – the economic characteristics that make national economies different.
- The second is to achieve *economies of scale*.
- The third is to exploit *economies of scope*.

The term *national differences* refers to what economists call factor conditions or differences in factor costs between different countries. According to international trade theory, a country will export those goods that make use of the factor conditions with which it is relatively well endowed. Thus a country like China is concentrating on modern assembly plants in which the low cost of Chinese labor plays a significant role in reducing costs. Multinational enterprises (MNEs) seek to locate their activities in regions with specific factor advantages. For example, BT along with many UK-based banks have relocated their call centers to India to take advantage of low costs but a skillful labor force. The Netherlands is the world's leading exporter of flowers. It has maintained its position by creating research institutes in the cultivation, packaging, and shipping of flowers. Therefore any company wishing to compete in this industry has to have an operation in the Netherlands. Similarly, in Formula 1 racing the central cluster of activity is to be found in Motor Sport Valley in the south of England, which has skilled labor and craftsmen in engineering, advanced materials, software, and project management. For Ferrari to become successful again in F1 racing it had to gain access to these skills by first establishing an operation in England, and then finding ways to transfer this knowledge throughout their Italian home base.

From this framework Ghoshal is able to articulate the nature of the TRADE-OFFS between alternative strategy choices. In other words, the framework is not deterministic, but it does enable consistencies and contradictions among different moves.

See also *globalization; global strategies; value chain analysis*

Bibliography

Ghoshal, S. (1987). Global strategy: An organizing framework. *Strategic Management Journal*, 8, 425–40.
Ohmae, K. (1985). *Triad Power: The Coming Shape of Global Competition*. New York: Free Press.
Porter, M. E. (1985). *Competitive Advantage: Creating and Sustaining Superior Performance*. New York: Free Press.
Prahalad, C. K. and Doz, Y. L. (1986). The dynamics of global competition. In C. K. Prahalad and Y. L. Doz (eds.), *The Multinational Mission: Balancing Local Demands and Global Vision*. New York: Free Press.
Yip, G. (1995). *Total Global Strategy*. Englewood Cliffs, NJ: Prentice-Hall.

global strategies

John McGee

There are four basic strategies that companies use to enter and compete in the international environment. Bartlett and Ghoshal's well-known work (1989) depicts these in figure 1.

Multidomestic strategies are country-centered with extensive customization for local markets and with an almost full set of value chain activities in each major market. They do transfer skills and products developed at the home base, but high degrees of local discretion are given to meet local conditions. Typically, these strategies cannot realize value from centralized, scale-effective, experience-rich production facilities. Bartlett and Ghoshal describe multidomestic companies as decentralized federations (see figure 3) and regard them as historically European, being conceived in days of higher transport and communication costs and higher tariffs.

International strategies create value by transferring key skills, capabilities, and products to local markets. The degree of differentiation developed in the home base is advanced and the

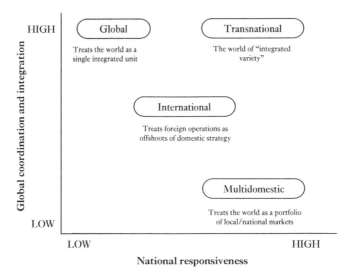

HIGH

Global coordination and integration

LOW

Global
Treats the world as a
single integrated unit

Transnational
The world of "integrated
variety"

International
Treats foreign operations as
offshoots of domestic strategy

Multidomestic
Treats the world as a portfolio
of local/national markets

LOW   HIGH

National responsiveness

Figure 1   International strategic environments: late 1990s (adapted from Prahalad and Doz, 1986)

intent is that the differentiation delivered in each local market reflects this. Thus, local differentiation is complementary to that from the center. However, the organization is usually country-centered and local managers have important degrees of discretion in deciding what product portfolio to offer and how it should be presented locally. Product development and R&D tend to be centralized in the home base, but other value chain activities are usually closer to market. Head office retains close control over marketing strategy and product strategy, and also exercises close financial control. Bartlett and Ghoshal regard this as typically North American – born in the 1950s and 1960s, as US companies began to realize the benefits of the scale and technological achievement of 50 years of distinctively large, progressive markets. They see this form as a coordinated federation (figure 3), the degrees of coordination (especially in marketing and finance) being distinctive American contributions to management practice in the postwar years. Many writers are tempted to place international strategies into the bottom left corner of figure 1. This would be to deny the distinctive coordinating power of these companies (e.g., Procter and Gamble, IBM, Kellogg, McDonald's, Merck). Moreover, with low coordination and low responsiveness, there would not appear to be a sustainable strategy.

Global strategies focus on increasing profitability through product standardization, and capturing the cost reductions that come from location economies (exploiting COMPARATIVE ADVANTAGE in Ghoshal's framework shown in table 1 in the entry on GLOBAL STRATEGIC ADVANTAGE), ECONOMIES OF SCALE and experience effects (*see* EXPERIENCE AND LEARNING EFFECTS), and the organizational focus on procedures and processes that support low costs. Bartlett and Ghoshal see these strategies as quintessentially Japanese, having emerged in the growth and tariff reduction years of the 1970s and 1980s. These companies are typically highly centralized, with little attempt to build local differentiation (marketing) activity. They do, however, often pursue global BRANDING and "quality" positioning, along with or after their initial focus on low cost (e.g., Sony). Toyota was a good example of a global strategy in the 1980s – its productivity (cars per employee) was about 37 compared to 20 at Ford, who would be regarded as having an international strategy. Many industries can be seen to be global in character. Thus, the semiconductor industry has global standards with enormous worldwide demands for standardized products. Not surprisingly, the players such as Intel, Texas Instruments, and Motorola pursue global strategies. Bartlett and Ghoshal describe global companies as centralized hubs (figure 3), reflecting the high degree of centralization.

Transnational strategies exploit experience-based cost economies and location economies, transfer distinctive competences within the company, and at the same time pay attention to pressures for local responsiveness. Bartlett and Ghoshal argue that the two dimensions of figure 1 are an incomplete description of the strategic choices. They offer a resource-based addition, suggesting that the need for innovation and learning should be a third dimension (figure 2). With this focus on capabilities, competences (Prahalad and Hamel, 1990), and strategic assets (Amit and Schoemaker, 1993) they argue that these characteristics do not simply reside in the home base. On the contrary, by careful investment, they can be developed anywhere appropriate in the company's worldwide operations. This is a locational economy (or comparative advantage), where the advantage is in the form of knowledge and capability rather than low cost. So the flows of skills and products can be in any direction within the worldwide configuration of activities – the organization can thus be described as an integrated network (see figure 3).

The role of the center is to provide an organizational and strategic context within which the complex flows and interactions can take place. Toyota is a good example, as are other Japanese auto manufacturers, such as Nissan and Honda. Toyota has moved from a focus on the "world car" to something more regional. This initially involved the development of manufacturing capabilities and sites in North America, Europe, and elsewhere in the world. Along with this goes a spreading of product development beyond Japan.

Unilever is another example. Once it was a classic multidomestic company in the European tradition. It has moved from 17 different and largely self-contained detergents operations in Europe toward a single European entity with detergents being manufactured in a handful of cost-efficient plants, and with standard packaging and advertising across Europe. Unilever's estimate of the cost savings is over $200 million per year. However, Unilever recognizes that there are major differences in distribution channels and that brand values and brand awareness vary a lot across Europe, and therefore, that local responsiveness must not be sacrificed for simple standardization benefits. In other words,

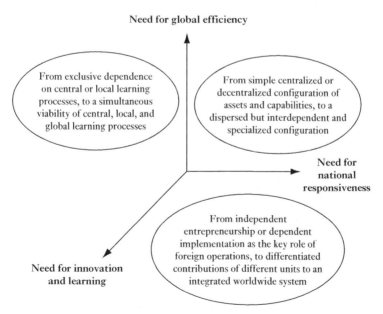

Figure 2 The strategic tasks (adapted from Bartlett and Ghoshal, 1989)

Centralized hub   Decentralized federation

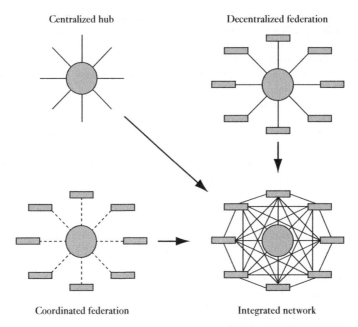

Coordinated federation   Integrated network

Figure 3   Alternative organizational solutions (adapted from Bartlett and Ghoshal, 1989: 50–2, 89)

Unilever intend to move from multidomestic to transnational.

By contrast, Procter and Gamble have seemingly moved more in the direction of a global strategy from an international position. Bartlett and Ghoshal maintain that the transnational company must have a network organization (see figure 3).

Strategic choice involves making TRADE-OFFS. It is not always clear what strategies should be followed, because it is rare that one choice will dominate all other possibilities. The advantage of a pure global strategy is the ability to become a low-cost player, but the disadvantage is the lack of local responsiveness (see the Matsushita example in Bartlett and Ghoshal, 1989). The multidomestic has the opposite trade-off. It is able to differentiate to local markets and respond to local conditions, but it cannot manage itself into a distinctive low-cost position. The international company is able to transfer distinctive competences to new markets, but it can be caught between the inability to differentiate enough locally or to be sufficiently low cost. It could be a case of "stuck-in-the-middle" – this seems to be

Procter and Gamble's own diagnosis. The transnational appears to solve all of these conventional trade-offs, but it clearly has major difficulties of implementation, because the network organization is so fundamentally different from more traditional "command and control" organizations.

See also *global strategic advantage; globalization*

Bibliography

Amit, R. and Schoemaker, P. J. H. (1993). Strategic assets and organizational rent. *Strategic Management Journal,* 14, 33–46.

Bartlett, C. and Ghoshal, S. (1989). *Managing Across Borders: The Transnational Solution.* Boston: Harvard Business School Press.

Prahalad, C. K. and Doz, Y. L. (1986). The dynamics of global competition. In C. K. Prahalad and Y. L. Doz (eds.), *The Multinational Mission: Balancing Local Demands and Global Vision.* New York: Free Press.

Prahalad, C. K. and Hamel, G. (1990). The core competence of the corporation. *Harvard Business Review,* May/June, 79–91.

globalization

John McGee

There is no doubt that globalization and internationalization have, as ideas, fired the imagination, even though the words themselves are cumbersome and awkward. Figure 1 portrays globalization in a broad economic context. "Global" refers, broadly speaking, to an entwined web of economic forces. The world dimension indicates the extent to which there is economic interdependence between countries, as indicated by the cross-border flows of goods, services, capital, and knowledge. At the country level, countries will differ in their degree of linkage between their economy and the rest of the world, using the same indicators. Our definition of global industry has thus to be seen in the context of the worldwide pattern and the role of individual countries. At the firm level, we are looking at the extent to which its revenue and asset bases are spread across borders.

GLOBAL INDUSTRIES AND MARKETS

International trade incorporates many different types of competition, and across industries we can observe marked differences in the patterns of international competition. On the supply side of industries, the dimension of competition and of strategic choice in which we are interested is geographic scope, the extents to which firms' activities extend across national borders. But it is the demand side that is more important. We use

the term *multidomestic* (or *multilocal*) to describe industries where the competition in any one country is independent of competition elsewhere. We use the term *global* when competition in one country is influenced by competition elsewhere. Multidomestic is the situation where markets are different in their consumer behavior patterns. Thus, the market for foods can be seen to be very different across the countries of the European Union (EU) and even wider across the countries of the world. By contrast, the market for Coca-Cola is broadly similar across the world, with consumers exhibiting similar if not the same utility functions and buying behavior. Global markets lead to standard products, whereas multidomestic markets lead to product differences and diversity. Multidomestic industries are, as the name implies, a collection of domestic industries. A global industry leads directly to international rivalry. In a multidomestic industry a firm can and should manage its worldwide activities as a portfolio of independent subsidiaries in each country – this is a country-centered strategy and relatively little coordination is necessary or valuable. In a global industry, to have a global strategy a firm must develop and implement a strategy that integrates its activities in various countries, even though some portion of the firm's activities must take place in each individual country.

The nature of globalization is complex and multidimensional, even without bringing in broader issues of culture, behavior, national

Degree to which a company's
competitive position within the
industry in one country is
interdependent with that in another

Growing interdependence among countries as shown by x-border flows of goods, services, capital, and know-how

Worldwide

Industry

Country

Extent of the linkages between a country's economy and the rest of the world

Company

Extent to which a company has expanded
its revenue and asset base across countries
and engages in x-border flows of capital,
goods, and know-how across its subsidiaries

Figure 1   Determinants of globalization

tastes, and so on. Accordingly, there have been many attempts to capture the term in a single definition. The original proponent of globalization was Theodore Levitt (1983), whose concept was that of *global standardization* – a single global market with standard products and a corporate focus on gaining efficiencies through standardization. Kenichi Ohmae (1985) introduced the idea of the "triad" – to compete effectively, firms should be present in each of the three major regions of the world. This has become known as *global localization*. Wisse Dekker, an erstwhile chairman of Philips, saw globalization as *assembly abroad* to *circumvent competition*. More recent commentators see *global niches* sitting alongside domestic redoubts.

We seem to be moving from a market-based focus on standardization (standard products and centralized production facilities) to a RE-SOURCE-BASED VIEW of standardization. This would argue for a common approach to knowledge, learning, resources, and capabilities across the world, but with products adapted to local or regional needs from a common core competence (*see* CORE COMPETENCES).

Figure 2 suggests what might be the deeper drivers. There are five forces at work. The first is a cultural homogenization – a "global village" argument. Two of the forces are from the demand side, convergence of markets and growing similarity of customers. Markets in this context are about the infrastructure and the processes by which markets work. This covers legislation, application of competition law, organization of selling and distribution systems, consumer protection laws, local tariffs, and so on. The markets for agricultural products are

---

- Cultural homogenization ("global village")
- Convergence of markets
- Globalization of customers
- Cost drivers
  - economies of scale and scope
  - increase in levels of fixed cost
- Fundamental changes in industry structure
  - deregulation, privatization
  - technological change

Figure 2   Why globalization?

vastly different between Russia and the US. The markets for packaged groceries are different between European countries, to the extent that the laws governing price promotions and use of television advertising are different, as is the extent to which superstores are allowed to develop, for example in France and Italy.

The customer argument is more plainly about the degree of similarity between the utility functions of customers in different locations and the impact this has on buying behavior. This can be exemplified by considering two buyers of auto components, one for Ford Motor Company's plants in Europe, the other for General Motors. Their buying criteria are likely to be very similar and component companies are very likely to be designing and selling very similar components across Europe. It is less clear that Italian and English shoppers in supermarkets will have the same attitudes and ideas about buying food products. To the extent that these buyers are fundamentally different in their behavior, suppliers will be adapting their products to reflect different requirements in Italy and in England.

On the supply side of industries, the cost drivers are very important. Other entries attest to the significance of *economies of scale, scope*, and *experience*. The costs of investment can be so high that single national markets, even those of the US, might be too small to support them. It is difficult to see how the design and development costs of large airplanes can be economically supported from even the US. The development costs of automobiles, prescription drugs, many high-technology new products, and much military hardware require a large international market. It is in the interests of companies, then, to make the offer of a standardized product across the world in competition with the more locally differentiated, but more expensive, options offered by local companies. From a cost point of view, the presence of significant scale and experience effects drives customers toward the cheaper, more standardized options. This is the basis of Levitt's approach to global standardization.

Finally, fundamental changes in industry structure can result in major changes to the underlying economics of industries (e.g., through technological change). Coupled with new management teams (e.g., through PRIVATIZATION and DEREGULATION), this can change the terms on which companies approach their marketplaces and their opportunities to move across borders. For example, the worldwide trend to the privatization of telecommunications and utility companies has challenged the presumption that the natural market for utilities is domestic only.

Scale is commonly considered to be a major characteristic of being global. But there are other benefits:

- Exposure to the world's "best" practice (*see* BEST PRACTICES).
- Learning and transfer opportunities of best practice.
- Access to technology.
- Ability to serve new customer groups.
- Ability to anticipate moves of global competitors.
- Ability to defend national profit sanctuaries through counter-attack.

In looking at global industries and the firms that compete in them, it should be possible to examine and test the proposition that industries do not go global by accident. They are global because of innovations in strategy. Global strategies can create advantage only if they:

- change the economics of the industry;
- serve local markets better than the local incumbents;
- are hard to emulate;
- are sustainable (*see* SUSTAINABILITY);
- are capable of further development.

As firms gain experience in operating within a global industry, some of the original strategic innovations become embedded into the INDUSTRY STRUCTURE and, thus, the industry economics will have characteristics like large-scale economies – high and rising R&D costs, extensive interaction with governments, and links with changes in country infrastructures. But there are still many strategy choices open to each firm: for example, how to increase local content without sacrificing global scale, how to increase product homogeneity through design, how to shape demand, how to develop systems to make coordination easier. Some firms will be striving to develop local/domestic niches, others will be focusing on global segments, and others might be attempting global standardization.

See also *global strategic advantage; global strategies; globalization of service industries*

Bibliography

Bartlett, C. and Ghoshal, S. (1989). *Managing Across Borders: The Transnational Solution*. Boston: Harvard Business School Press.
Douglas, S. P. and Wind, Y. (1987). The myth of globalization. *Columbia Journal of World Business*, Winter, 19–29.
Levitt, T. (1983). The globalization of markets. *Harvard Business Review*, May/June, 92–102.
Ohmae, K. (1985). *Triad Power: The Coming Shape of Global Competition*. New York: Free Press.
Porter, M. E. (1985). *Competitive Advantage: Creating and Sustaining Superior Performance*. New York: Free Press.

globalization of service industries

Susan Segal-Horn

Service industries are a very broad set of industries. They normally include: wholesale and retail trade, restaurants and hotels, transport and travel, construction, storage, communications (including telecommunications, media, and publishing), finance and insurance (both retail and commercial), property management and transactions, business services (cleaning, waste disposal, catering, computing, software), professional services (accounting, legal, consulting, engineering), community, social, health and personal services (from hairdressing, domestic cleaning, and plumbing to car repair and funerals). See figure 1 for an overview of the different types and range of service sector activity.

While much of the service sector in developing economies consists predominantly of relatively low-skilled services in wholesale and retail trades, restaurants, tourism, and personal services, in the developed economies, by contrast, the service sector contains a high proportion of high-skilled and high-technology jobs in media, software, financial, professional, and business services. The term *quartenary* sector describes these more sophisticated service jobs,

FINANCIAL SERVICES	COMMUNICATION SERVICES
e.g, commercial and retail banking, credit cards, brokerage, foreign exchange, portfolio management	e.g., postal, telecommunications, courier, news agencies, data transmission, film distribution
TRANSPORTATION SERVICES	INSURANCE SERVICES
e.g., passenger transport, freight, car rental, tour operators	e.g., life, pensions, property, actuarial, reinsurance
CONSTRUCTION SERVICES	EDUCATION SERVICES
e.g., site preparation, building, maintenance	e.g., schools, colleges, universities, language, training and development
BUSINESS SERVICES	HEALTH-RELATED SERVICES
e.g., property, equipment rental, professional services (accounting, legal, advertising, design, consulting, computer, surveying, engineering), cleaning, catering, packaging	e.g., dental services, hospital, medical, testing, counseling, advisory, psychiatric, non-human health (veterinary)
TRADE SERVICES	PERSONAL SERVICES
e.g., retailing, wholesaling, agencies	e.g., domestic cleaning and maintenance, plumbing, hairdressing
HOTEL AND RESTAURANT SERVICES	RECREATIONAL AND CULTURAL SERVICES
e.g., hotel, accommodation, food and beverage	e.g., entertainment (music, theater, cinema), parks and gardens, monuments, media

Figure 1　Services sector diversity (derived from World Trade Organization categories of international trade)

just as "tertiary" sector is the common term for any non-product economic activity. "Quartenary" is an attempt to separate out the enormous range of types of service activity. It recognizes the degree of difference between a chambermaid and a corporate financier or a judge. Service industries often suffer from a bad press in the advanced economies, which implies that only jobs in manufacturing are "real" jobs. Such comments exacerbate a widespread misunderstanding about the range and types of service jobs, since they draw their analogies from the tertiary sector whilst largely ignoring the power and sophistication of the quartenary sector in developed economies.

The Globalization of Services

Much of the historic pattern of competition in services occurred within domestic market boundaries as a result of the small-scale, fragmented structure of service industries, and their culture-specific patterns of demand and consumption. Under these conditions, clearly, scale and volume effects will be limited. However, in most service sectors restructuring has led to concentration, replacing fragmentation in INDUSTRY STRUCTURE. In addition, some homogenization of demand in services is also observable.

In the last 20 years many service industries have been transformed. They have become concentrated rather than fragmented; international rather than local; and capital-intensive rather than labor-intensive. This has occurred as a result of macroenvironmental factors, including technological innovations, which have had a profound impact on the range of services and service delivery channels. World market leaders have been created in banking, logistics and distribution, communication, consulting and business services, fast food, leisure companies, airlines, software and advertising agencies, telecommunications and media such as broadcasting and publishing, retailing, and professional services such as law, accountancy, and surveying. Indeed, the degree of concentration amongst professional service firms (PSFs) in accountancy has reached the point where genuine concern exists about lack of client choice. Many sectors resemble oligopolies, albeit with a long "tail" of smaller firms coexisting as local providers in most markets.

Many services (e.g., credit cards, automated teller machines, airline seats, software, Internet retailing, and automatic carwash) have emerged relatively recently. Therefore, in international terms, they have the advantage of no prior patterns of usage or acculturation, thereby making them more easily acceptable across national boundaries. However, alongside social, cultural, and technological changes affecting demand for services, there are additional economic and political pressures on governments to create, or remove, regulatory barriers (e.g., "open skies" policy in EU airline competition policy in Europe).

Despite their importance in job and wealth creation, the literature on global strategy (see GLOBAL STRATEGIES) has given relatively little attention to service industries (Porter, 1986; Yip, 1996). International agreement on a General Agreement on Trade in Services (GATS) to reduce trade barriers in services was reached only recently by the World Trade Organization. If successful, this will further simplify the internationalization of services. Such agreement is especially important to safeguard intellectual property, which is a high component of many services and is currently relatively unprotected from international infringements outside certain of the advanced economies. However, GATS is controversial and has encountered opposition particularly with regard to issues of freer international trade in services such as education and healthcare.

DRIVERS OF SERVICE GLOBALIZATION

In services it is often the customer who internationalizes first, with the service company

following to meet the needs of important clients who are themselves already global in their operations. The concentration in the advertising industry worldwide, resulting in multinational (MNC) agencies such as WPP or Interpublic, was needed to build international networks of agencies to service international clients, particularly those requiring the delivery of global campaigns. Large service firms can standardize and replicate facilities, methodologies, and procedures across locations. Specialization and standardization are leading to high-quality provision at lower cost to the client company or customer, in service businesses from car repair (e.g., exhaust, brake, and tire centers) to audits. BRANDING of services has become an important international guarantee of reputation, quality, and consistency around the world.

Global market segments (see SEGMENTATION) with homogeneous international needs have arisen (e.g., the business traveler). They make possible ECONOMIES OF SCALE, as well as branding, marketing, and reputation benefits. Such global segments provide attractive target markets for many service MNCs, since the business traveler is looking for consistency of service levels to minimize the risk and uncertainty of working in many and varied locations. International segmentation does not usually mean providing the same product in all countries, but offering local adaptations around a standardized core. The retail chain Benetton built its international strategy around the standardized core of Benetton's "one united product" of casual, color-coordinated leisurewear for the 15–25 age group. It has spawned many imitators (such as Gap). Table 1 gives a summary of the strategic issues and potential sources of international advantage on which the Benetton international strategy (first launched in 1982) was originally based.

However, in global strategy, standardization and adaptation always coexist. So Benetton does alter its color palette for different market preferences in different parts of the world. Similarly, in the fast food industry, global chains such as Pizza Hut, McDonald's, and KFC provide a standard core product around which local adaptations are made. For example, in France wine is sold in McDonald's outlets and tea in UK outlets. KFC adapted its large chunks of chicken

Table 1 Benetton's international strategy

Rationale behind globalization

- European domestic markets are relatively small and a successful concept can reach saturation coverage fairly quickly.
- The development of "lifestyle retailing" provided a clear global market segment.
- Identified international market segment of leisurewear for 15–25 age group.
- Proprietary technology – not in a technical sense, but in the interrelationship between the business activities in the value chain, this interrelatedness providing a potential source of advantage as it is not easily imitated.
- International information systems provide the channel for fast response to shifts in consumer demand and risk-free low inventory.

The strategy

- To put fashion on an industrial level.
- To develop "one united product": one product line of sufficient breadth to meet the needs of similar customers worldwide.

Putting the strategy into operation

- The concept: vertical integration, from design through manufacturing and distribution to retailing.
- The offering: good design and colors of universal appeal.
- Innovative merchandising: making space and inventory more productive.
- Control over store design and location.
- Inventory is replaced by information system links to factories.
- Inventory risk elimination: produce to firm customer orders.
- Financial risk elimination: agents and franchisees provide capital investment in stores.
- Logistics network: rapid access to information on demand.
- Innovative manufacture to allow "customized" batch production in response to demand.

Source: Segal-Horn (2003)

to bite-sized pieces for sale in the Japanese market.

Even education or medical services that have been highly domestic market based, regulated, and culture specific now have international chains (e.g., international campuses trading on well-known university brand names). Underlying these trends is what Levitt (1976) called "the industrialization of service." Services can be industrialized in a variety of ways:

- by automation, substituting machines for labor, e.g., automatic carwash, ATM cash machines, Internet e-tailing, or automatic toll collection;
- by systems planning, substituting organization or methodologies for labor, e.g., self-service shops, fast food restaurants, packaged holidays, unit trust investment schemes, mass market insurance packages;
- by a combination of the two (e.g., extending scope in food retailing via centralized warehousing and transportation/distribution networks for chilled, fresh, or frozen foods).

Such industrialization of service is based on large-scale substitution of capital for labor in services, together with a redefinition of the technology intensity and sophistication of service businesses. It also assumes a market size sufficient to sustain the push for volume.

Indeed, this is the most common driver for globalization. A firm is likely to shift to international operations when the domestic market provides insufficient volume to support minimum efficient scale. This may come earlier for service firms than for manufacturing firms since for many types of services the option of exporting is not available. Another related driver is "network effects." For many services such as telecommunications or credit cards or any travel-related service, the service will be more successful the more international presence and the wider network it has, since the service becomes more valuable to customers the more places they can use it.

CONFIGURATION OF THE GLOBAL SERVICES VALUE CHAIN

Service firms seek to benefit from the same sources of potential advantage as manufacturing firms in their international expansion. The issue is whether such benefits from international expansion are as attainable for service firms as for manufacturing firms.

Both firm-specific advantages (FSA) and location-specific advantages (LSA) may be available to the service MNC (Enderwick, 1989). Location decisions concerning particular parts of the value chain are key to the design of effective global strategies. These issues have also been conceptualized in international strategy by Porter (1986) as issues of configuration and coordination in the allocation of value chain activities by the firm. Historically, service firms have been bound to locate close to the customer as a result of the simultaneous production and consumption characteristic of services. However, in many services this problem in the provision of global services has been reduced and a greater range of service configuration is now possible.

FSA include factors concerning scale and scope in services. These include access to assets such as goodwill and brand name, particularly important in buying decisions for services (*see* SERVICE INDUSTRY STRATEGIES). Scale economies (*see* ECONOMIES OF SCALE) are obtainable from high fixed costs and from common governance of complementary assets. Scope economies (*see* ECONOMIES OF SCOPE) may be derived from extending the range of services, offering innovative or complementary services that reinforce a competitive position.

LSA factors are of two different types. One type of service is location specific because production and consumption are simultaneous and therefore wide international presence is mandatory (e.g., fast food chains). The other type are services that are tradeable and therefore the choice of international location would result from considerations of COMPARATIVE

ADVANTAGE just as in manufacturing MNCs (e.g., software houses located in India to take advantage of high skills and lower costs).

Central to global configuration issues in services refer to the important distinction between "back-office" and "front-office" activities in services. "Front-office" describes those activities that come into contact with the customer. They are front-line service encounter activities. "Back-office" refers to those operational activities that can be separated (disaggregated) from the customer and possibly performed somewhere else. *The larger the proportion of back-office value chain activities in the service that can be separated from the location of the customer, the greater the potential benefits of globalization for service MNCs.* It becomes possible to redesign the organization's value chain to secure scale and scope advantages in the same way as manufacturing MNCs. If most activities of a service organization cannot be separated from the customer in this way, then strategic flexibility remains low and the costs and service delivery problems of global strategy remain high. In particular it also means that service MNCs will remain unable to benefit from national differences in comparative advantage, which is one of Ghoshal's (1987) three major potential benefits from global strategies of firms. The more such disaggregation is possible, the greater the potential benefits from comparative advantage and scale and scope economies that become potentially available to service firms.

Figure 2 provides a simple illustration of some of these service design and reconfiguration possibilities. It reflects some of the rethinking of services that has occurred. For example, the location of retail banking in the top-left box reflects the capital-intensive, volume-driven, transaction-processing part of retail banking operations. These activities are usually now centralized and regionalized. At the same time, the retail banks have been closing many branches and redesigning remaining branch outlets to be more customer friendly, in order to cross-sell other higher-margin financial services. Software houses may sometimes appear in the top-left box also if they are selling standardized rather than bespoke software packages. However, the examples in figure 2 are inevitably oversimplified (e.g., it ignores the search by PSFs for

BALANCE OF RESOURCES

	Back-office	Front-office
STANDARDIZATION	Retail banking	Contract cleaning
CUSTOMIZATION	Reinsurance Courier services	Professional service firms PSFs

Figure 2   Service standardization (adapted from Segal-Horn, 1993)

methodologies to increase productivity and margins via back-office standardization). It is inevitable that continuous shifts such as those between standardization and customization should result in firms continually seeking optimization of such features at the highest level of scale and cost position available to them. It is also to be expected that these positions of optimum efficiencies will be continually shifting.

POTENTIAL PITFALLS IN THE
INTERNATIONALIZATION OF SERVICES

The "intangibility" and "simultaneity" characteristics of services make operational delivery of services across national boundaries a higher risk than for products. When the service network is extended globally, the management of the service encounter faces obvious quality control problems. It must accurately reproduce the service concept in different cultural, political, and economic environments and insure *consistency* rather than heterogeneity in the service offering at all transaction points. For example, in terms of the hotel industry, tangibles such as beds or televisions are relatively more straightforward to coordinate and deliver across borders than intangibles, such as the style and atmosphere of a hotel or how staff conduct themselves in their dealings with guests. The procurement and logistics strategies and processes that support the selection and supply of beds or televisions to

hotels around the world are far less complex than the shared values and tacit understandings needed to underpin the delivery of service encounter intangibles.

INTERNATIONAL SCALE AND SCOPE IN
SERVICES

The grid in figure 3 gives a historical representation of the spread of availability of scale and scope economies in different types of service businesses. The top-right corner of the grid is illustrated by information service firms such as Reuters, Bloomberg, and Dun and Bradstreet; by financial services companies such as American Express and VISA International; by the major international airlines; by travel firms such as Club Med. The top-left corner is illustrated by retailers (grocery/food and non-food). Electronic point-of-sale equipment (EPOS) and concentration of retailer buying power resulted in high scale effects for large retailers, initially combined with limited scope opportunities. However, many large food multiples also trade in clothing, homewares, and even financial services such as in-house credit cards (store cards), savings products, and, more recently, bank accounts. So the large retailers' position on the grid has been gradually moving from top left toward top right. Bottom right of the grid is illustrated by a wide range of PSFs such as accountants, lawyers, management consultants, surveyors, civil engineers, recruitment agencies ("headhunters"), and so on. PSFs may be high on potential scope economies from such factors as shared client and project databases or shared teams of expertise across national or regional offices, but with low potential economies of scale, since these services are frequently customized, often within different national regulatory frameworks. Bottom left on the grid consists typically of small-scale personal service businesses, which are highly location specific.

Figure 3 represents the traditional view of these varying types of service businesses. However, a migration is taking place. Large food (e.g, Wal-Mart, Aldi) and non-food (e.g., IKEA, ToysRUs) retailers are seeking scale benefits from volume purchasing and scope benefits from investments in information technology, logistics networks, and international branding. Another well-publicized example of such migration concerns the PSFs. It has given rise to a proliferation of large mergers amongst PSFs to try to capture these increasing benefits to scale from greater efficiencies in capacity utilization of scarce resources and for productivity gains from implementation of standardized methodologies. Insurance companies in Europe are building cross-border operations, as regulatory differences become less extreme and types of distribution channels develop and converge. Finally, many small service businesses, such as car repair,

are moving upward on the grid, for volume benefits in purchasing and operations arising from specialization and standardization (e.g., Kwik-Fit Euro specializing in repair of car exhausts or brakes only).

There is also potential benefit to diversified service firms from leveraging customer relationships across service businesses (Nayyar, 1990). Buyers of services already attempt to economize on information acquisition ("search") costs by transferring reputation (i.e., brands) effects to other services offered by a firm, thus enabling the service firm to obtain quasi-rents from firm-specific buyer–seller relationships. This supports the growing importance of the branding of services and reinforces, for services, two of the main competitive advantages of being MNCs: first, the ability of MNCs to create and sustain a successful brand image and its concomitant goodwill; second, the ability to monitor quality and reduce buyer TRANSACTIONS COSTS and uncertainty by offering services from multiple locations.

This may suggest that growth for service firms may not involve a deepening of asset structure as in manufacturing companies, but a horizontal accretion of assets across different markets and different industries (i.e., scope).

THE FUTURE

The separation of back-office and front-office activities, combined with the standardization of

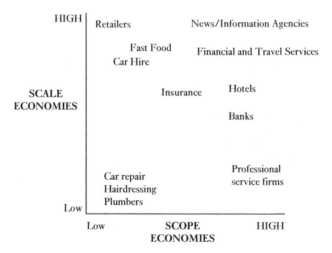

Figure 3   Potential for scale and scope economies in different service businesses (adapted from Segal-Horn, 1993)

many back-office processing functions, has created the opportunity for breaking out of the requirement for simultaneous consumption and production of a service and for greater potential sources of economies of scale and scope in services in international service firms. They allow for the reconfiguration of service value chains that can be disaggregated (just as for manufacturers) so that the activity may be located geographically for optimum scale, scope, or cost advantage. These types of international configurations for services are technology dependent rather than service encounter dependent. They signal a new set of opportunities for future strategies of service firms. Scale and scope are having considerable impact on the creation of international oligopolies in services. If such benefits are not available for service firms, it would usually mean that local service firms should have lower costs and provide higher service levels than service MNCs. In addition, core knowledge and information-based assets of service firms are codifiable and transferable across national boundaries, as is the consumer franchise from strongly branded services. Many services contain tangible components that are capital intensive, amenable to separation from the point of service delivery, and responsive to standardization.

Greater similarity between manufacturing and service firms now indicates that the special characteristics of services have diminished in significance at the industry level, although they remain critical at the level of the firm. For service firms, globalization still means that a mobile customer base (e.g., the tourist, the shopper, the business traveler) expects to experience a consistent service wherever it goes.

However, service industry dynamics are beginning to parallel those of manufacturing. Interestingly, with the emphasis on customer service in manufacturing, and the emphasis on efficient deployment of back-office assets in services, each is trying to capture the advantages the other has traditionally utilized.

See also *globalization*

Bibliography

Enderwick, P. (1989). *Multinational Service Firms*. London: Routledge.

Ghoshal, S. (1987). Global strategy: An organizing framework. *Strategic Management Journal*, 8 (5), 425–40.

Levitt, T. (1976). The industrialization of service. *Harvard Business Review*, September/October.

Nayyar, P. R. (1990). Information asymmetries: A source of competitive advantage for diversified service firms. *Strategic Management Journal*, 11, 513–19.

Porter, M. (1986). *Competition in Global Industries*. Boston: Harvard Business School Press.

Segal-Horn, S. (1993). The internationalization of service firms. *Advances in Strategic Management*, 9, 31–61.

Segal-Horn, S. (2003). Strategy in service organizations. In D. Faulkner and A. Campbell (eds.), *The Oxford Handbook of Strategy*, vol. 1. Oxford: Oxford University Press.

Yip, G. S. (1996). *Total Global Strategy*, 2nd edn. Englewood Cliffs, NJ: Prentice-Hall.

growth share matrix

Derek F. Channon

Derived from the early work of the Boston Consulting Group in the 1960s on experience curves, the growth share matrix became, and remains, the most widely used portfolio model for influencing investment and cash management policy in diversified corporations. The matrix is illustrated in figure 1. The horizontal axis is drawn to a logarithmic scale and identifies the relative MARKET SHARE of each of the businesses within the company's portfolio. In this system relative market share is defined as that of the company's business divided by that of its largest single competitor. By definition, therefore, only one company within a defined market can have a relative share greater than one. The vertical axis depicts the industry growth rate in real terms, with the impact of inflation removed.

Businesses are mapped on to the matrix, with the size of each business being reflected by the area of the circle used to depict it. The relative position of each business within the four quadrants indicates the expected cash flow to be generated and suggests an investment strategy. The cut line on the vertical axis is set at 10 percent real growth, while the relative share cut line is set usually at the 1.0× level.

A business in the bottom left quadrant is a CASH COW. A high market share coupled with slow real growth is expected to generate surplus

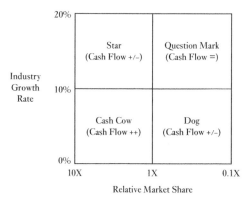

Figure 1   The Boston Consulting Group growth share matrix

cash as a result of high profitability due to lower cost. Moreover, future investment needs of such businesses are limited as growth has declined.

Those in the top left quadrant are STAR BUSINESSES with high relative share and high growth. While such businesses are profitable, they are largely cash neutral, since profits need to be continuously reinvested while the growth rate remains high in order to maintain market position.

Businesses in the top right quadrant enjoy high growth but low relative share. The objective for a few such QUESTION MARK BUSINESSES is to take the surplus cash flow from the cash cows in order to invest heavily while the growth rate is high, to convert them into future stars.

Those in the bottom right quadrant are said to be DOG BUSINESSES. These concerns have low relative share and low growth. They are expected to suffer a cost disadvantage as a result of their low share. However, it is anticipated that to convert such businesses into cash cows would take disproportionate effort in a mature market, where share gain would have to be obtained from established high-share rivals. Such businesses are therefore candidates for harvesting, exit, or disposal.

The underlying concept of the growth share matrix is the belief that, for the average business, there is an 80 percent experience effect (*see* EXPERIENCE AND LEARNING EFFECTS) and that relative market share can be used as a fairly easily

measured surrogate for cumulative production volume.

Businesses with a high relative market share should therefore enjoy a significant cost advantage compared with competitors:

relative market share	$4\times$	$2\times$	$1\times$	$0.5\times$	$0.25\times$
relative cost	64%	80%	100%	120%	165%

Similarly, real growth rate is seen as a surrogate for market attractiveness, with high and low real growth equating to high and low attractiveness, respectively. The rationale for this stems from the concept of the product life cycle.

The growth share model can be used in a variety of different ways. First, it permits the company to map its businesses in a way that enables management to rapidly visualize the position of its total portfolio. As a result, the strategic dynamics for the total corporation can be planned for its future development. The ideal sequence for development is depicted in figure 2. Surplus cash is siphoned off from cash cows and redeployed, first to any star businesses requiring it, and then to a carefully selected number of question marks with a view to building these into the stars of the future. Dog businesses, unless strong in cash generation, should be divested or closed. Good cash-generating dog businesses are due to low capital intensity and are candidates for harvesting rather than divestment.

By contrast, the sequence for disaster, illustrated in figure 3, indicates a failure to invest in star businesses due to a lack of positive cash-flow businesses. As a result, stars lose share to become question marks, which, in turn, are converted into dogs as markets mature.

It can be argued that the graphic presentation of the matrix represents a static snapshot of the business portfolio. This criticism has been addressed by the development of the share momentum graph illustrated in figure 4.

This graph is developed over a relevant time period (say, five years) and, by plotting the position of each business unit in terms of the two dimensions of total market growth versus growth in sales for the business, the businesses that have been gaining or losing share can be readily observed. Those businesses falling

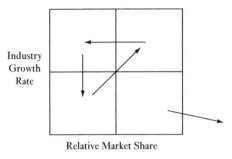

Figure 2   The growth share matrix cash flow sequence for success

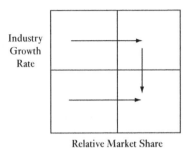

Figure 3   The growth share matrix sequence for disaster

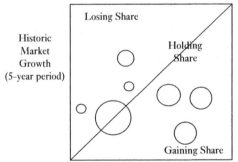

Figure 4   The share momentum graph

below the diagonal have been losing share, while those above it have been gaining share. The chart is a useful quick indication to management as to which businesses are succeeding or failing relative to the market; it also offers a useful correction in situations in which management may believe that it is performing well in achieving

growth in a business, whereas in reality it may be losing share.

The growth share matrix can also be a useful tool in evaluating competitive dynamics. This is illustrated in figures 5 and 6.

The relative market position of major competitors is illustrated in figure 5. The vertical cut line is in this case set at the industry overall growth-rate level. Those competitors above the cut line are growing faster than the market average, while those below it are losing share. A consequence of this analysis is that different competitors may classify businesses in different ways. Competitor A, with the largest market share, is clearly operating as a cash cow, but is also trading market share for cash by growing at less than the market, allowing competitors B and D to see their businesses as question marks and therefore investment opportunities. Only competitor C recognizes that its business is a dog.

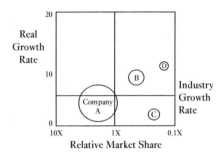

Figure 5   The industry growth share matrix

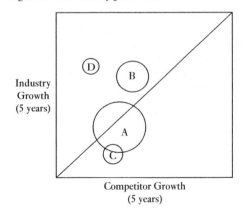

Taking the same industry over time, as shown in figure 6, clearly indicates that competitor B has been growing faster than competitor A, as well as faster than the market as a whole.

In addition to analysis at the level of the industry as a whole, further refinements of growth share analysis are to analyze businesses by product and by technology. For example, the 1978 product portfolio of Eastman Kodak is illustrated in figure 7. The figure shows that many of the company's activities are concerned with thin film coatings, yielding economies of scope and shared experience in this area of technology. As a result, product groups that might otherwise have been classified as dogs may well make a contribution to Kodak's overall position in a core technology. A similar analysis might well have been concerned with activities rather than technology. Share momentum charts can also be developed that reflect product-based portfolios over time.

The growth share matrix has therefore provided an extremely useful multifunctional management tool, both for diagnosing the position of the multibusiness and multiproduct firm and for understanding industrial and competitive dynamics.

However, the technique is also subject to a number of criticisms, which include the following:

- Growth share matrix positioning implies that relative market share can be used as a surrogate for cost. There is therefore a fundamental assumption that, on average, an 80 percent experience effect underlies market share. Evidence from the PROFIT IMPACT OF MARKET STRATEGY (PIMS) program suggests that the actual cost advantage derived from higher and lower relative shares is substantially less than this.
- Detailed experience analysis is rarely undertaken, due to the cost and the lack of appropriate data. Moreover, the impact of shared experience from technology, activities, and the like may not be adequately incorporated.
- The model assumes that only the two variables of relative market share and industry growth rate are necessary to establish the strategic position of a business. Evidence

Figure 6   The industry share momentum matrix

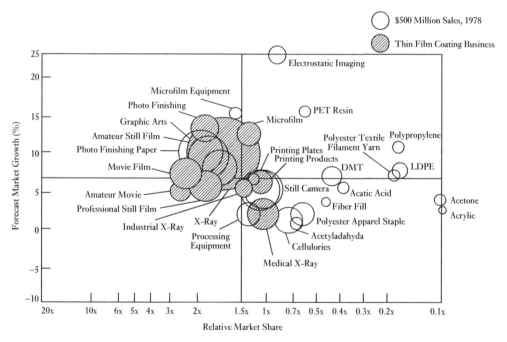

from the PIMS program and actual practice clearly indicates that these variables alone, while important, can be readily outweighed by other factors such as relative INVESTMENT INTENSITY, productivity, and so on.

- In calculating relative market share, it is assumed that "market" has been accurately defined. This need not be the case, especially in situations in which market boundaries are in a state of flux as a result of geographic, product, or customer segment changes.

Bibliography

Bogue, M. C. and Buffa, E. S. (1986). *Corporate Strategic Analysis*. New York: Free Press, chs. 2, 5.

Hax, A. C. and Majluf, N. S. (1984). *Strategic Management: An Integrative Perspective*. Englewood Cliffs, NJ: Prentice-Hall, ch. 7.

Henderson, B. D. (1973). *The Experience Curve Reviewed, IV: The Growth Share Matrix of the Product Portfolio*. Perspectives No. 135. Boston: Boston Consulting Group.

Lewis, W. W. (1977). *Planning by Exception*. Washington, DC: Strategic Planning Associates.

growth strategies

see LIFE–CYCLE STRATEGIES

H

holding company structure

Derek F. Channon

The conventional holding company structure, illustrated in figure 1, is usually found in companies that have attempted to expand or diversify by acquisition (*see* ACQUISITION STRATEGY). In its classical form, the central office plays no role in the strategy of the constituent member companies within the holding company, and, indeed, there may also be no central financial control.

In the 1970s such companies were common as an original strategy began to mature or be subjected to excessive pressure. As a consequence, almost invariably after the appointment of a new chairman or chief executive officer, such firms attempted to break out from the mature/decline strategic position by diversifying rapidly through acquisition, or by eliminating competition by buying them up. As the holding companies lacked the appropriate post-acquisition capabilities of integrating the new subsidiaries, they were allowed to manage themselves. A classic example would have been the development of GKN, a leading British manufacturer of screws, which expanded and at the same time

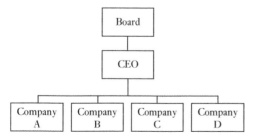

Figure 1   A holding company structure

attempted to eliminate competition by purchasing major competitors. There was no central control and, as a result, within the group the subsidiaries continued to compete with one another, so eliminating the expected benefits. The central office in this structure was virtually non-existent, consisting only of the chairman and a secretary.

The board structure of such holding companies tends to be made up of CEOs of a number of the subsidiary companies, operating under a chairman who might be a non-executive, or at least unable to intervene in the operations of the subsidiaries. In the absence of any formalized strategic plans, subsidiaries tend to pursue their own strategies, and are interested in preserving their autonomy rather than being subject to strict financial and strategic control from the central office. When a holding company is established, board membership may well change, and functional specialist directors of the original core company leave the board. This process is necessary in order to change the functional bias of the executive board members, who might otherwise concentrate on the original business to the detriment of new diversifications (*see* DIVERSIFICATION). However, where the original CORE BUSINESS is especially large, as, for example, in oil, banking, and tobacco, this change in board emphasis is especially hard to achieve.

A further form of the holding company structure is also current, in that some corporations exist in which, again, no attempt is made to influence the strategy of subsidiaries, although they are subject to tight financial control. Hanson Trust, for example, could be classified as a holding company. The difference between this form and the historic pattern is the sophisticated financial control systems, the central office strategic capabilities in acquisition search, post-ac-

Figure 2   A functional holding company structure

quisition rationalization, and the imposition of tight financial controls. Thus while no product market strategy is immediately apparent and the breakup and disposal of acquired companies is undertaken, the financial characteristics of the residual activities form part of an ongoing strategy. In the case of Hanson, therefore, disposals help to recover the financing of an acquisition, leaving the residual businesses to generate a high rate of return on a relatively limited capital outlay. The residual businesses also tend to be cash generators, allowing the buildup of a cash war chest to finance the next acquisition. This type of holding company, while apparently having no synergistic product market strategy, does have SYNERGY within a financial portfolio concept.

The traditional holding company strategy tends to be basically unstable. Without control there is a natural tendency for subsidiaries to undertake actions that may lead to financial imbalance. Acquisitions may not be adequately integrated or rationalized, and strategic moves may be undertaken which, while increasing corporate size, may also lead to reduced profitability. As a result, most of these holding companies have eventually been acquired by the second type, or have reorganized by adopting a DIVISIONAL STRUCTURE as consultants are brought in to establish greater control.

FUNCTIONAL HOLDING COMPANY

The functional holding company structure is an intermediate variant that is often used in the early stages of diversification away from the single business stage (*see* SINGLE BUSINESS STRATEGY). Diversification in the early stages normally occurs through acquisition and a new

subsidiary is usually grafted on to an existing functional structure, as shown in figure 2.

The constitution of the board of the new enterprise is usually modified to add the CEO – but not the functional directors – of the acquired company. The chairman and non-executive directors of acquired companies are often dismissed. The same is true of the CEO if the bid is contested.

This structure is rarely stable. First, in making a diversification, the acquiring company often underestimates the STRATEGIC FIT between itself and the acquiree. Second, the board culture still strongly reflects that of the parent, and board meetings tend to emphasize the affairs of the parent rather than those of the acquiree, even if the new arrival makes a substantial contribution to overall profitability. Third, the constitution of the board is predominantly made up of functional specialists, not general managers. As a result, it is common that the CEO of the acquired company may resign out of frustration. A serious common mistake then is for the parent company to install one of its own senior managers as the new CEO of the acquiree. Performance suffers further, and this tends to be compounded if further acquisitions are undertaken which lead to the establishment of a holding company structure.

Research indicates that, as diversification develops, one of the two traditional holding company structures is introduced. However, while corporate sales overall tend to expand sharply, profitability declines after a relatively short time. While the initial bout of diversification occurs after a change in the chairman and/ or the chief executive, the failure of the diversification moves to produce improved profitability

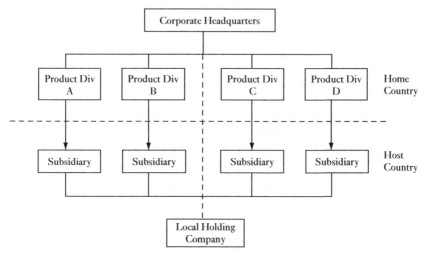

Figure 3 A local umbrella company structure (Channon and Jalland, 1979)

leads to a second change of leadership, which is often introduced from outside the company in order to establish a shift in corporate culture. This is often initiated by board changes and by the introduction of external consultants to rationalize and reorganize the business and to introduce a new structure. In the 1970s and 1980s this tended to mean the introduction of a divisional structure and/or a strategic business unit (SBU) structure. In the 1990s even more fundamental changes took place in strategy/ structure revisions, especially in industries in which changes induced by information technology transformed cost structures. Here the process of reengineering (*see* BUSINESS PROCESS REENGINEERING; VALUE-DRIVEN REENGINEERING) tended to convert conventional vertical organizational linkages toward customer quality-driven horizontal linkages.

Holding company structures may also be widely used for legal and fiscal reasons, which may or may not have organizational management implications. For example, an intermediate holding company might be used to avoid withholding taxes on dividends paid to shareholders resident outside the domicile of particular corporations. Thus Swiss corporations might operate with Panama-based holding companies, which receive dividends from some of their overseas subsidiaries which can be distributed to shareholders without withholding taxes.

Similarly, local umbrella holding companies, as shown in figure 3, are often required by multinationals to legally coordinate the individual interests of product divisions. Such a holding company can:

1 present a unified corporate face to local government and markets;
2 provide a communication channel for details regarding existing and future operations necessary for business unit coordination;
3 provide an overall corporate perspective on local opportunities;
4 achieve tax optimization;
5 insure consistent personnel policies; and
6 consolidate divisional funds to permit more local borrowing and to provide easier management control for centralized cash and foreign exchange management.

Bibliography

Channon, D. F. (1973). *The Strategy and Structure of British Enterprise*. Cambridge, MA: Harvard Division of Research.

Channon, D. F. and Jalland, M. (1979). *Multinational Strategic Planning*. New York: Amacon.

Goold, M. and Campbell, A. (1987). *Strategies and Styles: The Role of the Center in Managing Diversified Companies*. Cambridge, MA: Blackwell.

Rumelt, R. P. (1974). *Strategy, Structure and Economic Performance*. Cambridge, MA: Harvard Division of Research.

horizontal structure

Derek F. Channon

In traditional vertical organizations, work is divided into functions, then departments, and finally tasks. The primary building block of performance is the individual, with the chain of command rising through the function, and the manager's job is concerned with assigning individuals to tasks and then measuring, controlling, evaluating, rewarding, and sanctioning performance. Time and cost pressures have forced a reconsideration of the vertical structure and a move toward horizontal structures, organized around the core process.

In the horizontal form of organization, work is primarily structured around a small number of core processes or work flows, as shown in figure 1. These link the activities of employees to the needs of suppliers and customers, so as to improve the performance of all three. Work, and the management of work, are performed by teams rather than individuals. While still hierarchical, the structure tends to be flatter than traditional functional systems.

The processes of evolution, decision-making, and resource allocation shift toward continuous performance improvement. Information and training occur on a JUST-IN-TIME basis rather than "need to know," while career progression occurs within the process rather than the function, making individuals generalists rather than specialists. While individual rewards may be made, compensation also relates to team performance.

A number of key principles have been identified at the center of horizontal organizations. These include the following.

ORGANIZE AROUND THE PROCESS, NOT THE TASK

In a horizontally structured corporation, the focus of performance can be shifted by organizing the flow of work around company-wide processes. This involves selecting a number of key performance indicators (KPIs), quantitative but not necessarily financial measures, based on customer needs, and tying them to work flows. To achieve this, the corporation's activities need to be subdivided into around three to five "core processes." These might include order generation through to fulfillment, new product development, integrated logistics management, and branch management. The redesign of these processes can produce major one-off gains and then lay the basis for the introduction of continuous improvement strategies.

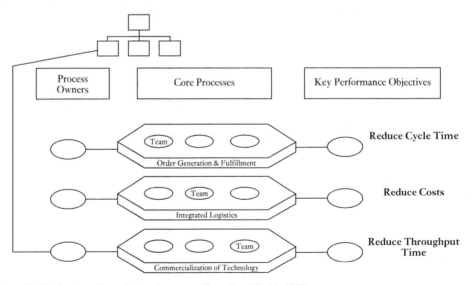

Figure 1   The horizontal organizational structure (Ostroff and Smith, 1992)

The structure for such a change involves the creation of a cross-functional team based upon the work flow, not on the individual task. These work flows are then linked to others, both upstream and downstream. Organizing mechanisms for the structure include:

- the appointment of a leader, or team of leaders, to "own" and guide each core process;
- assigning, to everyone involved in the process, objectives related to continuous improvement against "end of process" performance measures;
- establishing measurement systems for each process, to integrate overall performance objectives with those of all work flows within the process;
- reaching explicit agreement on the new staff requirements between upstream and downstream activities;
- creating process-wide forums to review, revise, and syndicate performance objectives.

FLATTEN THE HIERARCHY BY MINIMIZING THE SUBDIVISION OF WORK FLOWS AND NON-VALUE-ADDED ACTIVITIES

In horizontal organizations, hierarchy is still seen as necessary, although ideally core processes can be "owned" by a single team. In reality, effective teams rarely exceed 20–30 people, far fewer than the thousands involved in core processes in large corporations. As a result, some hierarchy is needed, although one or two layers of functional hierarchical structures are normally eliminated.

The mechanism of DELAYERING is used to combine related but formerly fragmented tasks, eliminating activities that do not add value or contribute to the achievement of performance objectives, and to reduce as far as possible the number of activity areas into which each core process is divided. While horizontal organizations are almost invariably flatter than vertical structures, this is not the key objective of restructuring; rather, this is to reshape the organization so that every element contributes directly to the achievement of the KPIs.

ASSIGN OWNERSHIP OF PROCESSES AND PROCESS PERFORMANCE

Leadership is still important in horizontal organizations. Thus teams or individuals are assigned "ownership" of each core process and are responsible for achieving performance objectives. Such individuals and/or teams are often responsible for the activities of thousands of employees engaged in the core process.

LINK PERFORMANCE OBJECTIVES AND EVALUATION TO CUSTOMER SATISFACTION

The primary driver in horizontal organizations may well be customer satisfaction rather than justifiability or shareholder value. These latter two terms might well be derived variables of the former.

Vertical organizations tend to drive for financial results and focus attention on the bottom-line contribution of each function. In horizontal organizations, by contrast, the primary measure may well be customer satisfaction. This is measured in a variety of ways, many of which are non-financial, such as relative MARKET SHARE, growth rate, and market penetration, in the sense in which these are measures of relative competitive position.

As teams develop a clear understanding of how to manage a core process, they often find it useful to evaluate activity areas from the perspective of the external customer. In this way, they use customer satisfaction measures to drive all the internal measures of performance.

MAKE TEAMS, NOT INDIVIDUALS, THE PRINCIPAL BUILDING BLOCKS OF ORGANIZATIONAL PERFORMANCE AND DESIGN

Managers who organize around work flows treat teams, not individuals, as the key organizational building blocks. Teams regularly outperform individuals owing to their greater skill base, broader perspective, and ability to solve complex problems. Moreover, many people find working in teams more rewarding than operating alone.

However, real teams need to be organized and motivated. As individuals they may offer a superior mix of skills, but unless these are orchestrated the result may actually be dysfunctional. For horizontal organizations to be successful, therefore, organization by teams is necessary, but leadership and orchestration of these skills are essential for them to be complementary.

COMBINE MANAGERIAL AND NON-MANAGERIAL ACTIVITIES AS OFTEN AS POSSIBLE

When teams are organized horizontally around work flows, it is important to make such teams as self-managing or empowered as possible. The premise behind this concept is that those who participate in the process know it best and, if so motivated, have the most to contribute to improving its productivity. Moreover, as problems develop, decisions can be made quickly and action can be taken in real time without interrupting critical work flows.

By contrast, in vertical organizations the benefits of self-management are constrained to within the function, where actions may ironically cause decreased efficiency in subsequent dependent functions. Moreover, lower hierarchical-level personnel may lack the authority to make changes, which need to be approved at senior levels within the organization. When such moves threaten the existing power system, changes may well be resisted.

Horizontal structures combine rather than separate managerial and non-managerial activities wherever possible. Teams must therefore be empowered to exercise training and information processing, and be motivated to evaluate and change when, how, where, when, and with whom they interact, and in so doing become the real managers of the process.

TREAT MULTIPLE COMPETENCES AS THE RULE, NOT THE EXCEPTION

In horizontal structures, the more skills that individuals bring to the team, the greater is the team's ability to manage the core process for which it is responsible. By contrast, in vertical organizations the trend is toward task specialization to maximize efficiency. This does not mean that horizontal structures can afford to ignore functional specialist skills; therefore, they also need to embrace such skills when they are identified as essential.

However, specialist skills are often illusory and may be used to reinforce the existing structure. It is therefore necessary to identify carefully what specialist skills are needed and which can be discarded. Often, this is a political decision rather than an operational one.

INFORM AND TRAIN PERSONNEL ON A "JUST IN TIME TO PERFORM" BASIS, NOT ON A "NEED TO KNOW" BASIS

In vertical organizations, information has often been used as a source of power rather than to improve the performance of a function or relationships between functions. Information has tended to flow on an "up-over-down-back" basis, leading to time delays and dispersed – and perhaps contradictory – decision-making. Despite training and attempts at improved coordination and cooperation in many corporations, interfunctional coordination is far from optimal.

In horizontal organizations, information is ideally made available on a "just in time to perform" basis, and is provided to those responsible for implementation. Moreover, the reward structure is linked to achievement of the core process activity rather than the function; hence it behoves the participants within the process to maximize rather than hinder efficiency.

MAXIMIZE SUPPLIER AND CUSTOMER CONTACT

In horizontal structures, corporations aim to bring their employees into direct, regular contact with suppliers and customers. Such contact increases their insight into the total value-added process within an industry. Done well, this provides opportunities for building supplier and customer loyalty and to improve cost efficiency. Managers sometimes resist this vertical integration because it reduces their power and influence over the business process. Evidence suggests, however, that overcoming such resistance provides an important means of strengthening customer-driven performance.

REWARD THE DEVELOPMENT OF MOTIVATIONAL SKILLS AND TEAM PERFORMANCE, NOT JUST INDIVIDUAL PERFORMANCE

In horizontal organizations, synchronizing the reward and sanction systems is important for successful implementation. The emphasis on developing the role of the individual within the core process team is very different from the narrow, individualistic competitive approach in the vertical functional system.

For teams to be effective, members must accept mutual accountability on agreed purposes and objectives. Within this structure some individual rewards are permissible; however, the competitive pressure imposed under the functional system, which may lead to suboptimal behavior, can be dampened. To maximize their rewards, team members must partially sacrifice their own position for the good of the team.

Conclusions

It is not easy to find the correct balance between vertical and horizontal structures. However, it is important to recognize that such a structural transformation may well be necessary, and will need to overcome the existing power structure for successful implementation. Horizontal structures are a natural consequence of reengineering strategies and, while accepted by top management, may well meet serious resistance in the ranks of middle management who may be "delayered" in the process of change (*see* REENGINEERING DISADVANTAGES).

Bibliography

Kaplan, R. B. and Murdock, L. (1991). Core process redesign. *McKinsey Quarterly*, **2**, 27–43.
Ostroff, F. and Smith, D. (1992). The horizontal organization. *McKinsey Quarterly*, **1**, 148–68.

hot desking

Derek F. Channon

Many companies are redefining the way in which office work is undertaken. These companies believe there is no longer a need for many of their staff to have an individual desk. This phenomenon has been termed "hot desking" because each desk can be used by more than one person. It is part of a wider redefinition of the workplace as a result of new technology,

customer needs, and drives to reduce non-productive labor and the cost of premises.

The logic of the approach is based on the fact that for sales, consultancy, and other activities involving face-to-face contact with external organizations and individuals, some 70 percent of working time is spent outside the office. The maintenance of full-scale accommodation means extra building/space costs and unnecessary "status" costs, and actually encourages attendance in the office rather than out in the field. These cost variants can be dramatic. In corporate banking, for example, making the relationship person's office a car, equipped with a laptop computer, fax machine, and telecommunications links, standardizing reporting formats, and eliminating the need for most dedicated secretarial backup can save up to 300 basis points – a dramatic saving in markets in which margins are often measured in unit basis points.

Crucial to the changes, however, is the need to install efficient support systems to service the mobile employee. Calls need to be channeled to mobile telephones or stacked; faxes need to be stored and easily retrievable on a screen or as hard copy, and similar considerations apply for email. However, the impact of office DOWNSIZING goes well beyond cost reduction. Many companies have dramatically reduced their use of paper, and filing systems have become electronic, further reducing space needs. Essential documents can be stored in secure, low-cost, off-site warehouses. In addition, many companies encourage their employees to work from home, as PCs also permit video conferencing.

The trend toward hot desking and accompanying change in work patterns and space utilization costs has become well accepted in corporations such as computer firms, accountancy practices, consultancy companies, and so on.

Bibliography

Becker, F. and Steels, F. (1995). *Workplace by Design*. San Francisco: Jossey-Bass.

industry structure

John McGee

ANALYSIS OF INDUSTRIES AND COMPETITION

In the entry on MARKET STRUCTURE perfect competition can be seen as the benchmark by which economists and others such as government departments and regulators judge the EFFICIENCY of markets. In general markets are seen as efficient if they are perfect in their principal characteristics, demonstrating price competition, ease of entry and exit, and wide distribution of relevant knowledge. Conversely, individual firms see it as in their own interest to have specific knowledge that enables them to build unique assets and offer distinctive products for which they can charge a price premium. In other words, firms have an interest in constructing imperfections that favor them in the marketplace. Firms may also have an interest in colluding together to create collective imperfections by which they can artificially limit competition and charge higher prices than otherwise. There is a very considerable literature on these monopolistic practices and the ways in which governments pursue pro-competitive policies in order to make industries more efficient and markets more competitive.

Firms actually compete on two levels. One level is in the marketplace where customers compare rival offerings and make choices; in doing so, prices emerge from these market processes. Firms also plan and invest for the future and in doing so they construct assets that they hope will be sufficiently distinctive for them to offer distinctive products. Thus, the R&D activities of pharmaceutical firms are intended to create new and unique products that can be protected by patents and that can then be sold as unique high-priced products in the market. Industry analysis is the analysis of assets, resources, and capabilities that set out the basic economic conditions under which firms collectively operate (the "industry context") and that condition their individual abilities to create distinctive individual positions in their industries.

For example, Ford and Toyota operate in the automobile industry. They share some common operating characteristics such as significant ECONOMIES OF SCALE in assembly operations, a largely common knowledge basis and technology characteristics, and a set of competing products that compete more on price than on product differences. To some extent they share common economic characteristics. However, they each conduct R&D and other development activities in order to gain points of difference with regard to each other. Toyota might claim a distinctive way of organizing its manufacturing activities with beneficial effects on quality and reliability. Ford might claim a better organization of distribution and servicing activities with beneficial consequences for the way in which consumers experience the service process. This mixture of common economic characteristics coupled with attempts at individual differentiation comprises the content of industry analysis. As we have seen in the entry on COST ANALYSIS, the nature of economies of scale in an industry (such as automobile assembly) affects the number of potential competitors in an industry (the greater the minimum efficient scale, the fewer competitors that can survive). Thus the economic characteristics of the industry shape the nature of competition in the market by affecting the number of players (in this example). More generally, the economic characteristics of an industry are shaped by the investment and planning decisions of firms and the extent to which firms can sustain uniqueness

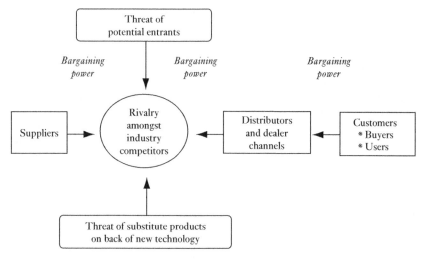

Figure 1   The Porter five forces frameworks (Porter, 1980)

affects the way in which competition then plays out in the marketplace.

Industry analysis is best known as Porter's five forces. This was first popularized by Michael Porter in his pathbreaking *Competitive Strategy* (1980). Figure 1 shows the celebrated diagram of the five forces of competition (often known as rivalry), entry, supplier power, buyer power, and power of substitutes. These are the five fundamental forces that determine the "attractiveness" of the industry, a term which is a surrogate for industry profitability. Thus the weaker/stronger are these forces, the more/less attractive will be the industry taken as a whole and the larger/smaller will be its profitability. On the whole, the more attractive the industry, the more likely it is that participants will enjoy "good" profits.

THE SUPPLY CHAIN

The heart of the five forces diagram is the horizontal line. Porter draws this as a force diagram with all the arrows pointing toward the central box, which represents the industry in question measured in terms of the competitors present. Alternatively, this can be shown as a supply chain representing the buildup and flow of goods to the final customer. Thus, for the food industry, goods flow from the farm, to food ingredients companies (such as flour milling),

to food manufacturers (such as cake and bread manufacturers), to wholesalers, to supermarkets, and then to final consumers. At each stage of the supply chain there is an industry that invests in assets, that accumulates fixed and variable costs, and then prices its goods to the next stage of the chain. The difference between its revenues and its material costs is its added value. This added value can be partitioned into three parts, labor costs, capital costs, and profits. The more attractive the industry, the greater the profits are likely to be, and vice versa. Where perfect competition is the norm, prices will tend to converge and profits will fall to a level that is the minimum rate of return on capital that will enable the capital to be retained in the industry. If profits fall below this level, there will be pressure to withdraw capital and place it in more profitable employment. If profits are higher, there will be an incentive for more capital to enter the industry. This is the basic mechanism behind the threat of entry in figure 1.

THE THREAT OF ENTRY

At each stage of the supply chain there is an industry that can be analyzed in terms of the five forces. Firms considering investment in an attractive industry will make an entry calculation. This takes the form of a conventional capital investment decision with three components.

The revenue stream depends on prices that can be charged (taking account of the price elasticity of demand; see ELASTICITY) and the volumes attainable. The costs depend on the unit costs of production and access to available economies of scale, scope (see ECONOMIES OF SCOPE), and learning, and on the level of marketing and other costs of getting the product to markets. Finally, the capital cost of the investment needs to be reckoned. If any of the cost elements (expressed in unit form) are higher than those of the incumbents, and if the prices relative to incumbents are lower, then the potential entrant faces "entry barriers," i.e., its profit margins are lower than those of the incumbents and it faces a cost disadvantage or barrier. If the cost disadvantages are high in relation to the profit margins, then they serve as an effective deterrent to entry. If for other reasons such as access to technology or to distribution systems the entrant is effectively barred from entry, we say that entry is *blockaded*.

THE POWER OF SUPPLIERS AND BUYERS

Suppliers have a natural interest in raising their prices at the firm's expense. To the extent that they succeed, they enhance their margins at the firm's expense. Under what conditions might this happen? Where there are relatively few suppliers the firm may not have many alternatives to an aggressive supplier. Where the supplier is providing a product that is very important to the eventual performance of the firm's own product, then he might be able to charge a "premium" price. Where a firm is accustomed to using a particular product, there may be costs of *switching* from this product to an alternative (see SWITCHING COSTS). This provides a price umbrella for the supplier in his negotiations with the firm. If there are no substitution possibilities, then price can go up. For example, if an electricity generator's power stations are configured around coal supplies and conversion to other supplies such as gas or oil is only a longer-term possibility, then coal suppliers have bargaining power. OPEC in pricing oil has to be aware that an over-aggressive pricing policy provides incentives for its customers to convert to other fuels and/or to invest in energy saving.

The analysis of buyer power is symmetrical. The greater the relative concentration of buyers,

the less important is an individual firm's product to the buyer; the more the product can be substituted by others (see SUBSTITUTE PRODUCTS), the less the firm's bargaining power and the greater is the buyers' bargaining power. In the UK the celebrated example of this is the power of supermarket chains over food manufacturers. The larger and more powerful the chain, the more it can force down its input prices. However, the principal defense of the manufacturer vis-à-vis the supermarket is its ability to differentiate its products. Thus, the more distinctive is Nestlé's Nescafe brand, the less will Tesco be able to force its price down. Tesco's calculation could be that customers will come into the store having already decided to buy the Nescafe brand regardless of any price differentials between Nescafe and other brands, including the supermarket's own brand. However, if Tesco could legitimately conclude that customers respond principally to Tesco's own branding and will therefore buy whatever Tesco put on the shelves (especially its own brand), then Tesco's buying power is strong and it will be more able to treat its suppliers as providers of commodity products. The threat of vertical integration (see VERTICAL INTEGRATION STRATEGY) can be very effective in disciplining suppliers. Some retailers such as Marks and Spencer have an own-brand policy that is a form of quasi-vertical integration that leaves strategic power effectively with the retailer. Conversely, the distinctiveness of luxury-brand purveyors such as Louis Vuitton and Gucci has enabled many of these players to invest in their own captive distribution and retailing systems so that they can extract every drop of the product differentiation premium for themselves.

The balance between supplier power and buyer power is a key issue in business. Very often the biggest threat to a firm's margins comes not simply from its competitors but from the adjacent (and sometimes even the more remote) parts of the supply chain. The biggest threat to food manufacturers probably comes from retailers. In the personal computer business the power in the supply chain lies upstream with the component suppliers, i.e., with Microsoft's operating systems and other software, and with Intel and its microprocessors. Estimates in Harvard Business School's case studies on Apple in the 1980s suggested that more than half of all the profits made in the personal industry supply chain were earned by Microsoft and Intel (Yoffie, 1992). Thus, the location of power along the supply chain is a key issue in understanding how profits can be earned. The well-known example of Dell shows how a strategic innovation downstream, close to the customer, has been able to create a defensible and profitable position in spite of the power of Microsoft and Intel.

The Threat of Substitutes

The pressure from substitutes tends to be longer-term pressure. If you conceive of the product from your industry as having a certain benefit-cost ratio to the immediate customer, then pressure from substitutes can be calibrated in terms of alternative benefit-cost ratios. A simple but powerful example concerns the substitution of fiber optic cable for coaxial cable in telecommunications in the 1980s. Fiber optic cable offered so many more benefits at relatively low marginal cost that the costs of investing in entirely new cabling systems could very quickly be earned back. Most technological changes can be assessed in the same way, trading off the added benefits, the added costs, and the required investments. Complications arise when the products involved are components within larger systems. The increased use of modularity of electronic components and the standardization of electronic interfaces have increased the incentives for substitution. Another problem arises when the scale and scope of substitution is so large as to effectively disrupt the existing supply chains. The advent of photocopying, the laser printer, and the personal computer demonstrate that there can be system-level substitutions that cause industries and supply chains to transform.

Competitive Rivalry

The intensity of competition is the fifth force in the list. This is regarded by economists as the first force in that it is the prototype of competitive force present in all economic textbooks. The propositions follow from the earlier discussion of perfect competition. Thus, competition will be the stronger (and profits the lower) the more competitors there are and the more commodity-like are the products. In addition, the supply-demand balance directly affects the market price. In declining markets, prices fall as excess supply chases deficient demand. The more the cost structure is fixed rather than variable and marginal costs are therefore low, then the more room there is to cut prices before contribution margins become negative. This explains why capital-intensive industries with low marginal costs suffer so much in recession. Prices can keep falling as long as cash flows remain positive, remembering that the capital costs are sunk (e.g., Eurotunnel) and fixed costs are programmed over a time period, so the only discretionary policy is to place price somewhere above marginal cost. In extreme cases cash flows might remain positive (and sufficient to pay cash costs including interest payments on capital) while accounting losses could be very high.

Porter's five forces model has been criticized for its essentially static approach. The analysis is presented as a one-time picture of an industry, thus neglecting the likelihood that the situation as observed is not stable. Industries and markets are not typically in equilibrium and we expect therefore that any observation takes a picture of an industry in motion. This might be retrieved by taking pictures regularly, but the point remains that an essentially dynamic situation is portrayed as static. Similarly, the role of innovation is slighted in this view. There is no evident return to innovation or indeed any other investments because they appear as costs without the attachment of any benefit stream. Concerns have also been expressed that the industry lens is too narrow; it excludes other relevant variables and in doing so exaggerates the importance of those that are included. This is exemplified by the famous debate about "does industry matter" (Rumelt, 1991). Rumelt famously found that industry structure only explains about 10 percent of the variance in profit rates across companies, the implication being that company differences (strategies) explain much of the remainder. This means that an industry analysis that concludes that an industry is attractive does not mean that all companies will or can make profits or that entering companies can necessarily make profits. The value of an industry analysis lies in its ability to portray the principal forces of competition in a concise and meaningful way. It is not an algorithm for predicting future profitability, although it does provide a basis for assessing potential future profit.

Bibliography

Porter, M. E. (1979). How competitive forces shape strategy. *Harvard Business Review*, **57**, 2 (March/April).

Porter, M. E. (1980). *Competitive Strategy: Techniques for Analyzing Industries and Competitors*. New York: Free Press.

Porter, M. E. (1985). *Competitive Advantage: Creating and Sustaining Superior Performance*. New York: Free Press.

Rumelt, R. (1991). How much does industry matter? *Strategic Management Journal*, **12**, 167–85.

Yoffie, D. (1992). *Apple Computer 1992*. Harvard Business School Case Study 9-792-081. Boston: Harvard Business School.

information goods

John McGee

Information and know-how are classic examples of public goods. A public good is a commodity or service in which the consumption of one agent (consumer or firm) does not preclude its use by other agents.

The cost structure of information goods is unusual and distinctive. The basic proposition is that information is costly to produce but cheap to reproduce. Music performances and concerts that cost hundreds of thousands of dollars can be copied and sold for tens; $100 million dollar movies can be copied onto videotape for cents. Thus, information has very high fixed costs but low to vanishing marginal costs. This means that cost-based pricing (based on markups over variable cost) does not make any sense. Pricing must be based on a direct assessment of value to the consumer.

Information is an "experience good," i.e., consumers need to experience it in order to value it. Thus the purchase of the *Wall Street Journal* or the *Financial Times* is based on previous experience even though one does not whether today's paper is as valuable as yesterday's paper. Information businesses devise ways to get people to give trials to information goods – trial subscriptions, for example. There are various forms of *browsing*, hearing music on the radio, watching trailers for movies. But the way information pro-

ducers really overcome reluctance to purchase is through brand and reputation.

The consequence of these characteristics of information goods is information overload. Information is available very quickly and in large quantities because of the low cost of reproduction of information. The experience good characteristics result in a reluctance to purchase. But the high fixed costs of information creation make information a risky proposition. Any rival to the UK's number one pay-TV channel (Sky) finds the fixed costs very high and customer attention difficult to gain given Sky's first-mover claim on the market. Thus On-Digital failed. The information goods business is therefore a risky business characterized by information overload as producers seek to gain the attention of consumers.

Information industries can be viewed as NETWORK INDUSTRIES. Since the marginal cost of information reproduction is low, sellers of information goods have to take into account the networks through which their information is distributed. Such networks may include legal and illegal copying, rental stores, and libraries. With the transition from printed to digital information, the transmission of information may cause congestion over the network resulting from overloading of the system by multiple information providers.

See also *network externalities; network industry strategies*

Bibliography

Shapiro, C. and Varian, H. (1999). *Information Rules: A Strategic Guide to the Network Economy*. Boston: Harvard Business School Press.

Shy, O. (2001). *The Economics of Network Industries*. Cambridge: Cambridge University Press, ch. 7.

intended strategy

see STRATEGY-MAKING

international business

John McGee

International business is the study of transactions taking place across national borders for the purposes of satisfying the needs of individuals and organizations. These transactions consist of trade (called *world trade*), which is exporting and importing, and capital transfers – foreign direct investment. Over half of all world trade and about 80 percent of all foreign direct investment is carried out by the 500 largest firms in the world. These companies are called *multinational enterprises* (MNEs). Typically, they are headquartered in one country but have operations in one or more other countries. In 2000 the MNEs that earned over $100 billion annual revenue were

- Exxon (US)
- Wal-Mart (US)
- General Motors (US)
- Ford Motors (US)
- DaimlerChrysler (Germany)
- Royal Dutch/Shell Group (UK/Netherlands)
- British Petroleum (UK)
- General Electric (US)
- Mitsubishi (Japan)
- Toyota (Japan)
- Mitsui (Japan)
- Citigroup (US)
- Itochu (Japan)
- TotalFinaElf (France)
- Nippon Telegraph and Telephone (Japan)
- Enron (US)

Each of these comes from one of three geographic locales: the US, Japan, or the European Union (EU). This group is called the *triad*. Of these 16 companies, seven are from the US, five from Japan, and four from the EU. The North American Free Trade Association (NAFTA) is a regional free trade agreement between Canada, the US, and Mexico. NAFTA is often used in place of the US as the North American element of the triad. Also Asia can be used in place of Japan to reflect the size and growth of markets such as China, India, and Indonesia. Table 1 shows the breakdown of world trade by region. World trade is the sum of all exports and imports. The EU is the biggest "trader" accounting for 35 percent of world trade, with Asia at 25 percent and North America at 22 percent.

Foreign direct investment (FDI) is capital invested in other nations by MNEs through their control of their foreign subsidiaries and affiliates. Most of the world's FDI is invested both by and within the triad. This has implications for the pattern of trade and industrial activity and is a highly controversial issue (see, e.g., the discussions at the Cancun meeting of the World Trade Organization about access by underdeveloped regions and countries to the rich markets of the OECD countries). The US is an excellent example of a country that is a major target of investment as well as a major investor in other countries. In 1999 nearly $990 billion was invested in the US, and the US itself (through its MNEs) invested over $1,132 billion in all other countries. Table 2 shows a breakdown of US inward and outward FDI by region. This demonstrates the concentration of Europe and Asia.

Trade and investment are subject to various rules and procedures. There are many international or supranational bodies that help to set trading rules and resolve trade disputes. For example:

Table 1 World trade, 2000

	Imports $ billion	%	Exports $ billion	%	World trade $ billion	%
North America	1692.8	25.6	1213.6	19.15	2906.4	22.4
EU	2284.9	34.6	2283.0	35.8	4567.9	35.2
Asia	1563.5	23.7	1742.6	27.4	3306.1	25.5
Others	1067.5	16.2	1129.5	17.7	2197.0	16.9
Total	66087.7		6368.7		12977.6	

Source: adapted from Rugman and Hodgetts (2003: 6)

Table 2 US: inward and outward FDI, 1999

$ billion	Into US	From US
Total	987	1133
Europe	686	582
Latin America	45	223
Africa	2	15
Middle East	7	11
Asia and Pacific	168	186

Source: adapted from Rugman and Hodgetts (2003: 8)

- *The Organization for Economic Cooperation and Development* (OECD) is a group of the 30 wealthiest countries that provides a forum for the discussion of economic, social, and governance issues across the world.
- *The World Trade Organization* (WTO) is an international body that deals with the rules of trade among member countries. One of its most important functions is to act as a dispute-settlement mechanism.
- *The General Agreement on Tariffs and Trade* (GATT) is a major trade organization that has been established to negotiate trade concessions among member countries.

The patterns of trade and investment are highly significant and are reflected in the nature of MNEs. The United Nations has identified over 60,000 MNEs, but the largest 500 account for 80 percent of all FDI. Of these 500, 430 are from triad countries (interpreted narrowly to mean the US, EU, and Japan); 185 come from the US, 141 from the EU, and 104 from Japan. This means that the triad is a basic unit of analysis for international strategy. It also means that for MNEs the actions and policies of a few key countries are highly important for their corporate strategies (*see* CORPORATE STRATEGY). Countries are concerned to maintain and foster their own economic competitiveness. Countries have strong incentives to invest in physical infrastructure and in human capital. In doing so, they hope to provide conditions under which business and trade can prosper and macroeconomic goals such as low employment, low inflation, and high growth can be sustained.

GLOBAL COMPANIES AND THE INTERNATIONALIZATION PROCESS

Table 3 indicates the degree of internationalization of Fortune 100 companies. Although we have a reasonably clear concept of what constitutes global at the industry level, it is much harder to distinguish a "global" firm from any other. From table 3 we can see that many firms have a high proportion of sales and production abroad. But there are deeper levels of internationalization. Table 3 picks out research and development, management style, and membership of boards of directors as indicators of the extent to which firms can transcend national boundaries.

The MNE has two areas of concern, its home country and its host country/countries. The linkages across these areas are in the end manifested by the cash flows across country boundaries. These are influenced by home and host government policies and by the actions of supranational bodies in setting trade rules and regulations. Rugman and Hodgetts (2003: 39–40) identify three main characteristics of MNEs:

1 MNEs have to be responsive to a number of forces across and within countries, some of which are competition-related (as per the five forces; *see* INDUSTRY STRUCTURE) and some of which are government related (as per the diamond; *see* NATIONAL COMPETITIVE ADVANTAGE);

Table 3 Degree of internationalization of Fortune 100 companies (early 1990s)

- ca. 40 companies generate > 50% of sales abroad
- < 20 companies maintain > 50% of production capacity abroad
- 13 companies have > 10% of shareholdings abroad
- R&D remains firmly domestic
- Executive boards and management styles remain solidly national
- Almost all highly internationalized companies originate from "small" economies:
  - Netherlands: Philips, Royal Dutch/Shell (60% Dutch), Unilever (40% Dutch)
  - Sweden: Volvo, Electrolux, ABB (50% Swedish)
  - Switzerland: Nestlé, Ciba-Geigy, ABB (50% Swiss)

2 MNEs draw on a common pool of resources that are typically found in the home country and that are made available throughout the MNE's affiliates;
3 MNEs link their operations through a common strategic vision and a unified international strategy (*see* GLOBAL STRATEGIES).

Figure 1 illustrates the stages by which companies enter into foreign markets and eventually become full-blown MNEs. Domestic firms go through a process of learning about foreign markets and minimizing the risks attached to them. Licensing, for example, gives access to the firm's standardized products for distribution by third parties in new markets. Similarly, export gains access to markets initially through independent local sales agents. If exports to particular countries become sufficiently large, then there is the possibility to set up one's own sales force. This is an important stage. It marks the arrival of sales in sufficient quantities to gain efficiencies from the fixed costs of own sales activities. It also represents a stage at which direct contact with customers becomes possible with potential for customization and differenti-

ation. It also results in familiarity at first hand with local conditions and could lead to direct investment in production and marketing and possible other value chain activities. This stage of FDI is what marks out an MNE from other domestically rooted companies. At this stage there is a risk investment in a new territory and the MNE has to manifest the three characteristics shown above, namely, local responsiveness, distinctive central resources, and an overarching strategy.

There are many reasons why companies decide to take the plunge and accept the new, often unfamiliar risks facing a multinational company. The usual reasons are:

- to diversify against the risks and uncertainties of the domestic (home-country) business cycle;
- to tap into new and growing markets;
- to "follow" competitors;
- to reduce costs by (a) building larger volumes and gaining scale effects; (b) gaining access to lower factor costs; and (c) "internalizing" control by eliminating intermediaries and other TRANSACTIONS COSTS;
- to overcome barriers to trade; and

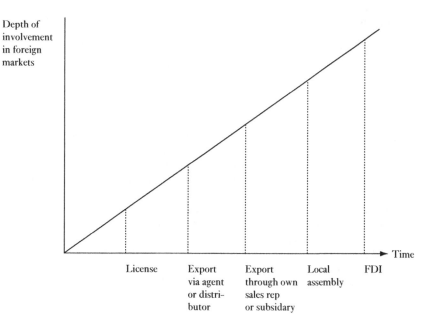

Figure 1 The internationalization process

- to protect intellectual property rights by undertaking value chain activities in-house rather than giving third parties access through licensing and sales agreements.

See also *competitive advantage; global strategic advantage; globalization; managing international organizations; national competitive advantage*

Bibliography

Rugman, A. M. and Hodgetts, R. M. (2003). *International Business*, 3rd edn. London: Financial Times/Prentice-Hall.

internationalization process

see INTERNATIONAL BUSINESS

investment intensity

Kevin Jagiello and Gordon Mandry

Over the long term many capital-intensive businesses, especially those involved in basic industries, achieve wholly inadequate rates of return on the capital they employ. Around the world examples abound in what are becoming known as SCRAP industries sectors, to which list could readily be added many businesses involved in construction materials such as flat glass; agricultural commodities such as palm oil or wheat; extractive industries such as tin, coal, and soda ash; and many fields of transportation, typified by the malaise in passenger airlines around the globe.

That these sectors have experienced periods of attractive return or that certain competitors manage to break out is not in question. What remains observable, however, is that over the long term the typical level of performance for the majority is totally inadequate.

The extent to which capital-intensive businesses underperform the norm in the PROFIT IMPACT OF MARKET STRATEGY (PIMS) database is explored in order to develop the reasons for that underperformance.

DEFINING INVESTMENT INTENSITY

Capital or "investment intensity" is defined as:

the net book value of plant and equipment plus working capital (i.e., total assets less current liabilities) expressed as a percentage of sales revenue or as a percentage of the value added generated by the business (where value added is defined as net sales revenue less all outside suppliers inputs).

In many instances, to obtain a balanced view on the underlying investment intensity of a business, both measures of investment intensity need to be employed. A business that has a low investment/sales ratio because it turns its asset base frequently may at the same time have a high investment/value-added ratio because its value added is low.

THE IMPACT OF INVESTMENT INTENSITY

What, then, is the typical profit performance of investment-intensive businesses when compared to the business universe? To answer this question, the 3,000 plus businesses in the PIMS database were divided into five equal groups on the basis of their average four-year level of investment/sales revenue and investment/value added and their profit performance observed in terms of pre-tax, pre-interest return on investment (ROI) and return on sales (ROS), as shown in figure 1.

It can be seen that, whichever measure of investment intensity is employed, ROI performance declines steeply as investment intensity rises. Businesses in the lower quintile of the distributions achieve approximately five times the ROI of their investment-intensive counterparts. When ROS is considered, the performance fall-off is again quite marked for the upper quintile of the distributions.

When taken at face value, the investment-intensity finding is not only of great importance for the business community, but also controversial in nature. Put simply, if profitability is the key concern, the argument runs that resources should be channeled away from investment-intensive businesses unless significant outperformance of the norm can be achieved.

WHY DO INVESTMENT-INTENSIVE BUSINESSES UNDERPERFORM?

What lies behind the investment-intensity finding? Is the effect more illusory than real? Several

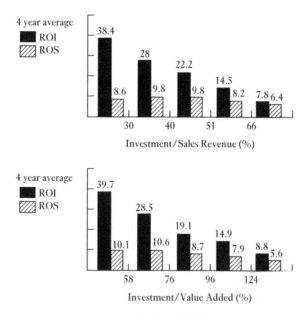

4 year average
■ ROI
▨ ROS

38.4

28

22.2

14.5

8.6 9.8 9.8 8.2 7.8 6.4

30   40   51   66

Investment/Sales Revenue (%)

4 year average
■ ROI
▨ ROS

39.7

28.5

19.1

14.9

10.1 10.6 8.7 7.9 8.8 5.6

58   76   96   124

Investment/Value Added (%)

Figure 1 Investment intensity is a severe drag on profitability (PIMS Associates)

plausible non-behavioral reasons can be put forward: the relationship is largely definitional; it reflects a managerial focus on ROS or absolute return; it captures the profit penalties of poor asset utilization or investing in new assets. Moreover, the relationship is exaggerated because it makes no allowance for investment grants, tax allowances or the like. Each hypothesis is examined in turn before considering possible behavioral explanators of the finding.

A definitional relationship. When the investment level in a business increases, it simultaneously increases the denominator of the ROI ratio, hence dragging down the value of the ratio. That there is more than a definitional relationship to the investment-intensity effect is demonstrated if we examine ROS in figure 1. If a business is to hold ROI as investment intensity increases, ROS should also increase smoothly. In practice, ROS is at best flat and in fact starts to tail off at higher levels of investment intensity. Moreover, "return" has been taken pre-tax, pre-interest, with no financial charge made on the amount of investment used in the business. If even a modest capital charge rate is applied to a business's returns to reflect its investment use,

the relationships in figure 1 would start to turn sharply down. If businesses with high levels of investment are not able to achieve profit margins sufficient to offset the higher level of investment that they need to sustain their sales, there must be more than just a definitial relationship at work.

Inappropriate managerial focus. It can be argued that management may be focusing on ROS or the absolute level of return achieved in the business irrespective of the heavier investment burden required to generate the sales. If this mindset is in place, it should be recognized that an adequate return on capital employed does not result. The more likely explanation is that management finds it cannot extract adequate returns over time because of the destructive nature of competition that typically accompanies high levels of investment intensity.

Poor utilization of investment. If a business is suffering from poor levels of capacity utilization, its investment intensity will rise and the finding may be capturing little more than businesses that are ineffectual users of their investment base. To check for this possibility, the average level of capacity utilization was tracked as investment

Table 1   Capacity utilization levels associated with investment intensity

	Values on PIMS database quintiles				
	Lower quintile		*Mean*		*Upper quintile*
Investment/sales revenue (%)	21	35	45	58	90
Capacity utilization (%)	75	75	76	76	75
Investment/value added (%)	44	67	86	109	163
Capacity utilization (%)	74	75	77	77	75

Source: PIMS Associates

intensity increased. As can be seen in table 1, no discernible differences were apparent.

This, of course, is not to argue that high-capacity utilization levels do not have a major benefit for investment-intensive businesses. When we examine the upper third of the PIMS database in terms of fixed capital intensity, businesses with utilization levels above 84 percent achieve on average an ROI of 19 percent, as opposed to an ROI of only 8 percent for those with utilization levels below 70 percent. Given this profit trap, it is readily apparent why management may adopt a defense of throughput mentality, even if margin has to be sacrificed and ultimately the return becomes inadequate to reflect the increased investment in the business.

Composition of the investment base.   Is the investment-intensity effect primarily due to the fixed capital or the working capital tied up in a business, or a function of both? It is shown in figure 2 that both drag on ROI in a similar manner.

The clear profit trap at 7 percent ROI is for businesses with high levels in each investment component. The double drag on profitability is mitigated when operating with low levels of one or the other.

The age of fixed assets may distort an investment measure taken at net book value. New fixed assets, especially if added at high replacement costs, would temporarily increase the ratio. No evidence of this effect is found in table 2.

In part, such effects will be smoothed because all analysis is based on four-year averages. Moreover, there may be a case that new fixed investment could in fact reduce the overall investment

ratio by generating a disproportionate amount of sales or value added.

Overstatement.   The magnitude of the investment-intensity problem may be overstated because of the measurement of "return" and "investment" employed here. Return has been taken pre-tax, pre-interest, hence making no allowance for tax breaks which encourage investment, and hence the after-tax return may be more favorable, notwithstanding interest charges. Investment in a business may be a harsh yardstick if part of that investment has been provided by grants or subsidies.

As PIMS data does not capture after-tax return or isolate the proportion of investment "given" to a business, no analysis to this end was

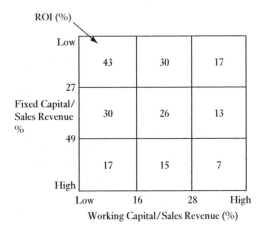

Figure 2   Both fixed and working capital drag on profitability (PIMS Associates)

Table 2   The nature of the investment base

	Values on PIMS database quintiles				
	Lower quintile		Mean		Upper quintile
Gross book value of plant and equipment/sales (%)	12	26	37	52	97
Newness of plant and equipment (net book/gross book) (%)	57	54	53	53	53
GBV replacement cost (%)	193	199	196	192	196

Source: PIMS Associates

performed. For this reason, the investment-intensity finding may or may not be overstated. The observation remains that as the investment used in a business increases, profitability declines. Managements who run businesses on the basis of tax breaks or investment allowances rather than on their intrinsic worth tread a dangerous path, running the risk of building on castles of sand.

The behavioral explanation.   The previous discussion shows that while there are definitional elements to the investment-intensity finding, there remains a significant element of the finding that is to be explained by behavioral factors.

With high levels of investment in a business, costs often become more fixed in nature with a high break-even resulting. The high levels of investment also raise exit costs. In this situation the key managerial task is to keep assets productive and highly utilized at adequate price levels. When marketplace occupancy levels sink below the break-even level, either because of too much capacity addition or because of a weakening in demand, the business becomes highly vulnerable to outside pressures in attempting to keep its investment working – it becomes a "buyers' market." Quite often under these conditions management has little alternative but to weaken on price to defend volume. Competitors faced with the same situation have little option but to match such moves, and profits spiral downward for all participants.

The problem is perhaps most acute, but not limited to, the base SCRAP industry settings, which are often caught by the twin pincers of

heightened investment intensity and reduced ability to differentiate. The situation comes about in low-growth markets, with technology played out and the ability to innovate and differentiate reducing. In order to become more cost competitive, managerial attention switches from product to process R&D. The change in emphasis further reduces the ability to differentiate, while process R&D invariably leads to a substitution of capital for labor. The twin pincers close; more investment intensive with a higher break-even without the ability to differentiate increases management's propensity to weaken on price. In its desperation to meet the new break-even, business is taken on the basis of contribution, with competitors readily able to respond on price. Destructive competition ensues and profitless prosperity results.

Once trapped it may be difficult to escape: the supply–demand imbalance may be long enduring; exit barriers are high; and competitors entrenched. Trying to escape the worst forms of price-based competition by seeking to differentiate the offer in some way is in the majority of cases no more than a comforting illusion. The incremental nature of innovation provides few opportunities to break out. Those that are found often require investment and cannot be "ring-fenced" from imitation – any edges achieved only give a short breathing space before being matched by competitors. If escape by price addition does not improve the margin equation, the hope is that a sustainable cost reduction on the back of a better technology will. With the technology largely played out, such leapfrogging is rare. Even where a step-wise technological advance is made, it remains difficult to keep it proprietary – the cost savings pass on to the market.

The management of an investment-intensive business also needs to be mindful of the potential double-profit penalty that can result when incurring substantial discretionary expenditure in its efforts to escape. Businesses in the upper third of the PIMS database in terms of investment intensity that incur heavy R&D (over 5.9 percent of sales revenue) or marketing (over 14.9 percent of sales revenue) expenditure achieve on average only a 4 percent ROI. The danger is that such high levels of expenditure are incurred but do not lead to a sustainable improvement in cost, price, or investment behavior which can be kept proprietary over the long term.

Overview

The investment-intensity phenomenon is real and damaging to business. It cannot be explained away as merely a definitional relationship. Heavy investment naturally leads to added anxieties about maintaining throughput. Faced with internal, market, and competitive pressures, management sacrifices margin and destructive forms of competition ensue. Once trapped, it is difficult to escape. Attempts to improve operating performance and marketplace position are difficult to sustain against able competitors in unfavorable market circumstances. The danger also remains that, in its efforts to escape the investment-intensity trap, management compounds its difficulties by its actions.

It should be recognized that while increased investment intensity damages a business, in many cases management has little choice but to do the "wrong thing" to stay competitive. When faced with this dilemma, management should not assume that increased investment will automatically improve profitability – rather, the reverse. Any increase in investment intensity that does not result in a major long-term advantage will exacerbate the problem. With heightened exit barriers the business is locked into a more unfavorable situation and management desperation increases.

The authors would like to acknowledge the assistance of John Hillier of the Strategic Planning Institute in researching the PIMS database.

Bibliography

Schoeffler, S., Buzzell, R. D., and Heany, D. F. (1974). Impact of strategic planning on profit performance. *Harvard Business Review*, 52, 137–45.

joint ventures

Derek F. Channon

Joint ventures may well prove to be a useful, and indeed necessary, way to enter some new markets, especially for multinational firms. In some markets that restrict inward investment, joint ventures may be the only way to achieve market access. Within joint ventures, clear equity positions are usually taken by the participants; such holdings can vary substantially in size, although it is usually important to establish clear lines of management decision-making control in order to achieve success.

A lesser form of participation, which may or may not involve equity participation, involves STRATEGIC ALLIANCES. Joint ventures do tend to have a relatively high failure rate. Nevertheless, they also enjoy a number of specific advantages.

ADVANTAGES OF JOINT VENTURES

First, for the smaller organization with insufficient finance and/or specialist management skills, the joint venture can prove an effective method of obtaining the necessary resources to enter a new market. This can be especially true in attractive developing country markets, where local contacts, access to distribution, and political requirements may make a joint venture the preferred, or even legally required, solution.

Second, joint ventures can be used to reduce political friction and local nationalist prejudice against foreign-owned corporations. Moreover, political rules may discriminate against subsidiaries that are fully foreign-owned, and in favor of local firms, through the placing of government contracts or through discriminating taxes and restrictions against foreign firms importing key materials, machinery, and components.

With the development of trading blocs such as the EU and NAFTA, intergovernmental negotiations have seen the introduction of tariff walls to protect the participants. As a result, despite the development of GATT, the use of joint ventures to gain access to trading bloc markets has increased, especially by firms from the Pacific Rim.

Third, joint ventures may provide specialist knowledge of local markets, entry to required channels of distribution, and access to supplies of raw materials, government contracts, and local production facilities. Japanese companies have actively exploited joint ventures for these purposes. Triad alliances have thus often led to Japanese manufacturers linking with European and/or North American manufacturers to provide badge engineered products, which have enhanced the global volume production of the Japanese suppliers and gained them access to western developed country markets without political friction. Similarly, after the first oil price shock, the Japanese moved swiftly to use joint ventures in order to gain access to secure supplies of oil. As a result, while western oil companies supplied some 80 percent of Japan's oil imports in 1973, by 1995 this had been reduced to around 25 percent, the balance being supplied via Japanese corporations operating via joint ventures.

Fourth, in a growing number of countries, joint ventures with host governments have become increasingly important. These may be formed directly with state-owned enterprises or directed toward national champions. Such ventures are common in the extractive and defense industries, where the foreign partner is expected to provide the necessary technology to aid the developing country partner.

Fifth, there has been growth in the creation of temporary consortium companies and alliances, to undertake particular projects that are considered to be too large for individual companies to handle alone. Such cooperations include new major defense initiatives, major civil engineering projects, new global technological ventures, and so on.

Finally, exchange controls may prevent a company from exporting capital and thus make the funding of new overseas subsidiaries difficult. The supply of know-how may therefore be used to enable a company to obtain an equity stake in a joint venture, where the local partner may have access to the required funds.

DISADVANTAGES OF JOINT VENTURES

Despite the advantages of joint ventures, there remain substantial dangers that need to be carefully considered before embarking on a joint venture strategy.

The first major problem is that joint ventures are very difficult to integrate into a global strategy (see GLOBAL STRATEGIES) that involves substantial cross-border trading. In such circumstances, there are almost inevitably problems concerning inward and outward transfer pricing and the sourcing of exports, in particular, in favor of wholly owned subsidiaries in other countries.

Second, the trend toward an integrated system of global cash management, via a central treasury, may lead to conflict with local partners when the corporate headquarters endeavors to impose limits or even guidelines on cash and working capital usage, foreign exchange management, and the amount, and means, of paying remittable profits. As a result, many multinationals that generate joint ventures may do so outside a policy of global strategy integration, making use of such operations to service restricted geographic territories or countries in which wholly owned subsidiaries are not permitted.

A third serious problem occurs when the objectives of the partners are, or become, incompatible. For example, the multinational corporation (MNC) may have a very different attitude to risk than its local partner, and may be prepared to accept short-term losses in order to build MARKET SHARE, to take on higher levels of debt, or to spend more on advertising. Similarly, the objectives of the participants may well change over time, especially when wholly owned subsidiary alternatives may occur for the MNC with access to the joint venture market.

Fourth, problems occur with regard to management structures and staffing of joint ventures. This is especially true in countries in which nepotism is common and in which jobs have to be found for members of the partner's families, or when employment is given to family members of local politicians or other locals in positions of influence. From the perspective of MNCs, seconded personnel may also be subject to conflicts of interest, in which the best actions for the joint venture might conflict with the strategy and objectives of the MNC shareholder.

Finally, many joint ventures fail because of a conflict in tax interests between the partners. Many of these could actually be overcome if they were thought through in advance; however, such problems are rarely foreseen. One common problem occurs as a result of startup losses. Due to past write-offs, accelerated depreciation, and so on, it is common for capital-intensive businesses to report operating losses in their first few years. It is therefore possibly more attractive for the local partner if these losses can be used to offset against other locally derived profits. To obtain such tax advantages, however, certain minimum levels of shareholdings may be necessary, and this may be in conflict with the aspirations of an MNC partner. The precise nature of the shareholding structure of joint ventures therefore needs to be considered at the formation stage in order to maximize fiscal efficiency and avoid this form of conflict.

THE JOINT VENTURE AGREEMENT

Because of the potential difficulties that can occur with joint ventures, they should be formulated carefully and the Articles of Association only drawn up after consideration of the objectives and strategies of the participants, both at the time of formation and as they might reasonably be expected to evolve in the future. Furthermore, such an agreement should set out, in clear language, the rights and obligations of the participants, taking care that differences in interpretation due to translation are not introduced when more than one language is used. The country of jurisdiction under which any disputes would be settled also needs to be clearly stated. The joint venture agreement should then cover the following points:

- the legal nature of the joint venture and the terms under which it can be dissolved;
- the constitution of the board of directors and the voting power of the partners;
- the managerial rights and responsibilities of the partners;
- the constitution of the management and appointment of the managerial staff;
- the conditions under which the capital can be increased;
- constraints on the transfer of shares or subscription rights to non-partners;
- the responsibilities of each of the partners in respect of assets, finance, personnel, R&D, and the like;
- the financial rights of the partners with respect to dividends and royalties;
- the rights of the partners with respect to the use of licenses, know-how, and trademarks in third countries;
- limitations, if any, on sales of the joint venture's products to certain countries or regions;
- an arbitration clause indicating how disputes between partners are to be resolved;
- the conditions under which the Articles of the joint venture agreement may be changed;
- consideration of how the joint venture can be terminated.

Bibliography

Channon, D. F. and Jalland, M. (1979). *Multinational Strategic Planning*. London: Amacom/Macmillan, pp. 200–6.

Farok, C. and Lorange, P. (1988). Why should firms cooperate? In C. Farok and P. Lorange (eds.), *Cooperative Strategies in International Business*. Lexington, MA: Lexington Books.

Harrigan, K. R. (1985). *Strategies for Joint Ventures*. Lexington, MA: D. C. Heath.

just-in-time

Derek F. Channon

In the face of substantially superior productivity and lower cost, as a result of low MARKET SHARE and high experience effect (*see* EXPERIENCE AND LEARNING EFFECTS) costs, Japanese car producers sought ways to gain COMPETITIVE ADVANTAGE against their major US competitors. On a visit to the US in the 1950s, the production director of Toyota Motors, Taichi Ohno, observed the replenishment pattern of shelves in US supermarkets, which were only refilled when they became empty. As a result, stocks could be significantly reduced, provided that deliveries of replenishments arrived at the moment of stockout. From this observation, the concept of "just-in-time" (JIT) production was born which, together with increasing labor productivity, resulted in Toyota ultimately gaining competitive advantage over the company's American rivals. The system developed at Toyota was also rapidly copied by other Japanese car makers, and by producers in many other indigenous industries.

The key to JIT is to produce (or deliver) the right items in the quantity required by subsequent production processes (or customers) at the time needed. As a result, buffer stocks of work in progress (WIP) and the like can be eliminated. The system also seeks to coordinate the final assembly activity to coincide with customer demand and so eliminate the need for finished goods stocks. While market share has been identified as an important factor in business unit profitability, other variables – notably fixed and working capital intensity – have been determined also to be powerful determinants of profitability such that they can eliminate the potential advantage of superior share. Thus Toyota, in competing against General Motors, used lower capital intensity brought about by JIT production systems as a key variable to establish competitive advantage.

However, the total JIT system involves more than simply inventory management. Rather, it is a comprehensive strategy to create competitor advantage via production. This is achieved as follows.

INVENTORY MANAGEMENT

A key element in JIT production is the reduction or elimination of WIP, so as to reduce the finished goods inventory. The result of successful implementation of such a strategy is a substantial reduction in capital intensity, which results in a

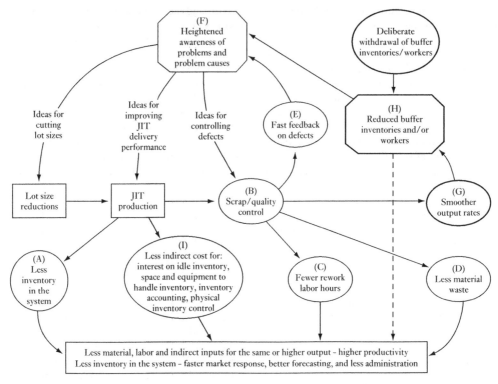

Figure 1　The effects of JIT production (Schonberger, 1982)

major improvement in return on equity. JIT exposes problems in identifying ways in which inventory can be reduced, and Japanese corporations aim for lot sizes that are considerably less than one day's supply. Moreover, small lot sizes reduce cycle inventory which, in turn, helps to cut lead times. While these reductions in WIP and stocks of finished goods reduce operating costs, potential problems with suppliers increase the element of risk. Hence a critical ingredient in JIT production systems involves the development of a close interdependence with important suppliers.

COMPETITIVE PRIORITIES

Low cost and consistent quality are the two production priorities that are emphasized most. As a result, Japanese producers seek to provide products such as automobiles with high-level specifications as standard, rather than slowing production lines by providing customized products.

POSITIONING STRATEGY

Under JIT, a product focus is selected to achieve high-volume, low-cost production. The workforce and capital equipment are organized around product flows which, in turn, are arranged to conform to work operations.

PROCESS DESIGN

The use of small lot sizes adds substantially to cost. This problem is especially important in fabrication industries. A solution is to design the process to minimize setup costs. Indeed, the implications of extra capital cost to carry EXCESS CAPACITY versus extra operating costs need to be carefully evaluated.

A further solution is to reduce setup frequency. Thus Japanese manufacturers may well be prepared to give away features on their products in order to reduce the cost of changeovers, rather than adopting a product line that has a number of variable features that require different production runs.

If costs are to be constrained, the workforce also needs to be flexible, thus helping to absorb shocks in production which are not dampened by inventory buffers. This may require significant investment in education and training.

A product focus also helps to reduce setup frequency and corresponding costs. This can be a significant ingredient in establishing the overall cost structure. When volume is insufficient to insure a revenue stream, technology may be used to reduce costs by producing components with common features on a common, small-volume production line. Changeover costs from one component to another are therefore reduced. A final method of reducing setup costs is to use an approach in which one worker operates several machines, each of which advances the production process by one step at a time. The Japanese also make considerable use of automation to reduce costs; they have installed around six to eight times the number of robots per head compared with other industrialized countries. The Japanese workforce is also trained to be flexible and, with enterprise unions, does not suffer from the restrictive practices found in some countries.

WORKFORCE MANAGEMENT

In the Japanese system, decisions normally undertaken in the West by management are influenced by the workforce. Virtually everyone is engaged in quality circles, which form one element in job enlargement. While the workforce is normally concerned with continuous operational improvements and management with planning investment improvements, inevitably the two spheres overlap. In some companies, meetings to discern methods of cost reduction actually take place on a daily basis. Workers are also rotated, with the best being trained as generalists rather than lesser performers. Decision-making in such an environment also tends to take place by consensus, rather than the confrontation that often occurs in the West. The status difference between all workers is also reduced, as are salary differentials.

EXCESS CAPACITY

As well as reducing inventory to the absolute minimum, Japanese concerns also attempt to eliminate excess capacity, which is seen as a form of waste.

SUPPLIER MANAGEMENT

Close relationships are forged between manufacturers and component suppliers. These too are expected to drive for continuous productivity gains and thereby reduced costs, to minimize stocks through the application of JIT systems, and to locate close to a manufacturer's plant. Any necessary buffer stock is the responsibility of the supplier. Similarly, suppliers take responsibility for component quality, so obviating the need for inward goods quality checks. In return, manufacturers maintain close relationships with suppliers and a steady level of production output.

PRODUCTION SCHEDULING

To reduce disruptions that might hinder inventory reduction, components are standardized as much as possible, even though final products may appear to be customized. Component standardization increases volumes, which provides experience gains as well as reducing inventory. Second, production schedules are standardized and lot sizes for final products are very small. Daily output for a month tends to be the same, and only then is adjusted for forecast errors and inventory imbalances.

PRODUCT QUALITY

Quality is seen as being everyone's concern and is paramount to the management of a JIT system. Workers are all given the opportunity to stop the production line at the first sign of a quality defect, while machines operate autonomation, or *jidoka*, whereby the machine will automatically stop if it begins to produce output outside specification. Under the line-stop system, supervisors and/or engineers rush to the trouble spot to correct the problem. While in the early stages of production setup this slows down production, ultimately the line speeds up, rework is minimized, quality is established, and productivity is improved.

Much control is established by correct plant layout rather than by sophisticated computerized control systems. For example, Japanese factories make considerable use of visual controls such as "*Andon*" or lantern lights which help to expose abnormal conditions, buzzers, video cameras, and "line of sight" to rapidly identify and relay information.

Production Control Boards

Throughout Japanese factories, the performance of work groups is made readily accessible through the extensive use of visual displays of performance, such as statistical control charts. These measure performance against agreed targets and are completed by workers themselves. In most western concerns, the collection of control data tends to be undertaken by accounting functions for management and the workforce is not kept fully informed about their performance.

Bibliography

Krajewski, L. J. and Ritzman, L. P. (1987). *Operations Management*. Reading, MA: Addison-Wesley.

Schonberger, R. J. (1982). *Japanese Manufacturing Techniques*. New York: Free Press.

Suzaki, K. (1985). Comparative study of JIT/TQC activities in Japanese and western companies. First World Congress of Production and Inventory Control, Vienna.

Suzaki, K. (1987). *The New Manufacturing Challenge*. New York: Free Press.

kaizen

Derek F. Channon

The Japanese term *kaizen* means "continuous improvement" and is an all-embracing concept covering JUST-IN-TIME, TOTAL QUALITY CONTROL (TQC), and KANBAN. It applies at all levels in Japanese corporations. A *kaizen* program can be subdivided into three areas based on complexity and hierarchical level:

- management-oriented *kaizen*;
- group-oriented *kaizen*;
- individual-oriented *kaizen*.

MANAGEMENT-ORIENTED *KAIZEN*

Under the Japanese system, continuous improvement is considered to be an activity that involves everyone. Managers are expected to devote half their time to seeking ways to improve their job, and the jobs of the personnel for whom they are responsible. Sometimes these tasks become blurred, as blue-collar workers also come up with ways of changing production processes as part of their own *kaizen* programs, whereas this task is technically the responsibility of management.

The *kaizen* projects undertaken by management involve problem-solving expertise and professional and engineering knowledge. Particular use is made of the "seven statistical tools." These are used by managers, but are also displayed within the factory and at the level of the work group. These tools (some of which are described in greater detail elsewhere) are as follows:

1 *Pareto diagrams.* These classify problems according to cause and phenomenon, nor-mally with 80 percent of cost being accounted for by 20 percent of factors (*see* PARETO ANALYSIS).

2 *Cause and effect diagrams.* Also called "fishbone diagrams," these are used to analyze the characteristics of a process and the factors that determine them.

3 *Histograms.* These display the data from measurements concerning the frequency of an activity, a process, and so on.

4 *Control charts.* Two types are in use; they detect abnormal trends with the help of line graphs. Sample data are plotted to evaluate process situations and trends.

5 *Scatter diagrams.* Data concerning two variables are plotted to demonstrate the relationship between them.

6 *Graphs.* These depict quantitative data in readily recognizable visual form: a variety of graphic displays are used. Graphic displays are widely used in Japanese culture, compared with western reliance on numerical tabulations.

7 *Checksheets.* These are designed to tabulate the outcome through routine checking of a situation.

These statistical tools are used by all levels within the organization, are prominently displayed throughout working areas, and all personnel are trained to use them.

Opportunities for improvement are to be found everywhere. However, *kaizen* is also the application of detail – each contribution may be small, but the cumulative effect is dramatic. In particular, *kaizen* is concerned with waste elimination, just-in-time, and TQC. Management-oriented *kaizen* may also involve group activities: ad hoc and temporary organizational units, such as *kaizen* teams, project groups, and task forces, may be created to undertake a specific task, and then dispersed upon its-completion.

GROUP-ORIENTED *KAIZEN*

In group work, *kaizen* is achieved via quality circles and other small group activities that use statistical techniques to solve problems. It also involves workers operating the full PDCA cycle and requires the groups to identify problems, analyze them, implement and test new practices, and establish new working standards. Groups are rewarded not so much with money as with prestige. Group achievements are communicated throughout the organization, partially via cross-functional structures: groups engaged in one business activity, and evaluating tasks similar to those of other groups, are expected to learn from one another in order to maximize productivity.

At all levels in the Japanese corporation, these small groups are no longer informal but, rather, have become an integral component of continuous improvement. The advantages of this practice are seen as follows:

- the setting of group objectives and working toward their achievement reinforces the sense of teamworking;
- members share and coordinate their respective roles better;
- labor–management communication is improved;
- morale is improved;
- workers acquire more skills and develop cooperative attitudes;
- the group becomes self-sustaining and solves problems that are normally considered the province of management;
- labor–management relations are significantly improved.

INDIVIDUAL-ORIENTED *KAIZEN*

At this level, *kaizen* involves the individual identifying ways of improving the productivity of the job. In particular, individuals contribute via the use of suggestion schemes. While in the West such schemes tend to be poorly supported, in Japan targets are now set for the number of suggestions to be contributed by work groups

and individuals. As a result, in large corporations the number of suggestions can amount to many millions, and each year the number increases. When sharp appreciation of the yen has taken place, as in 1987 and 1994–5, the number of suggestions has increased dramatically – in part because workers were hired under the assumption of permanent employment – in an attempt to maintain relative COMPETITIVE ADVANTAGE. The main areas for suggestions in the Japanese system have been identified as follows:

- improvements in one's own work;
- savings in energy, materials, and other resources;
- improvements in the working environment;
- improvements in jigs and tools;
- improvements in office working practices;
- improvements in product quality;
- ideas for new products;
- customer services and customer relations.

Kaizen policies are the norm in Japanese corporations. While sharp increases in the exchange rate make Japanese practices less competitive from time to time, the positive response of the workforce as a result of *kaizen* programs attempts to rapidly restore the Japanese productivity advantage. The low level of fear of forced redundancy has a significant impact on workers who, basically, may well suggest ideas which – if implemented – might actually eliminate their own jobs.

Bibliography

Cooper, R. (1994). *Sumitomo Electric Industries Ltd: The Kaizen Program*. Case Study 9-195-078. Boston: Harvard Business School.
Masaaki, I. (1986). *Kaizen*. New York: McGraw-Hill.

kanban

Derek F. Channon

Literally translated, *kanban* means "visible record." More generally, it is taken to mean "card." The system was developed by Taichi Ohno of Toyota Motors, the founder of JUST-IN-TIME (JIT), and based on the practice, within US supermarket groups, of replenishing stocks within stores only when they were approaching stockout.

In the *kanban* system developed at Toyota, every component or part has its own special container designed to hold a specific number of parts, preferably a small quantity. Each container has two *kanban* cards, which identify the part number and container capacity, amongst other information. The first of these, the production *kanban*, serves the work center producing the part, while the other, called a conveyance *kanban*, serves the user receiving center. Each container moves from the production area and its stock point to the using workstation and its stock point and back, with one *kanban* being replaced during the traffic flow.

Within the *kanban* system, the work section using a component effectively pulls through the next consignment in the following sequence:

1 The consuming work group picks up components as required.
2 The *kanban* cards are placed in a box.
3 These are sent to a warehouse or to a previous process. As components are picked up to resupply the using group, most cards are exchanged for the production cards attached to the components.
4 As the exchange takes place, production cards are collected in another *kanban* box.
5 The selected components are brought back to the user unit with move cards attached to them.
6 The production cards are brought back to the component manufacturing unit, where only the amount indicated by the production cards will be produced.
7 When production is completed, the production cards are attached to those goods produced.
8 Goods are transferred to the warehouse, thus ending the cycle.

Level/mixed production scheduling helps to smooth the flow throughout the factory. When *kanban* is introduced and a downstream process experiences fluctuating demand, all the upstream processes need to have adequate and flexible capacity to absorb such fluctuations. As a result, smoothing out any such fluctuations becomes an element in *kanban* management,

functioning as a tool for fine-tuning of production while linking all of the processes in a chain. For successful implementation, a number of factors need to be taken into account:

*   the sales/marketing function and production need to collaborate to determine the production schedule for final assembly to insure level/mixed production;
*   a *kanban* route through the factory needs to be carefully established;
*   to develop a steady flow and level/mixed production, usage of *kanban* should be tied to small lot production and frequent changeover;
*   for seasonal or promotional items, or in the startup phase of a new product, where substantial take-up volume fluctuations may occur, coordination with the sales/marketing function becomes essential;
*   the entire *kanban* system needs to be updated when long-term changes in demand occur;
*   a reliable rational production system is essential for the successful use of a *kanban* system.

In using the *kanban* system, a number of specific rules apply:

*   workers from a downstream process should obtain parts from the upstream process according to the information described on the *kanban* move card;
*   workers in the production process should produce parts according to the information on the *kanban* production card;
*   if there is no *kanban* card, there is no production and no transfer of components;
*   the *kanban* card must always be attached to the parts container unless it is in transit;
*   workers should insure that 100 percent of the parts produced are of the required quality; otherwise, the production line should be halted until defects are corrected;
*   the number of *kanban* cards should be gradually reduced in order to better link processes and to eliminate waste.

LIMITATIONS OF *KANBAN*

Kanban is feasible in almost any plant that produces goods in whole units, but not in process industries. It is beneficial in the following circumstances:

- *kanban* should be an element of JIT systems;
- the parts included in the *kanban* system should be used every day; companies using the system generally apply it to the high-use parts but replenish low-use items by means of conventional western techniques;
- very expensive or large items should not be included in *kanban*; such items are expensive to store and carry and should be regulated carefully.

Bibliography

Kiyoshi, S. (1987). *The New Manufacturing Challenge.* New York: Free Press.
Schonberger, R. J. (1982). *Japanese Manufacturing Techniques.* New York: Free Press.

keiretsu structure

Derek F. Channon

This is a specific structural form found in Japan. It occurs essentially in both horizontal and vertical forms, although groupings are also found in production and distribution. There are six main horizontal *keiretsu*: Mitsubishi, Mitsui, Sumitomo, Sanwa, Fuji, and Dai Ichi Kangyo. The first three of these are industrial groups which are based on the leading prewar Japanese ZAI-BATSU STRUCTURE, family-based industrial groups whose origins date back to Japan's initial industrialization. Originally each *zaibatsu* had a central holding company (*see* HOLDING COMPANY STRUCTURE) which set strategy. After World War II, the holding companies were eliminated, but the post-occupation Japanese government later allowed the industrial groups to reform, led by Mitsubishi. By the end of the 1950s, the historic *zaibatsu*-based groups had created Presidents' Councils as coordinating vehicles, and the groups had integrated, in part by taking cross-shareholdings in one another, as a protective device against possible hostile takeover bids. The other three major *keiretsu* groups developed during the 1960s, each based on the nucleus of one of the major city banks (strictly, the Dai Ichi Kangyo group is based on the

merger of two groups, following the creation of the Dai Ichi Kangyo bank from the merger of the Dai Ichi and Nippon Kangyo banks). A further industrial group also exists, centered on the Industrial Bank of Japan (IBJ). However, the participants in this group, which includes most major Japanese corporations, do not have the same relationship with the bank and are also members of one of the other horizontal groups. A horizontal *keiretsu* group is illustrated in figure 1.

There are several characteristics of these industrial groups that make them different to western structures.

First, they all contain financial service companies which can provide finance to other members when necessary: each contains a commercial bank, a trust bank, and a life insurance company. Historically, the commercial bank took in short-term deposits and lent short to medium term. In more recent times, and especially outside Japan, these organizations have mirrored their western competitors and added investment banking services. The trust bank took in long-term funds and would lend long. Similarly, the life insurance company would also provide long-term loan funds. While the internal financial concerns do not provide all of the funds needed within an industrial group, and there is a restriction of a maximum of 5 percent of total shares in any company that can be held by a bank, they do provide a special, formal relationship between the industrial members and the financial sector, quite unlike the position in western structures.

Second, each group contains at least one trading company, known as the SOGA SHOSHA. These act as trading companies, intelligence gatherers, financiers, and project coordinators in a way that can support other group members. In turn, the other group members form a cross-section of the economy: thus there will be a chemical company, a metal manufacturer, a heavy engineering concern, and the like.

Third, the cross-shareholdings between group members make it virtually impossible for external institutions to subject group members to predatory acquisition threats (*see* ACQUISITION STRATEGY). The linkages between a number of Mitsubishi Group companies are shown in figure 2. Shares in the trading

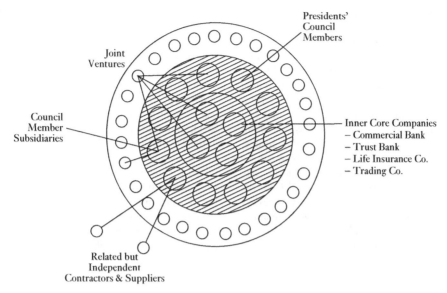

Figure 1   A Japanese horizontal *keiretsu* group

company Mitsubishi Corporation are held by member companies such as Mitsubishi Bank, Tokio Marine and Fire Insurance, and Mitsubishi Heavy Industries. In all, about one-third of the company's shares are held by other Mitsubishi Group concerns. In turn, the trading company owns shares in other Mitsubishi companies.

By contrast to western CORE BUSINESS strategies, *keiretsu* groups have tended to continue to increase their level of DIVERSIFICATION. Where new business areas develop, such as ocean mining, it would be quite natural for a *keiretsu* to enter the industry by forming a separate jointly owned subsidiary to exploit such a market opportunity; again, as in the case of fusion technologies, bringing together the elements of such a technology from across the group to create a new subsidiary.

Fourth, in the case of economic adversity in a particular member company, other group members will rally to its support, the financial members providing monetary assistance, while other group members might provide employment on a "loan" basis. In addition, personnel may be assigned to subsidiaries or affiliates. Usually, the major group companies send their managers to lower-order companies as senior

officers or directors. The bank in particular will often send a senior executive, as CEO, to any group member in financial difficulty. The average rates of directors sent by group members among the six major groups in 1990 were around 60 percent, with the highest rate being 97 percent for Mitsubishi and the lowest 41 percent for Mitsui. In addition to appointments from within, the leading group companies also employ senior retiring government civil servants (this process is known as *amakudari* or "the descent from heaven").

Fifth, while each group will have many hundreds of members, there is a leading group of

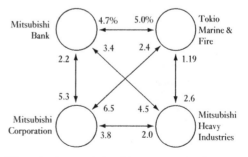

Figure 2   Japanese industrial group cross-shareholdings (Dodwell Marketing Consultants, 1992)

companies within the structure which form the Presidents' Council, or *Shacho-Kai*. The number of companies represented in such a structural element varies substantially, depending upon the roots of the *keiretsu*. Ideally, such a council should contain one representative from each industry. In the Mitsubishi Group this is approximately the case; but in the Dai Ichi Kangyo Group this is not so, as this group results from the merger of two major groups, each of which had its own set of companies. The councils meet regularly, on a specific day in each month. While the Presidents' Councils do not set specific group strategy, they do review external factors that affect member companies. The leader of the Presidents' Council in each individual group tends to come from one of a limited number of core companies, which varies

between groups. In addition, other regular meetings occur between group member companies at vice-presidential level, and between specialists in planning and public relations.

Vertical *keiretsu* are groups in which there is a vertical relationship between a core company and its supplying subsidiaries or associates. Typical examples would be the Toyota, Nippon Steel, and Matsushita Groups. The structure of the Toyota Group, which consists of the automobile manufacturer, its sales unit, and its suppliers, is shown in figure 3. While some of the subsidiaries are wholly owned, others are not; but Toyota may have a shareholding and an extremely close relationship. Such groups emphasize industries in which the parent companies are involved. Subsidiaries and affiliates are usually controlled by shareholdings and/or

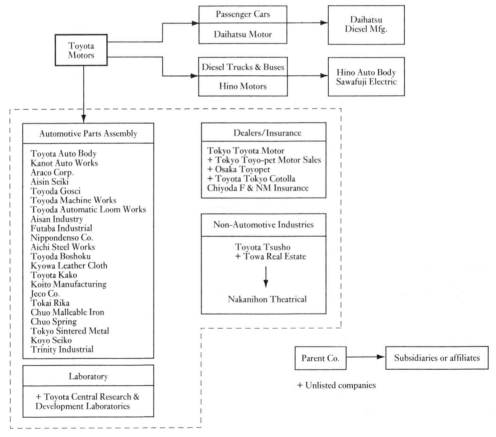

Figure 3 A vertical *keiretsu* group – the Toyota Motor Group (Dodwell Marketing Consultants, 1992)

the appointment of the CEO and/or other directors.

Keiretsu groups also occur in Japan within the service industry sector, such as the Seibu–Saison Group, which incorporates financial services, department stores, food retailers, entertainment, restaurants, hotels, and transportation.

The *keiretsu* form of organization found so extensively in Japan is unique to that country, and is a key element of the ability of Japanese companies to take a longer-term view. It contrasts with the stock market pressures experienced by western companies, which have forced them to modify strategy in many cases and adopt structures that emphasize short-term profitability. The nearest equivalent to the *keiretsu* is probably the CHAEBOL STRUCTURE of Korea.

Bibliography

Chen, M. (1995). *Asian Management Systems*. London: Routledge.

Dodwell Marketing Consultants (1992, 1994). *Japanese Industrial Groups*. Tokyo: Dodwell Marketing Consultants.

Tokyo Business Today (1989). Intimate links with Japan's corporate groups. *Tokyo Business Today*, January, 14–19.

knowledge-based view

Taman Powell

Research into the RESOURCE-BASED VIEW and dynamic capabilities perspective is increasingly seeing knowledge as a vital resource, so much so that a separate conceptualization of the firm has emerged in the form of the knowledge-based view.

It is argued that knowledge is a key reason for the existence of firms; "what firms do better than markets is the sharing and transfer of the knowledge of individuals and groups within an organization" (Kogut and Zander, 1992). This view is in complete contrast to the more traditional economics-based perspectives that view the firm as an option "of last resort, to be employed when all else fails" (Williamson, 1991). This traditional argument is advanced despite the "ubiquity of organizations" (Simon,

1991), which prompted Simon to ask "[w]ouldn't 'organizational economy' be the more appropriate term?"

Knowledge is seen as potentially the most strategically important resource, though also potentially the most difficult to define. What exactly is knowledge? As noted by Grant (1996), this is a question that has intrigued some of the greatest thinkers from Plato to Popper without the emergence of a clear consensus. Not wanting to enter this debate at this point, I shall simply claim, somewhat tautologically, that knowledge is that which is known.

What makes knowledge particularly interesting is that it can be either explicit, i.e., the knowledge that can be articulated to others, or tacit, i.e., the knowledge embedded in people that they are not able to articulate. Polanyi (1966) famously characterized tacit knowledge when he said that "we know more than we can say that we know."

In terms of strategy, both explicit and tacit knowledge can be very important. It is generally argued, however, that tacit knowledge is more strategically important as it is embedded in people and extremely difficult for competitors to replicate. In resource-based view terminology, it is inimitable. The valuable tacit knowledge of experts is also largely rare and non-movable, therefore satisfying all the characteristics of a valuable resource in the resource-based view.

If we take a cooking metaphor, a great chef can develop a recipe that, when followed by an amateur cook, produces a dish that is almost unrecognizable from the original dish on which the recipe is based. In developing the recipe, the chef has included all the information that he or she was able to articulate about how to cook the dish, but the recipe lacks the tacit knowledge that is embedded in the chef. It is this knowledge that is difficult to copy and therefore strategically valuable.

Additionally, when we look at the need for resources to change over time to maintain their market relevance (as is the case with the dynamic capabilities perspective), we are implicitly assuming a level of learning for this change to occur. This learning that facilitates the change relates to knowledge. Lastly, people and their knowledge are also one of the most flexible resources to which a firm has access. People can change their knowledge over time, this also tying strongly with the dynamic capabilities perspective.

While tacit knowledge can pose challenges for competitors to replicate, it can equally pose challenges for the firm that possesses this knowledge to replicate it. Often firms have only a limited understanding of how they perform an activity, and what knowledge is embedded in this performance that makes it special.

While there will always be tacit knowledge in a firm, this does not mean that all tacit knowledge cannot be made explicit. Indeed, organizations spend a large amount of time, effort, and money to better understand their tacit knowledge, and in turn convert this tacit knowledge to explicit knowledge to share with other members of the firm.

Nonaka (1994), one of the leading voices in the knowledge-based view of the firm, has popularized the focus of knowledge in the firm. He views converting between tacit and explicit knowledge as one of the key challenges for firms to remain competitive. He terms the four conversions in figure 1.

Nonaka claims that organizational knowledge creation takes place when all four modes of

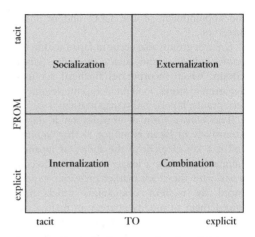

Figure 1   Converting between tacit and explicit knowledge (Nonaka, 1994)

knowledge creation are organizationally managed to form a continual cycle. This cycle is depicted in figure 2.

It is not argued that these knowledge conversions are easy, and indeed many organizations have been struggling with them in the form of knowledge management for a significant period of time. This difficulty, however, is one reason for the potential rewards that should accrue to

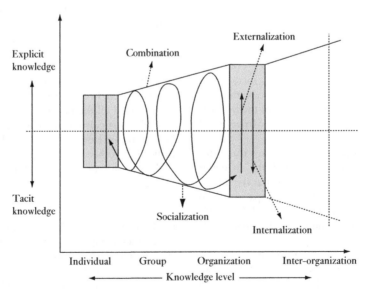

Figure 2   Managing the four modes of knowledge creation

those firms that are able to make positive steps in knowledge conversion.

Bibliography

Grant, R. M. (1996). Toward a knowledge-based theory of the firm. *Strategic Management Journal*, **17**, special issue, 109–22.

Kogut, B. and Zander, U. (1992). Knowledge of the firm, combinative capabilities, and the replication of technology. *Organization Science*, **3** (3), 383–98.

Nonaka, I. (1994). A dynamic theory of organizational knowledge creation. *Organization Science*, **5** (1), 14–37.

Polanyi, M. (1966). *The Tacit Dimension*. New York: Anchor.

Simon, H. A. (1991). Organizations and markets. *Journal of Economic Perspectives*, **5** (2), 25–45.

Williamson, O. E. (1991). Strategizing, economizing, and economic organization. *Strategic Management Journal*, **12** (8), 75–95.

leveraged buyouts

Derek F. Channon

Leveraged buyouts (LBOs) occur when the management of a company purchases it from existing shareholders and effectively becomes the owner. The target is typically a public company or a subsidiary of one which is taken private, with a significant portion of the cash purchase price being financed by debt. This debt is secured not by the credit status of the purchaser but by the assets of the target company. The debt used has usually been high-yield securities of substandard investment-grade quality, commonly referred to as "junk bonds." During the late 1980s and early 1990s in the US, and to some extent in western Europe, LBOs were very popular, and some financial institutions specialized in the issuance of junk bonds. With the arrival of the credit crunch of the mid-1990s and a number of highly visible failures amongst LBOs and investment banks, the movement lost ground.

An important criterion for an LBO is a gap between the existing market value of the firm and the value determined by a reappraisal of the assets or by the capitalization of expected cash flows. Moreover, after an LBO the incoming management is often able to achieve dramatic savings in the business's operating costs.

LBOs tend to be mature businesses with a demonstrable record of stable consistent earnings, a significant MARKET SHARE, and experienced in place management. Manufacturing and retailing businesses are attractive because they also contain a basis for asset-secured loans or stable income streams for unsecured or subordinated debt. Low capital-intensive service businesses are less popular because of their narrow asset bases.

LBOs are said to be attractive to all those involved. Typically, the target concern's top management approaches an investment banker with an LBO proposal. In some cases, specialist banks may take the initiative. The bankers then package an LBO deal, usually involving commercial bankers, insurance and finance companies, pension funds, and so on. The final deal will provide the incumbent management with the opportunity to purchase a stake in the common stock that is much greater than it would be able to obtain on the basis of its individual resources, provided that it can successfully secure the debt. Usually, however, the management group's resources still only provide a small percentage of the initial investment.

This equity gap led to the creation of a new form of financing known as mezzanine-level finance. Such lenders are often limited partnerships with wealthy investors, venture capitalists and pension funds as limited partners, supported by an investment banking firm acting as a general partner. In addition to investing in common equity, mezzanine lenders also hold securities senior to management equity but subordinate to secured debt. Most mezzanine financiers are short-to medium-term investors who expect to resell their share of the equity a few years after purchase to realize a substantial capital gain.

LBOs are far from risk-free. First, an LBO offer may serve to attract more bidders, although this is not a problem if the primary objective is to achieve the best value for existing shareholders. Second, and more important, is the risk of insolvency. Since revolving bank lending is a primary means of financing LBOs, they are very sensitive to increases in interest rates as a result of their highly leveraged position.

The risk of DIVERSIFICATION is also a potential problem. LBO firms tend to be relatively undiversified and from mature industries. The process of diversification, especially from a SINGLE BUSINESS STRATEGY or a DOMINANT BUSINESS STRATEGY, suffers a high failure rate. Furthermore, as LBOs revert to private status, results reporting becomes much less transparent than with publicly owned concerns, increasing the risk to lenders.

Bibliography

Diamond, S. C. (ed.) (1985). *Leveraged Buyouts*. Homewood, IL: Dow Jones Irwin.

Law, W. A. (1988). Leveraged buyouts. In J. P. Williamson (ed.), *Investment Banking Handbook*. New York: John Wiley.

Shaked, M. A. (1986). *Takeover Madness*. New York: John Wiley, ch. 3.

life-cycle strategy

Derek F. Channon

An alternative to the GROWTH SHARE MATRIX and COMPETITIVE POSITION–MARKET ATTRACTIVENESS MATRIX portfolio models was developed by Arthur D. Little, Inc. (hereafter, ADL) based on the concept of the life cycle, as illustrated in figure 1. As with the other portfolio models, the ADL approach first identifies the life-cycle position of a business as a descriptor of industry characteristics. Second, the competitive strength of a business is represented by six

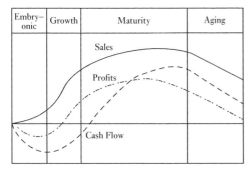

Figure 1   Yearly sales, cash flow, and profits through the industry life-cycle stages (Arthur D. Little, Inc.)

categories (dominant, strong, favorable, tenable, weak, and non-viable). The combination of these two variables is illustrated in figure 2 as a six by four matrix, on which the position of each business unit suggests a number of logical strategic alternatives, as shown. In using this system the corporation is first segmented into a series of relatively independent business units. Second, the life-cycle position of each business is carefully assessed (note that the product life cycle need not necessarily be the same as the business life cycle). Third, the competitive position of each business is carefully assessed.

The label "strategy center" was assigned by ADL to each business that others had defined as a strategic business unit (SBU) structure. To reach its conclusions on strategy centers, ADL defined them in terms of competitors, prices, customers, quality/style, substitutability, and DIVESTMENT or liquidation. The first four of these indicate that a strategy center contains a specific set of products for which it faces a specific set of customers and competitors that are also affected by price, quality, and style change. Moreover, all products within a strategy center should be close substitutes for one another. A strategy center could also probably survive as an independent business if divested.

The position of a business within its industry life cycle is determined by eight factors. These descriptions are market growth rate, market growth potential, breadth of product lines, number of competitors, distribution of MARKET SHARE among competitors, customer loyalty, barriers to entry (*see* BARRIERS TO ENTRY AND EXIT), and technology, as illustrated in table 1. Strategy centers do not usually fall into a single life-cycle phase for every descriptor, and some judgment therefore needs to be made as to the overall life-cycle position of a business. Embryonic businesses are usually characterized by high growth, rapid technological change, pursuit of a rapidly widening range of customers, fragmented and changing shares of market, and new competitor entries. By contrast, a mature industry is characterized by stability in known customers, technology, and market shares, with well-established and identifiable competitors. Interestingly, it is sometimes possible, usually as a result of technological change, to convert mature or emerging industries back into embry-

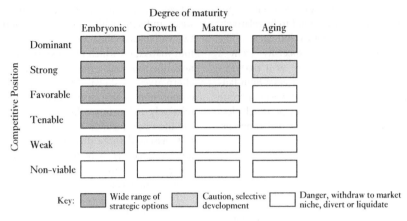

Figure 2   The life-cycle portfolio matrix (Arthur D. Little, Inc.)

onic industries. For example, in motor insurance, Direct Line Insurance transformed the industry over only eight years by selling policies direct and achieving a growth rate of ca. 70 percent per annum against the background of a relatively static growth rate for the industry as a whole. Most industries, however, work through the life cycle on a steady basis.

The competitive position of a business is assessed by ADL via a series of qualitative factors rather than the use of quantitative factors such as relative market share. Five categories of competitive position are identified: dominant, strong, favorable, tenable, and weak. The sixth position – non-viable – demands immediate or

rapid exit. A dominant position is rare, and comes about because a competitor has managed to establish a quasi-monopoly or has achieved technological dominance. Such positions could be claimed by IBM in computers and Kodak in color film. However, both positions have come under attack in recent years. IBM has failed to dominate the personal computer market which, because of technological advances, has become an increasing threat to IBM's core mainframe computer business (*see* CORE BUSINESS). Similarly, Kodak has begun to face a major threat from electronic digital imaging in its core business of amateur color film, a silver halide-based "wet" process activity. A "strong" business, by

Table 1   Factors affecting the stage of the industry life cycle for a strategy center

Descriptors	Stages of industry (maturity)			
	Embryonic	Growth	Mature	Aging
Growth rate				
Industry potential				
Product line				
Number of competitors				
Market share stability				
Purchasing patterns				
Ease of entry				
Technology				
OVERALL				

Source: Arthur D. Little, Inc.

contrast, enjoys a definite advantage over competitors, usually with a relative market share of greater than 1.5 times. "Favorable" means that a business usually enjoys a unique characteristic; for example, dominance of a specific niche, access to dedicated raw materials, or a special relationship with an important distribution channel. A "tenable" position means that the firm has the facilities to remain within a market but has no distinctive competence. Nevertheless, the position is such that survival is not a serious issue. Finally, a weak position is not tenable in the long term. Such businesses should either be developed to a more acceptable position or exited.

For portfolio balance using the life-cycle model, the firm needs a balanced mix of activities, with mature businesses generating a positive cash flow that can be used to support embryonic or growth operations. Success is also determined by having as many businesses as possible in dominant or favorable positions.

Once the portfolio of businesses has been determined, ADL has developed three further aids to assist managers of strategy centers in formulating strategy. The first of these concepts was labeled by ADL as *families of thrusts*. The consultants agreed that there were four families of activities which covered the spectrum of business development. These were "natural development," "selective development," "prove viability," and "withdrawal." The fit of each of these families is indicated in figure 3. A "natural development" position is likely to represent a position at industry maturity with a strong, competitive position which, as a result, justifies strong support to maintain or enhance the stra-

tegic position. A "selective development" strategy implies concentration of resources into attractive industry segments or where the firm has destructive COMPETITIVE ADVANTAGE. "Prove viability" status requires management to come up with a strategy that enhances strategic position or exit. "Withdrawal" clearly suggests exit, the speed of which needs to be clarified to avoid undue haste.

Having identified the family of strategic thrust that is most appropriate for a specific business, management is now challenged to select a specific strategic thrust for the business. For example, the following thrusts have been applied to the natural development family:

- *Startup* could be applied in an embryonic stage business to achieve a high share position while the market growth is high.
- *Growth with industry* applies when the firm is content with its industry position and seeks to maintain market share. This position prevails under dominant or strong conditions and at industry maturity.
- *Gain position gradually* is a stance that is applicable when a modest share increase is required to consolidate industry position.
- *Gain position aggressively* is similar to the double or quit position or question mark business (*see* QUESTION MARK BUSINESSES). The firm seeks to aggressively build share in an attractive industry while the growth rate remains high.
- *Defend position* applies when the firm already enjoys a dominant or strong position. As part of a defensive strategy, spending should be at whatever level is necessary to maintain the existing position. The relative cost of defense tends to be much lower for industry leaders than for attackers, due to ECONOMIES OF SCALE and ECONOMIES OF SCOPE.
- *Harvest* is relevant at all stages of the life cycle. The key factor for consideration is the speed of harvest. From a strong position, harvesting may be slow, with the cash flows generated being deployed more effectively in newer businesses. Rapid harvesting occurs from positions of strategic weakness and may imply strategies of sale or closure.

Competitors' Position \ Stages of Industry Maturity	Embryonic	Growth	Mature	Aging
Dominant				
Strong		Natural Development		
Favorable		Selective Development		
Tenable				Profit Viability
Weak				Out

Figure 3 Natural strategic thrusts (Arthur D. Little, Inc.)

The third concept developed by ADL is that of generic strategy (not to be confused with Porter's concept; *see* GENERIC STRATEGIES). ADL conceived 24 generic strategies, which were then grouped into a series of subcategories as shown in table 2. The three concepts of families, strategic thrusts, and generic strategies were then linked into an overall matrix to demonstrate strategic position.

In the ADL methodology, the position of a business in the life cycle impacts upon its financial performance. A tool used by ADL to assess this is the ronagraph, which is illustrated in figure 4. This shows, on the vertical axis, the

Table 2 Grouping of generic strategies by main areas of concern

I	*Marketing strategies*
F	Export/same product
I	Initial market penetration
L	Market penetration
O	New products/new markets
P	New products/same markets
T	Same product/new markets
II	*Integration strategies*
A	Backward integration
G	Forward integration
III	*Go overseas strategies*
B	Development of overseas business
C	Development of overseas production facilities
J	Licensing abroad
IV	*Logistic strategies*
D	Distribution rationalization
E	Excess capacity
M	Market rationalization
Q	Production rationalization
R	Product line rationalization
V	*Efficiency strategies*
N	Methods and functions efficiency
V	Technological efficiency
W	Traditional cost-cutting efficiency
VI	*Market strategies*
H	Hesitation
K	Little jewel
S	Pure survival
U	Maintenance
X	Unit abandonment

Source: Arthur D. Little, Inc.

return on net assets (RONA) generated by each business in the corporate portfolio and, on the horizontal axis, the internal deployment of cash flows. At 100 percent all cash generated is redeployed within the business, which thus becomes cash neutral. Above 100 percent the business becomes a cash user, while below 100 percent a business is a cash generator. In addition, a negative value implies a divestment strategy. On the ronagraph each business unit is represented by a circle, the area of which is proportional to the net investment attached to the business.

In addition to RONA, a number of other indicators are also expected to reflect industry maturity. These include profit after tax, net assets, net working capital/sales, fixed costs/sales, variable costs/sales, profit after tax/sales, and net cashflow/sales.

The final step in the ADL methodology consists of assessing the level of risk associated with a business unit strategy. This involved a substantial level of subjectivity, but ADL have identified a number of factors that contribute to such risk, including the following:

- *Maturity and competitive position*: derived from the position of the business within the life-cycle matrix. The greatest risk occurs for embryonic businesses with a weak market position, and the lowest for a business with a dominant position in a mature industry.
- *Industry*: some are much less predictable than others at the same stage of maturity.
- *Strategy*: aggressive strategies tend to be inherently more risky.
- *Assumptions*: future predictions enjoy varying degrees of probability and hence greater or lesser degrees of risk.
- *Past performance*: while the past is no necessary predictor of the future, stable historic records tend to be less risky than no records or inconsistent ones.
- *Management*: historic management performance counts, although this can be subject to change by events such as mid-life crisis, illness, etc.
- *Performance improvement*: the gap between actual and predicted performance is also important. Dramatic improvements tend to be

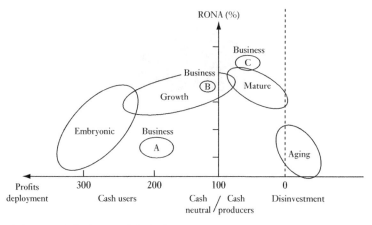

Figure 4   A typical ronagraph (Arthur D. Little, Inc.)

much more risky than gradual extensions of existing performance.

While the ADL model is a useful addition to the range of portfolio models, like the others it needs to be used with care. Criticisms of the approach include, first, the usefulness of the life-cycle approach, whose validity has been challenged by many. Second, where a life cycle can be accepted, the stages of each position vary widely in terms of time. Third, industry activity does not necessary evolve into a well-behaved S-curve. Markets can be rejuvenated and maturity can become growth through changes in fundamental industry characteristics. Firms can also fundamentally transform life-cycle positions by innovation and repositioning. Finally, the nature

of competition varies greatly from industry to industry. Thus fragmented industries may concentrate, while others go in the other direction. Nevertheless, used wisely, the life-cycle portfolio model provides a useful addition to the development of the STRATEGIC MANAGEMENT tool kit.

Bibliography

Arthur D. Little, Inc. (1974). *A System for Managing Diversity*. Cambridge, MA: Arthur D. Little, Inc.

Arthur D. Little, Inc. (1980). *A Management System for the 1980s*. San Francisco: Arthur D. Little, Inc.

Hax, A. C. and Majluf, N. S. (1984). *Strategic Management: An Integrative Perspective*. Englewood Cliffs, NJ: Prentice-Hall, pp. 182–206.

McKinsey 7S model

Derek F. Channon

While, historically, a relationship was established between strategy and structure, the concept has been broadened by McKinsey and Company to encompass a framework linking strategy and a number of other critical variables. It has been argued that the strategy–structure model is an inadequate description of critical elements in the successful implementation of strategy, and that a successful "fit" between those elements and CORPORATE STRATEGY is essential to insure successful implementation. The McKinsey model is illustrated in figure 1.

McKinsey and Company believes that there are seven broad areas that need to be integrated to achieve overall successful strategy implementation. Apart from strategy itself and formal organizational structure, the other variables that it has identified are as follows: shared values, attitudes, and philosophy; staffing and the people orientation of the corporation; administrative systems; practices and procedures used to administer the organization, including the reward and sanction systems; organizational skills, capabilities, and CORE COMPETENCES; and the management style of the corporation as set by its leadership. This model is called by McKinsey the 7S framework.

STRUCTURE

In the McKinsey model, it is argued that while formal structure is important, dividing up the organizational task is not the critical structural problem: rather, it is developing the ability to focus on those dimensions that are currently important to the evolution of the corporation, and being ready to refocus as critical dimensions shift.

SYSTEMS

By systems, McKinsey and Company means the procedures, formal and informal, that make the organization work. It is important to understand how the organization actually works: it is often reliant on informal rather than formal systems.

STYLE

Although it is often underestimated, management style, and especially that of the CEO, is an important determinant in what is strategically possible for the corporation.

STAFF

In the McKinsey model, the nature of the people factor is broadened and redefined. Consider-

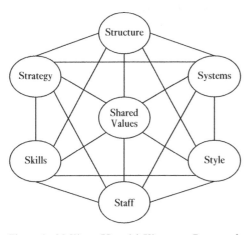

Figure 1 McKinsey 7S model (Waterman, Peters, and Phillips, 1980)

ation of people as a pool of resources, who need to be nurtured, developed, guarded, and allocated, is seen to turn this dimension into a variable that needs to be given close attention by top management.

SKILLS

Given a chosen strategy, this variable enables the corporation to evaluate its capabilities realistically in light of the critical factors required for success. One particular problem may actually be in weeding out old skills, which can be a significant block to necessary change and can prevent the development of new skills.

SHARED VALUES

At the core of the model are superordinate goals and shared values around which the organization pivots. These values define the organization's key beliefs and aspirations and form the core of its corporate culture. Corporations needing to change their values endeavor to undergo dramatic transformations which involve fundamental reappraisals of all aspects of activities. Sometimes such changes are introduced as reengineering projects (*see* BUSINESS PROCESS REENGINEERING; REENGINEERING DISADVANTAGES; VALUE-DRIVEN REENGINEERING). A major reason for the high failure rate of these projects is their lack of success in implanting new shared values that can embrace the radical changes required to achieve the dramatic stretch targets set by such programs.

Bibliography

Waterman, R. (1982). The seven elements of strategic fit. *Journal of Business Strategy*, 3, 68–72.

Waterman, R., Peters, T., and Phillips, J. (1980). Structure is not organization. *McKinsey Quarterly*, Summer, 2–20.

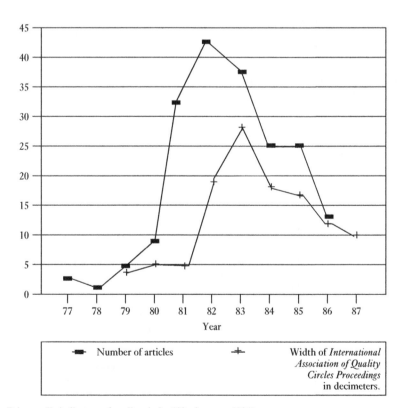

Figure 1 Print-media indicators of quality circles (Abrahamson, 1996)

management fashion

John McGee

Fashion can be thought of as vogues, fads, rages, and crazes that rise and fall with alacrity but in the process can have direct and substantial effects on everyday life. Theories of fashion focus more narrowly on fashions as aesthetic forms such as clothing or haute couture that gratify our senses and emotional wellbeing. Abrahamson (1996) argues that management fashions are the result of a management fashion-setting process. This is a process by which management fashion setters continuously re-define collective beliefs about which management techniques lead to rational management progress.

Quality circles (QCs) exemplify management fashion. During the early 1980s fashion setters promoted the transient belief that QCs were at the forefront of management progress. The rhetoric that fashion setters used to promote this belief survives in the popular management press articles as well as in the proceedings of meetings of fashion setters who actively promoted the QC fashion. Figure 1 illustrates the rapid growth and then decline of articles on QCs. The numbers peaked in 1982 from practically nothing in 1978 and then fell back by more than 50 percent within three years.

Bibliography

Abrahamson, E. (1996). Management fashion. *Academy of Management Review*, 21 (1), 254–85.
Castorina, P. and Wood, B. (1988). Circles in the Fortune 500: Why circles fail. *Journal for Quality and Participation*, 11, 40–1.

managing international organizations

John McGee

The international company has always had a tendency toward complex organization structure and difficulties of management control. Figure 1 demonstrates how multinationals tend towards matrix structures (*see* MATRIX STRUCTURE).

Multinationals historically have moved along the route of increasing product diversity, followed by geographic expansion, or geographic expansion followed by product diversity. A multiproduct firm with limited overseas commitment will naturally organize around product divisions. A multicountry, single-product firm will naturally organize around area or country divisions. The difficulty comes with multipro-

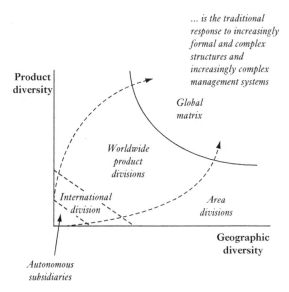

Figure 1   The global matrix (Stopford and Wells, 1972)

duct, multicountry operations – should it be organized around geography or around products? The pure strategies offer clear advice. A global company should operate product divisions, because of the imperative to standardize and achieve cost efficiencies. The multidomestic company should organize around countries, because the foundation of COMPETITIVE ADVANTAGE lies within the countries. TRADE-OFFS have to be made in international firms and in transnational organizations.

Where there is a fine balance to be struck, there has been much experimenting with matrix structures. The matrix attempts to substitute formal, vertically oriented control and planning processes with more direct contact between individuals. It does this by placing line managers in situations where they have two bosses and are required to meet the needs of both. Figure 2 illustrates this with reference to a global chocolate company. This example is inspired by the acquisition of Rowntree by Nestlé, when the new parent argued for the continuation of its country-centered structure, and Rowntree managers argued that because the chocolate industry was global (at least it was European), there should be a product division structure). However, many managers have been very uncomfortable with matrix structures because

- the time taken to make decisions may be too long;
- priorities may be confused, because equal priorities are implied in the matrix;
- responsibilities may not be clear, because of dual reporting lines;
- a matrix may engender conflict, because of the lack of vertical control processes.

Many multinational enterprises (MNEs) use matrix structures: some seem to work quite well, but in general they provoke much controversy. The dual line of reporting is the source of many problems and requires explicit procedures that can resolve the inherent tensions. There are three important criteria for making a matrix structure work well. These are clarity, continuity, and consistency. *Clarity* refers to how well people understand what they are doing and how well they are doing it. It is built on clear corporate objectives within which relationships in the structure have to be spelt out in simple, direct terms. *Continuity* means that the company remains committed to the same values, objectives, and principles of operation. This means that people know what is required, what the company stands for, and how it operates. *Consistency* relates to how well all parts of the company work in relation to one another. This means that different parts of

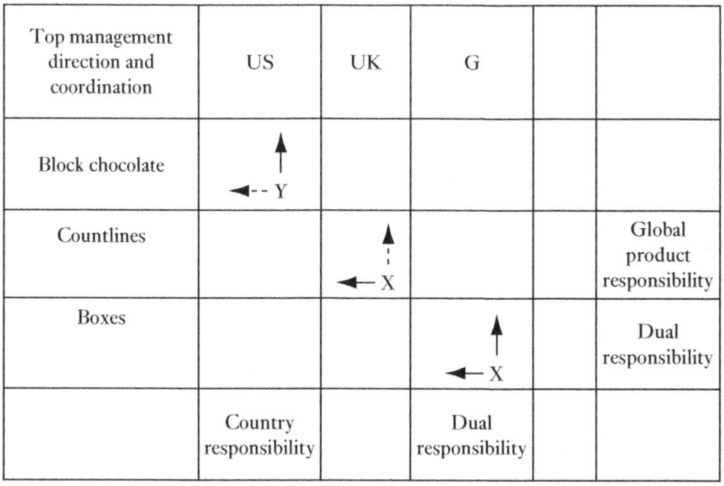

Top management direction and coordination	US	UK	G		
Block chocolate	↑ ◀-- Y				
Countlines		↑ ┆ ◀ X			Global product responsibility
Boxes			↑ ◀ X		Dual responsibility
	Country responsibility		Dual responsibility		

Figure 2   Managing the matrix, example: global chocolate company

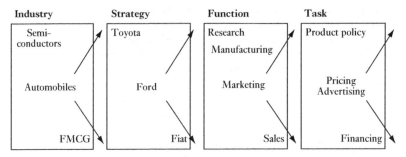

Figure 3   Integration and differentiation (adapted from Bartlett and Ghoshal, 1989: ch. 6)

the operation should work in the same way without (too many) unnecessary variations and adaptations.

One of the difficulties with organizational design and the management processes that support each design is that they have a "one size fits all" character. The multibusiness company has more complexity than any single organization structure can accommodate. Sometimes a central policy is needed, sometimes local discretion is required, often there needs to be a debate about how something should be done. The need for innovation, learning, and adaptation usually requires local discretion within a clear strategic intent. A useful approach is to seek to build the diagnosis of a company from the bottom up and not from the top down. Figure 2 implies that an overall judgment can be made about which type a company belongs to.

Alternatively, consider figure 3. This breaks down the unit of analysis into its constituent parts (rather like a parts explosion diagram). An international-type industry (automobiles) is broken down into its member companies, some of which are global, some international, etc. The Ford Motor Company, international in type, is broken down into its major functions. Research is seen to be global and centralized, sales are multidomestic and decentralized, and marketing is international (and it is probbly difficult to decide how it should be organized).

Breaking marketing into its constituents, we see that some parts, like product policy, should be centralized, whereas others, like advertising, still have a complex mixture of local and central contributions. In practice, the diagnosis can be

built from the bottom as well as from the top. Thus, the bottom-up approach identifies how things are done. The top-down approach can challenge this and ask how things should be done. The result might look like figure 4. In this we show the integration-responsiveness trade-off diagram for KFC (Kentucky Fried Chicken, now part of Tricon Global Restaurants, Inc.). The company is diagnosed in general as international in type. The vertical axis displays the tasks and functions that are to be done centrally, to gain the integration benefits. The horizontal axis displays those tasks and functions that ought to be carried out locally. Grouped around the origin of the diagram are those activities that require both central and local contributions. It is in these areas that a matrix-style structure would be relevant. Rather than adopting a one-size-fits-all structure, it would be appealing to be able to differentiate the structure according to needs.

See also *global strategic advantage; global strategies; globalization*

Bibliography

Bartlett, C. and Ghoshal, S. (1989). *Managing Across Borders: The Transnational Solution*. Boston: Harvard Business School Press.
Bartlett, C. and Ghoshal, S. (1990). Matrix management: Not a structure, a frame of mind. *Harvard Business Review*, **68** (4), 138–45.
Bartlett, C. and Ghoshal, S. (1992). What is a global manager? *Harvard Business Review*, **70** (5), 124–32.
Harvard Business School (1986). *Kentucky Fried Chicken (Japan) Ltd*. Case Study 9-987-043. Boston: Harvard Business School.

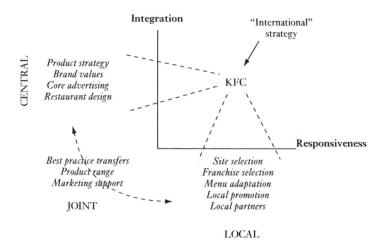

Figure 4 Integration and differentiation: KFC (adapted from Bartlett and Ghoshal, 1989: ch. 6)

Stopford, J. and Wells, L. T. (1972). *Management and the Multinational Enterprise*. London: Longman.

manufacturing strategy

Alan Harrison

Key decisions in manufacturing strategy fall into two categories:

- *Structure*: relating to the size and shape of the manufacturing facilities. Decisions in this area concern major investment decisions, the "hardware" of manufacturing strategy.
- *Infrastructure*: decisions relating to the systems and organization of running the manufacturing function. The combined effect of decisions in this area can be just as difficult and long term to change as decisions in the structural area.

A framework for developing a manufacturing strategy is shown in table 1.

ORDER-WINNING CRITERIA

Hill (1993) did much to develop this concept. Order-winning criteria (OWC) relate to column 3 in table 1.

Products gain advantage in the marketplace as a result of features that are better than those of the competition. The identification of such features (OWC) by marketing helps to set objectives that other business functions should meet. The responsibility for meeting such OWC is not always that of manufacturing alone. Some examples of OWC are described below.

Price. If marketing can define target prices, then other functions are given an objective:

$$costs = price - profit$$

Apart from controlling material overhead and labor costs, manufacturing can also plan for reduced costs by process innovation. Designing the product and its delivery system for low-cost manufacture and control can provide further payoffs.

Product quality and reliability. This OWC has been used by Japanese manufacturers of many different product ranges to win orders from western competitors. Price and design aspects are little different.

Delivery speed. Orders may be won by an ability to respond to customer requirements more quickly than the competition. Lead-time reduction in make-to-order businesses (and in others) is often a major strategy objective.

Table 1   Framework for developing manufacturing strategy

Business objectives	Marketing strategy	How do products win orders in the marketplace?	Manufacturing strategy	
			Structure	Infrastructure
Sales	Products: • launches • enhancements • terminations • range	Price Quality	Capacity: • amount • timing • type	Workforce: • skills • rewards • security
Profitability		Delivery: • speed • reliability	Facilities: • size • location • focus	Organization: • structure • control systems
Return on capital employed	Volumes			
	Level of customization	Color range		
Other financial measures		Product range	Process choice	Quality
	Market segments	JIT capability	Vertical integration: • direction • extent • balance	Production and materials control: • sourcing • systems
		Existing supplier		
		Design leadership		New product development Performance measurement systems

Source: derived from Hill (1993); Hayes and Wheelwright (1984)

Delivery speed in make-to-stock businesses is often achieved at the expense of high finished product inventories. Customer service and corporate objectives can, however, be enhanced by reduced throughput times and greater manufacturing flexibility.

Delivery reliability.   A company's reputation, and therefore its ability to win orders, can be greatly enhanced by consistently delivering the products by the date specified by the customer. Manufacturing considerations include capacity planning, scheduling, and inventory control.

Product range and color range.   In some markets, orders are won because the product range (and/or color range) is broader than that of the competition. Increased product range rapidly increases the complexity of the manufacturing task; but if it is necessary, then plans must be

developed to achieve this objective more economically than in other businesses.

Design leadership.   As a result of design innovation, the company's products may win orders because they perform better, or perhaps because they are the only products capable of performing a needed function. Manufacturing's role here is to support such design leadership by developing new in-house production processes and skills.

Qualifying Criteria

Any of the above OWC can change to something that is subtly different: qualifying criteria. These simply qualify the product to be in the marketplace at all. For example, manufacturers of 750 kV transformers who have not supplied working installations in their own countries will not qualify for export tenders, even if they claim to have design technology. Similarly, it is point-less to attempt to enter the toiletries market seriously without a wide product range. Qualifying criteria enable a product to enter or stay in a market; competitive products already possess such criteria.

If price is not the major order-winning criterion, then this does not mean that a company may charge what it likes. Price exploitation must be kept within limits; otherwise, a qualifying criterion may become an order-losing criterion. An important task for marketing is to identify criteria that are order-losing sensitive.

Regular reviews of the manufacturing strategy help to insure its relevance to corporate needs and to the strategic direction. Here, manufacturing strategy decision categories are checked regularly against each other and tested against "How do products win orders?" At each reiteration, the manufacturing strategy is more comprehensive and better understood. This process often identifies a demand for improvements in the company's marketing strategy.

Taking Stock

In table 1 it is proposed that manufacturing strategy can be developed in logical steps. Once business objectives and the marketing strategy (columns 1 and 2) have been developed, the following further action is needed:

- Marketing analyzes OWC and qualifying criteria for each product family.
- A detailed profile is produced to identify current key manufacturing and design capabilities. This should cover each product family, and relate to each division or facility of the company. It will cover aspects such as special skills and capacity for each product line.

Using the manufacturing/design profile, it is possible to conduct a review against marketing requirements in detail. Further valuable information would include:

- an assessment of current and future competitors worldwide, and their capability to manufacture products;

- an assessment of potential improvements in process technology.

From the marketing review and such additional considerations, a target manufacturing position relative to the competition should be identified as part of the business plan. The constraints in terms of manufacturing structure and infrastructure also need to be assessed.

Implementing Manufacturing Strategy

Having determined the manufacturing contribution to the business strategy, that position should be formalized through specific goals, such as the following:

- reduce the lead time for product A from four weeks to two weeks by the end of the current year;
- increase the inventory turnover from $2\times$ to $5\times$ over the next two years.

These objectives will be supported by a plan of how they will be achieved, as shown in table 1. The plan will cover the major elements of manufacturing strategy shown in table 2. It will be a formal document, circulated to the key contributors. Action will include:

- creating management awareness and commitment;
- prioritizing the tasks and assigning responsibilities;
- training employees.

The manufacturing strategy will be reviewed regularly (say, every six months). Major changes will only be made if fundamental business factors have altered.

Bibliography

Garvin, D. A. (1988). *Managing Quality*. New York: Free Press.

Hayes, R. W. and Wheelwright, S. C. (1984). *Restoring Our Competitive Edge: Competing Through Manufacturing*. New York: John Wiley.

Hill, T. J. (1993). *Manufacturing Strategy: The Strategic Management of the Manufacturing Function*, 2nd edn. Basingstoke: Macmillan.

Table 2   Manufacturing strategy presentation

1   Corporate strategy
2   Product strategy
3   Market priorities
  ● now
  ● future
4   The plant:
  ● general layout and process flow
  ● management control data
  ● human resources
    − special risks
    − reward systems
  ● inventory
  ● production and material control systems
  ● quality
  ● process automation opportunities
  Plant profile:
  ● capacity by product family
  ● focus
  ● vertical integration
5   Review of how well manufacturing supports current and future needs
6   Team meetings
  ● action plan development
7   Team presentations
8   Summary comments and guidelines for follow on assignments (accountability, target dates)

---

market share

Derek F. Channon

Widely believed to be a critical factor in the determination of competitive position, many firms focus on the achievement of market share gain as a critical strategic factor. However, great care must be exercised in the pursuit of market share. In the Boston Consulting Group (BCG) model, the GROWTH SHARE MATRIX, relative market share is used as a surrogate for cumulative production volume, a critical term in experience effect analysis (*see* EXPERIENCE AND LEARNING EFFECTS). It is assumed that the higher the level of market share, the more a firm will have produced of a particular product. The firm with the highest relative share should therefore enjoy a lower cost than its smaller rivals (assuming that all firms are on the same experience curve). As defined in the BCG model, relative market share is the share of the firm subdivided by that of the largest single competitor. By definition, therefore, only one firm within a market can enjoy a relative share greater than one. The widespread awareness and adoption of this model has contributed to the belief in the importance of market share. Note, however, that the model refers to *relative share*, not absolute share.

The PROFIT IMPACT OF MARKET STRATEGY (PIMS) model makes use of two market share terms, namely, absolute share and relative share. The PIMS definition of relative share is also different: it is the share of the business under analysis divided by the sum of the shares of the three largest competitors. The PIMS model's use of absolute share also avoids the problem with the use of the BCG model in that it has little meaning in fragmented industries. The PIMS model also argues that market share, although a significant variable in the determination of profitability, is actually a derived variable and that relative product quality is its driver. PIMS clearly supports the BCG contention that market share is an important determinant of business profitability. In the PIMS model, however, it is but one of a large number of variables. Moreover, for the variable to be of value, clear market identification is essential. While PIMS uses two market share terms in its analysis, it also emphasizes product quality, productivity, and capital intensity. As a result, making use of these latter variables, it is possible to eliminate the advantage of high market share. Japanese competitors have been especially successful at utilizing these variables as a way of countering the volume advantage of US-based competitors in industries, such as machine tools, automobiles, and electronics.

A major problem with the use of market share is its difficulty in measurement. First, it is essential to define exactly what the market is before a firm's share can be measured. This is actually extremely difficult in practice. The PIMS model expends great effort in defining the served market of a business. This is usually some combination of product, customer, and geography that a business chooses to serve. Serious problems of definition can, however, still occur. Moreover, market boundaries can and do shift. For example, in the early 1980s the US General Electric Company (GE) believed itself to be in a strong market share position in the US in product areas such as consumer electronics and appliances. While this was true, these markets were in the process of globalizing (*see* GLOBALIZATION), and if a global market definition had been adopted GE's position would have been recognized as much weaker. In some industries such as retailing, the correct market share is also extremely difficult to select. This could, for example, refer to national position, regional position, or that immediately surrounding an individual store.

While market share is therefore seen to be important, great care must be exercised in its definition and usage as a strategic variable. Nevertheless, different levels of market share have been shown to suggest alternate operating strategies. Businesses can thus be defined as high, medium, and low market share concerns. Dependent upon the position of a business, different strategies are suggested.

STRATEGIES FOR HIGH-SHARE COMPETITORS

While high market share does often generate lower costs in high experience effect markets, this may not always be the case. For example, although Kodak enjoys a worldwide volume advantage over Fuji Film, the latter is the lower-cost producer. Nevertheless, industry leaders are often able to maintain their position, especially when they control activities such as distribution and promotion. Three contrasting strategic positions have been identified for industry leaders.

(1) Stay on the offensive. Under this strategy, the best offense is the best defense. Leadership and COMPETITIVE ADVANTAGE are sustained by achieving FIRST-MOVER ADVANTAGE through continuous innovation and improvement. This forces competitors to adopt follow-on strategies. It also provides the possibility of locking up distribution channels and increasing customer SWITCHING COSTS.

(2) Fortify and defend. This strategy attempts to build barriers to entry for competitors (*see* BARRIERS TO ENTRY AND EXIT). The range of possible specific actions includes:

- raising the cost structure of competitors, as a result of increased promotion, customer service, and R&D;

- introducing alternative brands to match competitor product attributes;
- increasing customer switching costs;
- broadening the product line to maximize store shelf space, to reduce competitor distribution capacity, and to fill niche positions;
- introducing fighting brands to maximize price range offering;
- adding capacity ahead of the market to try to deter capacity investment, especially by smaller competitors;
- driving for experience gains as a result of greater cumulative production volume;
- patenting alternate technologies;
- signing up exclusivity deals with key suppliers and distributors.

This strategy is best for companies with a strong dominance position that are not subject to monopolies legislation. Such a business may well be a CASH COW but can be maintained with a long-term future by continuous adequate investment to maintain position. The critical danger from this strategy is the risk of flanking attacks which endeavor to shift the grounds on which the business is founded.

(3) Follow the leader. This strategy forces small-share competitors to conform to policies established by the industry leader. Clear signals are established for weaker competitors by: rapid responses to price attacks; heavy promotion spend when challengers threaten; special deals for customers and/or distributors; pressure applied to distributors to reduce competition shelf space availability; and the poaching of key competitor personnel from competitors attacking the leader. On occasion, such behavior can breach ethical standards, and care must be taken to insure that grounds for legal attack by smaller competitors are not provided. The "dirty tricks" campaign by British Airways against Virgin is a classic example, in which the industry leader, exasperated by the success of its smaller rival, adopted illegal tactics to try to limit Virgin's progress.

STRATEGIES FOR MEDIUM-SHARE COMPETITORS

Most product markets tend to be at least oligopolistic. Many have multiple competitors. As a result, most competitors are not industry leaders but, rather, medium-share concerns. Despite their medium-share positions, such businesses may operate a number of wholly viable strategies that are profitable and attractive. Some such companies operate as fierce challengers to industry leaders, while others appear content to accept their subordinate position. Those firms keen to strengthen their strategic position are recommended to adopt the indirect approach rather than engage in head-on confrontation.

In industries in which a substantial experience effect prevails, low-share competitors need to achieve similar cost positions by tactics such as lower capital intensity, higher productivity, use of debt leverage, and superior product quality. Alternatively, such firms should aim to achieve differentiation by technological leadership, alternate distribution systems, resegmentation of the market (see SEGMENTATION), and reconfiguration of the value chain. Where ECONOMIES OF SCALE or experience effects are more limited, the strategic options open to medium-share firms are greater and include the following.

(1) Vacant niche. Such a strategy involves focusing on customer segments that have been neglected by industry leaders. Ideally, such niches should be sufficiently large to justify specialization in product development, distribution, and the like, and to provide profitable opportunities. Such niches might include health foods in the food industry, feeder and commuter airlines, specialist magazines, and investment and insurance products targeted at the over-50s.

(2) Specialist. This strategy focuses on supplying the needs of specific market segments. Competitive advantage is gained through the differentiation achieved by specialization. Examples include Apple Computers in desktop publishing, Hewlett Packard in specialist calculators, and Baxter's in specialty soups.

(3) Superior quality. This strategy combines segment and/or product differentiation coupled with "superior" quality, where quality is based on customer perception. Customers are then prepared to pay higher prices for such product offerings. Examples include specialist foods from Marks and Spencer, Chivas Regal Whisky,

Smirnoff Vodka, Wedgwood china, and branded perfumes.

(4) Passive follower. Many medium-ranking competitors are content to maintain follower positions behind established industry leaders. Their strategies do not seek confrontation but react to the leader's moves rather than initiating attack policies. Under such stable market conditions – especially as growth slows but does not drift into decline – medium-ranking competitors are able to maintain satisfactory levels of profitability.

(5) Growth via acquisition. One strategy to rapidly strengthen market position is by the acquisition of or merger with competitors (see ACQUISITION STRATEGY; MERGERS AND ACQUISITIONS). Such moves may rapidly create high-share positions and reap economies of scale. Industries which have undergone such restructuring include pharmaceuticals, brewing, airlines, heavy chemicals, accountancy, and global media. The dangers in such a strategy stem largely from problems of integration, especially in supposed mergers, where potential clashes between the cultures of new partners may result in dysfunctional behavior.

Despite their non-leadership position, medium-ranked businesses often enjoy attractive profits and established market positions. In the food and drink product sectors, for example, food distributors offer at least two branded products, not least to maintain pressure on industry leaders. In many industrial and other consumer product areas, this is also the case. The handicap of lower market size can thus be circumvented by: segment-focused strategies in which price confrontation is avoided; superior technical and quality positions; lower costs, through reduced capital intensity and superior productivity; strategies that reinforce differences from the industry leader; and a focus on alternative distribution strategies and differentiation in advertising and promotion.

STRATEGIES FOR LOW-SHARE BUSINESSES

A number of strategic options are open to businesses with low-share positions. When a low-share position is coupled with low growth or a high cost of product development, unless the parent company can afford to attack and gain share by market means or acquisition, harvesting or rapid exit strategies seem to be recommended.

When it is possible, harvesting maximizes the cash that can be extracted from such a business. Under such a strategy, all unnecessary expenditure is cut, R&D is minimized, and new investment is limited to the maintenance of operations, provided that shareholder value is not destroyed. Prices are raised or maintained rather than cut in a trade-off (*see* TRADE-OFFS) of market share for cash flow. A number of indicators have been identified of when a harvesting strategy seems most appropriate:

- in industries with unattractive long-term prospects;
- when growing share would be too expensive and insufficiently profitable;
- when market share defense is too expensive;
- when share is not dependent on the maintenance of competitive effort;
- when resources can be deployed elsewhere to improve shareholder value;
- when the business is not critical to core activities (*see* CORE BUSINESS);
- when the business does not add special features to the corporation's overall portfolio.

Bibliography

Buzzell, R. D. and Gale, B. T. (1987). *The PIMS Principles*. New York: Free Press, ch. 9.

Buzzell, R. D., Gale, B. T., and Sutton, R. G. (1975). Market share: A key to profitability. *Harvard Business Review*, **53**, 97–108.

Hammermesh, R. B., Anderson, M. J., and Harris, J. E. (1978). Strategies for low market share businesses. *Harvard Business Review*, **56**, 95–103.

Kotler, P. (1978). Harvesting strategies for weak products. *Business Horizons*, **21** (5).

Kotler, P. (2003). *Marketing Management: Analysis, Planning, Implementation and Control*, 11th edn. Englewood Cliffs, NJ: Prentice-Hall.

Porter, M. E. (1985). *Competitive Advantage: Creating and Sustaining Superior Performance*. New York: Free Press, ch. 15.

Thompson, A. and Strickland, A. J. (1993). *Strategic Management*, 7th edn. New York: Irwin, pp. 226–68.

Woo, C. Y. and Cooper, A. C. (1982). The surprising case for low market share. *Harvard Business Review*, **60**, 106–13.

market structure

Ben Knight and John McGee

THE ANALYSIS OF MARKETS AND COMPETITION

The critical market-level influence on firm performance is the form and intensity of rivalry between the existing firms in a market. The economist's approach to market structure and the form and extent of rivalry is to use a taxonomy based on the number of firms in each industry. Figure 1 illustrates this.

At one extreme, we have *perfect competition*, in which products are not differentiable, rivalry is intense, and no firm has the power to alter market prices. In such a market the price is determined at the market level by the forces of supply and demand, so from the firm's point of view the price of its product is given. The forces of competition limit strategic discretion and drive profits down to the "normal" level, i.e., a level insufficient to attract new entrants to the market. Markets for agricultural products like wheat are often viewed as perfectly competitive, because no single producer can alter the market price. Perfect markets are not common. Firms have a huge incentive to adopt strategies that avoid the "strategic hell" of perfect competition.

At the other extreme, we have a *monopoly* in which one firm supplies the whole market. The firm is able to fix prices and hence enjoys control over its market environment and, as such, enjoys significant market power. Patents like that secured by the UK pharmaceutical company Glaxo in the market for ulcer drugs confer this kind of market power. A high level of market power enables the monopolistic firm to earn higher profits than the competitive firm, as Glaxo did with Zantac in the 1980s and until 1997.

In between these two extremes, we have *oligopolistic* markets, in which a few firms compete against each other, and *monopolistic competition*. Most economists would regard these intermediate cases as the norm. In the monopolistic competition case, there are many firms, each with small market shares (*see* MARKET SHARE), but each is able to differentiate its product to some degree and to obtain modest control over its prices and other aspects of its strategy, to build

Market Structure	Number of firms	Degree of differentiation	Comments
Perfect competition	many	zero	Fragmented, commodity-like
Monopolistic or imperfect competition	many	some	Multiple niches, Localised competition
Oligopoly– undifferentiated	Some to very few	Low	Commodity-like with scale economics e.g. steel
Oligopoly – differentiated	Some to very few	high	Strategic interdependence Large segments
Dominant firm	One to very few	high	Price leadership, high entry barricrs, competitive fringe
Monopoly	single	Not applicable	Natural monopoly due to very high scale economies

Figure 1   Market structure; the Broad Spectrum for Competition

COMPETITIVE ADVANTAGE over other players. The restaurant business in a big city like London or Singapore is a good example of monopolistic competition.

In oligopolistic markets, there are fewer players, each able to gain competitive advantage by exploiting scale economies (*see* ECONOMIES OF SCALE), by product differentiation, and so on. There are numerous examples of this kind of market, including, for example, the global car market and the EU steel market. In both of these cases, a handful of firms compete against one another. This competition could be muted because of collusion between firms aimed at reducing rivalry. Although this collusion is possible and gives market control to all colluding producers, improving both the financial performance of both individual firms and the sector as a whole, it is sometimes difficult to create and to sustain, and is usually illegal.

Intense competition could also occur in oligopolistic markets. Each firm knows that in this case, effective STRATEGIC MANAGEMENT may create competitive advantage, but also each needs to be aware that its rivals may copy any strategic move.

As well as the rivalry from existing players, it is important to take account of the threat of new entrants. This is technically known as "contestable markets." Sometimes the threat of new entrants is very low, because of the huge entry costs. These arise from the large fixed costs of installing plant, as well as the costs of acquiring the key competences of these businesses. The existence of static and dynamic scale economies arising from learning curve effects also creates market barriers for incumbent firms. In other sectors, this may not be the case.

See also *markets and imperfections*

Bibliography

Besanko, D., Dranove, D., Shanley, M., and Shaefer, S. (2003). *Economics of Strategy*, 2nd edn. New York: John Wiley.

McAleese, D. (2001). *Economics for Business*, 2nd edn. Englewood Cliffs, NJ: Prentice-Hall.

McGee, J., Thomas, H., and Wilson, D. (2005). *Strategy: Analysis and Practice*. Maidenhead: McGraw-Hill.
Scherer, F. M. (1970). *Industrial Market Structure and Economic Performance*. Chicago: Rand McNally.

markets and imperfections

John McGee

The foundation for strategic thinking requires an understanding of the nature of markets (*see* MARKET STRUCTURE). Perfectly competitive markets are characterized by free entry, perfect information, and identical commodity-like products. The consequence of such "perfect" competition is that price is the only competitive variable, that firms are essentially identical, and therefore, that there are no supernormal profits to be had. Profit is sufficient to provide a normal return on capital and any profits above this will be transitory, either through random shocks or because competition erodes the profit benefits of new initiatives. Thus, the perfectly competitive world is not conducive to super profits ("rents") and does not provide much incentive to entrepreneurial behavior.

However, imperfections in markets do provide the possibility for rents and rent-seeking activities. Imperfections could be differences in information about production possibilities, or consumer ignorance about product benefits. Some imperfections are market-wide, in that monopoly might prevail, perhaps because of government edict, or because of natural ECONOMIES OF SCALE, or perhaps through cartels (*see* CARTEL). These imperfections are associated with rents, because prices can be held artificially high without (much) fear of competition. The worldwide wave of PRIVATIZATION and DEREGULATION is usually marked by lower prices and greater competition. Figure 1 portrays the differences between the conditions under which perfect competition obtains and COMPETITIVE ADVANTAGE exists.

Imperfect competition can be characterized by one or more of the following:

- ability of sellers to influence demand by such practices as product differentiation, BRANDING, and advertising;
- restraints on the entry of competitors either because of the large scale of initial invest-

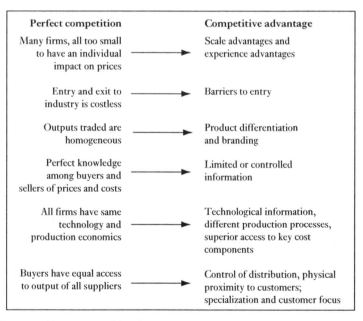

Figure 1 Perfect competition vs. competitive advantage

ment required or because of restrictive and collusive practices;

- the existence of uncertainty and imperfect knowledge about prices and profits elsewhere;
- the absence of price competition.

These are imperfections generic to a market. But, imperfections can be firm specific. Thus, a pharmaceutical company may, through its R&D activity, develop specific, proprietary knowledge that results in new products, which cannot be imitated without a significant time lag. An office equipment company might establish a worldwide service system that allows it to give 24-hour service response to clients. Competitors can only imitate after substantial delay. Firm-specific imperfections enable firms to be different from their competitors and to expect this difference to be sustainable (see SUSTAINABIL-ITY) over a non-trivial time span. If firms can be different, and if customers value such differences, then these firms can earn supernormal profits, at least for a time. In economic terms, this is the essence of strategy. Firms create ad-

vantage by creating assets and positions that are distinctively different from those of their competitors. The essence of these firm-specific imperfections lies firstly in the creation of different assets (either tangible or intangible), and secondly in the creation of distinctive, defensible positions in their chosen product markets. The "positioning" school (which could be known as the "market-based view") focuses primarily on the latter, with analysis of the nature and dynamics of competitive advantage. The RESOURCE-BASED VIEW is concerned with the former.

Bibliography

McGee, J., Wilson, D., and Thomas, H. (2005). *Strategy: Analysis and Practice*. Maidenhead: McGraw-Hill.

matrix structure

Derek F. Channon

Often found in complex multinationals, matrix structures involve a combination of geography and product, as illustrated in figure 1.

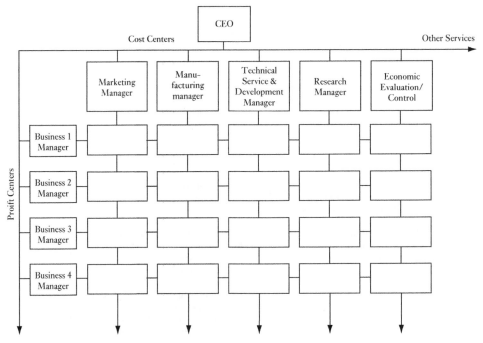

Figure 1   The form of a matrix organization

In multinational corporations (MNCs) that have multiple product lines, country organizations will normally have a manager, and may operate production units and certain sales and marketing teams for the corporation's product groups sold in that country. However, product divisions, to which geographic management will be subordinate, will tend to set strategy for each worldwide product division as a whole. Reporting relationships are therefore complex, with many executives reporting to more than one central unit.

Country managers report primarily to the area management and are responsible overall for the activities of the corporation within a specific country. They will also usually act as the corporation's representative for external affairs within a country. Each country may be treated as a profit center, but under some matrix systems and for a variety of reasons (e.g., tax treatment, location of high-cost facilities or services), the maximization of profitability by country may well be subordinate to regional or global product and profit considerations. In MNCs the management of international tax is especially important, as is management of exchange rate risk.

Below the country manager level, operations tend to be divided by product group. The management of such groups has dual reporting relationships to the country manager and to its own product divisions. In many matrix structures the latter relationship overrides the former, again increasing the difficulty of assessing country units on a pure profit basis. In the banking industry, for example, the use of worldwide account teams to service key global customers may well result in the sacrifice of profitability in one country in order to provide a superior customer service worldwide. Similarly, banks relinquish profits on scarce risk lending capacity in difficult countries in order to provide such capacity to selected worldwide key account customers at lower rates.

In general, the importance of the geographic component of matrix structures has diminished over time, and in some companies the position of an overall country manager has disappeared, with each main product division operating as a global business in its own right. Matrix structures are complex and difficult to manage. There is frequent rivalry between the perceived inter-ests of geographic units and product groups. The general trend, however, has been that the greater the degree of overseas product diversity, the more likely it has been that product considerations take precedence.

A specific problem that has affected corporations operating multinational matrix structures has been the dominance of headquarters operations staffed predominantly by home-country nationals in attempting to set the strategies of overseas subsidiaries. Where domestic product groups have attempted to set global strategy (*see* GLOBAL STRATEGIES), there has often tended to be a lack of knowledge of overseas conditions, and policies have often been established on the basis of domestic conditions. This is especially true of US multinationals, but also applies to MNCs from other countries. While, clearly, the US domestic market is usually paramount, the failure to appreciate international conditions and to allow non-US nationals sufficiently strong geographic inputs into policy-making has often led to the growth of overseas competition that has proved damaging. The contrast with Japanese corporations in this respect is marked. Japanese corporations very carefully examine local markets and design strategies to meet local product needs and minimize political friction, although foreigners have not been significantly accepted by these corporations.

The Japanese have also structurally attempted to coordinate not merely by product and geography but also by function. In this, production especially is coordinated on a worldwide basis and cross-functional product divisional teams endeavor to insure that any interdivisional rivalries are minimized, while gains made in one division are transferred rapidly to others. This elimination of rivalries leads to cooperation in the production of hybrid products, using fusion technology to cut across divisional boundaries. Marketing is less coordinated on a worldwide basis and localized marketing strategies may well be used. By contrast, in many western companies operating a DIVISIONAL STRUCTURE and/or a strategic business unit (SBU) structure, the boundaries between divisions or SBUs may well make such cooperation difficult, especially when reward structures are based on unit rather than corporate performance. In such circumstances sharing profits or accepting costs from another unit may apparently diminish unit performance despite actually or potentially improving overall corporate results.

Many multinationals use matrix structures but although some of these work out very well, many are reputed to be difficult to operate. Bartlett and Ghoshal (1990) suggest three criteria for success:

- *Clarity*: how well people understand what they are doing, how they are doing it, and why they are doing it.
- *Continuity*: where the company remains committed to the same core objectives, values, and strategies so that there is a well-understood unifying theme throughout the company.
- *Consistency*: how well all parts of the company are moving in relation to one another.

Bibliography

Bartlett, C. and Ghoshal, S. (1990). Matrix management: Not a structure, a frame of mind. *Harvard Business Review*, **68** (4), 138–45.

Davis, S. M. and Lawrence, P. R. (1978). Problems of matrix organizations. *Harvard Business Review*, **56** (3), 131–42.

Galbraith, J. R. (1971). Matrix organizational designs. *Business Horizons*, **15** (1), 29–40.

mature industries

see LIFE–CYCLE STRATEGIES

MBWA (management by walking about)

Derek F. Channon

This style of management is identified with corporate excellence. Leaders adopting MBWA do not wholly rely upon bureaucratic reporting systems but see for themselves, in one way or another, how the corporation actually works by personally meeting staff and customers. These informal channels involve talking to customers and suppliers, listening to junior employees, and making regular on-site visits. This enables the

leadership to avoid receiving filtered and sterilized information which otherwise may come through the conventional reporting procedures.

There are many examples of organizations in which MBWA has proved to be successful:

- Marks and Spencer directors regularly pay surprise visits to stores to observe operations at first hand and to meet customers.
- Apple Computer directors regularly operate customer complaints telephones to gauge customer reactions at first hand.
- Japanese companies provide expenses for regular superior/subordinate beer nights, to allow criticisms to be voiced without fear.
- McDonald's founder Ray Kroc regularly visited store units and did his own personal inspection on QSC and V (quality, service, cleanliness, and value).
- At Hewlett-Packard weekly "beer busts" in each division, attended by both executives and employees, create a regular opportunity to improve communications.

Such managers maintain their "feel" for a business which otherwise might disappear with increases in size, which bring with them increased bureaucracy and isolation.

Bibliography

Peters, T. J. and Peters, N. (1985). *A Passion for Excellence*. New York: Random House, chs. 2, 3, 19.

Thompson, A. and Strickland, A. J. (1993). *Strategic Management*, 7th edn. New York: Irwin, pp. 226–68.

mergers and acquisitions

Duncan Angwin

General reading of the business press and of academic writings suggests that mergers and acquisitions, although common, are not so tractable, and it is worth pausing to consider why this is so (see tables 1 and 2). Acquisitions touch all aspects of corporate life and so can be viewed from a multiplicity of angles. From a strategic perspective, much attention has been devoted to understanding the drivers for acquisition and identifying suitable targets. The underlying assumptions with this approach are that if one can correctly identify such targets, then the acquisition will be successful. This exposes us to Mintzberg's criticism of the planning school: Mintzberg questions whether successful results will inevitably follow from a good plan. Indeed, this author has often heard CEOs remark that if the acquisition failed, then it was due to a poor plan! This circular argument is not helpful, and indeed obscures the point that the causal link between plan and performance is weak at best – the relationship being substantially mediated by *implementation strategies*. As a consequence, strategy research efforts have turned to the post-acquisition phase, where "implementation is the bridge between the islands of plan and performance."

In focusing upon implementation, a new strategic agenda has arisen. Implementation has opened up the black box of the "messy" detail of organizations, which pre-acquisition planning frameworks largely overlook. This has implications for our view of strategy and the role of the HQ. Pre-acquisition frameworks tend to assume a top-down approach to strategy, whereas the latter is embedded within the organization, and is multilevel and complex. Focusing internally upon the resources and capabilities of the business echoes a shift in emphasis in the field of strategy itself, from the positioning school to the resource-based school (*see* RESOURCE-BASED VIEW). However, rather than being an "either/or" choice, this is really a question of emphasis, with the recognition that success in the latter is crucial to achieving the former.

Whilst 2002 saw a slump in activity from the record wave experienced in the previous five years totaling $10.84 million, 2003 saw an upturn. Interestingly, mega-deals, which characterized the boom of the late 1990s, continue, as do the large-scale cross-border transactions.

Acquisitions come in waves. The 1960s were characterized by a wave of DIVERSIFICATION activity designed to spread financial risk across a portfolio of businesses. Companies such as the tobacco giant BAT industries spent vast sums trying to establish sound footings in other industries, but with very poor results. The 1980s exposed the fallacy of diversification, as its supposed advantages were more than offset by the difficulties of managing such large, diverse groups. It was realized that shareholders could diversify more effectively themselves, and, with the rise of more aggressive financial techniques, such giants were no longer bid-proof (*see* BIDDING TACTICS). Breakups became the new order, as businesses streamlined, downsized (*see* DOWNSIZING), and generally "stuck to the

Table 1 Consultancy and business press evidence on acquisition failure

Consultancy	Date	Method	Failure rate (%)
Business	1975	400 postal questionnaires	49
International	1978	150 postal questionnaires	48–56
Coopers and Lybrand	1992	Qualitative in-depth interviews with senior executives in the UK's top 100 companies	54
Coopers and Lybrand	1996	125 companies. Low revenues, cash flow, profitability	66
Mercer MC	1995	150 companies. Poor returns to shareholders after three years	50
McKinsey & Co.	1995	Examined 58 acquisitions. Success was measured as financial return exceeding the cost of capital	58.6

Source: KPMG

Table 2   Academic evidence on failure rates

Types of academics	Conclusions	Author (date)
Financial economists	Target shareholders benefit by ca. 20% whereas acquirer shareholders do not, benefiting by ca. 0–2%	Jensen and Ruback (1983) Jarrell and Poulsen (1989) Sudarsanam et al. (1993)
Industrial economists		
• Using accounting data	• Bidders suffer an immediate decline in relative profitability	Hughes (1993)
• Subsequent market share	• Subsequent market share showed dramatic decline	Mueller (1985) Caves (1988)
• Divestment	• 58.5% of 2,021 acquisitions (1950–86) subsequently divested	Porter (1987)

knitting." The 1990s saw a massive resurgence in acquisition activity, spurred by DEREGULATION, GLOBALIZATION, and technological change. Differences from previous waves of activity are the number of mega-mergers to create global giants, such as Travelers/Citicorp forming the world's biggest financial services group, and Exxon and Mobil creating an oil behemoth.

In Europe, the drive toward a single market has encouraged internal, cross-border acquisitions. Free of the political barriers that have fragmented their markets, many European companies have sought to consolidate their efforts as a means of matching the advantages in economic scale of their US and Far East counterparts (Calori and Lubatkin, 1995). At the same time, the initial fears of Fortress Europe, as well as its size and sophistication, have made it an attractive hunting ground for non-European multinationals. This has not only resulted in a sharp increase in acquisitions on the continent, but also resulted in the rise of the almost unheard-of hostile takeover. Whilst almost a thing of the past in the US and UK, where they attract little attention, continental Europe is in the grip of such acrimonious deals, which regularly feature in its business press.

Another feature of this recent wave of acquisition activity is the rise in cross-border acquisitions. In the ten years 1985–1995, the value of cross-border acquisitions rose tenfold from 2 billion to some 20 billion, and the numbers of deals fivefold, to 655. (These figures undoubtedly understate the case, as the values of many cross-border deals are not publicly known. The numbers of deals, however, are a more reliable measure of activity.) Cross-border deals gained steadily in significance over that period from 15 percent to 30 percent of total deals.

Recent data (see figure 1) suggest that this trend in cross-border activity continues to surge forward, totaling $229.6 billion in 1998 (KPMG, 1998), an increase of 60 percent on the previous year. In the first quarter of 1999, European-wide deals amounted to $345 billion.

See also *acquisition strategy; post-acquisition integration*

Bibliography

Angwin, D. N. and Saville, B. (1997). Strategic perspectives on European cross-border acquisitions: A view from top European executives. *European Management Journal*, **15** (4), 423–35.

Calori, R. and Lubatkin, M. (1995). Euro-mergers 1993: Viewpoints and predictions. In G. von Krogh, A. Sinatra, and H. Singh (eds.), *Perspectives on the Management of Acquisitions*. London: Macmillan.

Capron, L. (1999). The long-term performance of horizontal acquisitions. *Strategic Management Journal*, **20** (11), 987–1018.

Haspeslagh, P. and Jemison, D. (1991). *Managing Acquisitions*. New York: Free Press.

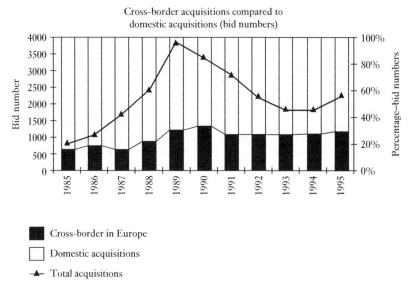

Cross-border acquisitions compared to
domestic acquisitions (bid numbers)

■ Cross-border in Europe

□ Domestic acquisitions

▲ Total acquisitions

Figure 1   The growing relative importance of European cross-border acquisition activity (Angwin and Saville, 1997)

KPMG (1998). *KPMG Deal Watch.*
McGee, J., Thomas, H., and Wilson, D. (2005). *Strategy: Analysis and Practice.* Maidenhead: McGraw-Hill.

mission

Derek F. Channon and John McGee

Large companies typically provide detailed statements of their strategic intent and their major goals in the form of mission statements. These are often criticized for their vacuity, but research (Campbell and Yeung, 1991) suggests that there are two schools of thought about mission statements. One expresses mission in terms of philosophy and ethics, thereby widening the band of actors that are relevant to the long-term future of the company and capturing the notion of stakeholders. It also captures those forms of corporate behavior that have implications for the social good and that are not reflected in the pricing mechanisms in marketplaces. Thus, Henry Ford aimed to "build a car for the great multitude" and Akio Morita intended Sony "to change the image around the world of Japanese products as poor in quality" (Collins and Porras, 1998).

The second school of thought expresses mission as strategy, an intellectual discourse that defines the firm's commercial rationale and target markets. Overall mission is supposed to answer the question "what is our business and what should it be?" Jack Welch offered a clear vision – "to become number 1 or number 2 in every market we serve." In this view the mission statement is an essential building block in establishing the strategy of the organization.

Establishing the mission itself is usually a difficult and demanding task. Top management tends to agonize for long periods of time over the development of a mission statement: the process involves negotiation and compromise, but is usually leadership led – and depends upon a critical input from the CEO. Surprisingly, perhaps, despite all the effort expended, many mission statements tend to seem full of platitudes and motherhood statements.

Mission statements need to be communicated throughout the organization. Top management must also demonstrate their importance by "living" them as an example. In this way, a clear mission statement can become an important inspiration to employees and can lead to commitment and loyalty to the corporation. Once established, missions are difficult to change, as they become critical ingredients in the corporate culture. For example, IBM attempted to change its mission several times, but the critical elements established by the company's founder, Thomas Watson, still encourage the IBM sales function to attempt to achieve "quota" by the year end, rather than seeking to provide customers with "solutions," or to promote non-mainframe sales.

Good mission statements tend to be simple and easy to understand at all levels of the organization. They stimulate enthusiasm and commitment amongst employees; they are challenging; they are short and easily absorbed and accepted; and they are frequently repeated. For example, in the US General Electric Company, the mission for each business is to "be number one or two in the world or sell it, close it, or fix it." Such a statement is readily understood and memorable.

Many Japanese companies have long emphasized a corporate mission or philosophy. Each strategic plan, lasting on average three years, has a clearly identifiable name which is well known throughout the organization. The key ingredients of such plans are fully communicated throughout the organization, and employees take on the corporate mission and values until such time as the strategy is changed.

A well-developed mission statement helps top management in a number of ways. First, it crystalizes top management's own view of the long-term strategic position of the firm. Second, it helps to insure that the behavior of lower-order personnel is directed toward achievement of the corporate mission. Third, it conveys a message to external stakeholders, such as financial institutions, that may influence their investment strategies. Fourth, it insures organizational confidence, in that top management knows where it wishes to drive the corporation. Fifth, it provides a pathway for establishing longer-term strategy.

Bibliography

Campbell, A. and Yeung, S. (1991). Creating a sense of mission. *Long Range Planning*, 24 (4), 10–20.

Collins, J. C. and Porras, J. I. (1998). *Built to Last*. London: Random House.

Thompson, A. A. and Strickland, A. J. (1993). *Strategic Management*, 7th edn. Homewood, IL: Irwin, pp. 24–7.

multinational enterprises

see INTERNATIONAL BUSINESS

national competitive advantage

John McGee

Why are some firms able to innovate consistently while others cannot? Michael Porter (1990) provided an intriguing answer to this question. He undertook a comprehensive study of 100 industries in ten countries. It is not simply due to the strength of individual corporate strategies (*see* CORPORATE STRATEGY). He found that the success of nations and their individual firms is determined by four broad attributes – factor (supply) conditions, demand conditions, related and supporting industries, and market (industry) structure (*see* INDUSTRY STRUCTURE; MARKET STRUCTURE). He called this the *diamond* of national advantage (see figure 1).

First, it is not just factor endowments and factor conditions that are an index of competitiveness – these are the typical concerns of government policy. Also on the supply side is the supporting, related industry infrastructure,

through which various EXTERNALITIES come into play. Thus, an automobile assembly industry is advantaged by a domestic infrastructure of auto component suppliers, who themselves have sustainable competitive advantages. Similarly, domestic rivalry and intensity of competition are seen to have a direct effect on competitiveness.

Finally, Porter points to demand conditions as a determinant of competitiveness. The size, growth, and character of demand shape the supplying industries. The sophistication of local demand will be reflected in the developing characteristics of domestic suppliers. The point to take away from Porter's diamond is that the companies are embedded in and influenced by their industries, and these industries are in turn embedded in a wider economic and social structure. However, it is not clear from this analysis, nor is it asserted in this analysis, that competitive advantage is necessarily determined by the broader economic context. It is possible to see

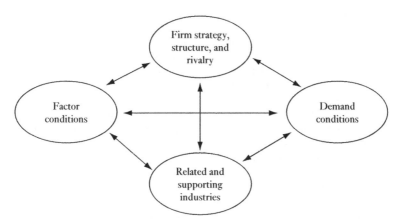

Figure 1   The determinants of national advantage (Porter's diamond)

that clusters of firms and clusters of industries might have shared benefits from a common location, at the expense of (in terms of competitive advantage) firms located elsewhere. Thus, it has been advantageous to be an auto assembler in Japan and a chemical manufacturer in Germany. It may also be the case that in these circumstances, it might not pay any one local player to attempt to be different from other local players. Strategically, any one firm can choose between shared local benefits ("nationality is destiny") and striving to create a unique and distinctive position.

See also *competitive advantage*

Bibliography

Dunning, J. H. (1993). Internationalizing Porter's diamond. *Management International Review*, 33(2), special issue, 7–16.
Porter, M. E. (1990). The competitive advantage of nations. *Harvard Business Review*, March/April, 73–93.

network externalities

John McGee

The entry on COMPETITIVE MARKET THEORY outlined the traditional economic model for the "old world," which was driven by ECONOMIES OF SCALE and ECONOMIES OF SCOPE. The "new world," characterized by information and communications technology, is governed by a different dynamic. Network externalities are the new drivers of the network economy (*see* NETWORK INDUSTRIES; NETWORKS). It is important to recognize that economies of scale/scope and network externalities represent the extreme ends of a spectrum of effects, and that the presence of one does not imply the exclusion of the other. Companies may experience the effects of both to varying degrees, with a tendency for network externalities to have more strategic relevance in the new network economy.

The concept of network externalities has attracted the attention of academics and practitioners alike. The extent to which network industries have proliferated in the economy is a recent phenomenon. The effects of network externalities, however, have been recognized for some time with the development of the older network companies such as the railroads and the electricity systems. In 1804 Trevithick constructed the first practical locomotive in England. In 1882 the Edison Electric Lighting Company completed the first commercial generating station at Holborn Viaduct in London. The first commercial telephone line was installed in Boston, Massachusetts, in 1877.

Network externalities are defined as the increasing utility that a user derives from consumption of a product as the number of other users who consume the same product increases. For example, the more people there are in a telephone network, the more users can be reached on the network, thereby increasing its usability. Fax machines, broadcast industry services, credit card networks, and computer hardware and software are examples of products exhibiting network externalities.

Networks were originally analyzed on the assumption that each network was owned by a single firm and research concentrated on the efficient use of the network structure and on the appropriate allocation of costs. With the antitrust cases against AT&T and its later breakup, attention shifted toward economies of scope, the efficiency gains from joint operation of complementary components of networks. This led to issues of interconnection and compatibility in parallel with the reduced role of IBM in the 1980s and 1990s in the setting of technical standards in computer hardware and software. As technology has advanced, there have been significant reductions in telecommunications costs and a shift toward fragmented ownership of telecommunications networks. MARKET STRUCTURE has shifted from natural monopoly to oligopoly. Similar trends are evident in other IT-intensive industries. Thus, the focus of interest in network economics has shifted from the analysis of natural monopoly toward issues of interconnection, compatibility, interoperability, and coordination of quality.

WINNER-TAKES-ALL STRATEGIES

For normal goods, the demand curve slopes downwards. As price decreases, more of the product is demanded. Other elements in the

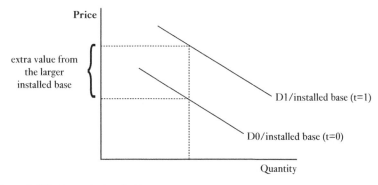

Figure 1   Demand shifts due to the installed base

demand function such as income or advertising serve as "demand shifters" and would elevate the demand to a higher level. Figure 1 illustrates the traditional role of a demand shifter. Higher levels of consumption are derived from higher incomes (positive income elasticities) or from lower prices (negative price elasticities).

This fundamental relationship is greatly distorted in the presence of network externalities because sales rise as accumulated sales (the installed base) rise. Therefore we observe a chicken and egg paradox. Customers may not be interested in purchasing because the installed base is small and/or not expected to grow. For example, imagine there may be reluctance to purchase complex software without Internet support, helplines, and user groups. Alternatively, there may be confident expectations that the installed base will grow substantially and therefore consumers will confidently make purchases. The paradox is that consumers will not buy if the installed base is too low. However, the installed base is too low because customers will not buy. The crux of the paradox lies in the management of expectations. In markets for normal goods, equilibrium is explained in terms of a balance between costs and demand, between marginal costs and marginal utility. In network markets, there is also equilibrium to be struck between actual demand and expectations of total demand.

This gives rise to an economic paradox. Almost the first law of economics is that value comes from scarcity. However, in the new world economy value comes from plenty: the more

something is demanded and the more it is expected to be demanded, then the more valuable it becomes. Expectations are so important in driving demand that a point exists where the momentum is so overwhelming that success becomes a runaway event and we observe a "winner-takes-all" phenomenon (see figure 2).

There exists a "tipping point" (*see* CRITICAL MASS) when the installed base (or size of network) tips expectations sharply toward one player (or one network) and away from its rival. We have experienced this effect when we moved toward Windows as our prevailing computer operating system, rather than OS2. Another example of tipping would be IBM-compatibles versus Apple, as shown in figure 3.

The exception to the winner-takes-all phenomenon would be a regulated network market with strong interconnections between competing platforms. The mobile telephone industry is a classic example. The standards are harmonized across the network providers, at least by continental region. The platforms are interlinked and the sales curves of the regulated network providers follow the pattern of the overall subscription curve for the industry.

Traditional economic thinking is based on negative feedback systems in which the strong get weaker at the margin and the weak get stronger, thus providing a drive toward a competitive equilibrium. This is captured in economics by the concept of diminishing marginal utility as consumption grows. In the new world of networks, feedback rules. In this world, the valuation of a product increases the more others

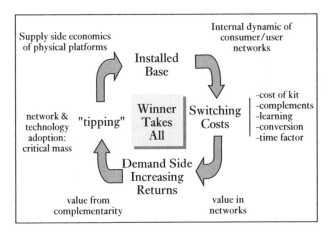

Figure 2   Winner takes all

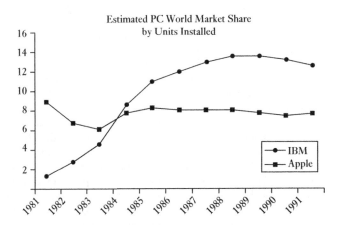

Figure 3   Market share of IBM and Apple

consume the product. Strictly speaking, it arises from the interdependence of consumer decisions whereas diminishing marginal utility dominates when consumer decisions are independent – the normal assumption in economics.

The price–quantity relationship is normally held to be downward sloping, but the demand curve for a network product should be drawn differently (figure 4). The value to the consumer of a network product is reflected in the price he or she is willing to pay – the vertical axis. The principal driver of value is the size of the network, also referred to as the installed base, and is shown on the horizontal axis. Quantity demanded does still have an effect on price,

but, for these products, this is secondary to the network effect.

The initial upward slope of the curve reflects a rising valuation at the margin, as consumers perceive that they gain value by virtue of other consumers having the product. Being on the Wintel standard gives value to new users. However, as the network grows, the extra consumers at the margin are less valuable – i.e., this shape assumes that those users with higher potential valuation of the network will join first. As the network gets very large, further growth has less value for future customers. The intercept on the vertical axis represents the value the network product has as a stand-alone product. Thus a

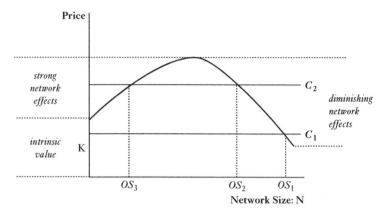

Figure 4 The network demand curve

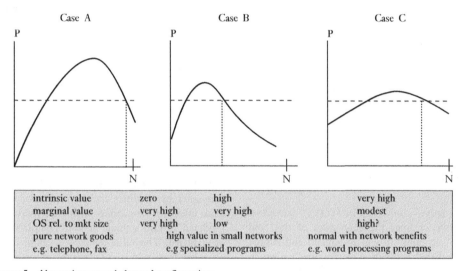

Figure 5 Alternative network demand configurations

Wintel computer has some stand-alone value, but a telephone has no value on its own and is a pure network good.

There is a notion of an optimal size of a network. This can be seen from the interaction of demand and cost so that, as less and less valuable customers join the network, there may come a time when the costs of acquiring and servicing new customers begin to exceed the price those customers are willing to pay. This determines the optimal size and has significant implications for competition.

The three configurations shown in figure 5 indicate the range of possibilities. The first is a pure network good, such as a telephone system, in which the optimal size of network is a very high proportion of the available market. This implies there is little or no room for rival networks. The second is a product with a significant intrinsic value that attracts a modest-size group of users. For example, this could be a corporate software package (e.g., enterprise solutions) that attracts dedicated user support from the supplier through the web. Alternative networks could coexist. The third case is one of very high intrinsic demand but extensive consumer interactions (small in size but several in number) providing a substantial total network value. The obvious example is word-processing software where the value from standardizing on Microsoft Word is very high, with the result that alternative standards (such as WordPerfect) are being frozen out of the market even though the intrinsic value of any word-processing package is high.

Bibliography

Baumol, W., Panzar, J., and Willig, R. (1982). Contestable markets and the theory of industry. *American Economic Review*, 72.

Economides, N. (1996). The economics of networks. *International Journal of Industrial Organization*, 14 (2), 675–99.

Katz, M. and Shapiro, C. (1985). Network externalities, competition and compatibility. *American Economic Review*, 75 (3), 424–40.

Sharkey, N. E. and Sharkey, A. J. C. (1993). Adaptive generalization and the transfer of knowledge. *Artificial Intelligence Review*, 7, special issue on Connectionism, 313–28.

network industries

John McGee

The entry on COMPETITIVE MARKET THEORY outlines the economics of the "old world" economy in which demand and supply are mediated through a market mechanism in which product demand is independent of other products and demand is not time dependent.

However, there is a class of markets and industries that do not conform to these assumptions. These are known as network industries (*see* NETWORKS). Networks are interconnected nodes that enable individual nodes to be linked, either in production or in consumption, with other nodes. Thus railroads and telephone systems are real, tangible networks, whereas virtual networks refer to nodes (individuals) connected by information, such as computer users.

Network industries are common. Many physical networks have been around for a long time, e.g., railroads, telephone, electricity. So-called virtual networks have arisen largely through information technology and include fax machines and computer operating systems. We can distinguish intuitively between pure networks and indirect or weak networks. Pure networks exist where it is an essential characteristic of the product that it is organized through complementary nodes and links, such as a railway network or the telephone system. A key element is the notion of complementarity, thus the value of a railway station is derived from the existence of other railway stations on the network. A weaker definition relies also on complementarity between products (or nodes, in network language) but allows the links to be created *by* the customer rather than *for* the customer. For example, the value of a washing machine is affected by the aggregate consumption of washing machines and the consumption level of the particular brand, since this determines the availability of parts, repair operatives, detergents, fabric softeners, and various other related goods and services. The value of a sporting event is influenced by the aggregate size of the audience, as this enhances the excitement level, analysis, discussion, and remembrance of the event.

The essence of this idea is that the demand for a product is influenced by total demand for the product class or by total demand in a complementary product class. Thus demand is conditioned by a consumer externality. Where these consumer externalities are powerful, the feedback effect on demand is such that there is a tendency toward a single network, or platform, or standard. The value for consumers of being on a common standard outweighs any specific differences between alternative standards. We see that the VHS standard was preferred to a "technically better" Betamax rival to the extent that the rival standard disappeared. The Wintel standard is greatly preferred to the Apple standard, although the rival does still exist as a small niche in the market. Where the externality is smaller and the intrinsic difference between standards is relatively larger, then we might observe multiple competing and coexisting "platforms" (where the term "platform" denotes an array of linked complementary products that together are compatible with other products). An example of a platform can be seen in the automobile industry, where a company might develop a core of components and subassemblies that can be used to support alternative body styling to create a product range. Such a platform can coexist with other platforms because the scale efficiencies associated with platforms are modest in relation to market size.

See also *network externalities; network industry strategies*

Bibliography

Economides, N. (1996). The economics of networks. *International Journal of Industrial Organization*, 14 (2), 675–99.

McGee, J. and Sammut-Bonnici, T. (2002). Network industries in the new economy: The effect of knowledge and the power of positive feedback. *European Business Journal*, 14, 3 (September), 116–32.

Shapiro, C. and Varian, H. (1999). *Information Rules: A Strategic Guide to the Network Economy*. Boston: Harvard Business School Press.

Shy, O. (2001). *The Economics of Network Industries*. Cambridge: Cambridge University Press.

network industry strategies

John McGee

"Firms that compete in markets where network externalities are present face unique trade-offs regarding the choice of a technical standard. Adhering to a leading compatibility standard allows a firm's product to capture the value added by a large network. However, simultaneously the firm loses direct control over the market supply of the good and faces (direct) intra-platform competition. Alternatively, adhering to a unique standard allows the firm to face less or no intra-platform competition, but it sacrifices the added value associated with a large network" (Economides and Flyer, 1997).

This trade-off (*see* TRADE-OFFS) is a key strategic decision that depends in part on the control that firms have in making their output compatible with competitors' outputs and complementary products. The ability to conform to a common standard opens the opportunity to make this trade-off. Where standards are proprietary, the decision rests with the owner of the standard. The owner's trade-off is the payoff associated with developing the existing network and its spillovers versus the introduction of more

intra-platform competition. Essentially the trade-off is the same: to adhere to a common standard or to seek uniqueness. This can be expressed as a sequential game: at the outset, one chooses the appropriate technical standard (and, therefore, the network to join), and later one chooses how to compete. Normal markets do not have this choice of network and there are consequences for MARKET STRUCTURE and competition of the presence of NETWORK EXTERNALITIES. Recent research models networks as coalition structures and analyzes the stability of coalitions under different standards regimes and varying levels of network externalities. There are a number of implications for market structure in the presence of network externalities.

First, it is intuitively clear that industry output will be higher when there are network externalities and when standards are open. Firms are free to choose which standard to adopt and are deterred only by the costs of adoption. Second, when standards are incompatible and the owners of standards can exercise proprietary control, incumbents are more strongly protected against the consequences of new entrants. Moreover, there will usually be considerable asymmetries between firms in terms of outputs, prices, and profits. (Under incompatibility regimes, firms are equivalent to platforms and constitute one-firm networks.) For pure network goods the asymmetries are particularly marked.

In general, with total incompatibility of standards, market concentration, output inequality, and price and profit inequality increase with the extent of the network externality. This is an important result because it explains why one or two firms so often dominate network industries. The mechanism is straightforward. The leading network establishes its CRITICAL MASS, leaving the second network to establish a critical mass across the remaining untapped market coverage. The third network follows in the same fashion, and so on. It follows that there will be a tendency to provide large incentives to organize customers into few platforms so as to maximize the added value from the available networks. Firms will be keen to abandon their own weak standards in favor of the higher value obtainable from a leading network.

There is a third implication. Where there are proprietary standards and strong network effects, there is no natural equilibrium in terms of network offerings. There are always incentives for at least one firm to move to a stronger network and the consequences of any one move is to shift the incentives for all other firms. However, equilibrium can be reinforced by the refusal of firms to make their proprietary standards available. Again, the mechanism is straightforward. Under strong externalities, the owner of a standard has a considerable incentive to exploit the standard by itself and to exclude other firms with weaker standards. Conversely, where the externality is weak, the owner will find a stronger incentive to admit other firms to its proprietary standard in order to grow the network through collective effort and thus generate more added value.

In summary, strong network externalities suggest the following conclusions:

1   Larger industry output.
2   Very large asymmetries between firms/platforms.
3   Likelihood of market dominance.
4   Enhancement and protection of proprietary standards.
5   Equilibrium market structures that are the reverse of the world without network externalities.

IMPLICATIONS FOR STRATEGY

This suggests some rules that govern the new economy:

1   The information economy depends on connectivity. Without connectivity, consumer interdependence is indirect. Positive feedback gives an economic law of plenty – more gives more.
2   The competition between rival networks/standards can be hard to call in advance. Management of expectations is key and "tippy markets" are common.
3   In the new world the upfront costs are very large and the revenues are substantially delayed and are significantly at risk.
4   As a result, this is a "winner-takes-all" world.

5   It is also a world of immense uncertainty where even the range of potential outcomes is not known, but also where there is a significant probability that future technological change might undermine an apparently winning position.
6   There is a law of inverse pricing. The best (i.e., the most valuable in the future) products are given away, such as web browsers, in order to create a consumer standard, and sheer volume causes both marginal costs and prices to fall over time as the product becomes more valuable. The cash flow machine consists of modest (even small) margins multiplied by gigantic volumes to defray massive investments. The machine is volume driven and protected by very large SWITCHING COSTS.
7   Open standards are the key to volume. Protected standards are only viable as small, high-priced niche markets.
8   The first strategic choice is what network to join. The second, and a long way behind, is how to compete within the network of choice.

A new set of strategies is emerging to offset the risks and pressures exerted by these rules. This is visible in the setting up of global standards and their ensuing platforms. For example, Group Speciale Mobile, commonly known as GSM, is an association of 600 network operators and suppliers of the mobile phone industry. Its primary objective is to set a common standard for mobile communications in order to create a homogeneous industry where equipment, software, and networks can seamlessly talk to one another. Strategies of standardization are stabilizing the markets and charting the course for research and development policies.

These economic characteristics of network industries are dependent in large part on the interconnectivity that is characteristic of the technologies of INFORMATION GOODS. Interconnectivity allows customers to view, use, and link products, giving rise to virtual networks of customers. In these networks, powerful demand-side increasing returns can operate. Where consumer-based externalities are powerful, there are strong pressures toward "winner-takes-all" phenomena (e.g., Wintel globally, and

Sky TV in the UK). In these circumstances, conventional economic laws are challenged. De facto monopoly can emerge, but uncertainty is high and markets may be intrinsically unstable. Successive waves of technology may outmode old monopolies and serve as the basis for new monopolies.

The rate of growth and now the sheer size of the ICT (information, computing, and telecommunications) industry has been the progenitor of major changes in the economy. We have seen major effects on other industries through the new value possibilities that information technology offers and through the substantial fixed costs and minimum scales required for effective deployment of these technologies. When linked to networks of interdependent customers, we see the potential emergence of "winner-takes-all" strategies and the emergence of new monopolies.

The ICT industry can be decomposed into its component parts in order to see who the players are and how they interact with one another. In doing this we begin to see a new type of industrial order – one marked by networked complementarities and cooperation in place of the traditional model of hierarchy and competition. We can also decompose the industry into four horizontal levels, technology, supply chain, platform, and network, to show that these have different economic characteristics and therefore that corporate strategies (*see* CORPORATE STRATEGY) have different dynamics. The examples quoted indicate the range and extent of the possibilities inherent in the new technologies and for the nature of rivalry in the form of preemptive strikes and technology races. We note particularly the pervasive changes that are taking places in supply chains generally. The increasing importance of connectivity and modularity is forcing a shift from competitive mode toward cooperative mode. This raises thoughts of self-organizing systems and the notion of co-evolution, rather a long way from the search for and exercise of crude bargaining power. The sheer size and cost of physical platforms also creates new dynamics. The pervasive use of alliances (*see* STRATEGIC ALLIANCES) is an obvious example. Less obvious is how the need for interoperability requires new attitudes toward complexity and requirements for agility.

Finally, note the significance of interdependence between consumers. This effect at its strongest completely shifts our thinking from the prevalence of oligopolistic competition (size matters but so do diminishing returns) to the possibility of winner takes all and the monopoly (size matters – full stop). Clearly, such network effects are not always going to be so extreme, but there is a real possibility that the combination of high fixed costs, significant ECONOMIES OF SCALE, and high degrees of knowledge specialization will, when taken together with consumer bandwagons, create massive new corporate structures to which the major (and perhaps only) discipline will be further developments in technology. However, the analysis of consumer lock-in suggests the real possibility that switching costs might inhibit the adoption of valuable new technologies.

Thus the brave new world has a sting in the tail. The pervasive development of the ICT industries has resulted in, and continues to promote, very substantial consequential changes throughout the economy. In doing so, industry economics and dynamics do change and significant adaptations have to take place in making responses to avoid getting run down by the juggernaut. But also changes are needed in the nature of the corporate strategies and in the mindsets required. Where the conjunction of certain technological and consumer circumstances takes place, then the strategy game becomes a very direct race to establish dominant position. Even where such games fail to achieve their objectives, the cost of unproductive investment could be enormous. Where they in fact succeed, many will nevertheless have failed and we would also face the difficulties in managing the consequences of de facto monopoly. The data available do not suggest that winner takes all is likely to be a frequent phenomenon. However, all the other indications suggest that various forms of scale-intensive, preemptive strategies will become much more common (see, e.g., the telecommunications boom and bust). But as a counterpoint, we can also see that there are very considerable forces promoting more cooperation and stronger incentives toward a much more subtle blending of cooperative and competitive modes of practice within industries.

230   networks

See also *competitive market theory; network industries; networks*

Bibliography

Arthur, W. B. (1989). Competing technologies, increasing returns, and lock-in by historical events. *Economic Journal*, 99, 116–31.

Arthur, W. B. (1990). Positive feedback in the economy. *Scientific American*, 262, 92–9.

Economides, N. (1996). The economics of networks. *International Journal of Industrial Organization*, 14 (2), 675–99.

Economides, N. and Flyer, F. (1997). Compatibility and market structure for network goods. Discussion Paper EC-98-02.

Garud, R., Kumaraswamy, A., and Prabhu, A. (1995). Networking for success in cyberspace. *IEEE Proceedings of the International Conference on Multimedia Computing and Systems*, 335–40.

Gottinger, H.-W. (2003). *Economics of Network Industries*. London: Routledge.

Henderson, R. M. and Clark, K. B. (1990). Architectural innovation: The reconfiguration of existing product technologies and the failure of established firms. *Administrative Science Quarterly*, 35.

Kelly, K. (1998). *New Rules for the New Economy: Ten Ways the Network Economy is Changing Everything*. London: Fourth Estate.

McGee, J. and Sammut-Bonnici, T. (2002). Network industries in the new economy: The effect of knowledge and the power of positive feedback. *European Business Journal*, 14, 3 (September), 116–32.

Quinn, J. B. (2001). *Services and Technology: Revolutionizing Economics*. Business and Education, Darmond College.

Sammut-Bonnici, T. and McGee, J. (2002). Network strategies for the new economy: Emerging strategies for new industry structures. *European Business Journal*. 14 (4), 174–85.

Shapiro, C. and Varian, H. (1999). *Information Rules: A Strategic Guide to the Network Economy*. Boston: Harvard Business School Press.

Shy, O. (2001). *The Economics of Network Industries*. Cambridge: Cambridge University Press.

networks

John McGee

A network is a set of connections (links) between nodes. A two-way network allows the links to be operated in both directions, whereas a one-way network has distinct directionality. Two-way networks include railroads and telephone systems. Figure 1 shows a simple star network where A can communicate with B through a switch, S. B can also communicate with A by reversing the direction of the link (e.g., a telephone call).

In figure 1 we have eight nodes (A through G) linked through a switch, S. If this were a two-way network, AB and BA would be distinct products (different telephone calls, different

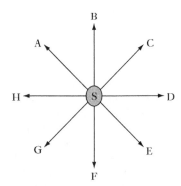

A star network has a collection of nodes clustered around some central resource. Movement of resources/products must pass through this central node, e.g., a local telephone exchange

Figure 1   A two-way network

rail journeys). The total number of products in the network would be 56, i.e., $n(n-1)$ where n is the number of nodes. If there were to be a ninth member (the dotted lines to H in figure 1), this would increase the total number of products to 72 (n is now 9), a total increase of 16 products available from the expanded network. If the value to each user of being in the network is proportional to the number of users, then the value of this network has just increased by 28.5 percent (16 as a percentage of 56), even though the size of the network has increased by only 12.5 percent (one added to eight). This is an algebraic characteristic of network ECONOMIES OF SCALE that the value rises disproportionately higher than the increase in network size as long as prices are constant and products are independent. Intuitively, we might expect that beyond a certain size an increase in network size beyond a certain point has little value. If this network were a one-way network, there would be half the number of products but the value of the network would nevertheless increase at the same rate, while achieving only half the value.

The analysis of complementarity is equivalent to the analysis of a one-way network. Figure 1 can be extended as in figure 2 to show a typical one-way network. Here we can interpret the A_i as automatic teller machines (ATMs) and the B_j as banks. The network runs only from A to B. The significance of the two switches S_A and S_B is that they have only one link. This means that there is compatibility between all ATMs and all banks. This maximizes the value of the network but increases the competition between banks for customers through ATMs. It is this compatibility that makes the complementarity actual and the network operational. For complex products, actual complementarity has to be achieved through adherence to specific technical standards. Other complementary products can be visualized in terms of figure 2. VHS tapes could be the A_i and VHS players could be the B_j. Think also of copier paper and copiers, or printer paper and printers, or car accessories and cars, or local and long-distance telephone networks.

Networks can be real or virtual. Real networks are found in industries such as telephony and railways where a physical network is present. Virtual networks are typified by computer and software platforms where the interconnection between users is intangible. In real networks the interconnection between users is tangible. Examples are cable networks for telephone

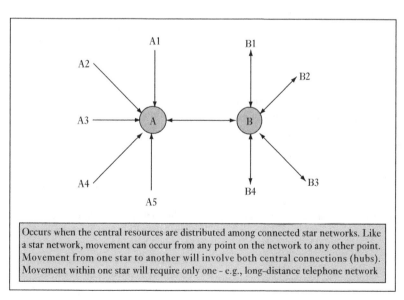

Occurs when the central resources are distributed among connected star networks. Like a star network, movement can occur from any point on the network to any other point. Movement from one star to another will involve both central connections (hubs). Movement within one star will require only one - e.g., long-distance telephone network

Figure 2   A one-way network

users and radio transmissions in mobile phones. Electricity grids and telecommunications networks, encompassing telephones, fax machines, online services, and the Internet, are typical examples of products or services within real networks. There are one-way networks such as broadcast television where information flows in one direction only. In two-way networks, such as railroads and telephone systems, links are operated in both directions. Any network may be viewed as a set of connections (links) between nodes. A two-way network allows the links to be operated in both directions, whereas a one-way network has specific direction.

In virtual networks the interconnections between users are intangible, but users remain interdependent. Computer systems are typical of virtual networks. For example, Mac users are part of the Mac network, with Apple as the sponsor of the network. Mac users are locked into a network determined by the technology standard of this platform. They can only use software that is compatible with the system and will exchange files with users within the system. Operating systems such as Windows and Unix are other examples of virtual networks. Virtual network dynamics also operate in the entertainment industry for Sony Playstation, Microsoft Xbox, and Nintendo's Gamecube networks.

Network size is still important in virtual networks in that a large consumer base makes production viable and usage possible. In addition, the value of a product increases as the number of, or the variety of, the complementary goods or services increases. Indirect network effects in the computer industry are referred to as the hardware–software paradigm. The success of an operating system for personal computers depends on the variety of software applications available in the market. Value may depend more critically on software applications.

See also *competitive market theory; network externalities; network industries; network industry strategy*

Bibliography

Economides, N. (1996). The economics of networks. *International Journal of Industrial Organization*, 14 (2), 675–99.

McGee, J. and Sammut-Bonnici, T. (2002). Network industries in the new economy: The effect of knowledge and the power of positive feedback. *European Business Journal*, 14, 3 (September), 116–32.

Sammut-Bonnici, T. and McGee, J. (2002). Network strategy for the new economy: Emerging strategies for new industry structures. *European Business Journal*, 14 (4), 174–85.

Shapiro, C. and Varian, H. (1999). *Information Rules: A Strategic Guide to the Network Economy*. Boston: Harvard Business School Press.

Shy, O. (2001). *The Economics of Network Industries*. Cambridge: Cambridge University Press.

non-financial performance indicators

Kaye Loveridge

These are measures of performance that do not appear in the company accounts. Although they are called "non-financial," this does not mean they have no financial impact. Moreover, it is argued that these are measures that drive financial performance, while financial measures themselves are focused on outcome.

Sales figures, for example, may depend upon a company's ability to deliver its products on time, to meet customer specifications. Similarly, the success of new product development may depend upon a company's ability to get a product to market before competitors. With ever-decreasing product cycles, time and delivery performance are clearly important non-financial measures that need to be monitored.

Traditional financial performance accounting measures, such as return on investment and earnings per share, have been criticized for giving misleading signals with regard to continuous improvement and innovation. While financial measures worked well in the past, they are out of step with the skills and competences that companies are currently trying to master (Kaplan and Norton, 1992; *see* BALANCED SCORECARD).

As the quality movement gained momentum in the 1980s, it stimulated the development of an array of techniques, as companies saw that quality could be used as a strategic weapon to differentiate themselves from their competitors. They committed substantial resources to developing new measures, such as defect rates, response times, and delivery commitments, to evaluate the performance of their products, services, and operations (Eccles, 1991).

According to Eccles, companies need to design their performance measures from scratch. They should begin by asking, "Given our strategy, what are the most important measures of performance?" If their strategy is to compete on quality, quality metrics will be needed to support them. Companies need to ask, "How do these measures relate to one another?" Defect rate, for example, is a quality measure that is presumed to affect customer satisfaction. Most importantly, "What measures truly predict long-term financial success in our business?" Customer satisfaction? If so, it needs to be measured. Basically, if it matters, the message is to measure it.

In the 1980s, companies that failed to notice a decline in customer satisfaction and the quality of their products saw their strong financial records deteriorate (Eccles, 1991). While many companies can honestly say they have been carrying out surveys of customer satisfaction for years, it is also true that these surveys were rarely examined at board level. Where companies describe their strategies in terms of customer service, innovation, or the quality of their products and capabilities of their people, non-financial measures need to reflect these strategic priorities and be monitored by the board.

In the UK, Bass Brewers Limited developed and implemented some new performance measures in 1993, to reflect its new way of working. It included a broader range of measures to summarize the overall state of health of the company, outside of finance. While quality and customer service, for example, had always been important to the company and had received attention, they were not measured as ratios. These measures were submitted to the board and became almost as important as financial statements.

In the past, while quality at Bass was measured throughout the brewing process, the aim was to get the brew right, to meet quality specifications, at the end of the brewing process. There were limits within which the condition of the beer could fall and, as long as the final package fell within those limits eventually, it would pass the quality test. Where beer had to be refiltered, an extra cost was generated, and so Bass began to look at quality on a "right first

time" basis and to measure how often it got it right first time. This is an example of a quality measure that has cost implications. The principle of getting it right first time, eliminating waste and rework, became much more important to Bass, along with the need to reduce costs in the business.

Current management accounting theory began to be widely criticized following the publication of Johnson and Kaplan's *Relevance Lost* (1987). The theme throughout this book is that performance measurement needs to be customer and market oriented, to measure external needs, not just internal requirements. It should support the organization's strategy, which needs to be customer driven.

At the beginning of 1992, IBM UK Limited changed its performance measurement system to focus on internal and external measures that it felt were important. Its business goals are now driven by five key measures: customer satisfaction, shareholder value, world-class quality on the Baldridge scale, employee morale, and a robust balance sheet. These measures represent the interests of its main stakeholders: its customers, shareholders, employees, and government.

IBM realized that it had to be customer driven, that unless it achieved its drive for customer satisfaction and world-class quality, it could forget its other measures. A customer service mentality is regarded by IBM as its number one critical success factor. It realized that getting its products to market quickly, working together in teams, and developing a service-based culture would be critical to its success in the future. It believed that performance measurement was fundamental to making its new organizational structure work.

However, measures of customer satisfaction are only important in so far as they ultimately end up as cash flow. Customer satisfaction, for example, may be maximized if a company gives its products away, but of course the company will go out of business. The appropriate balance has to be found, one that attempts to maximize customer satisfaction while at the same time minimizing the cost of providing it.

Following the takeover of United Distillers by Guinness in 1986, the company grew faster than it had ever grown before. Its success was largely attributed to the single-mindedness of

234 non-financial performance indicators

the Guinness personnel, who quickly agreed that its objective was to make a profit and focused on making its brands more profitable. United Distillers believed that a company had to determine its criteria for success; then it could measure its success on the basis of whether it met its performance objectives. However, success had to be measured in a commercial sense. At United Distillers, success means making money, because, as it emphasized, if it does not make money, it runs the risk of being taken over by a company such as Hanson and asset stripped.

While, in the past, the production workers were considered to be the most important, United Distillers brought in more marketing personnel, with an understanding of brands, and they carried out a large amount of qualitative research to find out what their customers wanted. Thus the company·shifted away from being producer focused to become more customer focused.

By being more responsive to its customers' needs and gaining a better understanding of its brand activities, United Distillers was able to hold on to MARKET SHARE, even at a time of changing consumer tastes, increased awareness of health and fitness, and changes in fashion and mixing of spirits, and it was very successful. It quadrupled the profits of many of its brands and increased overall profit by 28 percent. This is an example of where responsiveness to customers – not accounting costs – was necessary for competitive excellence in long-term profitability.

Being responsive to customers involves being flexible, reducing lead times, and removing constraints from the business (Johnson, 1992). Non-financial performance indicators form part of a broader set of measures and help to motivate improvements in critical areas of the business to determine the overall health of a company.

Measures that include the quality of a firm's products, the level of service to customers, and the customers' satisfaction with that service, help – together with a range of other measures – to predict a company's long-term performance and strength in the marketplace. The use of a balanced set of measures can motivate breakthrough improvements in critical areas such as product, process, customer, and market development (Kaplan and Norton, 1993). These factors are crucial to a company's success in the marketplace.

Performance measures need to be grounded in strategic objectives and competitive demands (Kaplan and Norton, 1993). Performance measurement is an integral part of the management system. It is no longer the sole responsibility of the accounting function, but the responsibility of everyone in the company.

Bibliography

Eccles, R. (1991). The performance measurement manifesto. *Harvard Business Review*, **69**, 131–7.

Johnson, H. (1992). *Relevance Regained: From Top-Down Control to Bottom-Up Empowerment*. New York: Free Press.

Johnson, H. and Kaplan, R. (1987). *Relevance Lost: The Rise and Fall of Management Accounting*. Boston: Harvard Business School Press.

Kaplan, R. and Norton, D. (1992). The balanced scorecard: Measures that drive performance. *Harvard Business Review*, January/February, 71–9.

Kaplan, R. and Norton, D. (1993). Putting the balanced scorecard to work. *Harvard Business Review*, **71**, 134–47.

Singleton-Green, B. (1993). If it matters, measure it! *Accountancy*, May, 52–3.

organization structure

Chris Smith

The modern, hierarchical business enterprise arose in the 1850s in the US and Europe, to administer the new railroad and telegraph companies. An organizational structure based on a split into functional responsibilities (the "U-form" – unitary form) was the norm at this time (see figure 1).

Expanding size, however, particularly where expansion included DIVERSIFICATION, compromised the effectiveness of the U-form.

> The inherent weakness in the centralized, functionally departmentalized operating company … became critical only when the administrative load on the senior executives increased to such an extent that they were unable to handle their entrepreneurial responsibilities efficiently. This situation arose when the operations of the enterprise became too complex and the problems of coordination, appraisal and policy formulation too intricate for a small number of top officers to handle both long-run, entrepreneurial, and short-run, operational administrative activities. (Chandler, 1962: 299)

To overcome such problems, the large American companies Du Pont, General Motors, Jersey Standard, and Sears Roebuck pioneered a movement to an innovative organizational form in the early 1920s. This innovation, which became known as the "multidivisional" or "M-form," divided tasks and responsibilities into semi-autonomous operating units (profit centers) organized on brand, product, or regional lines (see figure 2).

After slow early growth, the spread of the M-form increased dramatically following World War II. In 1949 fewer than a quarter of the Fortune 500 companies were divisionalized (*see* DIVISIONAL STRUCTURE). This figure had risen to just over a half in 1959. By 1969 only one fifth of companies in the top 500 were not divisionalized (Hill, 1994). Similar trends have been evident in Europe and the UK and today the multidivisional form is the most prevalent organizational structure in large companies in western economies.

> The basic reason for its success was simply that it clearly removed the executives' responsible for the destiny of the entire enterprise from the more routine operational activities, and so gave them time, information, and even more psychological commitment for long-term planning and appraisal. … Thus the new structure left the broad strategic decisions as to the allocation of existing resources and the acquisitions of new ones in the hands of a top team of generalists. Relieved of operating duties and tactical decisions, a general executive was less likely to reflect the position of just one part of the whole. (Chandler, 1962: 309–10)

The M-form has several positive attributes. It enables business managers to maximize economies of specialization, by allowing them to focus on their products and markets, whilst freeing corporate managers from the distractions of day-to-day operations. It makes it easy for corporate management to measure and compare the performance of business units through financial statements, and facilitates the addition (acquisition; *see* ACQUISITION STRATEGY) or deletion (DIVESTMENT) of businesses. On top of this, the stand-alone business ethos fits well with western values of individualism and accountability, and encourages the development of autonomous general managers.

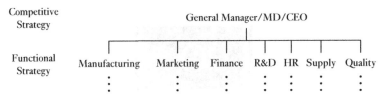

Figure 1　The U-form organization

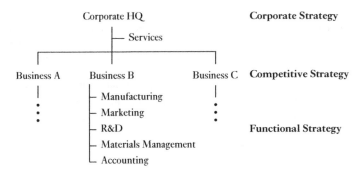

Figure 2　The M-form organization

Alfred Chandler, the eminent business historian, chronicled the rise of the M-form organizations in the US in his celebrated book *Strategy and Structure* (1962). He also provided a telling and powerful argument for the benefits of size in papers like "The Enduring Logic of Business Success." He argued that ECONOMIES OF SCALE and ECONOMIES OF SCOPE were the motive power behind large organizations. These enable large plants to produce at much lower costs than small ones (*scale*). Large plants use many of the same raw and semi-finished materials and intermediate production processes to make a variety of different products (*scope*). To capitalize on the new, larger scale of manufacturing investment, firms needed to make two further, related sets of investment. The first was to create national, then international marketing and distribution organizations (both scale and scope effects). The second was to develop new management teams. The lower/middle levels were to coordinate flow of products through production and distribution. The top level was to coordinate and monitor current operations and to plan and allocate resources for future activities. The new levels of investment

thus require an integrated and balanced economic and managerial infrastructure to insure constant flow of product and high-capacity utilization. In simple economic terms, the scale-and scope-driven savings in operations have to be balanced in part by higher administrative and managerial costs. But these too offer scale and scope benefits as long as volumes are maintained.

Chandler took the argument further. He observed that first movers quickly dominated their industries and continued to do so (for decades). Those who failed to make the right scale of investments rarely became competitive at home or in international markets, nor did the home-based industries in which they operated. But success was not simply a matter of cost efficiencies and competing on price. Competition took place through strategic positioning and innovation. The largest organizations were able to compete on quality improvement, innovations in marketing and market development, and on systematic R&D. At the same time, they made continuous improvements in production and distribution, product and process improvement, and better sources of supply. Competitive strategy was a blend of cost and differentiation. The

CORPORATE STRATEGY objectives of the emerging giants were growth by expansion into related products (mostly *scope*-driven), or by moving abroad (mostly *scale* effects). These were based on the organizational capabilities acquired in the process of domestic oligopolistic competition. There were also some horizontal movements (acquisitions) and some vertical integration (*see* VERTICAL INTEGRATION STRATEGY) to control material supplies or distribution outlets.

This is the history of the emergence of international oligopolies founded initially on scale and scope advantages in production and distribution but enhanced and secured by scale and scope effects in marketing, R&D, supply management, and organization. However, large is not always logical. The giants can and do stagnate, with Ford Motor Company providing the leading example in the 1920s. In its case the direct competition between two giants, Ford and General Motors (GM), was to leave at least one of them injured. In postwar years, particularly the 1960s, the compulsion for growth led companies to much broader-based diversification. This became known as conglomerate-style diversification (*see* CONGLOMERATE STRATEGY) and was, and is, highly controversial.

The economic argument for large size required an organization structure that was capable of managing both scale effects (which require specialization and depth) and scope effects (which need variety and breadth). The

divisionalized corporation, M-form in style, was clearly appropriate for the task in comparison to the earlier U-form. Figures 3 and 4 illustrate the strategy–structure choices. The term *U-form* has given way to *functional*, emphasizing the focus on functional specialization as the source of managerial economies. Figure 4 indicates the value of the divisionalized (M-form) in that it allows for both operational decentralization as well as strategic direction.

However, there are also manifest drawbacks to the M-form. Because corporate managers are free from operational distractions, they can also get out of touch with business and divisional issues, and hence are reliant on the input of their politically aware general managers. The clear structural split does not necessarily mean there is a clear split of responsibilities, and confusion often reigns as to which level is accountable for various outcomes or processes. Further complications arise due to the (rational) tendency of business units to compete rather than cooperate with one another for the limited resources available. This leads to general managers "selling" their business needs to the corporate level, with the resultant blurring of reality that selling frequently entails. Perhaps the most significant problem with the M-form is its tendency to impede the development of transfirm competences.

The relationship between strategy and structure has been established for a long time. The concept has been broadened to include other

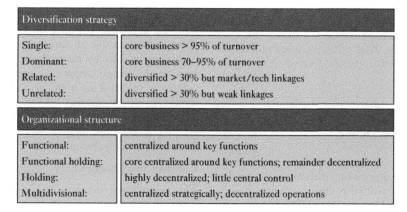

Diversification strategy	
Single:	core business > 95% of turnover
Dominant:	core business 70–95% of turnover
Related:	diversified > 30% but market/tech linkages
Unrelated:	diversified > 30% but weak linkages
Organizational structure	
Functional:	centralized around key functions
Functional holding:	core centralized around key functions; remainder decentralized
Holding:	highly decentralized; little central control
Multidivisional:	centralized strategically; decentralized operations

Figure 3   Strategy and structure

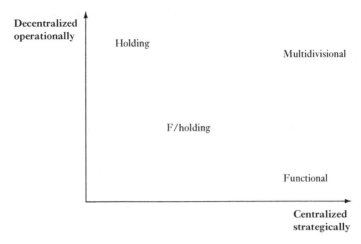

Figure 4   Structural types (Goold and Campbell, 1987)

variables with a further extension that a success-ful "fit" between these elements and corporate strategy is essential for success (*see* STRATEGIC FIT).

See also *McKinsey 7S model*

Bibliography

Campbell, A., Goold, M., and Alexander, M. (1995). Corporate strategy: The quest for parenting advantage. *Harvard Business Review*, March/April, 120–32.

Chandler, A. D. (1962). *Strategy and Structure: Chapters in the History of the Industrial Enterprise*. Cambridge, MA: MIT Press.

Goold, M. and Campbell, A. (1987). *Strategies and Styles: The Role of the Center in Managing Diversified Companies*. Cambridge, MA: Blackwell.

Hill, C. W. L. (1994). Diversification and economic performance: Bringing structure and corporate management back into the picture. In R. Rumelt, D. Schendel, and D. Teece (eds.), *Fundamental Issues in Strategy*. Boston: Harvard Business School Press, pp. 297–321.

organizational culture

Michael Brocklehurst

The interest in organizational culture during the 1980s – to practitioners and researchers alike – was stimulated by two factors. The first of these was the impact of Japanese enterprises in inter-national markets, and the search to identify a possible link between national culture and or-ganizational performance. The second factor was the perceived failure of the "hard Ss" – systems, structure, and strategy – to deliver a COMPETITIVE ADVANTAGE, and the belief that this elusive success was more a matter of delivering the "soft Ss," such as staff, style, and shared values. However, the early attempts to prescribe a specific culture and manipulate cul-tural change met with little success, and have led to a reappraisal of what the concept of "culture" involves.

Smircich (1983) provides a useful framework for reappraising the concept. She classifies the perspectives of culture as falling into two broad camps. In the first perspective culture is seen as a "product," something an organization "has." In such an approach, organizational culture is deemed to be capable of classification and ma-nipulation (usually by management). By con-trast, in the second perspective organizational culture is regarded as more of a "process," something an organization "is." According to this perspective, "culture" is much more diffi-cult to pin down and pigeonhole, and does not lend itself to manipulation.

CULTURE AS A "PRODUCT"

This perspective generates a spectrum of defin-itions, ranging from those that emphasize the surface indicators to those that try to tap some deeper meaning. The surface manifestations include definitions such as "how things get done around here," or culture as a "stock of values, beliefs, and norms widely subscribed to by those who work in an organization." In this vein, an influential approach has been Handy's division of cultures into four types: power, role, task, and person (Handy, 1978). Deeper definitions refer more to culture as "mental processes or mindsets characteristic of organizational members."

Hofstede (1990) defines culture as the "software of the mind." His work, conducted in over 50 countries, has concentrated on unearthing national cultural differences and determining how these influence organizational life. He claims that organizations have to confront two central problems: how to distribute power and how to manage uncertainty. He then identifies five value dimensions which, he claims, discriminate between national groups, and which influence the way in which people perceive that an organization should be managed to meet these two key problems. The dimensions are as follows:

- power distance, i.e., the extent to which people accept that power is distributed unequally;
- uncertainty avoidance, i.e., the extent to which people feel uncomfortable with uncertainty and ambiguity;
- individualism/collectivism, i.e., the extent to which there is a preference for belonging to tightly knit collectives rather than a more loosely knit society;
- masculinity/femininity, i.e., the extent to which gender roles are clearly distinct (masculine end of the spectrum) as opposed to those where they overlap (feminine end of the spectrum);
- Confucian dynamism, i.e., the extent to which long termism or short termism tends to predominate.

Hofstede's work is based only on employees of one organization. Furthermore, the extent to which one country can be said to have a homogeneous culture is problematic. Nevertheless, Hofstede's work has been highly influential. It attempts to explain why differing national cultural mindsets will cause difficulties when a manager from one country goes to work abroad. Difficulties can also be predicted when two organizations from countries with different cultural mindsets attempt to merge (*see* MERGERS AND ACQUISITIONS). Adler's work (1991) on differing national negotiating styles is also useful for gaining an understanding of cultural differences between nations. It is interesting to speculate whether GLOBALIZATION will increase the need to understand national cultural differences (as multinationals seek to manage diverse workforces) or whether the need will decrease as globalization brings about homogenization of national cultures.

In terms of the desire to "learn from Japan," it is possible to identify specific cultural values in Japanese society that might influence economic performance, such as the importance attached to reciprocity between those of different status. However, there are successful organizations in other parts of the world in which these conventions are flouted. Indeed, even within Japan, there is a range of organizational practices as to how employees are treated. It is also difficult to disentangle the effects of culture on performance from other factors, such as INDUSTRIAL STRUCTURE, manufacturing practices, and the role of the state (Dawson, 1992). The evidence on the attempts to introduce Japanese practices in other countries is also mixed (for the UK experience, see Oliver and Hunter, 1994).

The "culture as a product" perspective has also focused on the role of comparative organizational cultures within a country. Here an attempt has been made to provide a rigorous test as to what sort of a culture will lead to high performance. Denison (1991) argues that the four specific variables that influence performance are involvement, consistency, adaptability, and mission. Denison notes how these variables are, to some extent, contradictory: for example, consistency in terms of having agreement can sometimes inhibit adaptability. It is also important that a culture is appropriate to its environment, so it is unlikely that there is one universal culture that suits all environments. On the other hand, environments change much more rapidly than organizational cultures, which can take many years to develop. Kotter and Heskett's (1992) claim that in cultures in which there is a strong consensus that key stakeholders should be valued, leadership at all levels is seen as important, and the culture underpins an appropriate strategy, can serve as a valid generalization, but such claims have still to be put to the test. Brown (1994) carries a useful summary both of this issue and of the literature on models of organizational cultural change, of which Schein's model (1985) is the best known.

CULTURE AS A PROCESS

Smircich's other perspective sees culture as a root metaphor for understanding organizations. This perspective makes it difficult to define culture. Organizations do not so much *have* cultures; it is more that they *are* cultures. This has implications for those who wish to try to change a culture.

The "culture as root metaphor" concept sees culture as something that is collectively enacted, where all who experience a culture at first hand become part of its generation and reproduction. To assume that one group (usually management) can unilaterally modify a culture is thus to mistake its essential properties. This is not to deny that culture changes – indeed, its enactment is a continuous process – but it usually changes in unintended ways. It is important also to recognize that collective enactment does not mean harmony and agreement; the power to enact is not equally shared amongst all groups.

The concept also has implications for those who wish to research cultures: the researcher inevitably becomes part of the enactment process (Weick, 1983). Trying to fix a culture and establish typologies is just an interpretation, one more part of the enactment process. As Martin (1993: 13) puts it: "Culture is not reified – out there – to be accurately observed."

However, this does not mean that the concept of "culture" is valueless except as a stick to beat those who see it as a product. Morgan (1986) argues that culture can be a powerful metaphor for enabling thought about organizations, drawing attention to the importance of patterns of subjective meaning, of images, and of values in organizational life.

CONCLUSION

The life cycle of organizational culture mirrors that of many other alleged managerial panaceas, running through the stages of initial enthusiasm, followed by a critical backlash, and ending up with a more widely based consensus on the limited applicability of the concept, which often highlights the complexity of management as a discipline.

Culture as a "product" has already gone through this cycle. It soon became clear that "culture" is not something that can easily be manipulated. Indeed, culture as a "process" seems a more powerful perspective in that it recognizes that culture depends upon human interaction – it is continuously being produced and re(created). To believe that one group can unilaterally change an existing culture according to some blueprint is mistaken. Culture does change – but often slowly and in unpredictable ways. Managers who wish to establish a blueprint might be better advised to go for a greenfield site and then carefully control recruitment and selection (Wickens, 1987). There is also the danger of thinking of culture as a monolithic entity to which all organizational members subscribe. Martin (1993) terms such a view "integrationist" and contrasts it with a "differentiation" focus, which stresses the importance of subcultures and the potential for conflict between these subcultures.

Even if a particular culture could be established by managerial fiat, the links between culture and organizational performance are not well established. Assuming that cultures can be measured and pigeonholed, there is no clear evidence that one particular type of culture is always associated with success – indeed, some of the features that are claimed to be linked with success are themselves contradictory. Furthermore, the sheer complexity of the factors involved in organizational performance makes it difficult to pinpoint the exact contribution made by culture alone.

Bibliography

Adler, N. (1991). *International Dimensions of Organizational Behavior*. Boston: PWS-Kent.

Brown, A. (1994). *Organizational Culture*. London: Pitman.

Dawson, S. (1992). *Analyzing Organizations*, 2nd edn. London: Macmillan.

Denison, D. (1991). *Corporate Culture and Organizational Effectiveness*. New York: John Wiley.

Handy, C. (1978). *The Gods of Management*. Harmondsworth: Penguin.

Hofstede, G. (1990). *Cultures and Organizations: Software of the Mind*. Maidenhead: McGraw-Hill.

Kotter, J. P. and Heskett, J. L. (1992). *Corporate Culture and Performance*. New York: Free Press.

Martin, J. (1993). *Cultures in Organizations*. Oxford: Oxford University Press.

Morgan, G. (1986). *Images of Organizations*. London: Sage.

Oliver, N. and Hunter, G. (1994). *The Financial Impact of Japanese Production Methods in UK Companies*. Paper No. 24. Cambridge: Judge Institute of Management Studies.

Schein, E. H. (1985). *Organizational Culture and Leadership*. London: Jossey-Bass.

Smircich, L. (1983). Concepts of culture and organizational analysis. *Administrative Science Quarterly*, **28**, 339–58.

Weick, K. (1983). Enactment processes in organizations. In B. Staw and G. Salancik (eds.), *New Directions in Organizational Behavior*. Malabar, FL: Robert E. Krieger.

Wickens, P. (1987). *The Road to Nissan: Flexibility, Quality, Teamwork*. London: Macmillan.

organizational learning

David Wilson

As the competitive environment has become more dynamic, strategic management as a discipline has widened its scope to include the internal resources of firms and how these might create competitive advantage. De Geus (1988) argues that learning is the key internal resources of the firm. He argues that learning is a fundamental strategic process and the primary way in which sustainable advantage can be secured in the future. The 1990s has seen an increasing interest in the dynamics of the learning organization as a means of configuring value. Senior managers in many organizations have come to believe that the way in which an organization learns is key to its effectiveness and potential to innovate and grow (Garavan, 1997). However, the concept of organizational learning is by no means clear or consistent (Vera and Crossan, 2003) and finding work which builds cumulatively is very difficult indeed. Different authors use different concepts or different terminologies to describe learning. This entry outlines the key authors and approaches in the field and presents an overall framework by which we might interpret and understand organizational learning.

Garvin (1993) defines a learning organization as one able to create, acquire and transfer knowledge and to change its behaviour to reflect new knowledge. Organizational learning involves experimentation, creative moments, learning from experience, as well as best practice and transferring knowledge quickly and efficiently throughout the organization.

However, as Senge argues:

> Human beings are designed for learning... children come fully equipped with an insatiable drive to explore and experiment. Unfortunately, the primary institutions of our society are oriented predominantly toward controlling rather than learning, rewarding individuals for performing for others rather than for cultivating their natural curiosity and impulse to learn. (Senge, 1990: 285)

Here, Senge is pointing out two important aspects of learning:

- learning can be viewed from different levels of analysis, ranging from individual learning to organizational learning;
- organizations appear rather less adept at learning than individuals.

For an examination of these different levels of analysis see McGee et al (2005). For the moment, it is necessary first of all to examine the generic features of the processes of learning. Only then can we sensibly examine learning across different levels of analysis.

Senge (1990) suggest that learning is both an *adaptive* process and a *generative* process. Adaptive learning describes the processes whereby an organization can adapt to its environment and to accelerating or decelerating rates of change. Adaptive learning can thus best be described as the processes organizations engage in to cope with changing external conditions. But the learning process is much deeper than a desire to respond and adapt to external changes. Such responses may render an organization more efficient or effective in the short term, but cannot generate increased or new capabilities –

the bedrock of innovation and creativity. Only generative learning can provide this. Generative learning requires new ways of looking at the world whether making sense of the external environment or understanding how to manage internal business processes better. Such learning is important for the visionary aspects of strategy formulation. To achieve new ideas, an organization needs to develop its capacity for strategic thinking, which is the generative (or creative) learning to which Senge refers. However, in order to understand an organization's capacity to implement strategy as well as to formulate it (thinking and acting strategically), it is necessary to engage and develop both adaptive and generative learning.

These two types of learning originate from what Argyris and Schon (1987) termed single- and double-loop learning. This has been variously referred to in the literature as first- and second-order learning, exploitation, and exploration, or convergence and reorientation. When learning enables the organization to carry out its present activities and goals without disturbing existing cultural values and norms, it is termed single-loop learning. Single-loop learning is important for increasing effectiveness in implementing strategy because it ensures that organization is becoming better at undertaking its existing strategies. In the terminology of Peters and Waterman (1982) this form of learning helps an organization to "stick to the knitting." Single-loop learning is embodied in the experience curve of an organization. The more experience a firm has of an activity, the greater its efficiency and effectiveness become *in that activity*.

However, single-loop learning does not expose an organization to new activities or new ways of conceptualising old activities. When learning involves modification of an organization's underlying cultural values, assumptions, and norms, it is termed double-loop learning. In terms of complexity, single-loop learning is relatively simple to achieve while double-loop learning is far more complex. This is because individuals are constrained by their mental models to identify familiar patterns for solving problems. As existing patterns are within the managerial comfort zone of tacit knowledge and experience, this occurs even when the problem is

significantly different and requires new solutions. The longer an organization has been using an existing set of practices, the harder it is to conceptualise new ways of doing things. Thus, paradoxically, single-loop learning, which involves existing mental models, is necessary for improving efficiency and effectiveness in existing strategic practices, but poses a barrier to developing new ways of learning.

Double-loop learning may occur when a change in strategy is so difficult to implement that it exposes the problems in existing practices, causing fundamental changes in the way the organization approaches strategic problems. Senge (1990) provides a classic example of this at Shell. Realising "that they had failed to change behaviour in much of the Shell organization," Group Planning set about altering the mental models of managers. They developed tools, such as scenario planning to encourage managers to envision alternative futures. In this way, managers learned flexibility in their current practices. Using scenarios, they could work backwards from a series of anticipated futures to change the practices in the current organization. The capacity to learn enabled Shell to be more responsive than its competitors to changes in the political environment, such as the development of OPEC.

However, for many organizations, the gap between efficient current practices, which involve single-loop learning, and the capacity to double-loop learn, that is to create viable futures, is only exposed during a performance downturn. An organization needs to engage in both types of learning; single-loop learning to improve familiarity with existing practices, aiding strategy implementation, and double-loop learning to encourage exploration of new opportunities. A firm that can manage to encompass both has the capacity for continuous learning, thus potentially improving performance and avoiding crisis. Table 1 summarizes some of the major authors and their conceptual orientation to the field of organizational learning.

Bibliography

Argyris, C. and Schon, D. A. (1987). *Organizational Learning: A Theory of Action Perspective*. Reading MA: Addison-Wesley Publishing Company.

Table 1   Theories and approaches to organizational learning

Learning type (Key authors)	Definitions/Key words	Advantages	Disadvantages
Adaptive (Senge, 1990) Single loop (Argyris and Schon, 1987) First order (Lant & Mezias, 1992) Exploitation (March, 1991) Convergence (Tushman and Romanelli, 1985)	Increases effectiveness Incremental adaptation Refinement Efficiency Implementation Execution Stability Routine Conservative	Increases familiarity with existing strategy and routines Improves short-run effectiveness Improves capacity to make decisions and act Enhances strategy implementation	Provides a barrier to conceptualising new ways of evaluating strategies Becomes rigid and resistant to change May result in performance downturn in the long-term
Generative (Senge, 1990) Double loop (Argyris and Schon, 1987) Second order (Lant and Mezias, 1992) Exploration (March, 1991) Reorientation (Tushman and Romanelli, 1985)	Expanding capabilities New paradigms Reflexivity Exploring alternatives Discontinuity Risk-taking Experimentation Flexibility Discovery Innovation	Encourages creative thinking Improves flexibility and speed in changed environments Associated with innovation and redefining products/ markets Prevents long-run myopia	Risky, new ventures have potential to fail Difficult to 'manage' In excess, can lead to dilution of distinctive competences

Source: Adapted from Jarzabowski (2003)

De Geus, A. (1988). Planning as learning. *Harvard Business Review*, **66** (2), 70–74.

Garavan, T. (1997). The learning organization: A review and evaluation. *The Learning Organization*, **4** (1), 18–29.

Garvin, D. A. (1993). Building a learning organization. *Harvard Business Review*, July-August, 78–91.

Jarzabkowski, P. (2003). Strategic practices: An activity theory perspective on continuity and change. *Journal of Management Studies*, **40** (1), 23–55.

Lant, T. K. and Mezias, S. J. (1992). An organizational learning model of convergence and reorientation. *Organization Science*, **3** (1), 47–71.

McGee, J., Wilson, D., and Thomas, H. (2005). *Strategy, Analysis and Practice*. Maidenhead: McGraw-Hill.

March, J. G. (1991). Exploration and exploitation in organizational learning. *Organization Science*, **2** (1), 71–87.

Peters, T. and Waterman, R. (1982). *In Search of Excellence*. London: Harper Row.

Senge, P. (1990). The leader's new work: Building learning organizations. *Sloan Management Review*, Fall.

Tushman, M. L. and Romanelli, E. (1985). Organizational evolution: A metamorphosis model of convergence and reorientation in Cummings, L. L. and Staw, B. M. (eds), *Research in Organizational Behaviour* (7th edition). Greenwich: JAI Press.

Vera, D. and Crossan, M. (2003). Organizational learning and knowledge management: Towards an integrative framework, in Easterby-Smith, M. and Lyles, M. (eds), *Handbook of Organizational Learning*. Oxford: Blackwell.

organizational life cycle

Derek F. Channon

While it is possible to identify the formal structure of a corporation, at any moment in time this picture is static. In reality, organizations actually evolve, and the pattern of their progress has been observed by many researchers, leading to a number of similar models of evolution which may be termed organizational life cycles. Two such models are illustrated in figures 1 and 2.

Initially, firms tend to be created by individual entrepreneurs or groups. Such firms tend to operate a relatively undiversified product market strategy. Most decisions are taken by the owner-entrepreneur and such firms cannot usually afford professional management skills in most

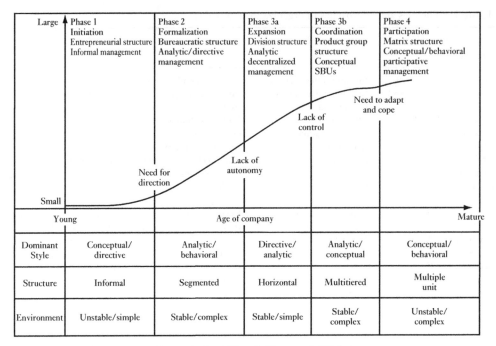

	Phase 1 Initiation Entrepreneurial structure Informal management	Phase 2 Formalization Bureaucratic structure Analytic/directive management	Phase 3a Expansion Division structure Analytic decentralized management	Phase 3b Coordination Product group structure Conceptual SBUs	Phase 4 Participation Matrix structure Conceptual/behavioral participative management
Dominant Style	Conceptual/ directive	Analytic/ behavioral	Directive/ analytic	Analytic/ conceptual	Conceptual/ behavioral
Structure	Informal	Segmented	Horizontal	Multitiered	Multiple unit
Environment	Unstable/simple	Stable/complex	Stable/simple	Stable/ complex	Unstable/ complex

Figure 1   Match of management with organizational life cycle (Rowe et al., 1994)

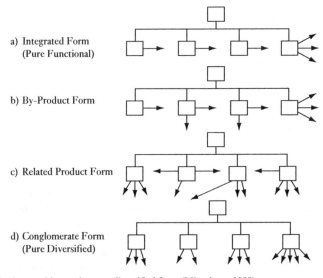

a) Integrated Form
(Pure Functional)

b) By-Product Form

c) Related Product Form

d) Conglomerate Form
(Pure Diversified)

Figure 2   Stages in the transition to the pure diversified form (Mintzberg, 1989)

functions. As a result, the organizational structure is informal and there is a lack of professional standards. Most small firms do not progress beyond this stage: this is often by design, in addition to the fact that they do not enjoy strategies that are capable of substantial growth. In such firms it is also difficult for founding entrepreneurs to give up decision-making authority to others, and this also tends to block growth prospects. Board structures in such concerns tend to be dominated by the founder and his or her family, and since such concerns are usually privately owned, few have non-executive board members.

For those firms that do grow, however, size usually adds some complexity although, as long as the historic product market strategy remains viable, DIVERSIFICATION is limited. Nevertheless, size makes some delegation of decision-making necessary and professional management is usually added to create a FUNCTIONAL STRUCTURE. Decisions, while usually still dominated by the founding entrepreneur until his or her death or retirement, involve functional specialists operating under direction.

The first major corporate crisis usually occurs with the death or retirement of the founder, unless, of course, he or she is unable to prevent the firm from entering an operational crisis, which also usually results in the removal of the founder. The organizational structure then tends to become a centralized bureaucracy and continues to pursue the original strategy established by the founder, but it lacks the original streak of imagination shown in the creation of the firm.

Eventually, the original strategy tends to mature and – often after the appointment of a new leader – the firm searches for new areas of activity into which to diversify. Such strategic moves usually occur through acquisition (see ACQUISITION STRATEGY; MERGERS AND ACQUISITIONS), and by this stage many such firms may well have become public companies. Most firms attempt to diversify into product market areas perceived by management to be related to the historic core activities. Unfortunately, this often turns out not to be the case, and many such diversification moves fail to achieve the expectations of the acquirer.

The organizational changes that accompany such strategic moves tend to result in the adoption of a HOLDING COMPANY STRUCTURE. Initially, a functional holding company system is usually introduced, with the board consisting of the original functional executives together with the CEO of any newly acquired concern. While such diversification moves may well lead to significant increases in corporate sales, profits usu-

ally do not grow commensurately. As a result, a further crisis may well develop and the share price may decline, often leading to a change in either the chairman or the chief executive, or both.

At this point it is common for management consultants to be brought in to help the company introduce a divisional or business unit structure (see DIVISIONAL STRUCTURE), together with suitable management information planning and control systems: the firm is ill equipped to introduce these on its own. The new structure also assists in the development of a cadre of general managers capable of continuing the strategy of diversification. A particular problem occurs with diversification away from a DOMINANT BUSINESS STRATEGY position, especially where the main business is significantly larger than the diversification moves. In these circumstances the main focus of the board remains centered on the functions of the traditional CORE BUSINESS or on geographic areas of operation.

While most diversification strategies move from a single or dominant business to related diversified areas, some firms adopt a CONGLOMERATE STRATEGY. While both strategies involve divisional or business unit structures, historically, conglomerate businesses operated with a very small central office, while related diversified concerns tended to have larger central offices, which were required to coordinate activities between operating units. Improved information technology and reengineering (see BUSINESS PROCESS REENGINEERING) have tended to result in reductions in the size and scope of the central office of all diversified concerns.

Concurrently with higher levels of product market diversification, many larger firms have also adopted multinational strategies, or environmental and technological factors have required the integration of cross-functional activities. In such firms, a form of MATRIX STRUCTURE has therefore tended to be adopted.

Different leadership styles also tend to be needed at the different stages of the organizational life cycle. In the initial phase, the successful executive is entrepreneurial and creative, usually with a strong dominant personality.

Many such individuals tend to come from socially depressed backgrounds and have ethnic origins that involve Jewish, Muslim, or Asian ethics.

In phase 2 (see figure 1) the successful executive focuses on pursuing growth with the original strategy, while introducing a formal functional structure coupled with appropriate financial controls and rudimentary planning systems. The management style tends to be analytic, but to lack the imagination necessary to evolve new strategies.

At the start of phase 3, a new chairman and/or chief executive is charged with breaking out of the historic strategy, usually through acquisition. This is generally accomplished by forceful leadership, with tight centralized control. As a result, the new strategy often fails to achieve its objectives; newly acquired executives find it difficult to work under such a leadership style, and the acquiring firm lacks the appropriate information and control systems to manage a diversified enterprise. As a result, a further leadership change often occurs, to introduce a style embracing a combination of analytic and behavioral skills. Such a leader has a broad strategic vision, a capacity to deal with complex situations, and the ability to achieve results by operating through other managers.

In phase 4, the best leadership style tends to be a combination of analytic, conceptual, and behavioral skills, together with a clear vision for the future direction of the corporation. Such leaders are capable of dealing with high uncertainty, coping with rapid change in the environment and technology, and delegating responsibility across a complex matrix structure.

Bibliography

Channon, D. F. (1973). *The Strategy and Structure of British Enterprise*. Cambridge, MA: Harvard Division of Research.

Galbraith, J. R. and Kaganjian, R. K. (1986). *Strategy Implementation*. Los Angeles: West.

Greiner, L. E. (1972). Evolution and revolution as organizations grow. *Harvard Business Review*, 56 (August/September).

Hansen, A. H. (1985). CEO management style and the stages of development in new ventures. Unpublished

paper. Sasem, OR: Atkinson Graduate School of Management.

Mintzberg, H. (1979). *The Structuring of Organizations*. Englewood Cliffs, NJ: Prentice-Hall.

Mintzberg, H. (1989). *Mintzberg on Management*. New York: Free Press.

Rowe, A. J., Mason, R. O., Dickel, K. E., Mann, R. B., and Mockler, R. J. (1994). *Strategic Management*, 4th edn. Reading, MA: Addison-Wesley, ch. 11.

Scott, B. R. (1971). The stages of corporate development, part 1. Unpublished paper. Boston: Harvard Business School.

outsourcing

Derek F. Channon

This occurs when a firm contracts with an outside organization for it to undertake specific activities which, historically, were undertaken by the firm itself. Some activities, such as cleaning and maintenance, have long been contracted out by many organizations; increasingly, however, activities which many might claim are strategic are being outsourced.

In particular, the areas of data processing and information technology management are being outsourced. The financial services industry has been a major user of outsourcing, with companies such as Banc One and American Express undertaking processing activities for many other organizations. Furthermore, in the UK for example, many government functions, including revenue collection, have been outsourced to private corporations.

Apart from providing specialist service at lower cost, outsourcing helps to reduce capital intensity in a business. Amstrad, for example, was able to grow at over 70 percent per annum compound because it outsourced all its assembly and component production to Far Eastern manufacturers, concerning itself basically with the design of its range of consumer electronics products and computers. The company did, however, maintain quality control by regularly inspecting supplier plants. On a larger scale, Marks and Spencer also manufactures nothing but rigorously lays down specifications against which its suppliers must produce. This reduced capital intensity can help to improve profitability and, in particular, shareholder value.

However, overuse can lead to potential technological dependency. Canon, for example, supplies some 80 percent of the engines for laser beam printers. As a result, western suppliers have become dependent upon the supply of a strategic component from a company which may eventually turn out to be a fierce competitor. Akio Morita of Sony thus described the effect of outsourcing as the "hollowing of American industry where the US is abandoning its status as an industrial power."

The key advantages of outsourcing include the following:

- reduced capital intensity;
- transformation of fixed costs to variable costs;
- reduced costs due to supplier ECONOMIES OF SCALE;
- encourages a focus on customer needs and product development rather than manufacturing;
- benefits obtained from supplier innovations;
- focuses resources on high value-added activities (in any manufacturing market value chain, some 40–50 percent of value added occurs at the distribution end).

It is a most effective strategy when:

- process technology is unavailable;
- competitors have superior technology;
- suppliers enjoy superior efficiency and quality;
- capital for investment is scarce and expensive;
- there are enough suppliers to insure security of competitive supply.

The critical assumptions made by companies adopting outsourcing strategies are as follows:

- a strong market position is a critical strategic success factor;
- a brand name is sufficient to negate the need for manufacturing capacity;
- manufacturing can be separated from design;
- manufacturing knowledge is not critical to an understanding of the market.

Bibliography

Bettis, R., Bradley, S., and Hamel, G. (1992). Outsourcing and industrial decline. *Academy of Management Executive*, **6** (1), 7–22.

Rowe, A. J., Mason, R. O., Dickel, K. E., Mann, R. B., and Mockler, R. J. (1994). *Strategic Management*, 4th edn. Reading, MA: Addison-Wesley, pp. 345–6.

Welch, J. P. and Ranganath, N. (1992). Strategic sourcing: A progressive approach to the make or buy decision. *Academy of Management Executive*, **6** (11), 23–41.

parenting advantage

see PORTFOLIO MANAGEMENT

Pareto analysis

Derek F. Channon

A number of criteria exist for evaluating the desirability of alternate economic and social states, and the desirability of a change from one such state to another. One such criterion was developed by the nineteenth-century economist Vilfredo Pareto and states that "in order for a maximum welfare position to be reached then the 'ophelimity' (utility) of some should not increase to the detriment of others."

Pareto efficiency, then, will be achieved when it is not possible to make anyone better off without making someone else worse off. From this perspective, perfect competition transactions (given no EXTERNALITIES) are Pareto efficient, as no one would voluntarily enter such a transaction if their welfare would be reduced by so doing. In practice, this is a very strict criterion with limited use. Even if it was possible for the person benefiting from a transaction to fully compensate the one who was losing out, such compensation might never be paid. A less restrictive criterion was, therefore, developed by Hicks and Kaldor, stating that a transaction is desirable if it leads to a potential Pareto improvement; that is, if the gainers could in principle fully compensate the losers and still have a net gain, even though in practice they do not pay compensation at all.

In many industries, the Pareto effect is commonly found along many dimensions. This is illustrated in figure 1. It follows from the obser-

vation, for example, that 20 percent of products will account for 80 percent of sales. This is illustrated on what is sometimes called an ABC analysis chart. It shows all of the expenses as bar graphs, arranged in order of size. Its purpose is to group relatively large-cost items so as to highlight them for management and control. Group A expenses account for 80 percent of total expenses, group B for 15 percent, and group C for the residual 5 percent. Usually the number of cost categories tends to be in inverse number to their importance. Such a chart enables management to focus attention on critical costs rather than devoting disproportionate service time to less significant factors.

The Pareto effect also applies to many other dimensions, such as customers, sales force, and critical machinery. Combining more than one significant variable, rather than using each variable alone, can therefore produce a useful guide to strategy. This is illustrated in figure 2.

In many businesses there is a strong tendency to add new products and customers while failing to eliminate those which are obsolete or unprofitable. When faced with the need for rationalization of unattractive products and/or customers, the sales function in most businesses is extremely reluctant to undertake such actions. This is so despite the fact that, at worst, 20 percent of customers and products may well account for the majority of costs in areas such as stocks, production costs, computer facilities, and administration. Conducting Pareto analysis of a business along the major strategic dimensions is therefore a significant exercise, and one that needs to be undertaken periodically to insure that inefficiencies are not repeated.

For further discussion of the Pareto principle, see Baumol (1977).

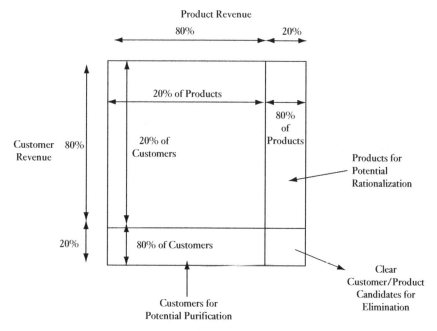

Figure 1   The customer/product Pareto matrix (Channon, 1986)

Bibliography

Baumol, W. J. (1977). *Economic Theory and Operations Analysis*, 4th edn. Englewood Cliffs, NJ: Prentice-Hall, ch. 21.

Channon, D. F. (1986). *Bank Strategic Management and Marketing*. Chichester: John Wiley.

Nagashima, S. (1992). *100 Management Charts*. Tokyo: Asian Productivity Organization, pp. 36–7.

PEST analysis

David Norburn

A number of major variables lie well outside the control of the organization: PEST analysis is a broad-brush instrument that can be used in attempts to define and measure their effects. PEST is an acronym of the four categories of change factor: political, economic, social, and technological. It is therefore essentially an environmental checklist of those external elements that both influence and constrain the attraction of industry profitability. Often used in conjunction with Porter's five forces model (*see* INDUS-

TRY STRUCTURE), it has become a powerful tool for reducing the parameters of risk.

POLITICAL CHANGE AND INTERVENTION

In most western countries, political legislators are expressly forbidden to benefit commercially from their legal enactment. How, then, should the business world influence and forecast likely political intervention? Each situation requires careful evaluation to determine strategic risk and opportunity. Who will be the decision-makers? Who will be the key influencers? How can the top manager reduce the lead time from early warning to strategic modification?

DEPENDENCY ON THE ECONOMIC CYCLE

Demand for every product or service is to some degree dependent upon the economic cycle. Is demand within any product/market segment a leader or a laggard relative to GNP momentum? Some show increased demand during the first phases of the economic cycle downturn, for example, gourmet convenience food. Some, such as two-star restaurant bookings, show the reverse. Relative to the economic cycle, what

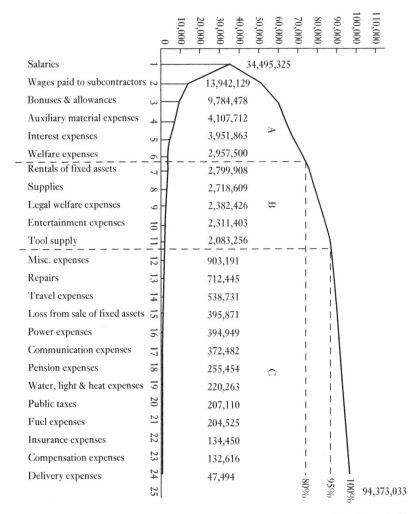

Figure 2 Pareto analysis of production cost, manufacturing expenses, and expenditure (Nagashima, 1992)

fiscal and monetary mechanisms are likely to be chosen by central government? Specifically, how will this affect disposable income expenditure patterns, or the cost of funding working capital? Would it be prudent to take on fixed-interest long-term debt rather than a floating rate shorter-term facility?

In response to this economic uncertainty, much progress has been made in both macro- and sectoral econometric model-building, leading, *inter alia*, to better inventory control and to a reduction in the cost of corporate capital.

SOCIAL DEMOGRAPHIC, ATTITUDINAL, AND RELIGIOUS CHANGE

From a corporate perspective, what social changes will affect contemporary strategic positioning and – given robust forecasting – what COMPETITIVE ADVANTAGE could be established? Take, for example, the falling reproduction rates in western Europe. When combined with an increase in life expectancy, who will fund the retirement pension? Can the state fulfill historic provision from the public purse? This social trend has led to the private sector developing new products, particularly private portable pensions, private medical schemes, sheltered housing developments, "third age" holidays, and vocational courses within the university sector.

Consider the rise of pressure groups: the anti-smoking lobby has recorded successes in restaurants, on hotel floors, and on public transport. The strong positive correlation between smoking and heart disease has been linked to a marked reduction in western adult male consumption of tobacco products, while – perversely – it has had no impact on female teenagers. Should the tobacco companies refocus their advertising and promotional activity on a smaller niche and/or diversify more rapidly into related products – see, for example, Philip Morris and Miller?

The third, and increasingly important, category is that of religious fundamentalism, often associated with extreme nationalism. Should western oil and gas companies invest for the long term in Kazakhstan? Will the Parsees of India, a minority religion who dominate much of private-sector enterprise, be better long-term joint venture partners than the majority Hindus?

TECHNOLOGICAL VULNERABILITY

It is axiomatic that we live in a world of rapid technological change – all the more reason to be proactive in corporate response. Organizations should regularly review the commercial impact of emerging new technologies upon activity costs along the value chain. Take the example of constant-velocity joints: GKN, who claim a 35 percent world market share, invest heavily in friction research (tribology) in the major technological universities. The reasoning behind this strategy is that, since the 1960s, engine brake horse power, from the same cubic capacity, has quadrupled – and vehicle top speed has doubled. Correspondingly, automobile manufacturers demand component technology of equivalence. Consider advances in data compression and transmission. Will this reduce the need for as many medical general practitioners, or for legal experts? Will neural networks replace branch bank managers? How soon will interactive video disk technology replace aging professors!

Any company that fails to monitor technological advance within the area of its existing CORE COMPETENCES exacerbates the risk of product/market obsolescence.

CONSTRUCTING A PEST FRAMEWORK

PEST analysis is an attempt to reduce strategic risk by scenario planning. It is not intended to be a precise technique in quantification but is specific to individual products and/or markets. It therefore follows that each PEST, although following the same general outline, will specify different item variables, to which different weightings will be allocated. Given the enormous number of potential variables, it is sensible to limit the PEST analysis to no more than five items within each of the main PEST headings in the first instance. The first step is to determine the probability rankings of each item variable, and the second is to evaluate the quantitative and qualitative effect of these occurring upon the achievement of corporate objectives. By multiplying probability by effect, a crude ranking index of corporate vulnerability – or opportunity – is established. This index is next refined by eliminating those items with insufficient impact, so that more detailed analysis can be conducted of the significant variables.

Bibliography

Fahey, L. and King, W. (1977). Environmental scanning for corporate planning. *Business Horizons*, **20** (4).

Hofer, C. W. and Schendel, D. (1978). *Strategy Formulation: Analytical Concepts*. St. Paul, MN: West.

Rowe, A. J., Mason, R. O., Dickel, K. E., Mann, R. B., and Mockler, R. J. (1994). *Strategic Management*, 4th edn. Reading, MA: Addison-Wesley.

Utterback, J. (1979). Environmental analysis and forecasting in strategic management. In C. Hofer and D. Schendel (eds.), *A New View of Business Policy and Planning*. Boston: Little, Brown.

William, R. E. (1976). *Putting It All Together: A Guide to Strategic Thinking*. New York: Amacom.

portfolio management

Chris Smith

Adding value through buying and selling businesses has been one form of CORPORATE

STRATEGY. The corporate center acts as a funds investor and seeks opportunities to buy companies that are undervalued by the market and then waits until the inherent value is recognized and sells them on at a profit. A more active role than this entails buying companies that are underperforming, and hence are available at a relatively low price, and acting to improve performance and selling price. A variant of this was undertaken by the so-called "raiders" and "asset strippers" of the 1980s, who bought conglomerates and then sold off the component parts for a total price far in excess of the overall purchase price. Opportunities to profit from this mode of corporate strategy are now rare, as the general market is more attuned to such opportunities, as are potential targets. The trend for conglomerates to become focused on fewer core businesses (*see* CORE BUSINESS) was a consequence of such threats.

Porter (1987) terms this corporate buy-and-sell approach *portfolio management*. The Ashridge researchers (Campbell and Goold, 1994; Campbell, Goold, and Alexander, 1995) call it *corporate development* and include the reshaping of existing businesses by amalgamation or division and the creation of new businesses by internal venturing. Both sets of authors agree that this is no longer a viable value-generating corporate strategy, as the market now anticipates the potential undervaluation and reflects this in the (speculative) premium in the price paid. Such premiums insure that profitable acquisitions must now be based on better management of the acquired business, or other forms of synergistic benefits of belonging to the new corporation.

In discussing the aspect of corporate strategy that is to do with the management of the multibusiness organization, Porter (1987) identifies three organizational/process concepts of corporate strategy: *restructuring*, *sharing activities*, and *transferring skills*.

- *Restructuring* occurs when businesses are acquired with the specific intent of achieving value by active intervention and improvement. The center needs the capability to effect such transformation and thus it exerts strong direct influence on business performance and processes. In Porter's view, once restructuring has been successful, the business should then be sold to capture the new value, unless it benefits in some way from ongoing membership of the corporation.

- *Sharing activities* is a value activity that is based on the component businesses using the same facilities, services, processes, or systems and thereby reaping utilization, learning curve (scope) scale or differentiation benefits. Management is based on interrelationships, but not necessarily interdependencies between the business units, that is, the shared facility can be a corporate-level activity.

- *Transferring skills* is managing ongoing interrelationships between the businesses. In this case, the corporate center actively fosters the sharing of expertise or skills among the businesses, even though they might have different value chains. As with "sharing activities," the center is actively involved, but this time it develops and promotes linkages and interdependencies between business units.

Campbell et al. (1995) have spent a considerable time focusing on the multibusiness company and how its corporate strategy adds (or subtracts) value (the general thrust of their findings is that *value destruction* is the norm in multibusiness companies). Consistent with the well-known COMPETITIVE ADVANTAGE, they coined the intuitively attractive term *parenting advantage* to denote the additional value that an insightful parent company can add to its component businesses through appropriate orientation and management. They suggest three requisites for parenting advantage:

1. the corporate advantage must translate into more competitive advantage in at least one business or membership of each business in the portfolio must create extra value somewhere in the portfolio;

2. it must create more value than the cost of the corporate overhead;

3. it must add more value than any other possible parent otherwise the market for corporate control might eventually challenge your ownership and parenting credentials.

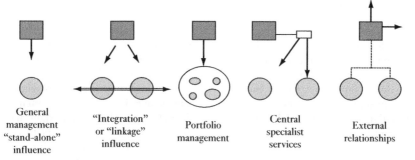

Figure 1 Sources of value creation

Campbell and Goold (1994) also identify three classes of value-adding corporate strategy, *stand-alone influence, functional and services influence*, and *linkage influence*, which parallel Porter's categories. They emphasize that these are not either/or choices but can all be in operation at the same time. Figure 1 illustrates the range of sources of value creation.

- *Stand-alone influence* is the value created by the influence on the individual business strategy and performance. The major focus is on vertical linkages, mainly between the chief executive officer and the managing directors of the businesses. In this category, successful corporate parents have to overcome the "10 percent versus 100 percent paradox" – the idea that part-time, organizationally removed managers can enhance the performance of the business's dedicated management.
- *Functional and services influence* is again a vertical process, with the focus on adding value through the influence of a range of centrally controlled staff functions. These may replace or augment those already in place in the businesses. The problem the corporate center faces here is offering a higher value-added service than specialist outsiders – the "beating the specialist" paradox.
- *Linkage influence* aims to increase value through the relationships between the businesses. The focus is on horizontal processes and incorporates both the "shared activities" and "transfer of skills" categories of Porter.

It is difficult to explain, however, why the managers of the businesses would not do this themselves if extra value would accrue as a result, that is, the "enlightened self-interest" paradox.

The general management influence is generally reckoned to be the key (only) justification for long-term survival of conglomerates. Linkages, portfolio effects, and specialist capabilities are all part of the SYNERGY and relatedness themes. The external relationship management theme harks back to much earlier thinking about the role of the top team and the board. This maintains that the specialist skills at the top are about understanding the external environment and finding ways to cope with it and to position against it. Modern thinking has focused very much on the internal management and dynamics of the organization, perhaps to a fault.

See also *corporate styles; divisional structure; organization structure*

Bibliography

Campbell, A. and Goold, M. (1994). Adding value from corporate headquarters. In B. De Wit and R. Meyer (eds.), *Strategy: Process, Content, Context*. New York: West.

Campbell, A., Goold, M., and Alexander, M. (1995). Corporate strategy: The quest for parenting advantage. *Harvard Business Review*, March/April, 120–32.

Porter, M. E. (1987). From competitive advantage to corporate strategy. *Harvard Business Review*, May/June, 2–21.

post-acquisition integration

Duncan Angwin

It is in the post-acquisition phase that value from the acquisition is created or destroyed. Many attempts have been made to produce diagrams that show clearly how the strategic intention behind an acquisition translates into post-acquisition integration actions. One such diagram is shown in figure 1.

Whilst diagrams such as figure 2 indicate how the level of complexity may increase with different types of deals, it is clear that the class of acquisitions labeled "horizontal," for instance, can give rise to almost all of the types of functional change suggested.

We are now shifting from issues of STRA-TEGIC FIT to issues of organizational fit, from viewing companies holistically to looking at the complexities within. As figure 3 shows, strategic fit offers the potential upon which organizational fit acts as a series of constraints.

Acquisitions are often associated with substantial redundancies. For this reason, there are numerous articles on the psychological impact of being acquired (Buono and Bowditch, 1989; Mirvis and Marks, 1992; Cartwright and Cooper, 1996). There are many layers to culture and the number affected by acquisition will depend upon the differences between the companies in terms of nationality, regionality, industry, corporate structure, history, and managerial style. A further important dimension is the relative importance of employees to the organization's offering. Where employees are an integral part of the offering, for instance consultants are not

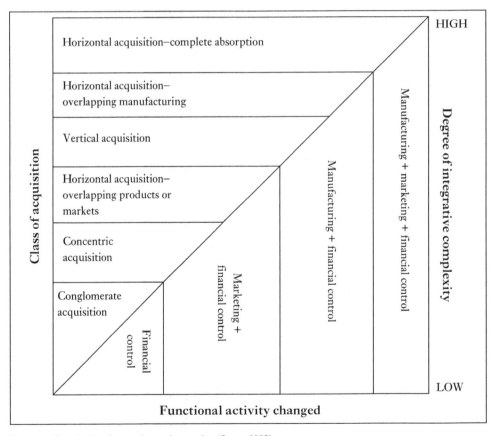

Figure 1   Complexity of post-takeover integration (Jones, 1982)

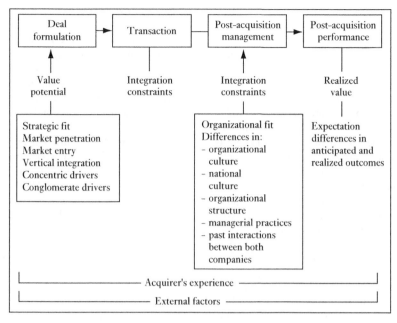

Figure 2 The tension between strategic and organizational fit (adapted from Angwin, 2000: 4)

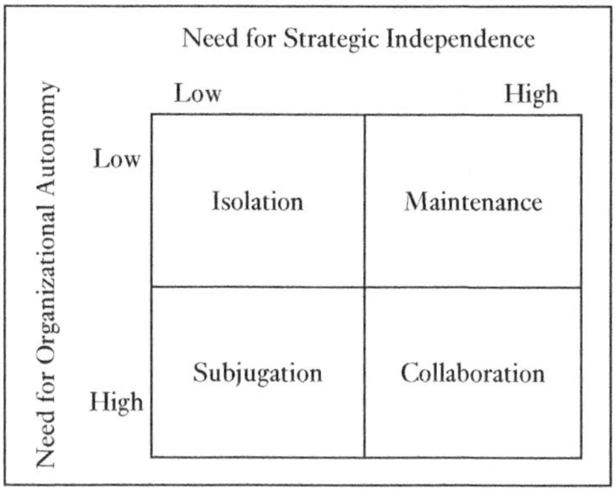

Figure 3 Types of acquisition integration approach (Angwin, 2000)

separable from their advice, then cultural differences can have serious outcomes. In the words of one chief executive of a service firm, if the key employees walk out, what have you got?

The impact of organizational constraints, such as a culture clash, is largely a function of, firstly, the inherent differences between the companies and the extent of integration pursued (the need for organizational autonomy in figure 3), and, secondly, the extent to which

value can be created from the acquisition is a function of the extent to which resources can be transferred or shared between the two businesses (the need for strategic independence in figure 3). The interaction between these two dimensions results in four distinct types of integration.

- *Maintenance*: Acquisitions that are maintained at arm's length are most often in unfamiliar business areas – perhaps classic unrelated takeovers. Acquirers avoid interfering in the running of these acquisitions and instead try to learn from the acquired company's achievements. There may be a modest amount of financial/risk sharing, but essentially the way in which value is created in the acquired business is by the parent company encouraging greater professionalism and positively influencing the ambition of the management group. The post-acquisition phase tends to be rather gentle and it can take years for real benefits to show.

- *Isolation*: These acquisitions are often in poor financial shape at the time of acquisition, and are usually held in isolation to avoid infecting the group. In most cases, a TURN-AROUND STRATEGY will be employed to restore them to a healthy condition. Owing to the poor state of the acquired company, post-acquisition actions tend to occur very rapidly, with the post-acquisition phase being relatively short. As an acquisition technique, isolation acquisitions are quite risky, but, as with all turnarounds, success can be very marked.

- *Subjugation*: Acquisitions that are subjugated rapidly lose their identity and structure and are subsumed within the parent group. Such acquisitions are often based upon clear similarities between both companies, so that amalgamation will bring ECONOMIES OF SCALE and ECONOMIES OF SCOPE. The integration process is complex, potentially occurring throughout all aspects of the business. The post-acquisition phase of subjugation acquisitions tends to occur quickly and bring rapid results.

- *Collaboration*: Acquisitions of a collaborative nature show the acquired company having considerable independence from the new parent. The acquired company has its own head, but future projects and arrangements show joint efforts for the benefit of the group. Over time, there is substantial interchange of capabilities, but this is a gradual process. Collaborative acquisitions are difficult to manage, have substantial risks, and the benefits are long term.

In theory, collaborative acquisitions offer the greatest potential for gain. However the gains require the acquired company to retain a high degree of strategic independence, to retain the configuration of its core capabilities, whilst at the same time experiencing interaction of resources with the parent. This is something of a paradox, as the acquired company, in order to receive resources from the acquirer, loses some of its precious independence and has its capabilities threatened.

The framework in figure 3 is important for making sense of different post-acquisition styles and attempting to integrate this backwards into the pre-acquisition process. There is now a growing literature on the mechanics of creating value through resource sharing and transfer. This RESOURCE-BASED VIEW is based on an enhanced utilization of CORE COMPETENCES and resources. Resource redeployment is the dominant value-creating mechanism of acquisition, primarily through capability enhancement, but also to a lesser extent through cost savings. Interesting recent research suggests the acquirer is better skilled at rationalizing its own assets and redeploying its own resources than those of the target.

See also *acquisition strategy; bidding tactics; mergers and acquisitions*

Bibliography

Angwin, D. N. (2000). *Implementing Successful Post-Acquisition Management*. London: Pearson Education.

Buono, A. F. and Bowditch, J. L. (1989). *The Human Side of Mergers and Acquisitions: Managing Collisions Between People and Organizations*. San Francisco: Jossey-Bass.

Cartwright, S. and Cooper, C. (1996). *Acquisitions: The Human Factor*. Oxford: Butterworth-Heinemann.

Jones, C. S. (1982). *Successful Management of Acquisitions*. Glasgow: Beattie.

Mirvis, P. H. and Marks, M. L. (1992). *Managing the Merger: Making it Work*. Englewood Cliffs, NJ: Prentice-Hall.

pricing strategy

Derek F. Channon

Historically the main determinant of buyer choice, pricing strategy produces revenue in CORPORATE STRATEGY. The choice of pricing strategy is therefore a key determinant in achieving corporate success. There are many options open to the firm in assessing pricing strategy, which are significantly influenced by a number of key factors. Buyers are less price sensitive under the following conditions:

- unique value effect – when products are unique;
- substitute awareness effect – when they are unaware of realistic alternatives;
- difficult comparison effect – when they are unable to differentiate between product offerings;
- total expenditure effect – when the purchase use is a low part of discretionary expenditure;
- end-benefit effect – when the cost is a small proportion of the total cost;
- shared cost effect – when costs are shared with another party;
- sunk investment effect – when costs are related to a cost which has already been incurred;
- price quality effect – when the product is seen by consumers as having higher quality, prestige, etc.
- inventory effect – when they cannot store the product.

Given the customers' demand schedule, the cost function of the business, and the pricing strategy of competitors, a number of pricing strategy options are available, including the following:

- *Markup pricing.* The most common strategy used in the West involves adding a markup to the cost of a product. Many companies compute the cost of producing a product and add a specific margin. This strategy, while widely used, has the serious disadvantage that competitors may reconfigure the value chain (*see* VALUE CHAIN ANALYSIS) and attack cost-plus suppliers.
- *Perceived value pricing.* Many companies presently base their pricing on perceived value as identified by the buyer. The price is set to maximize perceived buyer value by using both price and non-profit features. Companies such as Dupont

and Caterpillar have made heavy use of this method.

- *Target pricing.* The price is based on a target position within the market. This method is widely used by Japanese companies and in industries such as automobiles. From the target price, given a desired rate of return, the required production cost can be calculated and steps taken to remove cost at all stages in order to achieve the target.
- *Value pricing.* A number of companies have charged a low price for high-value products, representing a particular bargain for consumers. In automobiles in recent times, the Lexus was specifically priced lower than comparable Mercedes Benz models, despite its high value. Other examples might include Virgin Airways, Wal-Mart, and Direct Line Insurance.
- *Going rate pricing.* In this form of pricing, prices are decided in relationship to those of the competitors. Such a method may well apply to medium-share companies competing against high-share competitors. Typical examples also apply in relatively undifferentiated products such as gasoline.
- *Sealed bid pricing.* This is widely used in industries such as construction, and increasingly in industries in which OUTSOURCING is becoming important.
- *Penetration pricing.* This is often used to maximize rapid market entry by discounting and special deals. It has been used by entrants in automobiles from countries such as Malaysia and Korea.
- *Skimming pricing.* This is used by some competitors to maximize profit returns by maintaining the highest possible price for as long as possible. Examples might include compact discs.
- *Experience curve pricing.* Some companies have made extensive use of experience effects (*see* EXPERIENCE AND LEARNING EFFECTS) to set future pricing tactics. Texas Instruments has been a major exponent of this technique, and the effect is important in industries such as electronics in which substantial experience effects operate.

FACTORS IMPACTING EXTERNAL PRICE
STRATEGIES

The choice of pricing strategy adopted by the
firm will also depend on a number of criteria. It
should:

- be consistent with overall CORPORATE
  STRATEGY;
- be consistent with buyer expectations and
  behavior;
- be consistent with competitor strategies;
- be monitored and modified to reflect industry changes;
- be monitored for changes in industry boundaries.

There are also constraints on the range of pricing
options that are available. These include the
following:

- *Corporate image*. The external image of the
  corporation affects its ability to adopt a specific pricing strategy. For example, a producer of low-cost automobiles would find it
  extremely difficult to successfully be perceived to be a producer of luxury cars: a
  downmarket low-priced supermarket chain
  would find it difficult to move upmarket in
  price. The corporation also needs to consider
  the impact of its pricing strategies on others,
  such as shareholders, consumer pressure
  groups, regulatory authorities, and government agencies.
- *Geography*. Many companies charge different prices for goods and services in different
  parts of the world, depending upon local
  market conditions and regulations.
- *Discounts*. Many corporations offer discounts
  based on demand for both volume and value.
  Large users can usually command significant
  discounts. Discounts may also be offered for
  early payments and penalties imposed for
  late payments.
- *Price discrimination*. Many companies differentiate between customers, product or service form, place, and time.

Bibliography

Channon, D. F. (1986). *Bank Strategic Management and
Marketing*. Chichester: John Wiley.

Forbis, J. L. and Mehta, N. T. (1981). Value-based strategies for industrial products. *Business Horizons* (May/
June), 32–42.

Kotler, P. (2003). *Marketing Management: Analysis, Planning, Implementation and Control*, 11th edn. Englewood
Cliffs, NJ: Prentice-Hall.

Kotler, P. and Armstrong, G. (2004). *Principles of
Marketing*, 10th edn. Upper Saddle River, NJ: Prentice-Hall.

Nagle, T. T. (1987). *The Strategy and Tactics of Pricing*.
Englewood Cliffs, NJ: Prentice-Hall.

privatization

Stephanos Avgeropoulos

Privatization is the transfer of a controlling
interest in a state-owned organization to private
ownership. A wider definition also embraces
any substantial transfer of state asset ownership
or control to the private sector, including
any government activity intended to reduce the
role of the state, or of central or local government, in any particular industry or organization.
This can include the issue of new equity in the
capital market, the setting up of independent
holding companies to distance government
from the management of state enterprises, competitive purchasing practices, or even non-inter-
ference pledges made in relation to state
holdings.

As most privatized organizations used to
provide goods or services on behalf of the
state while they were part of its administrative structure, it is important to make the
distinction between the state's obligation to
make available and its obligation to be involved with all aspects of such provision. The
logistics of postal services may be delegated, for
example, while the financing (subsidy) of uniform national tariffs can remain the responsibility of the government, if this is considered to be
desirable.

In summary, although privatization is a concept that, strictly, only has to do with ownership
of assets, it is very difficult to understand and
explain it without consideration to the related
organizational matters of control and the setting
of organizational goals, priorities, and constraints, and the type and methods of management.

RATIONALE

There exist a number of different reasons to privatize, and these can typically be understood in ideological, financial, or political terms. Although not necessarily mutually exclusive, TRADE-OFFS are often involved; and the ranking of reasons depends, among other aspects, on the country and industry involved, and the place of any particular privatization in the privatizing country's program.

The ideological rationale is based on the neo-liberal view that the market is superior to government planning as a means of allocating resources. Therefore, exposure to the market for corporate capital and control in substitution to the allocation mechanisms employed by most governments encourages the development of a closer link between consumer and producer, and enhances the flow of information as well as accountability, leading to higher allocative efficiency. In addition, such exposure can enlarge a small national capital market in terms of both size and the number of participants and, in the extreme, be used to convert a planned economy into a market-based economy. Also, privatization can offer the opportunity to introduce or enhance competition in the product market (as the existence of a privileged state-owned competitor may mean that competitive production is unfeasible), with all the beneficial implications that this can have according to the same ideology. Finally, privatization segregates many activities from the all-encompassing state, and this permits more precise measurement of the rationality and cost of government involvement.

The financial rationale for privatization, increasingly implemented by administrations holding a wide range of political beliefs, is based on short-term monetary considerations and justifies the exchange of state assets for liquid funds by the need to raise revenue for the vendor government, often to finance current expenditure and reduce the public sector borrowing requirement (PSBR). In financial terms, privatization can be seen as the exchange of a perpetual series of cash flows for an up-front payment. A short-termist government would always be willing to sell below value, while the private sector would only pay more if it believed that it could undertake the management better.

Another associated reason to privatize is to allow financial decision-making in the organization to be carried out without regard to public spending, thereby often allowing the undertaking of investments which, although sound in their own right, may be deferred in view of more urgent government priorities.

The final privatization rationale involves political and electoral considerations. The ability of the government to reallocate wealth and resources, and through pricing and method of sale to strongly influence the composition of many organizations' ownership, enables it to attack opposition strongholds and form interest groups who benefit from the process (or would be expected to suffer as a result of its discontinuation or reversal), thereby creating a captive electorate.

RELATED ACTIONS

A number of government actions are often associated with privatization. Although they can often take place without privatization, and privatization can conceivably be implemented without them, these actions are frequently interlinked with privatization in critical ways, particularly as they take an active role in dissipating its effects.

The first such action is liberalization (see DE-REGULATION). In a deregulated market, state-owned firms have no justification for receiving subsidies or any other preferential treatment, so they can only survive if they are as efficient as any other competitor. Public ownership in a deregulated market, therefore, becomes irrelevant. Therefore privatization, although not strictly necessary, may well follow. Similarly, a privatized company cannot be allowed to maintain strong monopoly powers, so it must be controlled by means of competition and/or regulation. As a result, privatization is likely to lead to a combination of REGULATION and deregulation.

A second action is the decoupling of the organization's finances from those of the state, enabling the organization to raise funds directly from the markets. A state-owned organization may be able to raise some project funding directly from the market to circumvent some of the problems of combined funding which have already been discussed but, ultimately, this is likely to lead to loss of state control and, if carried out to any great extent, loss of ownership and privatization. Similarly, and almost by definition, a privatized enterprise ought to have its finances separated from those of the state.

The third action is a change in the employment status of the organization's personnel, who cease to be part of the traditionally strongly protected civil servant family and become private employees. This typically implies reduced job security. Civil servant status for employees of public sector organizations is often a matter of legal necessity, although it may be possible to alter the employment status of the employees concerned by moving them to private companies which are contracted to perform the same tasks. In essence, however, this is tantamount to partial privatization. Privatization, in turn, is associated with the drawing up of new employment contacts on a private basis.

ECONOMIC THEORIES

A number of economic theories are useful in the analysis of the merits of a particular privatization, and contribute to the understanding of the changes taking place. Three are of particular relevance, and they deal with the relationship between ownership and control.

The public choice theory stipulates that the public sector is unable to efficiently run an enterprise because politicians and state bureaucrats pursue their own objectives rather than the public interest. Government departments, the theory says, tend to implement policies designed to maximize votes and reduce risk, and pursue such goals as budget maximization, higher salaries, overstaffing, protective public regulation, power, patronage, and the like, such conduct being facilitated by the fact that bureaucrats tend to have better information about the consequences of budgetary changes than taxpayers do. Opponents of the theory believe that disinterested state officials do indeed pursue the public interest because, like their private sector counterparts, they find satisfaction in a job well done and, moreover, they have both developed in the same social and cultural backgrounds.

Such inappropriately self-serving behavior may be the result of a poor link between the interests of those who have the right to control and those who are entrusted to exercise it. This link is the field of interest of agency theory. The relevance of agency theory for privatization lies in the fact that a change in ownership implies a change in the requirements placed upon management and, similarly, a change in ownership concentration implies a change in the ability of owners to control management; so that, consequently, the incentive mechanisms that should be employed must also change. Incentives such as performance-related pay, for example, or share options, and disincentives such as the threat of bankruptcy, may become possible and necessary to use for the first time.

The final theory to be discussed is property rights. This essentially views ownership as the right to exercise control over assets in any way other than as specifically provided for by contracts or legislation. Two elements of the theory are of particular relevance.

First, the transferability of the organization's stock implied by privatization enables the market for corporate control to constrain management activity that significantly deviates from profit maximization, thereby aiding the agency mechanisms by establishing the threat of takeover as another disincentive for inadequate performance. Nevertheless, the applicability of the mechanism is limited for practical purposes by TRANSACTIONS COSTS, free-rider problems, and information imperfections; and, moreover, it is difficult to imagine the takeover of a utility which may be the largest capitalized group in the market.

Second, property rights coupled with private ownership can be useful in helping the government abide by its own or its predecessor's agreements, allowing organizations to receive the ex post return required to compensate for their ex ante investment. Because government holds legislative power and may possibly influence the judicial sphere too, it may find it difficult to commit itself to a particular policy, particularly so across parliamentary terms, and this can result in the inability of the organization to plan for the long term. This problem is less acute in private organizations, in which the holder of property rights (which are frequently guaranteed by constitutional laws that are more powerful than common legislation) is more clearly identified.

IMPLICATIONS

The planning and implementation of a privatization are affected by the country, industry, and company involved, and the rationale for the particular privatization. The ordering of privatizations within any single country also bears some significance. As a result, different privatizations can have different results. Nevertheless, some key effects are frequently encountered.

Ownership.   First of all, widespread trading of the organization's stock allows, in principle, its ownership to be optimized with regard to constitution and concentration. In practice, many privatizations disperse stock to a considerable extent, for reasons that are related to political and privatization success factors rather than to any considerations of economic optimization.

Strategy-making and government interference.   Another factor has to do with management. When a concern is state owned, particularly as governments and government officials tend to become involved in the operational matters of the industries for which they are responsible – frequently for reasons beyond the benefit of the particular organization – it is often the case that organizations are unable to set clear, long-term strategic goals and to prepare plans to achieve them. This should no longer be the case after privatization, when direct government involvement is restricted to the most important matters and is only justified to take place for the most important reasons. Moreover, as a result of the barriers between government and organization which are erected with privatization, such intervention becomes more explicit, opening the rationale for the intervention for debate.

Strategic choice.   One of the most significant influences that privatization can have is on the strategy of the organizations concerned. Assuming that the new owners are more profit oriented, the organization itself will have to adjust and comply with their requirements. As a result, it will begin to look for ways in which to reduce its costs, raise its efficiency, and increase its profits and turnover.

The first two of these aspects are reasonably straightforward and, once the appropriate motives are set in place by privatization, efforts to achieve them should be no different than they would be in any other enterprise, using methods such as reduction in the number of unnecessary employees, use of the most appropriate technology, use of best practice methods, and others. The third aspect, however, brings into the discussion the possibility of DIVERSIFICATION. Public sector organizations in many countries have historically been denied the ability to venture into markets other than those which they were set up to serve. There are many reasons for this. For example, if they were allowed to diversify, they would get in one another's way, or they would start to face competition from private companies. Under their new ownership and profitability culture, however, diversification seems an option that they are eager to explore, even though this may lead them to national and international markets of which they initially have little knowledge. Similarly, privatized businesses are likely to be keen to prune any activities that they find unprofitable.

Having said that, it should be made clear that diversification need not strictly follow privatization, as public sector organizations can, in theory, be allowed to grow in unrelated ways. Historically, however, very few governments have ever decided that it would be worthwhile to give them this kind of strategic decision-making freedom; so diversification does, in practice, often follow privatization. Similarly, there are very few cases in which, given the opportunity to diversify, privatized companies do not take it up, so the association between privatization and diversification seems to be very strong. Where it may appear that is not, this is because the association is moderated by the retention of monopoly powers. Privatized companies which are not immediately threatened by competitors tend to take diversification less seriously, until competitive forces are strengthened.

Structure, systems, and skills.   In order to be able to service the new strategies, and to reflect the newly adopted profit orientation, structure and management methods must also change. The kinds of changes involved include the establishment of market-facing divisions (*see* DIVISIONAL STRUCTURE) – as opposed to the use of functional integrated structures (*see* FUNCTIONAL STRUCTURE) – the proliferation of profit centers, and so on.

These changes also bring about a requirement for different skills, so privatization is often accompanied by major internal reorganization and the installation of new management teams. The latter, however, is often delayed in order to insure the incumbent management's cooperation in the process of privatization.

The need for regulation. A problem which emerges in the privatization of an organization possessing monopoly power (such as many of the traditionally state-owned utilities) is that the profit orientation of the private sector may lead to socially suboptimal pricing and output levels. In such cases, and until effective competition can be achieved, if ever, it is necessary for the government to establish an authority to oversee the organization concerned and to insure that it refrains from using its power in undesirable ways. The management of the relationship between such a regulator and the regulated company requires considerable skill, as the regulator is able to influence and perhaps determine the overall profitability and other key variables of the organization, yet the latter may wish to circumvent any restrictions placed upon it. This, in turn, means that regulation can have its own implications quite apart from those of privatization leading, for example, the regulated organization to adopt strategies that reduce the impact of the regulatory authority on itself.

Finally, regulatory authorities often possess considerable legal powers over the organizations that they oversee and have the right, and indeed the obligation, to request sensitive information to enable them to perform their duties effectively. As a result, regulation is a very potent mechanism for intervention in the organization's affairs, in substitution of direct government involvement, and regulatory regimes may easily become the new instruments of political intervention, this time with the private sector bearing the costs.

Implications for performance. Perhaps the most actively sought outcome of privatization is an improvement in organizational performance, and evidence generally suggests that such improvement is indeed compatible with privatization. This, however, is not sufficient to justify privatization. Financial performance has, with some exceptions, typically and historically been only one of the lower-ranking goals of state enterprises, and there is evidence to suggest that state-owned enterprises can perform equally well under certain circumstances.

One of the most important factors influencing the ability and intent of an organization to stretch itself in order to perform well is product market competition, and this often explains much of post-privatization performance variation. This means that liberalization (stronger competition in the product market) becomes at least as plausible an option as privatization (stronger competition in the capital market) if it is just a performance improvement that is required, although privatization usually leads to it anyway. In any case, it should be kept in mind that this is quite distinct from the ability of firms to profit from exploiting their markets, which leads to socially undesirable allocative inefficiency and also promotes productive inefficiency.

This, however, is not sufficient to explain all performance variations associated with privatization. Another factor at work is that the desire to privatize itself acts as a spur to improve the performance of state-owned enterprises in preparation for flotation, in order to maximize revenue for the government, and so performance improvements can also be observed during the period leading up to privatization. These improvements can be achieved not only by better productivity and efficiency, but also by means of simple price increases, particularly in monopolistic markets.

The above discussion is intended only to be a brief introduction to some of the mechanisms that link privatization to performance improvements, and it does not determine whether privatization is the only way to achieve such improvements, nor whether it can be relied upon to deliver them. What can be said, however, is that although it is possible for a determined government to provide strong efficiency and profitability incentives for public enterprises, this outcome remains a matter of discretionary choice. Privatization and deregulation turn this into a matter of necessity. Put another way, it can be argued that privatization, while not strictly necessary for the introduction of enhanced performance incentives, is an effective way of insuring that these incentives are put in place and remain there.

In summary, privatization is a strategy that may be adopted by government in order to re-allocate a considerable portion of a country's wealth, with the added bonus of raising revenue by means of the process. It can be used to accomplish a large variety of governmental and political goals, and enables the confrontation of lazy enterprises with competitive pressures in their capital and, indirectly, their product market.

Bibliography

Dunsire, A., Hartley, D., and Dimitriou, B. (1988). Organizational status and performance: A conceptual framework for testing public choice theories. *Public Administration Review*, **66** (4), 363–88.

Goodman, J. B. and Loveman, G. W. (1991). Does privatization serve the public interest? *Harvard Business Review*, **69**, 26–38.

Jensen, M. C. (1989). Eclipse of the public corporation. *Harvard Business Review*, **67**, 61–74.

Kay, J. A. (1988). The state and the market: The UK experience. Occasional Paper No. 23. Group of Thirty, London.

Kay, J. A. and Thompson, D. (1986). Privatization: A policy in search of a rationale. *Economic Journal*, **96**, 18–32.

Vickers, J. and Yarrow, G. K. (1988). *Privatization: An Economic Analysis*. Cambridge, MA: MIT Press.

product market diversification matrix

Derek F. Channon

Originally developed by Ansoff, the product market diversification matrix, shown in figure 1, originally divided a company's product market activities into four key areas, each of which suggested a particular strategy.

Current products produced for current markets suggest strategies of attempting to maintain or increase existing levels of market penetration.

The introduction of current products into new markets suggests strategies aimed at extending product reach. Many new products when first introduced have actually ended up being most successful in markets for which they were not originally conceived. One particular strategy that has proved effective in opening new markets has been the exploitation of new or unused distribution channels.

	Current Products	New Products
Current Markets	Market Penetration Strategy	Product Development Strategy
New Markets	Market Development Strategy	Diversification Strategy

Figure 1 The product market diversification matrix (Ansoff, 1987: 109)

New products for existing markets suggest a strategy of new product development. These should be introduced taking full cognizance of actual market needs, rather than attempting to force products developed internally, without paying due attention to customer needs.

The diversification cell, that of new products for new markets, is the most dangerous, as the company knows little about either the products or the markets. As discussed elsewhere (*see* DIVERSIFICATION), many diversification moves have therefore resulted in strategic failure, and thus great care needs to be taken when embarking on such a strategy. While a related diversified strategy (*see* RELATED DIVERSIFICATION) might gain greater stock market acceptance, the concept of relatedness needs careful attention, as experience indicates that what is initially thought of as a related activity may indeed turn out differently. For example, until fairly recently banking and insurance were seen as separate industries, but by redefining industry boundaries both can be categorized as "financial services" and hence related. The ability of each specialist function to absorb the culture and methods of the other is often difficult and fraught with danger.

Ansoff subsequently refined his original concept to include the added complexity of geography (see figure 2). In this three-dimensional format, the matrix can be used to define the strategic thrust and the ultimate scope of the business. As shown, the firm can opt for one of a number of variations of market need, product/service technologies, and geographic scope to

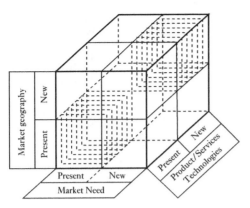

Figure 2   Dimensions of the geographic growth vector
(Ansoff, 1987)

define a SERVED MARKET. The second component of portfolio strategy, as defined by Ansoff, is the COMPETITIVE ADVANTAGE that the firm seeks to achieve in each served market. The third component consists of the synergies that might be achieved between businesses (*see* SYNERGY), while the last is the degree of strategic flexibility that can be achieved.

Strategic flexibility can be achieved in two ways. The first method is external to the firm, through diversifying the firm's geographic scope, needs served, and technologies, so that any sudden change in any of the strategic businesses areas does not produce serious repercussions.

Second, strategic flexibility can be achieved by making resources and capabilities easily transferable among the businesses. Ironically, optimizing one of the four components of the portfolio strategy growth vector is likely to depress the firm's performance with regard to the other components. In particular, maximizing synergy is very likely to reduce strategic flexibility.

Bibliography

Ansoff, I. (1987). *Corporate Strategy*. Harmondsworth: Penguin, pp. 108–11.

Profit Impact of Market Strategy (PIMS)

Kevin Jagiello and Gordon Mandry

Profit performance varies enormously from business to business and within a business over time. In developing strategy, both corporate and business unit management need to be able to realistically appraise the level of performance that should be expected for a given business, and to be clear as to what factors explain variations in performance between businesses, and within a business over time. Important guidelines that help address these questions have been developed from the Profit Impact of Market Strategy (PIMS) program. For a fuller description of the background of the PIMS program, see Schoeffler, Buzzell, and Heany (1974) or consult the PIMS website: www.pimsonline.com.

BACKGROUND TO THE PIMS
METHODOLOGY

At the heart of the PIMS program is a business unit research database that captures the real-life experiences of over 3,000 businesses. Each business is a division, product line, or profit center within its parent company, selling a distinct set of products and/or services to an identifiable group of customers, in competition with a well-defined set of competitors, for which meaningful separation can be made of revenue, operating costs, investment, and strategic plans. The business's SERVED MARKET is defined as the segment of the total potential market which it is seriously targeting by offering suitable products and/or services and toward which it is making specific marketing efforts. On this basis each business reports, in standardized format, over 300 items of data, much of it for at least four years of operations.

The information collected covers, *inter alia*, the market environment, competitive situation, internal cost and asset structure, and profit performance of the business. A full listing of the information captured by the PIMS database is given by the Strategic Planning Institute's *PIMS Data Manual*. A useful summary of the manual is given in Buzzell and Gale (1987).

The businesses in the database have been drawn from some 500 corporations, spanning a wide variety of industry settings. These corporations are based for the most part in North America and Europe.

The distribution of return on investment (ROI) in the database is shown in figure 1. As can be seen, profit varies widely among the

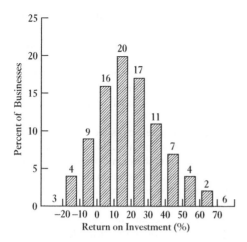

Figure 1 The distribution of return on investment in the PIMS database (PIMS Associates). ROI is defined as follows: pre-tax after deduction of corporate expenses but prior to interest charges divided by average investment where this is equivalent to the historic net book value of plant and equipment plus working capital (i.e., total assets less current liabilities). Note that four-year averages are used for all figures

businesses, with 16 percent of the sample showing negative returns and 12 percent consistently achieving in excess of 50 percent ROI. An understanding of why one business should be loss-making while another achieves premium returns lies at the heart of strategy formulation. To explain this variance, cross-sectional analysis is carried out on the database to uncover the general patterns or relationships that account for these profit differentials. The fundamental proposition that underpins this approach is that the name of a business has no bearing on its level of performance. What matters are the structural characteristics that describe the business, factors such as MARKET SHARE, growth rate, customer concentration, product quality, and INVESTMENT INTENSITY.

Research on the database has identified some 30 factors that are statistically significant at the 95 percent probability level or better in explaining the variance in profitability across businesses. These factors, which operate in a highly interactive way, collectively explain nearly 80 percent of the variance in ROI across the database. The more powerful factors are listed in table 1 under four categories: marketplace standing, market

environment, differentiation from competitors, and capital and production structure.

It should be noted at the outset that part of the explanation of variance is definitional. This comes about because some of the profit-explaining variables, such as investment/sales revenue, contain elements which are also present in the construction of the dependent variable, ROI. However, the emphasis is on behavioral relationships. Definitional elements are included in the independent variables only when it is impossible to separate out the behavioral and definitional effects of a particular factor.

Table 1 Key determinants of ROI in the PIMS database

Category of factor	Impact on ROI as factor increases
Marketplace standing	
Market share	+
Relative market share	+
Served market concentration	+
Market environment	
Real market growth	+
Selling price inflation	+
Market differentiation	+
Purchase amount immediate customers	−
Importance of purchase to end user	−
Differentiation from competitors	
Relative product quality	+
Relative price	+
Relative direct cost	−
% Sales new products	−
Marketing/sales revenue	−
R&D/sales revenue	−
Capital and production structure	
Investment/sales revenue	−
Investment/value added	−
Receivables/investment	+
Fixed capital/investment	−
Capacity utilization	+
Unionization	−
Labor effectiveness*	+

* Based on a productivity submodel.

Source: PIMS Associates

ROI (%)

Market Share (%)

Figure 2 Marketplace standing and profitability are closely related (PIMS Associates)

KEY RESEARCH FINDINGS FROM THE PIMS DATABASE

The more powerful relationships listed in table 1 are now considered one and two variables at a time in relation to the dependent variable ROI. While this approach sacrifices the insights contained in multifactor interactions, it has the benefit of reducing complexity and helps to develop an understanding of the basic building blocks. To this extent it provides insight and guidelines to aid business judgment rather than hard dogma.

MARKETPLACE STANDING

There are several measures of a business's marketplace standing: market share (the business's sales expressed as a percentage of total sales made within the served market), market share rank, and relative market share (the business's market share divided by the sum of the shares of its three leading competitors). Whichever measure is adopted, a strong positive correlation between marketplace strength and profitability is observed. Figure 2 shows the relationship between market share and profitability. Businesses with strong market share (above 38 percent in the upper quintile of the distribution) achieve on average a 38 percent ROI, compared to only 10 percent for their low-share counterparts (below 8 percent in the lower quintile of the distribution).

While the data in figure 2 show that strength of marketplace standing and profitability are strongly related, the question remains as to why we observe the effect. The numbers are a fact, but hypothesis and further examination are required to explain the relationships. It should be remembered that market share in and of itself is not important: it is an output measure that

reflects a business's historic and potential ability to gain substantive competitive advantages within its activities and in the marketplace. Factors that explain the underlying reasons why share may help profitability are shown in table 2. For a fuller discussion of the benefits of market share, see Buzzell, Gale, and Sultan (1975).

Powerful as these factors are, the fact remains that there is nothing inevitable about the relationship between share and profitability. Over 30 percent of the businesses in the database with market shares above 40 percent have ROIs below the average of 22 percent. These businesses have often become victims of their own success, wedded to historic investment decisions and burdened with complexity costs. For a fuller discussion of below-average performance for high-share businesses, see Woo (1984).

The benefits of market share are particularly marked in marketing and R&D-intensive environments, as can be seen in figure 3. The two variable cross-tables divide the database into equal thirds on the basis of relative market share and then into low and high marketing and R&D environments. Each cell contains approximately 300 businesses, and the numbers in the cells refer to the average ROI achieved by the businesses that fall into that cell over a four-year time period.

When marketing expenditure is below 5 percent of sales revenue, the ROIs achieved by low-share businesses are 14 percent, as compared to 30 percent for their high-share counterparts – a differential of 16 points. On the other hand, in marketing-intensive environments the importance of market share on profit is much more pronounced, with ROI going from 7 percent to 36 percent, a 29-point differential. A similar relationship manifests itself in the case of market share and R&D expenditure.

What the PIMS data highlight is the danger of low market share in an environment which is either marketing or R&D intensive. This is because both marketing and R&D have many of the characteristics of a fixed cost. Businesses with small market shares often find that they have to spend as much as their larger competitors on these activities, but do not have the same volume over which to spread the costs. The result is that they are trapped in the low-profit cells. When

Table 2   Potential benefits of strong market standing

"Experience curve" and "learning curve" benefits
Widely publicized by the Boston Consulting Group, the experience curve effect sees cost per unit come down in a
fairly predictable manner as cumulative volume doubles.

* *Economics of scale and scope*
Can drive down cost per unit throughout the cost structure of a business as well as benefitting balance sheet
productivity. Key areas for potential benefit are seen to be:
   – purchases: stronger negotiating stance with suppliers leads to preferential terms
   – manufacturing: plant scale and run length
   – distribution: drop size and drop density
   – marketing/R&D: spreading fixed-cost component over a larger number of units
   – investment productivity
      • improved asset utilization
      • improved ability to control all current asset components and extend current liabilities

* *Relative perceived quality*
Higher market visibility offering the "low-risk" option for buyers in many instances. Scale benefits should give
ability to establish stronger brand and better control distribution.

* *Competitive ability*
   – potential to act as "industry statesman"
   – opportunities to set and administer prices
   – size may deter competitive attack
   – size will heighten ability to control the chain from supplier to customers
   – better ability to spread risk and explore more competitive avenues

Source: PIMS Associates

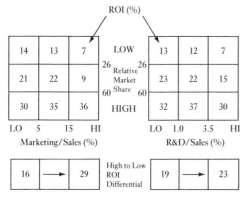

Figure 3   Share tends to have more leverage in
marketing and R&D-intensive settings (PIMS Associates)

faced with such a trap, the strategic alternatives
appear to be to reduce the role of marketing and
R&D, to strengthen share either organically or
by merger/alliance (*see* MERGERS AND ACQUI-
SITIONS; STRATEGIC ALLIANCES), or to

resegment to dominate a niche within the
market. If none of these possibilities appears to
be feasible, the small-share competitor will be
faced with the large-share competitor's "virtuous circle," shown in figure 4.

DIFFERENTIATION FROM COMPETITORS

A business's value-for-money position versus
competitors is a critical determinant of competitive advantage. PIMS assesses this position by
judging a business's relative competitive standing in terms of quality and price. It then examines how that offer is supported by new product
activity, marketing, and R&D expenditure and
the extent to which price is underpinned by the
relative direct cost position of the business.
"Relative perceived quality" is seen as the key
driver of business performance under this
category of factor.
   Quality in the PIMS database is defined from
the perspective of the external marketplace.
Customers evaluate the total benefit bundle of
products and services offered by the business

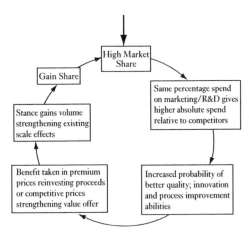

Figure 4   High-share competitors' "virtuous circle" (PIMS Associates)

and rank it relative to leading competitors as being superior, equivalent, or inferior. The "relative perceived quality" measure used by PIMS is then computed by subtracting the percentage of product and service attributes that are judged as being superior to competitors from the percentage that is judged as inferior.

Relative perceived quality has a major positive impact on profitability, as can be seen in figure 5. Businesses whose offer is judged as clearly superior to that of competitors on average achieve

more than twice the ROI of businesses whose offer is judged as inferior.

Not only is the relationship between quality and return one of the key determinants of performance in the database, but it is extremely robust in all types of business and marketplace situations. Businesses that achieve a significant quality advantage relative to their competitors can choose to benefit in one of two ways: either they can charge premium prices or grow market share at competitive pricing levels, or some combination of both.

The relationship between market share, quality, and profitability is shown in figure 6. The combination of share and quality is extremely powerful, with ROI in the high-quality/high-share cell averaging 39 percent.

Figure 6 also shows that quality and share are correlated. Thus, although the database was split into equal thirds on both quality and share, 45 percent of businesses lie on the top-left to bottom-right diagonal. The implications appear to be that high-share businesses that offer poor quality weaken in position, while weak-share businesses that offer high quality strengthen in position – both extremes may be transitory in nature and represent only 13 percent of the sample.

CAPITAL AND PRODUCTION STRUCTURE

Within this category of factor, the most powerful of the PIMS findings relates to investment

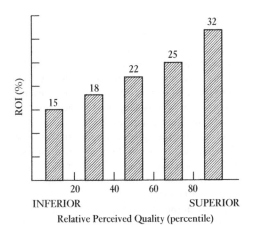

Figure 5   Relative perceived quality is closely related to profitability (PIMS Associates)

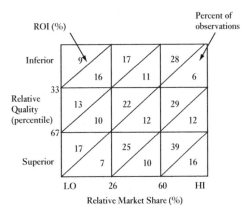

Figure 6   Market position and quality are partial substitutes for each other (PIMS Associates)

intensity. The definition of investment in this context is fixed capital, measured on a historic basis as the net book value of plant and equipment, plus working capital, defined as current assets less current liabilities. Investment intensity itself is measured in two ways: first, investment is ratioed to sales revenue in the conventional manner; and, second, investment is ratioed to the value added actually generated by the business (where value added is defined as net sales revenue less all outside suppliers' inputs).

Both measures are simultaneously employed to assess investment intensity, as many businesses have low levels of investment to sales (turn their asset base frequently) but, because of a high bought-in component, have high levels of investment to value added. Having cautioned that a balanced view on the overall investment intensity of a business is only achieved by using both measures in combination, on an individual basis each measure is similarly related to profit performance in the PIMS database, and here the more familiar investment/sales revenue ratio is employed to illustrate the investment-intensity effect.

As the investment intensity in a business rises, so the ROI that it achieves falls dramatically. This finding is the most powerful negative relationship in the database, with ROIs averaging only 8 percent for investment-intensive businesses, compared to 38 percent for low investment-intensity businesses. The finding is consistent with the experiences of many businesses in sectors such as airlines, shipbuilding, base chemicals, low alloy steel, refining, smelting, and commodity pulp and paper, which in large degree achieve at best modest rates of return.

Part of the reason for the relationship is definitional. As the investment level in a business increases, it simultaneously increases the denominator of the ROI ratio, hence dragging down the value of the ratio. That there is a behavioral element to the investment-intensity effect is vividly illustrated if the return on sales (ROS) achieved at different levels of investment is considered. If a business is to hold ROI as investment intensity increases, ROS should increase smoothly. In practice, ROS is at best flat, and in fact starts to tail off at higher levels of investment intensity. Moreover, it should be

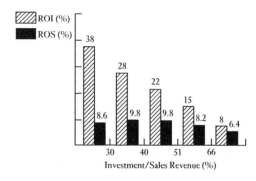

Figure 7 Investment intensity is a major drag on profitability (PIMS Associates)

remembered that return has been taken pre-tax and pre-interest, with no financial charge made on the amount of investment used in the business. If even a modest capital charge rate is applied to a business's returns to reflect its investment, the relationship would start to turn sharply down. If businesses with high levels of investment are not able to achieve profit margins sufficient to offset the level of investment that they need to sustain their sales, there is indeed a powerful behavioral element to the ROI/investment-intensity finding.

What explains this behavioral element? Part of the reason may lie in the fact that management often focuses its attention on profit margin on sales, rather than on the more important criterion of return on investment. The more substantive explanation, however, relates to the destructive nature of competition that typically accompanies high levels of investment intensity.

When a business is capital intensive, management not unnaturally becomes concerned about capacity utilization. When this drops, either because of a weakening in demand or because of new capacity addition by competitors, the knee-jerk reaction is to cut price. When one competitor cuts price, the rest of the industry typically follows, and the result is a price war. The tendency to cut price is particularly marked in fixed capital-intensive businesses, because the value of the marginal sale always appears to be so attractive.

The problem is compounded because fixed capital intensity frequently represents a major barrier to exit (*see* BARRIERS TO ENTRY AND

EXIT). When a company has sunk a lot of money into a business, it is often reluctant to exit: it becomes desperate to make the investment come good. It convinces itself that the problems of the business are transitory and that all it needs to do is "hang in" and better times will follow. This is a comforting illusion that does little for a business.

OVERVIEW

At the start, it was observed that profit performance varies enormously from business to business and within a business over time. Several of the key research findings arising from the PIMS database that help to explain this variance in performance have been discussed.

Given the richness and diversity of the PIMS database, the findings – when taken individually – direct attention to important areas of strategic strength and flag classic strategic traps faced by businesses. However, care must be cautioned in interpretation. Comprehensive insight is not obtained by examining one or two factors at a time: it requires a multifactor approach in order to start to capture the complexities and TRADE-OFFS in business. To this end, PIMS researchers have developed several models that help assess the level of ROI, cash flow, productivity, and so forth that should be expected for a business, given its structural makeup. Once these benchmarks have been established, atten-

tion can be focused on the next stage of strategy formulation, that of managing change. It can be extremely misleading to use the *general* findings presented for this purpose. That market share is generally closely related to profitability is observable; but that is not to argue, of course, that a business should try to grow share in all instances – the feasibility and cost-benefit trade-off of such a move need close examination. To this end, other modeling techniques and the database itself, via matched sample analysis, provide important empirical vehicles for the identification and evaluation of particular strategy moves by researchers and practitioners alike.

The authors would like to acknowledge the assistance of John Hillier of the Strategic Planning Institute in researching the PIMS database.

Bibliography

Buzzell, R. D. and Gale, B. T. (1987). *The PIMS Principles*. New York: Free Press, Appendix A.

Buzzell, R. D., Gale, B. T., and Sultan, R. G. M. (1975). Market share: A key to profitability. *Harvard Business Review*, 53 (1), 97–106.

Schoeffler, S., Buzzell, R. D., and Heany, D. F. (1974). Impact of strategic planning on profit performance. *Harvard Business Review*, 52 (2), 137–45.

Strategic Planning Institute (n.d.). *PIMS Data Manual*. Cambridge, MA: Strategic Planning Institute.

Woo, C. (1984). Market share leadership: Not always so good. *Harvard Business Review*, 62 (1), 50–6.

question mark businesses

Derek F. Channon

In the Boston Consulting Group's GROWTH SHARE MATRIX model, such businesses are seen to indicate opportunity. They are businesses that need to gain share by generating additional market share and hence lower cost via experience gains, while the growth rate in the industry is high. As a result, the primary objective of such businesses should be to gain share rather than maximize short-term profitability. Indeed, starving such businesses of their capital needs is a major reason for failure in companies operating such a strategy. For success, it is imperative that capacity additions and expansions should be added at a rate faster than growth in the market, to allow for share gain. This may mean poor financial performance – or even losses – and cash flow will be considerable and negative. Many companies are very reluctant to tolerate such poor performance and, as a consequence, fail to achieve the cost gains required to convert question mark businesses to STAR BUSINESSES. Due to overall group cash-flow capacity, few corporations can support more than a small number of question mark businesses. It is therefore important to carefully select from the range of new business opportunities that are available and to support those selected few to the full.

R

radar mapping

Derek F. Channon

The radar chart permits management to see at a glance the financial status of the firm. On the chart, the financial factors influencing strategy are broken down under five key headings of profitability, growth, financial stability, capital activity, and productivity. Many of these measurements are similar to those identified as critically important in the PROFIT IMPACT OF MARKET STRATEGY (PIMS) program.

Within each of these five key headings are a number of lesser measures. Overall, the position of the firm is plotted as a "snowflake" diagram. Circles for "normal," "bad," and "very bad" are shaded to emphasize the critical values and to identify areas for urgent management actions for improvement. The area outside the critical lines can be marked in green to indicate corporate strengths that might form the basis for strategic focus. Comparison of radar charts over time is also useful, to indicate trends that may be focused on or may call for corrective action.

Some companies have developed charts that illustrate different critical variables. Kodak, for example, has developed its measures matrix, or M-squared chart, illustrated in figure 1, as part of its BENCHMARKING process. In this system:

- Each radial line or spoke represents a measure.
- Concentric circles range from 1.0 at the center to 0.0 at the outermost circle.
- Data are normalized.
- Benchmarks for each measure are set in the center of the chart on its respective line. Consequently, the better an operation's performance, the nearer it is to the center and

the further away the greatest opportunity for improvement.

As they allow opportunities to observe performance for an operation from a single graphic, radar charts:

- highlight performance gaps between the company's measures and best practice;
- provide a tool to check performance over time;
- make management focus on best practice comparison (*see* BEST PRACTICES'), allowing a series of strategic measures rather than just one.

Bibliography

Bogan, C. and English, M. (1994). *Benchmarking for Best Practice*. New York: McGraw-Hill, pp. 58–61.
Nagashima, S. (1992). *100 Management Charts*. Tokyo: Asian Productivity Organization, pp. 44–5.

reengineering disadvantages

Kaye Loveridge

Reengineering is defined by Hammer (1990) as "the fundamental analysis and radical redesign of business processes, to achieve dramatic improvements in critical contemporary measures of performance such as cost, quality service and speed." Research suggests that while reengineering has had great success, it has also seen great failures (Hall, Rosenthal, and Wade, 1993). The benefits of reengineering are often emphasized, but little is said about its disadvantages, some of which are outlined below.

While the purpose of reengineering, at a meta-level, is to improve overall performance,

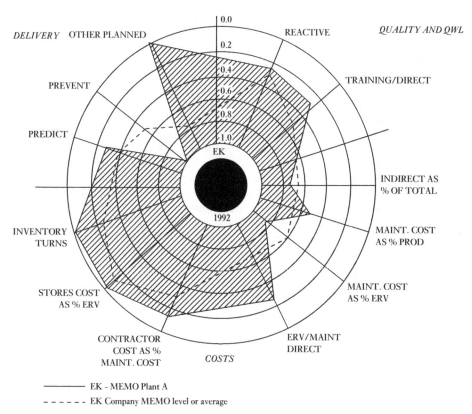

Figure 1   Kodak class MEMO benchmarking M-squared chart (Bogan and English, 1994)

in some cases after months, even years, of careful redesign, companies find that they achieve dramatic improvements in *individual* processes, only to watch *overall* results decline. Research shows that reengineering projects often fail to achieve real business impact, that the resulting improvements in performance are often disappointingly low (Hall et al., 1993).

If a firm is to function effectively, radical changes in business processes require correspondingly radical changes in a whole range of other organizational design variables. These changes cost money and are difficult to implement, while the length of time they take to achieve is uncertain. Companies that rely simply on "reengineering" as a universal panacea to achieve dramatic improvements in performance are deluding themselves. The dramatic improvements promised are often offset by huge costs, in

terms of disruption, retraining, and reworking of systems.

The implementation of reengineering is easier said than done and a successful outcome is not guaranteed. Indeed, the ingredients needed to insure success still remain unclear (redesign requires careful experimentation). There are no rules and we are told no certain formulas (Ostroff and Smith, 1992).

While companies know that they have to change in order to adapt to changing market conditions, they are often unsure how they should change, what their new organizational structure should look like, and how it should work in detail. They know they want to become more market oriented and customer focused, but do not know how to bring about the desired new behavior (Ostroff and Smith, 1992). They are equally unsure about how the new structure will actually fit together. While the board may have a vision of how this is to be accomplished, it is often not clearly understood at lower levels of the organization. Diagrams may look good on paper and impress the chief executive, but no one really knows what their impact will be.

Where initiatives are ill thought through, at best they only achieve modest levels of success, if any at all. At worst, they lead to failure, disruption, expense, and erosion of employee faith in management (Hall et al., 1993). Where initiatives continually fall by the wayside, they are seen merely as the management's "flavor of the month" and no one takes them seriously.

Many of the changes that are implemented are countercultural. They represent a threat to people's working environment and are often met with strong resistance. Many people are reluctant to give up their heritage and that which has always been held sacred to them in the past. Others may appear willing to change, but persuading them to pay more than just lip service is often a major problem.

Reengineering involves challenging the way in which things have always been done in the past and looking for new, more efficient ways of doing them. However, long-instilled behavior patterns are difficult to alter. A huge amount of management time has to be spent trying to convince people of the virtue of change. This requires a great deal of communication and reinforcement, a massive amount of effort and commitment of resources. Time has to be spent reinterviewing people for their jobs, reskilling them, and retraining them, often with uncertain results.

The fact that reengineering is being undertaken at all is a latent signal to everyone that cutbacks are to be made and almost certainly jobs will be lost. Critically, the way in which reengineering is carried out and seen to work will both affect and be affected by the culture and climate of trust within the organization.

Reengineering threatens current jobs, status, and future job opportunities, especially those of long-serving, middle-aged managers, in middle management positions. Indeed, the middle management layers are removed from the organization, as they are no longer perceived to be adding value to the business. However, where reengineering has not been carried out properly and there are simply fewer people in

the company, together with a flatter structure, people can find themselves with a broader job role and an expanded workload. Some may end up with more interesting and varied work, with more responsibility, while others, who are unable or unwilling to cope, may leave the organization.

People become cynical about reengineering and see it simply as an exercise to reduce the headcount and take costs out of the business. They fear they will be reengineered out of a job. They feel insecure and resentful, as hard work and loyalty no longer appear to be regarded as important. Indeed, people who have been rewarded for good work in the past can find themselves out of work. In a new, "slimline" reengineered company, there are no longer the same number of jobs to go round. Fewer people are needed. Redundancies are on a scale that would not have occurred in the past without the company having received bad press. It is a situation in which companies find themselves ill equipped and lacking in experience.

Where there are fewer middle management positions, the value system and compensation structure has to be changed. Whereas managers would once have come directly from school or university and been expected to stay with a company for a long time, this is no longer the case. Companies can no longer offer lifetime employment. People's careers are uncertain and their jobs insecure. The view of a career in the future has to change. In the past, it meant going up through the levels of the management hierarchy, whereas in a flat organizational structure these levels no longer exist.

Often, reengineering is not a once-and-for-all effort, but a series of waves washing over the organization for a period of years (Hall et al., 1993). It takes time and a huge amount of resources to effect fundamental change.

While companies scramble to take costs out of the business – much like throwing sandbags out of a hot air balloon, to see who can be the lightest and fly the highest – they are unsure about how far they should go. How many managers are really needed to manage effectively? What is the optimum size of their workload? Those companies that shed too many people may save on the payroll, but find themselves unable to cope if they secure a large contract.

A flat organizational structure often depends upon the implementation of new technology. While IT is an enabler for successful reengineering, it can also be a major constraint. The sheer variety of available IT solutions adds to the complexity of a reengineering project. The initial capital investment is often high, adding to the net risk of a project. Those who choose to go down the route of reengineering may find themselves committed to long-term investment in new technology.

A key to successful reengineering must surely be an appreciation of its disadvantages and weaknesses. In fact, some managers privately conclude that the best way to build a new organization is to start from scratch, and that the best way to change all the people is to do just that – change all the people. Companies' visions of the future can be held back by their memories of the past. It is important to remember that these visions are determined by the realities of today.

Bibliography

Hall, G., Rosenthal, J., and Wade, J. (1993). How to make reengineering really work. *Harvard Business Review*, 71, 119–31.

Hammer, M. (1990). Reengineering work: Don't automate, obliterate. *Harvard Business Review*, 68, 104–12.

Ostroff, F. and Smith, D. (1992). The horizontal organization. *McKinsey Quarterly*, 1, 148–68.

regulation

Stephanos Avgeropoulos

Regulation is the institution of a set of administrative and legal processes which are designed to insure that the purposes of particular groups are served and that such groups are protected from forces which tend to threaten them. There are essentially two types of regulation, economic and social. Regulation is typically set up by the government, which appoints a regulatory agency to set the terms for and to implement regulation, although self-regulation – whereby the members of the regulated industry form some sort of organization to regulate themselves – is also common, predominantly in the financial services industry.

Economic regulation, which includes public utility and antitrust regulation, can be further subdivided according to whether it serves to insulate producers from the vigor of market forces (in which case the regulator is said to act as an "environmental buffer"), or to protect consumers from the power of producers (in which case the regulator acts as a "change agent"). Sometimes, however, regulation that has initially been instituted to protect consumers is redirected to the benefit of producers as a result of the latter's actions, in which case the regulator is said to have been "captured by the industry" (Bernstein, 1955). More commonly, economic regulation is instituted to limit excessive competition, to insure that a critical industry is maintained in a healthy condition, or to deal with market imperfections such as asymmetric information, market failures, missing markets, predation, CROSS-SUBSIDIZATION and other monopolistic practices.

Turning to social regulation, this is an increasingly popular activity that often has a scope which goes beyond individual industries and aims for greater social justice overall, addressing matters such as EXTERNALITIES (e.g., pollution) and social change.

THE POLITICAL PROCESS OF REGULATION

The distinction between regulation in favor of an industry and regulation constraining an industry was explored in Stigler's (1971) seminal paper, in which a political theory of regulation was advanced which suggested that regulation may not necessarily be the result of forces originating from government to protect groups under threat, but could instead be the outcome of a political process of bargaining whereby pressure groups demand regulation, and government dispenses it to the benefit of those groups for a price, which could be in the form of help with reelection. The pressure groups that are powerful enough to obtain government action to their benefit prefer to receive their benefits in the form of regulation, e.g., by setting up barriers to entry (*see* BARRIERS TO ENTRY AND EXIT), import tariffs, or other mechanisms to retard the growth of new entrants, and not in more direct ways such as subsidies, as the latter can attract new companies into their market.

The Role and Methods of the Regulator

Because of the difficult nature of their task, regulators are often empowered to interfere at many levels of the regulated firms' decision-making, including decisions regarding major investments, the determination of market strategy, and the like. For much of the time, however, the purposes of regulation can be adequately served by controlling a few key variables such as prices and the quality of output. This is likely to be preferable because it allows the regulated firm to complete its own decisions, albeit within the framework that the regulator sets, minimizing unwanted side-effects.

As far as price controls are concerned, there are two main methods through which these can be imposed, namely, rate of return pricing and price limit control. Rate of return regulation involves the determination of a reasonable cost base, and the firm is then obliged to price no higher than to meet these costs, plus a fair rate of return that is set by the regulator. This type of regulation allows shareholders to expect a predictable, yet constrained, return and shifts uncertainty from the producer to the consumer. A resultant problem, however, is that management has no incentive to cut costs and, indeed, it may tend to extend the firm's capital base and distort its choice of inputs, particularly if the entire company's activities are grouped together for the purposes of cost determination. Also, rate of return regulation tends to push prices toward being based on average (rather than marginal) costs, and this can prevent the firm from price discriminating and using multipart tariffs.

Price limit regulation, on the other hand, involves the determination of a range of allowable real prices (an upper bound is typically established), leaving the benefit of cost reductions over a set amount with the organization. This system minimizes the incentive to inflate costs and the asset base, but it creates an incentive to reduce the quality of service. This is because a price-capped monopolist may reasonably expect that it can get away with a reduction in the quality of service without significant concurring loss of revenue. To combat this, a combination of price and quality targets may have to be set. In general, because the price limit regime requires the regulator to monitor its industry more closely than under a cost-plus regime, in order to obtain the additional information necessary to set maximum prices, it is more appropriate when technology is changing slowly. Another characteristic of the regime is that the shorter the interval is between the rate reviews, the more the regime resembles rate of return and cost-plus systems, as the firm does not have enough time to enjoy cost reductions before these lead to price cuts.

In general, the timing and scope of regime reviews, in which rates of return and price limits are regularly reevaluated, are very important because of their effect on EFFICIENCY and innovation. As far as efficiency is concerned, determination of the review frequency involves a TRADE-OFF between productive and allocative efficiency, as the longer the regulator allows prices to diverge from marginal cost, the more the regulated firm will have an incentive to reduce its costs and improve productive efficiency. Similarly, if the benefits of innovation are taken away from the firm too quickly, then the incentive to develop new products and processes will be reduced. In the longer term, the credibility of the regulator becomes as important as its current conduct. High sunk-cost projects, in particular, involve the threat that the regulator will modify its policies as soon as much of a company's (irreversible) investment has been completed and, if the regulator cannot be relied upon to maintain reasonable policies in the future, then the investment may not be undertaken at all.

The Costs and Impact of Regulation

Regulation cannot be implemented without costs. The administration of regulation itself is expensive, and each regulated firm must also incur the costs of negotiating and complying with the regulator. Its impact can be felt at both the industry level and the company level and, indirectly, it can also affect an entire economy.

Impact on market structure. At the industry level, regulation can have a considerable impact on MARKET STRUCTURE and the level of competition, as it may exclude certain competitors from a particular sector, it may segment a market, place specific limits on geographic expansion, or impede innovation. In addition, it can stifle competitiveness by reducing the surprise element of competition due to disclosure requirements, and it enables firms to contest the actions of their competitors in regulatory hearings.

Impact on the strategy development process. As far as individual organizations are concerned, the effects come through many directions. For a regulated firm, many environmental conditions are articulated through the regulatory agency which, therefore, becomes the focus of organizational attention, to the exclusion of the customer. Similarly, the number of relevant stakeholders is reduced (*see* STAKEHOLDER ANALYSIS), as is the ability of the firm to develop its strategy simply by balancing them off. Instead, the firm must become adept in political analysis and negotiating skills and, in time, traditional planning capabilities are weakened. Characteristics such as centralization, bureaucratic delays (e.g., the need to produce proposals for approval), and the need for procedural uniformity also appear.

Impact on optimal ownership. Another implication of regulation is related to optimization of ownership. As far as control of management is concerned, regulation provides some subsidized monitoring and disciplining as the regulatory agency also keeps an eye on management. This implies that regulation should reduce the need for ownership concentration. Nevertheless, this effect may be counterbalanced by the fact that limited competition reduces the incentive to hold down costs and, with cost-plus pricing in particular, as has already been discussed, management may resort to substantial amenity consumption. This danger is all the more realistic as shareholders know that, if alerted, the regulator may squeeze the firm's margins, so they have little to gain by discussing such practices in public. In turn, senior management may tolerate excessive wages, overstaffing, and so on as a means of taking out in cost what cannot be expropriated as profit, given the regulatory environment, so the implications of regulation for ownership do vary in practice.

Impact on strategic outcome. One of the most significant ways in which regulation can affect an organization is through its influence on strategic outcome, and DIVERSIFICATION in particular. As long as the interests of the regulated firm and the regulator remain convergent, the firm is likely to remain close to its main line of regulated businesses and may even integrate vertically (*see* VERTICAL INTEGRATION STRATEGY). When their interests diverge, however, for example due to high contract monitoring costs (*see* TRANSACTIONS COSTS), the firm may diversify into unregulated businesses, to the extent that is permissible.

Impact on structure. Organization may also be affected, although this is not necessarily the case. Where the regulated enterprise is also active in non-regulated markets, however, practices such as cross-subsidization become possible, so the regulator may require that any non-regulated business is undertaken through separate subsidiaries, to insure that any transactions between the two companies become more visible.

Performance. It is generally acceptable that regulation, by virtue of reducing competition, allows firms to charge higher prices and, consequently, enjoy artificially high levels of profit, although this may be diminished in situations in which manager control is more relaxed, as has already been discussed. Nevertheless, the regulatory process has also been observed to retard price adjustments during inflationary periods, and this can result in diminished performance and increased risk. Overall, however, the risk of a regulated firm is generally lower than for an unregulated one.

Other implications. Finally, certain social priorities (such as cross-subsidization of high-cost areas or low-income groups, or the provision of a universal service) imposed by means of regulation are likely to introduce a number of distortions (even though they may be correcting others), as can other constraints imposed on regulated firms, such as the requirement for uninterruptible service (guarantees of constant adequate electricity supply regardless of demand, for example, require companies to prepare for levels of output that may never be required). Technological innovation can also be discouraged with the burden of environmental impact statements, and the regulator's ability to categorize costs in a price ceiling regime can also influence the choice of technology.

SUCCESSFUL REGULATORY REGIMES

In order to judge the success of a regulatory setup, the criteria set out by Braeutingham and Panzar (1989) can be used: one can consider, for example, incentives for cost misreporting, choice of technology and levels of cost-reducing innovation, choice of price and output levels, and diversification into competitive markets.

Regulation may be unsuccessful:

- if the regulator possesses imperfect information, knowledge, or foresight;
- because of rigidities (regulatory rules are hard to change, yet technology and economic circumstances change constantly);
- because of insufficient means (government may fail to choose the least costly means of solving a problem);
- because of myopic regulation (if regulators are forced to specialize, regulation may become too forced or rigid);
- because of political constraints (political realities may prevent the "right" policy from being adopted); or
- due to inappropriately set objectives.

Finally, it is worth mentioning that where regulation is instituted in association with PRIVATIZATION, so that direct government involvement is minimized in the relevant industries, the regulatory framework may easily be converted to become the government's instrument for ad hoc political intervention in the industries involved.

See also *deregulation*

Bibliography

Bernstein, M. H. (1955). *Regulating Business by Independent Commission*. Princeton, NJ: Princeton University Press.

Braeutingham, R. R. and Panzar, J. C. (1989). Diversification incentives under price-based and cost-based regulation. *RAND Journal of Economics*, **20** (3), 373–91.

Littlechild, S. C. (1983). *Regulating British Telecommunication's Profitability*. London: Department of Industry.

Stigler, G. J. (1971). The theory of economic regulation. *Bell Journal of Economics and Management Science*, **2** (1), 3–21.

related diversification

Derek F. Channon

Businesses adopting a related diversification strategy are defined as corporations that had diversified into activities with some apparent similarities to their original activities. Such DIVERSIFICATION centered on a "core skill" such as a technology. Technologies of this kind included chemical, electrical, and mechanical engineering, and firms in these industries were natural and early diversifiers. They were also early adopters of the multidivisional structure form of organization (*see* ORGANIZATION STRUCTURE) in response to the growing complexity of the business as product market diversity increased. In the Harvard studies of the early 1970s, such businesses were defined as those in which fewer than 70 percent of sales were generated from any one concern.

Firms in technology-or skill-based industries, where the skill or technology led naturally to the production of a wide range of end products meeting the needs of a variety of markets, were amongst the earliest diversifiers. While acquisition (*see* ACQUISITION STRATEGY) was an important element in their diversification strategies, significant growth also occurred as a result of internal development. In chemicals and electrical engineering the level of research expenditure was relatively high, although it was low in mechanical engineering. Nevertheless, the skills of metal manipulation proved to be readily transferable to a wide variety of different end uses.

While overall concentration and capital intensity was high in specific segments, the wide market scope of these industries had not precluded new competitive entries. Furthermore, the constant rapid change of technology frequently transformed the pattern of strategic advantage. In general, despite technical SYNERGY or STRATEGIC FIT, the degree of integration between the different corporate activities was low. There were cases in which one unit supplied raw materials or components to another, but usually all activities had a direct interface with outside markets. Therefore, while some central coordination of interdependent activities might be desirable, this was usually low, relative to the product flow of the corporation as a whole. As a result, while these concerns were early adopters of a multidivisional form of structure and were latterly converted to a strategic business unit (SBU) structure, the large central office predicted for such businesses was sharply reduced during the 1980s and 1990s.

In industries that were historically relatively specialized, such as food, textiles, paper and packaging, and printing and publishing, and without a readily transferable technology, diversification occurred largely by acquisition. While a number diversified to conglomerate strategies (*see* CONGLOMERATE STRATEGY), most firms in these sectors of industry endeavored to achieve a strategic fit in which relatedness occurred more through efforts to service common customers, use of common distribution channels, and the like. In addition, as in the textile and paper industries, a number of firms adopted vertical integration strategies by entering additional stages in the processing of materials.

Growth rates and profitability within the non-technological diversifiers tended to be low. In specific segments, however, there were high-growth segments, such as convenience foods, plastic packaging, and synthetic fibers. Furthermore, competition tended to increase in these sectors as a result of new market entrants, many of which were international operators.

In the 1970s and 1980s, diversification occurred within both the manufacturing industry and service sectors. Moreover, there was a significant volume of activity between these sectors, such that by the mid-1990s it tended to be increasingly misleading to classify businesses as either manufacturing-or service-dominated.

By the mid-1990s, related diversification had become the most important single diversification strategy amongst large corporations throughout the developed world. This applied to both manufacturing-based and service-based businesses, and hybrid strategies also became common. Concurrently with product market diversification, many of these concerns have also adopted international – and an increasing number, global – strategies (*see* GLOBAL STRATEGIES), dependent upon the industries in which they are engaged. The management of such businesses now almost invariably corresponds to some form of DIVISIONAL STRUCTURE, SBU structure, or MATRIX STRUCTURE amongst western concerns, while, in the East, Japanese concerns are usually participants in vertical and/or horizontal *keiretsu*, or *chaebol* in Korea (*see* CHAEBOL STRUCTURE; KEIRETSU STRUCTURE).

As identified by Chandler (1962), it was believed that such businesses needed a large central office to coordinate interrelationships between the related divisions, and this was indeed normal until the late 1970s. The impact of improved information technology and the use of the SBU structure led to DELAYERING and reduction in the size of such central offices. By the late 1980s, pressures on cost had therefore led to sharp reductions in the central overheads of related diversified corporations, with a strong focus on strategic control and finance. Such thin head office structures should not, however, be confused with the traditional HOLDING COMPANY STRUCTURE, in which no central strategic control was exercised.

Bibliography

Chandler, A. D. (1962). *Strategy and Structure: Chapters in the History of the Industrial Enterprise.* Cambridge, MA: MIT Press.

Channon, D. F. (1973). *Strategy and Structure of British Enterprise.* Cambridge, MA: Harvard Division of Research.

Channon, D. F. (1976). *The Service Industries: Strategy, Structure and Financial Performance.* London: Macmillan.

Wrigley, L. (1970). Divisional autonomy and diversification. Unpublished doctoral dissertation, Harvard Business School.

replacement demand

Derek F. Channon

In the early stages of the product life cycle, most demand is primary or first purchase. However, as markets move toward maturity, to maintain demand it becomes likely that a growing proportion of sales will result from replacement, as initial purchases wear out or new purchases are stimulated by the introduction of product variants, improvements, and the like. The classic strategic example of this was the early development of the US automobile industry. Henry Ford created a mass market for automobiles by cutting cost through mass producing only one model. Unable to compete with the production cost of Ford because of the latter's volume, Alfred Sloan – in rescuing General Motors – decided that each of the different automobile marques that made up the company should be price-and feature-positioned in overlapping ranges that would encourage consumers to trade up when replacing their automobiles. In addition, regular model changes would be made, to stimulate consumers to change their cars more frequently. Therefore, unable to compete head to head, Sloan positioned Chevrolet at a price somewhat above Ford, but offered the consumer the opportunity to have variations that could be personally selected rather than being strictly standard. This strategy stimulated replacement demand, which Sloan further encouraged by helping to create the second-hand car market and introducing credit finance.

The philosophy remains current today, especially in the US, where the concept of the model year continues to lead to the introduction of new product variants. Manufacturers of many other product categories, including consumer electronics, electrical appliances, and computers and computer software, endeavor to make use of the principle. In a number of these examples, the development of follower strategies is an interesting variant. For example, Amstrad built its consumer electronics and computer business by offering well-tried and tested but semi-obsolescent hardware and software to the mass market at markdowns in price, thus opening new and unsuspected market segments via alternate distribution channels. Japanese producers have also stimulated the process of miniaturization, which has encouraged mass market penetration by cost reduction and product portability.

See also *demand analysis in practice*

Bibliography

Chandler, A. D. (1962). *Strategy and Structure: Chapters in the History of the Industrial Enterprise*. Cambridge, MA: MIT Press.
Channon, D. F. (1987). *Amstrad "A" Case*. Imperial College, University of London.
Sloan, A. P. (1963). *My Years at General Motors*. New York: Anchor.

resource-based view

John McGee

Economists see the firm as a bundle of productive resources where resources are defined as inputs into the firm's operations so as to produce goods and services. In this view resources are generic and specific categories are not suggested. But typical examples include patents, capital equipment, and skilled and unskilled human resources. Strategists go further and distinguish capabilities from resources. A capability is the ability to perform a task or activity that involves complex patterns of coordination and cooperation between people and other resources. Capabilities would include research and development expertise, customer service, and high-quality manufacturing. Skills, by contrast, are more specific relating to narrowly defined activities such as typing, machine maintenance, and book-keeping.

Strategists are interested in those resources and capabilities that can earn rents (a surplus of revenue over cost). These collectively are known as *strategic assets* or CORE COMPETENCES and are a subset of, but distinct from, those other resources and capabilities that do not distinctively support the COMPETITIVE ADVANTAGE. The strategic task for the firm is to sustain these rent streams over time by creating and protecting the competitive advantage and the strategic assets that together underpin them. The inherent value of the strategic assets for the firm depends on the ways in which the firm combines, coordinates, and deploys these assets in concert with the other firm-specific and more generic resources and capabilities.

The internal economy of the firm can be seen as sets of discrete activities (e.g., a product line), each of which leads to market positions and each of which is supported by assets of resources and capabilities. *Similar* activities (e.g., the Ford Mondeo and Ford Focus product lines) share some common strategic assets and some common generic assets. This sharing can lead to ECONOMIES OF SCALE (if different components share the same production line), to ECONOMIES OF SCOPE (where products might go through common distribution channels), and experience effects (*see* EXPERIENCE AND LEARNING EFFECTS). *Complementary* activities require dissimilar sets of strategic assets which would then require degrees of coordination (e.g., marketing activities and production activities). The skills of coordination and internal cooperation are in fact high-level capabilities with considerable strategic significance.

In the real world of uncertainty and imperfect information the firm may have (and usually does have) considerable problems in knowing which particular configurations of its strategic assets will maximize profits. Managers do not have perfect knowledge of future states of the world, of alternative actions that could be taken, nor of the payoffs from adopting various alternatives. Moreover the way a manager chooses to allocate resources will be a function of past personal experience, the firm's experience, values, biases, and personality. Accordingly, even if two managers were given identical bundles of resources, they would use them in different ways. The result is that a firm's set of resources and capabilities will diverge from those of its competitors over time. Managers in competing firms in the same markets do not face the same sets of choices – rather, they have different menus with different choices. The future, as firms sees it, is to a greater or lesser degree uncertain and unknowable and their capacities for addressing the unknowable are diverse. Further, no amount of information gathering can resolve this fundamental uncertainty of what the future will hold. Thus, STRATEGY-MAKING is a long way from the simplistic assumptions of the economic model. Strategies tend to be unique and idiosyncratic and simplistic theories for success are usually "magic theories," i.e., theories which explain everything but predict nothing (Lave and March, 1993). Nor are there simple rules for riches, i.e., there are no automatic rules that provide benefits in the long run.

This means that STRATEGIC MANAGEMENT is not captured in the form of a strategic theory of the firm in a way that enables equations to be identified, data collected and analyzed, and simple rules inferred. Strategic management is much more eclectic and diverse. Contexts external to the firm and internal to the firm are highly idiosyncratic. This places a premium on the ability to diagnose situations and formulate options. The specific routes to high performance are many and varied and not readily susceptible to simple generalizations. This goes some way to explaining why the resource-based view is widely seen as lacking specificity and definable concepts, and having no traceable connection to real performance improvements.

THE LANGUAGE OF THE RESOURCE-BASED VIEW: WHAT IS CORE COMPETENCE?

We can introduce the resource-based view with figure 1. The top line of this diagram shows how the firm's investment programs are directed toward the creation and development of resources and capabilities, and that these underpin the positional advantage from which superior value can be delivered to customers. The bottom line shows the value and financial consequences, in terms of the capacity of the firm to finance its investment programs. The resource-based view focuses on the resources and capabilities of the firm, asserting that it is the distinctiveness of these that enables sustainable positional advantages to be constructed. The added element in this diagram is the presence of core competences as representing those resources and capabilities that are distinctive to the firm. As a result, competitive advantage is seen as the joint product of core competences and positional advantage. What many writers observe is that imperfections in the resource and capability markets are more in number and larger in size than those in product markets. This places the burden on firms to pay attention to the underpinnings of competitive advantage in resource and capability terms. What many writers have also observed is that markets are changeable and even volatile, whereas it is quite difficult to get firms to change their internal cultures and processes quickly enough to keep pace with market changes.

Here we follow Grant's (1991, 1998) lead in using "resources" to describe inputs that can in

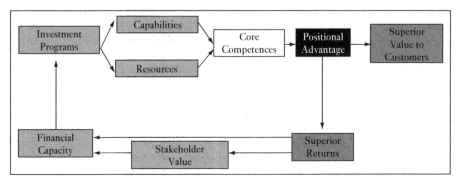

Figure 1   Competitive advantage and core competence

general be purchased on open markets and customized for use by the purchasers. Thus, production capacity might be generally available, but will be configured for specific use by each purchaser. The activities of individual purchasers may lead to imperfections in supply markets. For example, a company may seek to monopolize certain raw materials through acquisition, or maybe through offering long-term supply contracts. But, on their own, few resources are immediately productive. By contrast, the "capabilities" described here are firm specific. They are developed internally against the specific needs and ambitions of each company. They often depend on tacit knowledge, are path-dependent in that they emerge and develop over time, and are not in the form of assets that can be traded. These resources and capabilities have individual characteristics, but a large part of their value-in-use to a firm is related to their configuration and their coordination. Table 1 compares typical resources and typical capabilities. The distinctiveness of the firm's specific set of resources and capabilities is a function of which resources to acquire and what capabilities to develop (the *configuration* issue), the way in which each of these is developed (the *firm-specificity* issue), and the way in which they are internally managed to create positional advantage (the *coordination* issue).

PRAHALAD AND HAMEL ON CORE COMPETENCE

The language of assets, resources, and capabilities can be confusing. The Grant (1998) distinction between resources and capabilities is an easy

distinction as any to maintain. However, it is laborious to keep referring to strategic resources and capabilities as those that systematically and uniquely underpin the competitive advantage relative to those other resources and capabilities that do not. Thus it is attractive to refer to these as core competences, the language popularized by Prahalad and Hamel (1990). They provided an unusual metaphor:

> The diversified corporation is a large tree. The trunk and the major limbs are core products, the smaller branches are business units; the leaves, flowers, and fruit are end products. The root system that provides nourishment, sustenance, and stability is the core competence. You can miss the strength of competitors by looking only at their end products, in the same way you miss the strength of a tree if you look only at its leaves. . . .
>
> Core competences are the collective learning in the organization, especially how to coordinate diverse production skills and integrate multiple streams of technologies.

BCG AND CAPABILITIES-BASED COMPETITION

Prahalad and Hamel's approach is to define core competence as the combination of individual technologies and production skills that underlie a company's product lines. Sony's core competence in miniaturization allows it to make everything from the Sony Walkman to video cameras and digital cameras. Honda's core competence in engines and powertrains allows it to compete from lawnmowers to racing cars. But this latter example shows a difficulty in Prahalad and

Table 1   Resources and capabilities

Resources	Capabilities
• Distribution coverage • Financial capacity • Shared expertise with related businesses • Low-cost manufacturing and distribution systems • Production capacity • Ownership of raw material sources • Long-term supply contracts • Fast, flexible response capability	• Specialized knowledge • Customer service orientation • Design expertise • Application experience • Trade relationships • Ability to utilize relevant technologies • Systems design capability

Table 2   Strategic resources and capabilities

Speed	• the ability to respond quickly to customer or market demands and to incorporate new ideas and technologies quickly into products
Consistency	• the ability to produce a product that unfailingly satisfies customers' expectations
Acuity	• the ability to see the competitive environment clearly and thus to anticipate and respond to customers' evolving needs and wants
Agility	• the ability to adapt simultaneously to many different business environments
Innovativeness	• the ability to generate new ideas and to combine existing elements to create new sources of value

Source: Stalk et al. (1992)

Hamel's approach in that Honda's dealer network would be invisible – because of the focus on competences that lead directly to products. A development of their idea is contained in a Boston Consulting Group (BCG) paper (Stalk, Evans, and Shulman, 1992) on "capabilities-based" competition. This contained four basic principles:

1 the building blocks of strategy are not products and markets but business processes;
2 competitive success depends on transforming these key processes into strategic capabilities that consistently provide superior value to the customer;
3 companies create these capabilities by making strategic investments in a support infrastructure that links together and transcends traditional strategic business units;
4 because capabilities necessarily cross functions, the champion of a capabilities-based strategy is the chief executive officer.

This approach has the real merit of focusing on business processes as the integrative glue that binds together the various lower-level ingredients and on the investments that are required to make this effective. Unfortunately, the continued use of capabilities makes for some confusion. The essence of the idea here is that these business processes should connect to real customer needs. Things are only strategic when they begin and end with the customer because that is where value is sensed and created. Table 2 summarizes the five dimensions on which a company's strategic resources and capabilities should aim to outperform the competition.

BCG present this discussion in the language of strategic capabilities in an attempt to avoid an overuse of the term competences which is a feature of the Prahalad and Hamel approach.

AMIT AND SCHOEMAKER ON STRATEGIC ASSETS

A similar approach can be seen in another classic paper from the same era. Amit and Schoemaker

(1993) build on the resource and capability language to create "strategic assets." By resources they mean stocks of available factors of production that are owned and controlled by the firm. Capabilities refer to the firm's capacity to deploy resources, usually in combination, using organizational processes to effect a desired end. They are information-based, tangible and intangible processes that are firm specific and are developed over time through complex interactions with one another and with the firm's resources. Unlike resources, capabilities are based on developing, sharing, and exchanging information through the firm's human capital – as information-based assets they are often called "invisible assets." The authors describe "strategic assets" as "the set of difficult to trade and imitate, scarce, appropriable and specialized resources and capabilities that [underpin] the firm's competitive advantage." In practice it is difficult to draw clear distinctions between the core competences of Prahalad and Hamel, the capabilities-based competition of BCG, and the strategic assets of Amit and Schoemaker. They all convey the sense of firm-specific assets that are typically process and information based and intangible in character.

There are other assets and activities in the value chain, notably complementary assets that, when linked to strategic assets (core competences), are necessary for the existence of the competitive advantage. Thus, a research-based pharmaceuticals company like Merck or SmithKlineGlaxo would identify research expertise as a core competence but management of government regulations as a complementary asset, essential but not unique. Many other assets and activities in the firm can be classified as "make-or-buy," i.e., the firm makes a financial calculation as to make or buy. Figure 2 distinguishes "strategic assets" from "complementary" assets and "make-or-buy" assets. Strategic assets are those that are truly distinctive and unique to the firm and provide the underpinning of positional advantage in product markets. Complementary assets are those assets that are jointly required with the strategic assets in order to produce and deliver the product or service. Thus, product development might be a strategic asset, but production capacity is required for product trials and for product adaptations, even though that capacity is not unique to the firm. These assets are sometimes called

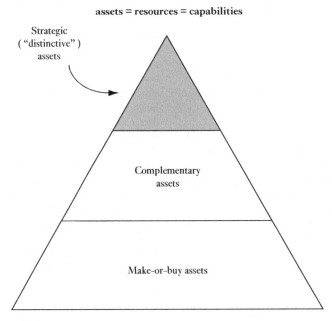

Figure 2   The asset triangle

co-specialized assets, in that they are complementary to the specialized assets and (lightly) customized to interface with them. Make-or-buy assets are those that are chosen to be included in the assets portfolio solely on the basis of financial calculations. For example, the decision to own or lease company cars might be made solely on financial criteria, because there are no strategic implications. In principle, if there are no strategic implications (which means that there is no need to customize the assets for specific purposes), then there will, in general, be a free outside market. This in turn generally means that the market is able to supply more cheaply than is possible internally. From this it can be seen that the pressure to outsource (*see* OUTSOURCING) can be very high and depends critically on the characteristics of supply markets.

CORE COMPETENCE = DISTINCTIVE CAPABILITY = STRATEGIC ASSET

The language of core competences is abstract and hard to put into practice. This reflects not only the idiosyncratic and unique nature of the strategic problems faced by individual firms, but also the need to have a clear concept upon which to base strategic thinking. The two building blocks of strategy identified so far are competitive advantage and core competence. They are both intellectual constructs. Each relies on situational characteristics for their application in practice. Each provides a way of thinking so that strategists can develop a "theory in use" that applies to their own situation. Gary Hamel (1994) has attempted to codify the idea of core competence further. He offers the following essential characteristics of a core competence:

1 A competence is a bundle of constituent skills and technologies rather than a discrete skill or technology and a core competence is the integration of a variety of individual skills.
2 A core competence is not an asset in the accounting sense of the word. A factory, a distribution channel, or brand cannot be a core competence, but an aptitude to manage that factory, that channel, or that brand may constitute a core competence.
3 A core competence must make a disproportionate contribution to customer-perceived value. The distinction between core and non-core competence thus rests on a distinction between the relative impacts on customer value.
4 A core competence must also be competitively unique. This means either that (a) a competence is held uniquely by one firm in the competitive set, or (b) a competence that is ubiquitous across an industry must be held at a superior level in the firm (e.g., power-trains are ubiquitous in the automobile industry but one could argue that Honda has unique strength in this area and thus it is a core competence for Honda).
5 From the corporate (multibusiness) perspective a core competence should provide an entrée into new markets. A particular competence may be core from the perspective of an individual business, but from a corporate perspective it will not be core if there is no way of imagining an array of new product-markets issuing from it.

The language of core competence has become widespread. Core competence and competitive advantage together have become the central conceptual terms in the analysis of competitive strategy. We define core competence quite simply as "the underlying capability that is the distinguishing characteristic of the organization."

- It is the way we do things.
- It is how we organize the way we do things.
- It is how we systematically *communicate* this knowledge and build upon it.
- It is understanding the difference, and building bridges, between tangible and intangible assets, tacit and explicit knowledge, and individual and team knowledge and skill.

More formally, we define core competences as "the set of firm-specific skills and cognitive processes directed towards the attainment of competitive advantage" (McGee and Segal-Horn, 1997).

Core competence is a fundamental concept in our understanding of what strategy-making is. It is *only* through core competence that the firm attains competitive advantage and is therefore the mainspring of sustainable distinctiveness. But it is also the lens through which the world is seen and interpreted. Different firms (and people) see different things in their environments and this is a function of the inheritance and their experience. In the same way, firms (and people) differ in the way in which they see themselves and therefore in their understanding of what they might achieve. Thus we can see core competences as the link between managerial cognition and the economics of the firm (see figure 3). The key tasks of strategy analysts are interpreting the external environment, understanding the dynamics of markets and of competition, and understanding the internal dynamics of one's own organization. Core competences provide the links to these economic assessments through a clarity of perception about the shared values and beliefs in the firm (often explicit in the MISSION statement), through tacit knowledge and understandings (that are possibly unique to the firm), and through flexible routines and recipes that enable non-standard challenges to be comprehended.

WHAT DETERMINES THE VALUE OF A CORE COMPETENCE?

Figure 4 summarizes the conditions that determine the value of a core competence (strategic asset). The basic foundations of value are *imit-*

ability, *durability*, *substitutability*, and *appropriability*. The ability of competitors to imitate a firm's assets is in part to do with *physical uniqueness*. More subtle issues around inimitability are:

- *Path dependency* – cumulative learning and experience over time, which is difficult to replicate over short periods.
- *Causal ambiguity* – not really knowing what it is that is the important element in a complex asset.
- *First-mover advantage* – the preemption of a market by being the first to create scale-efficient assets (*see* FIRST-MOVER ADVANTAGE).

Substitutability is often an unknown, in that new technologies can emerge that very quickly outdate older solutions. For example, the battle between satellite and cable television systems is still raging – substitutability is high, but it is not clear which standard will prevail. Appropriability is an important but subtle issue. A central question about a strategic asset is: Who can capture the value that is created? Is it the firm? Could it be the skilled technicians? Might it be patent owners? Perhaps there are long-term supply contracts?

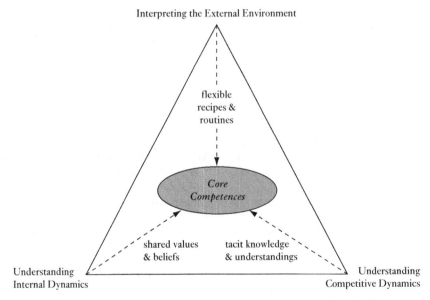

Figure 3   Core competences as the link between managerial cognition and the economics of the firm

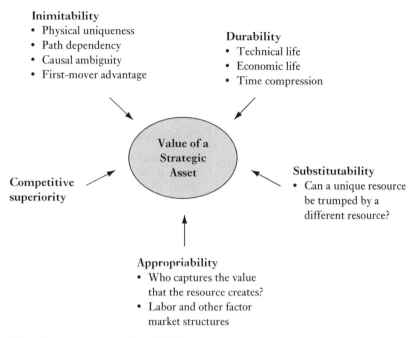

Inimitability
- Physical uniqueness
- Path dependency
- Causal ambiguity
- First-mover advantage

Durability
- Technical life
- Economic life
- Time compression

Value of a Strategic Asset

Competitive superiority

Substitutability
- Can a unique resource be trumped by a different resource?

Appropriability
- Who captures the value that the resource creates?
- Labor and other factor market structures

Figure 4   Value of a core competence (Peteraf, 1993)

Bibliography

Amit, R. and Schoemaker, P. J. (1993). Strategic assets and organizational rent. *Strategic Management Journal*, **14**, 33–46.

Grant, R. M. (1991). The resource-based theory of competitive advantage: Implications for strategy formulation. *California Management Review*, Spring, 114–35.

Grant, R. M. (1998). *Contemporary Strategy Analysis*, 3rd edn. Oxford: Blackwell.

Hamel, G. (1994). The concept of core competence. In G. Hamel and A. Heene (eds.), *Competence-Based Competition*. Chichester: John Wiley, pp. 11–33.

Lave, C. and March, J. (1993). *An Introduction to Models in the Social Sciences*. New York: University Press of America.

McGee, J. and Segal-Horn, S. (1997). Global competences in service multinationals. In H. Thomas and D. O'Neal (eds.), *Strategic Discovery: Competing in New Arenas*. Chichester: John Wiley, pp. 49–77.

Peteraf, M. A. (1993). The cornerstones of competitive advantage: A resource-based view. *Strategic Management Journal*, **14** (2), 179–91.

Prahalad, C. K. and Hamel, G. (1990). The core competence of the corporation. *Harvard Business Review*, May/June, pp. 79–91.

Stalk, G., Evans, P., and Shulman, L. E. (1992). Competing on capabilities: The new rules of corporate strategy. *Harvard Business Review*, **70** (2), 57–69.

risk

David Wilson

The concepts of risk and uncertainty are difficult to define precisely. This is made even more difficult because many authors define one aspect (risk) in terms of the other (uncertainty). For example, Hertz and Thomas (1983: 9) note that many authors define risk as "degrees of variability or uncertainty." This does not help distinguish the key elements of risk and uncertainty. Uncertainty is relatively easier to define. In this entry, we take uncertainty to mean:

> The limits to the precision and the extent of knowledge about a subject or an event.

For decision-makers, phrases they associate with uncertainty include "it is likely" or "the chances are" or, in the case of little uncertainty, decision-makers may say "it is quite certain that." All of these phrases, while in themselves imprecise, cluster around the notion of probabilities. Another way of defining uncertainty, therefore, is to describe uncertainty as:

> The subjective interpretations of probability by decision-makers and analysts of problems in organizations.

Risk is harder to define. Dictionaries typically describe risk in terms of the possibility of destruction, loss or damage. In business organizations, however, risk also takes on other characteristics. For example, insurance companies categorize risk into at least two distinct categories: pure risk and speculative risk. Examples of a pure risk are the likelihood of damage to assets and liabilities through fraud or criminal acts. It either will happen or it will not. However, speculative risks are characterized by the likelihood of gains *and* losses from which decision-makers hope profit will eventually accrue (Hertz and Thomas 1983). Risk and reward are the essence of business. Investment in marketing, production, and financial underpinning for a project are all risks undertaken by decision-makers – and are risks from which they eventually hope to make some profit. Knight (1921) argues "The only 'risk' which leads to a profit is a unique uncertainty . . . profits arise out of the inherent, absolute unpredictability of things."

This takes us nearer to defining risk. It is about the degree and type of unpredictability (rather than the notion that unpredictability exists, which is closer to describing uncertainty). We may say, then, that risk can be defined generically as:

> The assessment, severity, amount, and nature of losses which an action may incur, whether such actions are generated within an organization (such as a decision,) or are imposed upon it (such as a natural disaster). Risk is the measurable consequence of uncertainty for an organization.

Taking risks appears endemic to human behavior in social groups. In the 1960s social psychologists such as Stoner (1968) showed that individuals will accept higher levels of risk when taking decision in groups. He found that there was tendency for groups to go for risky and high pay-off decisions, while individuals favor relatively safe decisions with moderate pay-offs. Groups do not represent the average risk of their members. Stoner called this tendency for higher risk taking in groups "risky shift" decision-making.

DIFFERENT IMAGES OF RISK

From one perspective, risks faced by organizations can be viewed (and defined) as a set of wholly exogenous influences or shocks which they have to face. These could include changes in the natural environment or macro-economic stability. Natural disasters such as hurricanes, earthquakes or tornados would fall into this category as would disruptive technological changes which force decision-makers to make choices not of their own making (technologies may be invented outside the organization, forcing decision-makers in the organization to respond reactively). However, few analysts of risk maintain that uncertainties due to these exogenous shocks are wholly key to understanding how organizations both create and deal with risk. A noticeable movement has taken place over the last 20 or so years toward viewing risk as man-made (Turner, 1978) or manufactured (Beck, 1992). Both these authors argue that these organizationally-created risks influence the social and natural environments. Furthermore, they may also influence national and global economic systems. The number of completely exogenous shocks to organizations is very small indeed, according to these theorists.

Events which seem to be natural are argued to have an organizational origin. For example, the risks posed by earthquakes have been argued to have an organizational component, namely poor or disregarded building regulations. However, the occurrence of the earthquake itself is undeniably an exogenous risk. Technological failures, such as the Bhopal disaster, or the Challenger space shuttle, are argued to be rooted deeply in organizational processes. Perrow (1984) argued that one common factor in disasters which place people at risk, is the mismatch between organizational structure and its technology in use. The explosion in the Union Carbide plant in Bhopal, India, was argued to be a result of the firm growing in size but not adapting to new technologies. When a fault occurred in the plant, it was not immediately noticed since the specialization of roles together with the remoteness of the manufacturing process (relying on arm's-length safety checks) did not accommodate inter-role communication which would have been needed to avert disaster. When a switch was thrown (accidentally) giving a false "all systems OK" message, role specialization meant there was no possibility of checking this, despite it being obvious that something was wrong. By the time the problem was recognized it was too late. No individual had the capacity to stop the inevitable explosion which caused long-term damage to human and plant life.

Alexander (1996) accounts for the bursting of a gas pipeline in New Jersey in March 1994 as being attributable to the structure of the Texas Eastern Transmission Company, which was traditional, centralized and inflexible, unable to cope with the demands of gas transmission. Greening and Johnson (1996) argue that highly interactive, tightly coupled and high-risk technologies can spell high risk in an organizational structure which is bureaucratic and inflexible. They argued that one of the problems of such

organizations is the inability of top-level managers to cope with (or to prevent) disasters. This was seemingly prophetic, given the economic disasters which were to follow as a result of top-level failures (such as Enron). The events of September 11, 2001 and the subsequent invasion of Iraq have also been blamed on organizational failures, in this case the paucity of information exchange between security agencies worldwide. Therefore, we can view risk as being something organizations create, as well as have to manage, when external events (such as natural disasters) are imposed directly upon them.

To try and bring some order to understanding risk in an organizational context, it is useful to break down risk into sub-categories which correspond to organizational activities. This allows decision-makers to assess the risks internal to the organization and those external to it. Table 1 gives some examples of how this might be done.

Table 1 is not intended to be exhaustive. There are many more risks than those illustrated above, but breaking down risks into these (or similar) categories allows decision-makers to assess what would happen in the worst case if one or more of these were to occur. In that way,

Table 1 Categories of risks facing organizations

Risk Category	Examples	Endogenous/ Exogenous to the Organization
Strategy	Changing Patterns of Demand	Mostly exogenous
	Competitor Actions	Mostly exogenous
	Changing Markets	Mostly exogenous
	Business/Government Relationships	Endogenous and Exogenous
	New Disruptive Technologies Introduced	Exogenous
Operations	Manufacturing/Process Systems	Endogenous
	Financial/Accounting Controls	Endogenous
	Regulators	Exogenous
Economic	Poor cash-flow	Mostly exogenous
	Changes in interest rates	Exogenous
	Currency exchange	Exogenous
	Poor credit	Exogenous and endogenous
Hazards	Natural disasters such as earthquakes or volcanoes	Exogenous
	Terrorist attacks	Exogenous
	Criminal Activity	Exogenous and Endogenous
	IT Failure	Exogenous

decision-makers can rate each risk for severity and potential loss. In total, such a rating can produce an overall risk assessment score for an organization.

It is difficult for many of these risks to label them either as endogenous or as exogenous. In the majority of cases, they are a combination of both. For example, new technologies and scientific developments (such as genetic engineering or gene therapy) have been described as the new risks by a number of commentators. Mostly these are seen as exogenous risks to organizations (and to individuals in society). Nuclear power and biotechnology are developed "out there" and provide sources of cheap energy or improved crop production for organizations. But they are considered risky since the downsides of each are well-known. Yet, decision-makers inside organizations can actually increase (or multiply) these risks. For example, decision-makers in Monsanto ignored public anxieties about the testing of gene technologies and the company incurred heavy financial losses as a result. What began as an external risk was badly managed internally and resulted in Monsanto facing even greater levels of risk.

However, even narrowing down risk to categories and origin (endogenous or exogenous) is not without its problems. Several strands of research have emphasized different attributes and meanings to risk. The main difficulties stem from the difficulties in disentangling *organizational* risk from *managerial* risk.

ORGANIZATIONAL RISK AND MANAGERIAL RISK

Many authors have grappled with the many different definitions and descriptions of risk. Baird and Thomas (1990) argue that risk is multi-dimensional and that it is important to distinguish between *managerial* and *organizational* risk. Managerial risk-taking is where managers make choices associated with uncertain outcomes. Organizational risk is where organizations face volatile income streams that are associated with turbulent and unpredictable environments. It is important not to confuse the two. If, for example, we use organizational risk as a substitute term for managerial risk, we make the unwarranted assumption that managerial risk-taking leads to variations in organizational performance. This may not be the case. There is little empirical evidence on the relationships (if any) between organizational and managerial risk. Miller and Bromiley (1990) did find that risk loaded on three separate factors (managerial, firm performance, market performance) but their study concluded little about the possible inter-relationship of these factors.

Despite the relative lack of empirical evidence and the theoretical confusion, Palmer and Wiseman (1999) provide some clear and concise definitions of risk at the managerial and organizational levels. These are summarized in Table 2.

Differentiating between these two levels of analysis (organizational and managerial) allows decision-makers a clearer analysis of both the location and source of risks. Hazards, clearly identified as being at organizational level, help decision-makers focus on (say) environmental characteristics and help avoid needless and perhaps pointless examination of managerial processes (such as the composition of top teams). Clarity, not only over the source of risk (Table 1), but also its levels of analysis (Table 2), helps decision-makers begin the process of assessing risk.

However, the inter-relationships (if any) between organizational risk and managerial risk are much more in dispute. Some authors (for example, Fiegenbaum and Thomas, 1988) assume managerial risk taking to be congruent with organizational risk. The one and the other are essentially the same. Others (for example Palmer and Wiseman, 1999) argue that decisions that have high levels of uncertainty (such as R&D investments) provide only a partial explanation of organizational risk. There is presently too little empirical evidence to support one view or the other. It is clear that there are some inter-relationships between managerial and organizational risk, but the extent of that relationship is, as yet, unknown.

Bibliography

Alexander, C. B. (1996). Planning for disaster. *American Gas.* 78 (2), 24–27.

Baird, I. S. and Thomas, H. (1990). What is risk anyway? Using and measuring risk in strategic management in Bettis, R. A. and Thomas, H. (eds), *Risk, Strategy and Management*. Greenwich: JAI Press.

Table 2 Organizational and managerial risks

Organizational Risk Factors	Characteristics
Complex–simple environments	The more complex the environment, the greater the degree of organizational risk. Complexity corresponds to industry size as well as the number and heterogeneity of competitors. Simple environments, such as oligopolies, have institutional rules of behaviour. Complexity is likely to lead to blind spots, making it difficult for organizations to calculate risk or prepare for the responses of rivals – since not all are understood or even known.
Scarcity–munificence	Munificence refers to the abundance of resources, which include human, financial and capital. Abundance provides a context in which greater risk can be tolerated more easily. For example, mergers are tolerated to a greater extent in periods of growth rather than period of economic closure. The reverse is true of scarcity, when firms face less risk as they all look inward to tighten controls and to reduce costs.
Dynamism	Dynamism refers to the stochastic characteristics of the environment. These include, for example, discontinuities caused by the introduction of new technologies or novel products from competitor organizations.

Managerial Risk Factors	Characteristics
Aspirations and expectations	Aspirations are used to judge the quality of actual performance. Expectations indicate the level of anticipated future performance. Higher aspirations induce higher risks. Higher expectations mean better performance is more likely and this will induce lower levels of risk-aking. The framing of a situation as either a gain or a loss may also influence propensity to take risk. For example, when mangers/decision-makers are faced with the likelihood of failing to meet their objectives, they are likely to accept greater levels of risk in order to try and reach their objectives and to avoid losses. When managers/decision-makers are faced with the likelihood that they will achieve objectives, they are likely to favor safer options and avoid risk.
Top team characteristics	High levels of heterogeneity in top teams are likely to promote greater risk-taking. Managers with varied backgrounds (educational, international, other companies) will bring different perspectives and interpretive schema to bear upon decisions. Such groups are more likely to consider and take action on more risky, uncertain, and non-routine decisions. High levels of homogeneity will induce a greater tendency to preserve the status quo and only take action on less risky decisions.
Ownership	Managers/decision-makers who do not hold an equity stake in their organizations are less likely to take risky decisions than managers/decision-makers who do hold a stake. Equity ownership prompts owner-managers to make decisions that are in line with shareholder goals through carefully calculated risk taking. Other things being equal, equity ownership mitigates the risk aversion of managers who hold risk neutral preferences held by diversified shareholders. Non owner-managers may feel that taking risks puts their employment at risk, because gambles that don't succeed can result in their being fired or in the extreme, firm bankruptcy. They also have a less strong interest in the outcomes of successful risky decisions.
Slack	Slack means an organization has spare resources which can provide a buffer against fluctuations in environmental conditions. It acts to absorb shocks, which could otherwise detrimentally harm performance. Slack allows managers/decision-makers to avoid risky decisions and major strategic changes. Low levels of slack induce more risky decisions. This hunger-driven view of risk-taking is shared by some authors and not by others. For example, Wiseman and Bromiley (1996) provide evidence that supports the argument. On the other hand, Singh (1986) found a positive relationship between slack and risk-taking by managers. Firms do not necessarily have to be hungry for managers to take risks in this perspective. Palmer and Wiseman (1999) however found evidence in favour of the hunger driven view of risk taking, showing that organizations which have greater levels of slack take fewer risks.

Source: Adapted from Palmer and Wiseman (1999)

Beck, U. (1992). *Risk Society: Towards a New Modernity.* London: Sage.

Greening, D. W. and Johnson, R. A. (1996). Do managers and strategies matter? A study in crisis. *Journal of Management Studies*, 33 (1), 25–51.

Hertz, D. and Thomas, H. (1983). *Risk Analysis and its Applications.* New York: Wiley.

Knight, F. H. (1921). *Risk, Uncertainty and Profit.* Chicago: University of Chicago Press.

McGee, J., Wilson, D., and Thomas, H. (2005). *Strategy: Analysis and Practice.* McGraw-Hill: Maidenhead.

Miller, K. D. and Bromiley, P. (1990). Strategic risk and corporate performance: An analysis of alternative risk measures. *Academy of Management Journal*, 39, 91–122.

Palmer, T. B. and Wiseman, R. M. (1999). Decoupling risk from income stream uncertainty: a holistic model of risk. *Strategic Management Journal*, 20, 1037–62.

Perrow, C. (1984). *Normal Accidents: Living with High Risk Technologies.* New York: Basic Books.

Singh, J. V. (1986). Performance, slack, and risk-taking in organizational decision making. Academy of Management Journal, 29, 562–85.

Stoner, J. (1968). Risky and cautious shifts in group decision: the influence of widely held values. *Journal of Experimental Social Psychology*, 4, 442–59.

Turner, B. (1978). *Man-Made Disasters.* London: Wykeham.

Wiseman, R. M. and Bromiley, P. (1996). Toward a model of risk in declining organizations: An empirical examination of risk, performance and decline. *Organization Science*, 7, 524–43.

S

scenario planning

Derek F. Channon

This technique has become relatively widespread as a way of visualizing alternative futures, and thus of designing flexible strategies that can be developed to cope with these visions of the future. The success of the method owes much to Royal Dutch Shell's use of scenarios, one of which successfully predicted the first oil-price shock in 1973. Other organizations that make use of future scenarios include the White House, the Pentagon, the Economic Planning Agency, Volvo, and Inland Steel. One definition of a scenario is "a tool for ordering one's perceptions about alternative future environments in which one's decisions might be played out."

Key characteristics of scenarios are that they implicitly incorporate the subjective assessments of individuals or groups, and that they recognize that decision-makers have some influence on future development. Scenarios tend to be constructed upon facts and proven assumptions that have been accurate in the past. These positions are then extrapolated to create a series of alternate futures which, in themselves, are mutually consistent.

Within Royal Dutch Shell, every two to three years a series of usually three scenarios about the future is prepared, against which line managers are required to test their own business unit strategic plans. Historically, these scenarios have tended to predict optimistic, most likely, and pessimistic futures. Most recently, the most optimistic scenario has tended to be dropped, as this has never actually come to pass. Indeed, even the most pessimistic scenario has usually tended to be more optimistic than actual reality.

Most scenarios begin in the present and make assumptions about the future. The process of scenario development is illustrated in figure 1. It commences with a PEST ANALYSIS, which identifies the critical political, economic, social, and technical factors that influence both the present and the future.

From this analysis, the critical indicators of the future environment are selected and any potential future events are impacted against these key trends. The use of a Delphi analysis, and consultations with relative experts, may well be a useful process through which to gain enlightened opinion on likely futures.

For each historical performance indicator, past trends are examined and analyzed to identify the reasons for the past behavior. The future is then assessed and tested against the opinions of the Delphi review panel. As a result, future events may be forecast subject to clearly defined assumptions and an established rationale for the prediction of forward values.

A series of usually no more than three scenarios can then be developed on the basis of alternate predictions. Cross-impact analysis should also be undertaken to examine the effect of contrary variables on alternate futures. At the end of this process, a series of scenarios can be established for issue to line business units, as a background against which they can develop alternate strategic plans for their operations.

To insure that these scenarios will be useful in strategy formulation, it is important that the following criteria are applied:

- The scenarios must be internally consistent. Any internal contradiction may negate any SWOT ANALYSIS undertaken.
- The scenario must be possible. Any scenario that is seen as highly implausible will tend to be ignored by line business units.

294   segmentation

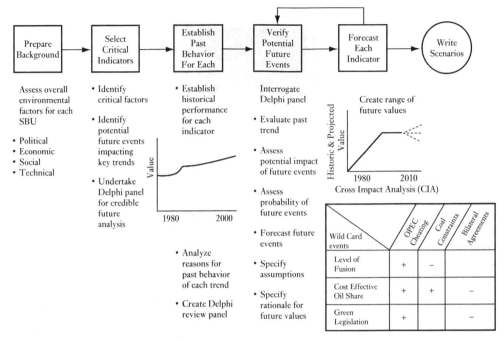

Figure 1   The process of scenario creation

Bibliography

Schwartz, P. (1991). *The Art of the Long View*. New York: Doubleday.

Wack, P. (1985). Scenarios: Uncharted waters ahead. *Harvard Business Review*, **63**, 72–89.

World Business Weekly (1980). Shell's multiple scenario planning: A realistic alternative to the crystal ball. *World Business Weekly*, April 7.

segmentation

Derek F. Channon

The choice of which markets to address is a critical strategic decision for the firm. Therefore, the SERVED MARKET is some combination of customers, products, and geography. This choice is based on the segmentation of markets into smaller groupings. Moreover, the development of relational databases and data mining allows firms to define their markets even more tightly. Successful segmentation of markets has proven to be a key source of strategic advantage, especially where this might involve reconfigur-

ation of the value chain (*see* VALUE CHAIN ANALYSIS).

BASES FOR MARKET SEGMENTATION

A range of variables can be used for segmenting both consumer and business markets. Typically these involve geographic, demographic, and psychographic factors. Normally more than one variable is used to try to identify a served market segment. Some researchers use consumer response variables such as quality, usage patterns, usage time, and BRANDING. A typical segmentation breakdown is shown in table 1. The main variables are described briefly below.

Geographic segmentation. In geographic segmentation, the market is broken down into differing geographic units, such as nations, regions, countries, cities, and neighborhoods. The company may decide to operate in many or few areas, or to differentiate between regions or districts. For example, the insurance industry may operate differential pricing policies based on the demographics of different neighborhoods, crime rates, property values, and so on. Some food retailers

Table 1 Major segmentation variables for consumer markets

Variable	Typical breakdowns
Geographic	
Region	Pacific, Mountain, West North Central, West South Central, East North Central, East South Central, South Atlantic, Middle Atlantic, New England
County size	A, B, C, D
City or MSA size	Under 5,000, 5,000–20,000, 20,000–50,000, 50,000–100,000, 100,000–250,000, 250,000–500,000, 500,000–1,000,000, 1,000,000–4,000,000, 4,000,000 or over
Density	Urban, suburban, rural
Climate	Northern, southern
Demographic	
Age	Under 6, 6–11, 12–19, 20–34, 35–49, 50–64, 65+
Sex	Male, female
Family size	1–2, 3–4, 5+
Family life cycle	Young, single; young, married, no children; young, married, youngest child under six; young, married, youngest child six or over; older, married, with children; older, married, no children under 18; older, single; other
Income	Under $10,000, $10,000–$15,000, $15,000–$20,000, $20,000–$30,000, $30,000–$50,000, $50,000 and over
Occupation	Professional and technical, managers, officials and proprietors; clerical, sales; craftsmen, foremen; operatives; farmers; retired; students; homemakers; unemployed
Education	Grade school or less; some high school; high school graduate; some college; college graduate
Religion	Catholic, Protestant, Jewish, other
Race	White, black, Asian, Hispanic
Nationality	American, British, French, German, Scandinavian, Italian, Latin American, Middle Eastern, Japanese
Psychographic	
Social class	Lower lowers, upper lowers, lower middles, upper middles, lower uppers, upper uppers
Life style	Belongers, achievers, integrateds
Personality	Compulsive, gregarious, authoritarian, ambitious
Behavioristic	
Purchase occasion	Regular occasion, special occasion
Benefits sought	Quality, service, economy
User status	Nonuser, ex user, potential user, first time user, regular user
Usage rate	Light user, medium user, heavy user
Loyalty status	None, medium, strong, absolute
Readiness stage	Unaware, aware, informed, interested, desirous, intending to buy
Attitude toward product	Enthusiastic, positive, indifferent, negative, hostile

Source: Kotler and Armstrong (1989)

may divide cities into different areas on the basis of age and/or ethnic mix.

Demographic segmentation. In demographic segmentation, markets are subdivided into groups on the basis of demographic variables such as age, sex, life cycle, education, income, and ethnic background. Historically, demographic variables have been most widely used in consumer marketing segmentation. They are also used in business market segmentation to determine, for example, the size of company that should be attacked, the industry mix to be achieved, and the location areas to be selected. Demographic variables are also amongst the easiest to measure:

- *Age and life-cycle stage*. Consumer needs and wealth change with age and position in the life cycle. Historically this was relatively predictable, but it is becoming more difficult to use as a variable. For example, historically, family life cycle could be assessed using the following sequence: single; married with no children; married with young children; married with children up to 18; married, children departed; retired married; retired single. Presently, marriage is a poor predictor due to the high rate of divorce, the growing preponderance of single-person households, and the growing number of working professional women. Nevertheless, age and life cycle still are important variables for segmentation and the mix of individuals is shifting, particularly toward aging populations in the developed economies.
- *Gender*. Segmentation by gender has long been an important variable in areas such as cosmetics, magazines, and clothing. It has also been applied in areas not normally associated with gender, such as cigarettes, do-it-yourself materials, automobiles, and liquor.
- *Income*. Income segmentation has always been an important variable for many industries, such as automobiles, clothing, cosmetics, travel, and banking. It is not, however, necessarily a good predictor of profitability or of volume markets. For example, compact discs were originally sold to the market of audio *aficionados* or status seekers, but the market turned out to be driven by young people interested in listening to pop music.
- *Multiple-attribute segmentation*. For most companies, markets are segmented by combinations of more than one demographic variable, such as age, income, and education. Thus in banking the young professional has a high income but also a high borrowing requirement in order to establish a professional practice, a mortgage, and so on. Such grouping can be further subdivided by ethnic, locational, and other variables. It is therefore important to attempt to combine variables in a way that clearly identifies an attractive target group profitable for the corporation to service.

Psychographic segmentation. In this form of segmentation, which has become increasingly widely used in recent times, buyers are divided upon the basis of social class, lifestyle, and personality. This form of segmentation has to a degree been used to replace demographic segmentation, as market researchers have discovered wide variations in behavior between subgroups within demographic profiling.

Behavioral segmentation. In this form of segmentation, which is widely used, purchasing behavior may vary significantly according to knowledge, attitude, usage rate, time of use, and attitude to the product.

REQUIREMENTS FOR EFFECTIVE SEGMENTATION

To be useful, market segments should:

- be measurable;
- be sufficiently large for products or services to be marketed profitably;
- be accessible – distribution/delivery system channels should be open;
- be differentiable – segments must be distinguishable from other elements of the market;
- be actionable – it must be possible to design strategic marketing programs that permit the segmentation strategy to be implemented.

Bibliography

Kotler, P. and Armstrong, G. (2004). *Principles of Marketing*, 10th edn. Upper Saddle River, NJ: Prentice-Hall.

Kotler, P. (2003). *Marketing Management: Analysis, Planning, Implementation and Control*, 11th edn. Englewood Cliffs, NJ: Prentice-Hall.

Roberts, A. A. (1961). Applying the strategy of market segmentation. *Business Horizons*, May, 65–72.

Robertson, T. S. and Barish, H. (1992). A successful approach to segmenting industrial markets. *Planning Forum*, 5–11.

served market

Derek F. Channon

The served market is that segment of the total market that the firm actively attempts to serve. It is difficult to define, but the concept is essential

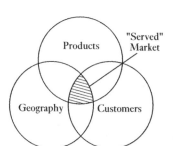

Figure 1 The "served" market concept (Channon, 1986)

to the measurement of variables such as relative and absolute MARKET SHARE and growth rate. It is therefore imperative that this task is undertaken creatively before embarking on precise strategy formulation.

Many observers cite market share and relative market share as key determinants of business and profitability, but fail to define the market. As illustrated in figure 1, the served market is defined as the intersection between a class of customers and the firm's product or service offering, and the desired geographic coverage.

For each market in which the firm is engaged, it should be sufficiently defined such that the following questions can be answered:

- Who precisely are the customers?
- What are their needs?
- What products or services does the firm offer to meet these needs?
- Can these be provided efficiently, profitably, and at an acceptable level of risk?
- What resources does the firm need to deliver these products or services?
- How will these resources be managed?

In order to evaluate the potential of a served market, it is desirable to complete a customer/product needs grid, on which segments are subdivided and the needs established for each key customer class. An adequate description of a market segment should constitute a set of boundaries on which strategies can be specifically targeted and where a defendable position can be sustained. Geographic boundaries for served markets may also differ sharply. For example, private banking tends to be a regional or global

business, while retail banking is mainly a local or national activity.

Bibliography

Buzzell, R. D. and Gale, B. T. (1987). *The PIMS Principles.* New York: Free Press.
Channon, D. F. (1986). *Bank Strategic Management and Marketing.* Chichester: John Wiley.

service industry strategies

Susan Segal-Horn

Most of the frameworks that dominate STRA-TEGIC MANAGEMENT research and teaching have been derived from research into manufacturing industries. However, services do differ from products. Therefore the concepts and frameworks with which strategists analyze industries, firms, and competition should not be applied unchanged to services.

Service industries are those whose output is not a physical good or product but an intangible "experience." The International Monetary Fund (IMF) defines international transactions in services as "the economic output of intangible commodities that may be produced, transferred and consumed at the same time" (IMF, 1993).

This definition suggests a set of specific differences between products and services. Service firms are "upside-down" firms. They can best be understood as inverted pyramids. The most important focus for service firms, and where a major proportion of resources are allocated, is at the borderline of contact between the firm and its customers. Although all organizations state as a matter of course that they are customer focused, with manufacturing organizations their major activity occurs away from the eyes and ears of customers. With service firms, their major activity occurs in combination with customers, and that is part of the definition of what we mean by a service.

THE PARTICULAR CHARACTERISTICS OF SERVICES

There are four distinct characteristics that define the most important differences between products and services: *intangibility, heterogeneity, simultaneous production and consumption,* and

Table 1   Services are different

Products	Services	Implications
Tangible	Intangible	Services are difficult to describe, exhibit, or communicate.
Easy to standardize	Heterogeneous; difficult to standardize	Guaranteeing a standard experience to the customer is problematic. Final implementation of the strategy is dependent on employees. Quality of service delivery is always partly personality dependent.
Production and consumption occur separately	Simultaneous production and consumption	Customers cannot "test drive" a service. Services are higher-risk purchases for customers. Both customers and employees participate in and affect the service outcome. Some parts of a service always need to be decentralized close to the customer.
Durable	Perishable	Services cannot be kept in stock, returned or resold. Capacity utilization is problematic but critical.

Source: Segal-Horn (2003)

perishability. Table 1 provides a summary of each of these characteristics, contrasts them with the comparable characteristic for a product, and explores some of the consequences of each difference. Each will then be more fully discussed.

INTANGIBILITY

Intangibility is probably one of the most influential factors in relation to services. As a result of intangibility, many services have no second-hand or part-exchange value since there is nothing tangible to sell. The nature of a service therefore may be best understood as an "experience," or "outcome" of an interaction, rather than a thing. For this reason one of the most effective ways of selling a service is through word-of-mouth recommendation. Since a service cannot be inspected before purchase, the most reliable way of making the purchasing decision is on the recommendation of someone who has already experienced it.

However, "intangibility" in services is only accurate up to a point. There are many services that contain a large amount of tangible content wrapped up with the intangible part. In fact services may be tangible or intangible or a combination of both (Levitt, 1986: 74). Figure 1 represents a different way of understanding the significance of intangibility for services. Although it illustrates degrees of intangibility for

different types of products and services, it represents intangibility by means of how easy or how difficult it is for consumers to evaluate the product or service that they think they have purchased. To do this, figure 1 draws on the economic concepts of *search, experience*, and *credence* goods. A search good is one that can be researched or tested by the potential consumer *before* deciding whether to buy it or not (e.g., going for a test drive in a car or sitting in an armchair before buying). An experience good is one that customers need to have *already experienced* or consumed before they can judge whether it was satisfactory or not (e.g., a meal in a restaurant). For credence goods, even *after* they have been bought *and* consumed, consumers are unsure as to whether they are satisfactory or not (e.g., insurance policies or pensions or hiring a lawyer). These are credence goods because consumers have to believe that they are fit for the purpose for which they were bought.

The implication of figure 1 is that services are mostly either experience goods or credence goods. This creates a particular relationship between the service provider and the customer that the strategies of service firms must embrace. In particular it means that establishing and retaining trust between the service provider and the customer has great strategic significance

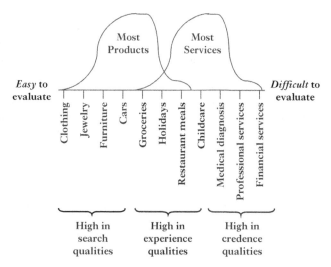

Figure 1 Continuum of evaluation for different types of products (adapted from Zeithaml and Bitner, 1996)

in service organizations. This point extends also to the important role of BRANDING in services.

HETEROGENEITY

Services are "personality intensive," i.e., they commonly rely on people to deliver them by means of a face-to-face (or telephone) interaction with the customer or client. In the services literature this is known as "the service encounter" or "the moment of truth" (Bowen, Chase, and Cummings, 1990; Normann, 1991) and it is by the quality of outcome for the customer of this service encounter that a service strategy is judged. Service encounters may be notoriously *heterogeneous*, i.e., they are difficult to standardize and guarantee because the encounter relies on the personality or mood of the individual responsible for that service encounter, in that organization, at that point in time, on that day. Whether a particular service business is capital intensive or labor intensive (and services may be either or both) is not the significant factor. What matters in services is how to manage the quality of service delivery to the customer at *the moment of truth* that occurs for each organization thousands of times each day. That is why so many service firms (including the public sector) have training based around what are often ironically called "smile" programs – intensive customer care programs that try to teach staff the importance of their manner and personal behavior in relating to customers.

What is interesting strategically about heterogeneity is that service strategies depend least on the quality of the analysis going into the design of the strategy in the first place, and most on the implementation of that strategy by the front-line staff of the organization. That is what is meant by calling service organizations "upside-down" organizations. They have to find ways to allow front-line staff, those in direct contact with customers, to drive the organization, with everything else in support.

Paradoxically, such front-line service staff are usually relatively junior within the structure of the organization, at a modest level in the reward structure, and with relatively little influence on strategic decision-making. Yet they are critical to the strategy implementation and, hence, to the service experience for customers.

Thus for strategies in service industries, strategy implementation takes on a new and powerful dimension. In implementation terms, control of the offering at the transaction point with the customer is critical. It is at that point that the service characteristic of heterogeneity occurs and makes its impact.

SIMULTANEOUS PRODUCTION AND CONSUMPTION

With a product, production of the product and then consumption of that product by a customer occur at different times. They follow the sequence of production, distribution, and then consumption. With many services it works rather differently. The sequence is more likely to be distribution, followed by production and consumption occurring simultaneously. For example, a hotel is built first then the customers and staff stay in it together, co-producing the service experience of staying in that particular hotel. For most professional service firms (PSFs), the accountant, or consultant, or lawyer interacts directly with the client to discuss the service required and how it will meet that client's needs.

Consider further personal services such as hairdressers. First the hairdressing salon is established, clients then make appointments and arrive to have their hair cut. They have to physically be present to participate in the delivery of the service and it is certainly an experience good, since clients will not be sure until it is over whether they like the haircut or not. This illustrates another aspect of simultaneous production and consumption of a service: risk. Since customers cannot "test drive" many services, purchasing a service is a higher risk for the customer than purchase of a product. It is also more difficult to return a service if dissatisfied. Customers can only decide to go to a different provider next time, e.g., change accountant, or not stay in that hotel again. Ways of attempting to reduce the risk arising from simultaneity of production and consumption of a service (especially experience or credence services) include the recommendation of someone else who has used it, or to buy a service brand. The service brand should represent to the consumer some form of trust and guarantee of standards of service delivery. The growth of service brands has been a feature of service strategies in the last decade. This has even been occurring in personal services such as hairdressing, where chain brands (e.g., Toni and Guy) have also been spreading internationally.

The final point to consider in relation to simultaneous production and consumption of services is that it has implications for the design of international strategies for service firms (*see* GLOBAL STRATEGIES; GLOBALIZATION OF SERVICE INDUSTRIES). If the main part of the service has to be delivered close to the customer and the service firm provider must therefore be located close to the customer for reasons of simultaneity, this will inevitably limit the scope for international strategies in that service sector. This service delivery characteristic of simultaneous production and consumption of services has begun to bite in the delivery of international services via the Internet. For example, there has been much discussion of the gradual realization by e-tailers that unless their product can be delivered by pure Internet transaction (e.g., downloading a software program or a piece of music), at some point service companies like amazon.com have to provide channels for local delivery of the service output.

PERISHABILITY

The first point to make about *perishability* of services is that it is difficult to apply the concept of inventory or stock to services. A meal in a restaurant or a holiday or an hour of billed time with a lawyer cannot be stored. Although they are part of the total capacity of that restaurant, that holiday company, or that law firm, if they are not sold (i.e., used) on a particular day and time, they cannot be stored and shown tomorrow to another potential customer. Therefore capacity utilization in service organizations is crucial. Optimal capacity must be sold today because if not, it is gone forever. That is why PSFs focus on "utilization" of their professional staff, i.e., the number of billable hours of their time they have sold in a given period. That is the PSF equivalent of productivity output, except unlike a car or a chair, it is impossible to attempt to sell the same hour tomorrow. If it remains unsold today it is lost. The hour sold tomorrow is a different hour, a different unit of output.

That is the perishability issue for the service organization. For the customer the problem is slightly different. As referred to above in discussing intangibility, services cannot be returned or resold. They have a fragile exchange value and no second-hand value. There are no car boot sales for services, except to a very limited degree, e.g., there is a secondary market in insurance policies and endowment policies. However, these are credence goods (as are all financial products), so the buyer and seller must agree on a future worth of the policy well in advance of its maturity and at some risk. Also, even though most services cannot be stored, some parts of a service (e.g., software programs or some of the research or design for one advertising campaign may be reusable for a different campaign) certainly have a shelf-life and can be stored and reused even if the service as a whole cannot.

The strategic issue regarding perishability is that service firms must be aware of how far it applies to their business and which, if any, of the firm's activities are reusable and tradeable. It also has massive implications for the operational systems and procedures within a service firm. They must be designed for optimal capacity utilization since for most service firms that is what both revenue and margins are dependent upon.

It is important too that many modern service businesses contain a shifting mixture of "hard"/tangible and "soft"/intangible elements. The "hard" elements are increasingly amenable to management by means identical to a manufacturing business. The "soft" (i.e., the service encounter) elements retain the distinctive needs of service management and service delivery. Thus the role of management in services is particularly demanding, especially for complex services with a high intangibility content.

THE VALUE CHAIN APPLIED TO SERVICES

An issue of general concern for strategic management in service organizations is that sometimes, existing strategy frameworks have to be reconsidered when applied to services. For example, consider the well-known strategy concept of the value chain and the issue of simultaneous production and consumption in services. The point has already been made that manufacturing organizations follow one sequence of business activities: production, distribution, and then consumption; while many services follow the sequence of distribution, followed by production and consumption occurring simultaneously. Consider the implications of that sequencing of activities for the traditional construction of the value chain in strategic management. In the traditional value chain applied to manufacturing businesses, marketing, sales, and service occur last. When used for a service business these activities should come *first*, since services are sold first and then produced and consumed afterwards. Consider the simplified indicative value chain for a hotel given in figure 2 to illustrate this important point.

It becomes highly inappropriate to apply a VALUE CHAIN ANALYSIS of a service starting with inbound logistics as in the traditional model. The traditional model was designed for manufacturing businesses and needs adapting for services, as with many frequently used strategy frameworks.

SCALE AND SCOPE IN SERVICES

More capital-intensive asset structures and high fixed costs have resulted in a prolonged process of concentration and restructuring of service industries for the last 20 years. High levels of merger and acquisition activity (*see* MERGERS AND ACQUISITIONS) have been commonplace in many service sectors, (e.g., hotel chains, accountants and management consulting firms,

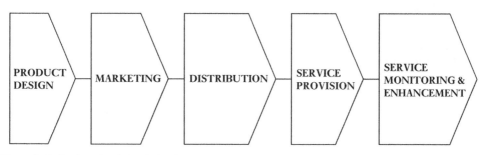

Figure 2 Indicative value chain of a hotel (Segal-Horn, 2000)

airlines, software, information services, telecommunications, media, financial services). Increased concentration has generated increased potential for ECONOMIES OF SCALE and ECONOMIES OF SCOPE. This has great significance for the potential strategies of service firms.

Teece (1980) specified two important circumstances when integration of activities across a multiproduct firm would be needed to capture scope economies: (1) if two or more products depend on the same proprietary know-how; (2) when a specialized indivisible asset is a common input into two or more products. Both of these conditions are now routinely to be found in service firms (see table 2).

An example of the interaction between scale and scope benefits deriving from the same proprietary know-how and indivisible asset is the central role played by computer reservation systems (CRS) in the activities of airlines, hotel chains, or car rental firms. These not only support the geographic spread of the business and the rapid processing of volumes of transactions, but also provide customer databases for cross-marketing of services and the capability to design and deliver completely new services. Airlines use sophisticated software to maximize yield from higher-revenue seats on all flights, a major contribution to profitability in a service business with high fixed costs. Database management provides potential for economies of scope for retail chains and financial services to

target cross-selling of additional products. In the retailing sector, the Italian leisurewear retailing group Benetton created a new retailing model by its innovative use of information systems. Twenty years ago Benetton became the first retailer to use real-time information from point-of-sale (EPOS) systems to tailor seasonal production to demand. This model is now commonplace within the retail sector.

Knowledge is often a special asset in services. The capability to acquire, process, and analyze information is the key asset or core competence (*see* CORE COMPETENCES) of many services (e.g., financial, software, brokerage, professional, and the agency function of computerized reservation systems linking many service businesses). "Know-how" here literally consists of the knowledge of how to combine human and physical resources to produce and process information. Service firms (e.g., management consultancies and other PSFs, fast food chains, hotel chains) are increasingly attempting to codify this inherited knowledge as the basis of standardization of their products, to achieve cost reduction and increased productivity, as well as reliability of service levels. Some of the strongest brands in services are based on perceived accumulated know-how, e.g., McKinsey, Reuters, Disney, McDonald's. Information-intensive assets are absorbing heavier investment in fixed costs, which in itself exerts pressure to lower unit costs by spreading output over larger

Table 2   Potential sources of economies of scale and scope in services

Economies of scale	*Economies of scope*
Geographic networks	ICT and shared information networks
Physical buildings or equipment	Shared knowledge and know-how effects
Purchasing/supply	Product or process innovation
Marketing	Shared R&D
Logistics and distribution	Shared channels for multiple offerings
Technology/ICT	Shared investments and costs
Operational support	Reproduction formula for service system
	Range of services and service development
	Branding
	Training
	Goodwill and corporate identity
	Culture
	Privileged access to parent services

Source: adapted from Segal-Horn (1993)

markets (for scale economies) and a wider variety of products (for scope economies).

These structural shifts in the supply of services are echoed on the demand side. Economies of scope in service firms can lower TRANSACTIONS COSTS for customers. Common examples of such customer benefits include: the effect of retailer buying power and Internet price transparency and search availability on quality and price in multiple retail chains; worldwide, integrated reservation systems of hotel chains, car hire, and airlines; cheaper products in banking and insurance; and the undercutting of all brokerage services such as travel agents or investment analysts.

POTENTIAL PITFALLS

Despite the evidence of benefits available to both service firms and service customers from economies of scale and scope in services, a cautionary note must be sounded. Attempting to deliver multiple services through a single service delivery channel may sometimes have unintended negative consequences. For example, many people will have experienced some annoyance at booking a few days' holiday retreat for a special break at a quiet hotel, only to find on arrival that most of the other guests are groups of business delegates using the hotel's "conference" facilities. In the evenings large noisy groups of delegates wearing name badges fill the bar and the "intimate" restaurant. Of course the hotel is only trying to obtain economies of scope by making the fullest use of its rooms and other facilities by selling them to different types of guests for different purposes. The problem arises from the different expectations and needs of the two types of customers/guests and their essential incompatibility in the close proximity within the same delivery channel of a service business.

THE FUTURE

Many services once regarded as highly specialized (e.g., airline seats, bank accounts) have become commodities, leading service providers to simultaneously push down costs and also add value (e.g., longer bank opening hours and a range of channels). Similarly, since manufacturing firms are seeking to add value through additional service features (Vandermerwe, 1993),

clear product–service distinctions may gradually be eroded. Greater automation and contracting out of mundane and repetitive service tasks could humanize rather than dehumanize services, by leaving service staff freer to serve customers (Quinn and Paquette, 1990). The inverted service organization, based on expert systems and interactivity, may in future end up looking more like a spider's web, with each employee able eventually to tap into the firm's collective knowledge via its computer networks. Pine and Gilmore (1998) go further. They describe not services but experiences as the next stage of service industry development, and the next great transition that of shifting from selling services to selling experiences. As more services follow products eventually into becoming commodities (as telephone calls already have), then experiences may offer the next route to added value.

Finally, it is important to distinguish service industries from service firms. At the level of the firm, service strategies continue to be about implementation. Successful service strategies are a result of how people carry out their responsibilities at work. In a service business, bridging the interface between strategy and operations is critical because *how* this interface is bridged defines the nature of the service experience for the customer.

Bibliography

Bowen, D. E., Chase, R. B., and Cummings, T. G. (1990). *Service Management Effectiveness*. San Francisco: Jossey-Bass.
International Monetary Fund (IMF) (1993). *Balance of Payments Manual*, 5th edn. New York: IMF.
Levitt, T. (1986). *The Marketing Imagination*. New York: Free Press.
Normann, R. (1991). *Service Management: Strategy and Leadership in Service Businesses*, 2nd edn. Chichester: John Wiley.
Pine, B. J. and Gilmore, J. H. (1998). Welcome to the experience economy. *Harvard Business Review*, July/August, 97–105.
Quinn, J. B. and Paquette, P. C. (1990). Technology in services: Creating organizational revolutions. *Sloan Management Review*, Winter.
Segal-Horn, S. (1993). The internationalization of service firms. *Advances in Strategic Management*, **9**, 31–61.
Segal-Horn, S. (2000). The search for core competencies in a service multinational: A case study of the French

hotel Novotel. In Y. Aharoni and L. Nachum (eds.), *Globalization of Services: Some Implications for Theory and Practice*. London: Routledge.

Segal-Horn, S. (2003). Strategy in service organizations. In D. Faulkner and A. Campbell (eds.), *The Oxford Handbook of Strategy*, vol. 1. Oxford: Oxford University Press.

Teece, D. (1980). Economies of scope and the scope of the enterprise. *Journal of Economic Behavior and Organization*, 1 (3), 223–47.

Vandermerwe, S. (1993). *From Tin Soldiers to Russian Dolls: Creating Added Value Through Services*. Oxford: Butterworth-Heinemann.

Zeithaml, V. A. and Bitner, M. J. (1996). *Services Marketing*. New York: McGraw-Hill International.

signaling

Stephanos Avgeropoulos

The purpose of signaling is to transfer information from one party to another in a credible way. Early work on signals included Schelling's essay on bargaining, which discussed the matter of promise, observed that "bargaining may have to concern itself with an 'incentive' system as well as the division of gains" (Schelling, 1956: 300), and also dealt with bargaining tactics such as "tying one's hands" and offering and accepting hostages.

Signaling finds two main applications. The first is in competitive situations, such as where one firm wishes to notify others that it does not welcome them in its market. The second has to do with the provision of information as to the nature and characteristics of a product, service, or even a company for sale, so that the party receiving the information will be convinced to buy or, if such a decision has already been reached, so that a higher price can be extracted from the buyer.

SIGNALING TO EXISTING OR POTENTIAL COMPETITORS

In its entry-deterrent capacity, therefore, signaling can act as a barrier to entry (*see* BARRIERS TO ENTRY AND EXIT) (the reverse is also true, and raising other barriers to entry may act as a very effective signal). In order to indicate that entry is unwelcome and that the entrant will be attacked, the incumbent can commit himself to such an attack (by building up EXCESS CAPACITY to credibly indicate readiness to lower prices upon entry, by guaranteeing to match any competitor innovations, or otherwise); it can indicate a low-cost function to scare off higher-cost producers (by permanently pricing low); and it can accumulate resources to prepare for retaliation, making such accumulation visible.

In the shorter term, the incumbent may just wish to provide a signal to some particular company which it knows is planning to enter its market. This can be done by means of an announcement of an impending product launch, or a new process or investment, and such actions may well be sufficient to delay entry until the incumbent has had more time to prepare, using methods including those just discussed.

Turning to signals toward existing rather than potential competitors, a firm may wish to indicate its willingness to collude (*see* CARTEL). Such activity may be illegal, particularly as far as stronger forms of collusion are concerned, but certain modes of independently devised behavior such as promises to match prices, or advance price change notifications, are often observed (it should be noted that practices such as promises to match prices can act both as a signal to indicate willingness to collude and as a signal of willingness to protect one's share of the market).

SIGNALING TO BUYERS

Having examined signaling to competitors, the discussion now turns to signaling to buyers. Nevertheless, some of the theoretical arguments presented here can also be used in the context of signaling to competitors.

In asymmetric information situations, parties will be induced to generate information as long as the marginal cost of such generation does not exceed the marginal expected payoff. A consequence of this is that when information is relatively expensive, buyers will refrain from information generation. As a result, the seller of a product whose characteristics (such as quality) cannot be observed at the time of the sale (even though these may eventually become apparent) may be unable to receive the full value of his product, potential buyers only being willing to accept a price that reflects their beliefs about expected or average characteristics.

One result of this is that sellers in such a situation are unable to sell high-quality products at prices higher than they can sell low-quality ones, so they have an incentive to reduce their costs and sell low-quality products.

To circumvent this problem and allow sellers of high-quality products to inform buyers of the characteristics of their products, signaling can be used to transmit the information required, so that the buyer is no longer required to generate it. Among the methods that are available for use are: the development of a brand image which conveys the desired characteristics; advertising; the use of sales force and product demonstrations to educate buyers; giving products away to opinion leaders for use and evaluation; or even relying on methods not under the seller's control, such as word-of-mouth. In principle, the more information there is about a product, and the more its producer/seller spends on signaling, the more its perceived value will tend to coincide with its real value.

A more generalized view of signaling has been provided by Spence (1973). He observed that if the seller of a high-quality product could find some activity whose marginal cost was lower for him than for a seller of a lower-quality product, it might pay him to undertake this activity to signal high quality. Offering warranties could act as a such a signal, for example, as this would be cheap for the sellers of reliable products, but more expensive for the sellers of lower-quality products. Similarly, assuming that education is cheaper for productive employees to acquire than for less productive ones, getting an education may act as a signal of higher productivity to employers, and may thus be worthwhile even if it leads to no productivity improvement at all. The exact nature of the signal used is, therefore, not so important in itself, but its most common consequence – giving away money – most certainly is. In the context of stock pricing, for example (particularly when a company is sold in tranches), underpricing, high dividend payments (high tax contributions), the use of expensive bankers, auditors, and solicitors, and high advertising expenditure all help to differentiate a high-quality firm from a lower-quality one.

While the above discussion is valid in principle, the conditions under which signaling equilibria are, in practice, free of potential dynamic instability are rather more restrictive than Spence supposed. It has been observed, for example, that Spence's assumption that the potential signaling activity should have a lower marginal cost for high-quality workers is a necessary rather than a sufficient condition. Instead, it appears sufficient for the proportional rate of decline in the marginal cost of signaling with respect to product quality to be sufficiently large.

Moreover, the success of any signaling strategy is affected by several other factors, including the length of time for which agents are committed to announced strategies. Signaling can, for example, be used to deceive the recipient of the information in the short run, where the long-run implications are of no concern. If a seller possesses information that is unfavorable to herself, she may still wish to provide the same signals that she would provide if she had favorable information, albeit at a higher cost. A government, for instance, may underprice bad as well as good companies in a PRIVATIZATION, for fear that investors will infer its private information if it does otherwise. By the time information emerges to prove these signals misleading, the privatization program may already be complete, so it may suffer little harm when its credibility in signaling the quality of stock is dented.

Bibliography

Hart, O. and Holmström, B. (1987). The theory of contracts. In T. Bewley (ed.), *Advances in Economic Theory*. Cambridge: Cambridge University Press.

Porter, M. E. (1980). *Competitive Strategy: Techniques for Analyzing Industries and Competitors*. New York: Free Press.

Porter, M. E. (1985). *Competitive Advantage: Creating and Sustaining Superior Performance*. New York: Free Press.

Schelling, T. C. (1956). An essay on bargaining. *American Economic Review*, 46, 281–306.

Spence, A. M. (1973). *Market Signaling: Information Transfer in Hiring and Related Processes*. Cambridge, MA: Harvard University Press.

single business strategy

Derek F. Channon

Such businesses have been defined as those in which 95 percent or more of sales came from one business. During the period from 1950 onward, in the manufacturing sector, such businesses have declined dramatically in most developed economies, and in the US and UK they have been virtually eliminated. Such firms have either diversified (*see* DIVERSIFICATION) or been acquired by more diversified firms. Single business firms are, however, still found in the service industry sector. These service industry firms tend to be of two types. First, there are those for which the strategic potential of the industry makes it unnecessary to diversify by product line. For example, food retailers tend to expand by increasing geographic coverage rather than by entering new product market segments. Second, there are companies that are protected from stock market pressures by factors such as mutual ownership. Such companies include many smaller building societies and mutual life assurance concerns.

Concentration on a single business focuses the attention of management; top management must give its undivided attention to the business. Furthermore, all of the key managers can be given the opportunity to have hands-on experience in all the key functions of the business; most have normally spent time actively involved in field operations. The key danger for the single business firm occurs when the original strategy reaches maturity and, in particular, when opportunities for geographic expansion dry up. At this stage, single business firms usually attempt to diversify or are themselves acquired by diversified firms. This outcome can be especially difficult for the single business firm as the incoming new management may lack experience in purchasing or operating other businesses, which may be quite different from the one that they know. Equally, in the process of acquisition, the single business firm usually has no experience with regard to being purchased or being subjected to subsequent integration (*see* POST-ACQUISITION INTEGRATION).

Single business firms are usually managed according to a FUNCTIONAL STRUCTURE, in which each of the core activities of the firm is the responsibility of a specialized manager.

Interestingly, the process of PRIVATIZATION has (perhaps temporarily) added to the number of single business concerns. Artificially constrained from diversification, privatized firms have strategically sought to rapidly diversify, tending to face the market rather than integrating backward to restore their single or dominant business origins.

Diversification away from their CORE BUSINESS has been both by geography and product market. Moreover, because of their stable cash flows, in an open market economy many of these concerns have found themselves open to hostile attack by predators interested in gaining access to their attractive cash-flow profiles.

Bibliography

Channon, D. F. (1973). *The Strategy and Structure of British Enterprise*. Cambridge, MA: Harvard Division of Research.

Rumelt, R. P. (1974). *Strategy, Structure and Economic Performance*. Cambridge, MA: Harvard Division of Research.

Wrigley, L. (1970). Divisional autonomy and diversification. Unpublished doctoral dissertation, Harvard Business School.

soga shosha

Derek F. Channon

The origins of the *soga shosha*, Japan's massive international trading companies, date back in large part to the Meiji Restoration of 1868, when the government resumed international trade after over 200 years of self-imposed isolation under the Tokugawa Shogunate. The incoming government encouraged the development of Japanese trading companies to reduce the role of foreign traders; to develop secure supplies of raw materials for the newly industrializing economy, and to help to provide technology, machinery, and other equipment needed to produce manufactured products; and to separate production from supply and marketing, leaving these activities to the trading companies, with their knowledge of overseas markets.

With the exception of the Sumitomo Corporation, the other leading *soga shosha* were created before World War II. Two of these, Mitsubishi Corporation and Mitsui and Company, were associated with the Mitsubishi and

Mitsui *zaibatsu* (*see* ZAIBATSU STRUCTURE), respectively, and were already diversified concerns by the outbreak of war. Both were broken up after World War II by the occupying authorities, but rapidly reformed when this was legally permitted. The other leading groups continued to specialize in particular product markets until the postwar period, but rapidly diversified into general trading companies and associated themselves with the emerging bank-related *keiretsu* (*see* KEIRETSU STRUCTURE). The Sumitomo Corporation was only formed in 1945, as trading was not previously considered to be an ethical activity within the Sumitomo *zaibatsu*. By the 1950s, therefore, much of Japan's internal and external trade was handled by the top ten *soga shosha* (subsequently reduced to nine by mergers).

These major trading companies formed key components within the major Japanese *keiretsu* groups. The leading nine concerns also maintained a major role within the Japanese domestic economy. While primarily concerned with trade in commodity products, some – depending upon their backgrounds – had a greater focus in particular areas, such as Sumitomo in metals and chemicals, or Itochu in textiles and machinery. However, each was involved with a wide range of products (usually 20,000–30,000); the degree of product market diversity is illustrated in figure 1, which shows the organizational structure of a typical *soga shosha*. They have also been increasing their interests in operating in higher-value-added products, and in increasing their share in trade between third countries.

The soga shosha operate in a number of distinct ways. First, they operate as pure traders, buying and selling commodities and other merchandise. While they provide trade finance, they can also act as guarantors for banks and other financial institutions. To stimulate activity they might also pre-pay suppliers. In addition, the *soga shosha* are skilled at barter trading, which can involve several counter-parties.

Second, the *soga shosha* can act as project organizers and managers for complex projects. In this scheme, the *soga shosha* might help to develop an iron deposit by helping provide the necessary finance for infrastructure development, providing project management, arranging construction, providing mining machinery, guaranteeing exports, arranging shipping, insurance, and freight, taking the output back to Japan to be sold to steel producers who might be members of the same industrial group, acting as a steel stockholder for the distribution of the product within Japan, and acting as export agent for the manufacturers of finished equipment from the steel.

Third, the *soga shosha* operate as a market intelligence agent for both itself and members of its industrial group. Each operates extensive global communications networks which, each day, pass millions of words through dedicated lines between all of the world's leading trading centers and Japan, on all the product lines covered. Being trading companies (unlike banks), the *soga shosha* normally do not require a license to open in any particular country. Hence they normally operate in all of the major world trading, agricultural, and commercial centers.

Fourth, the *soga shosha* provide an access route for Japanese companies to overseas markets. Subsequently, such concerns might develop their own overseas distribution systems, but initially the *soga shosha* make it possible for smaller firms to gain access without the necessity to build expensive infrastructures. More recently, under pressure from western governments to open domestic markets, the *soga shosha* have provided a route for western companies to enter the Japanese market. Such moves have usually been organized as JOINT VENTURES between individual western concerns and specific Japanese companies.

Fifth, the *soga shosha* have been instrumental in helping to achieve Japanese government policies of obtaining supplies of strategic raw materials. At the time of the first oil-price shock, for example, around 80 percent of the oil being supplied to Japan was imported via the leading western oil companies. Keen to reduce this apparent dependency, the government encouraged the *soga shosha* to help establish energy subsidiaries responsible for achieving secure supplies. By 1993, the share of the Japanese market supplied by western oil companies had fallen to around 25 percent, with the leading *soga shosha* playing a major role in this transformation.

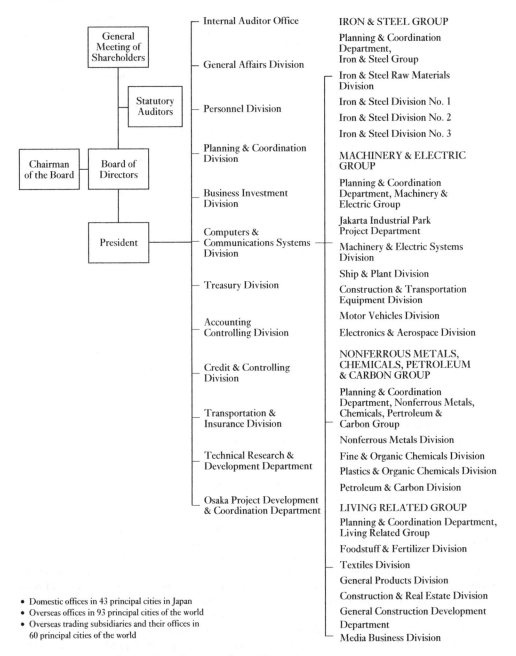

Figure 1   The *soga shosha* organizational structure (Annual Reports)

- Domestic offices in 43 principal cities in Japan
- Overseas offices in 93 principal cities of the world
- Overseas trading subsidiaries and their offices in 60 principal cities of the world

Sixth, the *soga shosha* are a source of trade finance or can act as a guarantor on the part of suppliers and customers. They are also skilled at barter trade in the case of situations in which financial credits are unavailable.

In terms of size and scale, this structural form is virtually unknown in the West. It has played – and continues to play – a significant role in Japanese economic and industrial success.

Bibliography

Yoshihara, K. (1982). *Soga Shosha*. Oxford: Oxford University Press.

Young, A. K. (1979). *The Soga Shosha*. Tokyo: Charles E. Tuttle.

specialized businesses

Derek F. Channon

In specialized businesses, clear market segments (*see* SEGMENTATION) can be defined which are distinct from one another and where overlap is limited. Within each segment, experience effects (*see* EXPERIENCE AND LEARNING EFFECTS) are important determinants of cost structure, but the segments themselves are discrete.

Industries in which this phenomenon occurs include pharmaceuticals, cosmetics, luxury automobiles, and designer clothing. Competitors may succeed by concentrating on a specific SERVED MARKET segment, in which dominance can lead to extraordinary profits. Within the industry there are typically a number of such successful competitors, each dominating a specific segment. Firms that are not market leaders tend to be less profitable.

While it is unusual, it is possible for competitors to serve more than one market segment and gain SYNERGY for a lower-volume market position. For example, Toyota has successfully penetrated the luxury automobile market with its Lexus brand, using its volume car division position to successfully lower costs relative to specialist producers of luxury segment vehicles such as Mercedes Benz or BMW.

See also *advantage matrix*

stakeholder analysis

Stephanos Avgeropoulos

Stakeholders are all the people (and organizations) that have an interest in a company, and that may influence the company or be influenced by its activities.

Stakeholders may be internal (such as employees) or external (such as suppliers or pressure groups). Most can be identified within the ranks of owners and stockholders, bankers and other creditors, suppliers, buyers and customers, advertisers, management, employees, their unions, competitors, local and state government, regulators, the media, public interest groups, the arts, political and religious groups, and the military. Others may also be identifiable, and their numbers and complexity of interdependence are likely to increase over the life span of the organization.

However, these groups are rarely sufficient to categorize stakeholders themselves, and stakeholders typically form groupings which are subsets of the above (such as secretarial personnel), or even cut across them (such as the group against the introduction of new factory automation technology, which may include some suppliers, some management, and many employees). In general, the population of stakeholder groups is unstable, with new groups tending to emerge and influence strategy as a result of specific current or expected events, while redundant groups disappear or, in some cases, the members of certain stakeholder groups diverge to such an extent in their views and opinions that the corresponding groups divide and split. It is important to recognize here that while some of the groups are explicitly formed, and may even have their own administrative organization, others may have no such organization, and their members may not even consciously view themselves as part of such a group. Most individuals are likely to belong to more than one stakeholder group.

THE ROLE OF STAKEHOLDERS

Stakeholders are important to the organization by virtue of their ability to influence it. As a result, their views must be a component of decision-making. It is rare, however, that all stakeholders agree on all issues, and some are more powerful than others, so the task of management is also a balancing act.

Given that management holds much of the decision-making power, that it needs some approval from some stakeholders to retain its power, but also that it is impossible for it to please all stakeholders, management has a variety of balancing methods from which to choose. In principle, it can attempt to balance all interests equally; or according to their weight and importance; or it can focus on just one group of interests, satisfying all others only to the extent that they permit them to continue in office. This leading stakeholder group could be the organization's owners and shareholders, or it could well be the managers themselves, as they also are a major stakeholder.

In addition to strategy formulation, an analysis of an organization's stakeholders is also a powerful tool for evaluating strategies, by ascertaining the existence of objecting stakeholders and the extent of their power on any issue in question. In addition, a stakeholder analysis can form the basis, if it is so desired, for greater participation in decision-making and better communication with stakeholders.

STAKEHOLDER MAPPING

Having established the importance of stakeholders, it is now necessary to find methods of obtaining an accurate picture of what the stakeholder groups are, which interests they represent in relation to the adoption of new strategies, whether they are likely to facilitate or inhibit change, how powerful these groups are, and how they should be dealt with (e.g., by means of side payments, the provision of information, and the like, to insure that they are sufficiently content so as not to take any action that could compromise the established strategies).

A typical stakeholder analysis would involve the identification of all stakeholders, a mapping of the significant relationships between them, an examination of this map for opportunities and threats, and the identification of the likely impact on the map of any proposed or likely change, so that the ground for this can be prepared.

Having identified who the most significant stakeholders are, a number of methods exist to decide how they should be dealt with. For example, the power/dynamism matrix, shown in figure 1, can be used to ascertain where political efforts should be channeled during the development of new strategies.

In this map, the most difficult group to deal with are those in segment D, since they are in a powerful position, and their stance is difficult to predict. In some cases, they can be dealt with by testing out new strategies with them before an

Predictability

		Low	High
Power	**Low**	A Fewer problems	B Unpredictable but manageable
	High	C Powerful but predictable	D Greatest danger or opportunities

Figure 1   Stakeholder mapping: the power/dynamism matrix (Johnson and Scholes, 1993)

irrevocable decision is made. Stakeholders in segment C are also important, although their stance is predictable and so their expectations can often be met. Groups A and B are reasonably easy to deal with, although their power may increase if it is aggregated on any particular issue.

Similarly, the power/interest matrix, shown in figure 2, classifies stakeholders in relation to the power that they hold and the extent to which they are likely to show interest in the organization's strategies, indicating the type of relationship that the organization will have to establish with each of them.

Level of interest

		Low	High
Power	**Low**	A Minimal effort	B Keep informed
	High	C Keep satisfied	D Key players

Figure 2   Stakeholder mapping: the power/interest matrix (Johnson and Scholes, 1993)

The acceptability of strategies to the key players D should be an important consideration in the evaluation of new strategies. Stakeholders in segment C are also very important as, although they are relatively passive in general, they may well emerge suddenly as a result of any specific event and become a very interested and significant party, moving to segment D on that particular issue. Similarly, the needs of stakeholders in segment B need to be addressed, largely through the provision of information, as these can influence the more powerful stakeholders.

Bibliography

Donaldson, T. and Preston, L. G. (1995). The stakeholder theory of the corporation: Concepts, evidence and implications. *Academy of Management Review*, 20(2), 65–91.

Freeman, R. E. (1984). *Strategic Management: A Stakeholder Approach*. London: Pitman.

Gardner, J. R., Rachlin, R., and Sweeny, H. W. A. (ed.) (1986). *Handbook of Strategic Planning*. New York: John Wiley, pp. 171–8.

Mendelow, A. L. (1991). Environmental scanning. Proceedings of the 2nd International Conference on Information Systems, Cambridge, MA.

Roberts, N. C. and King, P. J. (1989). The stakeholder audit goes public. *Organizational Dynamics*, Winter, 63–79.

Rowe, A. J., Mason, R. O., Dickel, K. E., Mann, R. B., and Mockler, R. J. (1994). *Strategic Management: A Methodological Approach*, 4th edn. Reading, MA: Addison-Wesley, pp. 134–44.

stalemate businesses

Derek F. Channon

In these businesses, ECONOMIES OF SCALE do not produce significant cost advantages, because a variety of factors – such as technology, raw material advantage – negate the value of high MARKET SHARE. Such industries tend to be low in differentiation and high in capital intensity, with heavy fixed capital – often in specialized plants. This makes exit from such businesses difficult, as the nature of the assets makes them difficult to resell. A further problem is the impact of environmental legislation, which also makes it difficult to close down such plants, as the cost of cleanup after closure may make it

more economic to continue production despite ongoing losses. Examples are petroleum refining, gas, aluminium, pulp and paper, shipbuilding, and commodity chemicals. Ironically, as part of a national portfolio strategy, the Japanese identify these businesses as SCRAP industries. Many of these businesses have been moved to emerging economies, such as India, South Korea, Indonesia, and Brazil. Japan tends to encourage overcapacity in these industries in order to lower prices. Stalemate occurs as strong competitors erode away any cost advantage in order to maintain capacity utilization, while weaker competitors may well be subsidized or protected by their governments and other parties not subjected to market forces.

See also *advantage matrix*

star businesses

Derek F. Channon

Such businesses are seen as having high MARKET SHARE in a high-growth environment. Because of their high share, they are expected to enjoy a lower cost structure than their lower-share competitors because of the experience effect (*see* EXPERIENCE AND LEARNING EFFECTS). However, cash flow is expected to be either marginally positive or negative, with any surplus being reinvested in the business to continue to add capacity, and thus to maintain or gain market share while industry growth remains high. Research evidence from the PROFIT IMPACT OF MARKET STRATEGY (PIMS) program supports this cash-flow expectation but high capital-intensity businesses with high growth may be cash negative, and may need to be supported by the funds generated by CASH COW businesses.

See also *growth share matrix*

strategic alliances

Duncan Angwin and Derek F. Channon

The poor performance record of MERGERS AND ACQUISITIONS has led to corporate disen-chantment with this method of expansion. Corporate indigestion meant that acquirers found the immediate advantages of acquisition to be frequently undermined by the trauma of integration (*see* POST-ACQUISITION INTE-GRATION). Acquirers often had difficulty in assimilating the expertise of the target company and, where the target company had considerable flexibility and innovative capacity, these characteristics were often lost in the subsequent bureaucracy. Added to this disen-chantment there has also been a shortage of appropriate targets to purchase. These twin con-straints led companies to search for alternative means of rapid, safer expansion so as to improve their control over the competitive environment.

Strategic alliances appeared to overcome many of the limitations of mergers and acquisitions. They seemed to avoid culture and organizational shock and yet achieve rapid presence in specific areas for the companies concerned. However, there does appear to be a growing backlash with companies recognizing problems of SUS-TAINABILITY with strategic alliances and some feeling strongly that acquisitions would have been preferable.

The term *strategic alliance* itself covers a multitude of different arrangements and there is no agreed typology in the literature. However, it is critical to understand the different forms in existence, as they have profound implications for the way in which the alliance is to be managed. In particular, there is an important distinction on the grounds of whether or not the partner is a competitor – note that even if the partner is a competitor, this may not mean collusion (*see* CARTEL).

STRATEGIC ALLIANCES BETWEEN NON-COMPETITORS

The following provides a useful way of linking alliance types amongst competitors to options for strategic expansion. These growth options may be grouped into three categories:

- *International expansion*: where a company extends its activities into a new geographic market, often after having established a dominant position in its domestic market.
- *Vertical integration*: where a company extends its activities upstream or down-stream to become its own supplier or cus-tomer (*see* VERTICAL INTEGRATION STRATEGY).
- *Diversification*: where a company expands outside its industry of origin (*see* DIVERSI-FICATION).

In figure 1 the implications for these expan-sion options for types of strategic alliance amongst non-competing firms are shown. There are three main types of strategic alliance amongst non-competing firms.

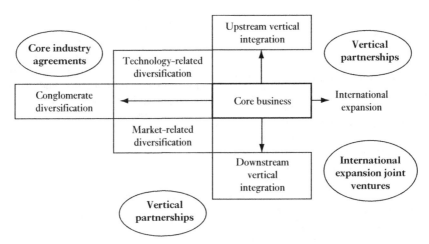

Figure 1   Expansion options and types of partnership between non-competing firms (Dussauge and Garrette, 1999: 51)

- *International expansion joint ventures*: these are formed by companies that originate in different countries (*see* JOINT VENTURES). One company often has a product that it seeks to market in another country in which the other firm has privileged access. The mutual benefits are that the local firm gains a product to distribute, whilst the manufacturer gains a foothold in a new country. Often these alliances are between partners with unequal skills and resources, one coming from the developed world with technical skills and considerable resources, and the other from the developing world without the ability to develop such a product on its own but having a profound understanding of the local market.

- *Vertical partnerships*: these bring together two companies that operate at two successive stages in the same production process. For instance, fast food chains are critical customers of soft drinks suppliers, so Coca-Cola has set up an alliance with McDonald's and Domino's Pizza.

- *Cross-industry agreements*: these are cooperations formed by companies from totally different industries to leverage their complementary capabilities. For instance, BMW forged an alliance with Rolls-Royce in aircraft engines in order to enter that market. Although for Rolls-Royce this meant the emergence of a new competitor, it also provided the opportunity to control its long-term development. This raises the issue of competing agendas, with the newcomer trying to close the expertise gap as rapidly

as possible, while the established company attempts the reverse. Such alliances may also occur where there is technical convergence between two industries. For instance, Philips has teamed up with Du Pont de Nemours for the production of surface coatings for data storage applications.

STRATEGIC ALLIANCES AMONGST COMPETITORS

Alliances amongst competitors seem rather paradoxical, but according to Morris and Hergert (1987), they account for approximately 70 percent of all cooperation agreements. Maybe it is in recognition of this that Hamel and Prahalad's (1989) article is entitled "Collaborate with your competitors and win." Whilst it is tempting to think of these alliances as collusive, it is a question of degree, with some being more collusive than others. Through the use of cluster analysis techniques on 200 alliances, Dussauge and Garrette (1999) have identified three main alliance types between competitors (see figure 2) in terms of balance of power between the partners (degree of symmetry) and impact upon competition.

The three types of alliance identified may be characterized in the following way:

- *Pre-competitive* or *shared supply alliance*: this may only cover one stage in the production process, so that whilst the final product contains inputs from both companies, these are specific to the parents and the alliance is not apparent to the market. These alliances

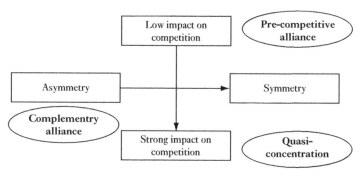

Figure 2   Mapping strategic alliances between competitors (Dussauge and Garrette, 1999: 61)

occur when the minimum efficient size at a particular stage in the production process is much greater than for the entire product and when neither firm produces enough volume to achieve this critical size. These sorts of alliances are mainly between firms of similar size, often intra-zonal, and in areas of R&D and manufacturing. Industries with such alliances are automotive, electronics, and data processing.

- *Quasi-concentration alliance*: this covers the entire production process and results in a common product marketed by all allies. The assets and skills brought by each partner are similar in nature and the goal is to benefit from ECONOMIES OF SCALE. Such an alliance is clearly visible to the customer, such as in the Airbus consortium or the production of the Tornado fighter aircraft. Clearly, such alliances eliminate competition between competitors, although there can be internal rivalry within the alliance. These sorts of alliances are found mostly in the aerospace and defense industries.
- *Complementary alliance*: when the assets contributed by the partner firms are different in nature. Most commonly, one may be a manufacturer and the other a distributor. For instance, Matra manufactures the Espace, a minivan, which is marketed in Europe by Renault. For such alliances to work, the product brought in by an ally must not compete directly with the products of the other firm. Complementary alliances are usually between two firms (unlike the other two styles) and the companies may be very different sizes. These alliances are often found in the automotive and telecommunications industries.

OUTCOMES

Assessing the outcomes of alliances is no easy matter (see tables 1 and 2). As we have shown, there are many different types and the partners have very different reasons for pursuing them. For alliances between competitors, the most frequent outcomes overall are either an extension of the alliance or premature termination – it seems it is unusual to have a natural end or be acquired. In most cases, alliances between competitors had significant strategic consequences for the partner firms, with one-way skills appropriation in particular, and such alliances tend to affect the levels of competition in the industry. However, there is considerable variation between the different types of alliance between competitors, as table 2 shows.

With an alliance strategy it has been possible for corporations to swiftly gain access to markets, exchange technologies, form defensive shareholding blocs, enter third markets in

Table 1 Outcomes of alliances between non-rival firms

Alliance type	Evolution of the alliance	Strategic consequences for each firm	Impact on competition
International expansion joint ventures	High mortality rate in their first years in existence, followed by stability	Stability in the partners' relative positions	Globalization
Vertical partnerships	Long-term relationship between the partners	New division of the value added within the industry	Concentration of the upstream industry and changes in the relative bargaining power of suppliers and buyers
Cross-industry agreements	Results are frequently disappointing when compared to initial expectations	Joint venture becomes independent or intensification of competition between partners	Creation of new activities and arrival of new competitors

Source: Dussauge and Garrette (1999: 209)

Table 2   The evolutions and outcomes of strategic alliances between competitors

Alliance type	Evolution of the alliance	Strategic consequences for each firm	Impact on competition
Shared-supply	Natural end or premature termination	No consequence	No impact on the intensity of competition
Quasi-concentration	Extension	Mutual specialization	Reduced intensity of competition
Complementary	Extension or continuation by one partner	One-way skill appropriation	Increased intensity of competition

Source: Dussauge and Garrette (1999: 220)

combination with other partners, and engage in otherwise prohibitively expensive technologies, production facilities, and so on. They have the advantage of being relatively easily formed and disbanded – more so than joint ventures – and by joining in multiple alliances firms may contain risk and hold down costs.

Despite these apparent advantages, however, their value has been seriously questioned by many corporations, and especially by those with proprietary technology, strategic cost advantage, and high market share. For such concerns it has been argued that the potential loss of technical skills, the provision of competitor access to markets, and organizational and cultural clashes may well outweigh any advantage. As a result, perhaps 50 percent of such alliances are therefore regarded as failures.

See also *cooperative strategies*

Bibliography

Child, J. and Faulkner, D. (1998). *Strategies of Cooperation: Managing Alliances, Networks, and Joint Ventures*. Oxford: Oxford University Press.

Dussauge, P. and Garrette, B. (1999). *Cooperative Strategy: Competing Successfully through Strategic Alliances*. New York: John Wiley.

Hamel, G. (1991). Competition for competence and inter-partner learning within international strategic alliances. *Strategic Management Journal*, **23**, special issue, 83–103.

Hamel, G. and Prahalad, C. K. (1989). Collaborate with your competitors and win. *Harvard Business Review*, **67** (1), 133–9.

Morris, D. and Hergert, M. (1987). Trends in international collaborative agreements. *Columbia Journal of World Business*, **19** (4), 319–32.

strategic change

David Wilson

Change is called strategic (rather than operational) when it involves relatively high level and pervasive changes to the structures, processes, and core businesses of the organization. Such changes are usually novel to the organization in question (although not necessarily novel in themselves). They are changes that set precedents for subsequent strategic decisions made in the organization, and they are difficult to reverse once in motion and tend to be capital hungry (in terms of both human and financial capital). Table 1 summarizes one way of viewing change along a scale which moves from status quo to revolutionary change, at the same time distinguishing between strategic and operational changes.

Researchers and practitioners in strategic management have all proposed various ways in which we might understand strategic change and, more importantly, which perspectives will yield the most useful results in making changes work successfully. Nutt et al (2000) provide a useful summary of the main approaches taken. They argue that there are five predominant ways to craft a strategy in the face of strategic change issues. These are:

- analytical approaches
- stakeholder approaches
- adaptive approaches
- gap analyses
- systems-based analysis of strategic tensions

Table 1   Levels and degrees of operational and strategic change

Degree of change	Level of change	Characteristics
Status quo	Can be both operational and strategic	No change in current practices. A decision *not* to do something can be strategic as well as operational
Expanded reproduction	Mainly operational	Change involves producing more of the same (for example, goods, and services)
Evolutionary transition	Mainly strategic	Sometimes radical changes occur but they do so within the existing parameters of the organization (for example, existing structures or technologies are retained)
Revolutionary transition	Predominantly strategic	Change involves shifting or re-defining existing parameters. Structures, processes and/or technologies likely to change

Source: Wilson (1999: 20)

Analytical approaches examine the strategic portfolio of the organization (services and products) to see how well its portfolio of activities fits with its commitment to find resources to change the mix to improve performance. Strategic change therefore is a constant process of aligning and shifting the mix of products and services, clients, funding sources, skills, and image (for example, brand strength).

Stakeholder approaches argue that strategies are crafted in line with those stakeholders in a position to be influential over strategic decision-making or who can place heavy demands on the organization. Strategic changes thus are designed to satisfy stakeholder interests.

Adaptive approaches take the view that strategic change is more a process of alignment of an organization's activities, structures, and cultures with the characteristics of the external operating environment it faces. Classic contingency studies of organizations fit into this category (for example, the nostrum that decentralized structures out-perform centralised structures in turbulent environments).

Gap analyses focus on assessing the current core competencies of the organization and seeing where there are gaps in competencies to provide a changed future portfolio of products and services. This current versus future thinking and the requirements in terms of organizational resources (human and financial) is the essence of gap analysis.

The strategic tensions approach attempts to move beyond position-based bargaining (as may characterize the stakeholder perspective for example) and attempts to see their wider interests in the context of the organization. Such a perspective also accords with that taken by Pettigrew and Whipp (1991) who argue that change can only be understood in terms of its content (what the change is about); its processes (how organizations craft strategies to get from state *a* to state *b*; and its context (the wider environment of infrastructure, culture, sector, nation, etc.). This approach relies on managers identifying as accurately as possible the various tensions in the wider system. Easy to say, but difficult to do! However, the approach argues that even a partial identification of wider tensions is better than a fuller analysis of more focused and local issues (but which ignore context). Examples of some common strategic tensions are illustrated in Table 2.

Nutt et al (2000) argue that the systemic tensions perspective gives a better chance of success in crafting change strategies than any of the other approaches. They cite examples from public and private sectors, showing that context (in the organization or the wider system) is crucial for facilitating win-win situations among competing interests. Like Pettigrew and Whipp (1991), he argues that a co-operative organizational culture (context) will create commitment and support for actions to be taken, since competing interests will always see something of value to them in the change.

Practical steps for managers crafting such change strategies would be to 'widen the arena' of the issues discussed (and hence of the change process). One way of achieving this is to communicate both the *how* and the *why* of change. Various techniques can be used for this, the most

Table 2   Examples of strategic tensions and their main characteristics

Examples of strategic tensions	Characterized by
Equity – Equity	Clashes between different interests (e.g. between clients, suppliers) all of whom call for a different set of actions to be taken. The key question is whose interests will be served?
Transition – Transition	Where several competing plans for what should change are in conflict. The usual characteristic of these tensions is disputes over diagnostics – that is, "my data is better than yours" arguments. The result is having to choose between several plans for change.
Preservation – Preservation	Difficulties in maintaining the status quo when it is unclear what are the organization's core values and strategic direction. Characterized by debates about what this organization *should* be doing and what is *appropriate*.
Preservation – Innovation	Where there are disputes over anticipated pay offs from strategic changes. The tensions are about who gets what out of the change, once implemented. The key danger here is that of inertia (that is nothing happens other than conflict).
Expansion – Contraction	Where departments (for example) are expected to produce more with less resources. This can happen to organizations, to sectors and to national economies.
Innovation – Tradition	The tension here is between values. There are those who argue that current practices are to be preserved and that what is being proposed violates central norms and values in the organization.
Change – Ethics	Similar to the above, but the urgency is to try and reconcile changes with ethical considerations such as commitment to environmental principles or to humanizing the workplace.

Source: adapted from Nutt et al (2000) and Wilson (1999)

popular being a simple laddering exercise. At the bottom of the ladder are placed the how-factors of strategies and then in logical ascending order the why-factors are listed. A simple example of such a ladder is given in Figure 1.

The objective of the change is to improve the standard and provision of health care over all the regions of a country. The ladder then begins at the bottom with three sets of actions (the how-factors) and then ascends through a series of why-factors to complete the loop, since the last why-factor very closely resembles the first objective.

The reason for using the laddering technique is to create a context in which the likelihood of buy-in to the change is increased. Buy-in is a much misunderstood idea. Many senior managers ask how they can achieve buy-in as if there were some kind of magic formula that they could apply to the organization after the fact, to win the hearts and minds of all individuals. The problem is that strategic changes are about meanings and interpretations, not simply process maps; and meaning grows from the opportunity to engage

at early stages in the formulation and discussion processes. Newsletters, corporate social events, prizes, and vision statements communicate facts and can provide a route map of the change but can never communicate behaviors or help individuals make sense of what is happening in the change process. Therefore, even a broad understanding of the wider context is only part of the answer to implementing change. We also have to understand the role of individuals in the process, both change initiators and those recipients of the process and the outcome.

Bibliography

McGee, J., Wilson, D., and Thomas, H. (2005). *Strategy: Analysis and Practice*. Maidenhead: McGraw-Hill.

Nutt P., Backoff, R., and Hogan, M. (2000). Managing the paradoxes of strategic change. *Journal of Applied Management Studies*, 9 (1), 5–31.

Pettigrew, A. and Whipp, R. (1991). *Managing Change for Competitive Success*. Oxford: Blackwell.

Wilson, D. (1999). *A Strategy of Change: Concepts and Controversies in the Management of Change*. London: International Thomson Press.

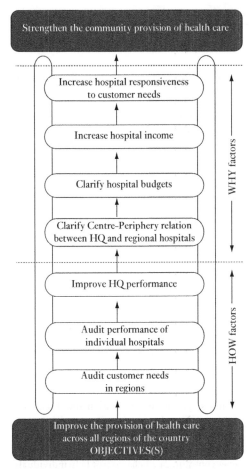

Figure 1   An example of a strategic outcome ladder

strategic decision-making

David Wilson

At the heart of strategy lies decision-making. Having analyzed the environment, assessed organizational capabilities, and investigated technological shifts, managers have to take preferred courses of action. They have to examine possible alternatives and choose amongst them. Strategic decisions are the handful of decisions that drive or shape most of an organization's actions, are not easily changed once made, and have the greatest impact upon organizational performance. Strategy may be a grand concept, but it is the individual strategic decisions that matter.

At its simplest, decision-making may be considered an instantaneous action, a choice between two or more known alternatives, made by individuals or groups. However, this "point of decision" approach is unable to capture the richness and complexity of the processes that lead up to the point of decision, the influences on putting the decision into action, and the ultimate performance of that decision. It also assumes that managers have full agency and control over decisions. Sometimes they may have very limited discretion to make decisions or choose amongst alternatives. This could be the case, for example, where strategic decisions in organizations are heavily constrained by interventionist government policies (such as PRIVATIZATION or DEREGULATION), where all strategic decisions are framed and shaped by this wider context. Nevertheless, managers still have some degree of strategic choice, even if the wider context (e.g., privatization) is firmly set in place. Managers can still make strategic decisions, for example, concerning such key topics as organizational design, choice of suppliers, choice and sophistication of information systems, and general product or service portfolios.

Of course, most people are aware that much of decision-making is not a simple process that happens in a linear sequence – a period of thinking followed by a period of acting. Decision-making – and the development of alternative courses of action – is fashioned in their doing. Therefore, factors such as previous experience or whether things "feel" right are likely to have as much influence over strategic choices (and what follows) as analysis and planning. Yet, these decisions are what will influence the fortunes or otherwise of any organization (from a sports club to a multinational enterprise) and understanding strategic decision-making processes therefore represents a key aspect of examining how strategies are put into practice. The entries on STRATEGY and STRATEGIC MANAGEMENT enable us to see how strategy, as an overall direction an organization might take, can be formulated by analytical and rational thinking. In this view strategy is a positioning process by which organizations chart their ways through the seas of competition, internationalization, and changing markets and technologies. Positioning alone, however, leaves open the question of how particular choices are made amongst a set of alternatives – however incomplete those alternatives might be. In short, to understand strategy fully we need to understand the processes of strategic decision-making.

DECISION-MAKING PERSPECTIVES

Five different (and sometimes mutually exclusive) perspectives on strategic decision-making have been identified:

- Decision-making as a *plan*: the decision is a consciously intended course of action. In the same way that you might intend to catch an airplane to a specific destination at a particular time, decision-making is a process which is carried out in advance of the action that follows and is developed with a clear purpose.
- Decision-making as a *ploy*: a decision from this perspective is a set of actions designed to outwit the competition and may not necessarily be the "obvious" content of the decision. For example, a decision to construct a new building in order to expand may not be the overt strategy, but is more concerned with increasing barriers to entry (*see* BARRIERS TO ENTRY AND EXIT) for potential competitors. There are obvious connections here with game theory, which examines the choices players make in every possible situation. Forcing one's opponent to move (to achieve a short-term win) so that this puts them at a longer-term disadvantage is an example of such a ploy. Equally, there are connections with strategy as conceived in its military roots, where the plans of campaigns may have similar intentions to the game analogy.
- Decision-making as a *pattern*: decisions are not necessarily taken with a planned purpose and decision-makers do not always have access to the range of knowledge required to plan wholly in advance. What happens is that multiple decisions taken over time form a pattern. It is this pattern of resulting (emergent) behavior that we call the strategy of the firm. Strategy is therefore characterized as a pattern which emerges from a stream of decisions.

- Decision-making as a *position*: decisions are less about the dynamics of planning or gamesmanship and more about trying to achieve a match between the organization and its environment. This position can be one of alignment, so that the organization matches its environment (e.g., highly decentralized structures to match a turbulent and unpredictable environment) or one of trying to secure COMPETITIVE ADVANTAGE (where the organization achieves a unique position in the market for some time). Positions, of course, can be planned, emerge, or be a combination of both emergent and planned processes.
- Decision-making as a *perspective*: decisions here are characterized as a reflection of how strategists in an organization see and perceive the world and their organization. For example, the strategic perspective of Nokia is one of continuous and sometimes radical change (Nokia began as a paper and pulp company); IBM favors a dominant marketing perspective, whilst Hewlett-Packard favors an engineering excellence perspective. This perspective, if pervasive enough, can influence the kinds of decisions taken, in respect of their content and their processes. We can see the effects of this embedded view of decision-making by observing that organizations in similar industries often choose similar strategic decisions. They become institutionalized. Universities tend to follow broadly similar strategies, as do large retailers or service organizations.

THE PROCESSES OF STRATEGIC DECISION-MAKING

The processes of making decisions can appear deceptively simple. Actions are formulated toward the solution of a particular problem. The problem with this approach is that there may be discernible actions and there may be observable outcomes, but they need not necessarily be wholly related to one another. Problems may be solved by factors other than strategic decisions and, sometimes, taking a strategic decision can create a whole new set of problems (without solving the initial problem the decision was supposed to address).

These polar views can be represented by the *planning* versus the *chaotic* processes of strategic decision-making. They are extremes and, although most decisions lie somewhere between the planned and the chaotic, both perspectives are useful for understanding the processes of strategic decision-making. Viewing processes as basically a set of planning tools allows *actions, procedures*, and *measurement* to be explicitly dddressed. Planning facilitates decision-makers in analyzing and codifying what appear initially as complex problems. Planning simplifies complexity and helps reduce uncertainty. Because of this, planning can also help decision-makers examine current planning practices in their organization and assess their utility in light of current problems. From a behavioral perspective, planning can insure that others in the organization are involved and are communicated with as fully as possible. Note that although involvement and communication can be explicit parts of the plan, this may not endow those participants with any influence over the process or its eventual outcome. Finally, planning processes help decision-makers identify key performance indicators by which progress of the decision can be monitored and judged.

Chaotic processes argue that organizations can be viewed as an "anarchy" or as a system with chaotic tendencies. Hence decision-makers can neither understand fully nor control decision processes. Means and ends are unlikely to be coupled, which implies that actions do not lead to expected outcomes and are swayed one way or another by other decisions, other actions, and unforeseen circumstances. The main components of a strategic decision-making process (problems, solutions, participants, and choice situations) interact in an apparently haphazard way, a stream of demands for the fluid attention and energies of managers. Participants move in and out of the decision-making process (every entrance is an exit elsewhere) and this can create discontinuity. At other times, participants fight for the right to become involved and then never exercise any influence they may have.

Viewing decision-making processes as chaotic also has some advantages for decision-makers. Unlike the planning approach, the chaos perspective does not seek to simplify and to reduce uncertainty. It avoids any oversimplification of

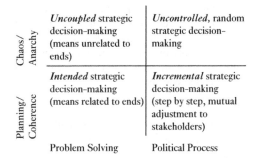

	Uncoupled strategic decision-making (means unrelated to ends)	*Uncontrolled*, random strategic decision-making
Chaos/Anarchy		
Planning/Coherence	*Intended* strategic decision-making (means related to ends)	*Incremental* strategic decision-making (step by step, mutual adjustment to stakeholders)
	Problem Solving	Political Process

Figure 1   A typology of decision processes

the process and allows decision-makers to appreciate and expect the role of politics and influence to be a natural part of the decision-making process. In theory, the chaos perspective should encourage decision-makers to think creatively around complex problems and help them to avoid thinking solely in linear sequences. Creativity and innovation may be enhanced by decision-makers being encouraged to take actions that seem unrelated to the decision under consideration. On the other hand, we should bear in mind that the distinction between creativity and madness is a rather fine line! From a decision-making perspective, this means that no one will know whether the tangential explorations were useful or folly until a long way down the track of the decision process. Figure 1 summarizes four polar types of decision process that can arise from counterposing planned versus chaotic and political versus planned perspectives.

strategic fit

Derek F. Channon

Strategic fit occurs usually in related diversified concerns (*see* RELATED DIVERSIFICATION) as a result of superior competitive position arising from overall lower cost and the successful transfer of core skills, technology, and managerial know-how between businesses. The earlier concepts of SYNERGY and shared experience have similar meanings.

Strategic fit, however, may apply in apparently unrelated businesses where financial synergy may be found. For example, a high-cash-flow business may financially complement a business that is a high capital user.

DIVERSIFICATION into businesses in which shared technology, marketing, and production skills are required can lead to ECONOMIES OF SCOPE when the costs of operating two or more businesses are less than operating each individually. The key to such cost reductions is therefore diversification into businesses with strategic fit.

Market-related fit occurs when the activity cost chains of different businesses overlap such that they attempt to reach the same consumers via similar distribution channels, or are marketed and promoted in similar ways. In addition to such economies of scope, it may also be possible to transfer selling skills, promotion and advertising skills, and product positioning/differentiation skills across businesses. Care must, however, be taken to insure that market-related fit is possible. Successful examples include Canon's strategic position in cameras and photographic equipment being logically extended into copying and imaging equipment, and Honda's position in motorcycles being extended into other activities using engines, including automobiles and lawnmowers. However, not all such moves are successful. Thus BAT found that selling branded cosmetics was different from selling branded tobacco items.

Operating fit is achieved where the potential for cost sharing or skills transfer can occur in procurement, R&D, production, assembly, and/or administration. Cost sharing amongst these activities can lead to ECONOMIES OF SCALE. Again, successes such as the sale of life insurance policies by retail banking branches can be identified. Similarly, failures are frequently due to inabilities to insure integration between activities from different businesses brought together by acquisition (*see* ACQUISITION STRATEGY; MERGERS AND ACQUISITIONS; POST-ACQUISITION INTEGRATION).

Management fit occurs when different business units enjoy comparable types of entrepreneurial administrative or operating problems. This type of gain is very difficult to achieve due to differences in corporate culture. Classic failures in achieving such fit gains occurred in the attempted diversification moves by the oil industry majors after the first oil-price shock in 1973. Redefinitions of their businesses

into "energy" and "raw materials" encouraged moves into minerals, coal, and gas. Most of these moves were serious failures, or the expected strategic fit did not materialize.

Ironically, the only strategic fit which is almost certain to be achieved is the financial one. The operational strategic fits have lower probabilities of success, that for marketing being higher than that for production, which, in turn, is higher than that for R&D.

The strategic fit concept has also been criticized as being too static and limiting, focusing as it does on existing resources and the existing environment rather than seeking out the future opportunities and threats that are the focus of firms with strategic intent.

Bibliography

Ansoff, H. I. (1965). *Corporate Strategy*. New York: McGraw-Hill, ch. 7.

Kitching, J. (1967). Why do mergers miscarry? *Harvard Business Review*, November/December, 84–101.

Ohmae, K. (1983). *The Mind of the Strategist*. New York: Penguin, pp. 121–4.

Porter, M. E. (1985). *Competitive Advantage: Creating and Sustaining Superior Performance*. New York: Free Press, pp. 318–19, 337–53.

strategic groups

Derek F. Channon

A strategic group consists of those rival firms with similar competitive approaches and positions in the market. The identification of strategic groups within an industry enables the competitive structure of the industry to be redefined to compare strategies of various competitors for similarities and differences. Thus some firms may have comparable product lines, be similarly vertically integrated, focus on similar customer segments, use the same distribution channels, sell with the same product positioning, and so on. If all competitors within an industry have similar strategic characteristics, then there will be only one strategic group. However, in most industries with a significant number of competitors, it is common for more than one cluster of competitors to emerge. This is illustrated in the strategic group map of the US

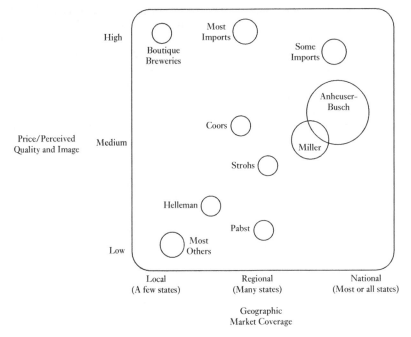

Figure 1   A strategic group map of the US brewing industry (Thompson and Strickland, 1993: 7)

brewing industry, shown in figure 1, which positions the major competitors along the two dimensions of price/perceived quality and image and geographic coverage.

To construct such a strategic group map, it is necessary to follow the procedure set out below:

1 Identify the key strategic characteristics which differentiate competitors, such as SERVED MARKET, product range, distribution channels used, price, and quality.
2 Plot firms on a two-dimensional map, using selected pairs of differentiating variables.
3 Cluster firms that fall in a similar strategic space into strategic groups.
4 Map the groups in terms of importance, by indicating the level of group total sales by the area of the circle surrounding clustered competitors.
5 If more than two significant strategic variables can be used for axes, draw a number of maps to identify alternate positions of competitive relationships.

This form of analysis helps to improve understanding of the degree and nature of competitive rivalry. As a generalization, the closer strategic groups are to one another, the greater is the likelihood of competitive rivalry between the firms within the group. Firms that are strategically distant from the main groups may be subject to much less competitive pressure. As a result, the profit potentials of different competitors may be radically different and not necessarily correlated with size. Thus, a large competitor, despite enjoying the advantage of a high MARKET SHARE, may operate within a group in which competitive rivalry is intense, thus leading to profit erosion. By contrast, a number of competitors operating in a smaller market of strategic space may enjoy superior margins due to the lack of other competitors. Thus competitive pressures will tend to significantly favor some groups over others.

Bibliography

McGee, J. and Thomas, H. (1986). Strategic groups: Theory, research and taxonomy. *Strategic Management Journal,* 7 (2), 141–60.

Porter, M. E. (1980). *Competitive Strategy: Techniques for Analyzing Industries and Competitors.* New York: Free Press, ch. 7.

Thompson, A. and Strickland A. J. (1993). *Strategic Management*, 7th edn. New York: Irwin.

strategic intent

John McGee

It has been argued that US firms seeking strategic fit have often found themselves overtaken by firms, especially the Asian conglomerates, driven by long-term visions of the future, which are then relentlessly and ruthlessly pursued. Companies like CNN, Honda, NEC, and Sony have succeeded (according to this argument) because of their sustained obsession with achieving global dominance in their industries. This obsession has been labeled strategic intent (Hamel and Prahalad, 1989). The significance of this is that the intent of these companies was out of proportion to their existing resources and capabilities. This gap between ambition and resources is known as *strategic stretch*. These companies had to expand and adapt their current stock of resources and create new ones. They were more concerned with "leveraging" resources than with achieving STRATEGIC FIT between their current resources and their industry environments.

Strategic intent can thus be used as a psychological target that provides a focus for all members of the organization to adopt. Becoming the industry leader or dominating a specific segment are frequent missionary goals. The fundamental focus of the firm's strategy commits well beyond its current resource profile. The prophecies can therefore become self-fulfilling, provided that employees have faith in their leadership and that, in many cases, the existing industry leaders fail to recognize that the challenge is on. The logic of expansion, coupled with ECONOMIES OF SCOPE, provides an economic basis for justifying strategic intent. However, there are limits to economies of scope that arise when industries and markets require more variety than the fixed factors that support scope effects can sustain.

Bibliography

Besanko, D., Dranove, D., Shanley, M., and Shaefer, S. (2003). *Economics of Strategy*, 2nd edn. New York: John Wiley.

Hamel, G. and Prahalad, C. K. (1989). Strategic intent. *Harvard Business Review*, **89**, May/June, 63–76.

Kontes, P. and Mankins, M. (1992). The dangers of strategic intent. *Marakon Associates*, April.

strategic management

Derek F. Channon

This concept consists of that set of decisions and actions that results in formulating a strategy and its implementation to achieve the objectives of the corporation. The process of STRATEGIC DECISION-MAKING is illustrated in figure 1. The process consists of a number of specific steps:

1 Determination of the MISSION of the corporation, including statements about purpose, philosophy, and objectives.

2 An assessment of the internal environment of the corporation, including an assessment of its culture, history, and informal as well as formal organization.

3 An assessment of its external environment by PEST ANALYSIS.

4 The matching of external opportunities and threats with internal strengths and weaknesses via SWOT ANALYSIS.

5 The identification of desired options from this analysis in light of the corporate mission.

6 Strategic choice of a relevant set of long-term strategies and policies required to successfully achieve the chosen options.

7 The development of short- and medium-term strategies and action programs that are consistent with the long-term strategies and policies.

8 Implementation programs based on budgets, and action plans based on budgeted resource allocations and monitored via appropriate management information, planning and control systems, and reward and sanction systems.

9   Review and evaluation systems to monitor the strategy process and to provide an input for future decision-making.

The process may or may not be articulated formally via a strategic planning system. In addition, strategic management occurs at a number of hierarchical levels within the firm, depending on the complexity of the corporations – this usually involves three levels. At the top is the corporate level, at which decisions are taken by the senior executive officers and, in particular, by the CEO in conjunction with the board of directors. This group is responsible for providing the vision of deciding where the company wants to go. It is also responsible for financial performance, legal structure, and for establishing overall corporate image and social responsibility, which reflect the views of the various stakeholders of the firm, including employees, shareholders, and society as a whole.

The corporate level also establishes an overall strategic perspective across the business activities of the firm. For multibusiness firms – which includes most large corporations – the corporate level determines the portfolio balance and the position of each business within it; sets performance objectives; allocates resources; makes key appointments and sets human resources policies; creates the formal ORGANIZATIONAL STRUC-

TURE (and influences the informal structure); sets the management information, planning, and control systems; and creates the reward and sanction systems. The corporate level is also usually responsible for the identification and implementation of any major acquisitions, although some companies delegate "fill-in" AC-QUISITION STRATEGY to the business unit level. Any new fields of activity, however, are normally determined at the corporate level.

The second main tier of strategic management occurs at the level of the business unit, although an intermediate division level may exist in some organizations, comprising a cluster of business units. At this level managers translate the general direction and thrust of the corporation into specific strategies relevant to their businesses and consistent with the overall portfolio investment strategy determined for them. At this level multifunctional strategies are formulated and implemented for the specific product market area in which the business operates. Such strategies might vary greatly in terms of commitment to growth. While some businesses may be expected to strive for growth, others may be expected to release resources by adopting harvesting or DIVESTMENT strategies. A number of portfolio models to position businesses, including the ADVANTAGE MATRIX, COMPETITIVE POSITION–MARKET

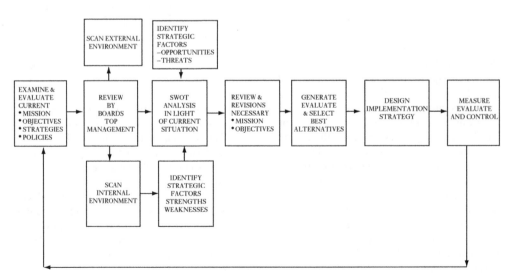

Figure 1   The strategic decision-making process

ATTRACTIVENESS MATRIX, DIRECTIONAL POLICY MATRIX, GROWTH SHARE MATRIX, LIFE–CYCLE STRATEGY, and VALUE–BASED PLANNING, are discussed in separate entries. All these models have been designed to aid the corporate center in identifying the appropriate position of each business within the corporate portfolio, and the development of appropriate strategies is discussed throughout many of the other entries in this volume.

The third tier of strategic management applies at the functional level of each business, at which managers from the principal functions of the business, such as marketing, production, operations, R&D, information technology, accounting, and human resources, develop operational strategies and tactics to implement the selected business-level strategy. The overall process thus represents a cascade approach.

The characteristics of strategic management decisions vary with the hierarchical level of activity (see table 1). Corporate-level decisions tend to be value oriented, conceptual, and less precise than those at lower level. In particular, the CEO's vision about how the corporation should develop is exceptionally important. This is especially true in large corporations that attempt to change direction, and in which overcoming the effect of historically established corporate inertia is perhaps the most challenging managerial task – unless the corporation is in crisis and a TURNAROUND STRATEGY is called for. Corporate-level decisions are also characterized by greater risk and determine future profit-

Table 1 Characteristics of corporate, business, and functional strategies

	Goals and Objectives	Strategy components	Major decisions	Coordination	Resource allocation
Corporate strategy	• Survival policy • Overall long-term direction	• Scope of business portfolio • Financial, organizational and technological competences • Financial, organizational and technological competences	• Financial policies • Organizational policies	• Among businesses	• Portfolio choice
Business strategy	• Constrained • Product market development • Growth and profit objectives	• Product market segments • Product market range (breadth) • Seek competitive advantages	• Value chain elements • R&D policies • Manufacturing policies • Marketing policies • Distribution policies • Systems policies	• Among functions	• Life-cycle issues
Functional strategy	• Constrained • Market share • Technological position	• Product market development • Branding • Packaging	• Pricing • Promotion campaigns • Production schedules • Inventory controls • Logistics	• Within functions	• Functional integration and balance of activities

ability and the ability of the corporation to survive and prevail. Such decisions also cover all aspects of financial strategy, including capital structure, dividend policy, growth priorities, and selection of the business portfolio.

By contrast, functional decisions are effectively made up of action programs which, hopefully, support the overall corporate position. However, this is not always so, and in conditions of corporate-level-led radical change, serious dysfunctional behavior may be experienced, especially when shifts in the existing power structure may be experienced during programs such as reengineering (*see* BUSINESS PROCESS REENGINEERING; REENGINEERING DISADVANTAGES; VALUE-DRIVEN REENGINEERING). Functional-level decisions are, however, normally concerned with relatively short-term, lower-risk, moderate-cost activities. They do not usually cut across businesses within the corporation unless interdependencies exist, and therefore tend to be confined to the individual business.

Decisions at the business level bridge those at corporate and functional levels. They are more risky and costly than those at the functional level and may involve significant changes in existing behavior, including factors such as plant location, SEGMENTATION strategy, geographic coverage, and the choice of distribution channel.

EVOLUTION TOWARD STRATEGIC MANAGEMENT

Relatively few companies can be said to have developed a full strategic management perspective, in which the whole corporation thinks strategically and has a clear vision of where it wants to go – and knows how to get there. Rather, companies evolve toward this position, as shown in figure 2.

McKinsey and Company believe that companies proceed through four stages of development. They start with simple financial planning (stage I), move through forecast-based planning (stage II), then externally oriented or

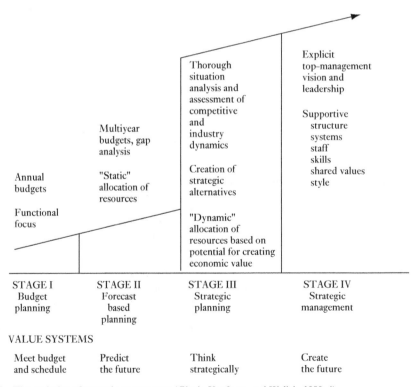

Figure 2   The evolution of strategic management (Gluck, Kaufman, and Wallek, 1980: 4)

STRATEGIC PLANNING (stage III), and finally arrive at stage IV, strategic management.

In stage I, budgets and financial objectives dominate the planning process, and managers and planners are preoccupied with setting an accurate budget and achieving it. In such companies, senior management assumes that the status quo will continue, that industry change will not affect the way things are done, and that industry boundaries are clear and will not be breached by new competitors or technologies. The question of change of corporate direction is seldom raised and the firm's approach is inward-looking and execution oriented. The process of planning is dominated by financial numbers rather than strategic variables and the development of budgets is usually undertaken by the finance and accounting function.

Movement of the company from stage I to stage II is an indication that management recognizes the need to extend the time horizon of the corporation beyond the single financial year and to think about the future. Usually, future forecasts extend for three years. In the 1970s and early 1980s such forward extrapolations often extended for longer periods, but the rapid growth of environmental turbulence, coupled with a recognition that future financial forecasts were relatively meaningless projections of the present position, has caused most managements to cut back to three-year projections. Even so, most such plans remain dominated by financial projections rather than strategic considerations. In many companies some managers also believe that senior management is mainly concerned with the first year of such a projection, and therefore tend to consider that extrapolations beyond this point are relatively meaningless. Again, the exercise tends to be dominated by the finance and accounting staff, with line management rarely participating in strategic decisions regarding operations, focusing instead on how to avoid or fill any profit gap.

A quantum leap in the effectiveness of strategic planning and decision-making usually occurs with the transition of the corporation from stage II to stage III. At this point the corporation becomes more focused on the external environment in which it operates, and the focus switches from the forecasting of volume and revenues toward obtaining a better under-standing of customer needs, competitive position, technological developments, and market characteristics. At this stage, line management becomes significantly involved in the development of strategy, professional corporate planning staff are introduced, and the system of developing strategy tends to become formalized with the introduction of detailed procedures and timetables.

The stage III company thus adds conceptual and analytic skills that theoretically enable it to develop strategies for sustainable COMPETITIVE ADVANTAGE. Many new variables are considered other than financial. Plans are sophisticated and resource allocations may be determined on the rational basis of the strategic positions of individual businesses. Despite these efforts, however, many such strategies fail to achieve necessary strategic changes in the corporation. This is due, in large part, to the fact that many line managers do not regard themselves as the owners of the plans and, as a result, fail to implement them. Moreover, many do not wish to change their perspective and in particular accept the organizational, cultural, and power relationship changes that may be necessary to transform the corporation when faced with major shifts in the external environment.

In examining the reasons why companies in leadership positions went into decline, McKinsey and Company concluded that such firms fell into one or more of three major traps. First, they used unrealistic or obsolete criteria to assess company strengths and/or weaknesses. Second, they became complacent about their leadership position – and as such became inflexible and assumed that the status quo would go on indefinitely. Third, they failed to recognize industry change and take action to respond to it.

Companies making the transition from stage III to stage IV did recognize these traps. They understood that change was continuous and permanent, and that unwillingness to meet the challenge would ultimately result in failure. Moreover, change within the corporation might be radical. Within corporations such as IBM, Citicorp, and GE, this acceptance has been clearly led from the office of the CEO.

In stage IV companies therefore, strategic management is inculcated throughout the corporation. The corporation is continually adjusting its competitive strategy in response to the market and competition. Such firms are also constantly changing the rules in the markets in which they compete, in order to win. They are also low on bureaucracy, with strategic responsibility passing throughout the corporation. Planning becomes a line rather than staff function and line managers own the plans.

Strategically managed companies are also experts in self-renewal. They do not, however, simply establish systems and procedures and then retreat into them. Rather, they constantly reevaluate and reassess the requirements for success, as in GE's Work Out method. They use BENCHMARKING to test themselves against the best, borrowing opportunistically the BEST PRACTICES of competitors and well-managed non-competitors wherever and whenever possible. They carefully blend strategic decision-making with operational execution. They are uncompromising in their commitment to competitive success and develop a management style and system to support this commitment. They are also able to both institute continuous incremental change and make that quantum leap when considered necessary. As such, their leaders are prepared to make big and bold decisions, while planners are expected to provide insights for adapting the vision rather than mere descriptions.

Bibliography

Andrews, K. R. (1980). *The Concept of Corporate Strategy*. Homewood, IL: Irwin.

Bowman, E., Singh, H., and Thomas, H. (2002). The domain of strategic management: History and evolution. In A. Pettigrew, H. Thomas, and R. Whittington (eds.), *Strategy and Management*. London: Sage.

Gluck, F. W. (1986). Strategic management: An overview. In J. R. Gardner, R. Rachlin, and H. W. A. Sweeny (eds.), *Handbook of Strategic Planning*. New York: John Wiley.

Gluck, F. W., Kaufman, S. P., and Wallek, A. S. (1980). Strategic management for competitive advantage. *McKinsey Quarterly*, Autumn, 2–16.

Hofer, C. W. and Schendel, D. (1978). *Strategy Formulation: Analytical Concepts*. St. Paul, MN: West.

Hunsicker, J. Q. (1980). Can top managers be strategists? *Strategic Management Journal*, 1, 77–83.

Pettigrew, A., Thomas, H., and Whittington, R. (2002). Strategic management: The strengths and limitations of a field. In A. Pettigrew, H. Thomas, and R. Whittington (eds.), *Strategy and Management*. London: Sage.

Saloner, G., Shepard, A., and Podolny, J. (2001). *Strategic Management*. New York: John Wiley.

strategic planning

Derek F. Channon

Most corporations today have some form of corporate plan. However, very few are successfully implemented. In theory, strategic planning is the mechanism whereby the corporation organizes its resources and actions to achieve its objectives. It is a formal rather than an informal process, the usual contents of which are illustrated in table 1, while the process of strategic planning is illustrated in figure 1.

Planning will be conducted at hierarchical levels within the corporation, depending on its complexity. For the multibusiness firm, plans will be established at the corporate, business unit, and departmental or market segment levels.

At the corporate level, for example, the overall MISSION is established consistent with internal resources and external opportunities and threats. The direction in which the corporation will go is determined in large part by a corporate vision of where it would like to be. The CEO plays a

Table 1   Strategic plan components

Mission	Defines the present and desired position of the corporation. Similarly, a mission will apply at the business unit level.
Objectives	Qualitative and quantitative statements of what the corporation wishes to achieve over a measurable future. These should be internally consistent and fit the mission.
Goals	Specific short-and long-term quantitative results which directly support the objectives measured as key performance indicators. They should also reflect the critical successful factors for each business within the corporation.
Strategies	These will apply at both the corporate and business unit levels.

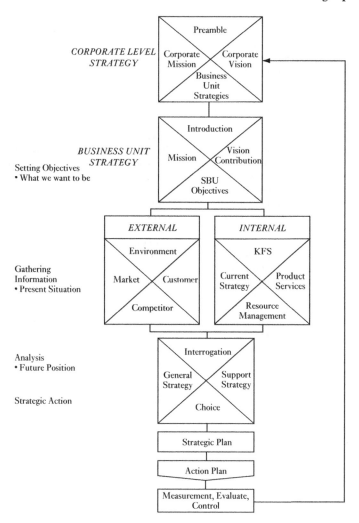

Figure 1   A strategic plan flowchart (Channon, 1994)

disproportionate role in the establishment of such a vision.

At the business unit level the concept of mission translates into the markets and activities that the business unit would like to address, subject to corporate-level constraints such as resource allocation. At the market segment level, mission is less ambitious and more constrained, being based on the scope of activities assigned to that segment. Similar cascades apply to the other elements of a plan, as shown in table 2. The system is an iterative process, involving a repetitious sequence of strategic developments, strategic planning, plan implementation, and strategic performance measurement. The cycle is normally repeated on an annual basis, with plan horizons tending to be around three years in western companies. Normally, the procedures are standardized with schedules also phased throughout the planning cycle. A typical cycle is illustrated in figure 2.

The main steps often consist of the following elements, although the precise timing and content vary from company to company.

Table 2   Hierarchical plan requirements

	Corporate level	*Business unit*	*Market segment level*
Mission	Corporate mission	Markets, activities assigned to divisional constraints	Scope of activities assigned to develop market segment
Objectives	Corporate objectives	SBU objectives supporting corporate objective	Segment objective
Assumptions	Specific to corporation capabilities, opportunities, threats	Specific to scope of divisional activities	Specific to market: demand, competition, service
Competitive strength	Corporate strength, weakness	SBU strength, weakness	Specific share, strength, weakness
Assessment of market opportunity		As evaluated and reviewed at all levels	
Market portfolio strategy	Overall corporate mix and priority, including new areas of interest	Mix for markets assigned to SBU	Specific investment priority for this segment
Changes desired in controllable variables	Attack plans for change in corporate capabilities	Attack plan for change in SBU capabilities	Attack plans to change factors
Programs to implement change, specific to corporation	Specific to corporation	Specific to SBU capabilities	Specific to segment
Expected financial results	Corporate financial measures	SBU financial measures	Segment financial measures

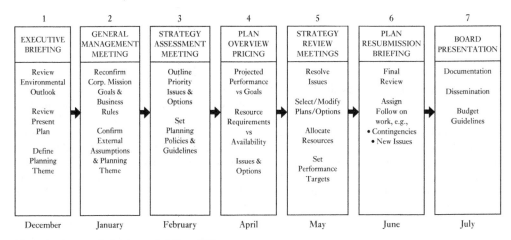

Figure 2   An annual planning cycle (King, 1986)

Executive briefing. The starting point of the plan commences with a senior management review, which includes:

- assumptions about the external environment;
- changes from previous assumptions;
- alternate futures/scenarios (*see* SCENARIO PLANNING);
- a review of progress against the existing plan and an update of performance against goals;
- a possible theme for the forthcoming plan cycle.

General management meeting. This establishes the mission, goals, and objectives of the corporation, and decisions reached are then broadly communicated to operating managers at business unit level and to other operating managers.

Strategy assessment meeting. Follow-up meetings are held between corporate and strategic business unit (SBU) executives to discuss issues and options, and policies and guidelines.

Plan overview. Plan submissions from SBUs are consolidated and reviewed with corporate management.

Strategy review meetings. The corporate center and SBU management negotiate to develop shared views on SBU plans by selecting strategic options, plan modifications, resource allocations, and performance targets.

Plan resubmission. Resubmitted plans by SBUs are then consolidated with any corporate-level adjustments and given a final review by corporate incentive management.

Board presentation. The final plan is then summarized in strategic terms, formally submitted to the board of directors for discussion, and usually approved.

The plan and planning cycle are never fully finalized in the sense that both internal and external events may cause them to change. Nevertheless, the plan should provide a blueprint for the development of the corporation over the next period of time.

One major consideration is the relationship between the plan and the budget. Theoretically, the two systems should coincide. However, many line executives tend to focus their attention more on the budget than the longer-term plan, and as a consequence there is often some cynicism about the plan unless it is clearly taken seriously by top management.

Interestingly, perhaps, the current literature on strategic management pays little attention to the practicalities of the mechanics of strategic planning, unlike in the 1970s, when formal systems were emphasized. Moreover, while during the 1980s many corporations built up substantial central planning units, these have lost considerable credibility, since line management believes that they are the operational component of the corporation needed to implement plans. In addition, many line managers believe that top management in the West has become relatively obsessed with short-term rather than long-term performance.

Interestingly, Japanese corporations have built significant planning departments. Employees in these departments, however, have rarely been trained as specialist planners; rather, they are assigned to planning departments as a regular element in their development, based on job rotation, and many come to such departments from anywhere in the company. While plans themselves tend to have a three-year time horizon, they are not seriously changed each year. Furthermore, such plans, all of which have a formal name, usually form elements in much longer-term "visions" established by the president of the corporation. These visions may have time horizons spanning 20 years or more, and rather than being driven by financial objectives, have broader technical and social goals.

Bibliography

Channon, D. F. (1986). *Bank Strategic Planning and Marketing.* Chichester: John Wiley.

Channon, D. F. (1994). Strategic management workbook. Working paper, Imperial College.

Chinn, W. D., Yoshihisa, M., and Vanderbrink, J. D. (1986). Strategic planning: A view from Japan. In J. R. Gardner, R. Rachlin, and H. W. A. Sweeny (eds.), *Handbook of Strategic Planning.* New York: John Wiley.

King, W. C. (1986). Formulating strategies and contingency plans. In J. R. Gardner, R. Rachlin, and H. W. A. Sweeny (eds.), *Handbook of Strategic Planning.* New York: John Wiley.

Toyohiro, K. (1992). *Long-Range Planning in Japanese Corporations.* Berlin: De Gruyter.

strategizing

John McGee

Strategizing has become a common word in the strategy lexicon, although it does not merit an entry in conventional dictionaries of the English language. In its simplest form it means the processes in the firm by which strategy is shaped (*see* STRATEGIC DECISION-MAKING; STRATEGIC PLANNING; STRATEGY; STRATEGY-MAKING), thus how goals are decided, what the scope of the firm should be, what COMPETITIVE ADVANTAGE should be constructed, and how the logic can be turned into practice.

STRATEGIZING AS STRATEGIC PLANNING

Strategizing has often been linked with strategic planning and has thus attracted the usual array of criticisms (Starbuck, 1992; Mintzberg, 1994). Following Starbuck's approach, these criticisms can be summarized under four main headings.

1 Planning is typically a formal process but formalization of planning undercuts its potential contributions.
2 Nearly all managers misperceive both their firms and their market environments.
3 No one can forecast accurately (enough) over the long term and thus strategy's consequences cannot be anticipated.
4 There is good reason to doubt that most firms will ever gain high profits from formal strategic planning.

Starbuck (and other authors) expands on this critique but also offers some rules-of-thumb suggestions for better strategizing. The remedy lies in preserving the essential uncertainty of the world in planning data and in planning for contingencies ("hope for the best, plan for the worst" is an old military axiom). Specifically:

1 Use simple forecasting methods, make sensible forecasts, and use them to motivate alertness to external conditions.
2 Exploit CORE COMPETENCES, entry barriers (*see* BARRIERS TO ENTRY AND EXIT) and market power, and proprietary information.
3 Broaden manager's horizons recognizing that the value of planning lies in its process,

which can signal contingencies, breadth of vision, depth of management inputs, and the value of internal routines and processes for effective implementation.
4 Inject realism – the planning process should educate managers.
5 Plan to change strategies later because forecasts are typically wrong. This means avoiding over-strong rationales that only serve to make behaviors inflexible, minimize formalization (because of the inherent magnitude of the potential errors), and emphasize informal communication (because it is better at reflecting reality and fostering understanding).

THE CONTRIBUTION OF CHAOS THEORY

The ideas of chaos theory have interesting implications for strategizing and any efforts that involve assessments of the future. The modern notion of chaos describes irregular and highly complex structures in time and space that *do* follow deterministic laws and equations, although these laws are often unknown. Chaos is not structureless – it only seems so because of our ignorance of the underlying logic. Chaotic systems are typically highly sensitive to initial conditions, thus leading to the well-known butterfly effect in which we see that not only are outcomes very sensitive to inputs, but the outcomes may also be highly unpredictable. This has implications for control of chaos in that excessive control can easily be destabilizing. It does not require too much imagination to speculate that firms in the modern economy may be subject to some of these characteristics. How should one approach the problem of controlling a non-linear dynamic system? Decision-makers can choose between types of model of the system to assist reasoning.

- Conceptual models use intuitive reasoning based on experience. They typically abstract the most relevant features from a sea of redundant information. They are very flexible in adapting to unforeseen changes and generalize to qualitatively new situations.
- Traditional analytical models try to anticipate as many factors as possible in as much detail as possible. Thereby they become very

inflexible and practically useless in surprise situations. These models are typically not very adaptive.

Chaos theory suggests the use of models with local, short-term predictability and high adaptability. Adaptability requires simple, low-dimensional, possibly intuitive models with fast and direct data access and efficient data retrieval and analysis capability (Mayer-Kress, 1995). If the hypercompetitive world of business is essentially "chaotic" in character (which it may be), then the strategizing approach should resemble the Starbuck conjectures above.

STRATEGIZING VS. ECONOMIZING

ECONOMIZING (Williamson,1991) behavior revolves around perfectly competitive equilibria where entrepreneurial profits are zero. Consequently, the best and only strategy for the firm is to pursue EFFICIENCY. This is a depressing and gloomy world for firms and for entrepreneurs. It has four assumptions:

1 that profits earned by firms capturing increasing returns from the reconfiguration of their value chains toward market conditions are reduced to zero in perfectly competitive equilibrium because constant returns prevail;
2 that profits earned by firms capturing synergies from their complementary resource bundles (*see* RESOURCE-BASED VIEW) are reduced to zero in perfectly competitive equilibrium because resources are perfectly substitutable;
3 profits earned by firms through treating markets as segmented are reduced to zero in perfectly competitive equilibrium because all customers are homogeneous; and
4 profits earned through innovation and learning are reduced to zero in perfectly competitive equilibrium because all technical possibilities are known and firms operate at these boundaries (i.e., no X-inefficiency).

In the world of strategizing firms we make different assumptions. Fundamentally, we take a disequilibrium approach where, in the absence of perfectly competitive equilibria, entrepreneurial profits can be made. We draw also on

three main perspectives or theoretical frameworks of competitive advantage. One is the market-based view (some call this the activity-based view; see Mathews, 2002, on whom much of this section is based) associated with Michael Porter, which seeks to locate competitive advantage in terms of industry position in relation to competitive forces where SUSTAINABILITY of advantage is achieved through creation of barriers to entry. The second is the resource-based view, which locates competitive advantages in terms of internal resources whereby advantage is defended through creation of resource barriers. The third is the STRATEGIZING ROUTINES perspective derived from Penrose (1959) and Nelson and Winter (1982). This was later supported by Teece, Pisano, and Shuen's (1997) dynamic capabilities approach. This focuses on the creation of advantage arising from the development of routines and processes that link resources and markets/activities. A holistic view of strategic advantage links these three perspectives together and thus provides a basis for describing strategizing formally.

Strategizing around markets and activities is the way firms strive to configure and reconfigure their value chains so as to capture increasing returns. The bundling of resources so as to capture synergies through complementarities is the focus of strategizing around resources. The emphasis lies on the overall bundle of resources because complementarities are available only in bundles. So it is the bundle as a whole that should conform to the conventional criteria of being valuable, rare, and hard to imitate. This was the original Penrosian insight that has been obscured in the conventional approach of the resource-based view (Mathews, 2002).

The twin firm-level concepts of resources and activities are tied together by routines (business processes). A prime function of management is to build routines through which resources are linked to activities, performance is monitored, and the routines are amended or modified as necessary. This has a clear dynamic element and incorporates organizational learning as an essential ingredient. Strategizing behavior here is the attention paid to the design of the architecture of routines, how discrete and low-level routines are monitored by and linked into higher-level routines.

Strategizing is about the management of the firm as a whole where a balance is struck between the market-focused activity set, the resources required, and the routines required to hold the firm together and to position it for future development. In this sense strategizing is not simply a business process like strategic planning. Nor is it a branch of futurology that might be consulted. It is a fundamental way of thinking about the future of a business. Strategizing behavior involves making creative changes in its configuration of activities, in the nature of its resource bundles, and in the routines and processes that link resources with activities.

Bibliography

Mathews, J. A. (2002). Strategizing vs. economizing: Theorizing dynamic competitive behavior in disequilibrium. Unpublished paper.

Mayer-Kress, G. (1995). www.santafe.edu/~gmkk? MFGB/node11.html; accessed July 15, 2004.

Mintzberg, H. (1994). The fall and rise of strategic planning. *Harvard Business Review*, January/February, 107–14.

Nelson, R. R. and Winter, S. G. (1982). *An Evolutionary Theory of the Firm*. Cambridge, MA: Harvard University Press.

Penrose, E. (1959/1995). *The Theory of the Growth of the Firm*, 3rd edition with new foreword by author. Oxford: Oxford University Press.

Starbuck, W. H. (1992). Strategizing in the real world. *International Journal of Technology Management*, special publication on Technological Foundations of Strategic Management, 8 (1/2), 77–85.

Teece, D. J., Pisano, G., and Shuen, A. (1997). Dynamic capabilities and strategic management. *Strategic Management Journal*, **18** (7), 509–33.

Williamson, O. E. (1991). Strategizing, economizing, and economic organization. *Strategic Management Journal*, **12**, special issue, Fundamental Research Issues in Strategy and Economics, 75–94.

strategizing routines

John McGee and Jonathan Menuhin

Routines are embedded, sanctioned behaviors. They adjust and evolve over time (Nelson and Winter, 1982). Routines as a concept are a way of expressing the conjunction of structure and process. In practice they are used to progress forward the administrative, operational, and strategic activities of an organization. *Strategizing routines* can be thought of as the natural, organic way in which an organization carries out its strategic thinking, STRATEGIC PLANNING, and the execution of strategic actions. Hence, in order to shape the firm's strategic path, it is important to better understand the firm's strategizing routines, to learn how to identify and characterize them, and to recognize both the potential and the limitations of their contribution to the development of the firm.

Nelson and Winter suggest that a firm's behavior is ruled by two levels of routines and a governance mechanism:

1   the operational routines that govern the short-run behavior of a firm and relate particularly to the use of production facilities;
2   the strategizing routines that determine "the period-by-period augmentation or diminution of the firm's capital stock." This second set of routines governs the strategic behavior of a firm and serves as a mediator between what are perceived as external variables (e.g., market conditions) and internal firm (state) variables (e.g., the organizational stock of machinery, knowledge, values, and techniques);
3   the governance mechanisms are "routine-changing processes."

There has been growing empirical evidence that routines can explain the heterogeneity between firms. Most of the empirical work on routines has been conducted with regard to operational routines. The main objective of these and other studies is to identify the knowledge or memory embedded in the firm's routines and to link this to observed differences in performance between firms.

Strategizing routines shape the long-term development of the firm. They include various types of routine, for example well-structured planning or budgeting routines or less structured product-oriented innovation routines. The strategy literature has long discussed the importance of the planning and budgeting processes for the long-term success of the firm. Nevertheless, it seems that these processes alone cannot explain the development of the firm, due to the limited ability of both planning and forecasting to anticipate and influence the future. Alternative approaches focus on the development of a product or technology. For example, Benghozi (1990) analyzes the innovation routines of France Telecom. He suggests that innovation routines consist of routines relating to "planning, monitoring scheduling and personnel movements and deployment function and so on" (Benghozi, 1990: 552). Moreover, his analysis highlights the explicit, formal process in which management arranges the organization in order to facilitate innovation.

Strategizing routines contribute to the firm's STRATEGY-MAKING because they store the firm's experience in such a way that it can be automatically used in new situations. They simplify the structure of decision-making processes and channel the organizational members into types of behavior that have brought the firm success in the past. The positive side of routines lies in capturing the firm's best practice (*see* BEST PRACTICES), thereby giving a sense of stability and control to the firm. However, routines also have a negative side. Over time, due to changes in the environment, gaps occur between the environment's requirements and the firm's capabilities. These gaps cause the firm's routines to become dysfunctional and to inhibit the development of the firm when they are applied to inappropriate situations.

The dysfunctional character of routines provides the basis for the dynamic processes of adjustment and evolution of routines. Nelson and Winter argue, in a somewhat deterministic manner, that the processes of change and the learning of new routines are configured in the firm's behavior. This inevitably narrows down the scope of the manager's actions. Although Nelson and Winter emphasize that there are managerial actions that are not considered to be routines, as they are not repetitive and can shape existing routines and create new ones, these events are rare and the process is difficult. This view shares a close affinity to population ecology, since it assumes that a firm cannot change its strategy or its structure easily or

quickly. Nevertheless, firms can and do learn new routines.

LEARNING NEW ROUTINES

New routines are built through experiential learning such as when members of the firm understand that the new context of operation is not adequate for the new situation, and a new type of behavior is needed. With the onset of realization that failure is linked to its routines, the firm begins to unlearn the ineffective routines. Unlearning is "a process through which learners discard knowledge" and opens up the opportunity for new learning to take place.

A firm derives its routines from its history and its experiences. Thus, routines serve as the memory in which the organization stores its "best practice." This raises the question of how the firm can learn new sets of routines. There are two main views, one cognitive, the other structural. The cognitive view emphasizes that learning occurs at an individual level, and thus research should focus on looking at individual perception and individual mental models. The structural view suggests that learning is an organizational phenomenon. Nonaka and Takeuchi (1995) combine these two views when they suggest that the knowledge-creation spiral begins within the individual and then proceeds through the socialization and integration processes, so that eventually the knowledge comes to be part of the organization. A similar view is suggested by Grant (1996) and Teece, Pisano, and Shuen (1997), who argue that learning occurs only at the individual level and not at the organizational level. However, learning involves "encoding inferences from history into routine" (Grant, 1996: 112). In that sense, we can identify an organization's learning through changes in its routines. This learning process might be described as a "sense-making" process (Weick, 1995), through which a firm's members construct a "common reality" that influences the way in which they seek to achieve an "objective" economic rationality.

Research offers sound explanations of how different operational routines lead to differences in performance. Research also has yielded some important theoretical insights on the key properties of strategizing routines. Nevertheless, since the discussion is conceptual, there is a need to explain what these strategizing routines actually consist of and how they shape the firm's strategy.

A Dynamic Capabilities Approach to Strategizing Routines

A comprehensive discussion of the nature of the organizational routines that shape the firm's strategy is found in Teece et al. (1997). They reject the term "routines" to describe the threads that link the firm's action in favor of "dynamic capabilities," since, according to them, the concept of routines "is a little too amorphous to properly capture the congruence amongst processes and between processes and incentives that we have in mind" (Teece et al., 1997: 520). However, their definition of dynamic capabilities as "the sub-set of the competences/capabilities which allow the firm to create new products and processes and respond to changing market circumstances" actually corresponds closely to the second set of routines set out by Nelson and Winter (1982). Eisenhardt and Martin (2000) link back the concept of dynamic capabilities to the routines as they argue that "Dynamic capabilities . . . are the organizational and strategic routines by which firms achieve new resource configurations as markets emerge, collide, split, evolve and die" (Eisenhardt and Martin, 2000: 1107).

Bibliography

Benghozi, P.-J. (1990). Managing innovation: From ad hoc to routine in French Telecom. *Organization Studies*, 11 (4), 531–55.

Eisenhardt, K. M. and Martin, J. A. (2000). Dynamic capabilities: What are they? *Strategic Management Journal*, 21, special issue, 1105–21.

Grant, R. M. (1996). Toward a knowledge-based theory of the firm. *Strategic Management Journal*, 17 (Winter), special issue, 109–22.

Menuhin, J. (2001). Strategizing routines analysis: The emergence of strategic initiatives. Unpublished PhD thesis, University of Warwick.

Nelson, R. R. and Winter, S. G. (1982). *An Evolutionary Theory of the Firm*. Cambridge, MA: Harvard University Press.

Nonaka, I. and Takeuchi, H. (1995). *The Knowledge-Creating Company*. New York: Oxford University Press.

Teece, D. J., Pisano, G., and Shuen, A. (1997). Dynamic capabilities and strategic management. *Strategic Management Journal*, 18 (7), 509–33.

Weick, K. (1995). *Sensemaking in Organization*. Thousand Oaks, CA: Sage.

strategy

John McGee

Strategy has always dealt with the future, usually a longish-term, rather uncertain future for which preparations have to be made, plans established, and actions taken together with provision for alternative actions should the future turn out to have unexpected characteristics. The word strategy itself derives from the Greek "strategos," meaning leader, reflecting military roots where strategy is concerned with "the science and art of military command as applied to large-scale combat operations" (*American Heritage Dictionary of the English Language*, 1992). Orientation to the future is an essential ingredient in the idea of strategy and we can best explore this by looking at the key characteristics of strategic decisions.

First, strategy is essentially about the future but quintessentially about that part of the future about which there is uncertainty. We don't plan for tomorrow because tomorrow is either essentially known and surprises are likely to be few, and/or there is little that can be done in preparation for tomorrow's surprise. What is important to us is how we might cope with an uncertain future by making preparations against future possibilities today.

Second, it follows that strategy is essentially about taking risk. We make preparations today against expected futures knowing that these futures might never materialize. Thus we plan to defend the country against floods and storms, not knowing when, if ever, storms and floods of critical magnitude might ever occur.

Third, strategic decisions are typically complex. The expected futures arise from complex social, technical, and other interactions. They are a joint product of many smaller events. Typically, the preparations and plans envisaged require the construction of complex assets (such as flood barriers or early warning weather forecasting systems), which themselves have a distinct risk of not working as required. These custom-built assets may require complex interactions between several human agencies. They may require extensive research and development.

Fourth, strategic decisions take time to bring to fruition and are irreversible. Strategy is typically delivered through capital investment that can take decades to complete. Investment is the process of creating assets customized for a specific purpose – once the process has begun, the assets cannot be deconstructed back to the original starting point.

Fifth, there is an internal logic attached to strategic decisions that requires the organization and coordination of large numbers of people within organizations. The intent is to create a STRATEGIC FIT between the resources and capabilities of the organization and the requirements asked of it. Strategic decisions typically require high degrees of coordination of activities and adaptation of behaviors.

Sixth, the future is uncertain with unknowable consequences, but strategies as bets against this uncertainty do have immediate implications for change that have at least some knowable (and often unpleasant) consequences. Thus, strategy makes demands that are often alarming and unpleasant, with further consequences none of which is conducive to the quiet life.

Finally, strategic decisions have significant scale and importance. They typically concern expenditures of large amounts of money in relation to our total resources. Thus a house purchase for a family is strategic in terms of the commitments out of income required to service the loan, whereas the purchase of a computer is much less strategic (but note that the control of multiple minor amounts of expenditure has strategic consequences if that control is ineffective). Strategic decisions are also important in that they may (or are intended to) make a big difference.

The classic definition of strategy is:

> the determination of the basic long-term goals and objectives of an enterprise, and the adoption of courses of action and the allocation of resources necessary for carrying out these goals. (Chandler, 1962: 13)

This definition stems from Alfred Chandler's seminal work on the development of large-scale enterprises in the American economy. It captures a sense of direction and plan of action and a sense of an organization being led toward its goal, but it is silent on issues of risk and uncertainty and only hints at the underlying complexities. A similar definition from another well-known American academic suggests more of the internal complexities: it is "a unified, comprehensive, and integrated plan designed to insure that the basic objectives of the enterprise are achieved" (Glueck, 1980).

Inherent in both definitions is the idea that strategy is the exercise of choice and the making of TRADE-OFFS between alternative courses of actions for the deployment of scarce resources. Missing from both definitions is a sense of the intrinsic uncertainty inherent in a modern economy, the situational complexity of different industries, and the variety of history and experience of real firms. Absent also is the notion that strategies might all be individual and situation specific, although consultants and academics do their best to search for regularities in experience and in the linkage of strategic behaviors to outcomes and performance.

A succinct way of describing strategy is shown in figure 1.

Step 1 requires a description of the underlying MISSION of the organization and the objectives (including financial performance) that it wants to achieve over a defined time horizon (see STAKEHOLDER ANALYSIS; STRATEGIC INTENT).

---

1   A clear set of long-term goals
    "Where are we going?"

2   The scope of the business
    "What are we going to do?"

3   Competitive advantage
    "How are we going to do it?"

4   The strategic logic
    "How do we know it will work?"

Figure 1 Describing strategy

Step 2 describes the scope of the organization – in which product markets does it choose to compete? Firms obviously cannot compete in any and every market. They must make some choices. However, the logic for making choices is not obvious in itself. Firms might choose to compete in closely related markets where, for example, the technologies and production methods are similar, where distribution channels are common, or where there are common customers for a range of products. But such "relatedness" or SYNERGY can be difficult to define or achieve and some firms have preferred to adopt more *conglomerate*-style approaches (*see* CONGLOMERATE STRATEGY) where the chosen businesses are apparently very diverse. Another facet of scope is geographic markets. Should one restrict the focus to the home market? Or are there arguments for adopting a more multinational posture? Ansoff's famous PRODUCT MARKET DIVERSIFICATION MATRIX shows the different types of DIVERSIFICATION. (*See* CORPORATE STRATEGY for an analysis of business portfolio choices.)

Step 3 articulates the benefits that the firm can bring to its customers and to itself by its positioning within its chosen product markets. Why should the customer buy this product? Why should he or she buy from us? What value can we gain from making this proposition to the customer? These are all ways of describing the nature of the COMPETITIVE ADVANTAGE that the firm can achieve.

This has implications for positioning choices in product markets. This takes us into step 4, the strategic logic behind competitive advantage. This has two parts. The first is the positioning logic – the market-based logic which underpins our competitive advantage ambitions. The second part is the *resource-based* logic (*see* RESOURCE-BASED VIEW) that states why we think our intentions and actions about resources and capabilities will lead to the products and services that can be positioned in markets in the desired way (*see* CORE COMPETENCES).

Bibliography

Chandler, A. P. (1962). *Strategy and Structure: Chapters in the History of the American Enterprise*. Cambridge, MA: MIT Press.

Glueck, W. F. (1980). *Business Policy and Strategic Management*. New York: McGraw-Hill.

strategy content

Taman Powell

The strategic content is the substance of a firm's STRATEGY. The strategic content is developed within the confines of the strategic context, with the view of taking advantage of the opportunities and minimizing the threats that are afforded the firm. There are numerous perspectives on how strategies should be and are developed (*see* DESIGN SCHOOL) and the concept of strategic content does not prescribe how the content should be developed.

Researchers have distinguished between three levels of strategy – business, multibusiness, and multinational – and have offered a typology for each. The dimensions used reflect the tensions of strategic choice. At the level of business strategy the dimension runs from cost-based to differentiation-based (cf. Porter's GENERIC STRATEGIES, 1980, 1985). At the multibusiness level (CORPORATE STRATEGY) there is tension between scale and scope, i.e., between vertical and horizontal specialization (in a way that Adam Smith would have recognized and George Stigler, 1951, would have analyzed) and vertical and horizontal integration, a process that Chandler described so vividly (1990). At the multinational level scholars such as Prahalad and Doz (1987) and Bartlett and Ghoshal (1989) distinguish between global integration and national responsiveness. This is an analogue of cost-based standardization versus differentiation at the business level.

Figure 1 presents a two-dimensional strategy space (S_1 and S_2) that can be used to represent these strategy tensions or TRADE-OFFS. The curved solid line represents a strategy frontier (in economics this would be an efficiency frontier) where those firms with best current practice (*see* BEST PRACTICES) are situated. Using this framework we can think of four different types of strategy with specific dynamic characteristics. *Improving and imitating* involves a move from within the frontier to a best practice

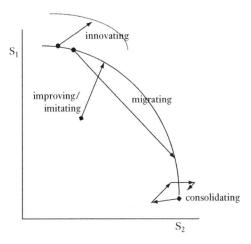

Figure 1 The dynamics of strategy content

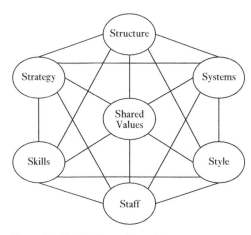

Figure 2 The McKinsey 7S model

position on the frontier. *Innovating* represents an attempt to move beyond the existing frontier to create a new best practice. *Migrating* is a shift of position from one strategy emphasis to another, such as moving from a cost-based strategy to a differentiation-based strategy. *Consolidating* is the shoring up and improving of an existing position, e.g., investing more in capital equipment to gain further ECONOMIES OF SCALE.

Practitioners, mostly consultants, have taken different views of the nature of strategy content. One of the more popular is the MCKINSEY 7S MODEL (Pascale, 1981). This model lists the seven factors that were believed to be critical for any strategy to include. These factors were based on research into Japanese management practice in the 1970s (see figure 2).

Another is the "enterprise transformation" model used by Andersen Consulting (now Accenture). This model proposes an approach of cascading the strategic intent of the organization into a number of different elements, these different elements then being implemented to deliver against the strategic intent (see figure 3).

Figure 3 The enterprise transformation model

Bibliography

Bartlett, C. and Ghoshal, S. (1989). *Beyond Global Management: Transnational Solutions*. Boston: Harvard Business School Press.

Chakravarty, B. S. and White, R. E. (2002). Strategy process: Forming, implementing and changing strategies. In A. Pettigrew, H. Thomas, and R. Whittington (eds.), *Handbook of Strategy and Management*. London: Sage.

Chandler, A. D. (1990). *Scale and Scope: The Dynamics of Industrial Capitalism*. Cambridge, MA: Belknap Press.

Pascale, R. T. (1981). *The Art of Japanese Management*. New York: Simon and Schuster.

Porter, M. E. (1980). *Competitive Strategy: Techniques for Analyzing Industries and Competitors*. New York: Free Press.

Porter, M. E. (1985). *Competitive Advantage: Creating and Sustaining Superior Performance*. New York: Free Press.

Prahalad, C. K. and Doz, Y. (1987). *The Multinational Mission*. New York: Free Press.

Stigler, G. J. (1951). The division of labor is limited by the extent of the market. *Journal of Political Economy*, **59**, 185–93.

strategy cycle

John McGee

STRATEGY is concerned with fashioning success in the long term, hence there is a performance dimension to the market-based view and the RESOURCE-BASED VIEW. This is demonstrated in figure 1, which shows how the real economy of the firm (the creation of resources and capabilities and the positioning within product markets) interacts with the financial economy of the firm. The top line shows schematically the transformation of "raw" assets (people, knowledge, and money) into resources and capabilities customized to create goods and services for the chosen product markets. The "output" of the real economy is cash flow conditioned by the scale of the COMPETITIVE ADVANTAGE achieved.

Competitive advantage has two dimensions, the extra value over competitors that customers receive, and the extra value in terms of real profits that are taken back into the firm. These profits, contained within the cash flow, are partitioned between those that are returned to shareholders and debt holders and those that are retained internally. The returns to shareholders and bondholders as dividends and interest payments serve to maintain the value of the firm in financial markets through two mechanisms. The first is the market value as represented by the share price, which itself is determined through the price earnings ratio by dividends and by shareholder expectations about future profitability. The second is the credit rating (e.g., an AAA rating by Standard and Poor's on the New York Stock Exchange), which influences the interest rates a company will have to pay for any new debt issues. Through these mechanisms the value of the firm and its financial capacity are established. Coupled with internal liquidity, this represents the ability of the firm to reinvest in resources and capabilities.

We can see the possibility of a virtuous circle in which the firm enjoys competitive advantage and superior profitability, has the financial capacity to reinvest in its assets, capabilities, and competences, from which it can further enhance its competitive advantage and its profitability, and so on. We can see also the possibility of a vicious spiral in which competitive disadvantage and poor profitability could be matched with limited financial capacity and consequent inability to reinvest to restore competitive advantage, and so on.

A key role for top management is to manage this balance between the firm's real and financial economy. The dynamics of markets and companies is such that there is rarely a balance; rather, there is continuous adjustment of the key decision variables so as to maintain competitiveness in markets, maintain cash flows, and maintain financial capacity. In this sense we see the firm as taking "actions" to influence the "context" in which it works in order to achieve superior "performance" (see figure 2). Context in this language has external dimensions such as markets and industry membership, and internal dimensions such as its assets and its ORGANIZATION STRUCTURE and processes. Strategy thus has a focus on actions to affect performance directly and indirectly through context.

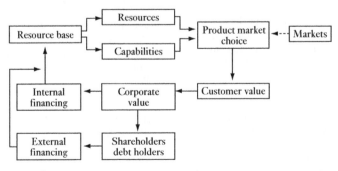

Figure 1   The strategy cycle

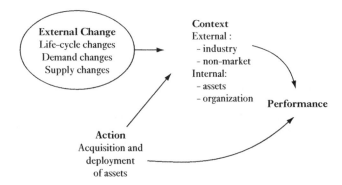

Figure 2 The dynamics of strategy

Bibliography

McGee, J., Wilson, D., and Thomas, H. (2005). *Strategy: Analysis and Practice*. Maidenhead: McGraw-Hill.

strategy-making

John McGee

How do strategies come about in practice? STRATEGY is essentially a practical subject and strategic decisions can be very individual in character. But we have also seen that the direction and purpose of the organization is very much the province of the general management team. On the other hand, the general managers cannot know everything. It is evident that strategy requires some form of directional input. This input might be to maintain continuity or momentum in strategy-making. It might be to create organizational frameworks within which strategy can be addressed. The kind of attention required by general managers can be understood through a simple distinction between *intended* and *emergent* strategies. Intended strategy refers to desired strategic direction deliberately planned or formulated, whereas emergent is the strategy or sequence of strategic decisions actually followed in practice. Mintzberg's notion of strategy is "a pattern in the stream of decisions." This idea enables us to see intentions as one source of patterning and (successful) emergence as another but equally valid source.

Intended strategies rest on systematic, comprehensive approaches to managing the whole business and are articulated through formal STRATEGIC PLANNING processes. This view of managerial intent includes the planning view, the command view, and the logical incremental view. The planning view (sometimes called the classical school) contains a logical sequence of activities, setting of objectives, the analysis of the environment and the resources of the organization, the generation of the strategic alternatives, and their evaluation. This has been codified in practice as SWOT ANALYSIS: analysis of strengths, weaknesses, opportunities, and threats in which the former two are matched against the latter two in order to obtain an appropriate STRATEGIC FIT. The command view is simply that of an autocratic leader. J. B. Quinn (1980) developed logical incrementalism as a way of explaining the combination of longer-term plans and targets with evolutionary, learning-based patterns of movement on the way. This is an attractive explanation because it seems to combine rational resource allocation thinking with practical learning by doing. Quinn argues that, "properly managed, it is a conscious, purposeful, pro-active, executive practice."

Emergent strategies are effective responses to unexpected opportunities and problems and are developed from the locations at which business-level strategies are usually implemented, i.e., within business units and not at corporate headquarters. The pure definition of emergence requires the absence of any intentions. This is too strong for most occasions but, as Mintzberg and Waters observe, organizations come close to pure emergent strategies when an environment directly imposes a pattern of actions on them.

The twin lens of intentions and emergence do come together mostly because neither as a pure form is likely to be observable. Instead there is a continuum on which different blends can be seen (figure 1). In this figure we see intentions being formulated as deliberate strategies, some of which come to fruition. But we also see a simultaneous pressure from circumstances producing a stream of emergent (but purposeful) thinking. *Realized strategy* is a blend of intentions and emergence which can be interpreted by reference to the strength of pressure from the external environment – a kind of environmental determinism. But it should also be interpreted in relation to the firm's strength of purpose in answering the four key questions (below) and thereby seeking to impose its will (its intentions) on the external environment.

STRATEGY-MAKING IN PRACTICE

The planning view of strategy (intended strategy) is not the only way of looking at strategy and, in the opinion of some, it might even be a distortion of the realities of strategic thinking and decision-making (*see* STRATEGIC DECISION-MAKING). Nevertheless, top–down strategic planning is still prevalent in many organizations and in very many cases one sees combinations of formal planning thinking with emergent, adaptive, and opportunistic activity.

Strategic management deals essentially with four questions:

1   How do we develop and formulate strategy?
2   How do we make choices between strategic options?

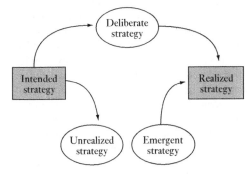

Figure 1   Intended and emergent strategies

3   How do put the strategy into operation and to sustain it over time?
4   How to manage the processes of strategic change and strategy renewal?

The first question raises issues of intended and planned strategies (typically top-down), versus emergent strategies that arise from experience and learning where the emphasis is on knowledge that is distributed throughout the organization, versus accidents, serendipity, and "muddling through" within which strategy is very much the junior partner to flexibility, operations expertise and tactical acumen, and speed of response.

The second question focuses on the nature of data and information required, the analytical processes used, and how TRADE-OFFS are made. It confronts the logic approach of economic and quantitative models with the uncertainty and risk endemic in long-term decisions and raises questions about criteria for decision-making and the nature and role of organizational influences.

The third question is widely regarded as the key to superior performance. This view is based on the nostrum that ideas are cheap but action is difficult. However, these questions are linked and, for example, difficulties in implementation are partly (not largely) to do with over-ambition and error in the first two parts. Nevertheless, implementation is distinctively difficult. It is complex in the range and the depth of detail, making operational planning and control highly complex. It often requires the adoption of path-breaking new knowledge beyond the known best practice (*see* BEST PRACTICES). Thus it is not clear that matters may not proceed as expected and contingencies have to be anticipated. If operational matters were clear cut and lacked complexity, it almost always follows that the strategy lacks distinctiveness and competitive advantage will not be attained. The points at which competitive advantage are delivered are generally through specific operations and activities. Where these are unique or at least new to the firm, successful implementation is clearly not assured. The issue of SUSTAINABILITY is to be seen in similar fashion. Keeping ahead of competitors involves continuous reinvestment and reappraisal of key operations. Thus the firm is continually having to prospect into new territory in order to keep ahead with all the risks and uncertainties that this implies.

The fourth question has provided significant employment and fee income for consultants. Strategies get out of date and performance suffers when markets change faster than organizations can respond. This gives rise to the need for strategic change and renewal. The management of strategic change has been one of the central practical and theoretical issues of the last 25 years. The era since 1979 has one of persistent and substantial external change resulting in radical changes to the business portfolios and activities of firms and to their traditional ways of doing business. The most common management responses have been to divest businesses and product lines (*see* DIVESTMENT) in order to refocus on sustainable core businesses (*see* CORE BUSINESS) in which competitive advantage can be pursued. The pressures for internationalization have been very strong and companies have used acquisitions, alliances, and organic growth in order to enter new markets (*see* ACQUISITION STRATEGY; MERGERS AND ACQUISITIONS; STRATEGIC ALLIANCES). This combination of retrenchment plus expansion has obliged firms to undertake major programs of change in which these changes in strategy have had to be matched by internal changes in ORGANIZATION STRUCTURE, habitual ways of doing business (culture), and management processes have also had to be adapted and reengineered (*see* BUSINESS PROCESS REENGINEERING).

Bibliography

McGee, J., Thomas, H., and Wilson, D. (2005). *Strategy: Analysis and Practice*. Maidenhead: McGraw-Hill.

Mintzberg, H. (1987). Crafting strategy. *Harvard Business Review*, **65** (4), 66–75.

Mintzberg, H. (1994). The fall and rise of strategic planning. *Harvard Business Review*, January/February, 107–14.

Mintzberg, H. and Waters, J. (1985). Of strategies, deliberate and emergent. *Strategic Management Journal*, **6**, 257–72.

Quinn, J. B. (1980). *Strategies for Change: Logical Incrementalism*. Homewood, IL: Irwin.

Whittington, R. (1993). *What is Strategy and Does It Matter?* London: Routledge.

strategy process

John McGee

The study of the processes of STRATEGIC MANAGEMENT (often summarized as strategy process analysis) is descriptive rather than prescriptive – it contains no suggestion that, because such processes exist, this is how they should be managed. Conversely, however, the prolonged survival of some types of strategic process implies a sustainable value and a reality of strategic development that has to be taken into account in any strategy-making endeavor. Some of the key facets of strategy processes are described below.

It is important to distinguish between *intended* strategy and *realized* strategy. This is particularly important in considering the fit between the external environment and strategy – it is likely that the fit with realized strategy is the more powerful.

Strategy also evolves *incrementally*. This means that change takes place through a process of continual, relatively small adjustments to existing strategy. This is most likely to be the case where there is an overall strategic direction and existing momentum that is persistent over time.

Formal planning processes may be important as an aid to analyzing strategic positions and strategic options but are not necessarily the processes by which strategy is actually developed. Very often managers are likely to assess the need for strategic change through essentially qualitative assessments of strong and/or weak signals that may have accumulated from inside or outside the environment. Thus dispassionate analysis of data (required by formal planning) may be the exception rather than the rule. Process views give more emphasis (1) to the perceptions of what (powerful) individuals in the organization see as important, and (2) on managers' reconciliations of the circumstances of the present with past experience and the received wisdom encapsulated in the core assumptions and beliefs of the organization. Therefore the *cultural web* of an organization – its political structures, routines, and rituals and symbols – is likely to exert a preserving and legitimizing influence on the core beliefs and assumptions that impede strategic change.

With such powerful forces of inertia mounted within the organization, it may become out of line with a changing organization leading to a process of continual weakening of STRATEGIC FIT: this is called *strategic drift*. Where strategic drift has accumulated over time, the gap between the external environment and the existing realized strategy may become so profound as to require fundamental or transformative strategic change. Where external environments are themselves unpredictable and discontinuous, then formal analysis of data may also be contraindicated and the reliance on managerial experience and on flexible learning organizations becomes especially important.

See also *strategic decision-making; strategic intent; strategic planning; strategizing; strategy content; strategy cycle; strategy-making*

Bibliography

Johnson, G. (1992). Managing strategic change: Strategy, culture and action. *Long Range Planning*, **25** (1), 28–36.
Mintzberg, H. (1987). Crafting strategy. *Harvard Business Review*, **65** (4), 66–75.
Mintzberg, H. (1994). The fall and rise of strategic planning. *Harvard Business Review*, January/February, 107–14.
Mintzberg, H. and Waters, J. (1985). Of strategies, deliberate and emergent. *Strategic Management Journal*, **6**, 257–72.
Pettigrew, A. M., Ferlie, E., and McKee, L. (1992). *Shaping Strategic Change*. London: Sage.
Porter, M. E. (1986). What is strategy? *Harvard Business Review*, November/December, 61–78.
Quinn, J. B. (1980). *Strategies for Change: Logical Incrementalism*. Homewood, IL: Irwin.

structuring organizations

Derek F. Channon

Mintzberg has suggested that an organization consists of five basic components that differ in size and importance. These components are illustrated in figure 1.

The first component, the *operating core*, consists of those personnel who undertake the basic work of the organization which is related directly to operations or the production of products/services. This component conducts four key functions:

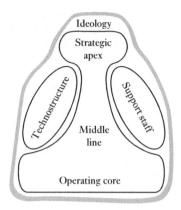

Figure 1   Five basic parts of the organization (Mintzberg, 1989)

- securing inputs;
- transforming inputs into outputs;
- distributing outputs;
- providing direct support to the production process.

The second main component is the *strategic apex*. This consists of managers responsible for the overall direction of the corporation. They manage the organization to achieve the objectives of those who own or control it. Their primary functions are as follows:

- direct supervision, resource allocation, structure planning and control system design, conflict resolution, and STRATEGIC DECISION-MAKING;
- managing and monitoring relations with the external environment;
- formulating organizational strategy.

The third component is the *middle line*. This comprises the chain of managers with formal authority and connects the apex with the operating core. Historically it was seen as essential, because the apex could not directly supervise all the line operators. In addition, the middle line:

- provides feedback to the hierarchy about performance in the operating core;
- makes some basically operational decisions and allocates some resources;

- manages the relations of business units or functions with the external environment.

As a result of reengineering (*see* BUSINESS PROCESS REENGINEERING; REENGINEERING DISADVANTAGES; VALUE-DRIVEN REENGINEERING) and the adoption of the horizontal structure, the role of the middle line has come under serious threat, as the span of control of the apex has been considerably enlarged as a result of improved IT systems. Moreover, there is some feeling amongst senior management in firms with operating horizontal structures that middle line managers act as an often undesirable block on the information flow between the apex and operations.

The fourth organizational component, *support staff*, provides support for line operations and includes functions such as property, social affairs, legal industrial relations, payroll management, and accounting. Historically, support staff were added to enable the firm to gain greater control over boundary activities in order to reduce perceived risk and uncertainty. These activities were usually loosely coupled to core processes and could be located at various levels in the hierarchy.

As the size and scope of support staff numbers and duties have come under serious scrutiny in many corporations as part of reengineering projects and cost-reduction drives, many concerns are turning to OUTSOURCING as an alternative to operating their own support functions. While this poses no serious threat in non-technical areas, a number of strategic and/or specialized functions have been outsourced, including computer systems.

The final component is the *technostructure*. This consists of analysts who evaluate and influence the work of others. Many technostructure personnel are control specialists who attempt to increase the level of operational standardization, so reducing the level of skill required in the operating core. Three types of analysts are identified:

- work study analysts, whose task is to standardize work processes;
- planning and control analysts, who attempt to standardize outputs such as planning, budgeting, and quality systems;

- personnel analysts, who seek to standardize organizational skills via training and recruitment.

In order to accomplish the total task of the organization, it is also necessary to integrate the activities of the key components. Mintzberg identifies five specific coordinating mechanisms that help to achieve this:

- mutual adjustment – whereby work is coordinated through direct informal communication between related personnel;
- direct supervision – a formal mechanism whereby an individual or manager is given authority over and takes responsibility for the work of others and for monitoring their activities;
- standardization of work processes – whereby the content of work is specified or programmed;
- standardization of outputs – which insures that the results of work conforms to predetermined standards and specifications;
- standardization of skills – which is accomplished via appropriate training and recruitment.

Bibliography

Galbraith, J. K. and Nathanson, D. A. (1980). *Strategy Implementation*. St. Paul, MN: West.

Mintzberg, H. (1979). *The Structuring of Organizations*. Englewood Cliffs, NJ: Prentice-Hall.

Mintzberg, H. (1989). *Mintzberg on Management*. New York: Free Press.

substitute products

Stephanos Avgeropoulos

Substitutes are goods or services that are consumed instead of one another. They can be identified by their positive cross-price ELASTICITY of demand (i.e., the quantity demanded for one product increases as the price of the other increases). Two products can be strong or weak substitutes, according to how easy it is to switch between the two, although substitutability is a continuous measure, and the distinction between the two is quite arbitrary. COMPLEMEN-TARY PRODUCTS are consumed together, and have a negative cross-price elasticity of demand.

Products offered by the same company can be substitutes, as can products offered by different companies in the same industry, or even those offered by different companies in different industries. There is no requirement that substitutes are in any way similar as far as their producers are concerned, except that they must broadly fulfill the same purpose as far as their buyer is concerned. Not only is the Channel Tunnel a substitute for ferry boats, therefore, and fizzy water for still water, but also restaurants for cinema, as they both often compete for the same entertainment budget.

Perhaps the most important function of substitutes is that they enhance the competitive forces in the industries concerned. By allowing the buyer to compare the attributes of the products involved, and switch between the two, the manufacturers or service providers involved are kept in check in terms of the prices they can charge, and the quality, performance, and other attributes of the products. Although good for competition, this may act to the detriment of the firms involved. Indeed, the threat from substitute goods is one of the forces in Porter's five forces model (see INDUSTRY STRUCTURE).

Another importance of substitutes lies in the fact that a measure of the degree of substitutability can be helpful in determining the likely impact on pricing and demand of a change in prices of a substitute product, whether under the control of the same firm or not.

MEASURING THE THREAT FROM
SUBSTITUTES

The strength of this danger for any given product is related to the cost, price, quality, and performance of the substitute, the buyer's propensity to switch, and his or her SWITCHING COSTS. These must be evaluated over the entire lives of the products concerned, as the running and maintenance costs of certain products are much higher than their initial purchase costs.

Even where switching costs for any individual buyer are prohibitive, the threat from substitutes remains. The costs of changing between electricity and gas for industrial and domestic heating, for example, are such as to lock in many con-sumers once they have made their initial investment in equipment. Over the long term, however, the two energy sources are substitutes for each other and as purchasing decisions are repeated (perhaps by other buyers), switching costs become less relevant and it is the attributes of the substitutes themselves that maintain the two industries in balance, and deserve the most attention.

When evaluating the threat of substitution, the entire value chain of the buyer must be looked at. In addition, covert threat from substitution can also be the result of substitution further downstream, a good secondary market for recycled or reconditioned goods or, at the extreme, from the buyer no longer requiring the product at all, or manufacturing it personally or performing its function internally. The threat of substitution varies by geographic area, product varieties, buyer segment, and channel.

In general, the number of substitutes in an industry increases over time, with young industries often tending to have fewer substitutes. As far as the proactive development of substitutes is concerned, it is often observed that substitutes are attracted by industries earning high profits. Substitute-producing industries are likely to enter into another market and become a threat if they become more competitive in their own right, or if they are still financially healthy although they have been forced out of their industry, and the target industry appears more accommodating. Early indication of substitute products which are about to become significant may be provided by growing sales and profits, and (planned) capacity growth.

IMPLICATIONS FOR STRATEGY

Substitute analysis can be used proactively in three main ways: to defend an industry's position if it is threatened by them; to increase its sales if it is producing them; or to determine their pricing if it is involved in the marketing of a range of products acting as substitutes for one another.

Where substitutes limit a company's flexibility, an attempt to develop strategies to minimize their influence will have to be made. This can be done by: (1) modifying the product's image, e.g., by means of differentiation in product design, innovation, quality enhancement, and careful marketing; (2) redefining competition away from the strengths of the substitute (e.g., by focusing on service rather than price); (3) finding new, unaffected uses for the original product; (4) raising buyer switching costs; or (5) in the short term, acting opportunistically to counter any attempts by competitors to enter the market. Retaining customers while a more fundamental improvement is being searched for along the lines of the above methods is more important where switching back costs are high. In addition, (6) other firms adversely affected by the substitute, such as competitors, suppliers, and other stakeholders, can be encouraged to organize themselves and help with the defense by such means as industry-wide advertising or R&D, the enforcement of standards, or getting regulatory or legislative approval or protection. Otherwise, the company may decide to enter the substitute industry itself, putting the company's future ahead of the business unit's, or to exit from that area entirely if it has become too unattractive.

In order to promote substitution, on the other hand, a firm may help its product by: (1) aggressively targeting the likely early switchers on the basis that it is they who will influence the subsequent take-up of the product, SIGNALING to them necessary information about the new product, and trying to lower their switching costs, and perhaps even subsidising them; (2) integrating forward in a limited way to create demand from the end users (especially where these face lower switching costs than any intermediate buyers), informing them, or helping them to lower their switching costs, or inducing limited backward integration to bypass intermediate parties unwilling to take on the new substitute; (3) insuring adequate capacity, perhaps in combination with other companies, to assure prospective buyers that this is a strong industry on which they can rely for a long time after switching; (4) promoting investment in complementary goods; or (5) otherwise acting to enlarge the substitute's market. The speed of entry is a function of barriers to entry (see BARRIERS TO ENTRY AND EXIT). Where there are first-mover advantages (see FIRST-MOVER ADVANTAGE), early entry on a large scale and the setting up of protective barriers is warranted, while if the firm faces high barriers, then it may be best to attack the high-value segments first.

As far as the management of product line substitutes is concerned (i.e., where a firm chooses to produce a number of products that may act as substitutes for one another), then the optimal rates of output for each good will be less than the rates that would maximize profits if there was no demand interdependence, as sales of one good preclude sales of the other.

Bibliography

Porter, M. E. (1979). How competitive forces shape strategy. *Harvard Business Review*, **57**, 2, (March/April), 137–45. Reprinted with deletions in H. Mintzberg and J. B. Quinn (1991). *The Strategy Process: Concepts, Contexts, Cases*, 2nd edn. Englewood Cliffs, NJ: Prentice-Hall, pp. 61–70.

Porter, M. E. (1980). *Competitive Strategy: Techniques for Analyzing Industries and Competitors*. New York: Free Press.

Porter, M. E. (1985). *Competitive Advantage: Creating and Sustaining Superior Performance*. New York: Free Press.

sunk costs

Taman Powell

Sunk costs are costs that have occurred and are not recoverable. An example of sunk costs could be advertising or research and development expense.

Sunk costs can be an effective barrier to entry (*see* BARRIERS TO ENTRY AND EXIT). If high sunk costs are required to enter a particular industry, new potential entrants may be more hesitant about entering than would otherwise be the case. The converse is also true. In the absence of sunk costs being required to enter an industry, firms may be able to easily enter and leave an industry. This could result in greater competition in the industry and lower profits to participants.

While it is important to consider the opportunity cost of an investment (*see* COST ANALYSIS), it is equally important to realize that sunk costs are lost and should not be considered in future investment decisions. As Peter Drucker commented in a popular *Harvard Business Review* article (1963):

> And while the job to be done may look different in every individual company, one basic truth will

always be present: every product and every activity of a business begins to obsolesce as soon as it is started. Every product, every operation, and every activity in a business should, therefore, be put on trial for its life every two or three years. Each should be considered the way we consider a proposal to go into a *new* product, a new operation or activity – complete with budget, capital appropriations request, and so on. One question should be asked of each: "If we were not in this already, would we now go into it?" And if the answer is "no," the next question should be: "How do we get out and how fast?"

Bibliography

Drucker, P. F. (1963). Managing for business effectiveness. *Harvard Business Review*, 41 (53).

sustainability

John McGee

Sustainability refers to the extent to which COMPETITIVE ADVANTAGE can be maintained over time. It may be regarded as normal that competitive forces will serve to erode competitive advantage over time through imitation and/or innovation. When the sources of competitive advantage resist competition, then the competitive advantage is said to be sustainable.

Positional advantage arises from the ability of a firm to locate itself in a position within an industry where it can resist the forces of competition and erect firm-specific entry barriers from which it can deliver a superior value proposition to customers and make above-average profits. Such positional advantage can be eroded in the following circumstances.

1   *A competitor can move into the same position and offer at least an identical-value proposition to the customer.* In the face of direct competitive challenge, sustainability depends on the strength of the underlying cost position and the strength of product differentiation. The cost position is the stronger for the presence of scale and scope effects that are large relative to the marketplace, thereby requiring significant and risky investments by competitors who wish to imitate. The strength of differentiation lies in the goodwill attached to the brand (or product) in the market in the sense that switching would require the new competitor to provide superior value before switching would take place. A good example of sustainability was the ability of Xerox in its photocopying business to defend itself against direct attacks by Kodak and IBM. Its position was defended by two (at least) barriers that proved insurmountable. One was the wall of patents that made it difficult and costly for new entrants to directly imitate the Xerox process. Second, the worldwide spread of service and distribution centers made it difficult for IBM and Kodak to challenge on either a global basis or a niche basis without making comparable investments. Similar examples are IBM 's installed base in mainframe computers and Microsoft's installed base of users of PC operating systems. Imitators find it difficult to imitate at a comparable level of cost.

2   *The position itself might lose its value.* A typical example is the lowering of trade barriers that results in incumbents being (suddenly) exposed to competition in such a way that the level of increased competition reduces prices and profits. Saloner, Shepard, and Polodny (2001) quote the example of domestic banks in Korea being historically able to exploit their position as domestic firms to earn attractive returns. As trade barriers were lowered, these firms found they had no advantage to protect themselves – the value of their position was destroyed when entry became possible. In the UK pay-TV (satellite) market, the battle between British Satellite Broadcasting (BSB) and Sky Television was one for position in a natural monopoly. The degree of increasing returns meant that the position itself was immensely valuable but only one company could occupy it – and then its position was likely to be highly sustainable. In the event Sky won, absorbed BSB, and became BSkyB and has continued as a powerful competitor in the pay-TV market (Maude, 2004).

Resource-based advantage rests on the key resources being expensive, difficult to imitate, and durable (Peteraf, 1993). Sustainability rests on the level of protection around these key resources. The argument for sustainability is stronger the more the key resources as a collective bundle are the differentiating feature and collectively difficult to imitate. The Prahalad and Hamel (1990) view of core competence (*see* CORE COMPETENCES) is as a collective asset of the corporation (see also Mathews, 2002). The difficulty of imitation is high where the firm has spent much effort in exploring resource complementarities and designing synergies. These core competences (or distinctive assets) are complex in character. This character of complexity has very many tacit elements and is thus difficult to define and imitate. Moreover, the routines (business processes) by which these core competences have been designed, implemented, and maintained are themselves firm specific, often tacit in nature, and difficult to imitate. The combination of complexity of core competence and complexity of supporting business processes creates a causal ambiguity which shrouds the source of advantage in mystery. Hence such core competences can be sustainable in nature.

See also *resource-based view; strategizing; strategizing routines*

Bibliography

Ghemawat, P. (1986). Sustainable advantage. *Harvard Business Review*, September/October, 53–8.

Mathews, J. A. (2002). Strategizing vs economizing: Theorizing dynamic competitive behavior in disequilibrium. Unpublished paper.

Maude, I. (2004). BSkyB: Embracing the digital revolution. Warwick Business School case study.

Peteraf, M. A. (1993). The cornerstones of competitive advantage: A resource-based view. *Strategic Management Journal*, 14 (2), 179–91.

Prahalad, C. K. and Hamel, G. (1990). The core competence of the corporation. *Harvard Business Review*, May/June, 79–91.

Saloner, G., Shepard, A., and Polodny, J. (2001). *Strategic Management*. New York: John Wiley.

sustainable growth rate

Derek F. Channon

A company's sustainable rate of growth depends in part on, and is limited by, the rate at which it can generate funds that can be invested to achieve growth targets while at the same time paying interest and dividends, accounting for depreciated assets and inflation. The sources of these funds are generally retained earnings, debt, and new equity capital. Improved EFFICIENCY, which reduces capital intensity by superior asset turnover and greater productivity, can also be an important source of new funds for growth.

Debt, risk, dividend, and return policies and intentions should therefore be determined before overall corporate goals are established. These factors will essentially determine the limits to growth. The sustainable growth rate of the firm can then be calculated as follows.

The rate of growth is equal to the firm's return on equity if no dividends are paid. This is the rate of return (profit) less interest on debt, as follows:

$$\text{profit} = r\,(TA) - iD$$

where r is the rate of return, TA is the total assets, i is the interest rate, and D is debt. Since total assets are equal to the sum of debt and equity (E), their expression may be rewritten as:

$$\text{profit} = r\,(D + E) - iD$$

or

$$\text{profit} = rD + rE - iD$$

Dividing through by E, this becomes:

$$\text{profit/equity} = (D/E)(r - i) + r$$

or

$$\text{growth rate } (g) = (D/E)(r - i) + r$$

However, the payment of dividends reduces this rate of growth due to the disbursement of funds.

The effect of dividend payout can be accounted for by multiplying the expression by the percentage of earnings retained by p, the dividend payout ratio. The growth formula thus becomes:

$$g = (D/E)(r - i)p + rp$$

Each of the financial variables in the growth formula can be used strategically to influence the growth rate of the firm. The sensitivity of the growth rate to the key variables of rate of return, interest rate paid, the debt : equity ratio, and the dividend payout ratio is demonstrated in table 1. In the table each of these variables has been changed in turn by 10 percent with other variables remaining constant.

As expected, the most sensitive variable is return on assets. Most surprising for most observers is that the dividend payout ratio is the second most powerful variable, and not the debt : equity ratio. Interest rates tend to be relatively inconsequential. As a result, a significant increase in the debt : equity ratio may be a viable strategic alternative, even if higher interest rates are incurred as lenders perceive the firm as be-

coming more risky. Interestingly, perhaps, high leverage has been a significant reason behind the success of Japanese corporations, where the strength of the yen has also provided low rates of interest. Similarly, reduced dividend payment ratios help to accelerate corporate growth – again a characteristic of Japanese concerns. Indeed, by operating with a high debt : equity, a low dividend payout ratio, and constant attention to improved asset turnover – the inverse of lower capital intensity – Japanese companies have been able to achieve superior investment performance compared to their nearest US counterparts during the past three decades.

The relationship between financial strategy and MARKET SHARE growth suggests several important conclusions: high margins do not necessarily indicate an attractive business while reported earnings are not always meaningful. However, since most managers perceive margins as an indication of market attractiveness, the aggressive-growth firm might seek to keep margins down in order to discourage competitive market entry.

Firms using debt aggressively and reducing dividend payouts can both cut price relative to competitors and finance an increase in market share. Provided that such growth achieves a satisfactory return, greater than the cost of equity, such a policy also builds shareholder value.

Table 1   Sensitivity analysis of four variables influencing corporate growth rate

Variable	Growth rate	Growth rate in response to 10% change in variable
Earning power		
6.3%	4.8%	
7.0%	5.5%	12.7%
7.7%	6.2%	
Interest rate		
3.3%	5.35%	
3.0%	5.50%	2.7%
2.7%	5.65%	
Debt: Equity ratio		
0.9:1	5.30%	
1.0:1	5.50%	3.6%
1.1:1	5.70%	
Dividend payout		
45%	4.95%	
50%	5.50%	10.0%
55%	6.05%	

Source: Boston Consulting Group (1971)

Bibliography

Boston Consulting Group (1971). *Growth and Financial Strategies*. Boston: Boston Consulting Group.
Rowe, A. J., Mason, R. O., Dickel, K. E., Mann, R. B., and Mockler, R. J. (1994). *Strategic Management*, 4th edn. Reading, MA: Addison-Wesley, pp. 375–6.

switching costs

Stephanos Avgeropoulos

Switching costs are the fixed costs that buyers face in order to change between SUBSTITUTE PRODUCTS (the costs of changing suppliers are typically excluded from the definition).

Switching costs arise from all impacts that a substitute can have on the buyer's value chain, including any linkages with the supplier's value chain. They can be the result of investment by the buyer in high-cost specialized equipment, investment in learning how to operate such equipment, or even the result of product specifications which tie the buyer to particular inputs.

Typical switching costs include the costs of identifying, evaluating, and testing the substitute, the costs of product or process redesign, the costs of purchasing additional equipment, employee retraining costs, and the costs of the technical help needed to effect the changeover. Other, indirect, costs may arise from the changing role of the user: these include resistance to the substitute, and the cost of failure, which includes any costs incurred in switching back.

Switching costs typically change and fall over time. Early adopters of a new substitute have to develop their own technologies, procedures, and standards, and so – in effect – they subsidize subsequent adopters, who may find it easy to copy the early work. Similarly, products and processes using substitutes can be redesigned to reduce the costs, and thus increase the demand for and acceptability of the substitute, and reduce its costs. The propensity to switch can also change over time, as success with a substitute will induce other companies to try it.

As switching costs can lock in buyers, they constitute effective barriers to entry (*see* BARRIERS TO ENTRY AND EXIT), so they are pursued by the company which already has the business, and reduced by the company which aspires to win the business. Establishing high switching costs, however, may foster inflexibility. IBM, for example, has long strived to make its systems incompatible with those of any other supplier. This strategy has meant that repeat business was almost guaranteed, but as open systems became more commonplace, buyers were reluctant to purchase IBM products for fear that they would be unduly restrained by the company. To overcome switching costs, suppliers of substitute goods may initially have to offer buyers considerable price concessions or extra quality of service, which can mean lower profit margins.

Bibliography

Porter, M. E. (1979). How competitive forces shape strategy. *Harvard Business Review*, **57**, 2, (March/April),

137–45. Reprinted with deletions in H. Mintzberg and J. B. Quinn (1991). *The Strategy Process: Concepts, Contexts, Cases,* 2nd edn. Englewood Cliffs, NJ: Prentice-Hall, pp. 61–70.
Porter, M. E. (1980). *Competitive Strategy: Techniques for Analyzing Industries and Competitors.* New York: Free Press.
Porter, M. E. (1985). *Competitive Advantage: Creating and Sustaining Superior Performance.* New York: Free Press.

SWOT analysis

Derek F. Channon

An acronym of strengths, weaknesses, opportunities, and threats, SWOT analysis provides a simple but powerful tool for evaluating the strategic position of the firm. It is especially useful for senior executives undertaking a fundamental reappraisal of a business, in that it permits a free-thinking environment, unencumbered by the constraints often imposed by a finance-driven budgetary planning system. It also allows a test of perceived common purpose within an organization when carried out at various levels within the firm. The requirements for undertaking such an analysis are relatively simple and, at the end of the exercise, key information needs can usually be identified which might prove to be the subject of further research.

A list of common strengths, weaknesses, opportunities, and threats is shown in table 1. This list is not comprehensive and other critical factors may be identified. In terms of usage, executives may be divided into groups to initially identify – first as individuals and second as groups – their views as to the firm's SWOT. It may well be useful to focus on only a prioritized list of these and also to assess the cross-impacts of strengths and weaknesses on threats and opportunities, utilizing a form such as that shown in figure 1.

For strategy formulation, the firm attempts to build upon its strengths and eliminate its weaknesses. When the firm does not possess the skills required to take advantage of opportunities or avoid threats, the necessary resources needed may be identified from the SWOT analysis and steps taken to procure the strengths or to reduce any weaknesses.

Table 1   SWOT analysis – potential key factors

Potential strengths	Potential weaknesses
Core skills	Lack of strategic direction
Adequate finances	Obsolete plant
Good customer perception	Weak IT systems
High market share	Weak control systems
High productivity	Lack of finance
High product/service quality	Lack of management skills
Low production costs	Internal power struggle
Superior R&D	Weak marketing skills
High innovation record	Lack of raw material access
Good top management	Poor access to distribution
Proprietary technology	High cost structure
Access to distribution	Poor product quality
Political protection	Poor record on innovation
Well established strategy	Others?
Others?	
Potential opportunities	Potential threats
Entry to new markets/segments	New low-cost competitors
Diversification to related activities	Technological substitutes
Vertical integration (forward or backward)	Slow growth
High growth prospects	New regulatory requirements
Export markets	Foreign exchange rates
Weak competitors	Bargaining power of customers/suppliers
Government contracts	Adverse demographic shift
Deregulation	Vulnerability to recession
Others?	Changing consumer needs
	Others?

Bibliography

Channon, D. F. (1986). *Bank Strategic Management and Marketing*. Chichester: John Wiley.

Channon, D. F. (1994). *Strategic Management Workbook*. Imperial College London, pp. 87–9.

Thompson, A. and Strickland, A. J. (1993). *Strategic Management*, 7th edn. New York: Irwin.

synergy

Derek F. Channon

As originally conceived by Ansoff, synergy was seen as one of the major components in a firm's product market strategy. It was the extra value added achieved when two businesses were integrated together such that the sum of the whole was greater than that of the constituent parts. It was popularly described as "2 + 2 = 5." The concept lost some credibility when expected synergistic effects were found to be elusive, and it became said that in many situations "2 + 2 = 3." More recently, the term has tended to be less widely used, its nearest modern equivalents being *relatedness* and STRATEGIC FIT.

Ansoff classified synergy in terms of the components of the formula for return on investment:

- *Sales synergy.* This could occur when products used common distribution channels, sales administration, or warehousing. Similarly, a full line of related products enhanced sales force efficiency, while advertising, promotion, and reputation were also enhanced.
- *Operating synergy.* This occurred as a result of higher facilities and staff utilization rates, spreading of overheads, shared experience effects, and greater purchasing power.

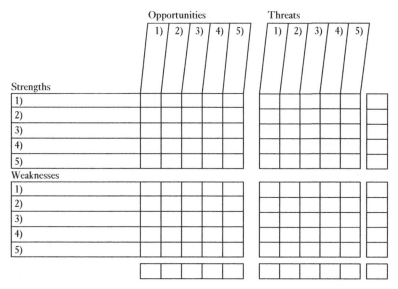

Figure 1 SWOT analsyis

- *Investment synergy.* This could result from joint use of plant, common raw materials stocks, R&D transfers, a common technology base, and common plant and equipment.
- *Management synergy.* Less apparent than the other forms of synergy, management synergy was seen as an important element in the total synergy effect. This could come about when entry into a new industry allowed managers to transfer their skills into industry structures and problems similar to those experienced in the firm's original areas of business expertise.

However, if problems in an acquired business are not familiar, not only can positive synergy be low, but it can actually have a negative effect. Ansoff has recognized, in a more recent version of his original work, that management synergy quickly becomes negative when a firm diversifies into a product market area in which environmental turbulence is significantly different from that to which it has historically been accustomed.

Ansoff originally did not discuss financial synergy, which has been reported elsewhere as the most easy form to release. For example, blending two balance sheets together is easily achievable and quick. Other functional synergies are much more difficult to release and, due to internal organizational conflicts and incompatible cultures, may never be attained.

Ansoff also differentiates between *startup synergy* and *operating synergy*. In the startup phase, apart from identifiable physical costs, such as facilities and working capital, there are one-off costs associated with setting up a new business, such as the creation of a new organization, new hirings, errors made due to lack of familiarity with the new business, and costs of establishing awareness in the market. Most of these costs are not capitalized but rather are charged as operating costs incurred during the startup phase.

The degree to which new activities are similar to the firm's existing operations, and for which there are transferable skills, in part determines the scale of these startup costs. When the new situation is very different from existing operations, the costs of startup are likely to be significantly higher. This is especially true when management believes that new activities are similar to existing ones and then belatedly discovers that this is not so, after market entry. In these cases, substantial diseconomies may result in many functional areas. Startup business situations may therefore exhibit negative or positive synergy effects, and firms with a positive effect may gain significant COMPETITIVE ADVAN-TAGE over those that do not.

Apart from setup costs in startups, new market entries often experience a penalty for the delay. Those firms which contain the required skills, such as production facilities, access to distribution channels, and sales force capabilities, are likely to be able to enter related markets much more rapidly than concerns that have to start afresh. Timing advantage synergy can therefore be especially significant in highly dynamic, fast-growth markets.

Ansoff also identifies a second category of costs incurred as a result of new market entry. This is concerned with the operating costs and investment required to support the new activity. Two basic effects can produce synergy in this area. First, there may be the advantage of scale, whereby overall costs may be reduced as a result of extra volume (such as volume discounts in purchasing, improved machine capacity utilization, and distribution cost savings).

Second, it may also be possible to spread corporate overhead over a wider range of activities. The use of ACTIVITY-BASED COSTING is important in insuring that overhead is correctly allocated, however, otherwise new activities may be disproportionately burdened with overhead, which is not in reality consumed in the new business.

Top management talent, which is usually a scarce resource, may be better employed by adding new businesses, provided that it is not fully utilized. The synergy generated from this resource is, however, difficult to measure. Moreover, in switching top management resources to new business activities, care must be taken to insure that existing operations do not suffer from excess withdrawal of any necessary attention. It is also important to insure that any such talent deployed is actually appropriate to the new activities. For example, the disastrous record of the attempts by oil companies to diversify can, in part, be attributed to the appointment of oil industry managers to new business activities for which they were poorly equipped in terms of their skills and understanding.

As a generalization, synergy effects during startup tend to complement operating synergy, although the respective effects may differ according to the specific circumstances.

Ansoff suggests that the effect of synergy should be measured and mapped on one of three variables: increased volume of dollar revenue to the firm from sales, decreased operating costs, and decreased investment requirements – with all three being viewed in perspective over time. In practice, such mapping is rarely possible, especially for unrelated DIVERSIFICATION moves. Here, although the primary variables affecting synergy can be identified, it is rarely possible to quantify and combine their effects. The same criticism can be leveled at the concept of strategic fit. Thus, while the concept of synergy is seductive, making the concept operational has proved to be more problematic.

Bibliography

Ansoff, I. (1987). *Corporate Strategy*. Harmondsworth: Penguin, ch. 5.

Capron, L. (1999). The long-term performance of horizontal acquisitions. *Strategic Management Journal*, **20** (11), 987–1018.

Kitching, J. (1967). Why do mergers miscarry? *Harvard Business Review*, **45** (November/December), 84–101.

target-based costing

Derek F. Channon

Japanese producers have made extensive use of target-based costing. Market research is undertaken to establish what consumers might be prepared to pay for the functions offered by a new product. Once this is established, the retail price minus any discounts is set. After allowing for the required level of profitability, this establishes the cost at which the company must produce in order to achieve a satisfactory level of profit. Sony calls such prices "magic price" points.

Having established the target price and corresponding costs, designers, engineers, and procurement officers set out to achieve the desired cost level using techniques described elsewhere, such as JUST-IN-TIME, KAIZEN, TEAR DOWN, TOTAL QUALITY CONTROL, and VALUE ENGINEERING. The process also involves techniques such as ACTIVITY-BASED COSTING and BENCHMARKING and is illustrated in figure 1. The process is conducted in extreme detail, with consideration given to component reengineering, changes in assembly methods, function elimination, pressure applied to suppliers, etc. If the target cost is not reachable, then the product may need to be aborted. A further practice by Japanese producers, however, is strategic miniaturization. This involves reducing the size of products, such as office

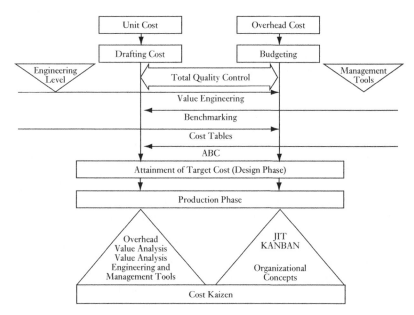

Figure 1 Attainment of target cost (production phase)

machinery and electronic products. A major result of this technique is to both reduce costs and increase market penetration. For example, the reduction in size of office photocopiers has encouraged distributed photocopying rather than centralized processing on large machines. The ultimate miniaturization is to make such equipment portable, or purchasable by the individual household. This has already occurred with fax machines, personal computers, personal copiers, and mobile telephones. This results in dramatically increased volumes, new purchasers, new distribution channels, and substantially reduced production costs as a result of shared experience, and deliberate attacks on costs due to target costing procedures.

Bibliography

Channon, D. F. (1993). *Canon B Case*. Imperial College, London.
Kotler, P. (2003). *Marketing Management: Analysis, Planning, Implementation and Control*, 11th edn. Englewood Cliffs, NJ: Prentice-Hall.

tear down

Derek F. Channon

This is a method of comparing products and components with those of competitors. Originating in the US automobile industry, the technique involves the systematic analysis of a competitor's product in terms of materials, parts, function, manufacture, coating, and assembly.

The approach used by the US General Motors Corporation (GM) was modified by Isuzu Motors and became the basis for the Japanese tear down method. The major difference between GM's original method and that of Isuzu is the scope of the Japanese approach.

The Japanese tear down program contains eight different methods. The first three of these were designed to reduce the direct manufacturing cost of a vehicle. The next three seek to reduce capital intensity by increased productivity, while the last two are integrations of tear down and VALUE ENGINEERING techniques. These techniques are as follows:

- *Dynamic tear down.* This method seeks to identify ways in which to reduce the number of assembly operations required to produce a vehicle in the time required.
- *Cost tear down.* The objective of this method is to reduce the cost of components used by comparing the components used with those of a competitor. Cost reduction techniques are then used when costs are higher and cannot be compensated for with greater functionality.
- *Material tear down.* This approach compares materials used and surface treatments. Any innovations observed in competing products are adopted.
- *Static tear down.* This basic approach consists of the disassembling of competing products to their components, which are then laid out for observation by design engineers.
- *Process tear down.* This process consists of comparing the manufacturing processes for similar parts and reducing the difference between them, with the long-term objective of producing multiple products or components on the same production line.
- *Matrix tear down.* In this method a matrix is developed of all components used in the company's products. This matrix is prepared on an as-needed basis and identifies the volume of each component used per month by model and the total usage across all models. Low-volume components are identified, designed out of existing products, and banned from future ones.
- *Unit kilogram price method.* In this method parts produced by similar production processes are treated as a product group and analyzed for possible savings. The efficiency of the product or component is expressed in terms of its value per kilogram. Products requiring further analysis are identified by plotting the value per kilo for all the products in the same group against their weight. Outliers are carefully examined with a view to identifying why their costs are higher than the group's average value.
- *Group estimate by tear down method (GET).* This method is a combination of basic value engineering and tear down procedures and a modified version of the unit-kilogram price method. The method consists of treating, as

a group, parts that have similar functions and analyzing them for possible cost savings.

Bibliography

Cooper, R. and Yoshikawa, T. (1994). *Isuzu Motors Ltd, Cost Creation Program*, Case No. 9-195-054. Boston: Harvard Business School.

technology and standards in network industries

John McGee

The significance of the economics of information is attributed to two key factors: the continuing reduction in cost of information technology hardware products and the scale effect of global standards. Gordon Moore, founder of Intel Corporation, created a corporate empire on his eponymous Moore's law, which states that every year and a half processing power doubles while costs hold constant. Moore's foresight proved prophetic and his law is expected to remain valid for the foreseeable future. Computer memory, storage capacity, and telecommunications bandwidth are all going through a similar pattern of cost reduction. This makes it very affordable for individuals and small businesses to be equipped with the electronic means to conduct commerce and transfer information as fast and freely as large corporations can. Hence, the demand for the products of the information, computing, and telecommunications (ICT) industries continues to grow (in spite of the feast and famine evident in the telecommunications industry reminiscent of the fragility of corporate structures during the railway boom of the 1840s).

However, the rapid growth of products from the ICT economy depends on operating technology standards as well as on production costs. For example, automated teller machines across the world must work on an agreed standard to insure customers can use one card in different countries. A technology standard is the important enabler to create wide reach and to capture a wide network of subscribers. With the GLOBALIZATION of commerce, national and regional boundaries blur and the need for international standards is more urgent and critical.

A new standard can be registered with organizations such as the British Standards Institute, the American National Standards Institute, or the International Standards Organization. But the process to determine the prevailing standard does not stop there. The path to achieving a de facto standard stems from three modes of selection process: market-based selection, negotiated selection, and a hybrid selection process where both market competition and negotiation operate jointly.

Market-based selection is reflected in standards wars such as that between VHS and Betamax where consumers decided on the dominance of the VHS standard. The marketing strategies of firms are key to which firm and standard is most likely to win. VHS gained a decisive advantage from a strategy of wider distribution channels and a range of complementary products (Hollywood films) as well as longer recording time than Betamax in spite of other more advanced features available only on Betamax.

Negotiated standardization is becoming more widespread. Organizations that determine prevailing standards are emerging to reduce the cost and the uncertainty associated with adopting new standards. Negotiated standard setting guarantees the smooth interchange of information, technical components and services along different networks. The telecommunications industry was able to keep up with the speed of technological development by opening up the negotiation process to market players (David and Steinmueller, 1994; David and Shurmer, 1996). Groupe Speciale Mobile (GSM), the current mobile technology in Europe, is an association of 600 network operators and suppliers of the mobile phone industry. The UMTS Forum is a similar association, developed to speed convergence between telecommunications, IT, media and content suppliers for the 3G industry. As with GSM, the name of the UMTS association is synonymous with the name for the industry technology standard.

The Internet has a different history of standardization to telecommunications. Standards were completely open and established within the research communities of universities. As the Internet has become a commodity for the domestic and the commercial communities, other players are increasingly influencing its evolution.

Hybrid standard setting emerges as private firms adopt strategies to undercut collaborative decisions taken in negotiated standardization. They introduce new products, which initiate unprecedented developments but also create incompatibilities, lock-in effects, and pockets of market power. Internet telephony is a typical example, where companies, standards organizations, and governments create a hybrid standard-setting environment (Vercoulen and Wegberg, 1998).

Standards organizations are playing an increasingly important role in the process of upgrading standards (called "versioning"). The GSM Association is guiding the evolution of the mobile industry through a family of wireless technology standards from today's standard through to GPRS, EDGE, and 3GSM. Each subsequent standard offers a higher level of service. GPRS provides open Internet. EDGE facilitates faster data streaming, and 3GSM will provide video streaming. The network of companies supporting the technologies will go through grades of service levels, in order to phase out older standards and introduce new ones (see figure 1). At the end of the life span of a standard the technology platform is decommissioned, with the exception of equipment and software that is forward compatible with the next generation of standards.

Software standards follow a similar versioning strategy. Microsoft publishes the *Windows Desktop Product Lifecycle Guidelines* to provide advanced notice of changes in product availability and support. Microsoft makes Windows licenses available for purchase for a minimum of five years and provides assisted support for a further four years. The guidelines are important so that companies can plan their investment through software upgrades of Windows 98, NT, 2000, ME, and the latest version of Windows XP.

Switching costs are minimized when standards are designed to evolve from one another. The introduction of revolutionary standards, however, is costly. The payoff is superior performance against the high cost of switching standards. The telling example is the price paid by mobile telephone operators to switch to third-generation technology. Mobile spectrum auctions earned European governments 200 billion, with Britain and Germany raising 22.5 and 60 billion, respectively. The mobile operators had to bid – to renounce third-generation spectrum was to opt out of the future (but did they have to pay so much?). The outcome of these auctions left mobile operators with increased debt, depleted cash flow, and delay in third-generation launches, all of which became the more significant as the stock market faltered and then stopped dead.

See also *network externalities; network industries; network industry strategies; networks*

Bibliography

David, P. A. and Shurmer, M. (1996). Formal standards-setting for global telecommunications and information

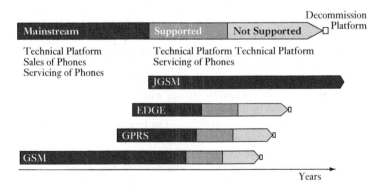

Figure 1   Standards versioning in the mobile telecommunications industry

services: Towards an institutional regime transformation. *Telecommunications Policy*, **20** (10).

David, P. A. and Steinmueller, W. E. (1994). Economics of compatibility standards and competition in telecommunication networks. *Information Economics and Policy*, **6**.

Shapiro, C. and Varian, H. (1999). *Information Rules: A Strategic Guide to the Network Economy*. Boston: Harvard Business School Press.

Vercoulen, F. and Wegberg, M. (1998). Standard selection modes in dynamic, complex industries: Creating hybrids between market selection and negotiated selection of standards. Maastricht: NIBOR Working Paper, NIB98006.

technology assessment

Derek F. Channon

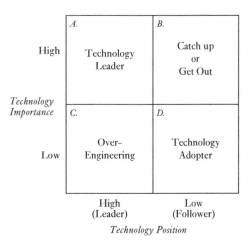

Figure 1   The technology evaluation matrix (Rowe et al., 1994)

In many industries, technology drives STRATEGIC DECISION-MAKING, with new products, and new production systems, distribution channels, and markets, often stemming from technological advances. Today, increasingly, industries may be transformed by the impact of information technology, provided that it is not used merely to automate the business practices of the past. The monitoring of technological development can therefore be a critical factor, and many companies have woken up too late to recognize that their historic COMPETITIVE ADVANTAGE has been rapidly eliminated by a technological bypass. For example, the camcorder eliminated amateur cine film in about three years, xerography eliminated diazo copying in a similar period, and automated teller machines now process over 90 percent of cash withdrawals and some 65 percent of deposits in Japan.

There are two basic components to technology. The first of these is tangible in the form of machines, tools, and materials. Second, which is more important, is the intangible component of technological knowledge. This factor drives skills and techniques that need to be learned and adopted by employees, plant layouts, machine operating procedures, computer software, etc. It also forms the basis for achieving competitive advantage via patents and distribution know-how.

Assessing technological capability involves collecting data on the firm's relative technological position (technology scanning) and analyzing this position (technology evaluation). The outcome of this analysis is shown in figure 1.

To undertake technology scanning:

- Divide the corporation into strategic business units (SBUs).
- For each SBU, determine (a) the technology currently in use and (b) the technology used by key competitors (potential new technologies). A widespread scan is important at this point and is where many companies succumb to BLIND SPOTS.
- Investigate sources of new technologies and their effects on all stakeholders.

To undertake technology evaluation, check the following:

- Is the technology important to the success of the business unit? Does it add value? Is it changing? Will it open new markets? Does it threaten existing markets? Does it significantly change cost structures?
- How strong is the company presently and in future with respect to the technology? This can be assessed by consideration of R&D expenditure, patents, R&D personnel employed, and adaptability to change. The company's relative position as a

technological leader or follower should be evaluated.

From this analysis the SBU's position is mapped on the technology evaluation matrix (see figure 1). Businesses which in general are high in both technology importance and technology position represent a strong position, which should be pursued aggressively in order to maintain competitive advantage. Businesses in which technology is important but the firm is in a follower position have several strategic alternatives. First, resources can be committed to strengthen the firm's technology position and attempt to gain competitive advantage. Second, the firm can exit and deploy released R&D resources to other businesses. Third, enough resources can be committed to maintain an adequate follower strategy position while monitoring opportunities for potential future technology shifts.

Businesses in quadrant C are probably guilty of over-engineering. The resource commitment is probably too high for the needs of the business, and consideration should be given to redeploying such resources to improve their effectiveness.

Businesses in quadrant D have a weak position in an important technology. Involvement in such an area should be reconsidered, and any technical requirements might be outsourced (*see* OUTSOURCING).

While technology alone usually does not sustain long-term competitive advantage, it can be a vital ingredient, especially during the early stages of the business life cycle. It may also be important in industries with short product life cycles. The role of technology at maturity might be one of transforming industry cost structure via substitution, rejuvenation by opening new market segments, and by product development to stimulate replacement demand.

Bibliography

Birnbaum, P. H. and Weiss, A. R. (1974). Competitive advantage and the basis for competition. Strategic Management Society Seventh Annual Meeting, Boston.

Gould, J. M. (1983). Technology change and competition. *Journal of Business Strategy*, 4 (2), 62–73.

Rowe, A. J., Mason, R. O., Dickel, K. E., Mann, R. B., and Mockler, R. J. (1994). *Strategic Management*, 4th edn. Reading, MA: Addison-Wesley, pp. 116–21.

technology fusion

Joe Tidd

This involves the combination and transformation of a number of different core technologies in order to create new product markets. The term was popularized by Fumio Kodama of Japan's Science and Technology Agency (STA) in the 1980s: "The fusion of technologies goes beyond mere combination. Fusion is more than complementaries, because it creates a new market and new growth opportunities for each participant in the innovation ... it blends incremental improvements from several (often previously separate) fields to create a product."

The key elements of technology fusion are that it is both complementary and cooperative. Typically, it is the result of reciprocal and substantial R&D expenditure by companies from a range of industries and with different technological competences. For example, in the 1970s, the fusion of research by companies from the mechanical and electronic engineering sectors created what the Japanese call "mechatronics." A group of Japanese companies from a wide range of industries combined efforts. Fanuc, a spin-off from the computer company Fujitsu, led the group with the development of an electro hydraulic servomotor and a new controller; Nippon Seiko (NSK), Japan's leading bearing manufacturer, developed a new type of ballscrew; and material suppliers developed a new low-friction coating. This spawned the Japanese robotics and numerically controlled machine tool industries, which now dominate world markets.

Technology fusion is of increasing importance in a wide range of industries in which American and European companies are currently strong. In the telecommunications sector the fusion of optics and electronics technologies has been critical. In the automotive industry the integration of electronic and mechanical systems has become a major locus of innovation, particularly in engine, transmission, and braking systems. In aerospace the development of fly-by-wire systems demands the fusion of electronics and hydraulics technologies – and the next generation of fly-by-light systems will also require expertise in optics technologies.

Significantly, Japanese companies have considerable expertise in electronics, opto-electronics, and hydraulics technologies and appear to be able to recognize and exploit the potential of technology fusion. Japanese companies are reflecting the importance of technology fusion in their slogans and company missions (*see* MISSION). For example, NEC uses "computers and communication," whereas Toshiba uses "energy and electronics." This is more than marketing alliteration, and reflects an explicit strategy of RELATED DIVERSIFICATION.

However, there are a number of potential problems with the concept of technology fusion that need to be resolved: the measurement of technology fusion; the level of analysis; and the organizational constraints. The first two issues are closely related. Most of the current analysis of technology fusion has been undertaken at the level of the industry or sector, and has been based on levels of R&D expenditure. In Japan, companies are required to report their R&D expenditure to the government, disaggregated into 31 different product fields. Studies suggest that a growing proportion of R&D expenditure lies outside the traditional CORE BUSINESS. Two ratios are of particular significance:

$$\frac{\text{R\&D expenditure by industry A in other industries}}{\text{R\&D expenditure by industry A in itself}}$$

and

$$\frac{\text{R\&D expenditure by other industries in industry A}}{\text{R\&D expenditure by industry A in itself}}$$

The ratio of R&D in outside industries to that in the core business can be used as an indicator of technology fusion. Similarly, the R&D from outside industries into an industry as a ratio of the R&D within that industry can be calculated. However, strictly speaking, these ratios may simply indicate diversification; but, by definition, technology fusion involves reciprocal investment by companies in the respective industries. Combining the two ratios for specific pairs of industries provides a better measure of reciprocal investment. For example, a coefficient of technology fusion (CTF) can be defined as follows:

$$\text{CTF} = vR_\text{A}R_\text{B},$$

where

$$R_\text{A} = \frac{\text{Total outside R\&D by A}}{\text{R\&D in B by A}}$$

and

$$R_\text{B} = \frac{\text{Total outside R\&D by B}}{\text{R\&D in A by B}}$$

Defined in this way, the closer the CTF is to unity (one), the greater the level of mutual R&D investment. Therefore one can construct year-by-year fusion maps based on the level of reciprocal R&D investment. Kodama has done this for several periods, and claims to have identified the emergence of mechatronics and biotechnology in the mid-1970s.

In Japan, the MITI now conducts fusion surveys on a periodic basis. However, there are several problems in applying this analysis. First, the standard industrial classification adopted may obscure occurrences of technology fusion. Second, the reliability of data on R&D is uncertain; for example, numerous studies suggest that the definition of R&D is variable, despite the OECD "Frascati" guidelines. Moreover, the precision of allocation into the different product groups is unknown. Third, only aggregate R&D expenditure by principal industries is published outside of Japan. Any attempt to allocate to different product groups would have to be based on primary data collection from companies, or estimates from annual reports and other sources.

For these reasons, other measures of technological capability and activity may be more appropriate at the level of the firm. Of the techniques available, patent analysis and bibliometric measurements based on publications are the most promising. Patent analysis will typically involve detailed study of between 1,000 and 10,000 patent applications, depending on the company and field of technology. For example, in the US 1,000 new patents are issued every day. A leading high-tech company such as Hitachi will be issued almost 2,000 patents each year. Patent data can be used in a number of ways, the most common being to measure changes in the number of patents granted in specific fields. In addition, maps of technology fusion and the associated organizational linkages can be generated by examining the cross-citation of related patents.

Finally, there may be significant organizational barriers to technology fusion at the level of the firm. Past strategic choices clearly shape existing organizational structures and processes, and these structures and processes may constrain future strategic options. For example, most large firms are organized into strategic business units (SBUs), based on past product market linkages, but these linkages may no longer be relevant, and may prevent technological synergies across SBUs. This suggests a potential barrier to the recognition and exploitation of technology fusion. Independent strategies to optimize the performance of each division may not necessarily produce optimum corporate performance.

Bibliography

Kodama, F. (1991). *Analyzing Japanese High Technologies*. London: Pinter.

time-based competition

Peter Dempsey and Ed Heard

The technique of time-based competition addresses the complete order to delivery cycle. It analyzes each element of time used and questions the right to use it. It involves much more than JUST-IN-TIME (JIT), ELECTRONIC DATA INTERCHANGE, or any single technology. It helps to compress time in the whole organization. This means that one has to change processes, information, and decision flows from the customer, to engineering, to procurement, through manufacturing, order processing, and distribu-

tion, and back to the customer. In all these stages of the business cycle, actions and the use of time are driven by the voice of the customer.

It is important to establish the relationship between time and money. The fact is that profit is typically reduced by one third for every six months by which a capital goods product is late to market. A computer game has only a six-month life anyway, so time is even more vital. The relationship between time and quality is also vital. Doing everything faster means doing this right first time. One cannot afford the time for rework. Quality is inextricably linked to customer satisfaction, which is a number one requirement of time compression management. Achieving the required quality standard first time does not mean rushing the job and cutting time out. Time compression management may mean deliberately taking longer on tricky aspects in order to insure that "right first time" is achieved.

Companies that compress time out of their business cycle or pipeline understand that, throughout it, materials, direct labor, handling and transportation, interest, and overheads contribute to overall costs. The longer the business cycle takes, the greater the costs are and the slower is the response to the customer. The trick is to speed up the flow of all events. The process flow consists of all of the operations of the business, the information flow consists of all of the data in the business, and the decision flow consists of all of the actions taken by people in the business.

Responsiveness refers to the ability to satisfy customer requirements quicker than one's competitors. However, satisfying customer requirements has a variety of interpretations, such as:

- filling an order from shelf stock;
- assembling to requirement;
- engineering to order;
- bringing a new product to market.

Other variations also exist, but what they all share is cycle time (elapsed time) as the common measure of performance.

As a result of the emerging competitive importance of responsiveness, cycle times are beginning to have unprecedented significance. As emphasis shifts from product-based competition, a major rethink of the roles of traditional functions is taking place. It is becoming increasingly clear that competitiveness is a "whole enterprise" problem.

In the past, it was relatively easy for non-manufacturing functions to abdicate responsibility for enterprise competitiveness. After all, their impact on product quality and price was thought to be quite minor. Product quality and price were regarded as "blue-collar" variables, whereas they were "white-collar" people. However, when various cycle times are seen as determinants of competitiveness, "white-collar" staff become extremely important in the enterprise competitiveness scheme (see figure 1). Therefore, let us examine a typical enterprise and identify the three main time cycles to be managed.

Three main activity cycles control the responsiveness of a manufacturing company:

- new product introduction;
- value-adding pipeline;
- customer service.

Their interrelationships with key functions of the business are shown in figure 1.

Low-cost, high-quality products are beginning to be simply the price of admission to some markets. Likewise, customers are beginning to think in terms of total enterprise cost, quality, and responsiveness. These changing market needs are on a conflicting course with current and past trends in traditional manufacturing enterprises. Meeting the responsiveness challenge depends on an enterprise's ability to identify and shorten the three primary business cycles – new product introduction, the value-adding pipeline, and customer service. Some approaches to shortening cycle times impact cost, quality, and capital requirements negatively. Short cycle management incorporates numerous JIT/total quality control/total quality management principles selected to complement one another. Those principles can be used to dramatically improve competitiveness by simultaneously improving white-collar and blue-collar processing cycle times, cost, quality, and capital requirements. In short, if a structured approach is taken to reduce wasted time in designing, developing, producing, and distributing, then: costs will decrease; less capital will be tied up;

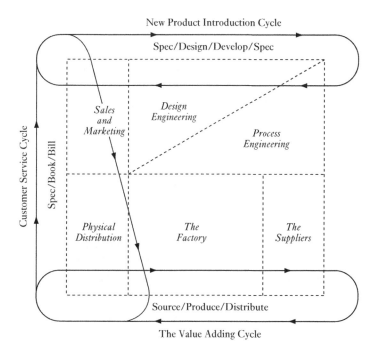

Figure 1   Responsiveness activities and business functions (Ed Heard and Associates)

and customer value will increase. This is so provided that capital is not substituted for intelligence, people are not thrown in at the deep end, and necessary activities are not eliminated. Time compression is therefore managed, and the vision of the customer as king is maintained.

Bibliography

Stalk, G., Jr. and Hout, T. M. (1990). *Competing Against Time*. New York: Free Press.

tipping point

see CRITICAL MASS

total quality control

Derek F. Channon

The founder of total quality control (TQC) as it has developed in Japan was the influential US quality expert, W. Edwards Deming. An annual award named after him, for the most significant quality performance in Japan, is still highly prized. Deming's work strongly emphasized statistical techniques of quality control, and although these are widely used and Japanese workers are highly trained in their use, TQC is today much more than this. It has become a fundamental philosophy which guides all aspects of Japanese manufacturing strategy.

TQC may stand alone but, more commonly, it may be used in conjunction with other concepts, such as KAIZEN and JUST-IN-TIME (JIT). To implement TQC, all plant personnel are inculcated into the philosophy, and implementation is achieved by the use of a cross-functional management structure and processes. In particular, under the Japanese system all individuals are responsible for their own actions rather than being overseen by quality inspectors and accountants. The concept has been widely used in Japanese industry since the early 1960s, and has been constantly elaborated on and improved.

An attempt is made in table 1 to group a number of TQC factors into specific categories.

Table 1   Total quality control: concepts and categories

TQC category	TQC concept
1 Organization	Production responsibility
2 Goals	Habit of improvement • Perfection
3 Basic principles	Process control • easy-to-see quality • insistence on compliance • line stop • correcting one's own errors • 100 per cent check • project-by-project improvement
4 Facilitating concepts	QC as a facilitator • small lot size • housekeeping • less than full capacity scheduling • daily machine checking
5 Techniques and aids	Exposure of problems • foolproof devices • $N = 2$ • analytical tools • QC circles

Source: Schonberger (1982: 51)

ORGANIZATION

This consists of the key concept of assigning the primary responsibility for quality to production workers rather than a staff quality control department.

After organizing for TQC, the rate of quality improvement can be accelerated by introducing the items in categories 2–5. These include new goals, principles, facilitating concepts, and techniques for successful implementation of TQC. Some of these concepts are alien to western production practice, while others have been copied from the West and adapted to Japanese business culture.

GOALS

The habit of improvement. While most western companies accept one-off improvement programs, Japanese companies have developed the habit of *kaizen* – continuous improvement, day after day, year after year, at all levels within the organization. For example, in some Japanese corporations the workforce meets each morning to confirm and consolidate productivity gains made the previous day.

Perfection. The goal of perfection is treated differently between Japanese and western concerns. There is agreement that quality needs to be regularly monitored to insure adherence to specification. However, while western concerns accept a given standard of defects, Japanese concerns continue to work toward absolute perfection. Similarly, both Japanese and western concerns accept that quality depends on the efforts of all functions within the corporation. However, while western concerns place a limit on the costs to be incurred in the pursuit of quality, Japanese companies believe that ever better quality will continue to improve MARKET SHARE and expand the overall market. It must also be seen that for Japanese concerns the TQC concept may well include continuous cost reduction as well as product perfection.

BASIC PRINCIPLES

A number of basic principles are listed as components of TQC. The first two of these are closely related and equally important.

Process control. The concept of process control is a standard western quality control technique. However, it is undertaken by the inspection of only a number of processes in the production system, together with final inspection. Moreover, this activity tends to be undertaken by the quality control department. In the Japanese system all processes are continuously checked, but by the workforce, who have been trained to undertake this task themselves, thus allowing every workstation to become an inspection department.

Easy-to-see quality. This principle, which is an extension of the Deming and Juran concepts that there should be measurable standards of quality, has been finessed by the Japanese such that display boards are located everywhere in Japanese plants. These convey to workers, management, customers, suppliers, and visitors what quality factors are measured, recent performance, and what current quality improvement projects are in progress, which groups have won awards, and so on. Many of the displays are graphic rather than numerical and are completed regularly by the workforce. These have much more impact than pages of computer printout, which may well be unread by western management and perhaps not even shown to the workforce.

Insistence on compliance. In many western concerns, while lip service is paid to achieving consistent quality standards, these may be sacrificed on occasions for short-term expediency. In most Japanese concerns, the pursuit of quality standards is paramount and takes precedence over output standards and pressures.

Line stop. Closely related to the compliance principle, in Japanese production systems every individual worker has the facility to stop the production line if quality standards are compromised. By contrast, in many western plants the production line is not expected to stop, and any production identified as deficient is despatched to rework areas. While the Japanese system is initially slow when a new production process is started, as quality problems are gradually resolved, the line speeds up, quality improves, and rework costs are eliminated.

Correcting one's own errors. When errors do occur in the Japanese system, unlike in the West, it is the responsibility of the worker or workgroup to correct its own errors by undertaking its own rework. While the output rate is unimportant in the Japanese system, with, for example, the line-stop system being open to all workers, daily output is important and in the event of line stops and needed reworks the workforce is expected to work late to make any necessary corrections. In this way, workers assume full responsibility for quality problems. In general, however, these are limited while JIT keeps lot sizes small, so that any defects detected apply to only a small number of units.

100 percent check. In Japanese systems this requires every item of output to be inspected – not merely a random sample. This principle applies rigidly to all finished goods and, where possible, to components. When it is impossible to inspect all components, the $N = 2$ concept is used (see below), with a long-term goal of achieving a 100 percent check. By contrast, in western companies statistical sample inspections are the norm. This technique, which was developed by the US military in World War II, was used initially by the Japanese but later rejected because the concept of a lot implied long production and hence the buildup of inventory – the antithesis of JIT. Second, the Japanese adopted much tighter standards of defects and ultimately were aiming for true zero defects, which made sampling tables irrelevant. Third, sampling itself was considered inadequate.

Project-by-project improvement. Schemes for project-by-project improvement are visible throughout Japanese production units. The displays may also show partly completed projects, on a type of "scoreboard." Western visitors find such displays impressive, but are skeptical when they understand the number of such projects being undertaken. While it is true that individual projects make little contribution, the overall number, coupled with the cultural environment induced toward quality, results in a massive continuous level of improvement which most western firms find impossible to replicate.

FACILITATING CONCEPTS

The effect of quality improvement can be enhanced by making use of the facilitating concepts once the organizational and quality principles are in place. These facilitators are as follows:

- *Quality control as facilitator.* In Japan, as responsibility for quality is assigned to the line function, specialist quality control departments are reduced in size and used as facilitators for the total process. As a result, they promote the removal of the causes of defects, keep track of quality achievements, monitor as standard procedures are followed, and observe procurement to insure that supplier factories have similar quality standards and conduct QC training. The inspection of goods inwards parts is also passed back to suppliers and, as such, goods inward are sent straight to the production line. One exception to this practice is that parts received from western suppliers may be inspected by the quality department.
- *Small lot sizes.* This is a key element in JIT production. It is also important in insuring that any defects are detected early. As such, it also forms a basic concept in quality control.
- *Housekeeping.* Japanese factories are carefully laid out to insure scrupulous tidiness and cleanliness. While individual workers are expected to keep their workplace tidy, any production workers not required for their line production jobs may be temporarily assigned to cleanliness and hygiene tasks elsewhere in the factory.
- *Less-than-full-capacity scheduling.* Having available spare capacity insures that the daily production schedules will be met. It is also a quality control concept, as it permits the line to be stopped for quality or other reasons. Moreover, capacity slack avoids over-pressuring the workforce, tools, and equipment – so reducing the probability of errors.
- *Daily machine checking.* Unlike in the West, where production machinery is used as hard as possible and maintenance is the responsibility of specialists, in Japan production workers are expected to perform routine

maintenance on their machines at the beginning of each day. Each morning, therefore, the Japanese normally go through a checklist, insuring that the machine functions correctly, oiling, adjusting, sharpening, and so on before operations commence.

TECHNIQUES AND AIDS

In Japanese TQC there are fewer techniques and aids than those found in the West, where specialists using various techniques and aids are common. In Japan, the commonly used tools are fewer and different. They include the following:

- *Exposure of problems.* In the TQC system, discovery of a defect triggers a detailed investigation to discover the cause of the defect and correct it. This process is so valued that management may deliberately remove workers or buffer inventories to expose problems affecting quality. Exposure of problems and correction of causes are also sought out before there is actual evidence of problems. This might involve very careful analysis of product designs and checks at the product startup phase, before volume production commences. Similarly, workers – both individually and in small groups or quality circles – are constantly seeking ways in which to improve quality.
- *Foolproof devices.* The work process can be redesigned to eliminate many mistakes. Many machines are fitted with *bakayoke*, which automatically check for abnormal production. When such defects are found, the machines stop automatically – the process of "autonomation." The monitoring mechanisms may therefore check for malfunction, excess tool wear, etc., in addition to dimensions and tolerances. Such devices are also sometimes used in final assembly or when manual systems are used via the line stop system or via worker-triggered warning lights.
- *N = 2.* While foolproof devices are useful for high-volume operations, for lower volumes manual inspection may be required. High percentages of production are inspected – even as high as 100 percent, in the case of unstable processes. For more stable processes, sample inspection may be used. Unlike in the West, where random sampling is normal, in Japanese TQC inspection is not random. In practice, the first and last pieces in a production run are inspected – hence the term $N = 2$. The argument is that in a stable process, if the first and last units are good, then those produced in between should also all be good.
- *Tools of analysis.* Statistical tools are used in both western and Japanese quality control systems. In Japan, however, these tend to be used by superiors and workers who have undergone extensive training in their preparation and use. Many Japanese variants of such tools, however, show greater detail. The cause–effect or Ishikawa diagram was less known in the West but is now a normal tool used in quality analysis.
- *QC circles.* QC circles are used throughout Japanese corporations and almost all employees are members. Such groups meet to develop ideas for quality improvements on a regular basis. Their output is prodigious, with ideas for quality and *kaizen* improvement often running into millions of suggestions each year per company. Most of these ideas are implemented. While successful ideas are rewarded, the gains in monetary terms are usually small, with prestige awards being more highly thought of.

The TQC concept has been accepted by a number of western companies, but few have adopted the depth of commitment to the principles and practice found in Japanese concerns. Without such commitment, the constant improvements in quality and costs experienced in Japan are unlikely to materialize in the West, leading to a continuous loss of COMPETITIVE ADVANTAGE.

Bibliography

Kusaba, I. (1981). Quality control in Japan. *Reports of QC Circle Activities*, 14, 1–5, Union of Japanese Scientists and Engineers.
Ishikawa, K. (1985). *What is Total Quality Control? The Japanese Way*. Englewood Cliffs, NJ: Prentice-Hall.
Juran, J. M. (1978). Japanese and western quality: A contrast in methods and results. *Management Review*, 26–45.

Monden, Y. (1983). *Toyota Production System*. Atlanta, GA: Institute of Industrial Engineers.

Schonberger, R. J. (1982). *Japanese Manufacturing Techniques*. New York: Free Press.

trade-offs

Taman Powell

Essentially, a trade-off is when more of one thing necessitates less of another. Trade-offs are important in STRATEGY, as in the words of Michael Porter (1996):

> a strategic position is not sustainable unless there are trade-offs with other positions. Trade-offs occur when activities are incompatible. Simply put, a trade-off means that more of one thing necessitates less of another. An airline can choose to serve meals – adding cost and slowing turnaround time at the gate – or it can choose not to, but it cannot do both without bearing major inefficiencies.

In developing a strategy, therefore, it is very important to be aware of the trade-offs that are being made. A firm simply cannot do all the things that it would like to do, so instead it needs to decide what it will, and therefore also, what it will not do.

To make these trade-offs it is important that the firm has a solid understanding of its positioning, as it is the positioning that defines what the firm is trying to achieve and therefore what trade-offs should be made. In essence, it is the trade-offs that a firm makes that are its strategy. For without trade-offs, all firms would be able to replicate any good idea. This would leave firm performance depending solely on operational efficiency.

Bibliography

Porter, M. E. (1996). What is strategy? *Harvard Business Review*, 74 (6), 61–78.

transactions costs

Stephanos Avgeropoulos

These are the costs involved in any transaction between two parties relating to the transfer or exchange of goods or services.

Initially, transaction cost principles were used in a debate regarding the role of government in promoting economic efficiency with respect to EXTERNALITIES. In 1920, Pigou took the view that common law needs to be applied to force the internalization of social costs in the quest for EFFICIENCY (Pigou, 1920). His view was contested by Coase (1937), who claimed that externalities are sometimes self-correcting, and suggested that holding the party that created the externality liable under common law was not necessarily efficient; instead, efficiency would be best achieved by balancing costs and benefits, to which the role of causality was not decisive.

The transaction costs theory was considerably extended and gained its widespread appeal through a series of publications by Oliver Williamson, who applied it to the organization of the firm. Williamson suggested that there are three generic governance structures, namely, the market (in which, e.g., a firm subcontracts a certain task to another firm), hierarchy (in which, e.g., a firm asks a salaried employee to undertake some task that is required), and a hybrid one which combines elements of both. According to this model, hierarchies (surrendering authority to a single party) are expected to emerge where the costs of drawing up an all-contingent contract are high, typically due to an unusually uncertain environment. These structures differ in two principal respects, namely, the form of contract law that they support (an employee, for example, has no access to the courts for most intents and purposes), and the applicable incentive and control mechanisms (from the automatic coordinating role of prices in a market, to the conscious and deliberate considerations in hierarchies).

NATURE OF THE COSTS

Transactions costs consist of two main components, namely, transaction uncertainty and performance ambiguity. Transaction uncertainty exists to the degree to which transactions are unstandardized and unpredictable, and is influenced by factors such as the frequency of transactions, their duration, and the degree to which parties to the transaction have made transaction-specific investments. Performance ambiguity refers to the ability of the parties involved to monitor and evaluate the performance of the other parties and to determine the value of the objects of exchange, and is influenced by the intangibility content of the objects of exchange, the simultaneity of production and consumption, and the involvement of skilled and specialized personnel.

Transactions costs relate to all aspects of a transaction, including negotiating, monitoring, and enforcing the exchange. Typical costs in a market organization are discovering what the relevant prices are, learning and haggling over the terms of the trade, and negotiating and concluding a separate contract for each exchange transaction; they typically increase with long-term agreements. Similarly, costs in an internalized (hierarchical) organization include increased organizational rigidity and often higher management costs too; these increase with the number of hierarchical levels involved, by virtue of the latter adversely affecting the quality and quantity of the information transmitted.

IMPLICATIONS

Transactions costs can affect a firm in many ways, and can even explain its existence. When the costs of determining market prices are substantial, a firm emerges and workers surrender the right to use their labor by contract (Coase, 1937). Similarly, high transactions costs (such as in the form of difficulty in forecasting input or output prices) may lead the firm to internalize activities further upstream or downstream (i.e., to integrate vertically; *see* VERTICAL INTEGRATION STRATEGY), can explain multinationalization (as a way of producing cost savings by internalizing markets across international boundaries), and can modify organizational structure so that the level of task interdependence is reduced to lower the transaction uncertainty and performance ambiguity and allow prices to emerge as the principal governance system.

In addition, high transactions costs may lead to allocative inefficiency, if they feed through to higher prices. Similarly, they may necessitate the establishment of rules and regulations, and the government may have to intervene to limit the impact of a harmful transaction cost (*see* REGULATION).

Bibliography

Coase, R. H. (1937). The nature of the firm. *Economica*, 4, 386–405. Reprinted in G. J. Stigler and K. E. Boulding (eds.) (1952). *Readings in Price Theory*. Chicago: Irwin.

Pigou, A. C. (1920). *The Economics of Welfare*. London, Macmillan; 4th edition, 1932; reissued 1952, New York: St. Martin's Press.

Williamson, O. E. (1975). *Markets and Hierarchies: Analysis and Antitrust Implications*. Glencoe, IL: Free Press.

Williamson, O. E. (1979). Transaction cost economics: The governance of contractual relations. *Journal of Law and Economics*, 22 (October), 232–61.

Williamson, O. E. (1981). The economics of organization: The transaction cost approach. *American Journal of Sociology*, 87, 548–77.

turnaround strategy

Duncan Angwin and John McGee

Hofer's (1976) classic article on turnarounds draws the distinction between operating and strategic forms. Operating turnarounds are about "doing things differently," so that the firm's EFFICIENCY can be improved. This may be achieved by a fundamental change in a firm's operations, by using advanced manufacturing technology, for instance. Strategic turnarounds are about "doing different things." In this instance, companies attempt to change their fortunes by fundamental adjustments to their strategy, e.g., in terms of acquisition (*see* ACQUISITION STRATEGY) and DIVESTMENT.

Hofer's distinction between strategic and operating turnarounds has been challenged by Hambrick and Schecter (1983). They argue that the difference becomes blurred as we move from the corporate to the business unit level. They suggest three categories: traditional asset cost surgery, product-market pruning, and, their largest category, piecemeal strategies. This suggests that there is such a difference between individual companies that it is difficult to establish a single turnaround framework.

Grinyer, Mayes, and McKiernan's empirical study (1988) of corporate turnarounds by UK manufacturing companies does find evidence to suggest that turnarounds have distinct stages. Figure 1 shows the different types of "sharpbender" identified.

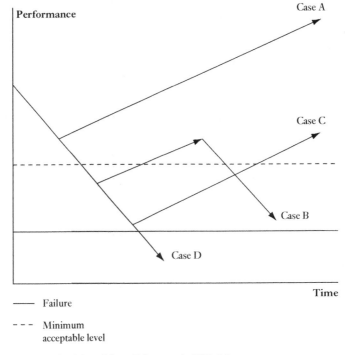

Figure 1   Types of sharpbender (adapted from Grinyer et al., 1988: 14)

Case A is the firm showing *early recovery*. The firm is aware of its decline in performance and *anticipates* that on such a trend, it is likely to breech its managerial-determined minimum acceptable level of performance. Although the firm is far from extinction, actions are taken in advance, the crisis averted, and a path of sustained improvement achieved.

Case B is the firm taking *intermediate* action to break through its line of minimum acceptable standards. Alarm bells are ringing and actions taken to recover. However, such actions are insufficient – perhaps superficial, addressing symptoms rather than causes – and the firm returns to its decline trajectory. At this point, the firm may countenance more sweeping changes to restore the firm to a trajectory of sustained improvement. However, should this step not be taken, it is likely that the firm will continue to oscillate around the line of minimum acceptable standards, with successive uplifts being more difficult to achieve than previously, before ultimately failing.

Case C is a firm which is late in reacting to the crisis. The firm has breached its managerial-determined minimum level of performance and has begun to approach the line of failure. It is the classic turnaround, as described by Slatter (1984). In this instance, the firm needed the spur of breaking its internal standards, as well as the threat of extinction to begin to take substantial action. By so doing, sustained recovery is achieved.

Case D is the firm that does not perceive the threat of extinction, despite breaking its own minimum acceptable standards, or is unable to make any changes before termination.

THE DECLINE PROCESS

Research gives a wide variety of reasons for corporate decline:

● *Over-expansion*: firms that have expanded too far find that they are stretched in both managerial and financial terms. This is the classic criticism of the DIVERSIFICATION boom of the 1960s in the UK, which led to massive underperforming conglomerates.

- *Inadequate financial controls and high costs*: these often occur when a business grows beyond the capability of its original systems, so that costs spiral out of control.
- *New competition entering the market*: the arrival of a new competitor can substantially distort the competitive dynamics of a market and damage a firm's health.
- *Unforeseen demand shifts*: the nature of the market may change dramatically. Where a firm has substantial and rigid asset configurations, this can spell disaster, the classic example being the impact on IBM of the widespread switch from mainframe to desktop computers. The area most on people's minds at the moment is the potential impact of the Internet.
- *Poor management*: managers may have a false sense of confidence in their own abilities. This can arise from experiencing a period

of success, causing an atmosphere of infallibility, and the screening of information. Of course, poor management may also just mean poor management.

How Do Managers React to a Crisis?

When the crisis is too obvious to ignore, managers tend to react in a sequential way, taking the least risky actions at first, and then becoming progressively more radical if the crisis worsens and they have time to act.

The stages of reactive behavior are well captured in figure 2. Comparisons are continually drawn between reference points such as competitor performance, share performance, and ambitions and aspirations for profit performance. Should this comparison be favorable, then the innermost loop will be followed with the current behavior being reinforced. Should the comparisons prove unfavorable, then the first stage will be followed. If desirable results are not forthcoming, then executives may

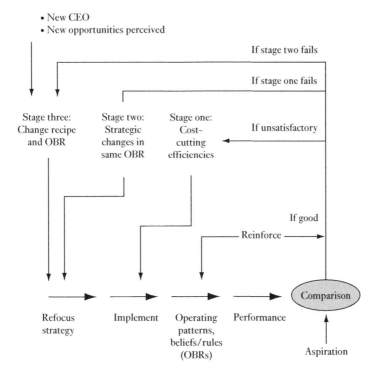

Figure 2 A conceptual model of the stages of reactive behavior (extended Cyert and March model) (McKiernan, 1992: 58)

move progressively outwards in figure 2 until the third stage of a fundamental review of strategy is undertaken.

TRIGGERS FOR ACTION

Whilst it may be clear that an organization is on a decline trajectory, it is vital that triggers are identified to bring about action. If triggers cannot be identified, then it is likely that nothing will change, despite the abundance of warning signs.

The important triggers for bringing about change are seen in table 1. A well-known example of an acquisition as a trigger prompting a strategic change is the Hanson bid for ICI. In fighting off the bid, ICI announced the demerger of Zeneca.

The main trigger identified is a new CEO. His/her importance is in terms of supplying a new vision and symbolizing that things need to change. Indeed, such a person has undoubtedly been appointed with a mandate for change.

In terms of early, intermediate, and late-stage recoveries, the broad pattern, as one might expect, is for the early stagers to have internal triggers and have a management able to perceive problems and opportunities. As we move to the late stagers, all triggers are important with an increased external emphasis.

ACTIONS TAKEN

If there are triggers in place, then the sorts of actions that might be taken to bring about a recovery are contained in table 2. We are interested to know the actions that sharpbenders took, and in particular those actions that are specific to them. For this reason we show the percentage of sharpbenders citing an action in column 1, the percentage of other randomly selected companies citing an action in column 2, and the difference between the two scores in column 3.

Table 1   Triggers for bringing about change

Triggers	Sharpbenders citing this factor (%)
1 Intervention from external bodies	30
2 Change of ownership or the threat of such a change	25
3 New chief executive	55
4 Recognition by management of problems	35
5 Perception by management of new opportunities	10

Source: Grinyer et al. (1988: 47)

Table 2   Actions taken to bring about recovery

% of firms citing factor	Sharpbenders	Control companies	% difference
Major changes in management	85	30	55
Stronger financial controls	80	70	10
New product market focus	80	80	0
Diversified	30	70	(40)
Entered export market vigorously	50	30	20
Improved quality and service	55	50	5
Improved marketing	75	30	45
Intensive efforts to reduce production costs	80	30	50
Acquisitions	50	80	(30)
Reduced debt	50	80	(30)
Windfalls	85	70	15
Other	25	20	5

Source: Grinyer et al. (1988: 64)

Table 3   Key features of sustained improved performance

Key features	Number of characteristics cited	% of firms cited
1 Good management	4+	90
2 Appropriate organizational structure	4+	75
3 Effective financial and other controls	4+	50
4 Sound product market posture	5+	45
5 Good marketing management	2+	55
6 High quality maintained	2+	35
7 Tightly controlled costs	3+	40

Source: Grinyer et al. (1988: 110)

The major difference between sharpbenders and control companies in terms of action taken are management changes: 85 percent of sharpbenders cited management changes, some 55 percent more than the control companies. They also devoted considerable efforts to improving marketing and reducing production costs. Unlike the control companies, they were very reluctant to diversify and there were markedly reduced levels of acquisition. Interestingly, they also were reluctant to reduce debt, and here there is a distinction with pure turnarounds in that the latter make considerable efforts to reduce debts. Sharpbenders are more likely to invest to improve performance.

CHARACTERISTICS OF SUSTAINED PERFORMANCE

Following the turnaround, sharpbenders needed to adopt characteristics that would enable sustained levels of performance – to refer back to figure 1, organizations want cases A and C, rather than B (where the recovery achieved is only short term). The characteristics identified in the sharpbenders (1988) study are contained in table 3:

- Good management is seen to be critical to sustained recovery.
- Appropriate organizational structure often meant a much leaner one, with fewer layers in the hierarchy.
- Tightly controlled costs meant better controls, rather than cutting costs.

GENERIC TURNAROUND STRATEGIES

Grinyer et al.'s (1988) academic study is consistent with the review of practitioners' work by Hoffman (1989) in identifying a three-stage process for recovery, although not all organizations need to go through all three stages (see figure 3 and table 4).

CONCLUSION

Turnarounds are just one example of crisis situations in CORPORATE STRATEGY, and it should be borne in mind that this has particular implications for how strategy is viewed in such circumstances. In the case of turnarounds:

- *A proactive top-down style of management* has been advocated as necessary and effective for turnarounds. For other strategy decisions, a Mintzbergian bottom-up view, or indeed a middle-up-down perspective, is more common.
- *Rapid change* is critical to survival in a turnaround, although currently dominant in STRATEGIC MANAGEMENT is the processual (Whittington, 1993) view, which emphasizes the complexity and difficulty of change, so that it is perceived as a long and involved process.
- *Structure* comes before strategy in so far as changes are made for the company's very survival before the luxury of a strategy can be considered. This is contrary to the strongly held Chandlerian view that structure follows strategy.

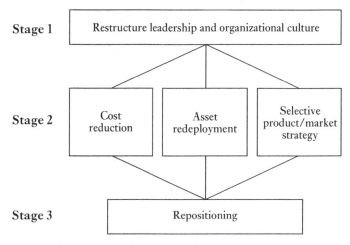

Stage 1 — Restructure leadership and organizational culture

Stage 2 — Cost reduction | Asset redeployment | Selective product/market strategy

Stage 3 — Repositioning

Figure 3 Five generic strategies of recovery (adapted from Hoffman, 1989)

Table 4 Three-stage process for recovery

Stage/Strategy	Action	Conditions
1 Restructuring	Replace top managers Use temporary structures Alter organizational structure Alter culture Culture change Structure change	Internal causes of turnaround Need to diversify Control and communications problems Aid repositioning
2 Cost reduction Asset Redeployment	Reduce expenses Institute controls Sell assets Shutdown or relocate units	Internal causes of decline Sales 60–80 percent of break-even Over-expansion/low capacity use Sales 30–60 percent of break-even Rapid technological change Rapid entry of new competitors
Selective product/ market strategy	**Defensive** Decrease marketing effort Divest products **Offensive** Increase marketing Increase prices Improve quality, service	 Over-expansion External causes of turnaround High capacity use Possessing operating and strategic weaknesses
3 Repositioning	**Defensive** Niche Market penetration Decrease price Divest products **Offensive** Diversification into new products	Over-expansion (defensive) Improved short-run profitability External causes for turnaround Major decline in market share Non-diversified firms faced with external causes of decline (offensive)

Source: adapted from Hoffman (1989)

Bibliography

Cascio, W. (1993). Downsizing: What do we know? What have we learnt? *Academy of Management Executive*, **7** (1), 95–104.

Gopinath, C. (1991). Turnaround: Recognizing decline and initiating intervention. *Long Range Planning*, **24** (6), 96–101.

Grinyer, P., Mayes, D., and McKiernan, P. (1988). *Sharpbenders*. Oxford: Blackwell.

Hambrick, D. C. and Schecter, S. M. (1983). Turnaround strategies for mature industrial product business units. *Academy of Management Journal*, **26** (2), 231–48.

Hofer, C. W. (1976). Turnaround strategies. In W. F. Glueck (ed.), *Business Policy and Strategic Management*, 3rd edn. Englewood Cliffs, NJ: McGraw-Hill, 1980, pp. 427–33.

Hoffman, R. C. (1989). Strategies for corporate turnarounds: What do we know about them? *Journal of General Management*, **14**, 3 (Spring), 46–66.

McKiernan, P. (1992). *Strategies of Growth*. London: Routledge.

Slatter, S. (1984). *Corporate Recovery*. Harmondsworth: Penguin.

Whittington, R. (1993). *What is Strategy and Does It Matter?* London: Routledge.

uncertainty

John McGee

In the long-running argument about the sources of profit economists have argued over the role of management (Alfred Marshall), risk-bearing (the Victorian classical economists), and change (J. B. Clark). The American economist Frank Knight argued that the cause of profit was *uncertainty*: profit arises not from change itself but from the unpredictability of change. In the absence of risk, every factor of production would have some minimum price at which it could be induced to supply. In the presence of uncertainty these minimum supply prices are increased by a "risk premium." In Knight's view, profits are earned by entrepreneurs (and firms) for bearing the brunt of uncertainty, i.e., from unpredictability and from imperfect foresight. Since the future is unknown and the outcomes of actions are uncertain, there are risks that the entrepreneur (and the firm) may have to meet unexpected costs, and, as a result, suffers unexpected losses. Entrepreneurs can relieve themselves of those risks that can be calculated and therefore insured against. But for many activities it is not possible to assign probabilities and it is impossible to insure against unexpected losses. For bearing these unexpected risks, the entrepreneur receives a profit when his or her actions (bets against the future) are successful. To the extent that entrepreneurs and firms can develop specific, sustainable competences in assessing future risks, they have sustainable competitive advantages (*see* COMPETITIVE ADVANTAGE) that can result in superior profits.

Strategy textbooks commonly identify four main sources of uncertainty – these are particularly prevalent in emerging and growing markets.

1. *Technological uncertainty* can create new markets and destroy old markets. The Schumpeterian notion of creative destruction catches the technological dynamic of the economy. Coaxial cable gives way to fiber optic cabling. Mini-computers give way to PCs. The information technology industry emerged from technological changes in computing. Sometimes technological change becomes predictable, as when Moore's law predicts the continual fall in the cost of computing (*see* TECHNOLOGY AND STANDARDS IN NETWORK INDUSTRIES). In other situations the uncertainties are much more prevalent. For example, technological racing (Gottinger, 2003) is based on (a) the idea that different firms can take very different technological paths to reach a common performance level, and (b) the interactive patterns of continuous contest among rivals to get ahead or not be left too far behind. Different patterns of development would not be observed where common views of future technology prevailed. The uncertainties concern (a) whether something will work, and (b) whether it will work better than others.

2. *Market uncertainty* concerns the difficulty of anticipating how big demand will be for the product class. How much demand will there be for pay-TV in Europe? How much will consumers pay for an electric car? Case studies contain dramatic miscalculations, such as IBM's original view of the demand for mainframe computers and EMI's underestimation of the demand for CT scan technology. Conversely, laser discs and other consumer gadgetry have failed to make an impact. What price levels can be sustained in a marketplace?

3 *Organizational uncertainty* concerns the capabilities and competences of firms and their organizational arrangements. The technology may be feasible but can many firms develop it? Should ventures be housed within existing units or hived off to an independent skunk works? IBM's famous separation of its new personal computer business from its existing divisions is a celebrated success story.

4 *Strategic uncertainty* is concerned with choosing the right business model and picking the right strategic logic. To specialize or to compete broadly? To pursue differentiation and ECONOMIES OF SCOPE (GM in the 1920s) or to pursue ECONOMIES OF SCALE (Ford)?

At the heart of the traditional approach to strategy lies the assumption that the economic method as suggested in Porter's five forces (*see* INDUSTRY STRUCTURE) allows the firm to analyze and to calculate the costs and benefits of alternative strategic approaches so as to be able to choose a clear strategic direction. As the above discussion implies, to the extent that all firms can apply this economic calculus, then intended competitive advantages are likely to be neutralized. In relatively stable environments the economic calculus can work because forecasts can be made and probabilities assigned to alternative futures. However, where environments are so uncertain, analysis has a limited payoff. In such situations a focus on the nature of uncertainty is indicated.

McKinsey's work in the McKinsey strategic theory initiative indicates four different levels of uncertainty. The uncertainties that remain after the best possible analyses have been conducted is called the residual uncertainty (similar to the idea of uninsurable risk).

1 *A clear enough future*: At this level managers can produce forecasts that are precise enough for formulating strategy. The traditional strategy toolkit can be deployed and a clear strategic direction can be identified. For example, in the airline industry in both Europe and North America, the strategy for a low-cost entry can be assessed in this way, as can the response by a major airline to a low-cost entry. This is possible because the four types of uncertainty above are relatively low and probabilistic judgments can be made with some security.

2 *Alternate futures*: The future contains a number of discrete possibilities that attract probability analysis and are reasonably certain in their feasibility. This future lends itself to decision analysis and risk analysis, to option valuation models, and to game theory. Many businesses facing major regulatory or legislative change confront this kind of uncertainty, for example, telecommunications businesses and mobile telephone companies plotting entry strategies into privatized markets. Also those industries marked by high capital intensity, such as chemicals, are prone to first-mover advantages (*see* FIRST-MOVER ADVANTAGE) where the nature of the first move is a critical event that will determine the future economic landscape of the industry.

3 *A range of futures*: A number of possible futures can be identified. These are driven by a small number of key variables, but as these variables are intrinsically uncertain, so no probabilistic forecasting can be developed. A range of possible outcomes or scenarios can be identified. This level of uncertainty can be handled through technological forecasting and SCENARIO PLANNING. Latent demand research can be useful in trying to assess underlying deep structures of demand and, from these, likely trajectories for consumer expenditure. This kind of uncertainty is prevalent in emerging markets – some levels of uncertainty are tractable, but typically market uncertainty and strategic uncertainty are very high.

4 *True ambiguity*: At this level the four main sources of uncertainty (above) interact to create an environment that is virtually impossible to predict. McKinsey call this *true ambiguity*, but Frank Knight would probably have called it *ignorance*. These are situations where the range of possible outcomes is unknown and there is no possibility of any probability analysis. Correspondingly, there are no analytical tools available apart from processes that simply organize and lay out facts, such as pattern recognition and

analogies. Companies facing major investments in the post-cold war world of Russia and China face this level of uncertainty. The legislative environment is unknown. Market infrastructures and supply chains are unknown. Macroeconomic and political shocks can be destabilizing.

The strategic analysis that follows from better assessment of uncertainty adds a new dimension to the traditional toolkit. The traditional method of *shaping the future* applies where outcomes and probabilities can be reasonably well understood. Shapers attempt to define the industry toward an economics that suits them. A second approach is to *adapt to the future*. Rather than set out to play a leadership role in the industry, one sets out to win through speed, agility, and flexibility in recognizing and responding to opportunities. This is more of a resource-based approach (*see* RESOURCE-BASED VIEW) that relies on developing abilities to recognize and respond to alternative futures. The third approach is to *reserve the right to play*. This is an option play where one invests sufficient to stay in the game but avoids premature commitments until the shape of the game can be seen. Again it requires company-specific abilities to read the political, economic, technological, and social indicators (*see* PEST ANALYSIS) so as to be able to move when the time is ripe, not too soon because of the risk of error, and not too late because of the loss of first-mover advantages.

Bibliography

Courtney, H., Kirkland, J., and Viguerie, P. (1997). Strategy under uncertainty. *Harvard Business Review*, November/December, 67–79.

Gottinger, H. (2003). *Economics of Network Industries*. London: Routledge, ch. 4.

McGee, J., Thomas, H., and Wilson, D. (2005). *Strategy: Analysis and Practice*. Maidenhead: McGraw-Hill.

Saloner, G., Shepard, A., and Podolny, J. (2001). *Strategic Management*. New York: John Wiley, pp. 280–1.

value-based planning

Derek F. Channon

Since the early 1980s, an increasing number of corporations have adopted the concept of value planning. An alternate model to other portfolio systems, value-based planning seeks to maximize the value of the corporation for shareholders. By examining the corporate portfolio with this objective, individual businesses may be seen as creating, sustaining, or destroying shareholder value. Those businesses that create value should be invested in, those sustaining value should be supported, and those destroying value should either be divested or closed.

THE CONCEPT OF VALUE PLANNING

The fundamental economic relationship underlying value-based management is that shareholder value in developed economies with established stock markets is determined by the net present value of the future cash-flow streams that can be expected from the corporation. At the same time, the value of the equity of the firm is given by the market value of the common stock. This assumes that the market is efficient, and that the market value represents a consensus of the expected present value of future cash-flow streams based on the portfolio of existing assets and the returns that can be expected from future investments. Over the long term, and despite short-term market fluctuations, there is strong evidence to support this view. This market value can be contrasted to the book value of the corporation, which is based on the accountant's view of the value of historic contributions by shareholders. The market to book model has been derived from the comparison between these two values of the firm. The market/book (M/B) ratio is calculated as follows:

$$\frac{\text{market value}}{\text{book value}} = \frac{\text{expected future payments}}{\text{past capital invested}}$$

From the calculation the basic message is as follows:

- If $M/B = 1$, all future payments are yielding the expected rate of return required by the market, and the firm is neither creating nor losing value.
- If $M/B > 1$, the rate of return is greater than that expected by the market, and the firm is creating value.
- If $M/B < 1$, the rate of return is less than that required by the market, and the firm is destroying shareholder value.

Utilizing this basic principle, a number of portfolio models have been developed which compare market to book with the rate of return on equity compared with the cost of equity. This latter factor is calculated roughly by the risk-free bond rate of return and adding a premium for equity risk. This in turn is finalized by multiplying by a beta value risk factor, which is based on the industry and the individual company. The precise calculation of the cost of equity varies slightly between consultancy company models. Comparing this calculated cost of equity with the full return on equity provides a term against which to compare M/B. Marakon Associates thus calculate the "spread," which is the actual return on equity minus the calculated return on equity. The combination of M/B versus spread is illustrated in figure 1, which indicates a positive association between the two. This model provides the basis for a useful comparison between competitors.

By contrast, McKinsey and Company use a different way of comparing the economic

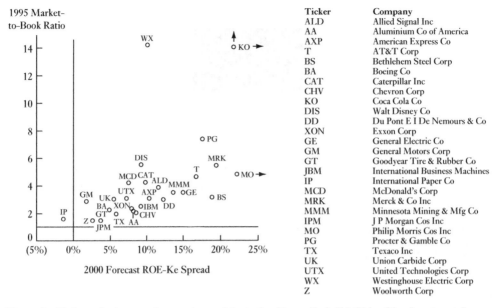

1995 Market-
to-Book Ratio

Ticker	Company
ALD	Allied Signal Inc
AA	Aluminium Co of America
AXP	American Express Co
T	AT&T Corp
BS	Bethlehem Steel Corp
BA	Boeing Co
CAT	Caterpillar Inc
CHV	Chevron Corp
KO	Coca Cola Co
DIS	Walt Disney Co
DD	Du Pont E I De Nemours & Co
XON	Exxon Corp
GE	General Electric Co
GM	General Motors Corp
GT	Goodyear Tire & Rubber Co
JBM	International Business Machines
IP	International Paper Co
MCD	McDonald's Corp
MRK	Merck & Co Inc
MMM	Minnesota Mining & Mfg Co
IPM	J P Morgan Cos Inc
MO	Philip Morris Cos Inc
PG	Procter & Gamble Co
TX	Texaco Inc
UK	Union Carbide Corp
UTX	United Technologies Corp
WX	Westinghouse Electric Corp
Z	Woolworth Corp

2000 Forecast ROE-Ke Spread

Figure 1   Market-to-book versus forecasted spread (note that K_e = Tech K_e) (Value Line Investment Survey, Marakon Associates, 1995)

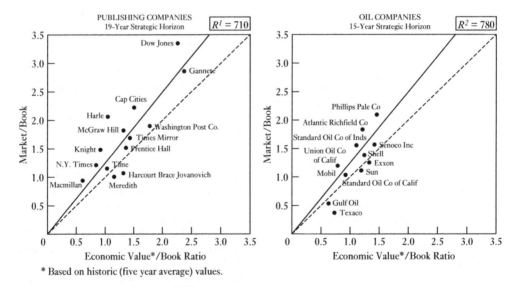

* Based on historic (five year average) values.

Figure 2   McKinsey's (M/B) versus (E/B) graph

performance of a group of firms. In this method M/B is plotted against an indicator called the economic-to-book value ratio (see figure 2). This is calculated on the basis of historic performance projected into the future but, again, the measure

is based on future cash-flow streams discounted plus a residual term.

Strategic Planning Associates, a pioneer of the technique but subsequently acquired and now Mercer Management Consultants, used a term

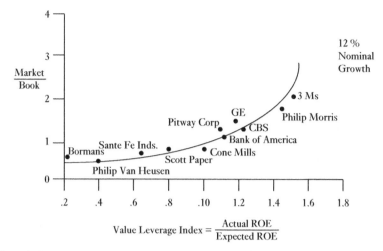

Figure 3   Across industries the higher the VLI, the higher the market/book (Mercer Management Consultants)

called the value leverage index (VLI) index, and by comparing this with the M/B one can construct the value curve illustrated in figure 3. The VLI is estimated by dividing the actual to expected return on equity. The implications of the value curve are similar to those from the Marakon calculations. Only when the actual to expected ratios of return are equal will the market value of the corporation be equivalent to the book value. When the VLI is less than one, the curve flattens out, which is assessed as an underlying value and thus a potential acquisition premium, while a VLI greater than one indicates a growth in shareholder value and the market essentially rewarding the performance with a share premium. As shown, these models are all static.

USING VALUE PLANNING AT THE SBU VALUE LEVEL

When growth is added it can have a positive, negative, or neutral effect on the market/book ratio. Corporations adding shareholder value enhance M/B, those sustaining it remain on the curve in the case of SPA, while those producing negative value have a reduced level of M/B. Growth itself, therefore, is not necessarily seen as attractive, except when it leads to increased shareholder value.

When applied within the multibusiness firm, these methodologies attempt to evaluate the con-tribution of each business unit to the overall value of the firm. When SBUs are free-standing and independent, the value of the firm is equal to the sum of the units.

The evaluation of the contribution of each business unit is critical to assessing the desired strategy at the SBU level. In particular, the impact of growth is critical. SBUs with a positive value contribution are candidates for investment, while those that destroy value should not be invested in, as further growth will accelerate this trend. However, the calculation of positive or negative value is complex, and may be subject to interpretation dependent upon how return on equity at the business unit level is calculated. Thus, if the capital structure of each business unit is seen as proportional to that of the parent, return on equity may be substantially affected by the allocation of debt, equity, and risk. However, if each SBU is treated as if it were a microfirm, its capital structure might reflect the nature of the industry in which it operates rather than that of the firm as a whole.

For example, as shown in figure 4, for two businesses with the same asset size and profitability, the return on assets value may be the same, while the return on equity value may be dramatically different, due to different capacities to generate free debt and apply leverage. Moreover, relative risk values may be quite different, and the future prospects of the business units

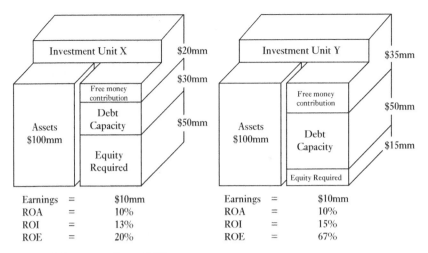

Figure 4   The capital structure effect on ROE

may also vary widely. Similarly, risk, while a function of industry, will also vary according to the competitive position of both the corporation and the business unit itself. For example, selective segmentation in insurance may result in reduced risk, which is unrecognized by industry regulators.

In assessing the portfolio position of each business, Marakon notes that its capability to generate value is determined by a combination of market economics and competitive position (see figure 5). Market economics are determined by competitors, that determine the average equity spread and growth rate over time for all competitors in its product market. Competitive position is based on factor 3, or on forces that jointly determine a specific competitor's equity spread and growth rate over time relative to the average competitor in its product market, where competitive position is defined in terms of a combination of product differentiation and economic cost position.

These two key variables can be used to assess the SBU's current and expected profitability of the business, as shown in figure 6. Business units with sustainable competitive advantages (*see* COMPETITIVE ADVANTAGE) in attractive markets will always be substantially profitable:

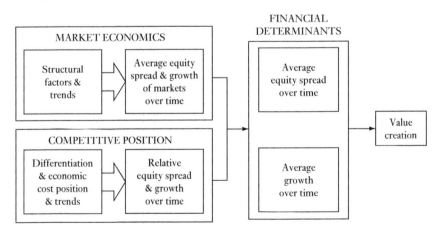

Figure 5   Strategic determinants of value creation (Marakon Associates)

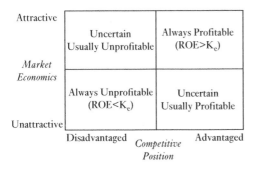

	Disadvantaged	Advantaged
Attractive		
Market Economics	Uncertain Usually Unprofitable	Always Profitable (ROE>K_e)
	Always Unprofitable (ROE<K_e)	Uncertain Usually Profitable
Unattractive		

Competitive Position

Figure 6 Linking strategic position to value creation (Marakon Associates)

ROE will always exceed the cost of equity capital and M/B will always be greater than one.

SBUs with weak competitive positions in unattractive markets will always be unprofitable: they will produce economic losses and they will destroy existing shareholder value.

In the remaining two cases the linkage is less clear, although competitive position tends to have a greater influence on profitability than market economics. Marakon notes that when a business enjoys substantial competitive advantage but participates in unattractive markets, it still tends to generate value over time, although long-term profitability tends to be a function of size and the SUSTAINABILITY of its competitive advantage. Those businesses with a competitive disadvantage in attractive markets are usually unprofitable.

From this form of financial and strategic analysis combination, value planning advocates that business units should be assigned one of four strategies – grow, hold, invest, or divest. Ironically, by eliminating portfolio losers, divestiture results in an increase in market capitalization despite a reduction in corporate assets, as future expected cash flows increase long-term shareholder value.

Bibliography

Copeland, T., Koller, J., and Murri, J. (1990). *Valuation*. New York: John Wiley.

Day, G. S. and Fahey, L. (1990). Putting strategy into shareholder value analysis. *Harvard Business Review*, 68, 156–62.

Hax, A. C. and Majluf, N. S. (1991). *The Strategy Concept and Process*. Englewood Cliffs, NJ: Prentice-Hall.

McTaggart, J. M., Kontes, P. W., and Mankins, C. M. (1994). *The Value Imperative*. New York: Free Press.

Rappaport, A. (1986). *Creating Shareholder Value*. New York: Free Press.

Strategic Planning Associates (1981). *Strategic and Shareholders' Value: The Value Curve*. Washington, DC: Strategic Planning Associates.

value-based strategy

John McGee

COMPETITIVE ADVANTAGE is about creating value both for the customer and for the firm. The first task is to define what this means in practice. Thus value to the customer can be crystallized as the firm's ability to:

1 position a product better than or differently from competitors;
2 persuade customers to recognize, purchase, and value the difference.

Value to the firm can be defined as the firm's ability to:

1 create and sustain capabilities that underpin the positioning at manageable cost premiums;
2 run (the rest of) the business efficiently and at best practice levels.

These definitions can be operationalized according the schema shown in figure 1. The four elements of valued are coded as positioning, customer persuasion, capability, and EFFICIENCY. Each of these requires strategic indicators by which performance can be measured. The figure suggests some starting points. Data should be collected to identify the firm's own performance on these measures, and then some benchmark comparisons should be made. To complement this strategic performance analysis, financial indicators can also be shown, remembering that these reflect the outcomes of previous strategies whereas the strategic indicators will presage future financial performance.

Competitive strategy will usually have a limited time scale over which assessments can be made reliably. This is usually related to the

Strategic Indicators		Company 1	Benchmark
price:performance segment maps	Positioning		
repeats; price premium; share	Customer		
peer ratings; tech benchmarking	Capability		
engineering studies cost analysis	Efficiency		
Financial Indicators	Sales Margins Asset T/o RoI		

Figure 1 Managing the business for value

tangibility of assets and to the speed with which the product life cycle operates. As a rule of thumb, firms can see to the end of the current product life cycle and are actively engaged in the planning and the next cycle. The cycle beyond that is much less clearly seen. Thus in practice one can expect firms to see one and a half life cycles ahead (subject to the life expectancy of their capital assets). Thus, if a car manufacturer has a product life cycle of four years, one would expect it to be able to see and forecast about six or seven years ahead. So how do firms plan beyond this if the numbers are missing? Figure 2 shows the break in the planning horizons.

The shorter period of competitive strategy horizon (shown as for example five years) should not and does not mean that there is no strategic thinking beyond that. One way of dealing with this is to compare alternative growth targets (shown in the figure). For each of these, the enablers and the blockers need to be identified and their nature assessed as either technical, internal, or external (see figure 3). An enabler might, for example, be a creative and productive research team and it would be internal in nature. A blocker might be the growth of low-cost manufacturing capability among competitors and it would be external in character. An example of a technical issue might be the development of new technical standards (such as for DVD rewriting), and this might either be an enabler or a blocker depending on the firm's capabilities.

Longer-term strategic thinking requires both enablers and blockers to be managed properly. Thus one would expect a focus on the key enablers to develop measures and information sources, to create an intelligence system to track their progress. The need is to assess and keep assessing the prior probability of these enablers occurring. The blockers are more difficult. The task is to identify the blockers, sort them into groups according o their common factors, discover the underlying forces and dynamics, and develop strategies to shift the blocks or to get round them (note how in the reprographics industry in the 1970s Canon developed an R&D strategy to get around Xerox's network of blocking patents). For blockers one need (as for enablers) to assess and track over time the prior probability of controlling the blockers and moderating their influence. This analysis should then be repeated for different growth targets. The outcomes will of course by quite qualitative and multidimensional, but figure 4 suggests a way of summarizing the outputs.

The vertical axis is the prior probabilities of facilitating the enablers and controlling the blockers (a joint probability of achieving a target would be one way of operationalizing this). The horizontal axis is time. The first part of this is a commitment period during which the foundations are being established (typically, the first part of a J-curve), shown here for example as four years. Beyond this period we are looking for

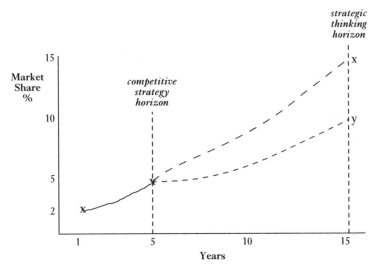

Figure 2   Positioning the business for growth

	Technical	Internal	External
Enablers			
Blockers			

Growth Target = %

Figure 3   Identifying enablers and blockers

a confidence that growth can be managed – *the ring of confidence* in the figure – or, if not, *the undesirable region*. More generally, one would expect to see a curve showing the prior probabilities rising over time. The key question is whether the probabilities are sufficiently high early enough. The bad position is when the probabilities remain low well beyond the commitment period. Conversely, happiness occurs when they rise quickly.

Approaches such as this one require considerable judgment and they often will defy the objective tests implied by quantification. However, the advantage here is of applying a systematic procedure that is rooted in the economics of the firm and in the nature of customer behavior, and that seeks to balance opportunity against risk.

See also *competitive strategy; value-based planning; value creation and value analysis*

Bibliography

McGee, J., Wilson, D., and Thomas, H. (2005). *Strategy: Analysis and Practice*. Maidenhead: McGraw-Hill.

value chain analysis

Derek F. Channon

The activities that a firm performs become part of the value added produced from a raw material to its ultimate consumption. Individual actors may operate over a greater or lesser extent of the total value generated within an industry. The value chain for the firm is shown in figure 1, in which are also illustrated many of the key issues associated with each of the main functions within the value chain. At the same time, the firm does not exist in isolation but merely forms part of the overall supply chain. Thus suppliers have value chains, as do customers and the channels that supply them. Moreover, in multibusiness firms there may well be a variety of value

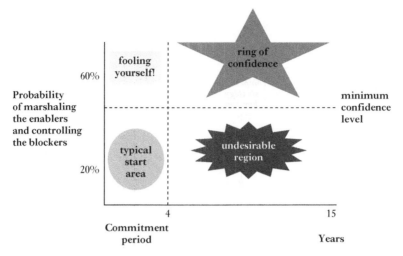

Figure 4   Positioning the business for growth: assessing feasibility

chains with different dimensions in which the firm is involved. The value system for single business and multibusiness firms is illustrated in figure 2.

The value chain concept allows the firm to be disaggregated into a variety of strategically relevant activities. In particular, it is important to identify those which have different economic characteristics; those which have a high potential for creating differentiation; and those which are most important in developing cost structure (PARETO ANALYSIS may be a useful tool for this purpose). The value chain concept thus helps to identify cost behavior in detail. As such, a number of the Japanese cost analysis techniques are useful in gaining this information. From this analysis, different strategic courses of action should be identifiable in order to develop differentiation and less price-sensitive strategies. COMPETITIVE ADVANTAGE is then achieved by performing strategic activities better or cheaper than competitors.

Value is the amount that buyers are willing to pay for the product or service that a firm provides. Profits alter when the value created by the firm exceeds the cost of providing it.

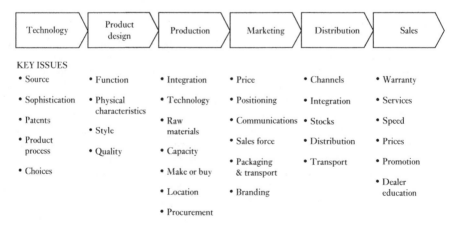

Figure 1   The business value chain

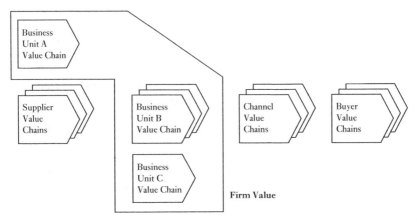

Figure 2   Competitive advantage value system for a diversified firm (Porter, 1985)

This is the goal of STRATEGY, and therefore value creation becomes a critical ingredient in competitive analysis. Every value activity employs costs such as raw materials, and other purchased goods and services for "purchased inputs," human resources (direct and indirect labor), and technology to transform raw materials into finished goods. Each value activity also creates information that is needed to establish what is going on in the business. Similarly, value is created by producing stocks, accounts receivable, and the like; while value is lost via raw material purchases and other liabilities. Most organizations thus engage in many activities in the process of creating value. These activities can generally be classified into either primary or support activities. These are illustrated in figure 3, which details the view of Michael Porter, who states that there are five generic categories of primary activities involved in competing in any industry. Each of these is divisible into a number of specific activities that vary according to the industry and chosen strategy of the firm. These categories are as follows:

- *Inbound logistics.* Activities associated with receiving, storing, and disseminating rights

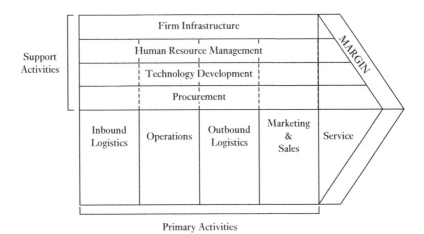

Figure 3   The generic value chain (Porter, 1985)

to the product, such as material handling, warehousing, and stock management.

- *Operations*. All of the activities required to transform inputs into outputs and the critical functions which add value, such as machining, packaging, assembly, service, and testing.
- *Outbound logistics*. All of the activities required to collect, store, and physically distribute the output. This activity can prove to be extremely important both in generating value and in improving differentiation, as in many industries control over distribution strategies is proving to be a major source of competitive advantage – especially as it is realized that up to 50 percent of the value created in many industry chains occurs close to the ultimate buyer.
- *Marketing and sales*. Activities associated with informing potential buyers about the firm's products and services, and inducing them to do so by personal selling, advertising and promotion, etc.
- *Service*. The means of enhancing the physical product features through after-sales service, installation, repair, and so on.

While each firm provides these activities to a greater or lesser degree, they do not do so to the same extent, nor is each function as important to all competitors, even within the same industry.

Porter has also identified four generic support strategies. These are broad concepts that support the primary activities of the firm:

1 *Procurement*. This concerns the acquisition of inputs or resources. Although technically the responsibility of the purchasing department, almost everyone in the firm is responsible for purchasing something. While the cost of procurement itself is relatively low, the impact can be very high.
2 *Human resource management*. This consists of all activities involved in recruiting, hiring, training, developing, rewarding, and sanctioning the people in the organization.
3 *Technology development*. This is concerned with the equipment, hardware, software, technical skills, etc. used by the firm in transforming inputs to outputs. Some such

skills can be classified as scientific, while others – such as food preparation in a restaurant – are "artistic." Such skills are not always recognized. They may also support limited activities of the business, such as accounting and order procurement, and in this sense may be likened to the value-added component of the experience effect (*see* EXPERIENCE AND LEARNING EFFECTS).

4 *Firm infrastructure*. This consists of the many activities, including general management, planning, finance, legal, and external affairs, which support the operational aspect of the value chain. This may be self-contained in the case of an undiversified firm or divided between the parent and the firm's constituent business units.

Within each category of primary and support activities, Porter identifies three types of activity that play different roles in achieving competitive advantage:

- *Direct*. These are activities directly involved in creating value for buyers, such as assembly, sales, and advertising.
- *Indirect*. These are activities that facilitate the performance of the direct activities on a continuing basis, such as maintenance, scheduling, and administration.
- *Quality assurance*. These are activities that insure the quality of other activities, such as monitoring, inspecting, testing, and checking.

To diagnose competitive advantage, it is necessary to define the firm's value chain for operating in a particular industry and compare this with those of key competitors. A comparison of the value chains of different competitors often identifies ways of achieving strategic advantage by reconfiguring the value chain of the individual firm. In assigning costs and assets, it is important for the analysis to be done strategically rather than to seek accounting precision. This should be accomplished using the following principles:

- operating costs should be assigned to activities where incurred;
- assets should be assigned to activities where employed, controlled, or influencing usage;

- accounting systems should be adjusted to fit value analysis;
- asset valuation may be difficult, but should recognize industry norms – particular care should be taken in evaluating property assets.

The reconfiguration of the value chain has often been used by successful competitors in achieving competitive advantage. When seeking to reconfigure the value chain in an industry, the following questions need to be asked:

- How can an activity be done differently or even eliminated?
- How can linked value activities be reordered or regrouped?
- How could coalitions with other firms reduce or eliminate costs?

Successful reconfiguration strategies usually occur with one or more of the following moves:

- a new production process;
- automation differences;
- direct versus indirect sales strategy;
- the opening of new distribution channels;
- new raw materials used;
- differences in forward and/or backward integration;
- a relative location shift;
- new advertising media.

Bibliography

Porter, M. E. (1979). How competitive forces shape strategy. *Harvard Business Review*, **57**, 2 (March/April), 137–45.

Porter, M. E. (1985). *Competitive Advantage: Creating and Sustaining Superior Performance*. New York: Free Press.

value creation and value analysis

John McGee

The concept of value is central to economics and to the understanding of COMPETITIVE ADVANTAGE. The theory of value in economics deals with the determination of final market prices (as opposed to factor prices, which are determined by the theory of distribution).

PERCEIVED BENEFIT AND CONSUMER SURPLUS

If you buy a car for $15,000 but, in terms of the services it renders, it is worth to you $20,000, then you are better off by $5,000. This is known as the *consumer surplus*. Given a choice of cars with identical service values, you would (rationally) buy the cheaper car – this would save you money and increase your consumer surplus. The idea of consumer surplus is a profit idea – it is the "profit" that the consumer makes from a purchase. If the "consumer" was a firm buying a machine for $15,000 but, as a result, lowering its costs by $20,000, the value created by the purchase (i.e., the profit) is $5,000.

In tabular form:

Perceived gross benefit
    less user costs
    less transactions costs
= Perceived net benefit
    less price paid
= Consumer surplus

VALUE MAPS

A firm must deliver consumer surplus to compete successfully. Value maps illustrate the competitive implications of consumer surplus analysis. The vertical axis shows the price of the product and the horizontal axis shows quality or performance characteristics of the product. Each point corresponds to a particular price quality combination. At any point in time, the series of price quality combinations available to consumers is shown by an upward-sloping schedule, an indifference curve. The slope shows the trade-off between price and quality: the steeper the slope, the higher the extra price to be paid for increased quality. This is an "indifference" curve because at each point on the curve the consumer surplus is the same. Above the curve is lower consumer surplus, because prices are higher. Below the curve is higher consumer surplus, because prices are lower. Without any innovations in product or process, any firm wishing to price below the indifference curve to gain volume will do so at the expense of profit. Genuine innovation might enable a competitor to make a different "offer" in the form of

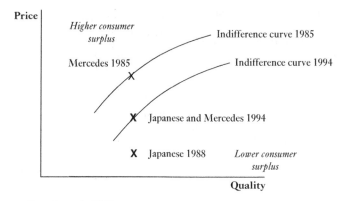

Figure 1   Value maps (Besanko et al., 2003)

a new indifference curve below the original one. This will offer higher consumer surplus, will divert volume toward the new competitor, and take volume and profit away from the non-innovating competitor.

This is illustrated in figure 1 by the luxury car market in the US. When the Japanese luxury automobiles Lexus, Infiniti, and Acura were introduced in the late 1980s, they offered comparable quality to Mercedes but at lower prices. Not surprisingly, they gained MARKET SHARE. Eventually the Japanese firms increased prices and Mercedes lowered prices, converging on a new and lower indifference curve. Overall, the consumer gained – consumer surplus increased.

The suppliers would have benefited if their costs had fallen by at least an equivalent amount.

VALUE CREATION AND PRICING

As goods move along the supply chain and into and along the firm's value chain, economic value is created. Firm A in figure 2 illustrates the different value creation packages.

- Consumer surplus is benefit less price paid: $B - P$.
- Firm profit (or producer surplus) is price paid by the consumer less costs: $P - C$.
- Total value created is consumer surplus and firm profit: $B - C$.

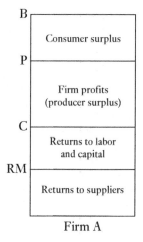

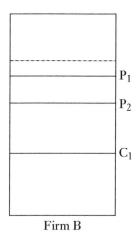

Figure 2   Pricing, consumer surplus, and profit

Table 1 Pricing, advantage, and profits

	Cost advantage	Differentiation (benefit) advantage
High price elasticity	SHARE STRATEGY Under-price competitors to gain share	SHARE STRATEGY Maintain price parity and let differentiation gain share
Low price elasticity	MARGIN STRATEGY Maintain price parity and gain profits through high margins	MARGIN STRATEGY Charge price premium relative to competitors

- Value added (as measured in the national accounts and used as a measure of output of the economy) is technically firm profit less costs of raw materials: P – RM.

The firm's pricing decision can be seen as critical in partitioning total value between consumers and firms. A high price claims more for the firm, giving less to the consumer running the risk that Firm B, for example, might opt for lower prices and attract volume away from Firm A. With similar costs, competitive forces will move the market toward a common price level, P. However, if Firm A is innovative and reduces costs to C1, then it has the option of various prices below P, such as P1 or P2. The choice of price depends on the price ELASTICITY of demand.

PRICING, PRICE ELASTICITY, COSTS, AND PROFITS

Table 1 illustrates the interactions between price elasticity for the firm (not the market) and type of advantage – differentiation (benefit) or cost. The four boxes tell different stories.

- With a cost advantage and high price elasticity, it pays to under-price competitors to gain share.
- With a differentiation (benefit) advantage and high price elasticity, it pays to maintain price parity and let the differentiation advantage increase volume and thereby pull profits through.
- With cost advantage and low price elasticity, the best option is a margin strategy whereby prices are maintained and profits are increased through the margin benefit.

- With a differentiation (benefit) advantage and low price elasticity, a margin strategy is again indicated where prices can be substantially raised because of the low elasticity and high benefits – profits accrue through increased margins with only small volume offsets.

In setting prices the task is to create a competitive advantage by (1) creating unique value to consumers (best possible consumer surplus) and (2) creating above-average profits for the firm. If every firm was like Firm A in figure 2, there would be no competitive advantage. If one firm can innovate and create lower costs like Firm B or higher benefits, then a competitive advantage is possible for a range of possible prices depending on the price elasticities of demand and the type and scale of advantage available to the innovating firm. In this situation, Firm B would wish to identify the "break-even price elasticity": that elasticity that would enable it to identify the borderline between a share strategy and a margin strategy.

Bibliography

Besanko, D., Dranove, D., Shanley, M., and Shaefer, S. (2003). *Economics of Strategy*, 2nd edn. New York: John Wiley.

value engineering

Derek F. Channon

Japanese companies have made heavy use of value engineering in their pursuit of cost reductions. One such approach, used by Isuzu Motors, has eight aspects to its value engineering program.

Value target. This term is used at Isuzu for its procedures developed to identify target costs of components purchased from suppliers. At the planning stage, the target cost of an entire vehicle at the concept proposal stage is distributed among the company's many thousands of component suppliers. Target costs for major functions and components are determined using monetary values or ratios. Monetary values are determined from customer-based market research, although factors such as technical, safety, and legal considerations are often used to adjust these values. Once target costs are established, outside contractors are invited to bid to supply. Creative suppliers can add value by increasing component functionality.

Zeroth-look value engineering. This involves the application of value engineering techniques to the earliest state of product development. By this process the company expects to find revolutionary solutions to improve the functionality of the firm's products.

First-look value engineering. Defined as developing new products from concepts, this method is applied during the second half of the concept proposal stage and during the entire planning stage. In the planning stage, the key components or major functions are identified, the commodity value is determined, a design plan submitted, target costs distributed to major functions, and a degree of component commonality set. The objective is to increase a product's value by increasing its functionality without a corresponding increase in cost.

Second-look value engineering. This technique is applied during the second half of the planning stage and the first half of the development and product preparation stage. In the development and product preparation stage, the components of the main functions are identified and a first handmade prototype produced. The objective is to improve the value and functionality of existing components rather than to create new ones. Improved components are then incorporated into new products.

Manufacturing value engineering. The objective of this approach is to identify the best method to produce a part, with the critical trade-off being quality versus cost. This approach is applied during the second half of the development and product preparation stage and the first half of the development and production–sales preparation stage.

Wate method. This is a mechanism to systemically incorporate value engineering techniques into small group activities such as quality control and industrial engineering. It is applied on a continuous basis during the development and product preparation stage, the development and production–sales preparation stage and the production–sales preparation stage. The method utilizes a working group approach, with each analyzing problems encountered with new products.

Mini-value engineering. This is a simplified approach to second-look value engineering and applies to specific parts or very small inexpensive parts. The technique is applied during the development and product preparation stage, the development and production–sales preparation stage, and the production–sales preparation stage.

Value engineering reliability program. This is designed to insure that the most appropriate form of value engineering is applied during the development and product preparation stage, the development and production–sales preparation stage, and the production–sales preparation stage.

Bibliography

Cooper, R. and Yoshikawa, T. (1994). *Isuzu Motors Ltd, Cost Creation Program.* Case Study No. 9-195-054. Boston: Harvard Business School.

venture capital

Taman Powell

Venture capital is essentially funds made available for investment in young, small companies that have good growth prospects but are short of funds. These investments are generally seen as being highly risky, but also as having the potential for very high returns. These funds are generally managed by venture capital firms (such as 3i, Apax Partners, and Kleiner, Perkins, Caufield, and Byers), who build funds from wealthy individuals, insurance companies, and pension funds and invest these funds in early-stage companies.

Venture capital emerged in the 1950/1960s from individuals and small groups of people who began to seek out early-stage companies in which to invest. These business "angels" saw very good returns on their investments and began to search and invest more systematically. They also started to look to source additional funds for investment in the firms that they identified. This was the emergence of the venture capital business.

Venture capital firms essentially offer the firms in which they invest capital in return for a stake in the company. The venture capital firms also often sit on the board of the companies in which they have invested. It is often believed that the key benefit from venture capital firms is not so much the funds as the expertise and network that they provide to the firms in which they invest.

In the UK, venture capital is a large business, with an investment of 55 billion in nearly 25,000 firms over the 1984–2002 period (BVCA, 2003). Over the same period, 35 percent of trading company flotations on the London Stock Exchange were venture capital-backed.

Bibliography

BVCA (2003). *The Economic Impact of Private Equity in the UK, 2003*. London: BVCA.

vertical integration strategy

Derek F. Channon

Vertical integration strategies aim to increase the firm's coverage of the value-added chain of an industry by extending backward into the production of components or raw materials or forward into wholesaling and distribution toward end users. Such moves can aim at full integration, participating in all stages of the value chain (*see* VALUE CHAIN ANALYSIS), to partial integration where the firm is engaged in part of the process.

ADVANTAGES OF VERTICAL INTEGRATION

It has been claimed that the only good reason for investing company resources in vertical integration is to strengthen the firm's competitive position. Thus, unless such a strategy produces COMPETITIVE ADVANTAGE or produces cost savings that create shareholder value, it should not be undertaken.

Backward integration is therefore only viable when the volume needed is sufficient to gain the same ECONOMIES OF SCALE as those of suppliers and when it can match supplier EFFICIENCY. This may be possible when suppliers achieve high margins, when the item supplied is a high value-added component, and when the firm possesses – or can readily gain access to – any necessary technology. The strategy can be valuable when, by producing its own components, the firm can achieve a competitive advantage for its primary product or gain industry dominance for a strategic component. For example, Canon holds some 80 percent MARKET SHARE in the production of laser beam engines, although the company's share of the market for laser printers is much lower.

Backward integration may also be advantageous when the firm is faced with dependency for critical components or raw materials from a monopoly supplier, or where there are few powerful suppliers bent on maximizing their own profitability.

Forward integration offers similar potential advantages. Poor access to existing distribution channels may lead to an expensive buildup in inventory and poor capacity utilization, so reducing economies of scale. Forward integration offers the firm greater control over the distribution function and may provide an opportunity to gain competitive advantage by opening new channels. When it is realized that some 50 percent of value added in consumer products can occur at the distribution stage, this option may well be attractive provided that the firm has the requisite skills to manage this function. For example, until the late 1980s personal computers were sold by professional sales persons or from specialized computer stores. By lowering prices and opening a mass volume segment, a firm such as Amstrad transformed the market by supplying its products through consumer electronics stores. In the early 1990s, however, this channel was superseded by manufacturers adopting a strategy of direct selling off the page, so dramatically weakening the position of the mass market retailers.

Integrating forward into production may assist raw materials producers to achieve product differentiation and higher value added while avoiding the price-competitive market for undifferentiated, commodity products. In high capital-intensity businesses with specialized fixed assets, in the early stages of the value chain products are sold primarily on specification. As a result, differentiation is often minimal and competitors compete away possible margins in order to maximize capacity utilization. Where EXCESS CAPACITY exists, therefore, margins are often too low to provide an adequate return on equity – as, for example, in oil products and bulk commodity chemicals. Forward vertical integration therefore may improve the possibility of differentiation and so avoid margin pressures. In areas such as refined oil products, backward integration by hypermarket and superstore operators has proven to be especially attractive, as the oil companies themselves have fought to supply the distributors because of their high-volume sites and in order to maintain or strengthen refinery capacity utilization.

DISADVANTAGES OF VERTICAL INTEGRATION

There are also a number of actual or potential disadvantages from the pursuit of a vertical integration strategy. First, vertical integration adds to the level of capital investment involved in a business, and unless the additional level of value added covers the extra capital required, overall capital intensity will be increased, with consequent pressure on margins and profitability, and shareholder value will be destroyed.

Second, integration introduces additional risk in that the firm's strategic scope across an industry is increased. Third, vertical integration makes it more difficult for a firm to exit an industry and to resist changing technology and production facilities because of losses likely from investment writedowns. Such firms are there-

fore vulnerable to shifts in technology or methods of production.

Fourth, vertical integration may well require careful coordination of each stage of an integrated activity chain. Efficient economies of scale may also vary significantly for different processes within the chain. One interesting characteristic of integrated strategies occurs when such a chain is broken or where each process is opened to the external market. In the aftermath of the first oil-price shock, for example, BP lost control of 94 percent of its crude oil supplies. While the company subsequently made important new discoveries on the North Slope in Alaska and in the North Sea, the integrated flow of the company's operations was severely disrupted. As a result, BP's tanker fleet was largely disposed of: it became a net purchaser of crude in some markets, and a crude supplier in other markets in which it lacked refining capacity and retail outlets to engage in downstream value-added activities. In other companies such as Booker McConnell, where similar sudden environmental shifts have broken up integrated strategies, companies have moved to create separate businesses from their previously integrated functions, thus essentially becoming conglomerates (see CONGLOMERATE STRATEGY).

Vertical integration as a strategy therefore has both strengths and weaknesses. The value of such strategy depends on how compatible it is with the long-term interests of the firm; how much it strengthens the firm's strategic position within an industry; and the extent to which it generates competitive advantage. Therefore, unless such a strategy creates shareholder value, it is unlikely to be attractive.

Bibliography

Harrigan, K. R. (1984). Formulating vertical integration strategies. *Academy of Management Review*, **9** (4), 638–52.

Harrigan, K. R. (1985). *Strategic Flexibility*. Lexington, MA: Lexington Books, p. 162.

Stuckey, J. and White, D. (1993). When and when not to vertically integrate. *McKinsey Quarterly*, 3, 3–26.

Thompson, A. and Strickland, A. J. (1993). *Strategic Management*, 7th edn. New York: Irwin, pp. 120–2.

volume businesses

Derek F. Channon

Identified as one of the environments in the BCG ADVANTAGE MATRIX, in volume businesses basic costs make up the key element in overall cost structure and, as a result of low product differentiation, the experience effect is important (*see* EXPERIENCE AND LEARNING EFFECTS). Moreover, margins tend to be reduced in the drive to maximize capacity utilization. Examples of volume businesses include basic consumer electronics products such as television sets, VCRs, and DVD players. Others include fast foods, microcomputers, commodity chemicals, and electronic banking.

For success in volume businesses it is imperative to achieve volume leadership, which is translated into a lower-cost structure. This allows the business to achieve COMPETITIVE ADVANTAGE. However, many industry leaders adopt umbrella pricing strategies, negating their potential cost advantage and encouraging low-share competitors, and this often leads to stalemate strategies. To maintain strategic advantage, therefore, it is imperative that leaders in volume businesses maintain share by investing in adequate capacity additions until market maturity occurs, to avoid undue cost increases due to business complexity, and to monitor the environment carefully to avoid any technology bypass or market redefinition, such as that caused by GLOBALIZATION.

vulnerability analysis

Derek F. Channon

An alternate method of evaluating the threat to a company is to conduct a vulnerability analysis. When executives undertake a SWOT ANALYSIS there is a tendency to play down the potential impact of threats. Vulnerability analysis assesses the potential damage to the firm of removing its key strategic underpinnings. These have been identified as:

- customer needs and wants served by the firm's products or services;
- resources and assets – people, capital, facilities, raw materials, and technology;
- relative cost position compared with that of competitors;
- consumer base – size, demographics, and trends;
- technologies required;
- special skills – systems, procedures, and structures;
- corporate identity – image, culture, and products;
- institutional barriers to competition – regulations, patents, and licensing;
- social values – lifestyles, common norms, and ideals;
- sanctions, supports, and incentives to do business;
- customer goodwill, product quality, safety, and corporate reputation;
- complementary products or services in the stakeholder system.

Conducting a vulnerability analysis involves the following steps:

1 Identify the key underpinnings.
2 Identify the threat caused by their removal.
3 State the most conservative consequence of each threat.
4 Rank the impacts of the worst consequence of each threat.
5 Estimate the probability of each threat occurring.
6 Rank the firm's capability to deal with each threat.
7 Determine whether the company's vulnerability to each threat is extreme or negligible.

Having conducted this assessment, rank the impact on a scale of 0 to 10, where 0 denotes no impact on the organization and 10 represents catastrophe. Similarly, the firm's ability to respond to each threat should also be ranked from 0 to 10, where zero represents defenselessness and 10 means that the company can easily absorb the threat.

From these assessments, the company's overall vulnerability to each threat can be plotted on a vulnerability assessment matrix, as shown in figure 1.

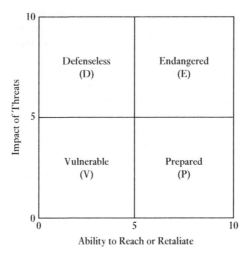

Figure 1   The vulnerability assessment matrix (Rowe et al., 1994)

The firm is virtually defenseless against threats that fall in quadrant D. Any entry falling in this box thus requires immediate management action to reduce the threat. This should be done by abandoning plans or strategies that might result in the threat materializing. In the event that this is not possible, the firm's ability to react must be appraised.

Threats in quadrant E are still dangerous, but the capabilities exist for the firm to react. For such threats, contingency plans should be developed, to be brought into play as and when such a threat materializes.

The firm is well prepared to deal with threats in quadrant P, and little monitoring is therefore required. While threats in quadrant V have limited impact, the company is not well prepared to deal with them. Such threats should therefore be monitored to insure that they do not escalate, although detailed contingency plans are not likely to be necessary.

Bibliography

Hurd, D. A. (1977). *Vulnerability Analysis in Business Planning.* SRI International Research Report No. 593.

Rowe, A. J., Mason, R. O., Dickel, K. E., Mann, R. B., and Mockler, R. J. (1994). *Strategic Management*, 4th edn. Reading, MA: Addison-Wesley, pp. 202–6.

Z

Z-score

Derek F. Channon

The Z-score was developed in the US by Altman (1968) as a predictor of corporate failure. The concept has been extended to other countries and provides a useful tool for predicting bankruptcy or financial difficulties largely in manufacturing businesses (or those with significant working capital intensity). The formula makes use of ratios derived from standard financial statements and can therefore be applied to the analysis of competitors, customers, suppliers, acquisition candidates, and so on. However, care must be taken to insure that financial statements provide a realistic estimate of the financial health of companies investigated. The tool can also be used as a predictor for business units or the corporation in multibusiness concerns.

A company's Z-score is calculated using the formula

$$Z = (1.2)X_1 + (1.4)X_2 + (3.3)X_3 + (0.6)X_4 + X_5$$

where X_1 = working capital/total assets, i.e., net current assets divided by total book value; X_2 = retained earnings/total assets (virtually by definition, retained earnings are less for younger companies, and the lower value of this ratio for such concerns can be seen as a higher risk effect of failure for them); X_3 = EBIT/total assets, i.e., earnings before interest and tax divided by all capital employed; X_4 = market value of equity/book value of total debt, i.e., market capitalization of all classes of equity divided by total short and long debt (this ratio is not available for companies that are not listed on the stock market); and X_5 = sales/total assets, a measure of capital term (note the similarity to the capital intensity term used in PROFIT IMPACT OF MARKET STRATEGY).

Using historic data from 85 failed US companies, Altman calculated that 95 percent of these had a score of less than 1.81 a year before failure and 72 percent up to two years before. However, only 4 percent of firms had such a low score three years prior to bankruptcy. By contrast, scores above 3 had a low likelihood of failure.

While Altman's model was essentially a short-term predictor of bankruptcy, many companies have used it as a trend predictor, plotting Z-scores on the vertical axis and time on the horizontal. A significant downward trend in Z-scores may therefore be a predictor of future trouble and potentially highlights the cause of such a problem. For private companies, for which the X_4 ratio is not relevant, such concerns will, by definition, tend to have a lower Z-score.

Bibliography

Altman, E. (1968). Financial ratios discriminant analysis and the prediction of corporate bankruptcy. *Journal of Finance*, September.

zaibatsu structure

Derek F. Channon

These concerns formed the basis for the foundation of Japanese industrialization. They developed from a variety of sources, but emerged as highly diversified, family-dominated concerns from the late nineteenth century. Today they would be defined as conglomerates (*see* CONGLOMERATE STRATEGY), although at the time DIVERSIFICATION moves tended to be seen as related, albeit opportunistic in some cases. The businesses within a *zaibatsu* were not necessarily legally independent concerns, but were sometimes organized as internal divisions (indeed, the Mitsubishi *zaibatsu* seems to have been the first recorded corporation to adopt a multidivisional structure in 1908, some 15 years before this structure developed in the US). Nor were *zaibatsu* necessarily large, although the largest formed the core of Japanese industry. Moreover, not all Japanese large corporations were *zaibatsu*, with joint-stock companies also being relatively undiversified in industries such as power generation and textiles. All of the large concerns were located in one of the major central cities – Tokyo, Osaka, Kobe, and Yokohama – with location being a subsequent influence on corporate evolution.

After the Meiji Restoration in Japan in 1868, eight major *zaibatsu* groups – Mitsui, Mitsubishi, Sumitomo, Yasuda, Furakawa, Okura, Asamo, and Fujita – had begun to develop. Two further groups, Kuhara and Suzuki, emerged around 1910. These ten concerns exerted substantial influence over the Japanese economy, both qualitatively and quantitatively, and in the industries in which they operated (and frequently dominated).

The rise of the *zaibatsu* was based around the concept of the family firm, despite the fact that the joint-stock company concept was introduced early in the Meiji period. The main sources of wealth for the founding families which enabled them to embark on their diversification strategies came from profits generated as a result of government patronage and mining. The families invested their fortunes in new activities because of strong internal pressures, in part from family members, such as in the case of the Iwasaki family in Mitsubishi, but mainly from professional managers employed by the concerns.

By the early 1920s all the major *zaibatsu* had a multisubsidiary form of organization. In this structure, each of the businesses into which the *zaibatsu* diversified took the form not of a division but of a subsidiary company and, as in a multidivisional structure, each subsidiary functioned autonomously within the framework of the *zaibatsu* overall policy. This was established by the central office, which controlled the subsidiaries via share ownership. Although historic-

ally family businesses, the leading *zaibatsu* were also progressive in employing more educated managers who guided the affairs of the organization.

The four leading prewar *zaibatsu*, Mitsubishi, Mitsui, Sumitomo, and Yasuda, accounted for around 24 percent of all Japanese industry. Created by Iwasaki Yatoro, a low-order samurai, the Mitsubishi *zaibatsu* was born out of shipping operations and diversified into trading, shipbuilding and heavy engineering, and banking and insurance. By 1945, Mitsubishi was engaged in virtually all sectors of manufacturing industry. The Iwasaki family still owned 55.5 percent of the Mitsubishi Holding Company, which in turn owned more than 52 percent of the subsidiary and affiliated companies. The Iwasaki family, however, owned directly only 0.4 percent of subsidiary and affiliated companies. Under Iwasaki management control was strongly centralized and this tradition continued with his sons. Professional managers were, however, given a great deal of power over operations.

Mitsui was initially concerned with the textile industry and money exchange, and dated back to the late seventeenth century. Following the Meiji Restoration, Mitsui developed with government encouragement as a bank, spinning off its dry goods retail business into a new family branch, Mitsukoshi, which – while outside the Mitsui clan – developed properly as a major retailing organization. Mitsui itself diversified by adding a trading company, which in turn diversified into mining and traded in a wide range of products. By the end of World War II, Mitsui had diversified substantially and consisted of some 22 subsidiary and affiliated companies. The Mitsui family owned some 67 percent of the group holding company and over 50 percent of the stocks of all subsidiaries and affiliates. As the group expanded and diversified away from its money exchange activities to become a major *zaibatsu*, management was passed to professional managers. Indeed, the family imposed a strict rule against the participation of family managers in company management.

The Sumitomo *zaibatsu* had its roots in copper mining and smelting, but after the Meiji Restoration diversification occurred into metal and commodities trading, shipping, warehousing, and financial services, and other areas of metal processing and timber. By 1946 the Sumitomo family held 29 percent of the group's holding company and 13 percent of the subsidiary and affiliated companies. However, the family had gradually dissociated itself from direct management of the businesses, and by the end of World War II Sumitomo was essentially managed by professionals.

The Yasuda *zaibatsu*, like Mitsui, had its origins as a privileged provider of fiscal services to the government. Founded by a low-rank samurai, Yasuda Zawjuro, at the end of the Tokugawa period, the organization began as a money-changing concern before becoming a political merchant. After the Meiji Restoration, Yasuda cooperated with the new government in introducing unconvertible paper money. In 1876, Yasuda created a bank, which became the foundation of the group. Non-financial businesses were less significant than in the other three major *zaibatsu*.

After World War II, the *zaibatsu* became a target for the occupying powers. Eighty-three *zaibatsu* holding companies were initially identified for dissolution. This focused on breaking their ownership of banks, subsidiaries, and affiliates, freezing their assets, and imposing a capital levy on their wealth. Where family interests remained, these linkages were also broken. The four largest *zaibatsu*, Mitsubishi, Mitsui, Sumitomo, and Yasuda, voluntarily made dissolution proposals and, to prevent the groups from reforming, US-style antimonopoly laws were introduced. The deconcentration of 1,200 companies was planned at the end of 1947, but this policy had to be abandoned in the face of Japan's critical economic condition.

In 1957 a final treaty was signed which restored Japan's independence. The post-occupation government, anxious to restore the economy, allowed the former *zaibatsu* to reestablish links with banks of their former groups; defensive cross-shareholdings began to be established as a protection against acquisition, and soon the former Mitsubishi, Mitsui, and Sumitomo *zaibatsu* began to come together in the late 1950s. Unlike the prewar *zaibatsu*, however, these newly emerging groups had no family ownership and no overall holding companies. These new groups were the first of the postwar horizontal *keiretsu* groups (*see* KEIRETSU STRUCTURE).

Not all of the prewar *zaibatsu* reestablished connections with former related companies. Partially in response to the emergence of the three leading former *zaibatsu* groups, other *keiretsu* groups formed around the major city banks, who were key providers of funds for redevelopment. The Yasuda *zaibatsu* thus reformed in part, to become a key element within the Fuyo group, centered on the Fuji Bank. The other leading *keiretsu* groups developed around the Sanwa and Dai Ichi Kangyo banks. By the mid-1960s the *zaibatsu* conglomerates had been superseded by *keiretsu* groups. The historic family structures of these groups, however, can be seen today to some extent in the evolution of *chaebol* groups in Korea (*see* CHAEBOL STRUCTURE) and the CHINESE FAMILY BUSINESS elsewhere in Asia. By contrast, the concept of family-or clan-based industrial conglomerates has not developed in the West, and an understanding of these two alternate structural modes helps to explain major differences in strategic evolution.

Bibliography

Bisson, T. A. (1954). *Zaibatsu Dissolution in Japan*. Berkeley: University of California Press.

Hattori, T. (1989). Japanese *zaibatsu* and Korean *chaebol*. In K. H. Chung and H. C. Lee (eds.), *Korean Managerial Dynamics*. New York: Praeger, pp. 79–88.

Min Chen (1995). *Asian Management Systems*. London: Routledge.

Morikawa, H. (1992). *Zaibatsu: The Rise and Fall of Family Enterprise Groups in Japan*. Tokyo: University of Tokyo Press.

Index

Note: Headwords are in bold type

Printed and bound by CPI Group (UK) Ltd, Croydon, CR0 4YY

23/04/2025

14660954-0002